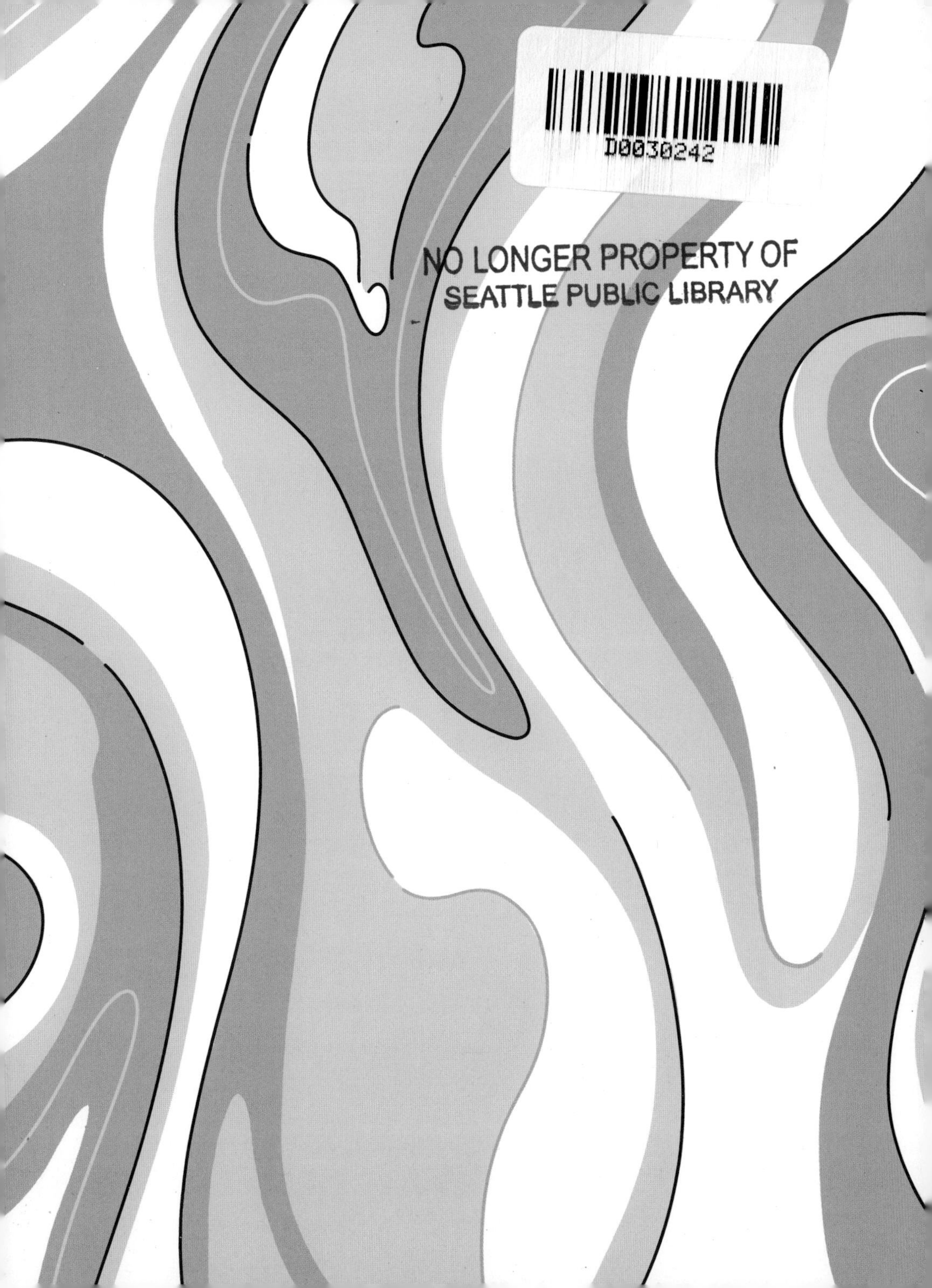

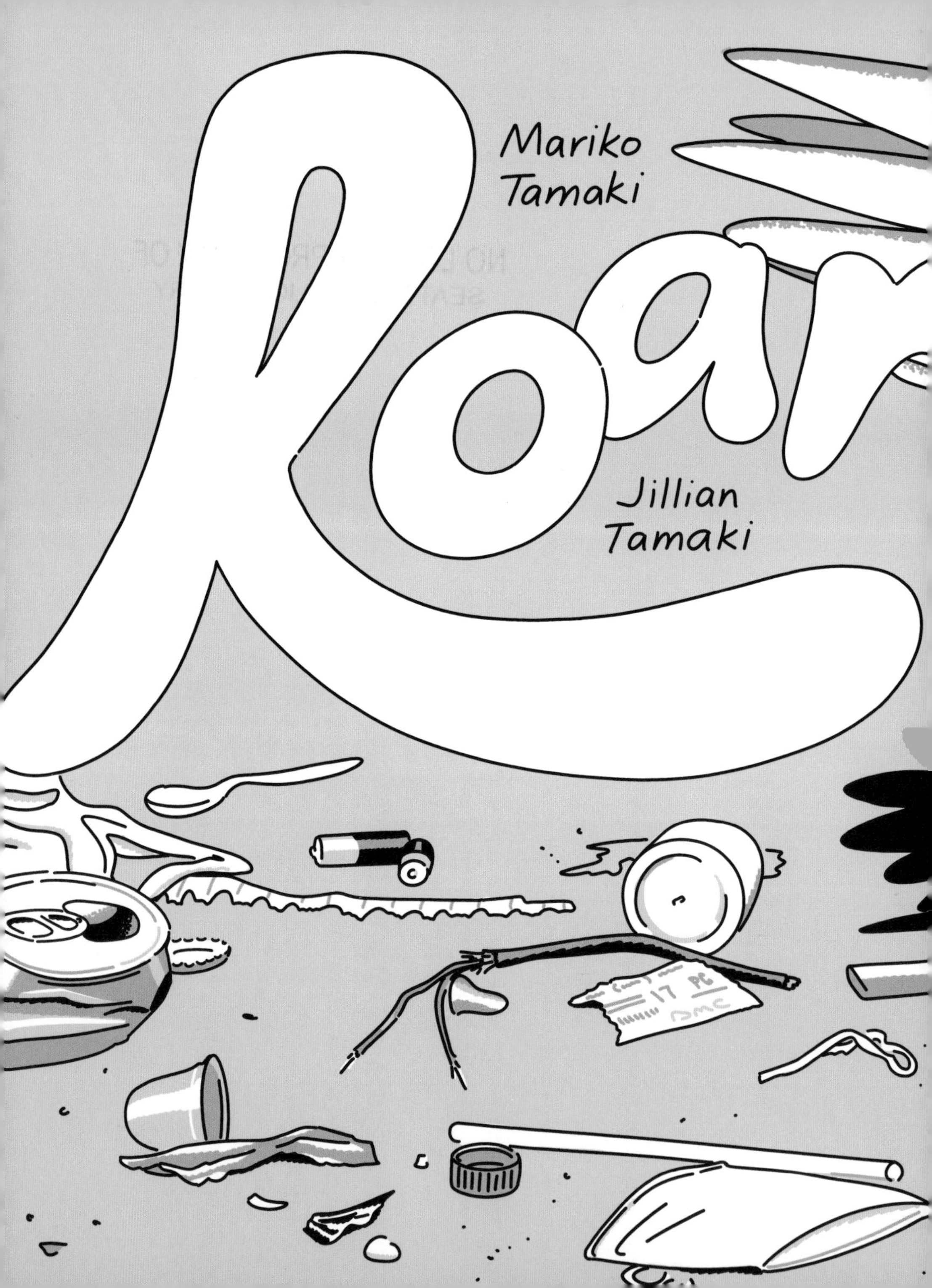
Mariko
Tamaki
Jillian
Tamaki

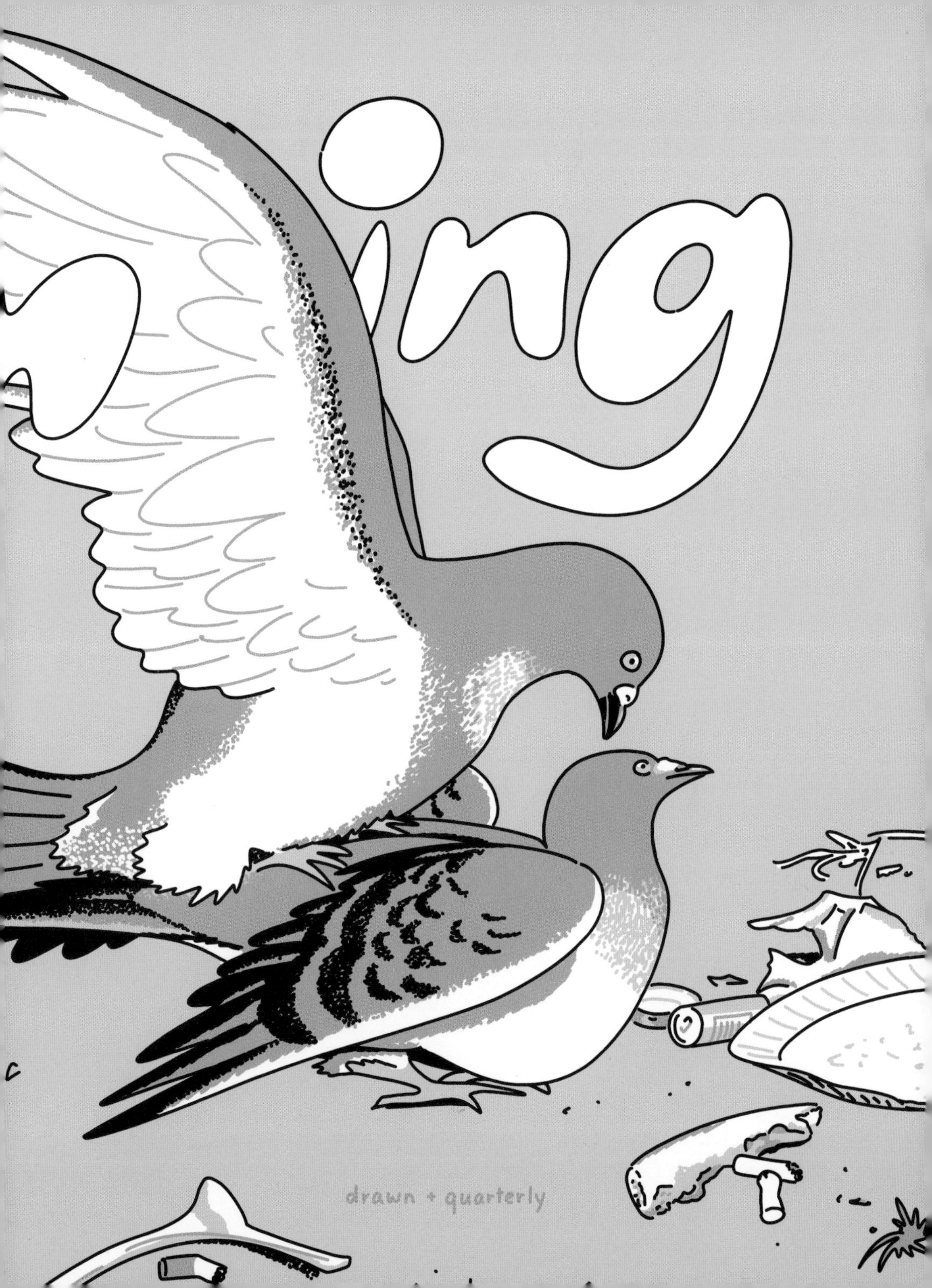
ing
drawn + quarterly

Day 1

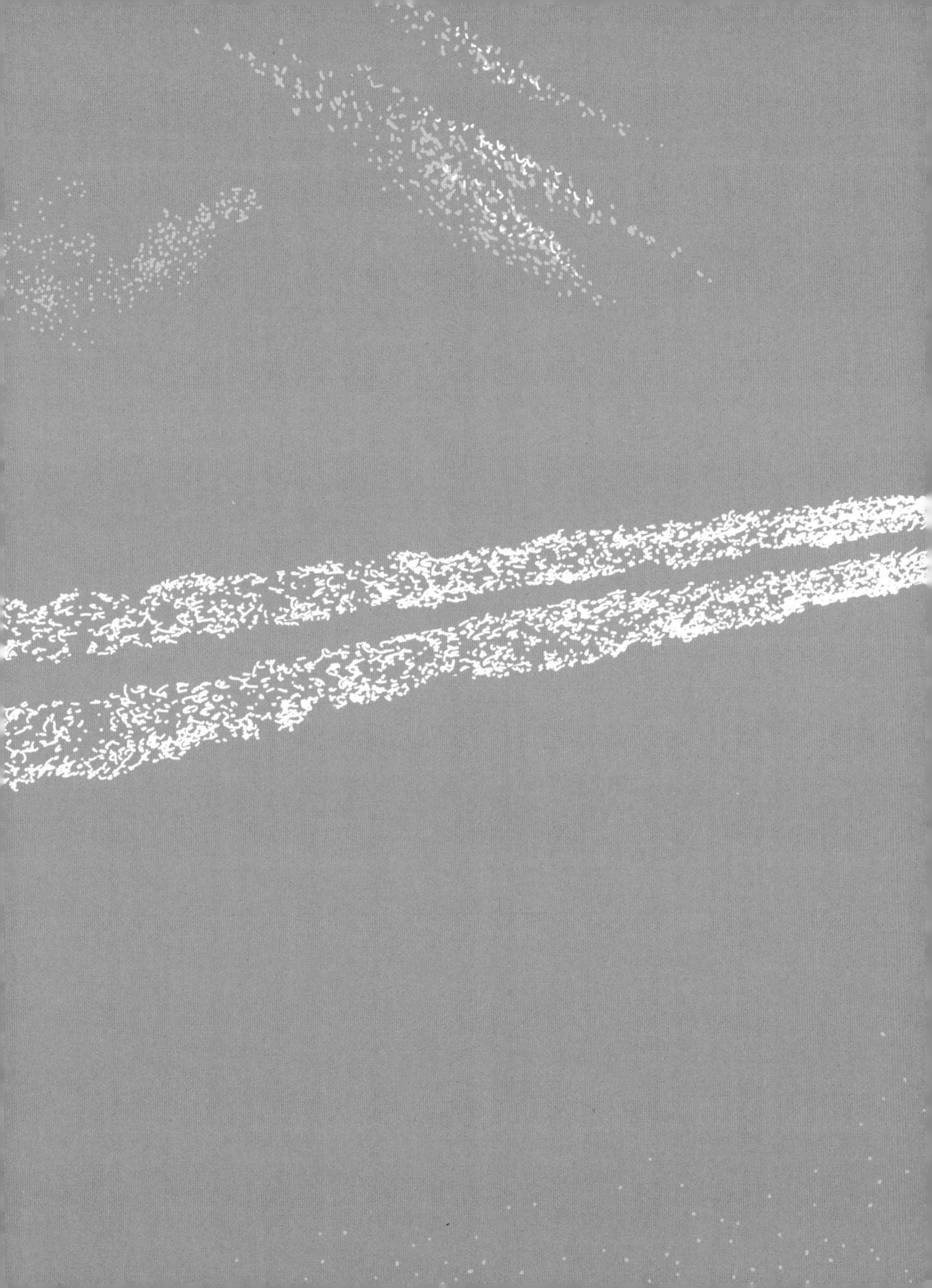

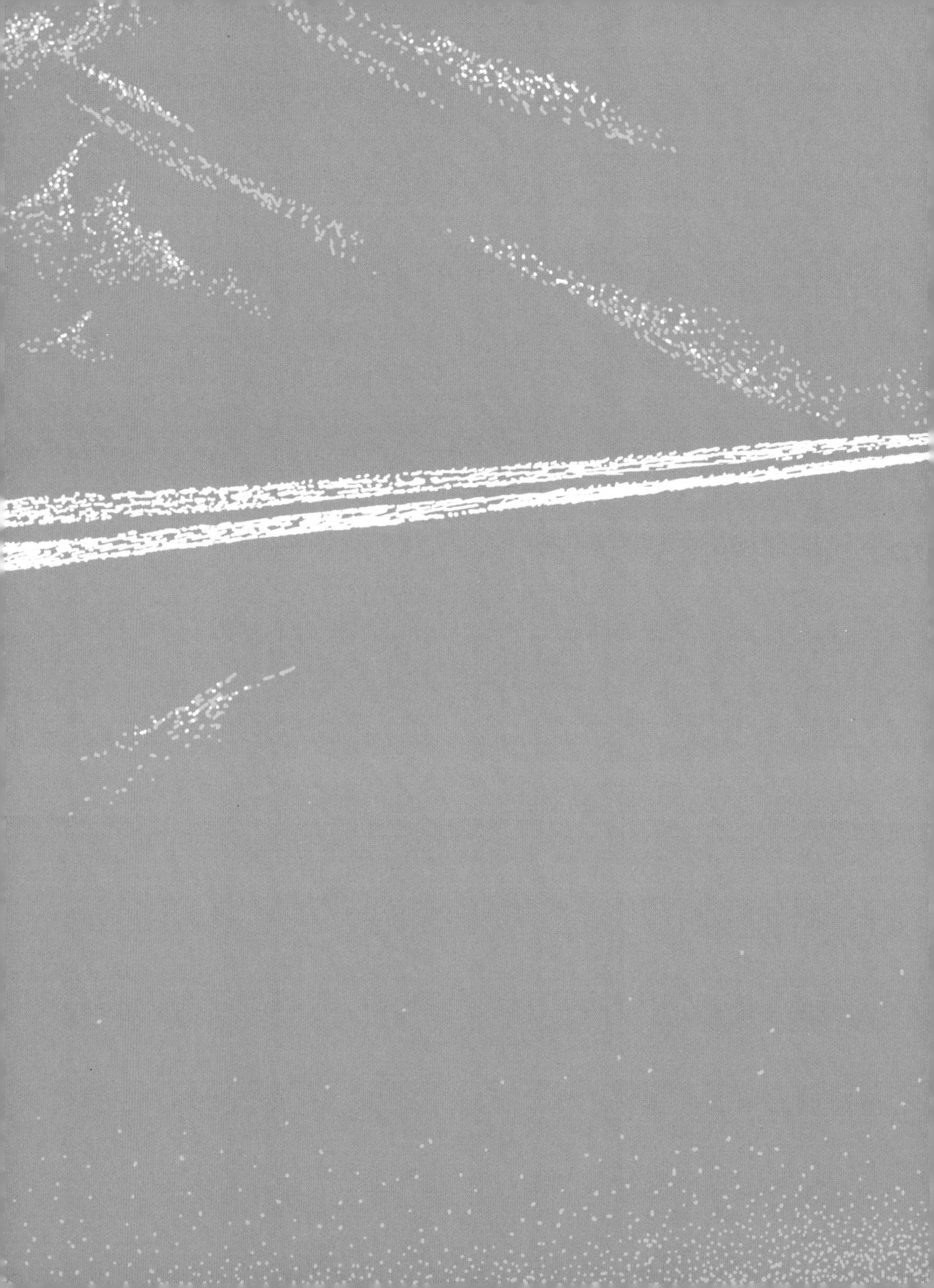

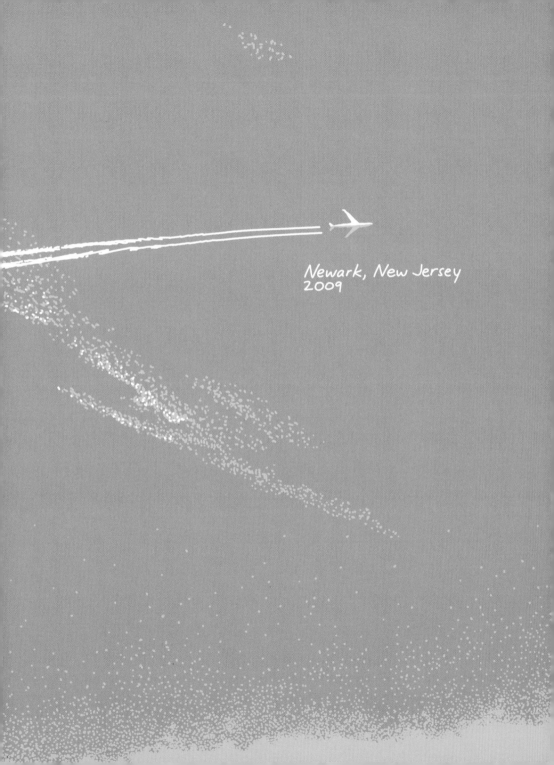

Newark, New Jersey
2009

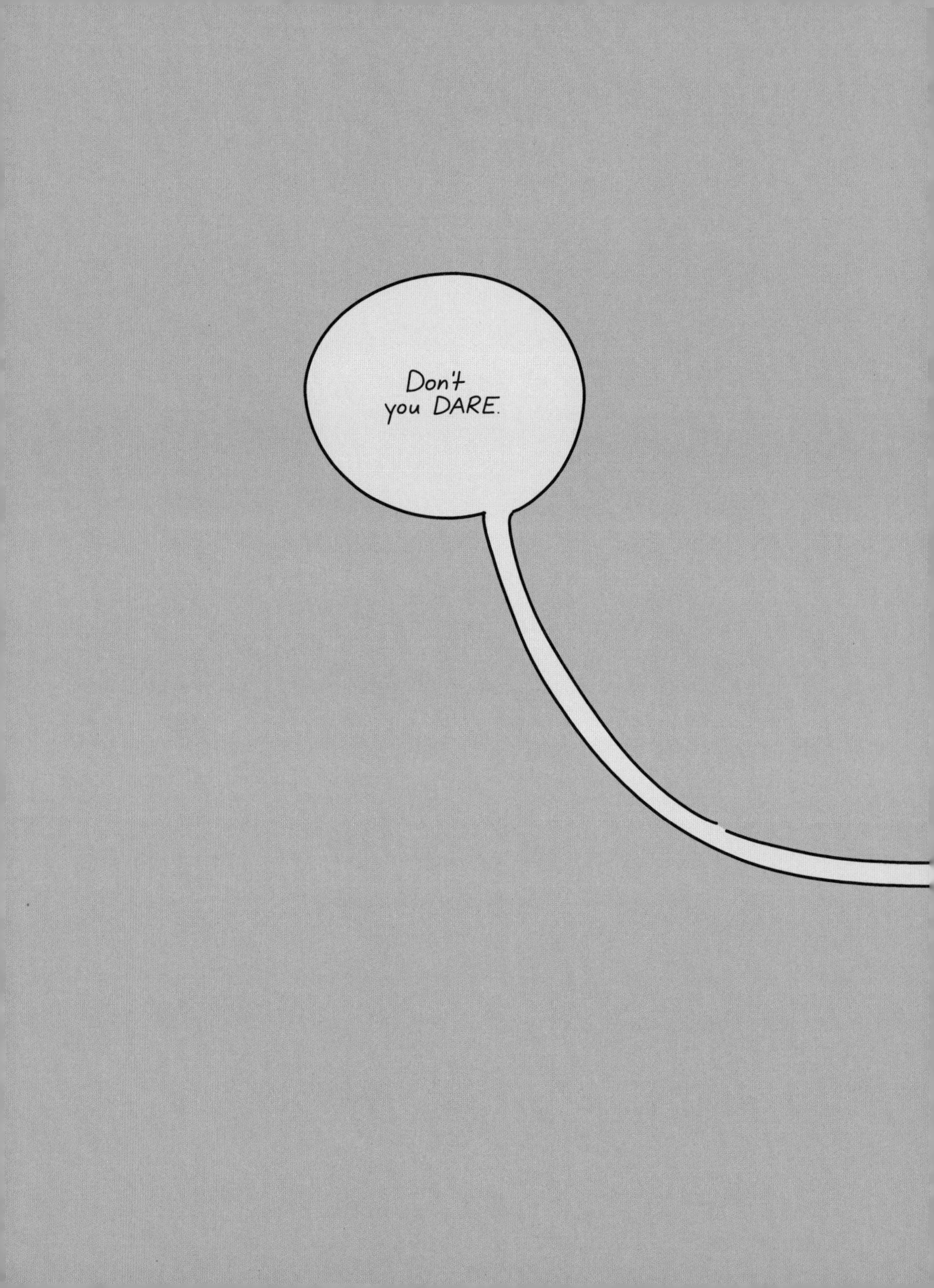
Don't you DARE.

No.

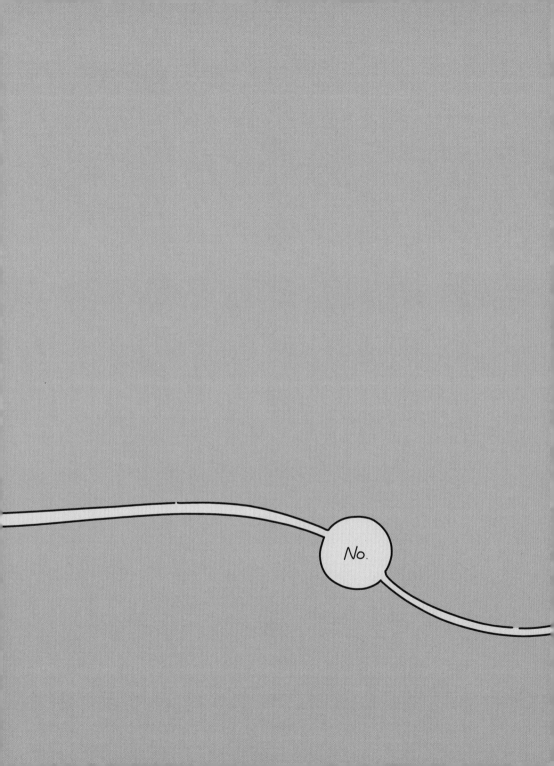

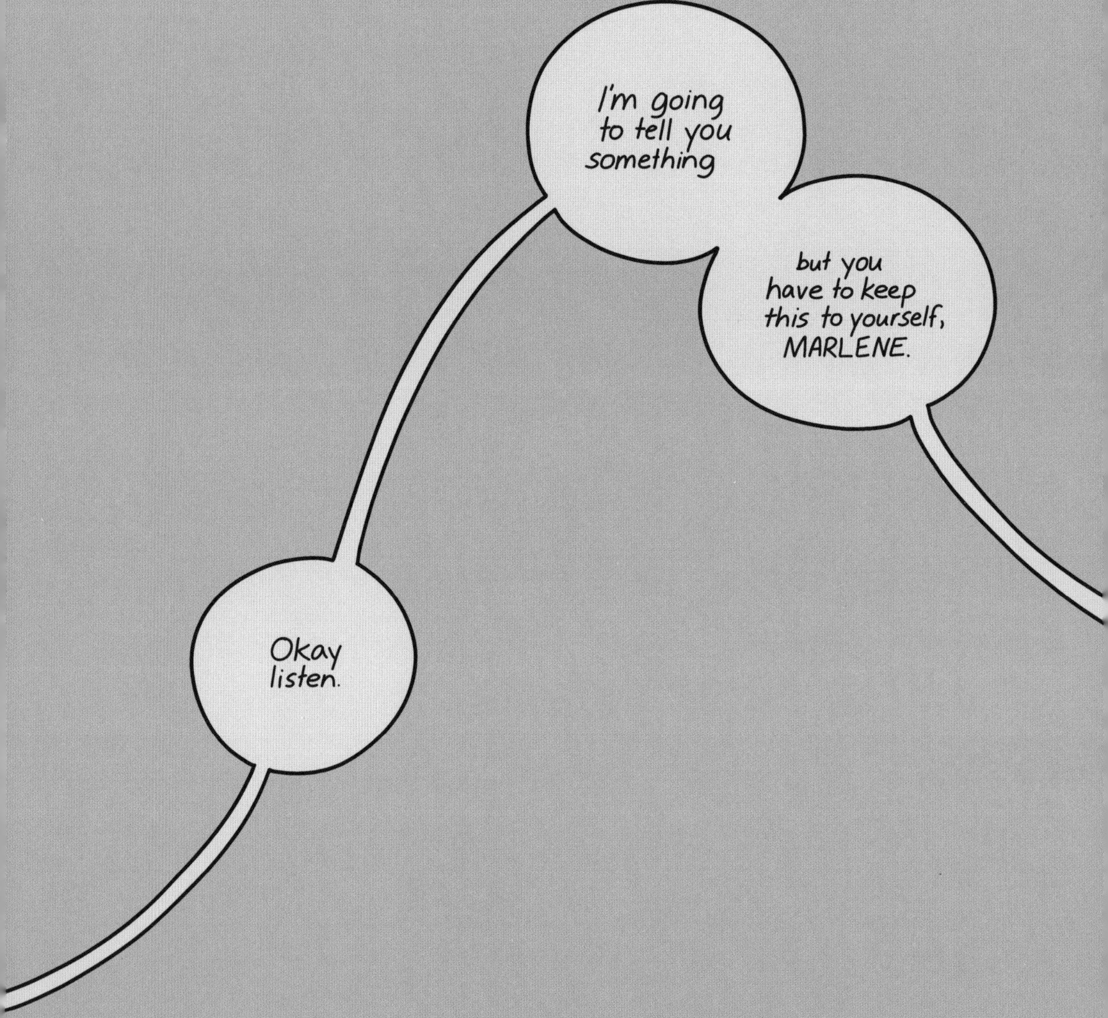
Okay listen.
I'm going to tell you something
but you have to keep this to yourself, MARLENE.

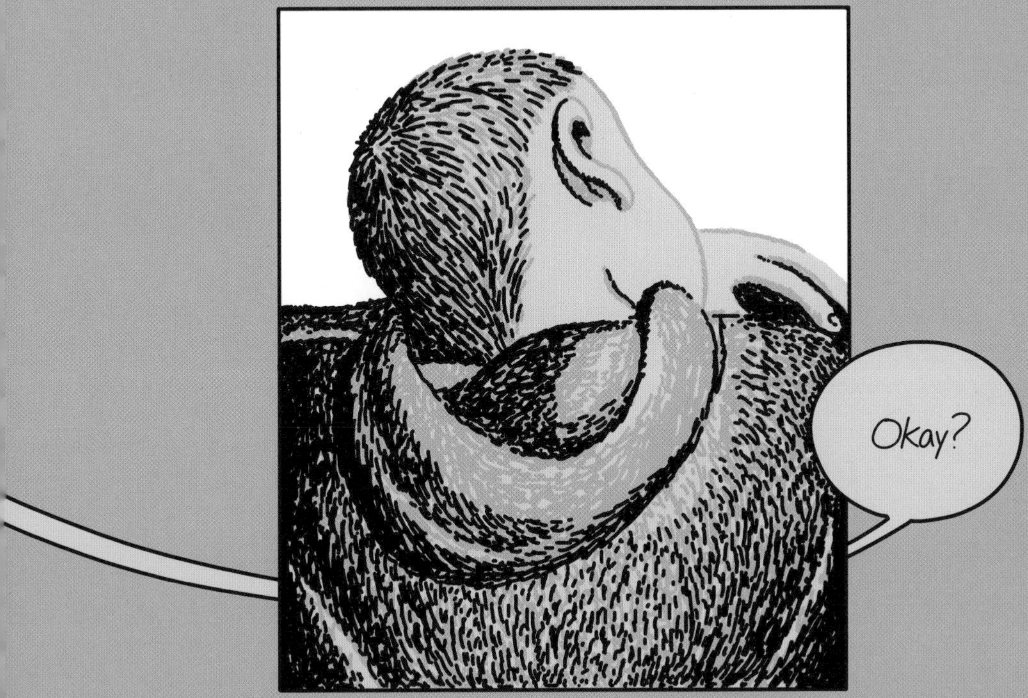
Okay?

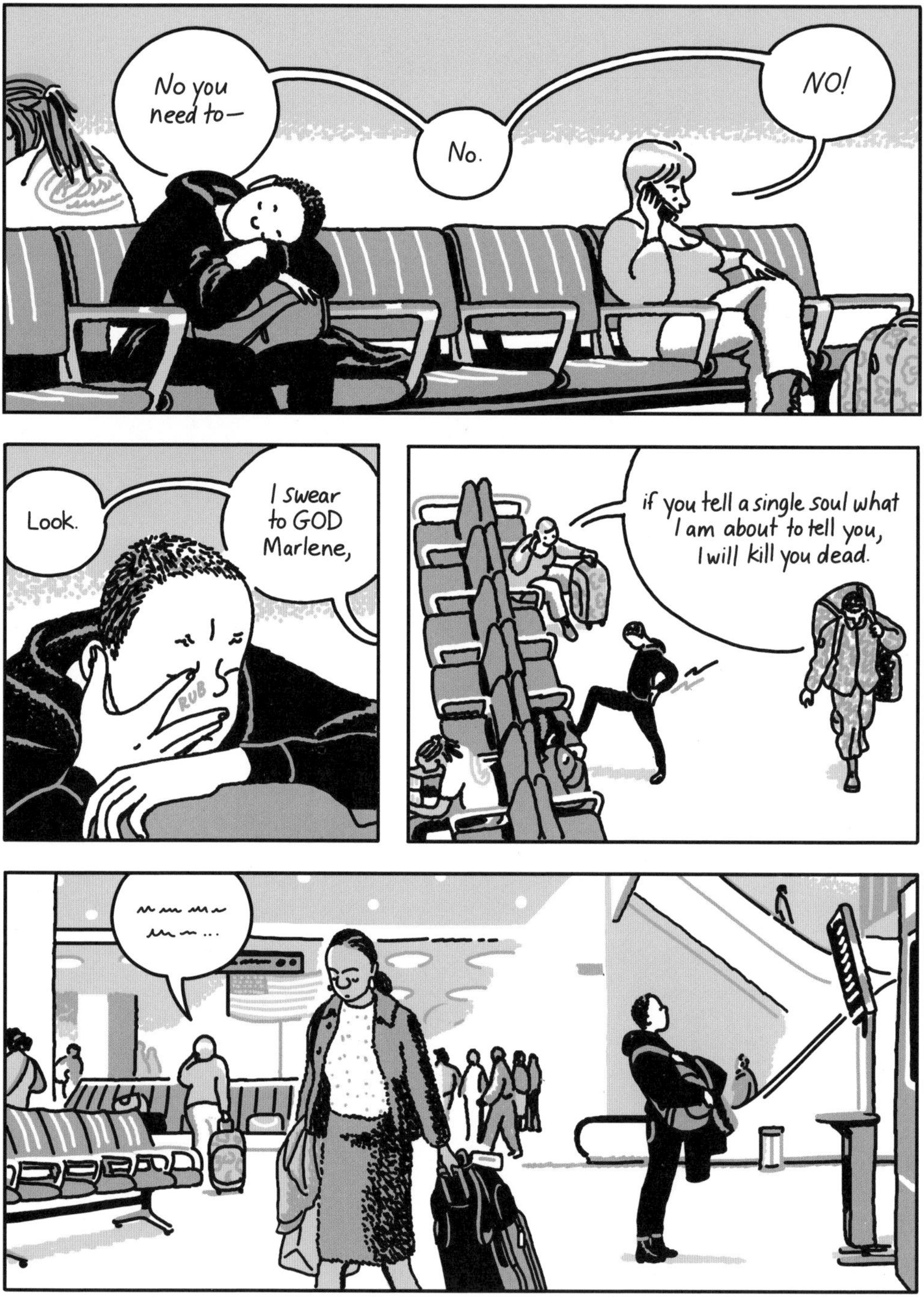
No you need to—
No.
NO!
Look.
I swear to GOD Marlene,
RUB
if you tell a single soul what I am about to tell you, I will kill you dead.

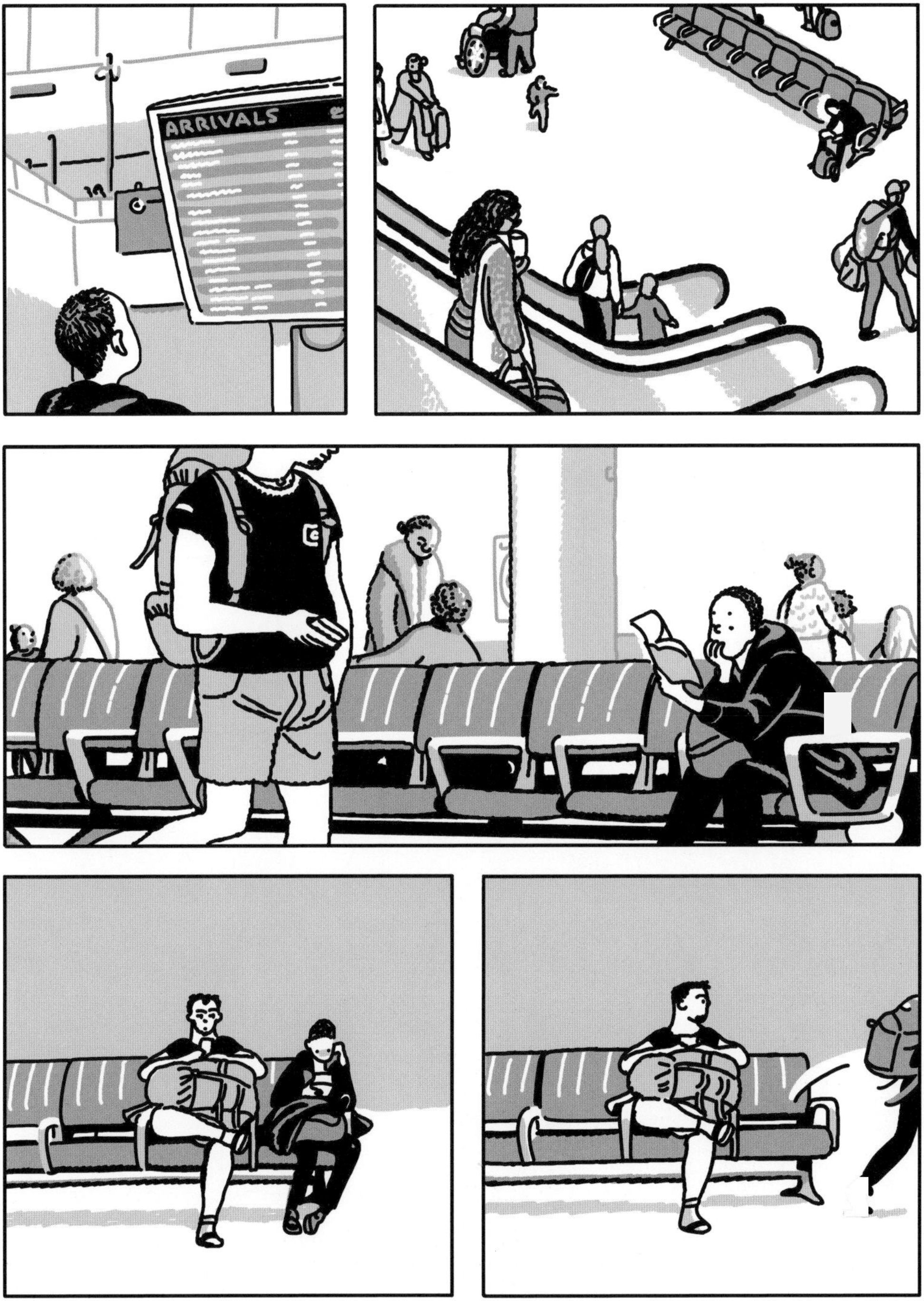
ARRIVALS

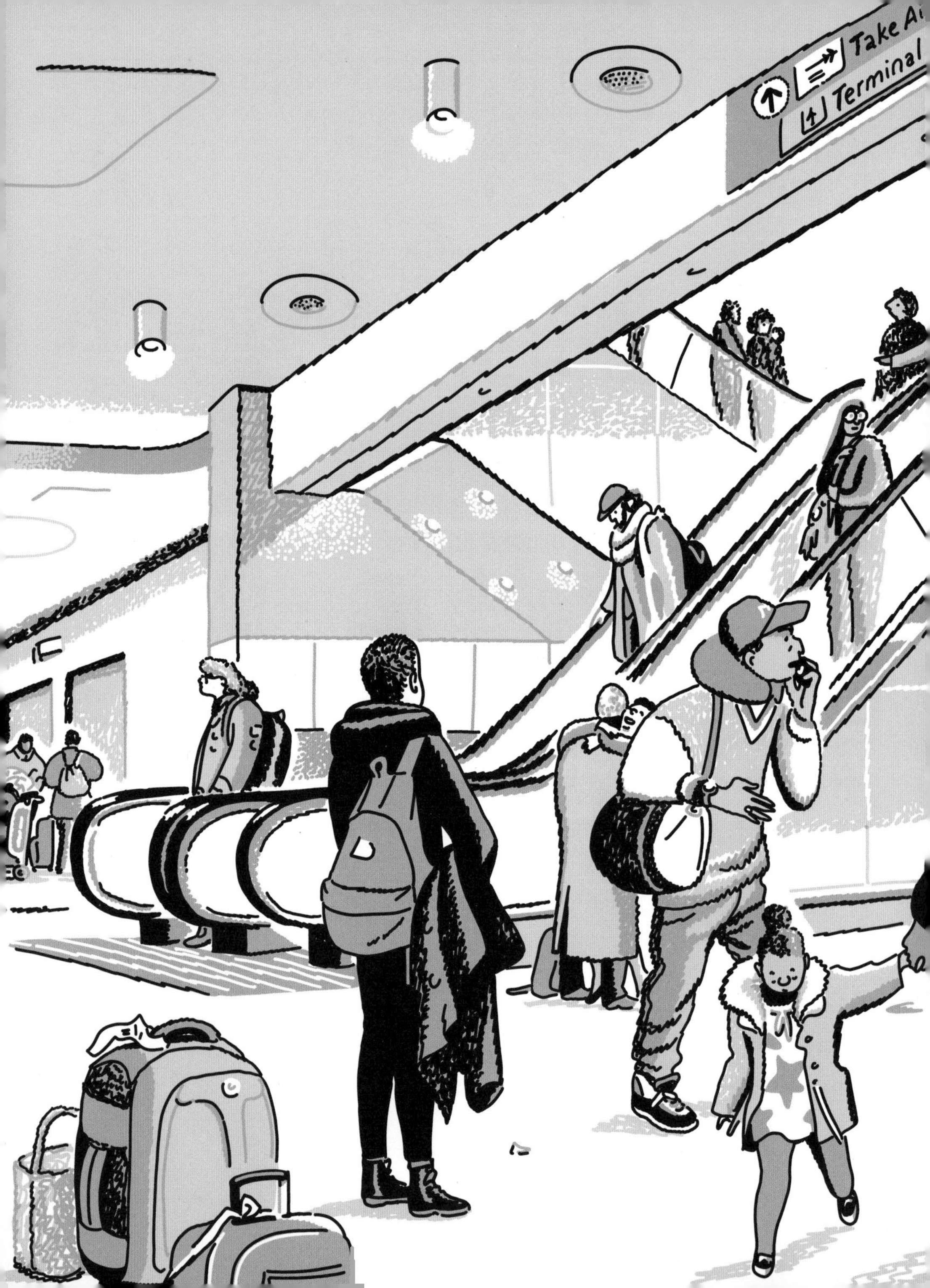
Take Ai
Terminal

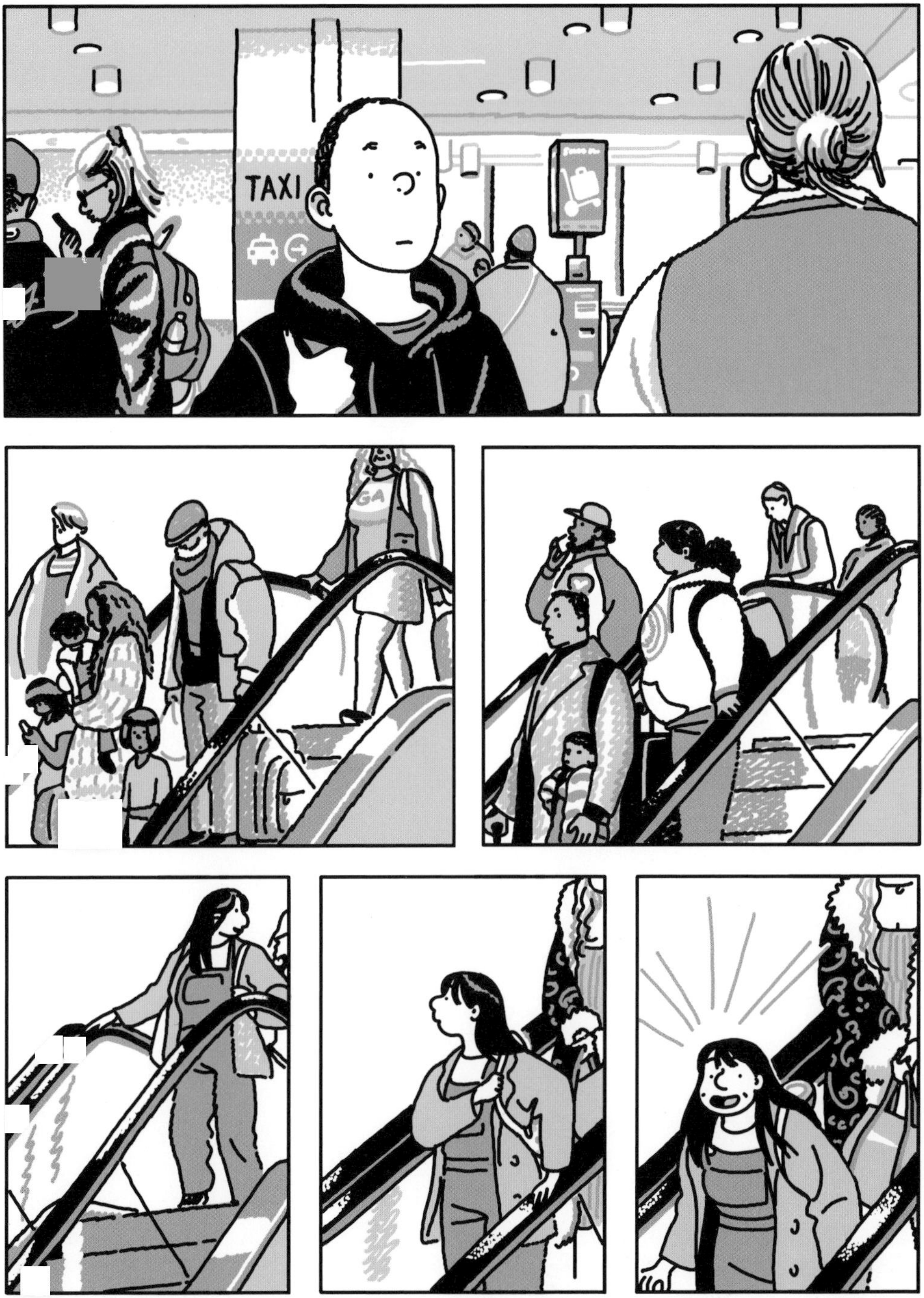
TAXI

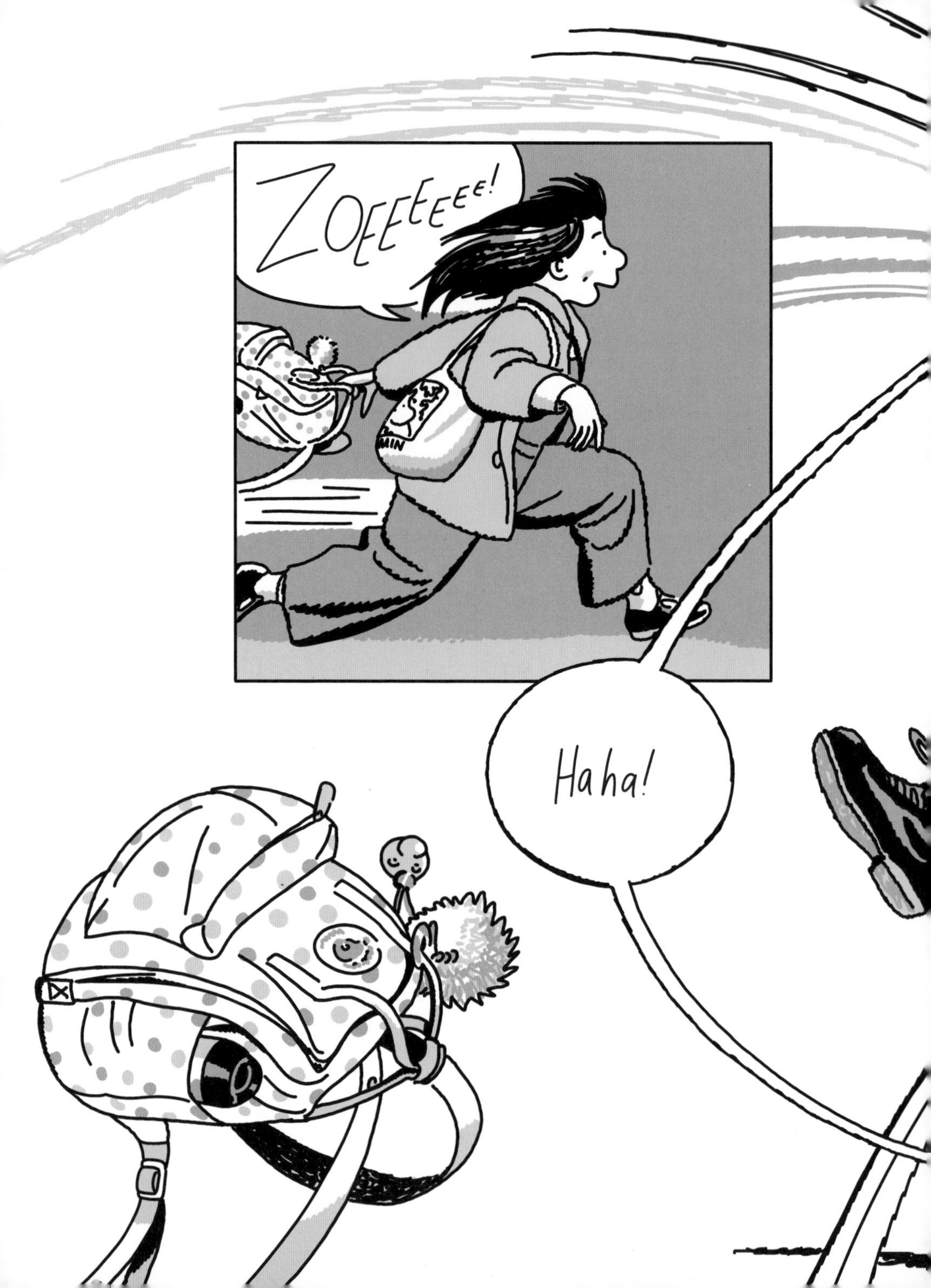
ZOEEEEEE!
Haha!

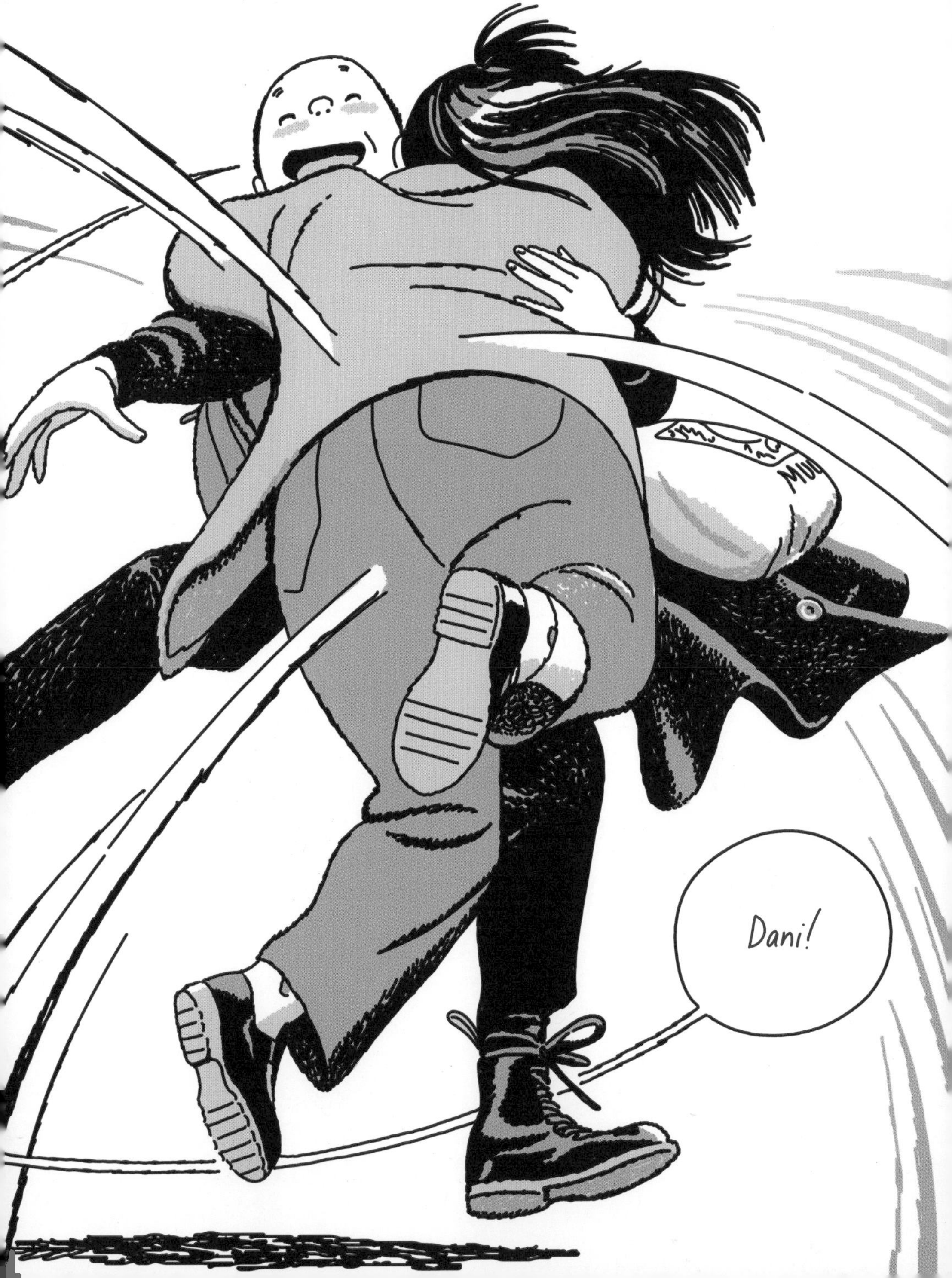
Dani!

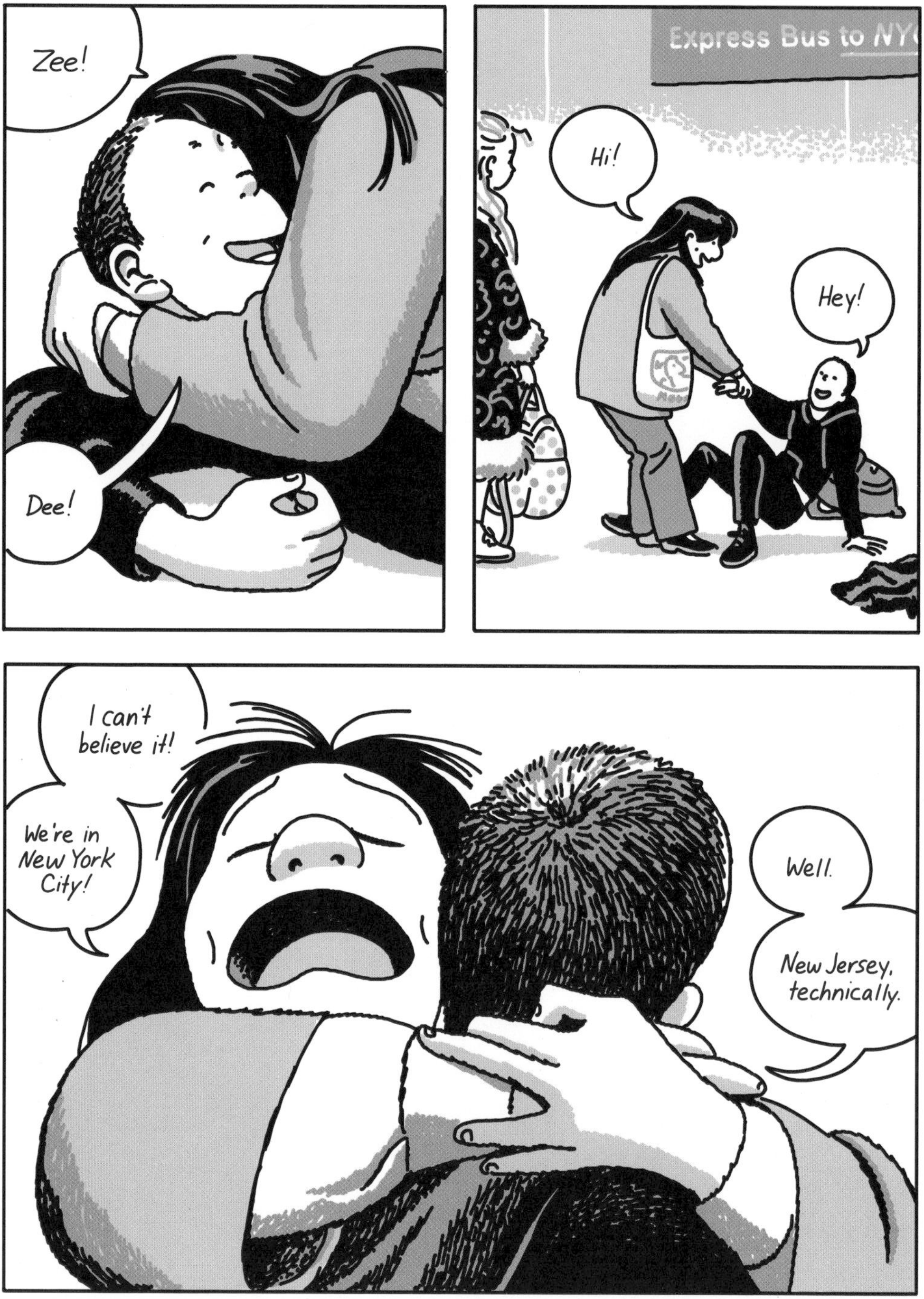
Zee!
Dee!
Express Bus to NY
Hi!
Hey!
I can't believe it!
We're in New York City!
Well.
New Jersey, technically.

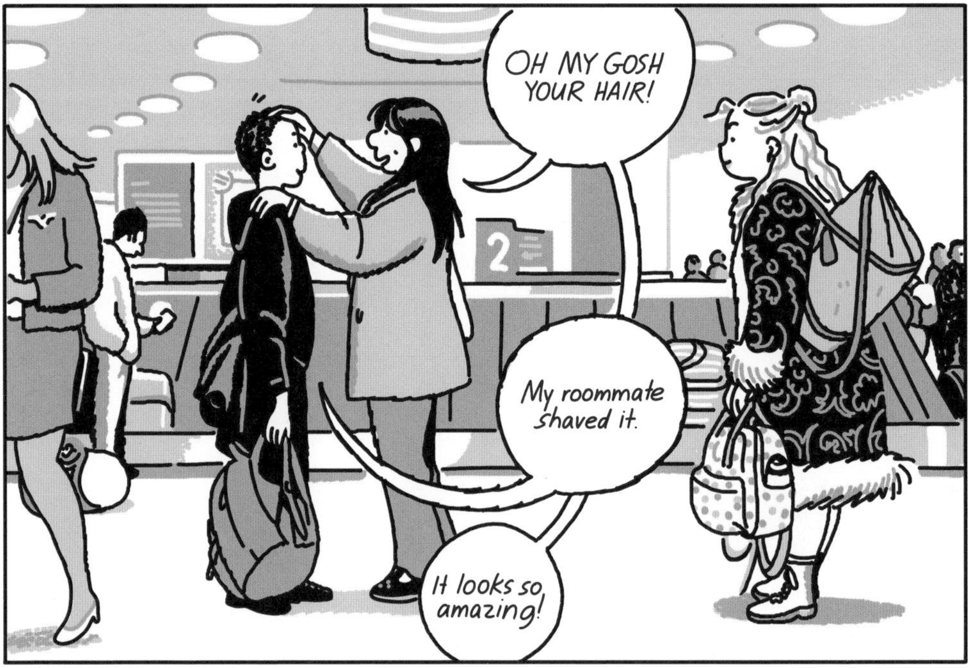
OH MY GOSH YOUR HAIR!
My roommate shaved it.
It looks so amazing!

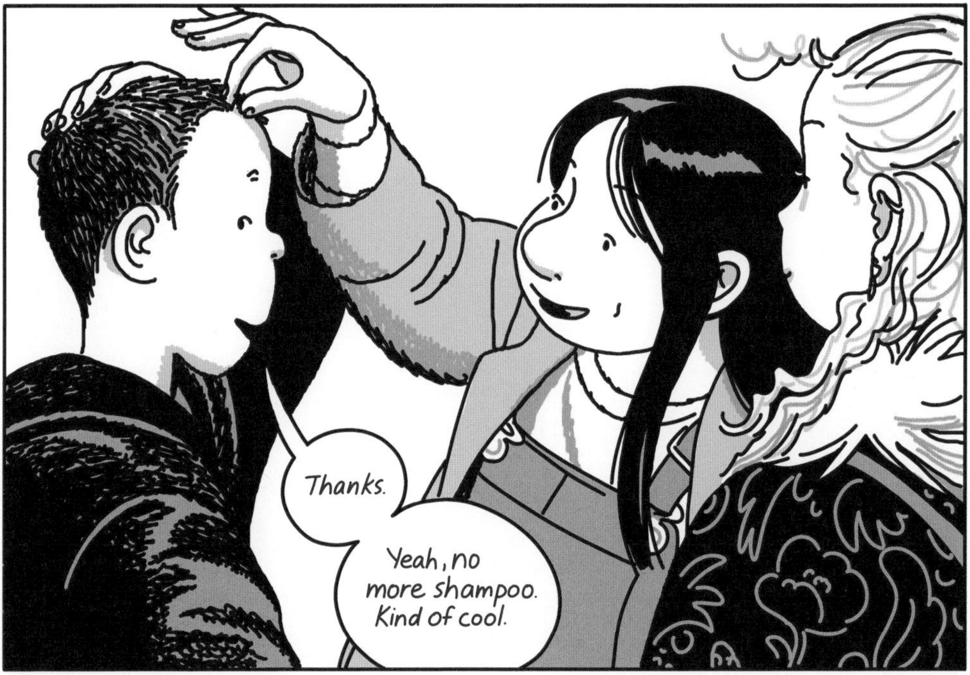
Thanks.
Yeah, no more shampoo. Kind of cool.

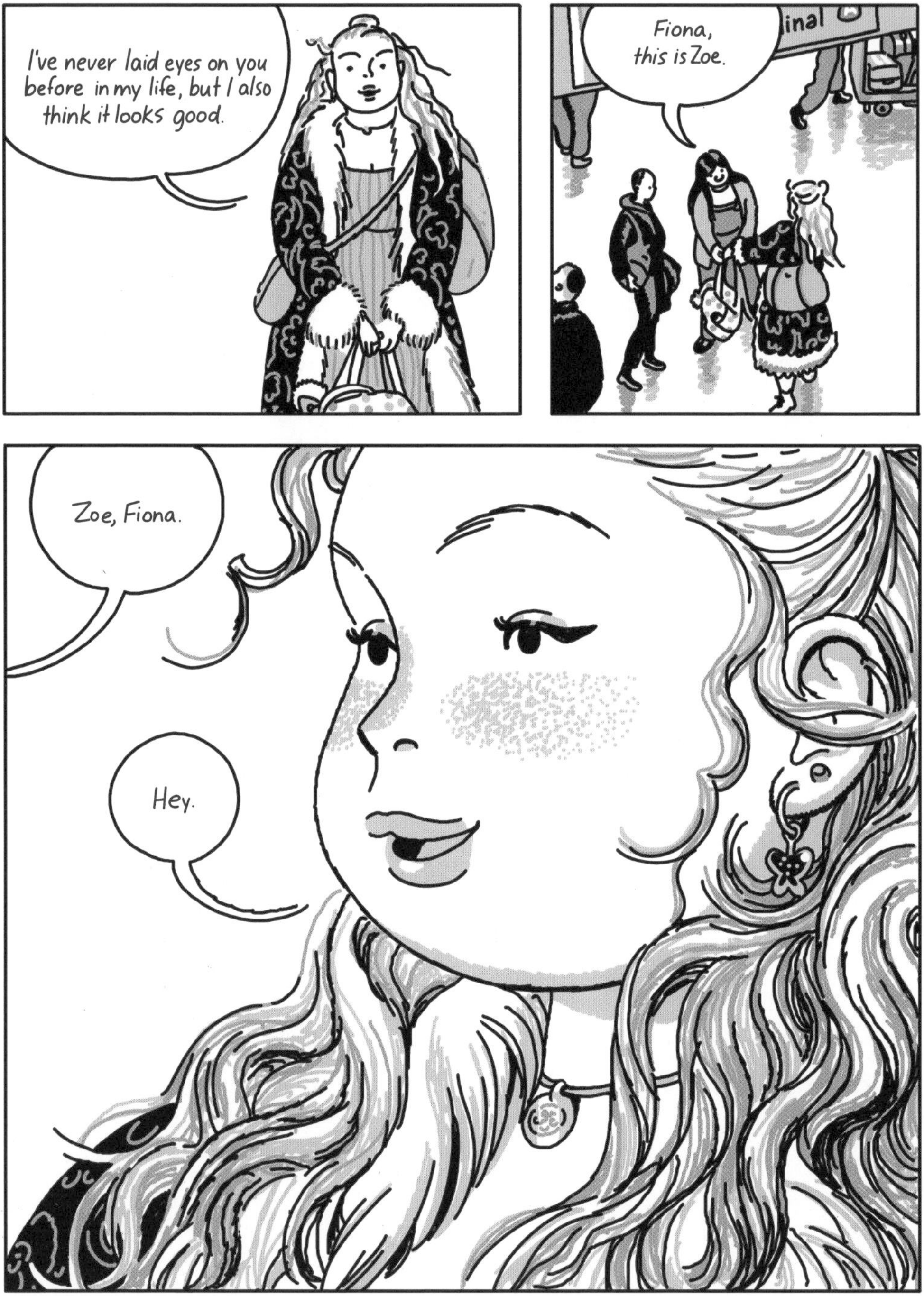
I've never laid eyes on you before in my life, but I also think it looks good.
Fiona, this is Zoe.
Zoe, Fiona.
Hey.

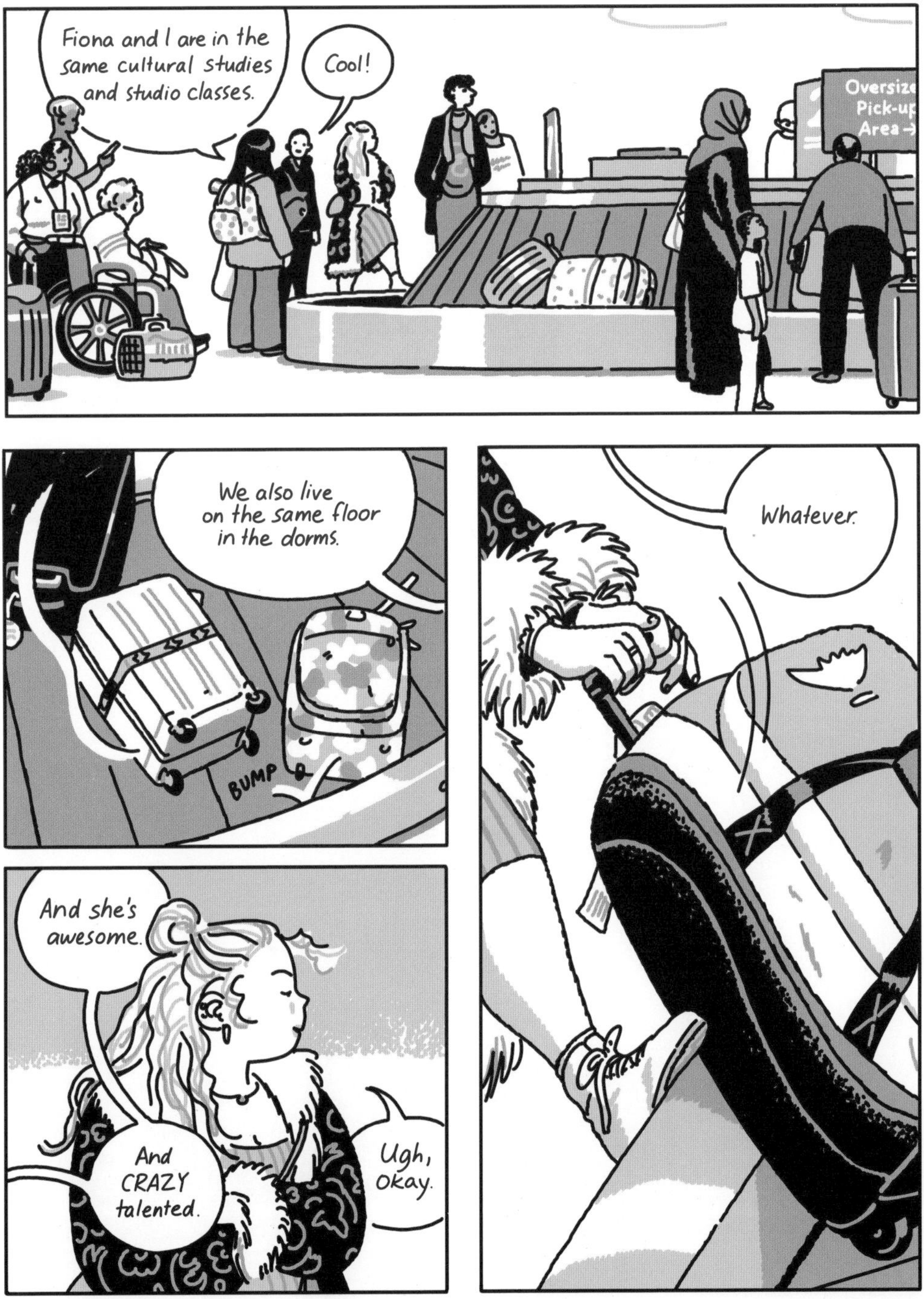
Fiona and I are in the same cultural studies and studio classes.
Cool!
Oversize Pick-up Area →
We also live on the same floor in the dorms.
BUMP
Whatever.
And she's awesome.
And CRAZY talented.
Ugh, okay.

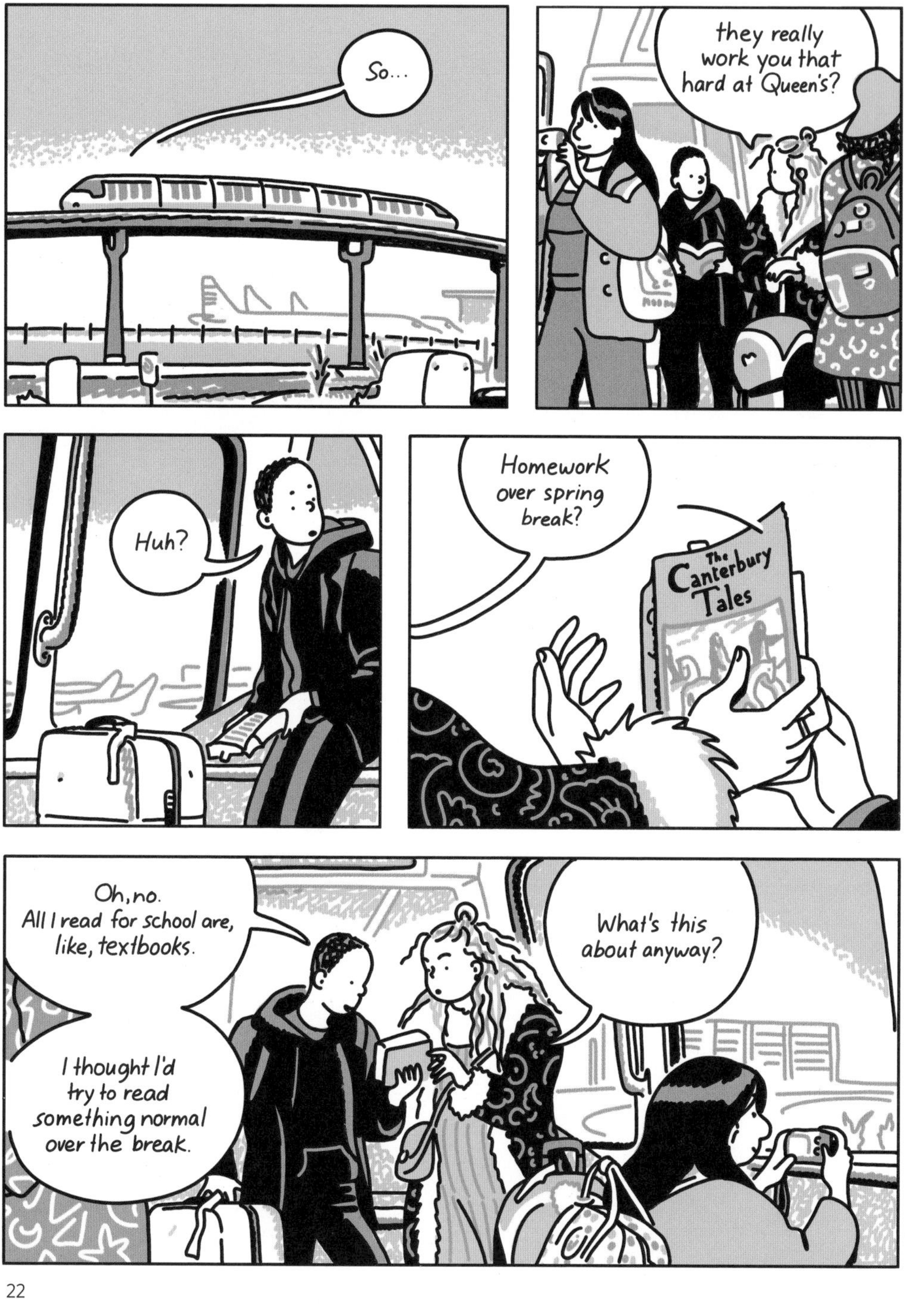
So...
they really work you that hard at Queen's?
Huh?
Homework over spring break?
The Canterbury Tales
Oh, no. All I read for school are, like, textbooks.
I thought I'd try to read something normal over the break.
What's this about anyway?

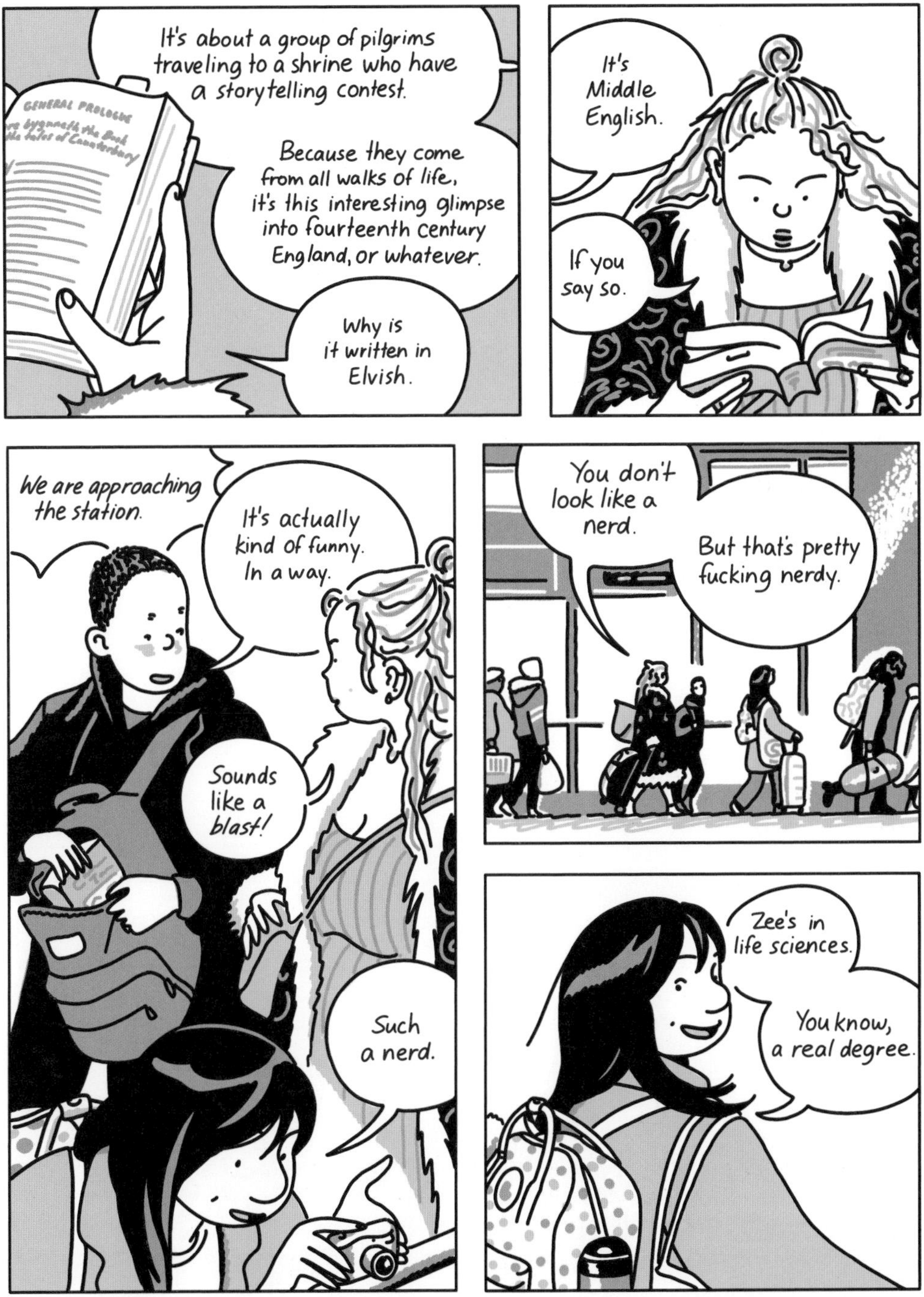
It's about a group of pilgrims traveling to a shrine who have a storytelling contest.
Because they come from all walks of life, it's this interesting glimpse into fourteenth century England, or whatever.
Why is it written in Elvish.
It's Middle English.
If you say so.
We are approaching the station.
It's actually kind of funny. In a way.
Sounds like a blast!
Such a nerd.
You don't look like a nerd.
But that's pretty fucking nerdy.
Zee's in life sciences.
You know, a real degree.

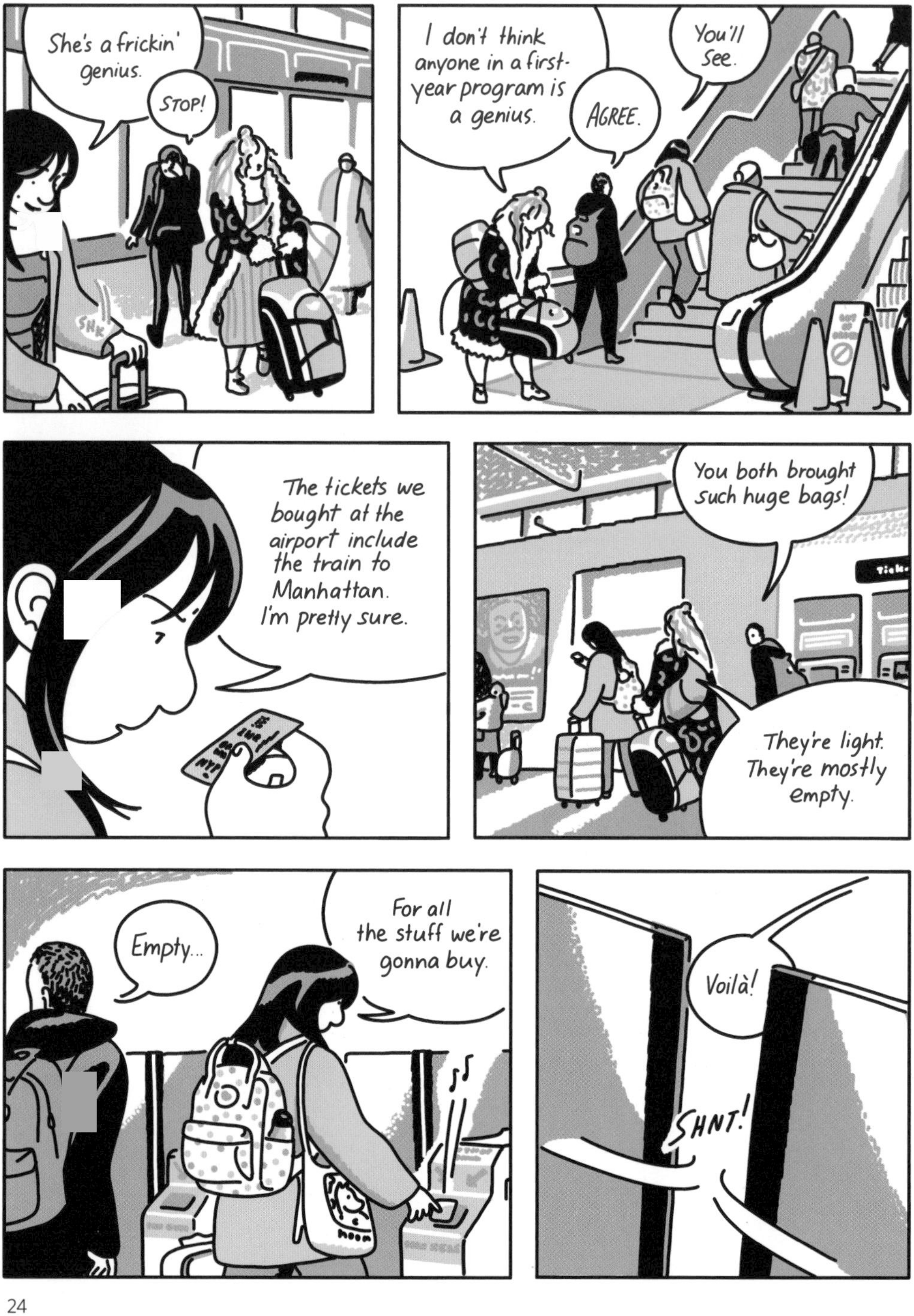
She's a frickin' genius.
STOP!
SHK
I don't think anyone in a first-year program is a genius.
AGREE.
You'll See.
The tickets we bought at the airport include the train to Manhattan. I'm pretty sure.
You both brought such huge bags!
They're light. They're mostly empty.
Empty...
For all the stuff we're gonna buy.
Voilà!
SHNT!

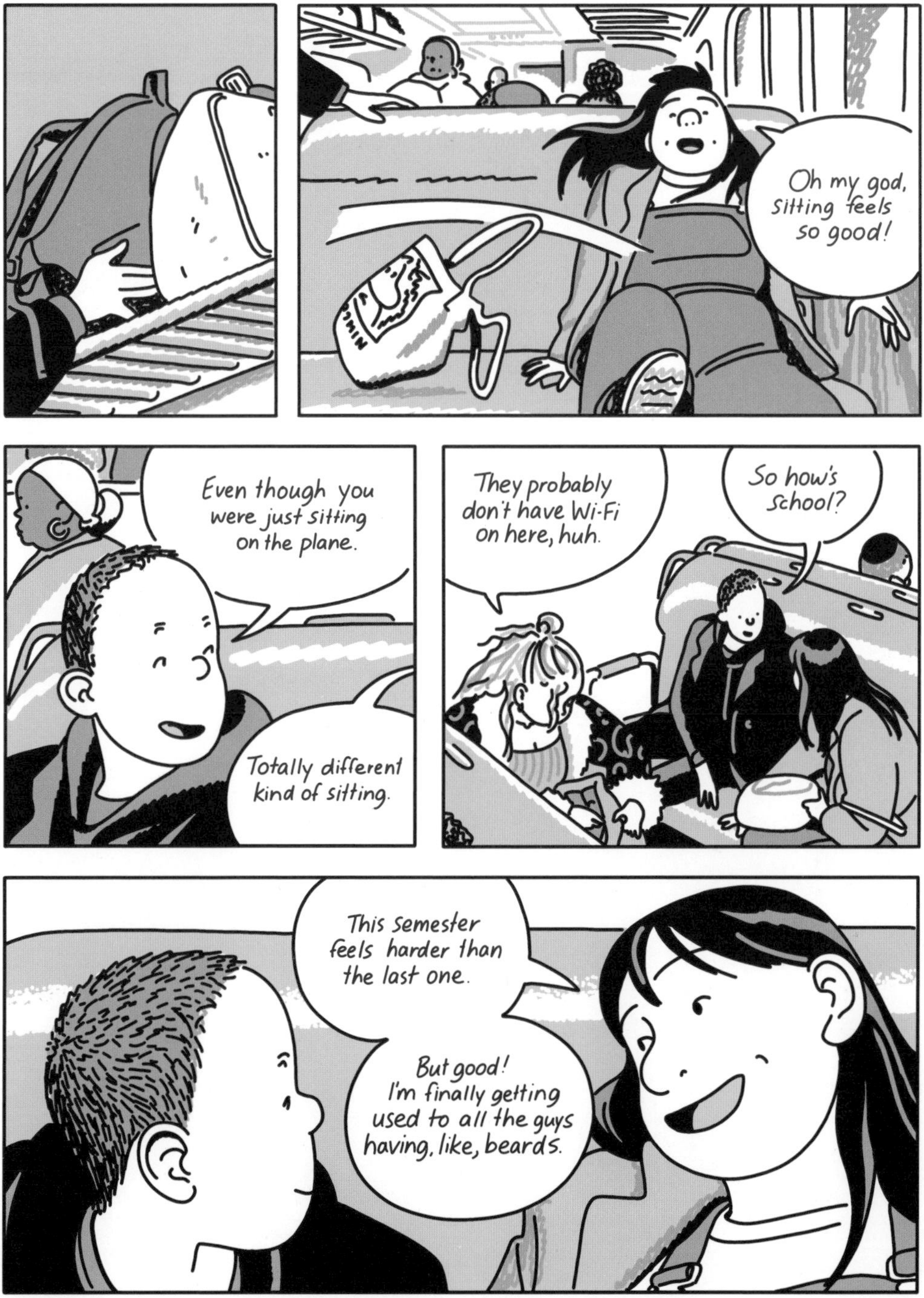
Oh my god, sitting feels so good!
Even though you were just sitting on the plane.
Totally different kind of sitting.
They probably don't have Wi-Fi on here, huh.
So how's school?
This semester feels harder than the last one.
But good! I'm finally getting used to all the guys having, like, beards.

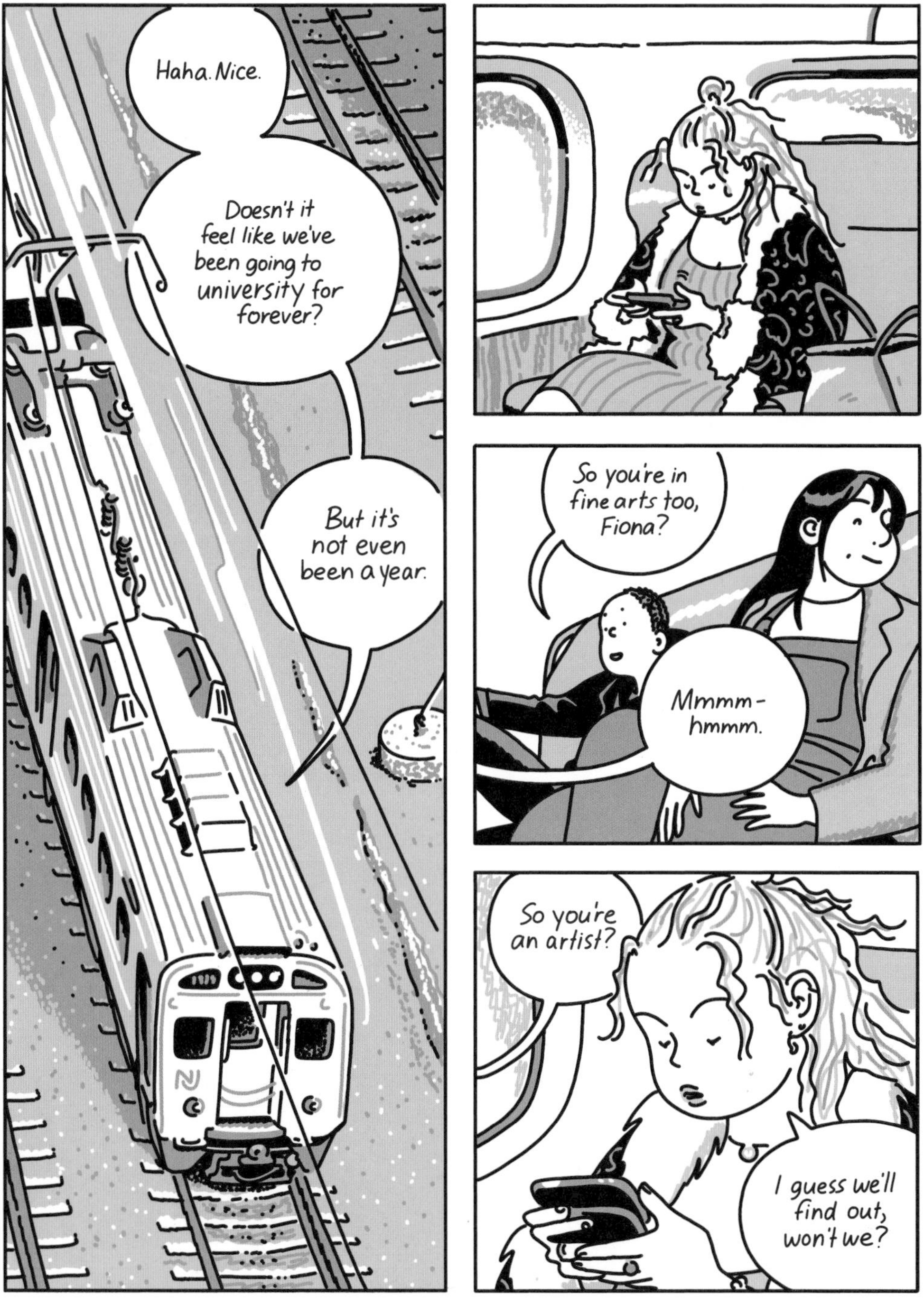
Haha. Nice.
Doesn't it feel like we've been going to university for forever?
But it's not even been a year.
So you're in fine arts too, Fiona?
Mmmm-hmmm.
So you're an artist?
I guess we'll find out, won't we?

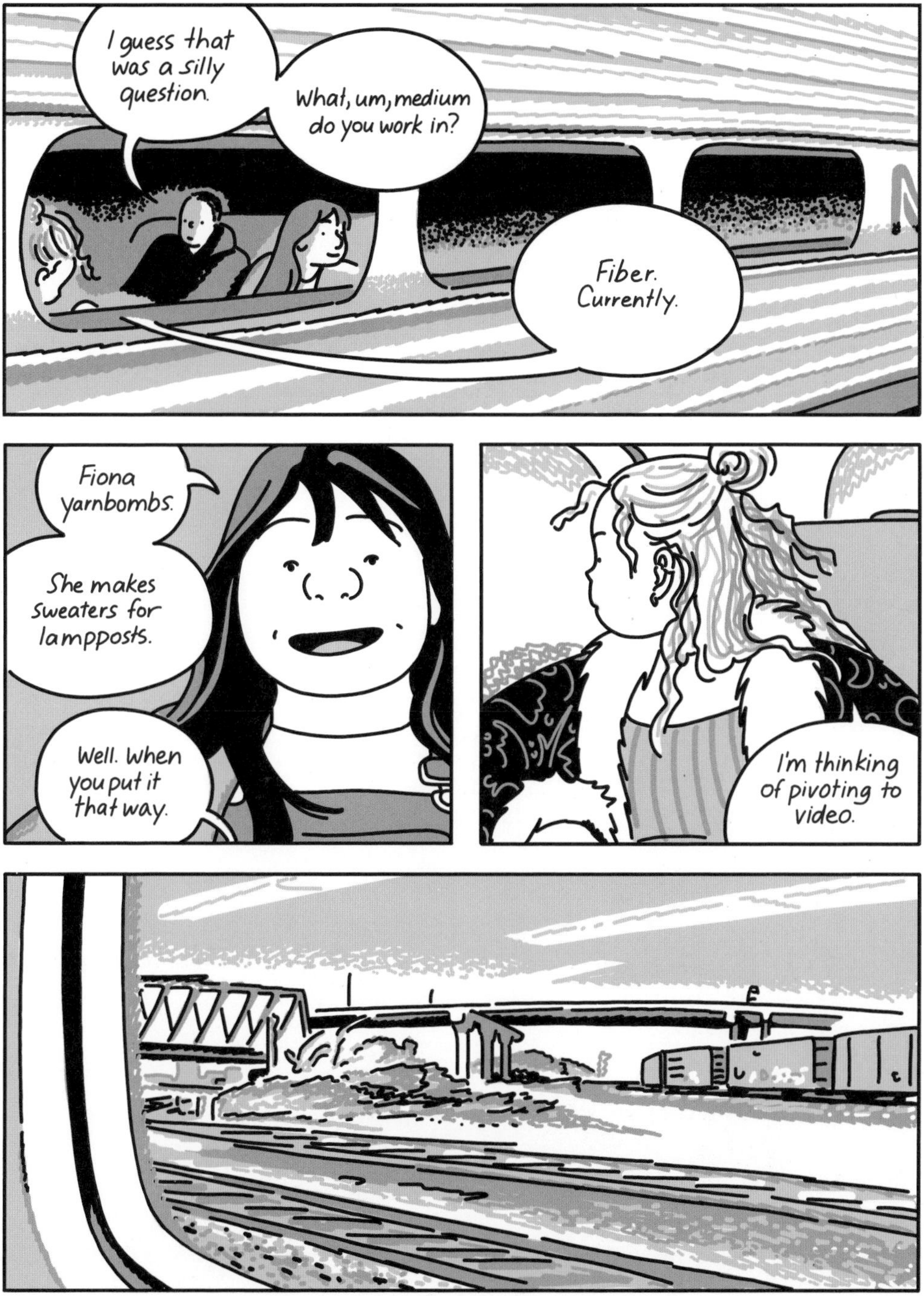
I guess that was a silly question.
What, um, medium do you work in?
Fiber. Currently.
Fiona yarnbombs.
She makes sweaters for lampposts.
Well. When you put it that way.
I'm thinking of pivoting to video.

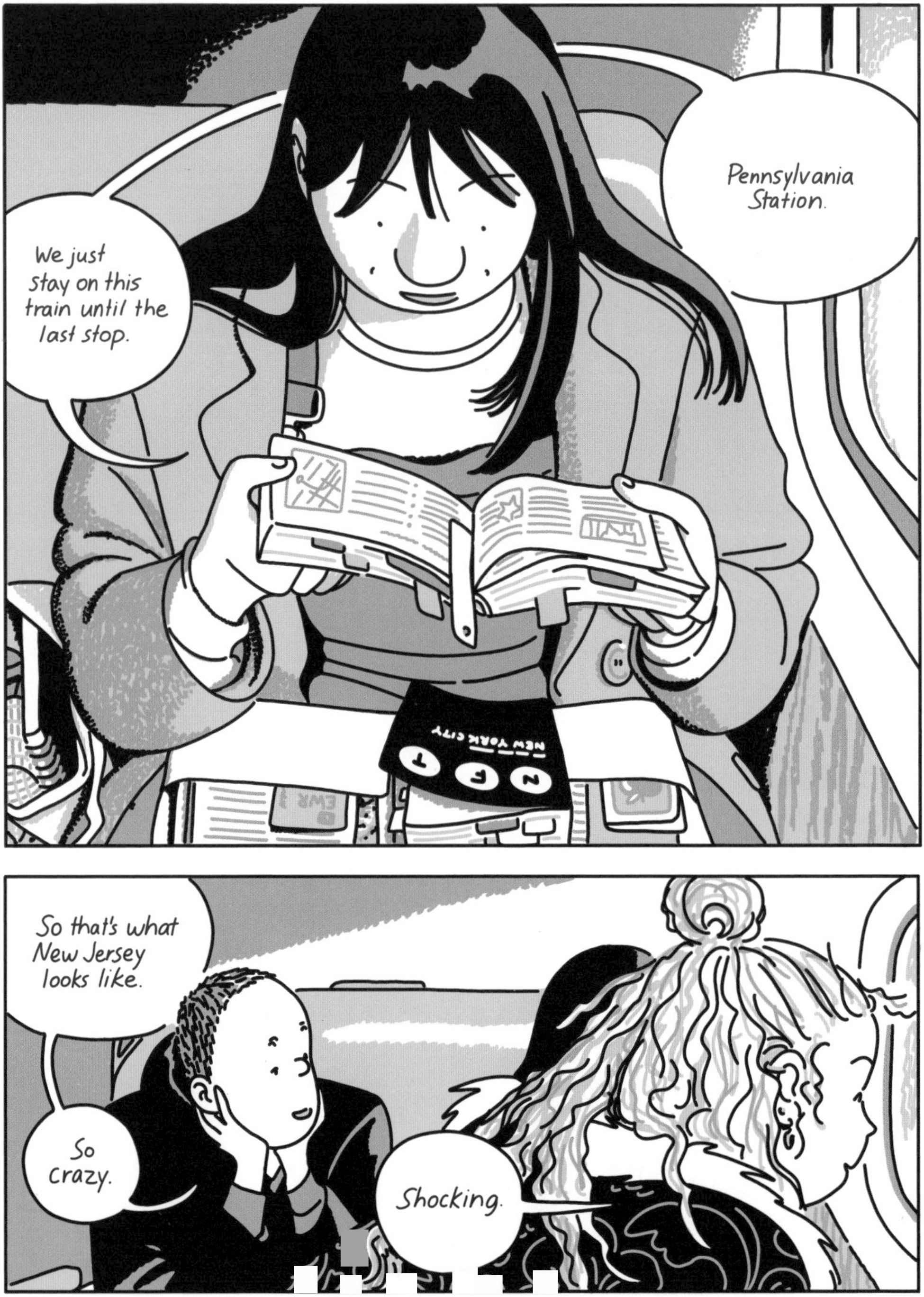
We just stay on this train until the last stop.
Pennsylvania Station.
So that's what New Jersey looks like.
So crazy.
Shocking.

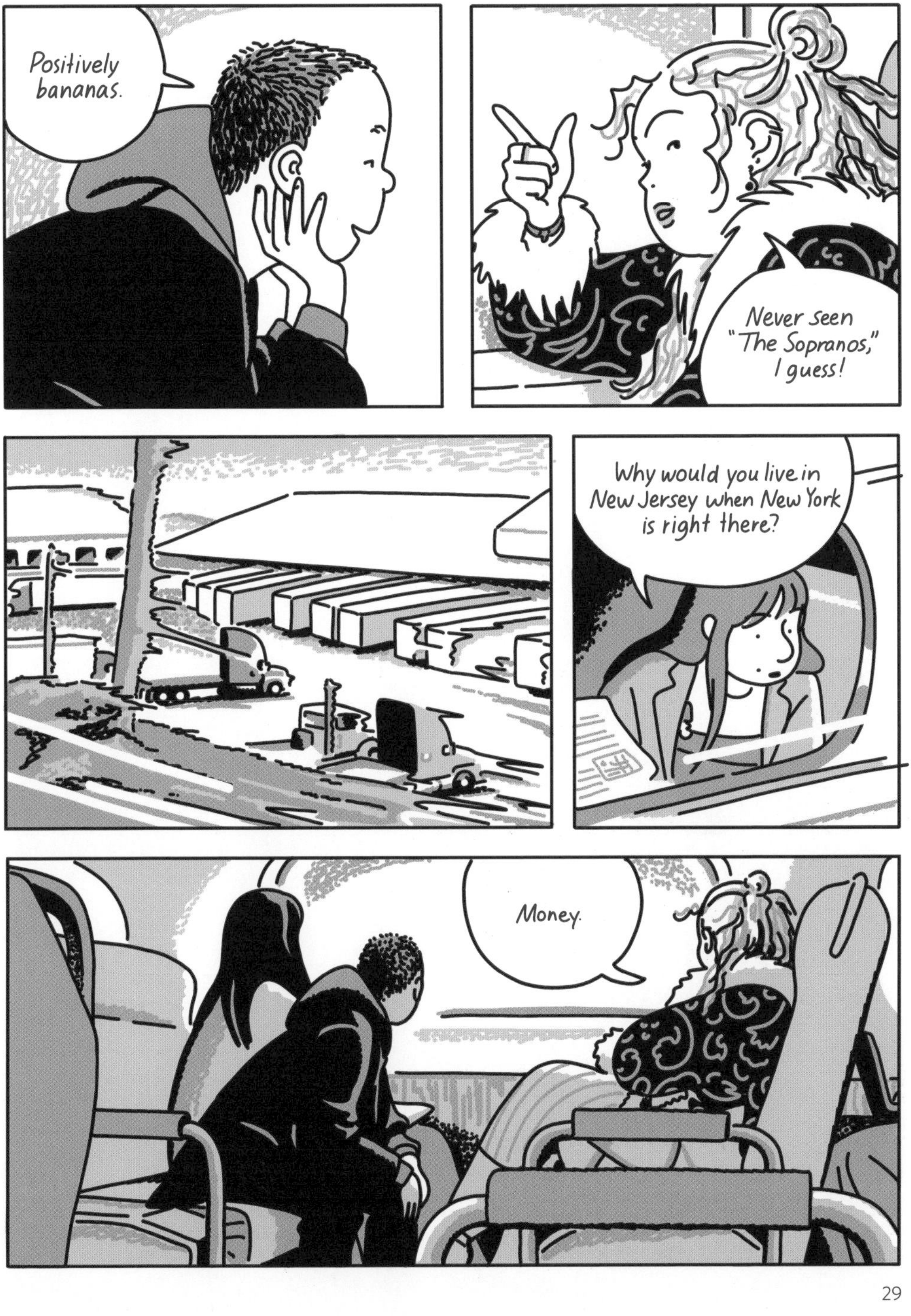
Positively bananas.
Never seen "The Sopranos," I guess!
Why would you live in New Jersey when New York is right there?
Money.

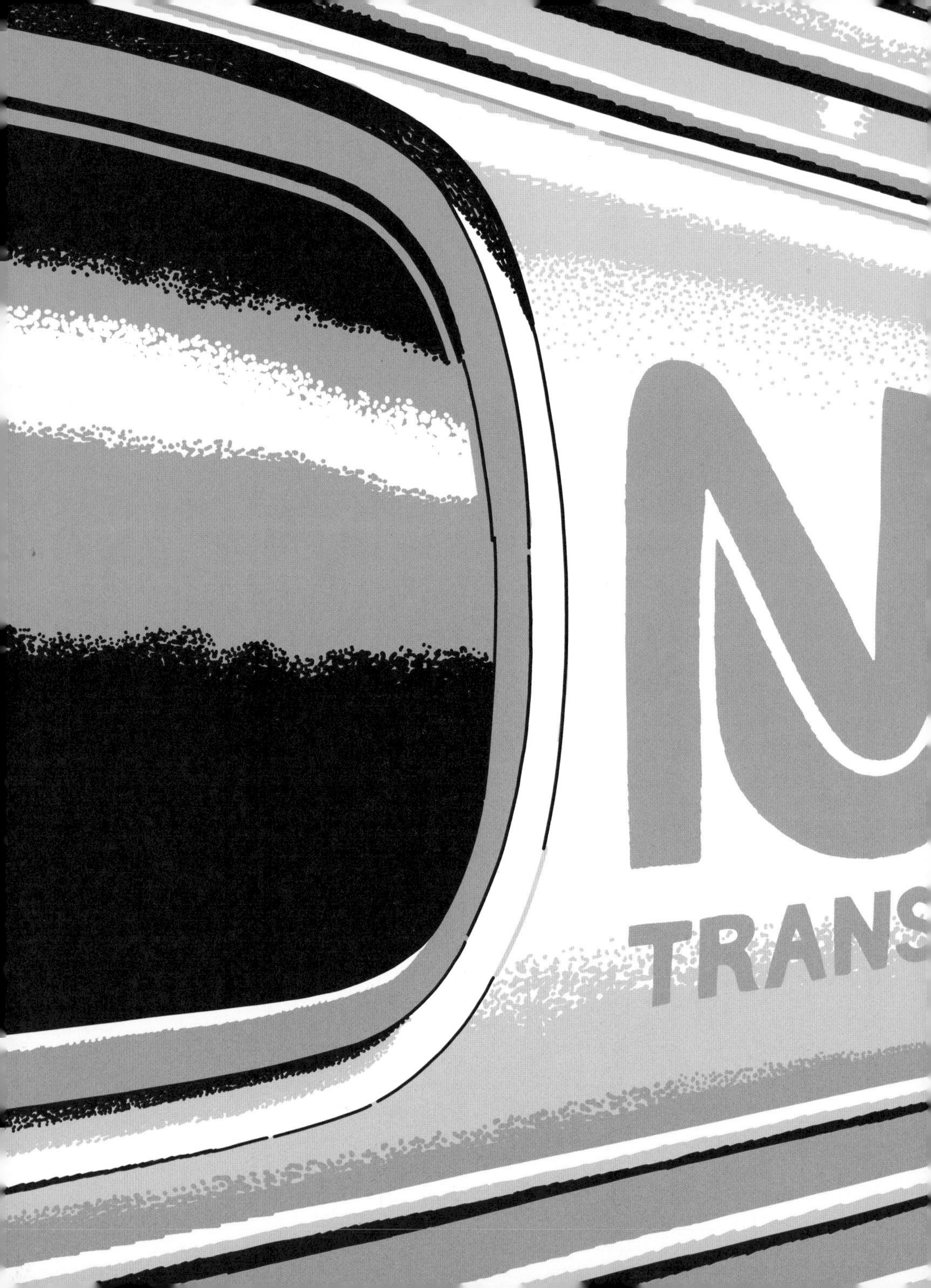
TRANS

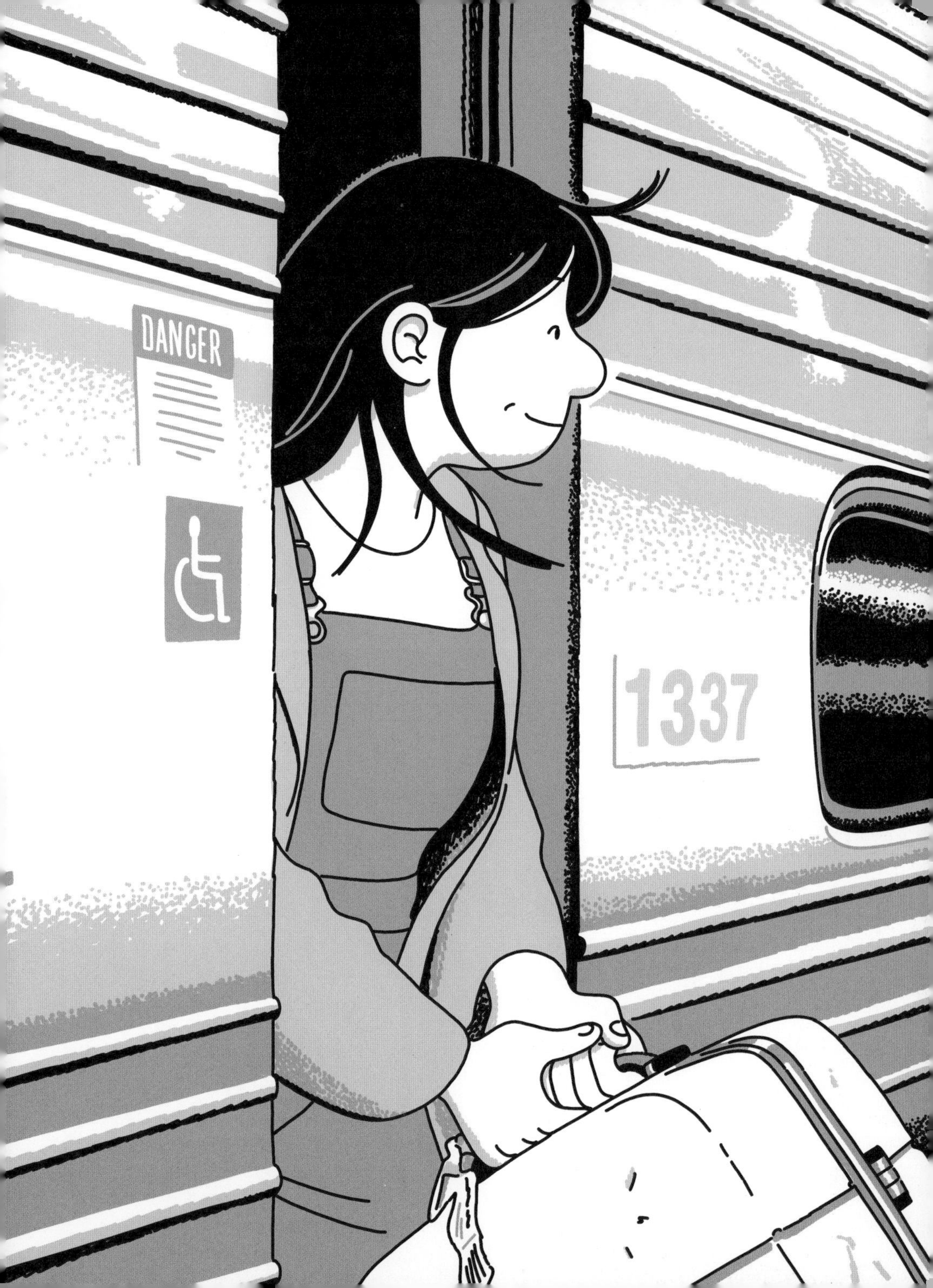
DANGER
1337

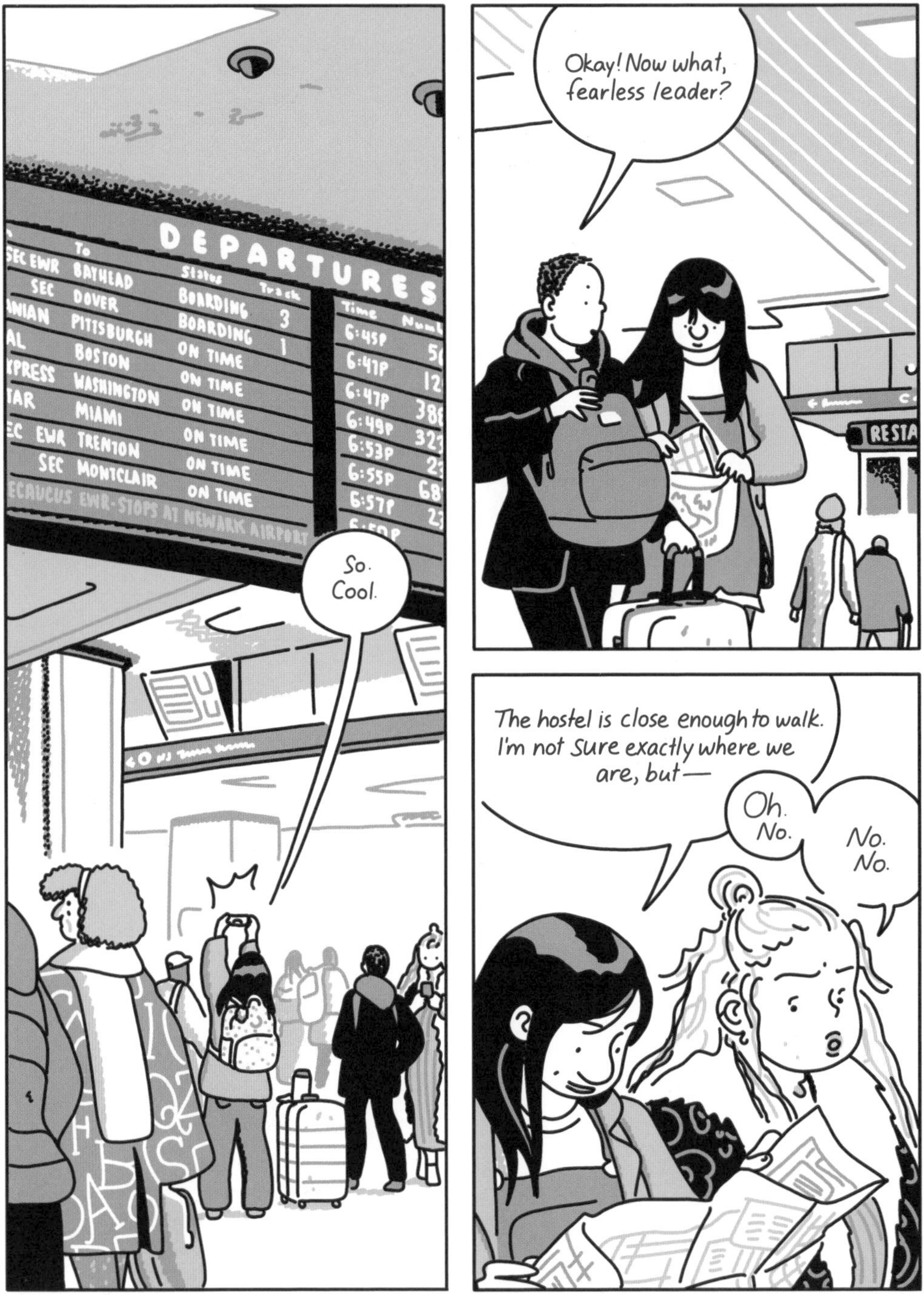
DEPARTURES
BAYHEAD BOARDING 3
DOVER BOARDING
PITTSBURGH BOARDING 1
BOSTON ON TIME
WASHINGTON ON TIME
MIAMI ON TIME
TRENTON ON TIME
MONTCLAIR ON TIME
So. Cool.
Okay! Now what, fearless leader?
The hostel is close enough to walk. I'm not sure exactly where we are, but—
Oh. No.
No. No.

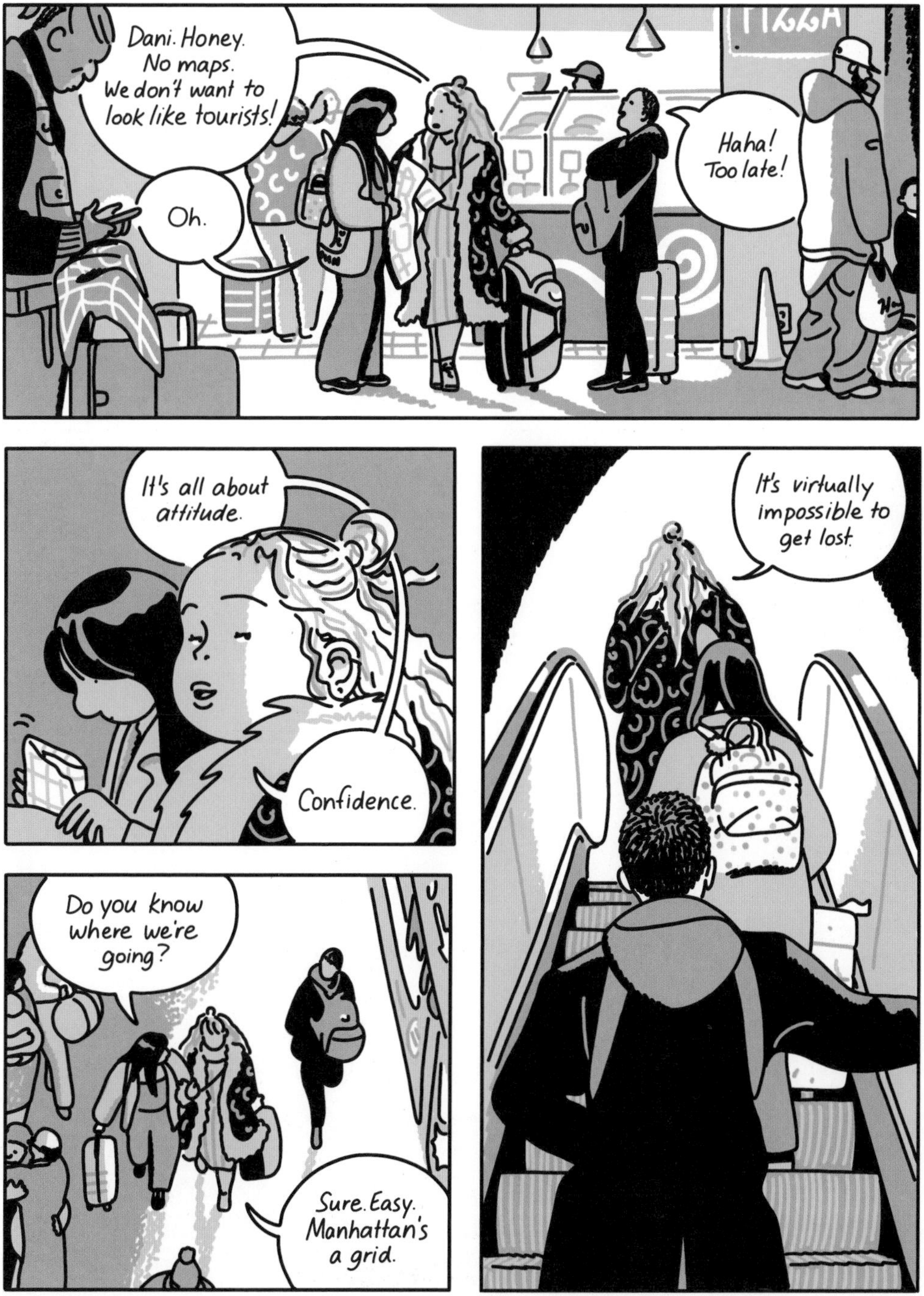
Dani. Honey. No maps. We don't want to look like tourists!
Oh.
Haha! Too late!
It's all about attitude.
Confidence.
It's virtually impossible to get lost.
Do you know where we're going?
Sure. Easy. Manhattan's a grid.

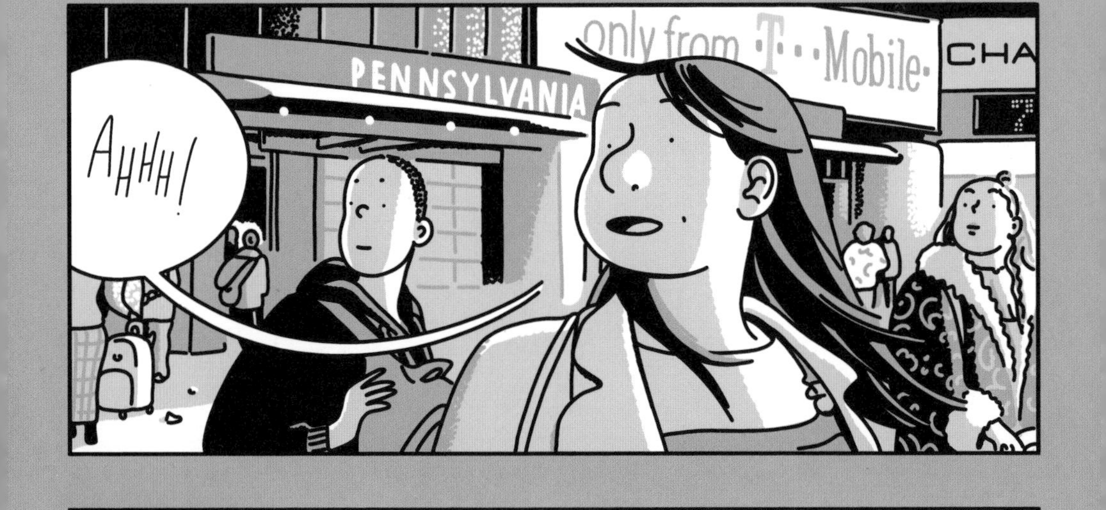
AHHH!
PENNSYLVANIA
only from T-Mobile

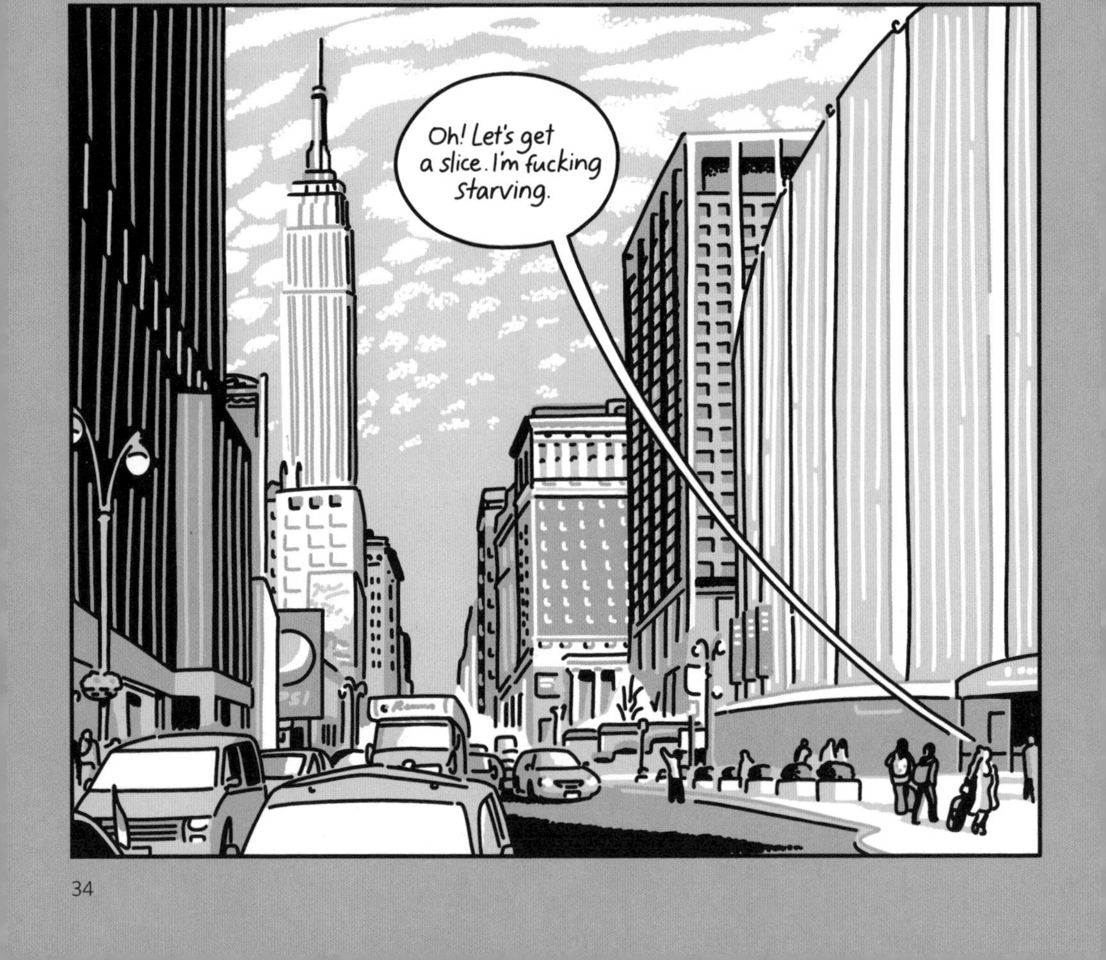
Oh! Let's get a slice. I'm fucking starving.

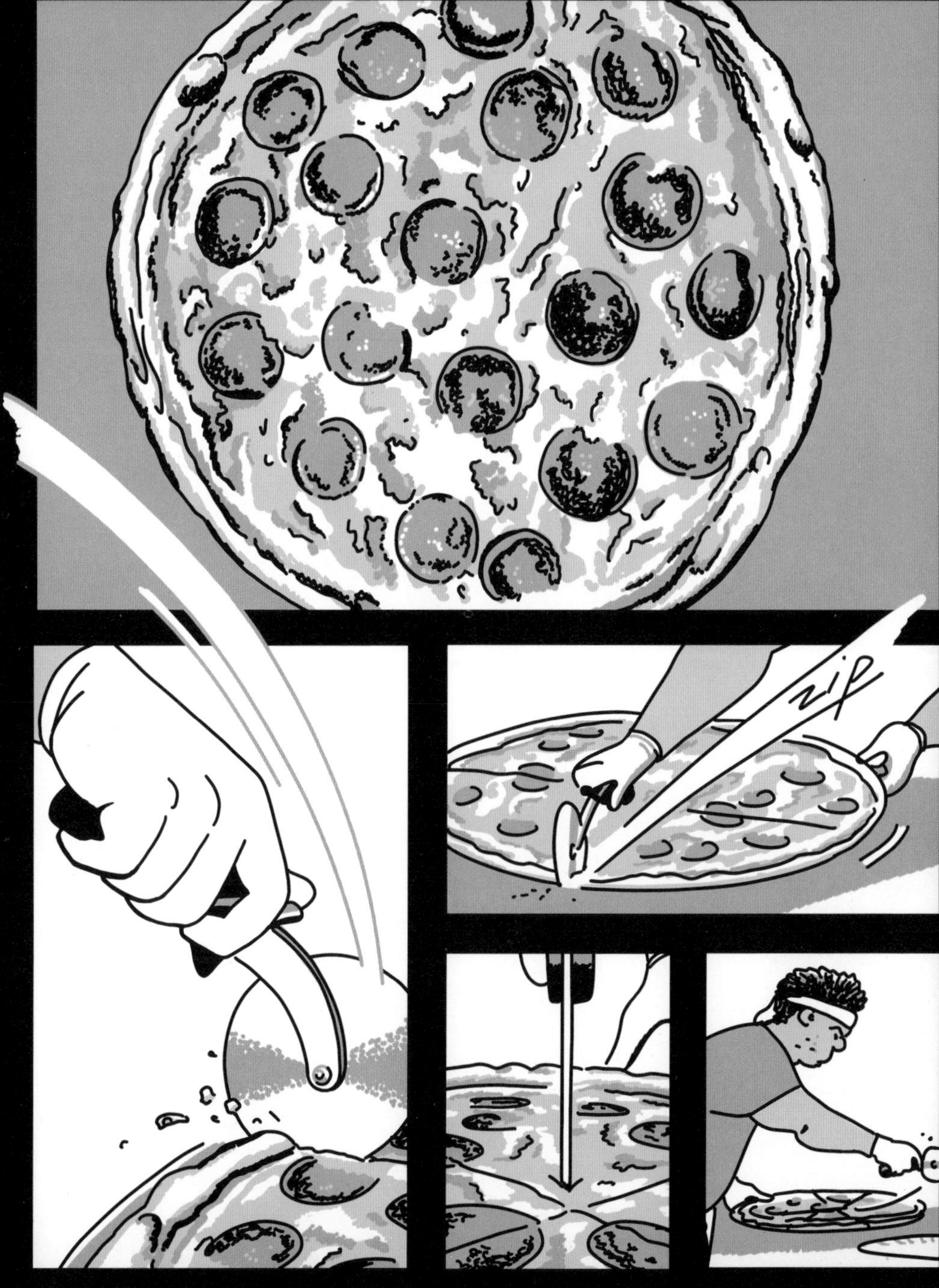
zip

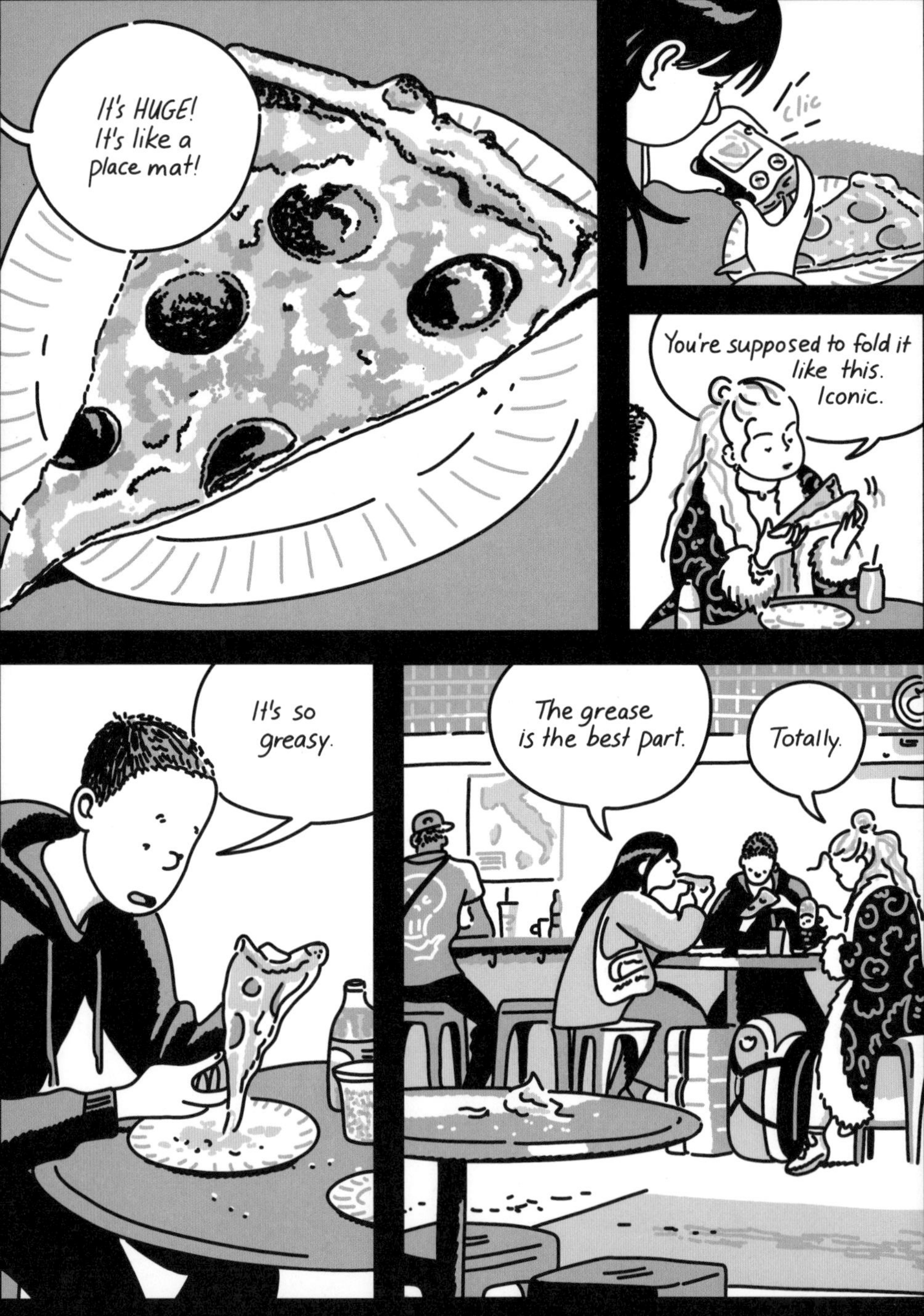
It's HUGE! It's like a place mat!
clic
You're supposed to fold it like this. Iconic.
It's so greasy.
The grease is the best part.
Totally.

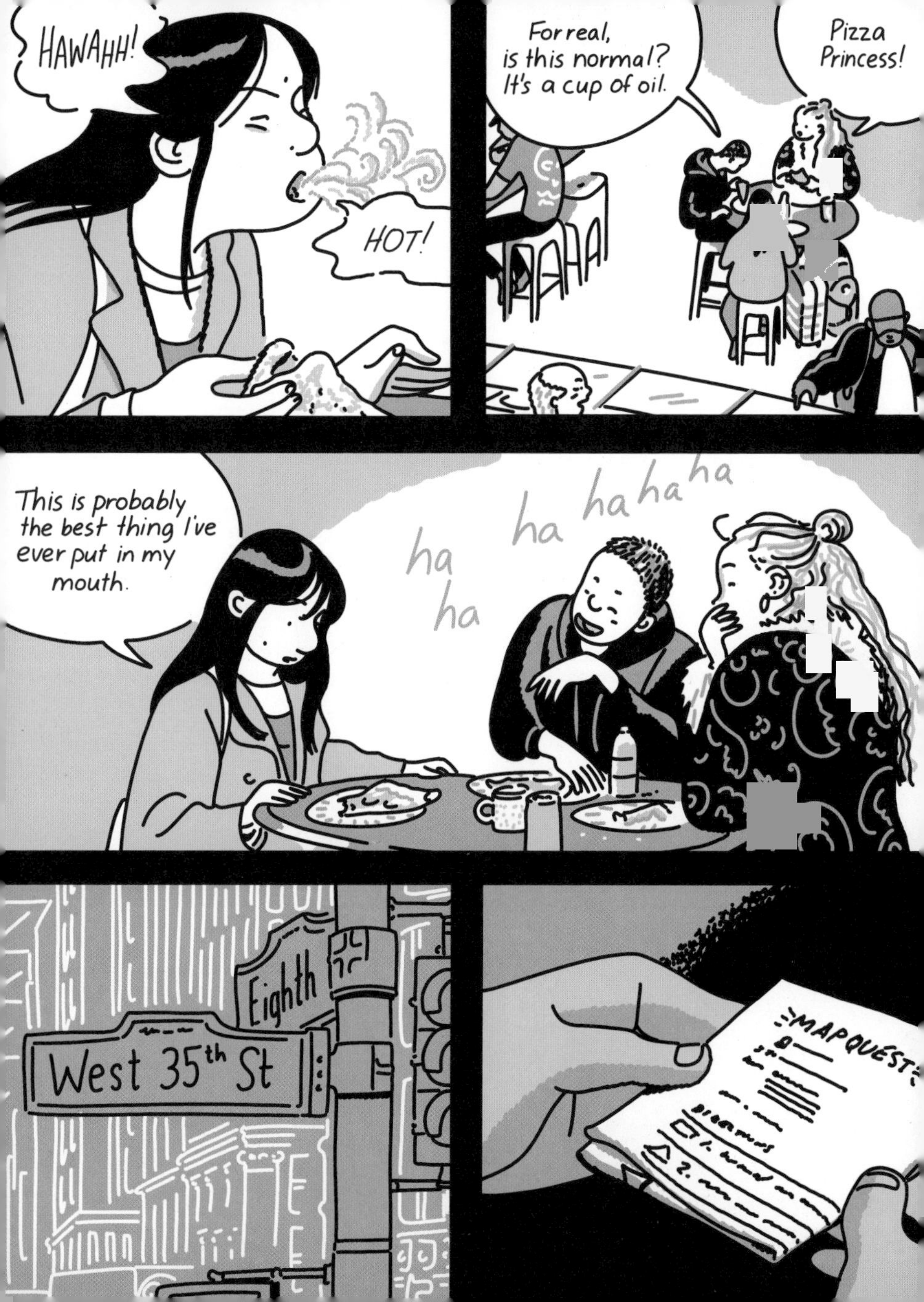
HAWAHH!
HOT!
For real, is this normal? It's a cup of oil.
Pizza Princess!
This is probably the best thing I've ever put in my mouth.
ha ha ha ha ha ha
Eighth
West 35th St
MAPQUEST

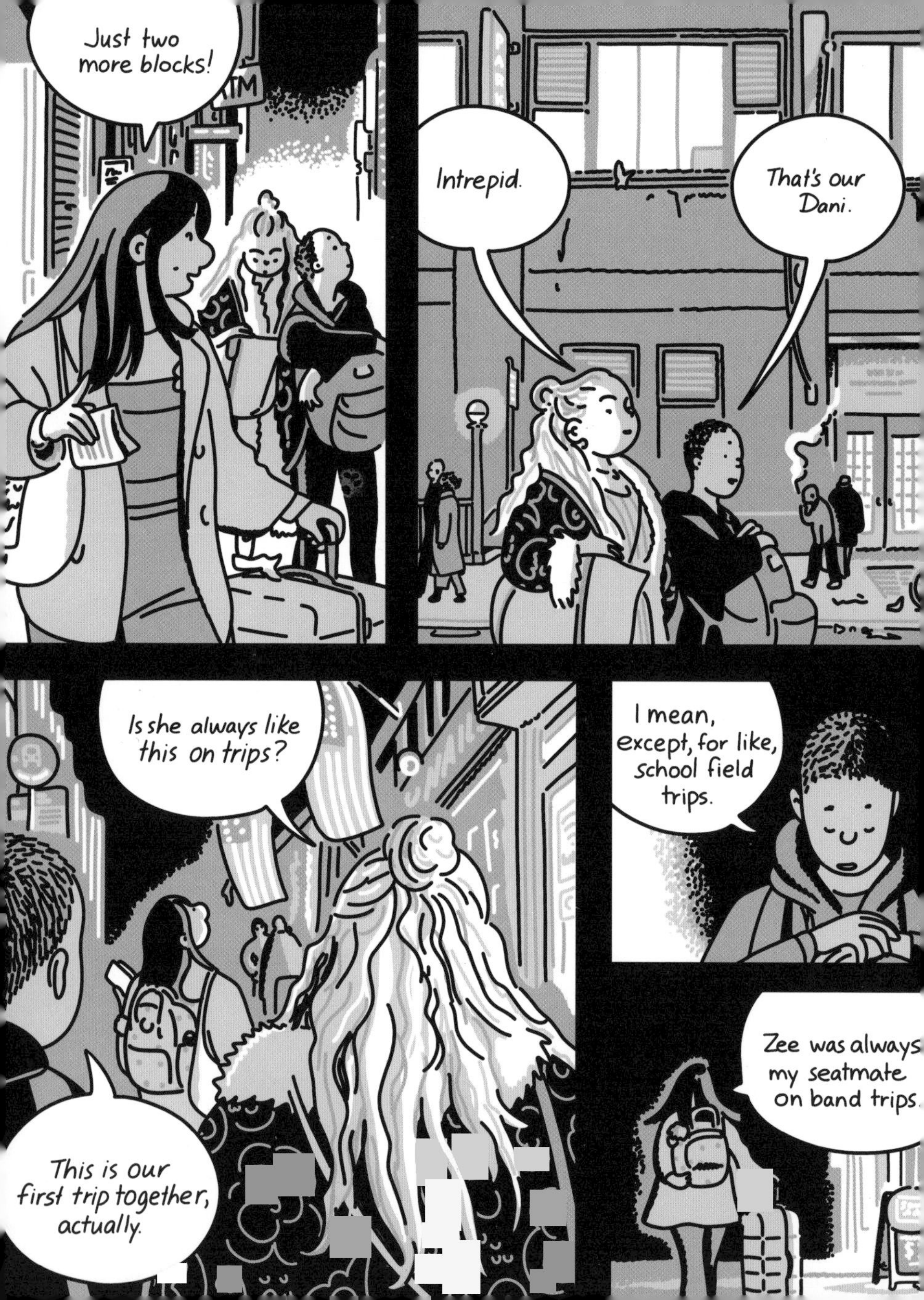
Just two more blocks!
ATM
Intrepid.
That's our Dani.
Is she always like this on trips?
This is our first trip together, actually.
I mean, except, for like, school field trips.
Zee was always my seatmate on band trips.

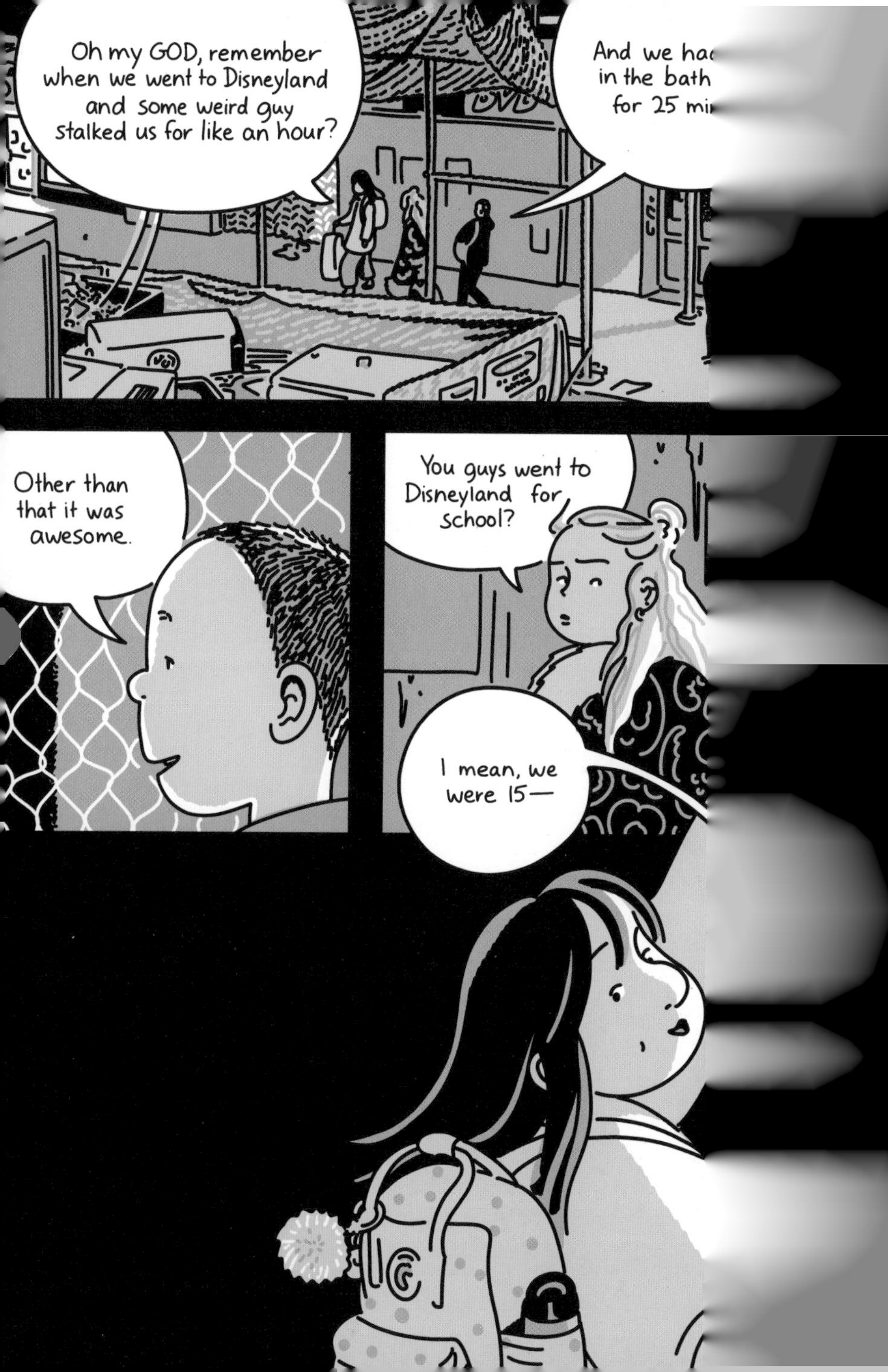
Oh my GOD, remember when we went to Disneyland and some weird guy stalked us for like an hour?
And we
in the
for 25
Other than that it was awesome.
You guys went to Disneyland for school?
I mean, we were 15—

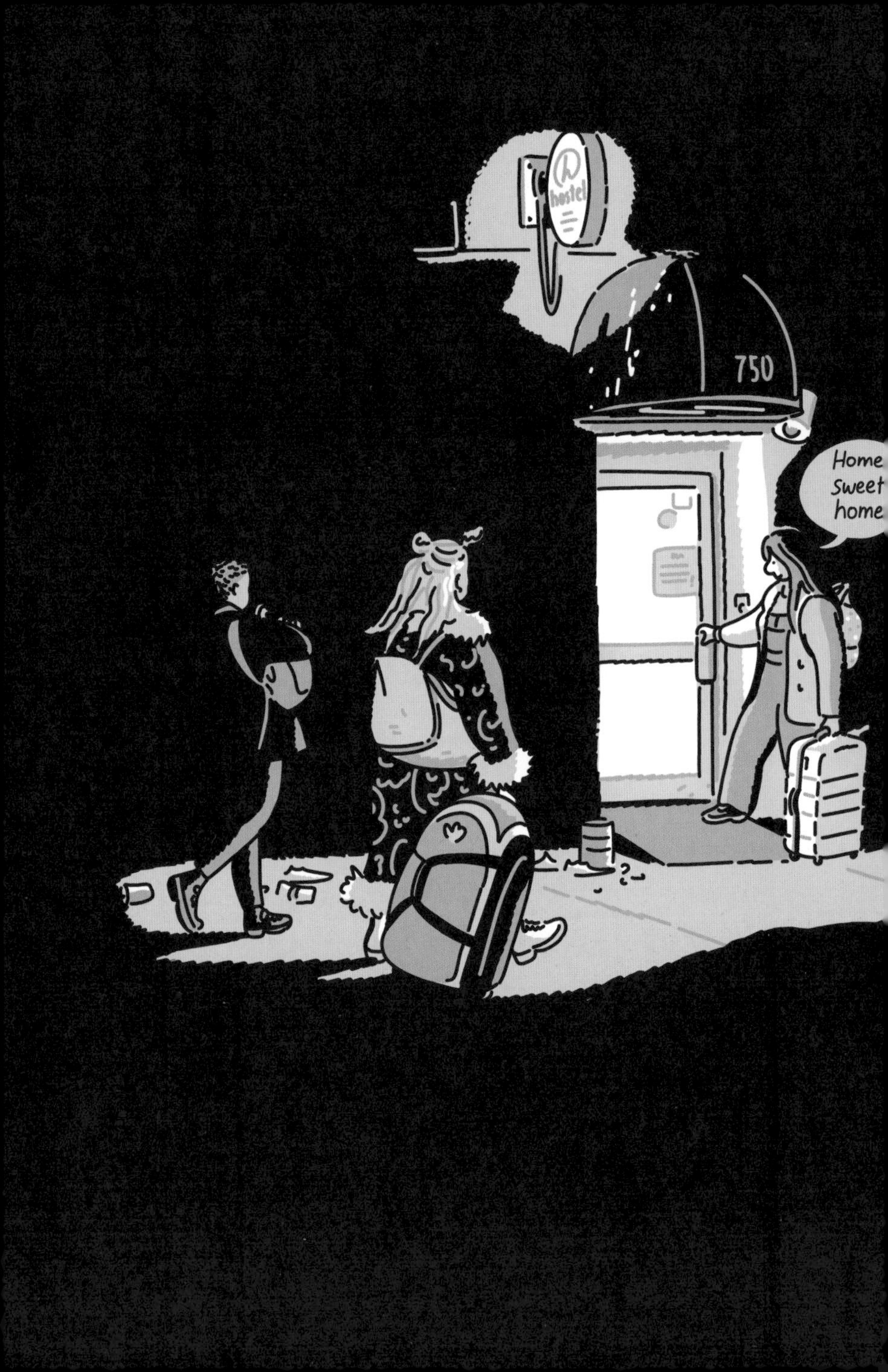
hostel
750
Home sweet home

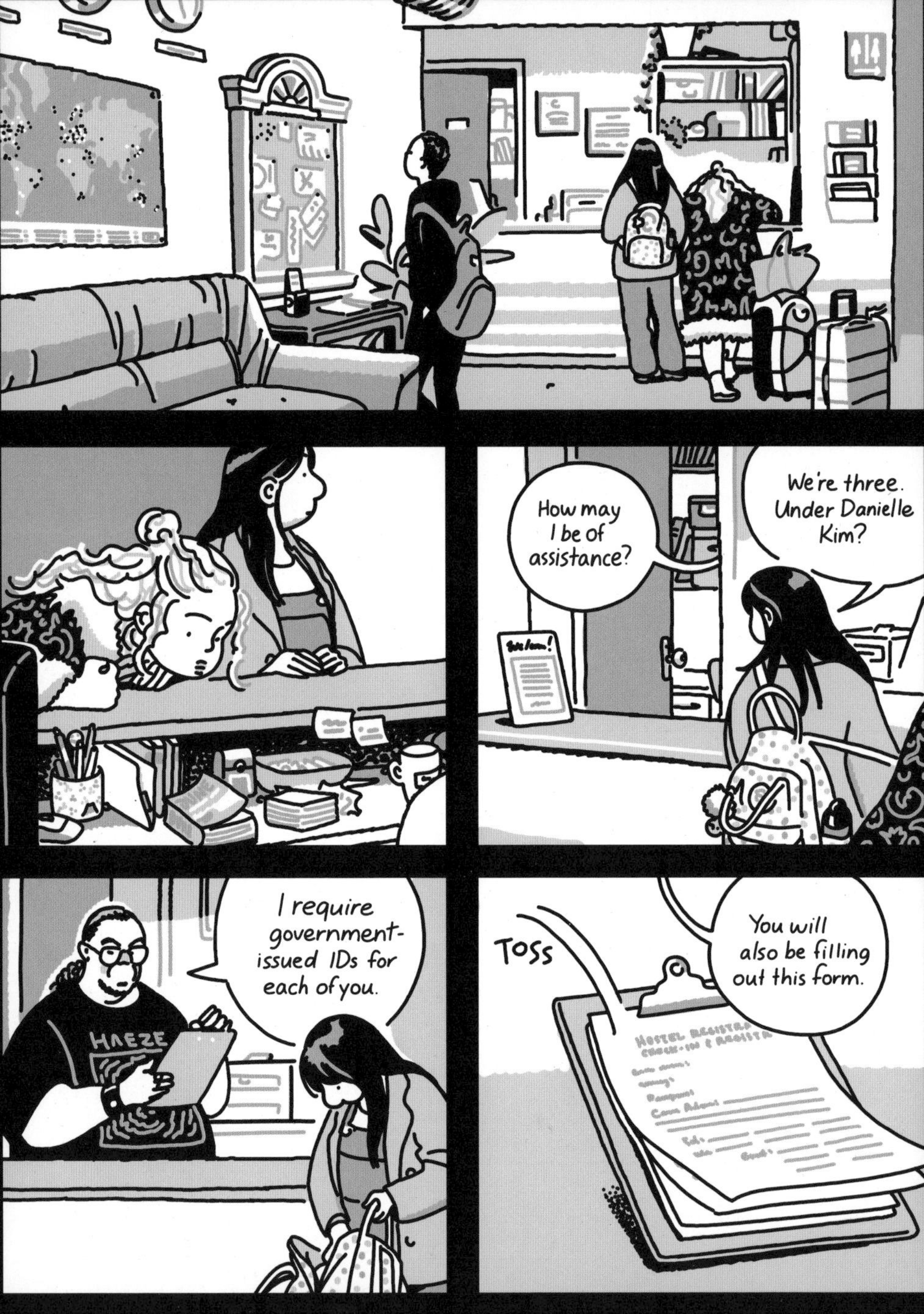
How may I be of assistance?
We're three. Under Danielle Kim?
I require government-issued IDs for each of you.
TOSS
You will also be filling out this form.

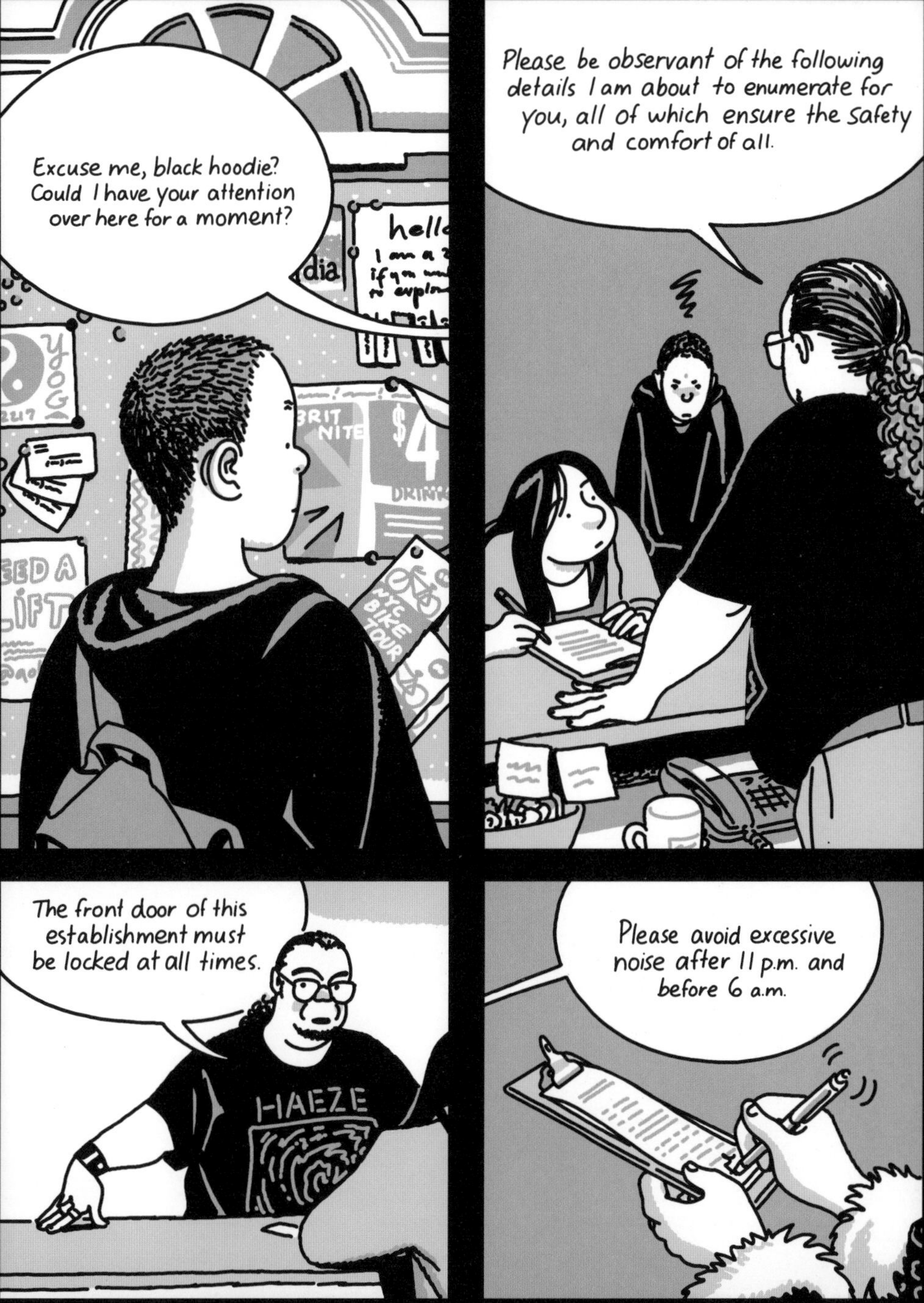
Excuse me, black hoodie? Could I have your attention over here for a moment?
Please be observant of the following details I am about to enumerate for you, all of which ensure the safety and comfort of all.
The front door of this establishment must be locked at all times.
Please avoid excessive noise after 11 p.m. and before 6 a.m.
BRIT NITE
$4
YOGA
NYC BIKE TOUR
HAEZE

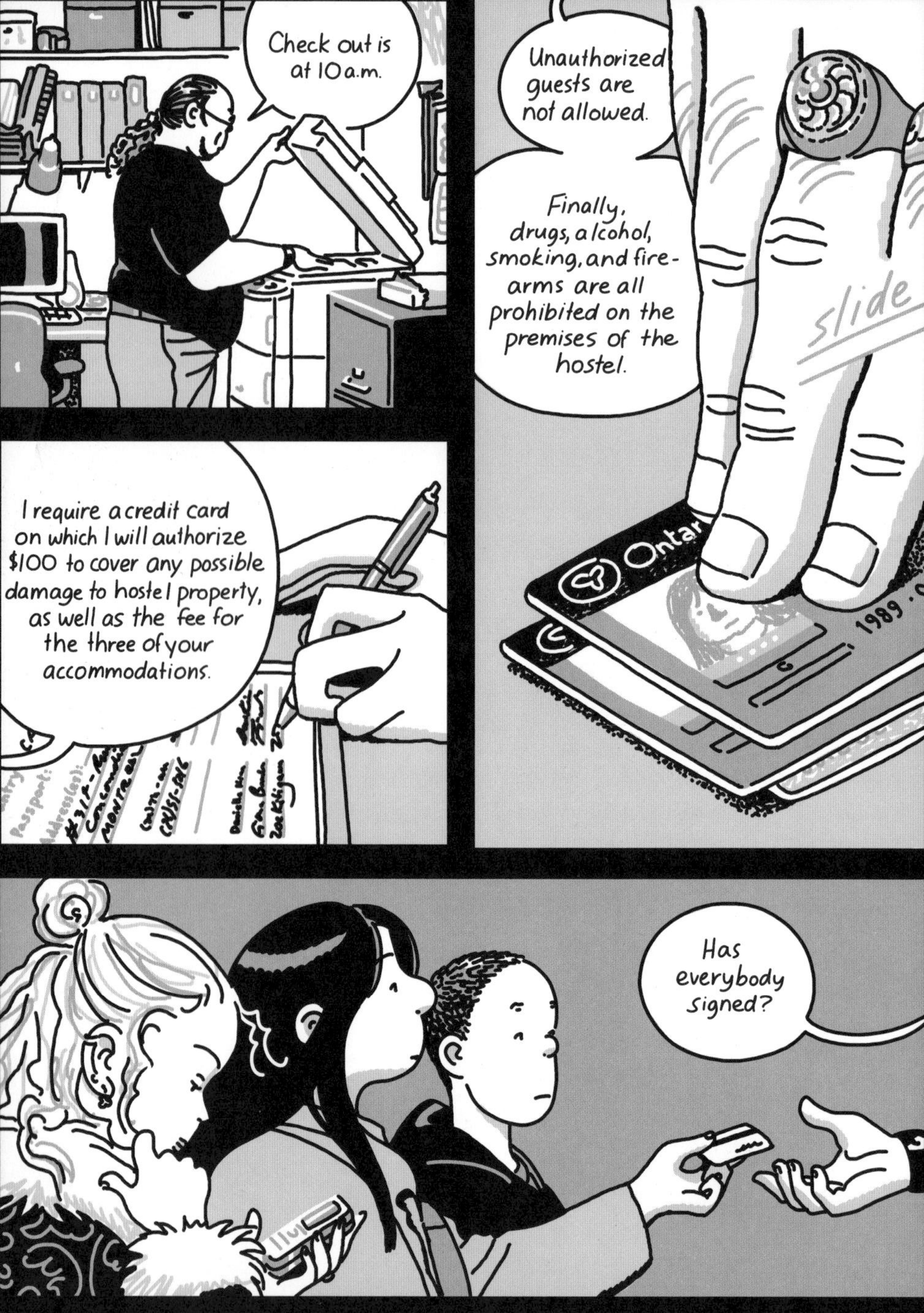
Check out is at 10 a.m.
Unauthorized guests are not allowed.
Finally, drugs, alcohol, smoking, and fire-arms are all prohibited on the premises of the hostel.
slide
I require a credit card on which I will authorize $100 to cover any possible damage to hostel property, as well as the fee for the three of your accommodations.
Has everybody signed?

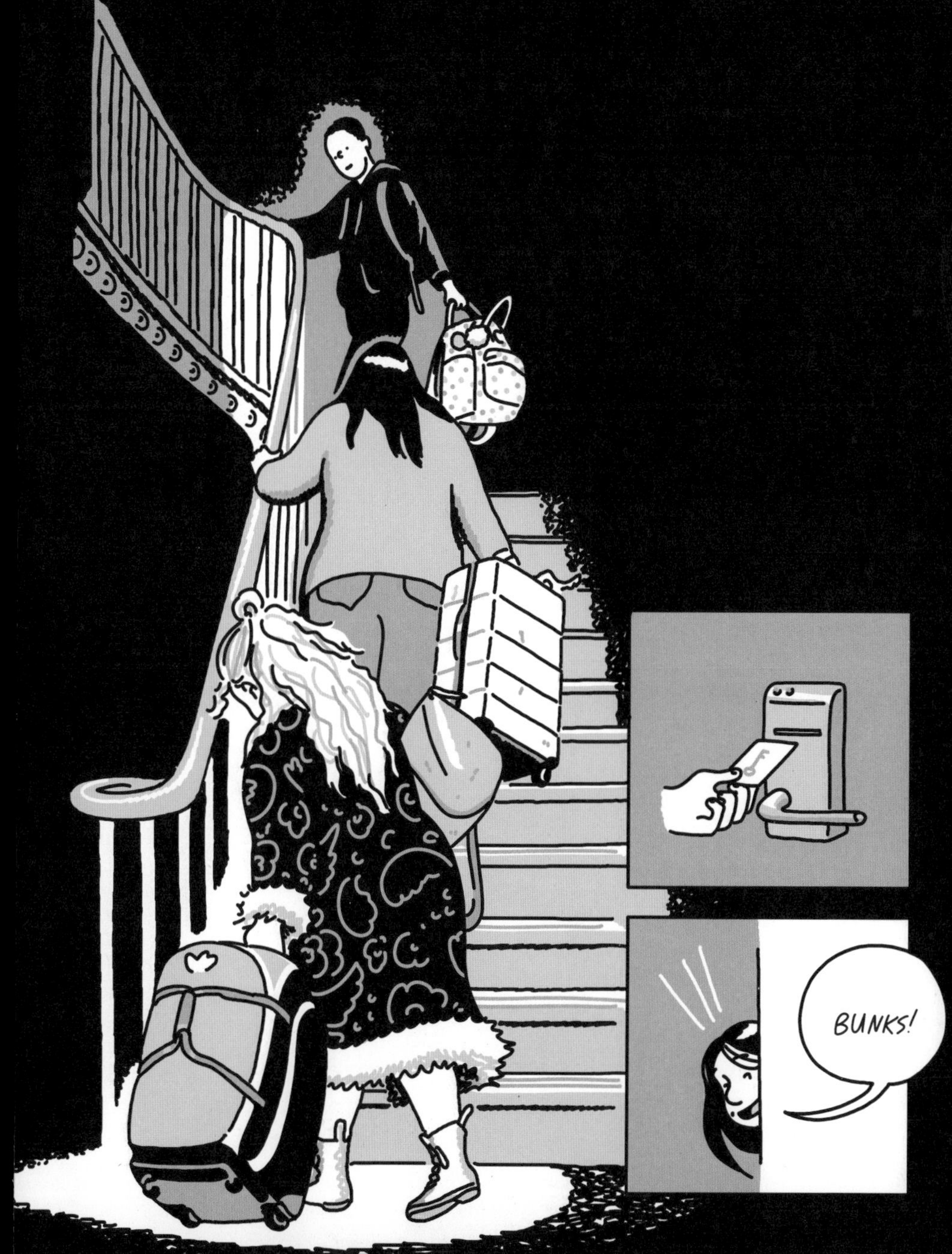
BUNKS!

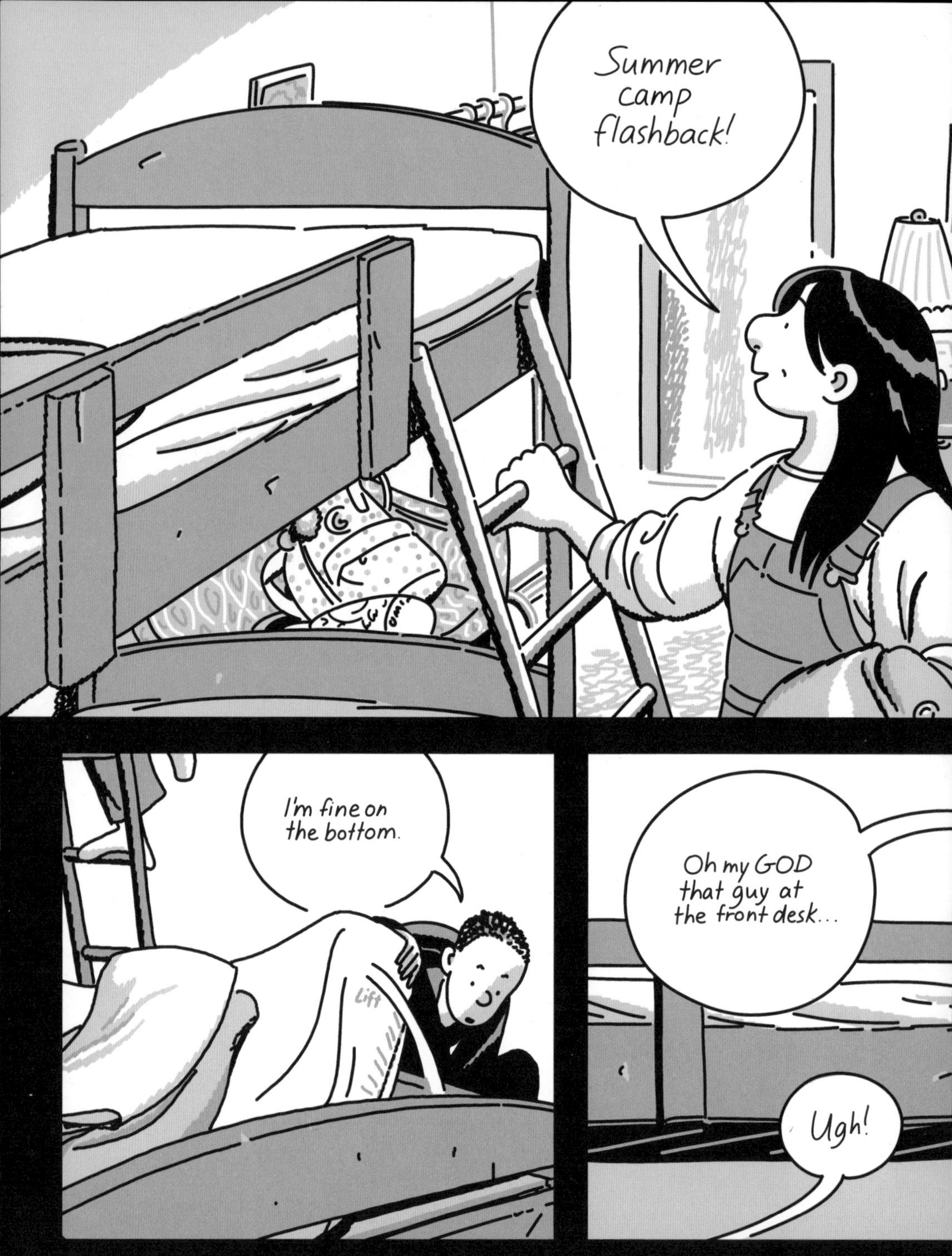
Summer camp flashback!
I'm fine on the bottom.
Lift
Oh my GOD that guy at the front desk...
Ugh!

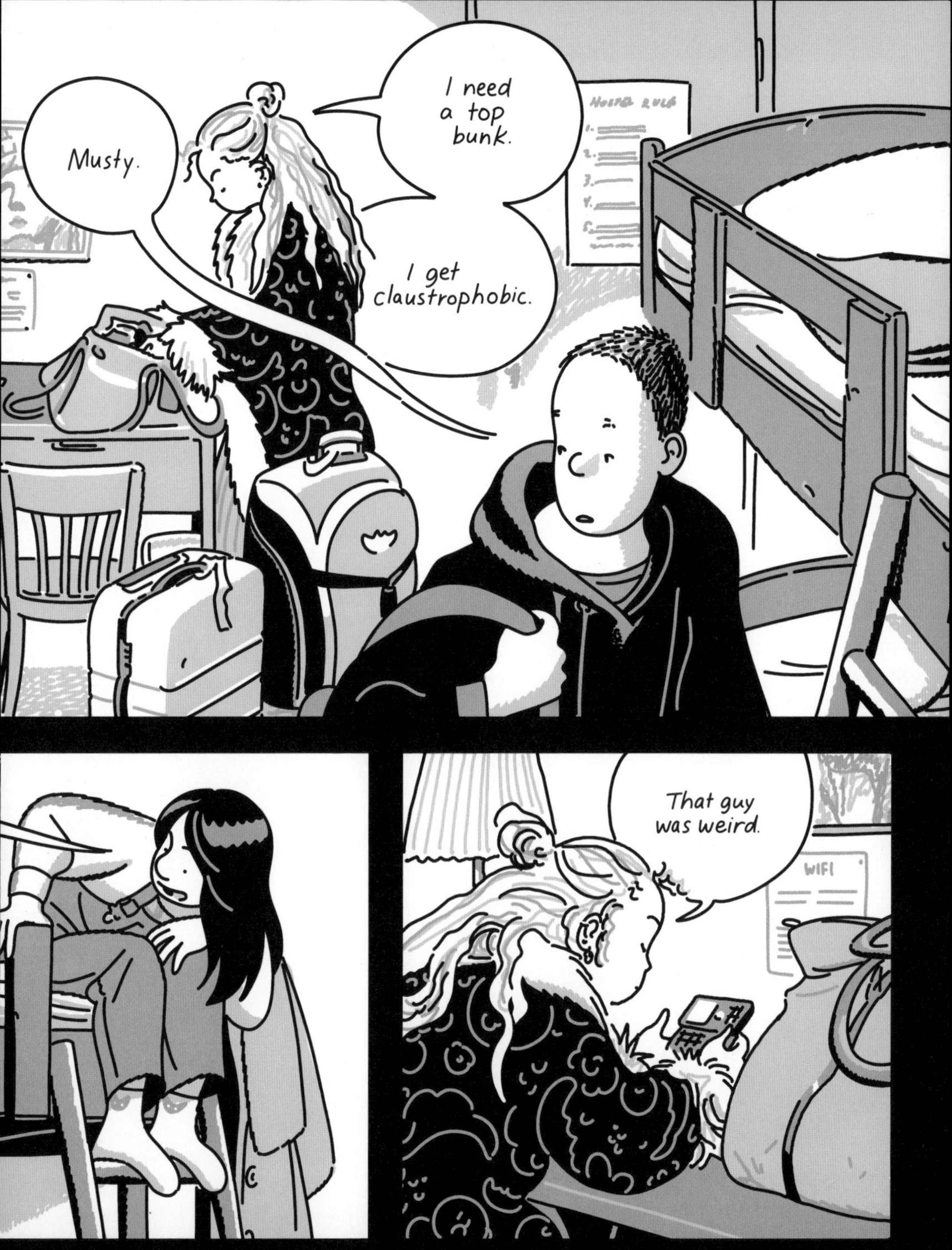
Musty.
I need a top bunk.
I get claustrophobic.
That guy was weird.
WIFI

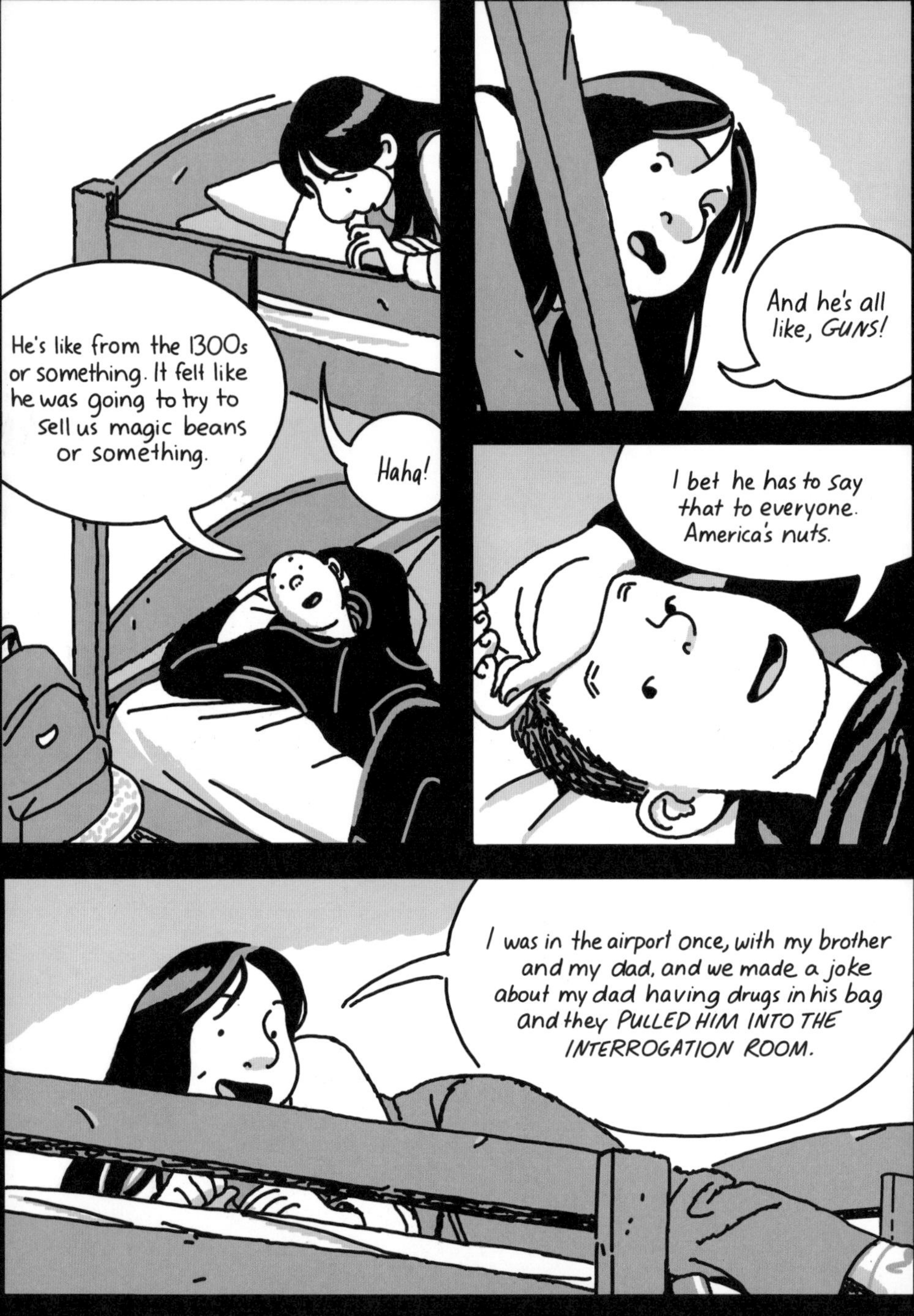
He's like from the 1300s or something. It felt like he was going to try to sell us magic beans or something.
Haha!
And he's all like, GUNS!
I bet he has to say that to everyone. America's nuts.
I was in the airport once, with my brother and my dad, and we made a joke about my dad having drugs in his bag and they PULLED HIM INTO THE INTERROGATION ROOM.

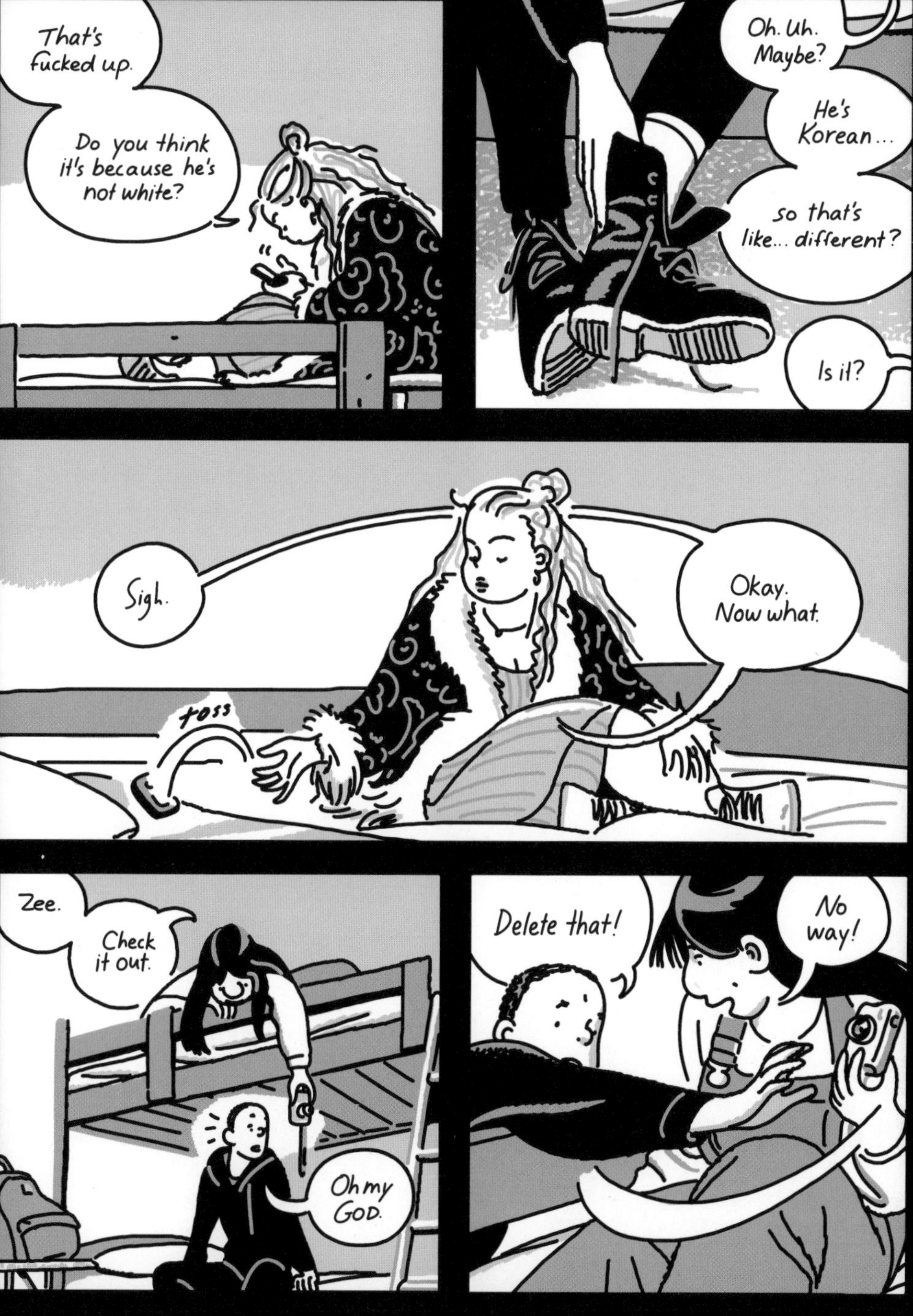
That's fucked up.
Do you think it's because he's not white?
Oh. Uh. Maybe?
He's Korean...
so that's like... different?
Is it?
Sigh.
Okay. Now what.
toss
Zee.
Check it out.
Oh my GOD.
Delete that!
No way!

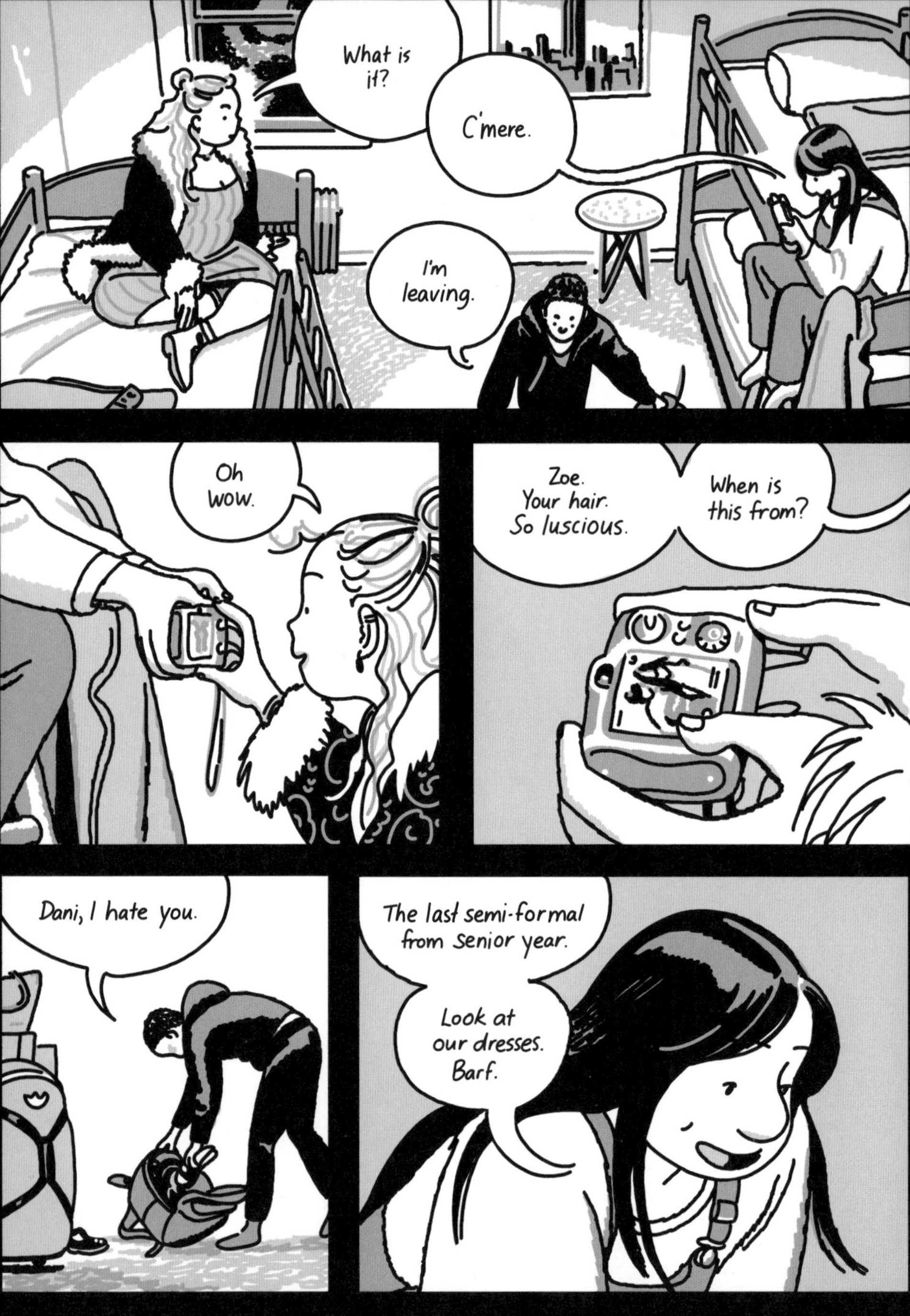
What is it?
C'mere.
I'm leaving.
Oh wow.
Zoe. Your hair. So luscious.
When is this from?
Dani, I hate you.
The last semi-formal from senior year.
Look at our dresses. Barf.

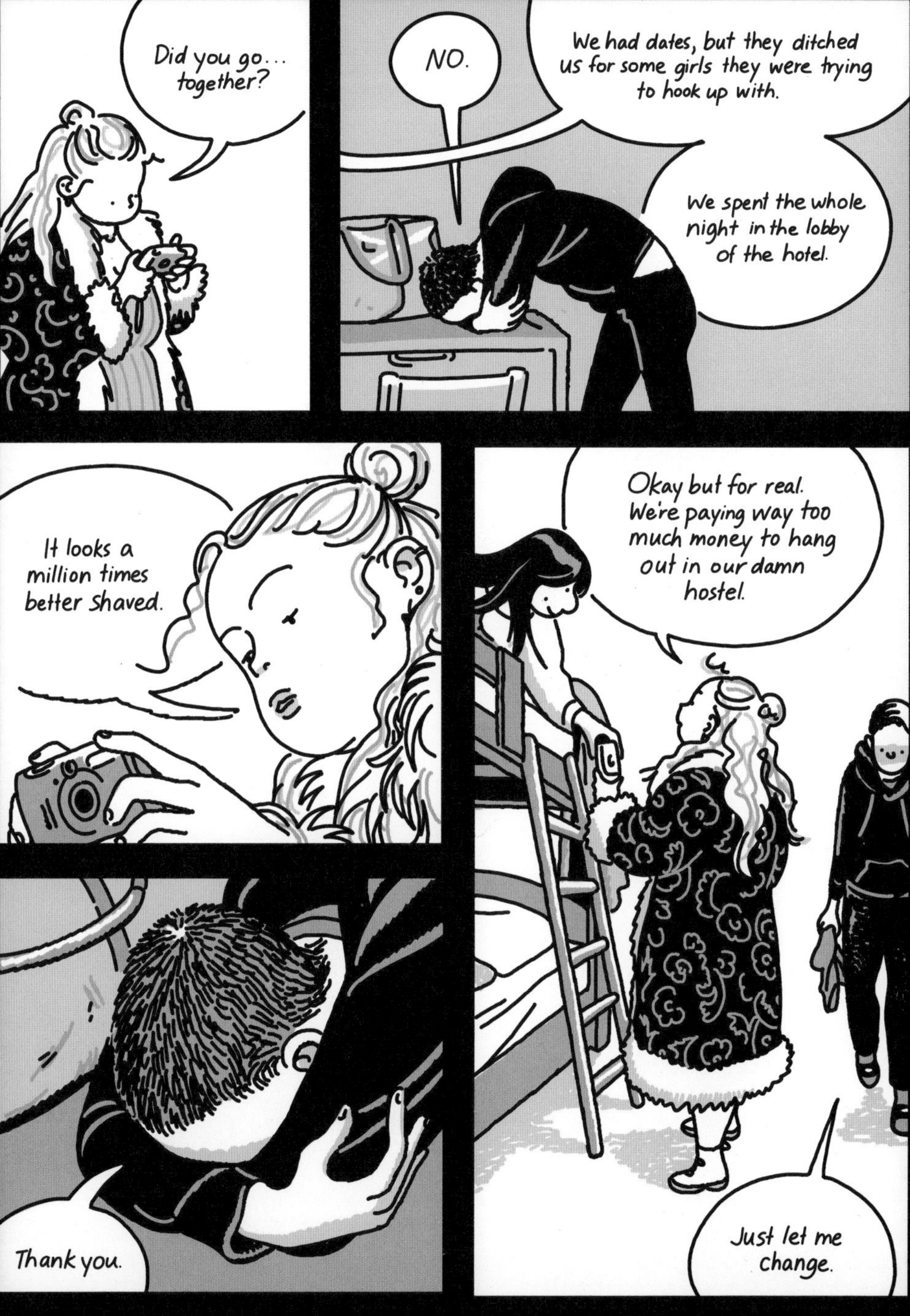
Did you go... together?
NO.
We had dates, but they ditched us for some girls they were trying to hook up with.
We spent the whole night in the lobby of the hotel.
It looks a million times better shaved.
Okay but for real. We're paying way too much money to hang out in our damn hostel.
Thank you.
Just let me change.

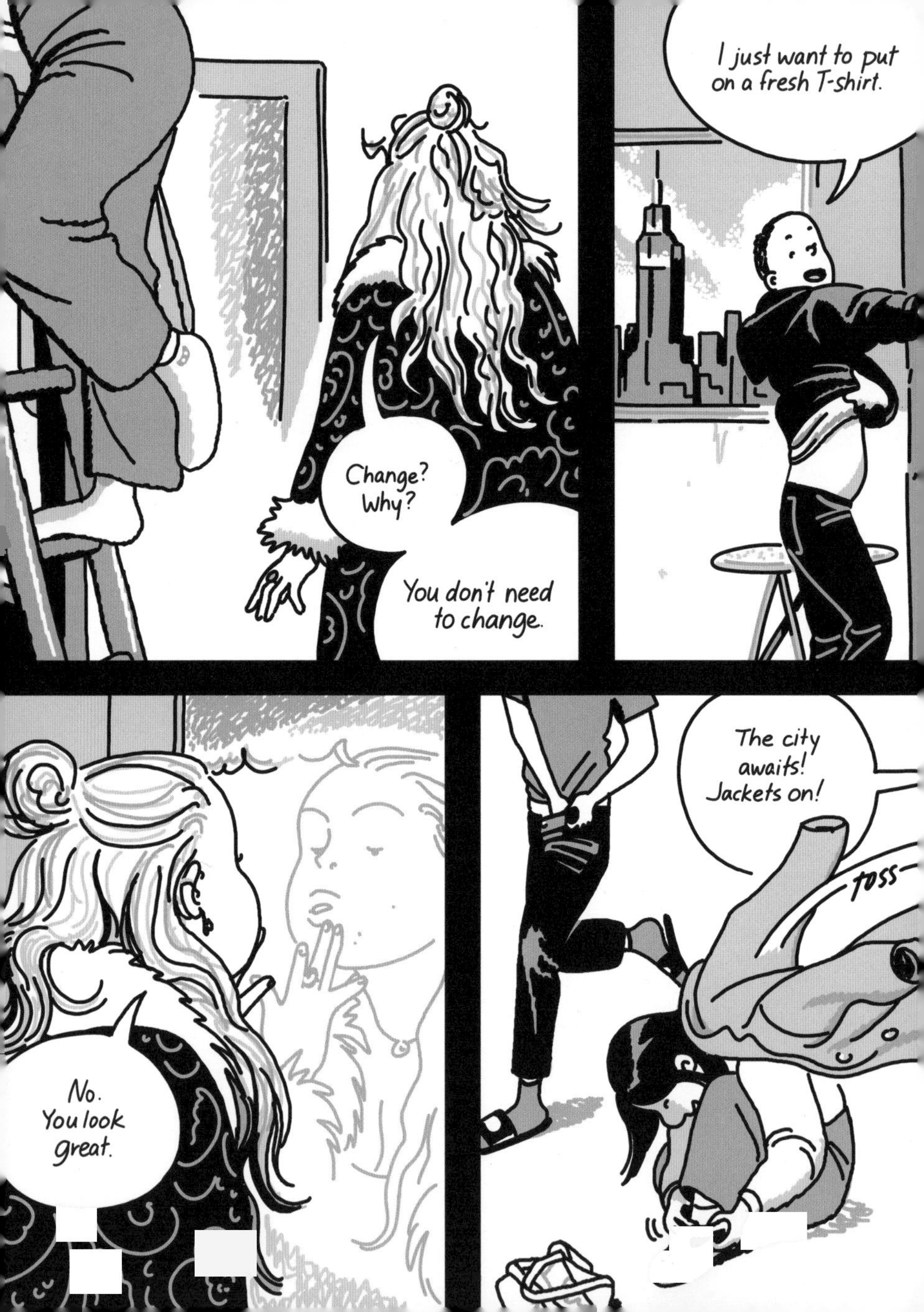
Change? Why?
You don't need to change.
I just want to put on a fresh T-shirt.
No. You look great.
The city awaits! Jackets on!
TOSS

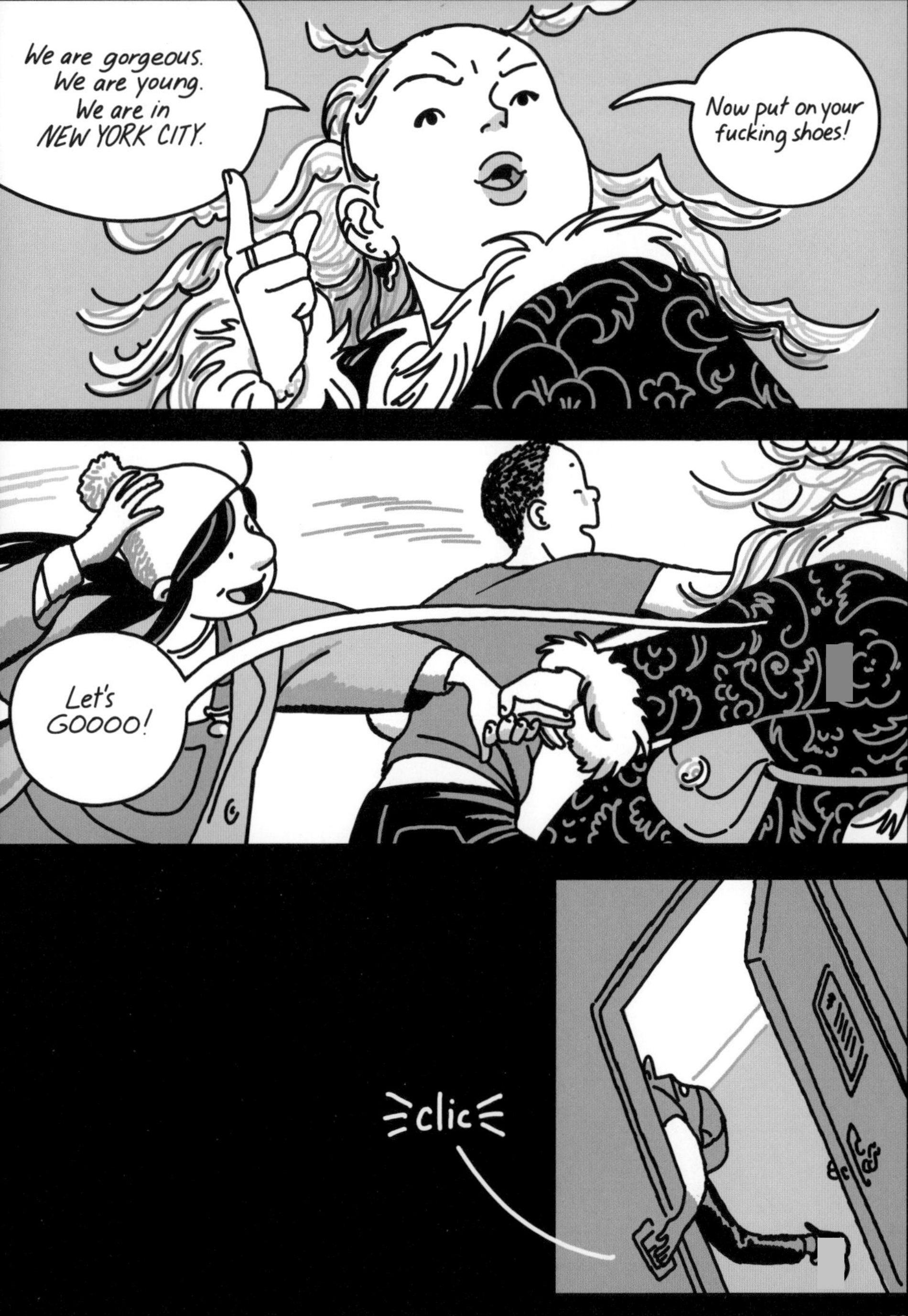
We are gorgeous. We are young. We are in NEW YORK CITY.
Now put on your fucking shoes!
Let's GOOOO!
clic

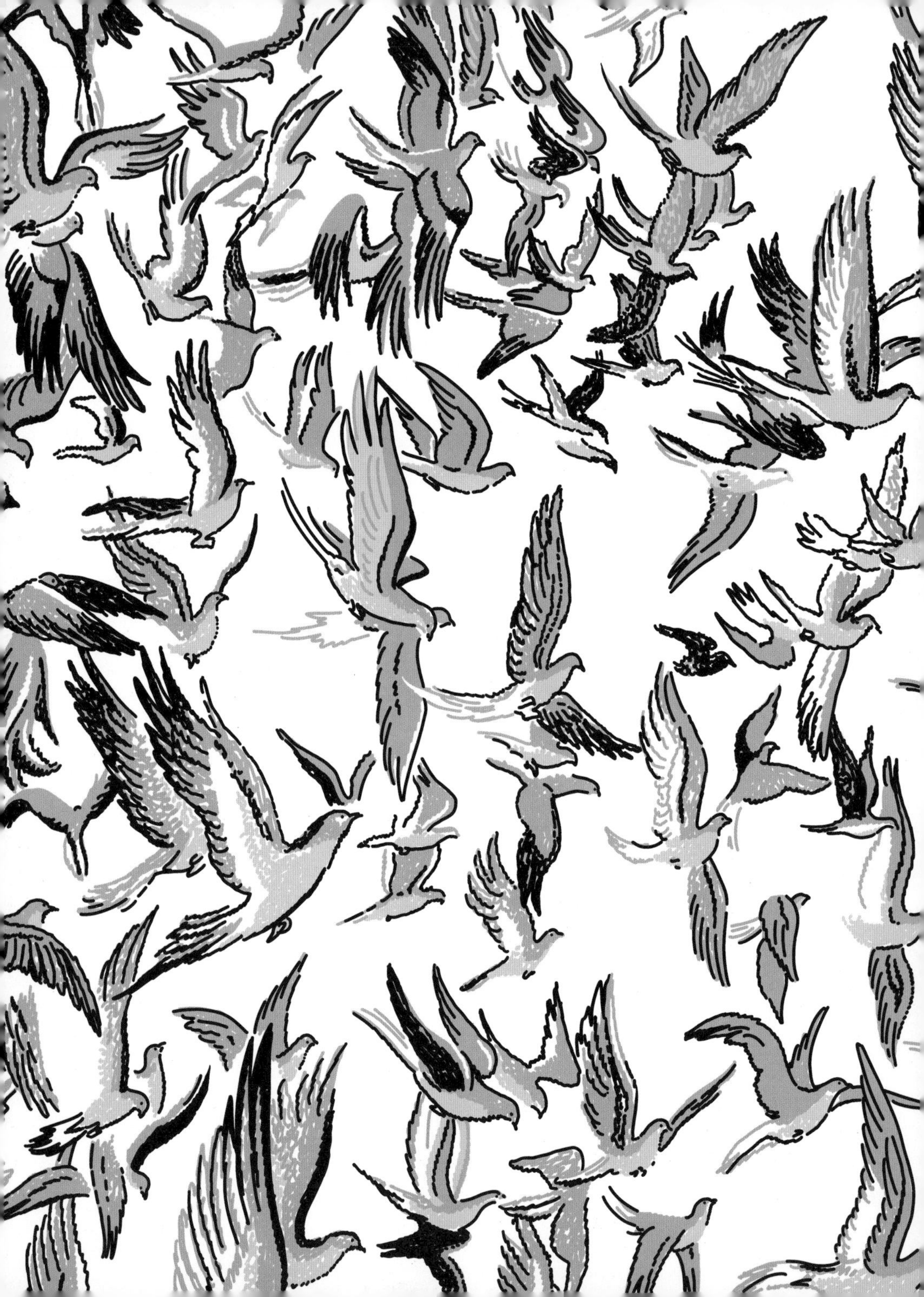

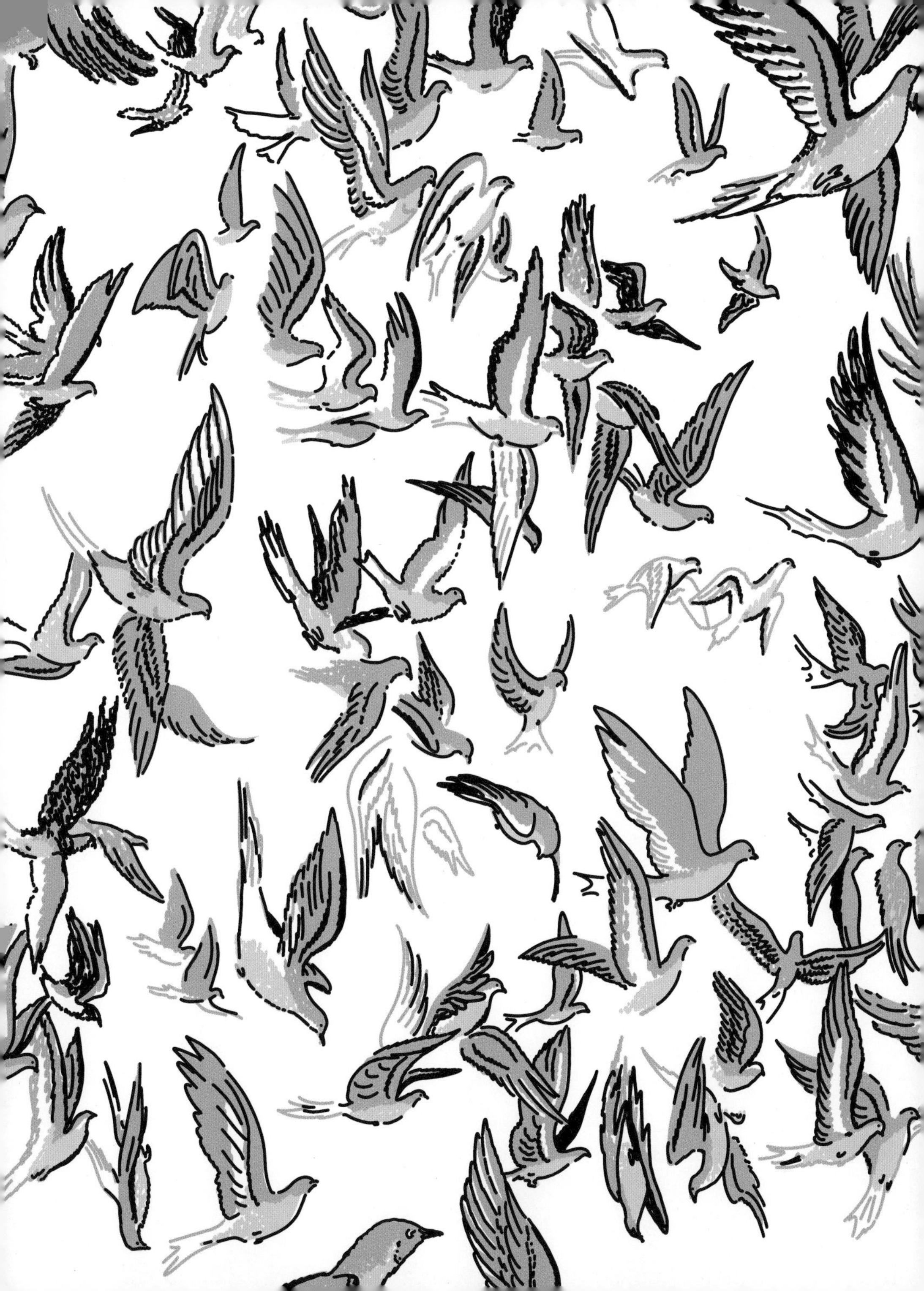

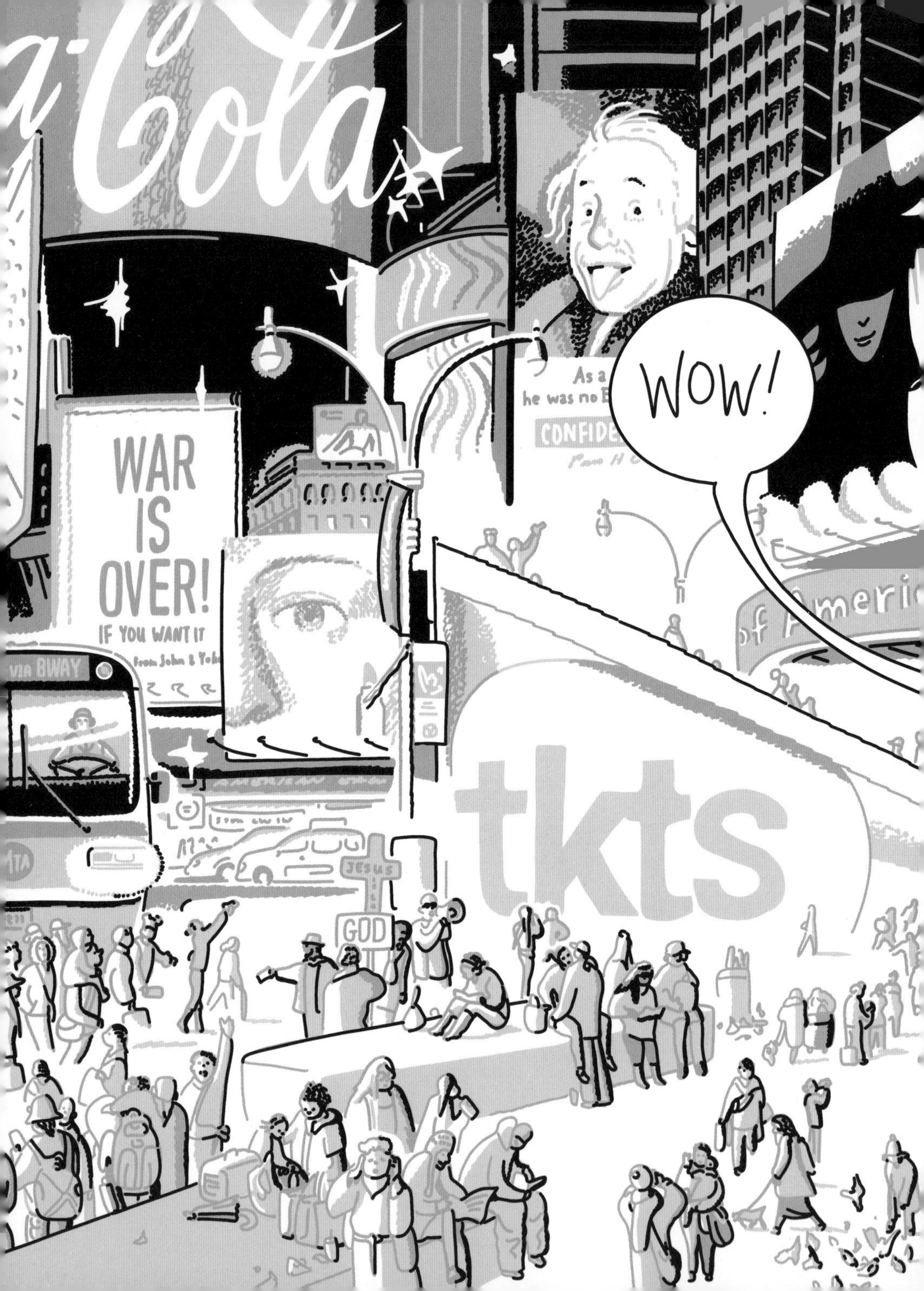
WOW!
WAR IS OVER!
IF YOU WANT IT
VIA BWAY
JESUS
GOD
tkts

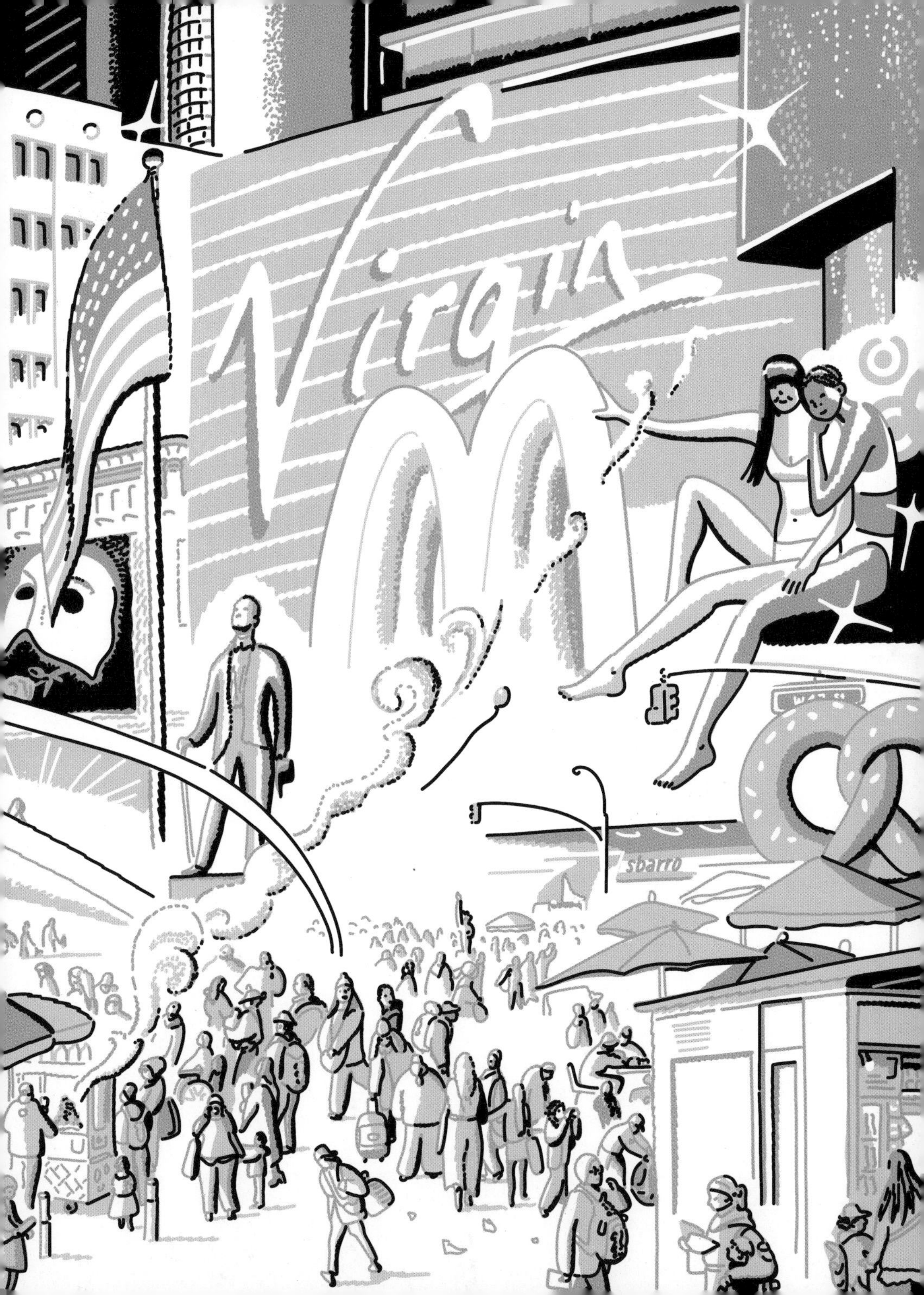
Virgin
sbarro

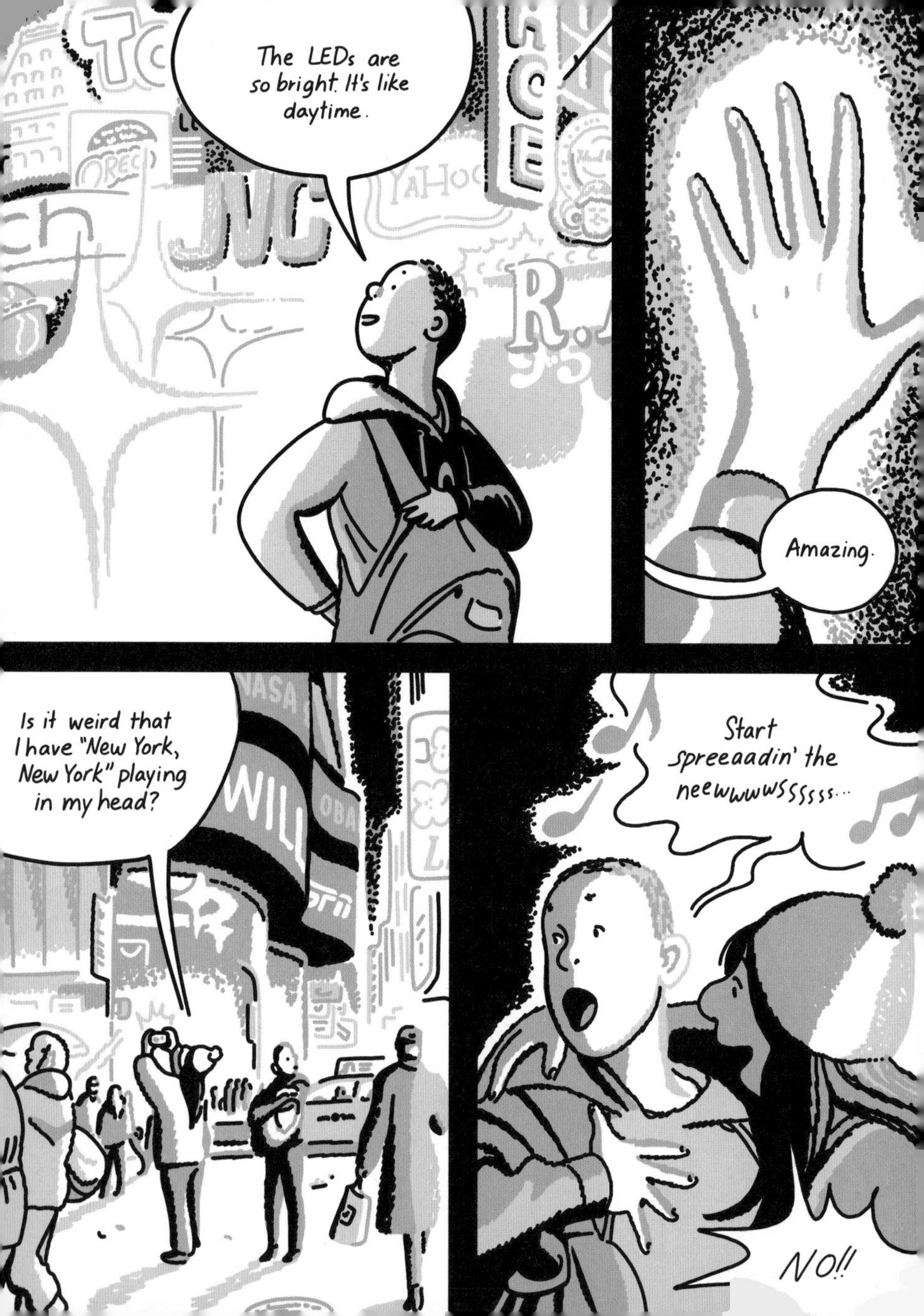
The LEDs are so bright. It's like daytime.
Amazing.
Is it weird that I have "New York, New York" playing in my head?
Start spreeaadin' the neewwwwwsssss...
NO!!

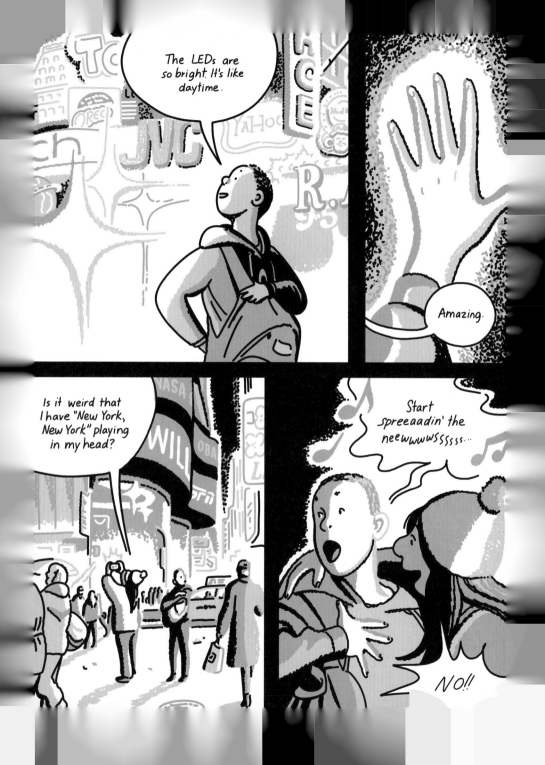

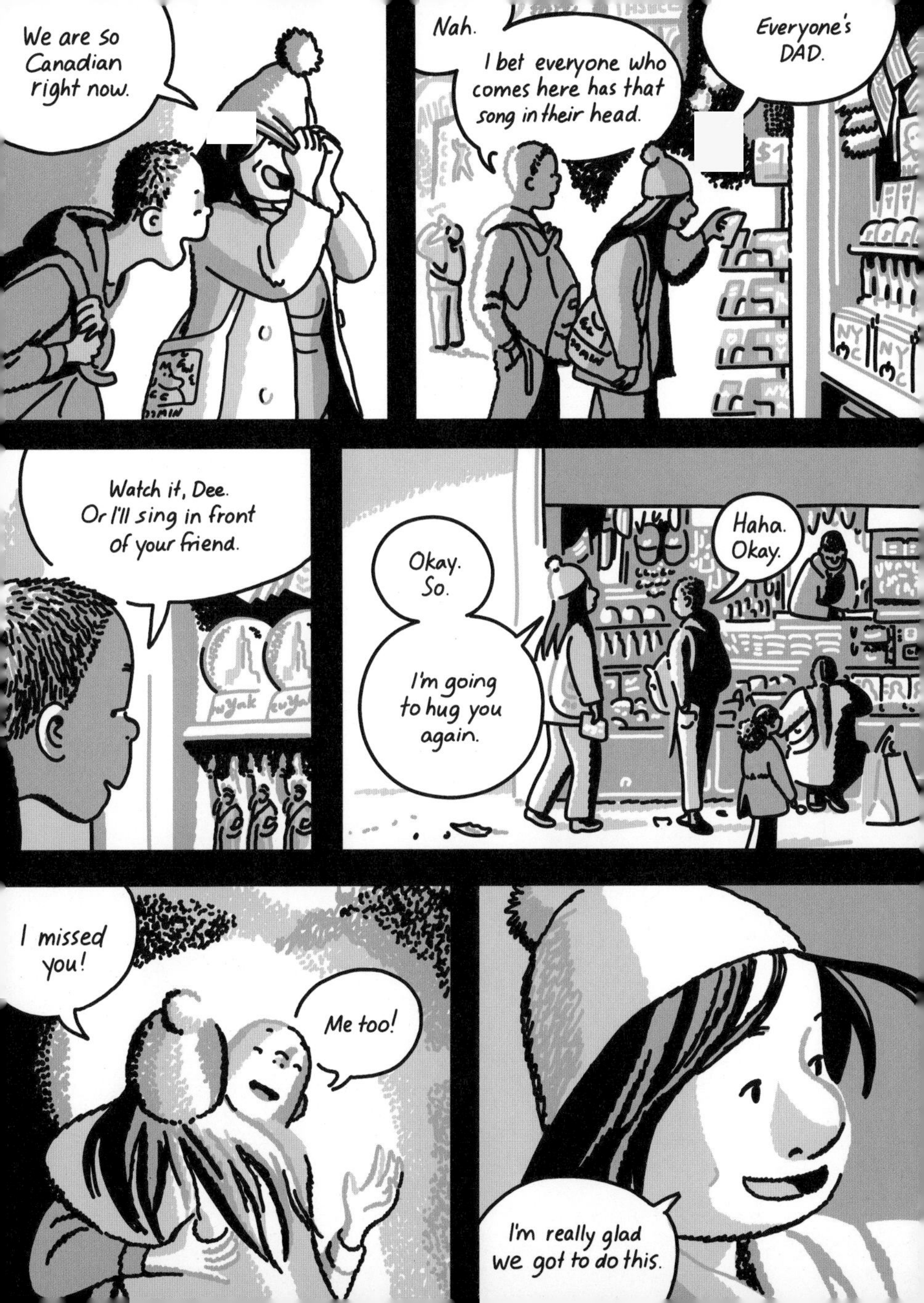
We are so Canadian right now.
Nah.
I bet everyone who comes here has that song in their head.
Everyone's DAD.
Watch it, Dee. Or I'll sing in front of your friend.
Okay. So.
I'm going to hug you again.
Haha. Okay.
I missed you!
Me too!
I'm really glad we got to do this.

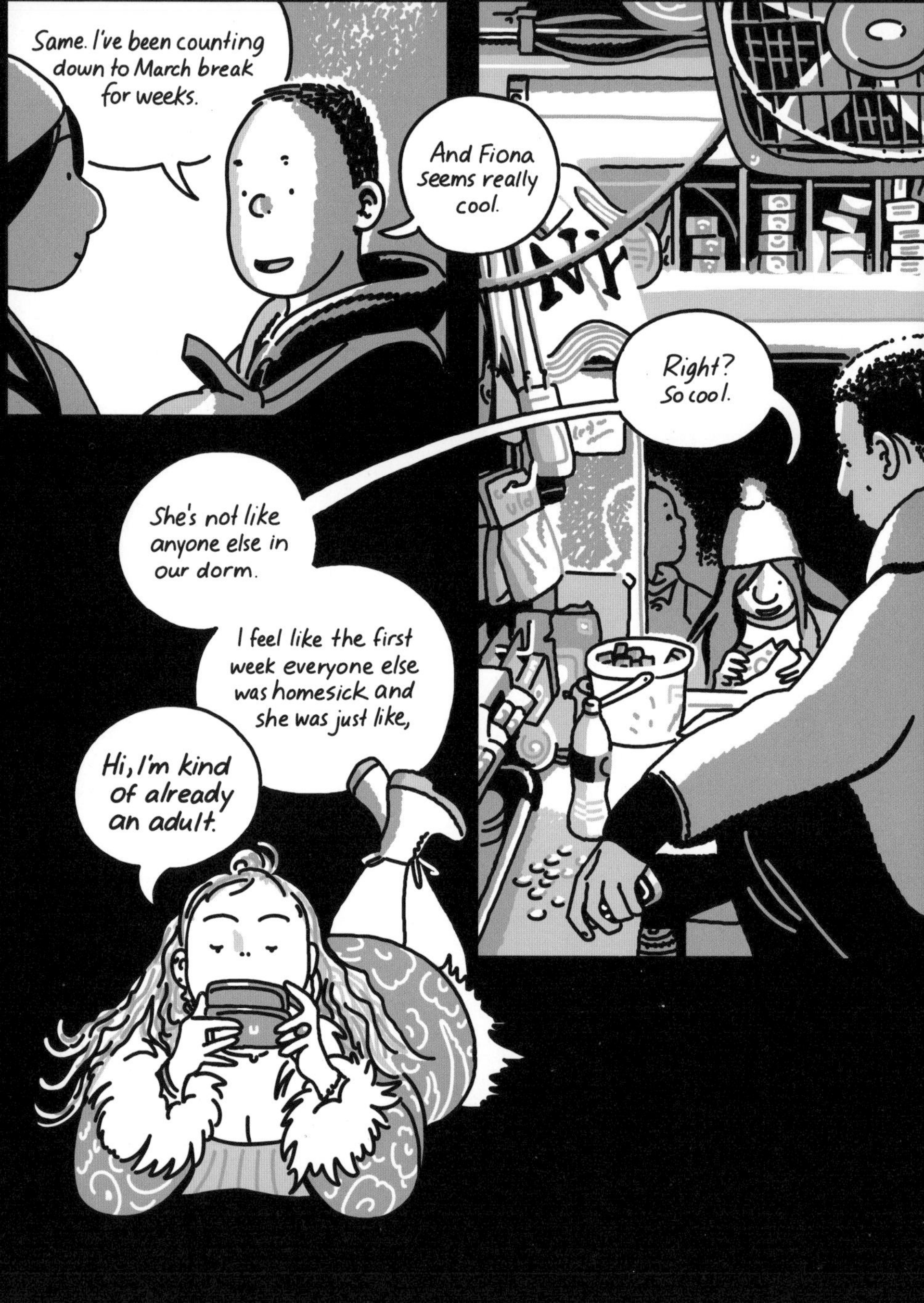
Same. I've been counting down to March break for weeks.
And Fiona seems really cool.
Right? So cool.
She's not like anyone else in our dorm.
I feel like the first week everyone else was homesick and she was just like,
Hi, I'm kind of already an adult.

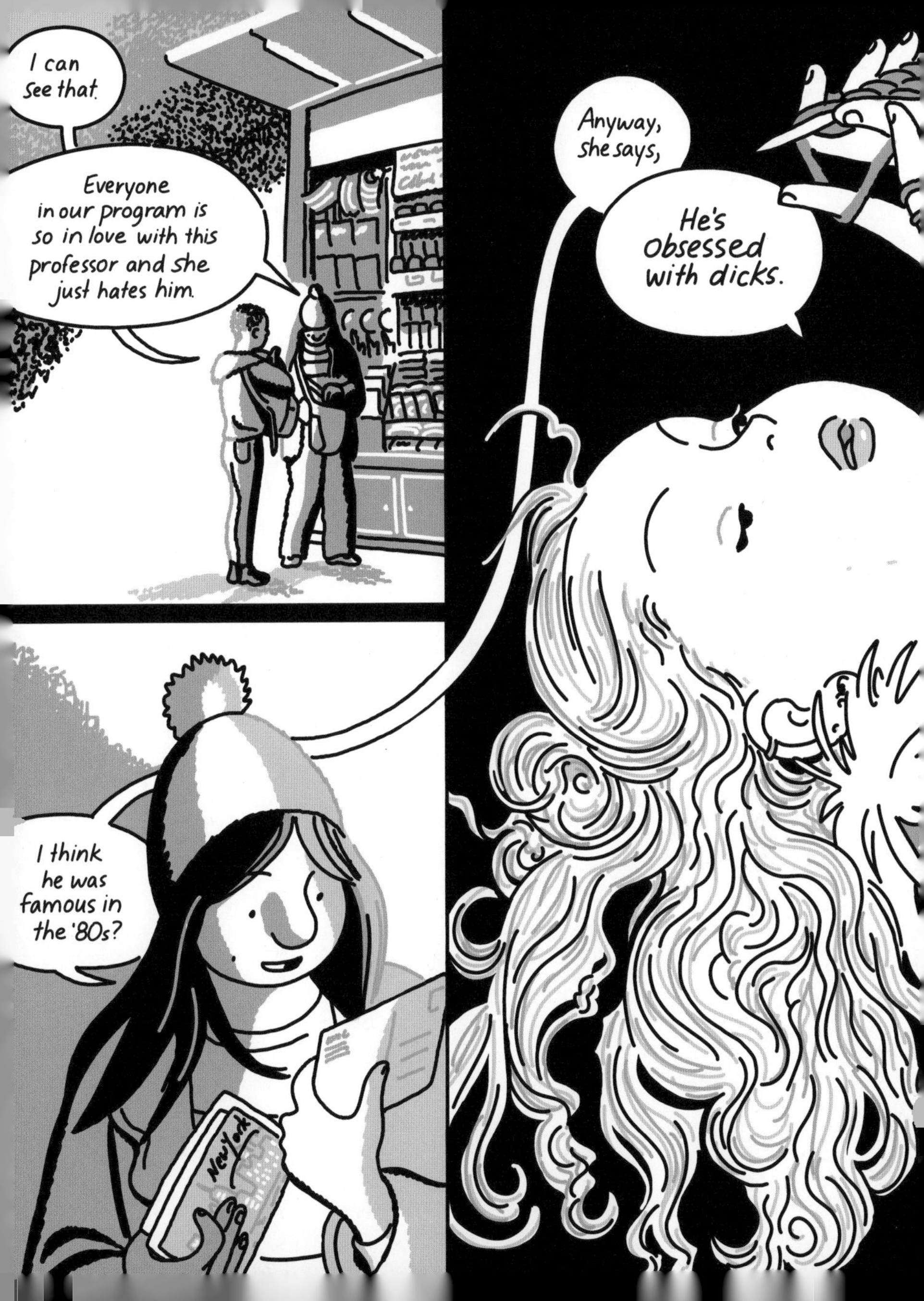
I can see that.
Everyone in our program is so in love with this professor and she just hates him.
Anyway, she says,
He's obsessed with dicks.
I think he was famous in the '80s?
New York

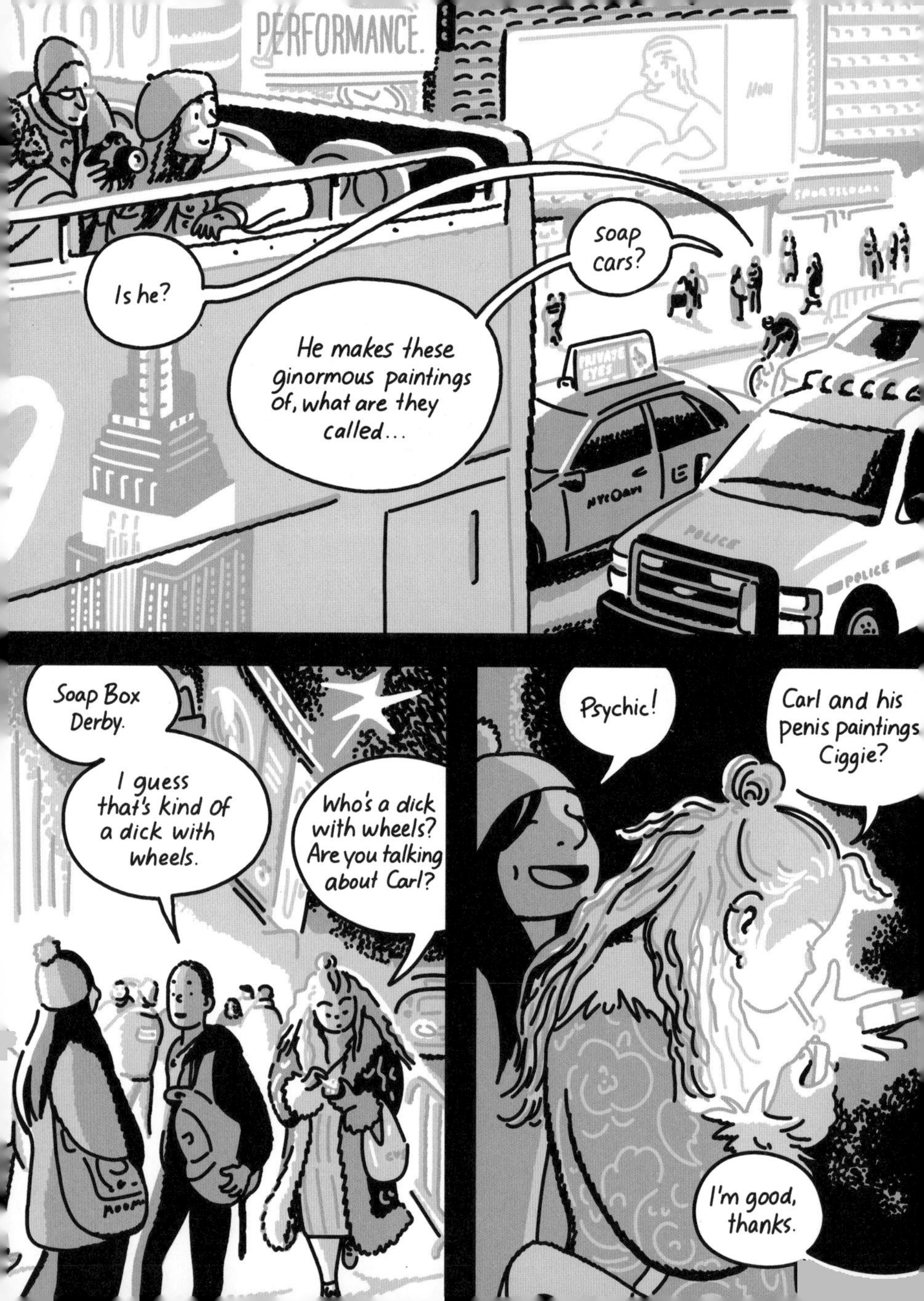
PERFORMANCE.
Is he?
soap cars?
He makes these ginormous paintings of, what are they called...
PRIVATE EYES
NYC TAXI
POLICE
POLICE
Soap Box Derby.
I guess that's kind of a dick with wheels.
Who's a dick with wheels? Are you talking about Carl?
Psychic!
Carl and his penis paintings. Ciggie?
I'm good, thanks.

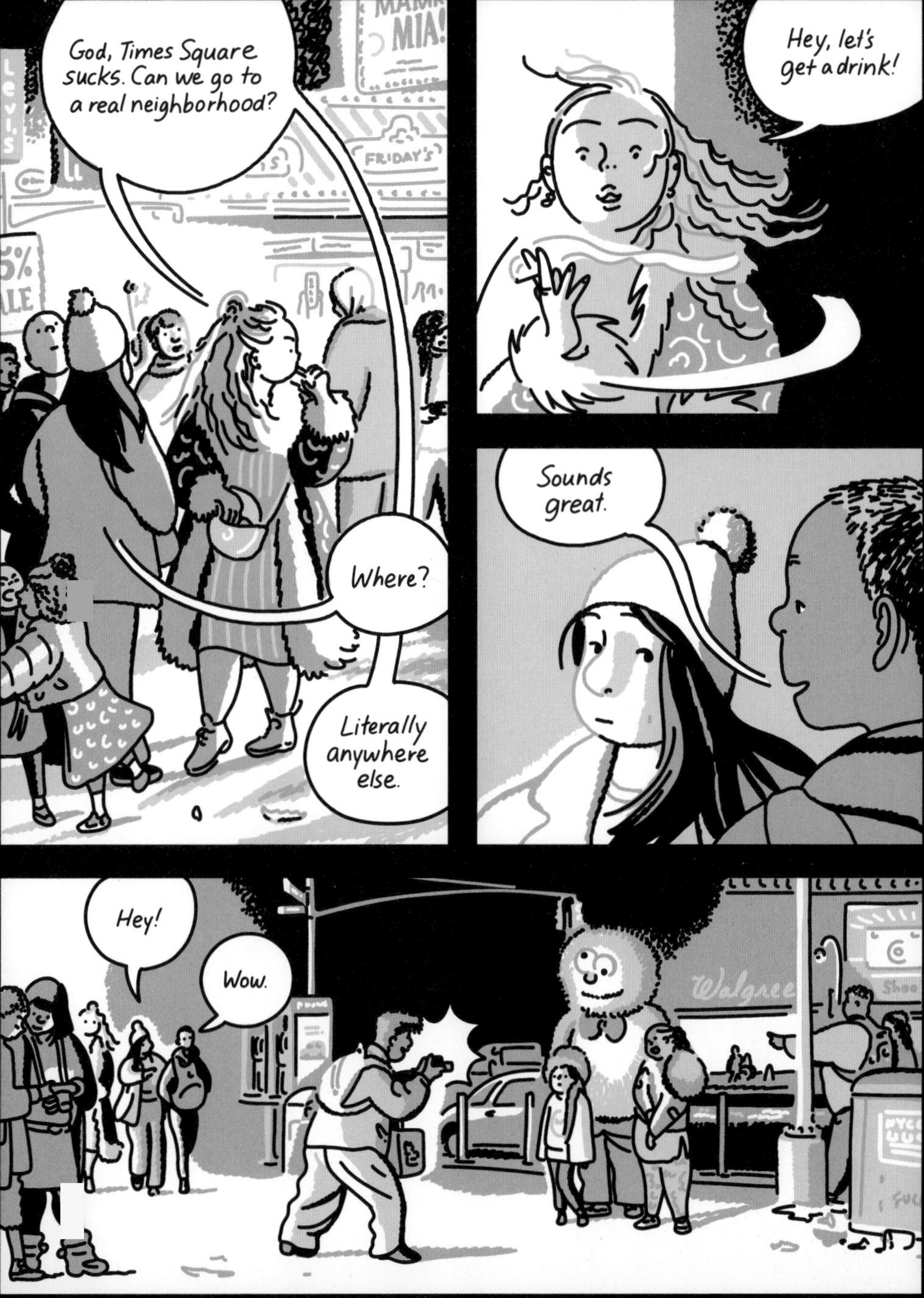
MIA!
FRIDAY'S
God, Times Square sucks. Can we go to a real neighborhood?
Where?
Literally anywhere else.
Hey, let's get a drink!
Sounds great.
Hey!
Wow.

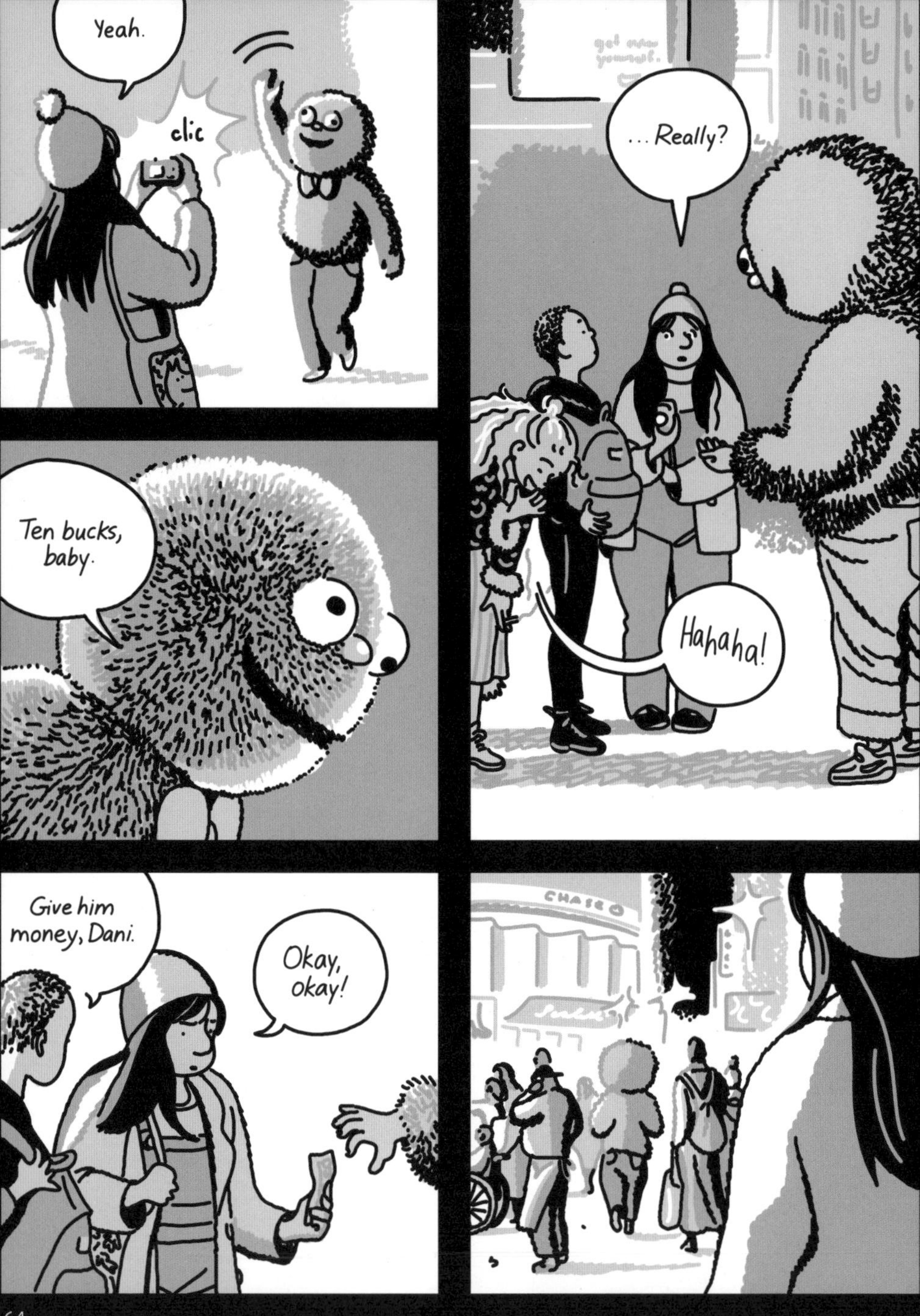
Yeah.
clic
Ten bucks, baby.
... Really?
Hahaha!
Give him money, Dani.
Okay, okay!
CHASE

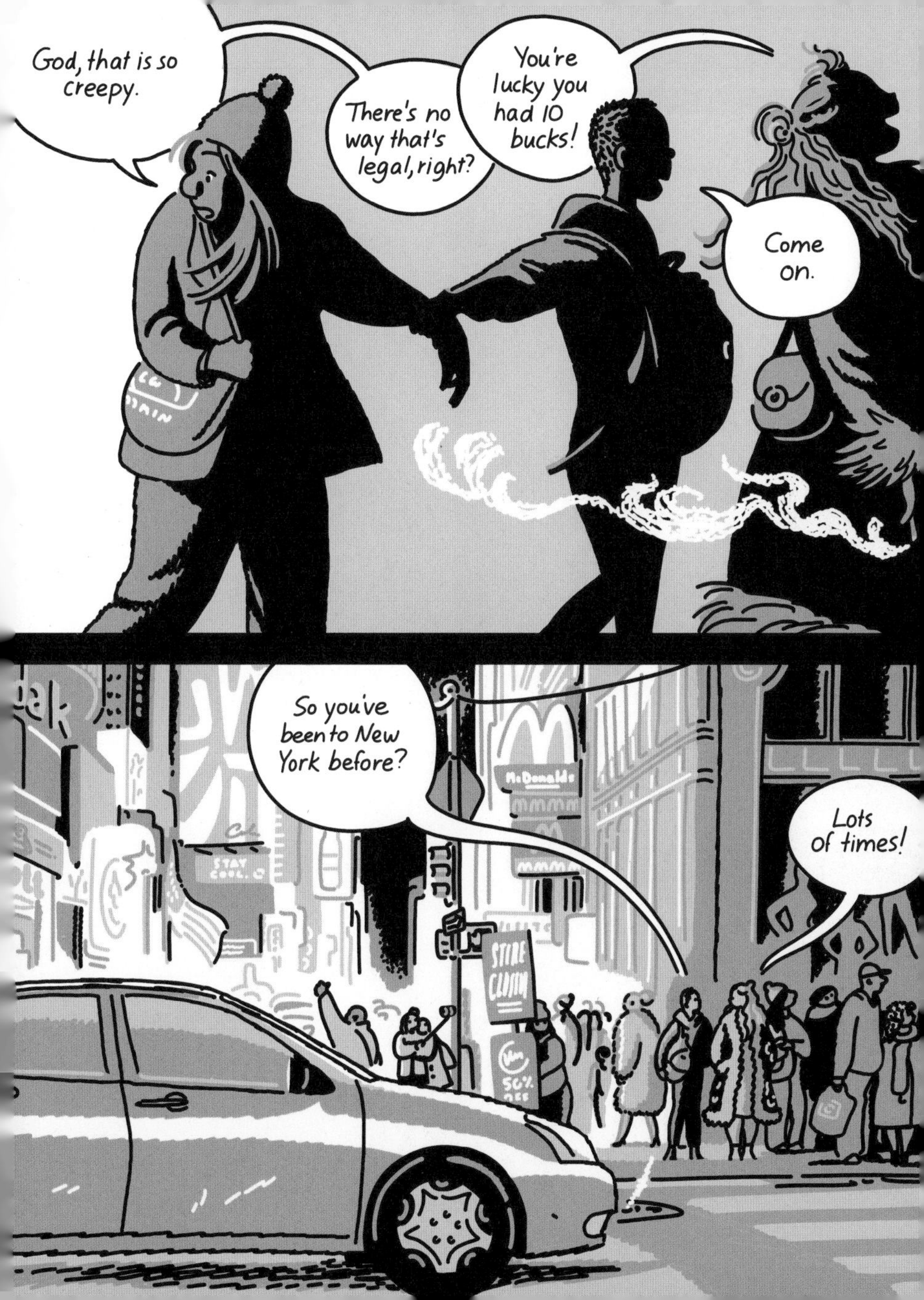
God, that is so creepy.
There's no way that's legal, right?
You're lucky you had 10 bucks!
Come on.
So you've been to New York before?
Lots of times!

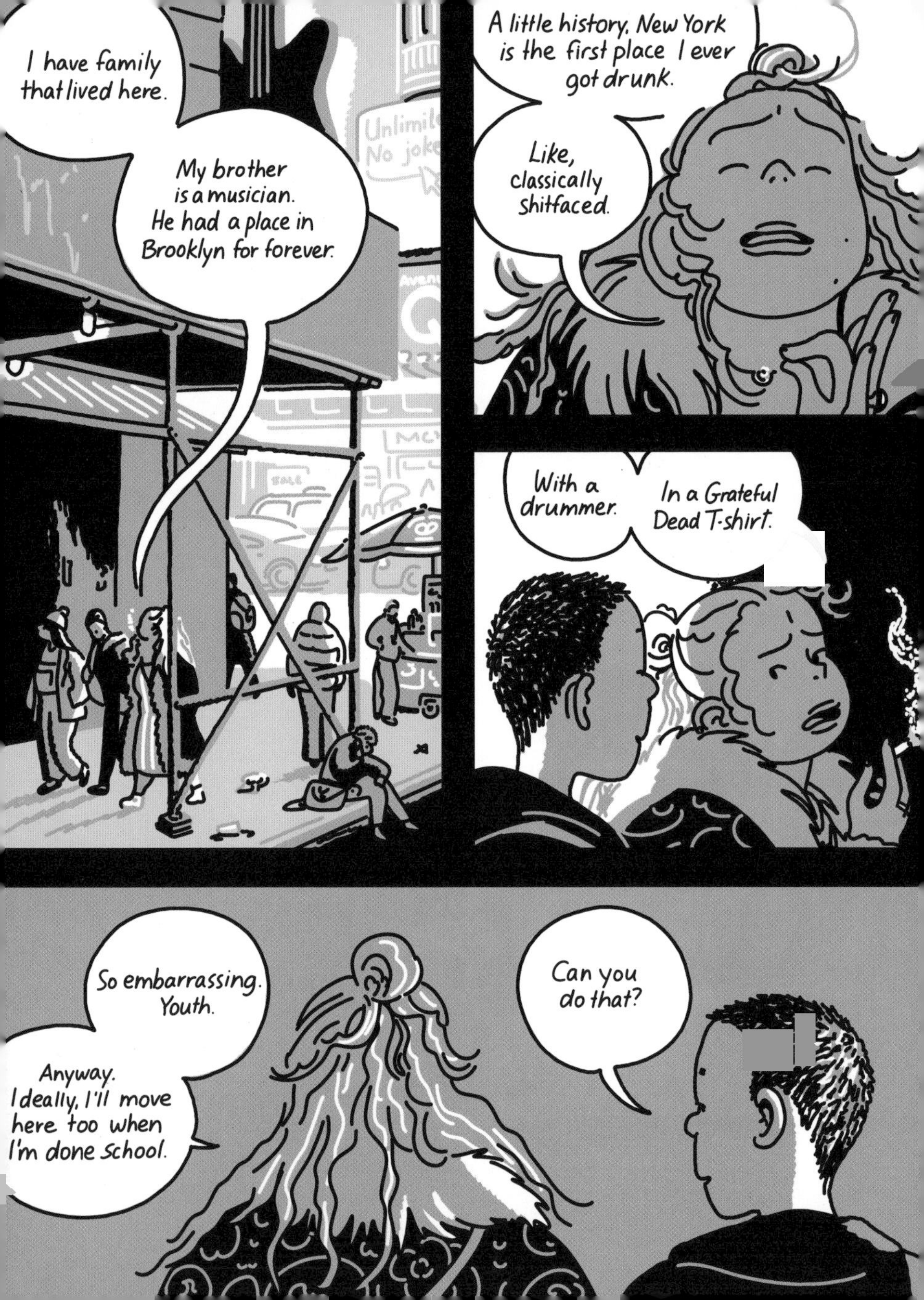
I have family that lived here.
My brother is a musician. He had a place in Brooklyn for forever.
A little history, New York is the first place I ever got drunk.
Like, classically shitfaced.
With a drummer.
In a Grateful Dead T-shirt.
So embarrassing. Youth.
Anyway. Ideally, I'll move here too when I'm done school.
Can you do that?

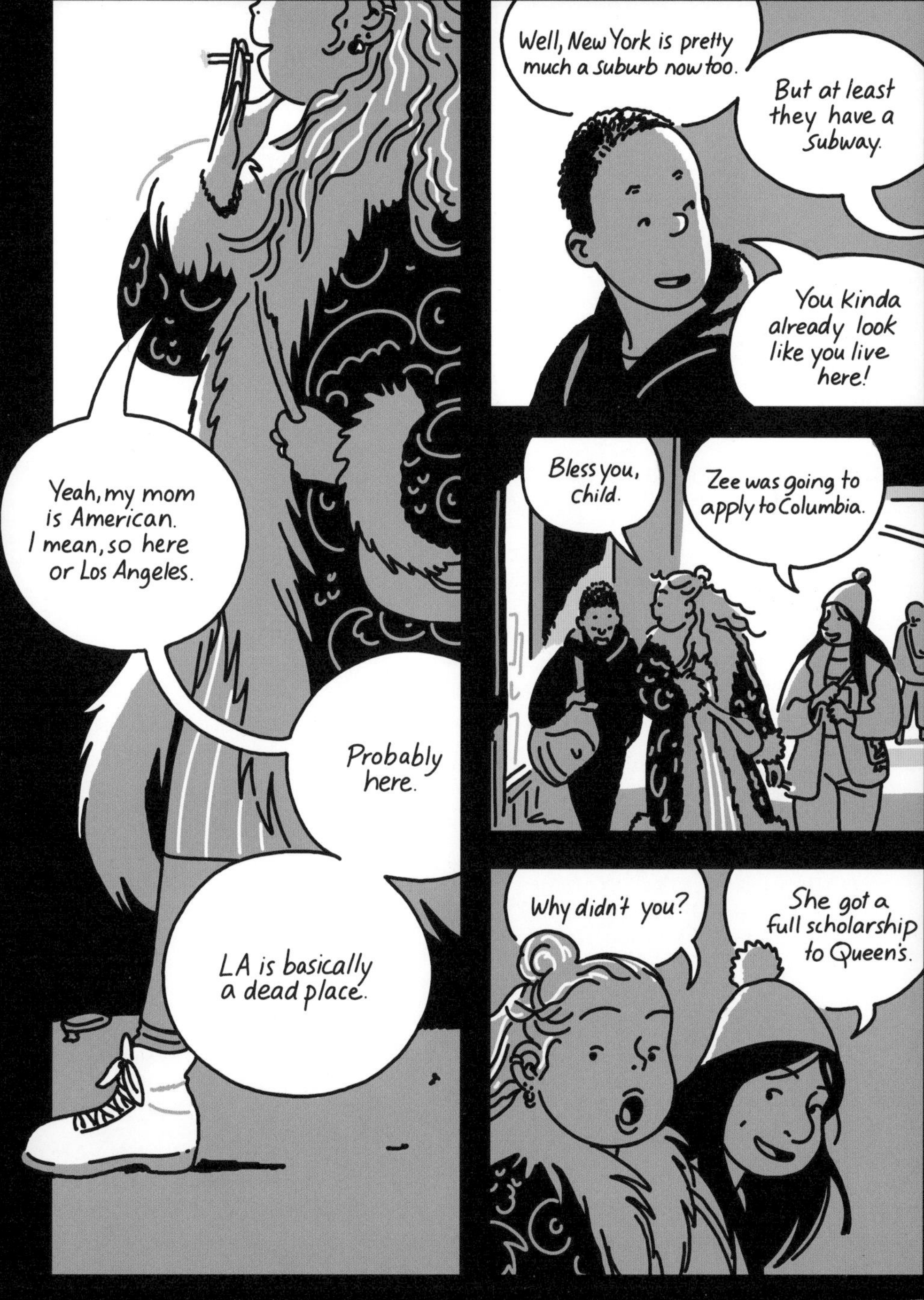
Well, New York is pretty much a suburb now too.
But at least they have a subway.
You kinda already look like you live here!
Yeah, my mom is American. I mean, so here or Los Angeles.
Probably here.
LA is basically a dead place.
Bless you, child.
Zee was going to apply to Columbia.
Why didn't you?
She got a full scholarship to Queen's.

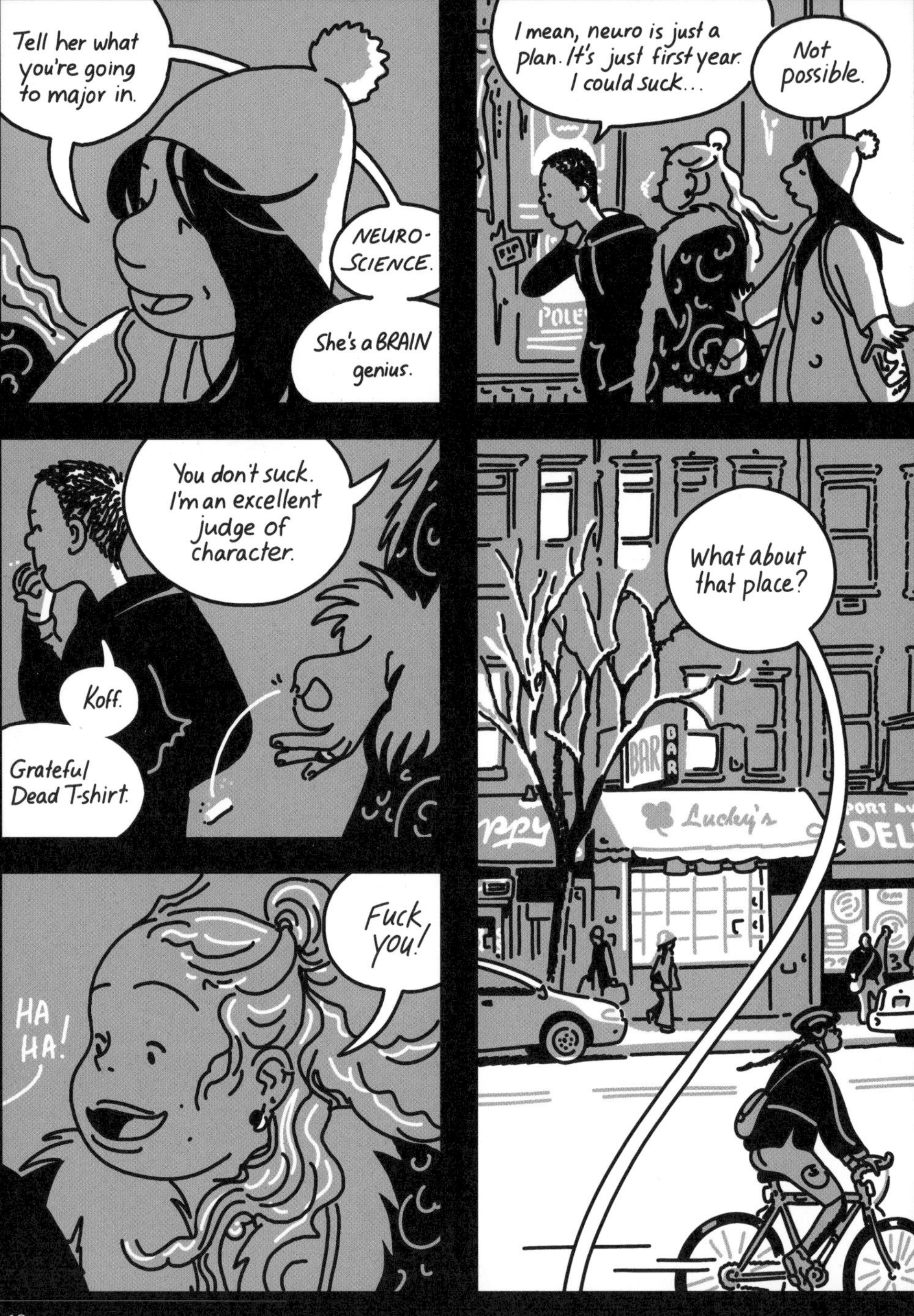
Tell her what you're going to major in.
NEURO-SCIENCE.
She's a BRAIN genius.
I mean, neuro is just a plan. It's just first year. I could suck...
Not possible.
POLE
You don't suck. I'm an excellent judge of character.
Koff.
Grateful Dead T-shirt.
What about that place?
BAR
BAR
Lucky's
DELI
Fuck you!
HA HA!

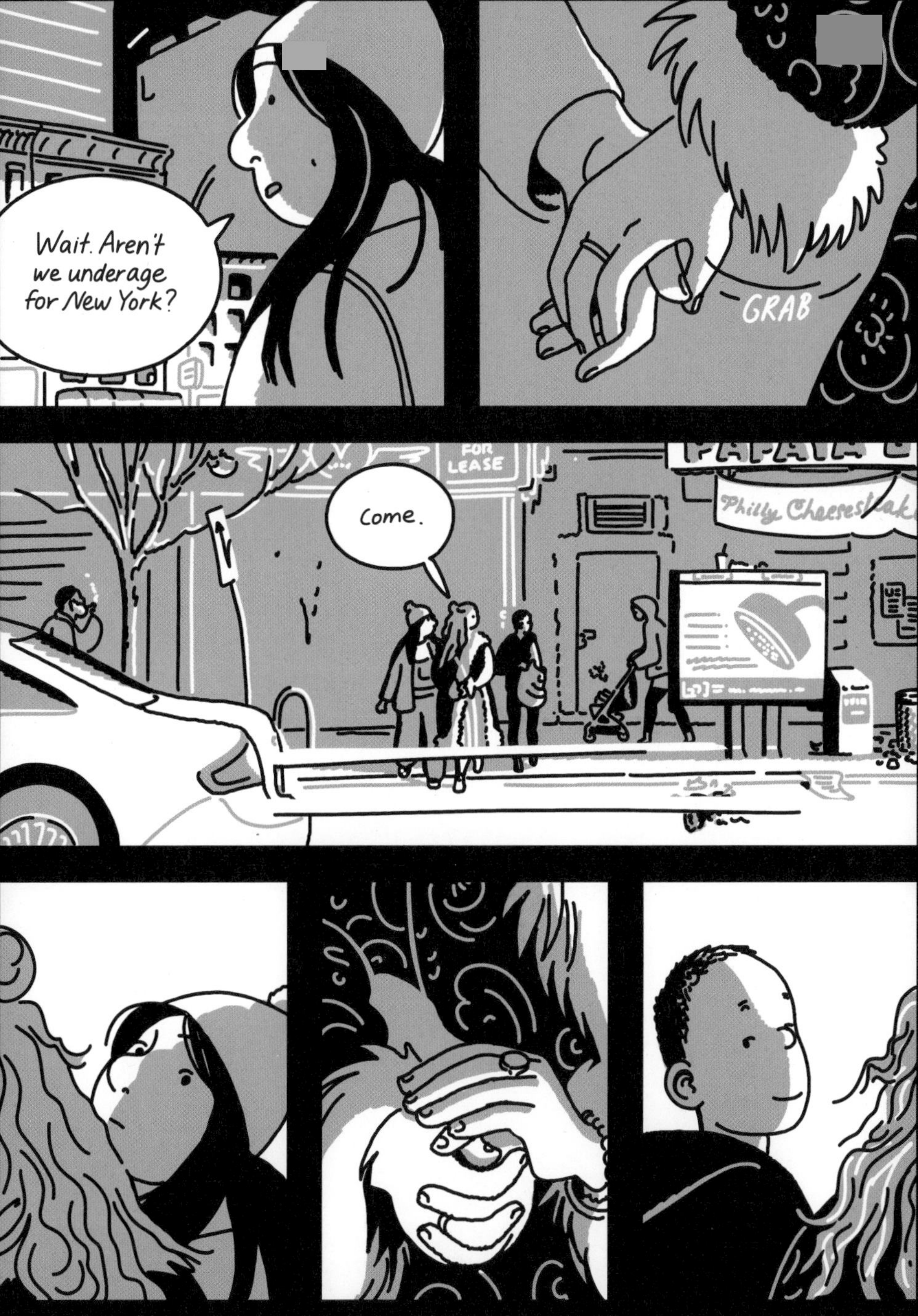

Wait. Aren't we underage for New York?
GRAB
FOR LEASE
Come.

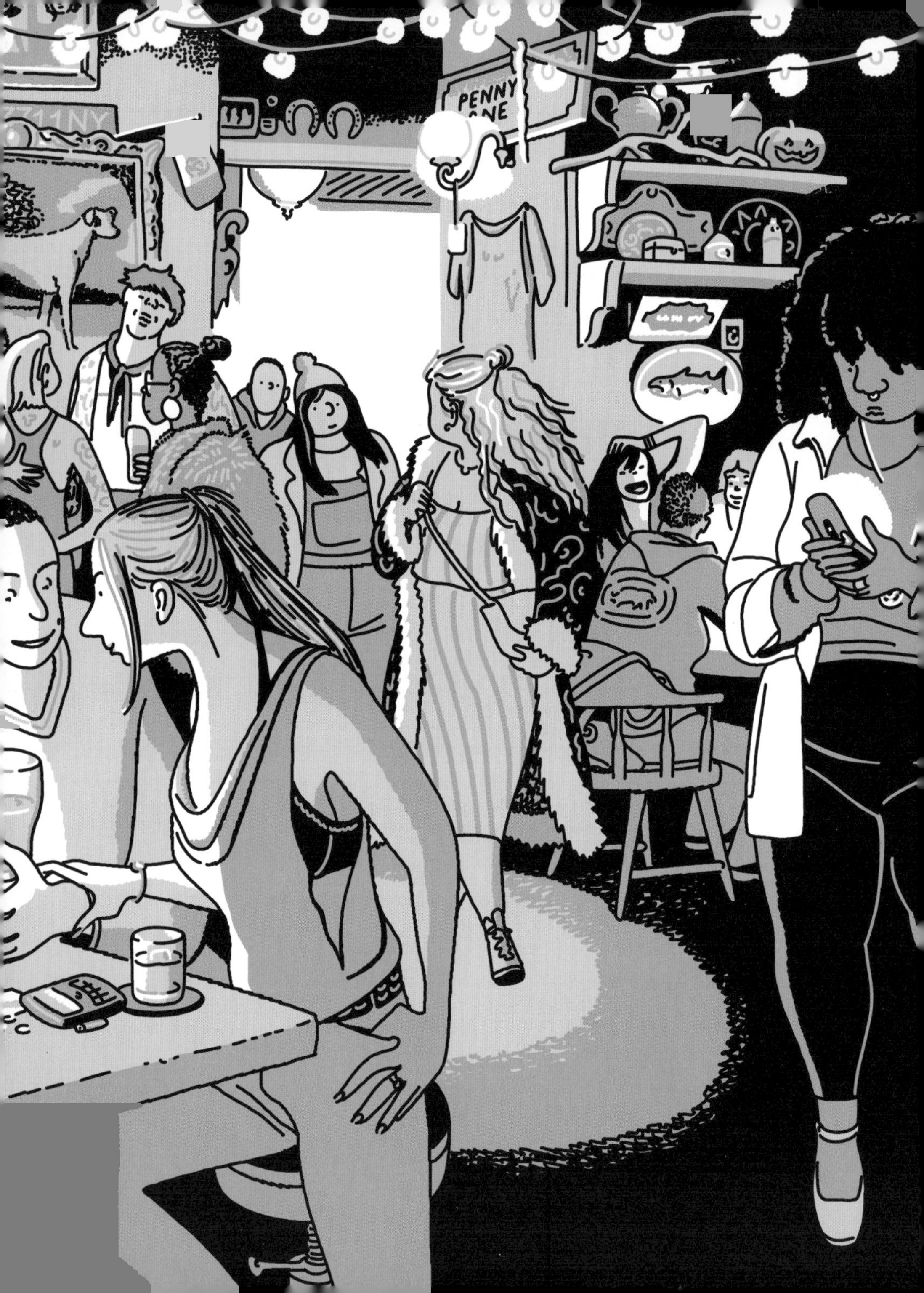
PENNY

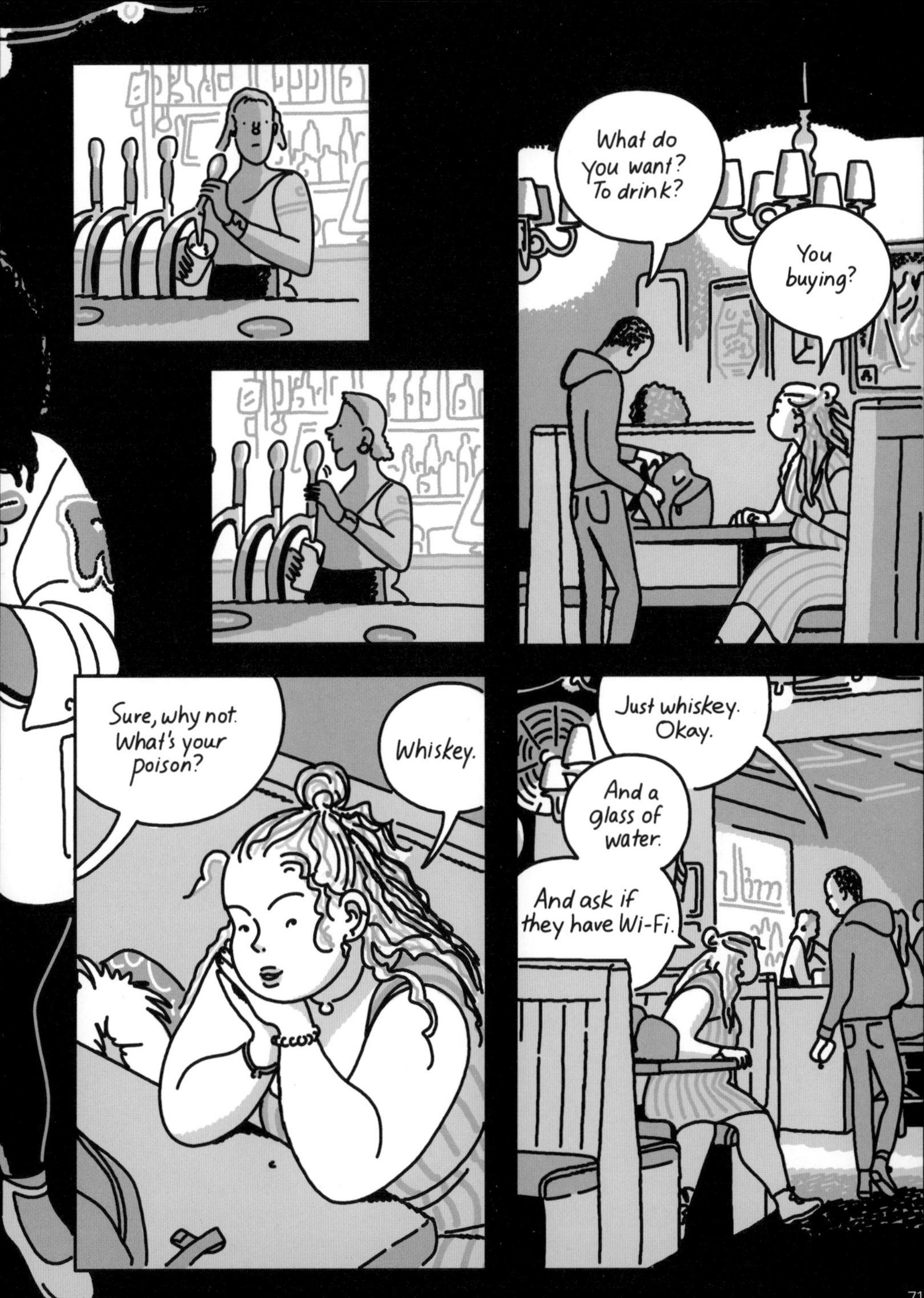
What do you want? To drink?
You buying?
Sure, why not. What's your poison?
Whiskey.
Just whiskey. Okay.
And a glass of water.
And ask if they have Wi-Fi.

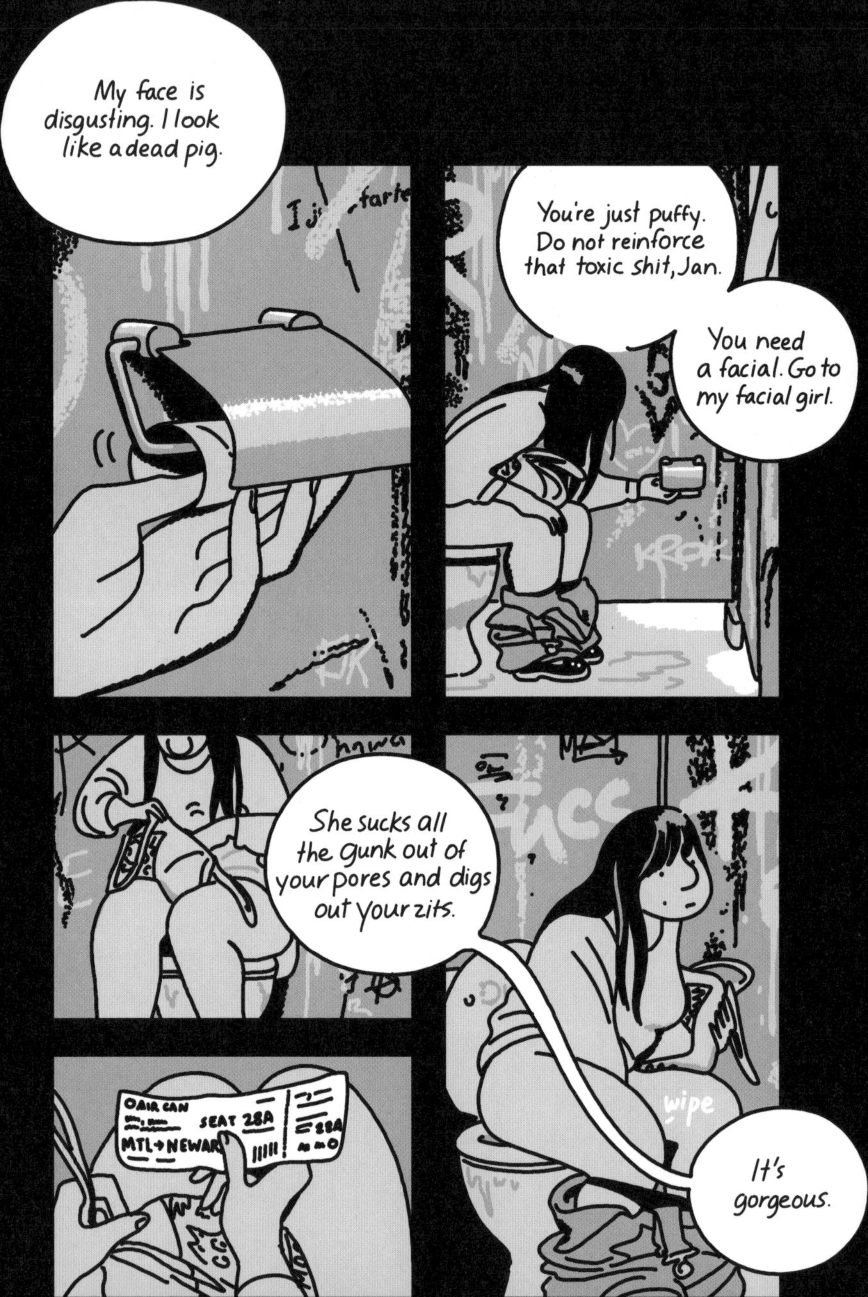
My face is disgusting. I look like a dead pig.
You're just puffy. Do not reinforce that toxic shit, Jan.
You need a facial. Go to my facial girl.
She sucks all the gunk out of your pores and digs out your zits.
wipe
It's gorgeous.
AIR CAN
SEAT 28A
MTL → NEWAR
28A

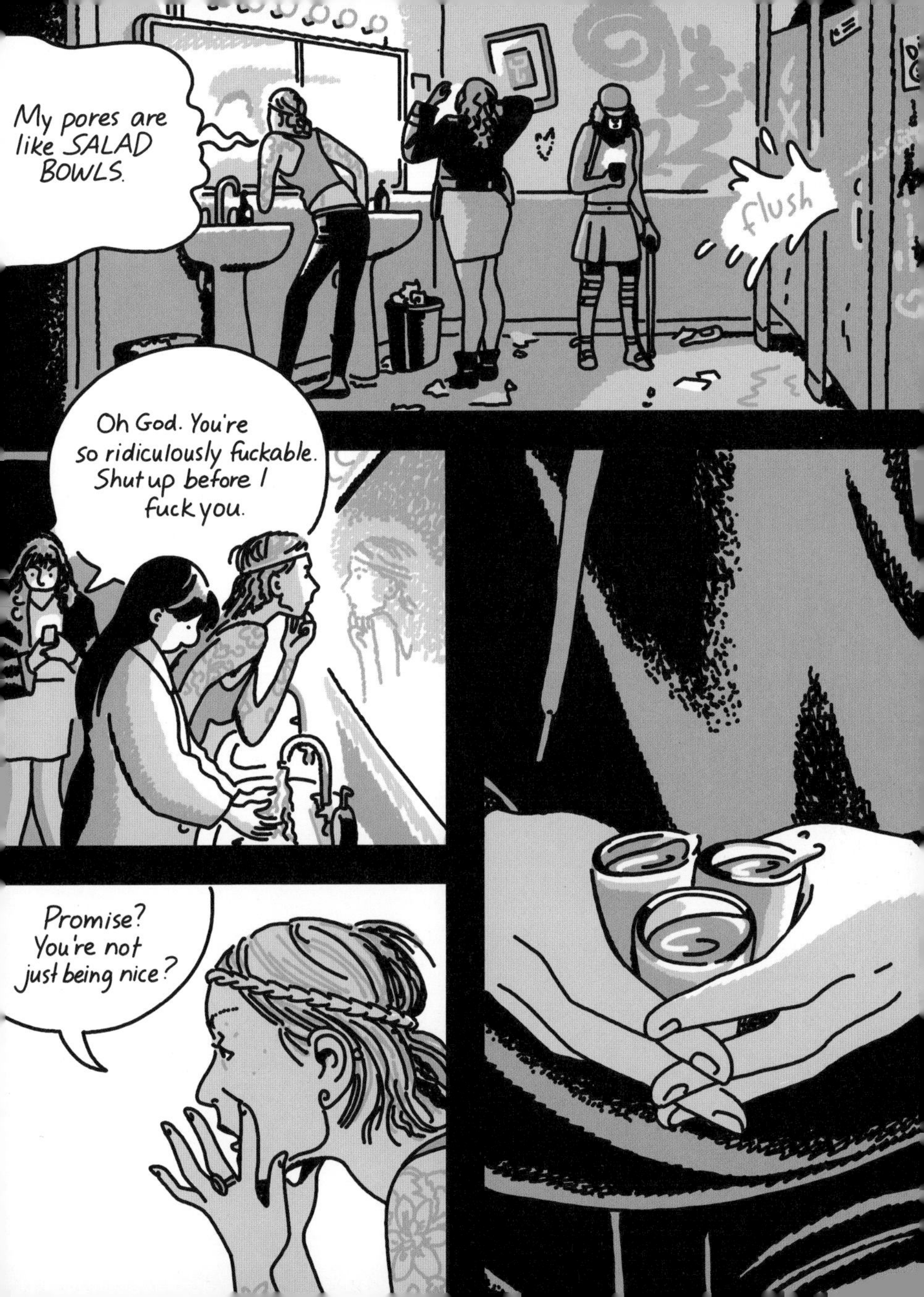
My pores are like SALAD BOWLS.
flush
Oh God. You're so ridiculously fuckable. Shut up before I fuck you.
Promise? You're not just being nice?

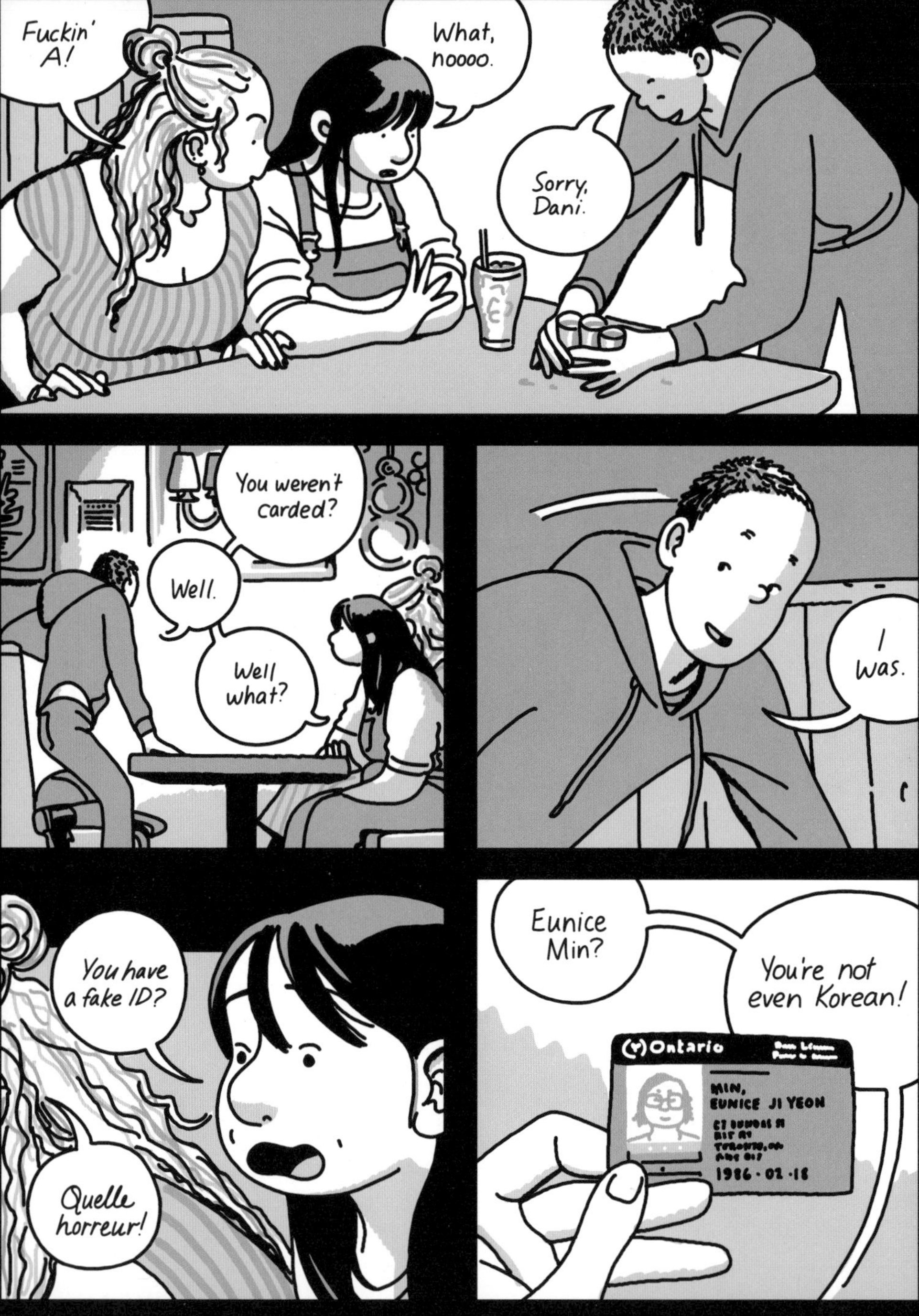
Fuckin' A!
What, noooo.
Sorry, Dani.
You weren't carded?
Well.
Well what?
I was.
You have a fake ID?
Quelle horreur!
Eunice Min?
You're not even Korean!
Ontario
MIN, EUNICE JI YEON
1986 - 02 - 18

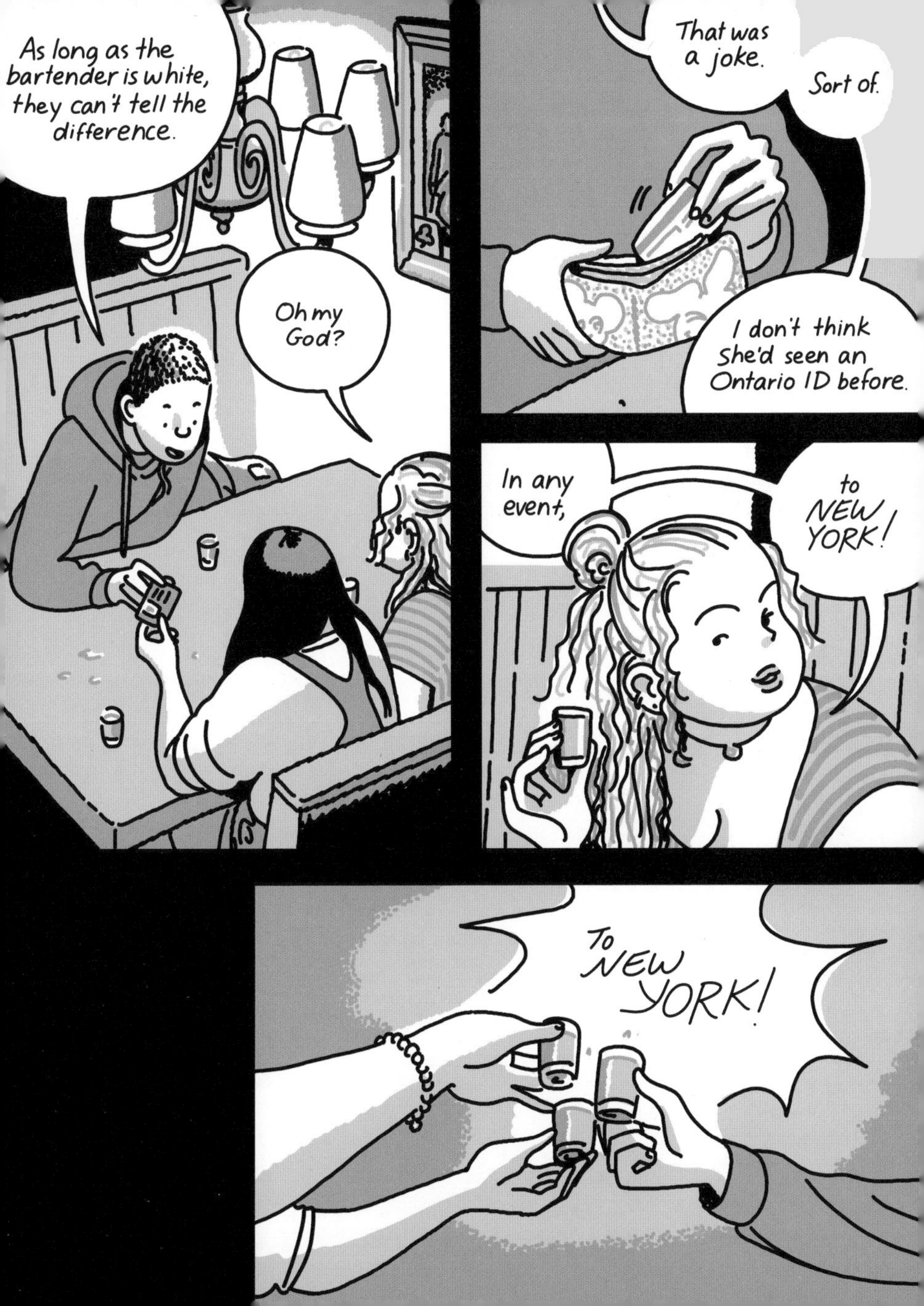
As long as the bartender is white, they can't tell the difference.
Oh my God?
That was a joke.
Sort of.
I don't think she'd seen an Ontario ID before.
In any event,
to NEW YORK!
To NEW YORK!

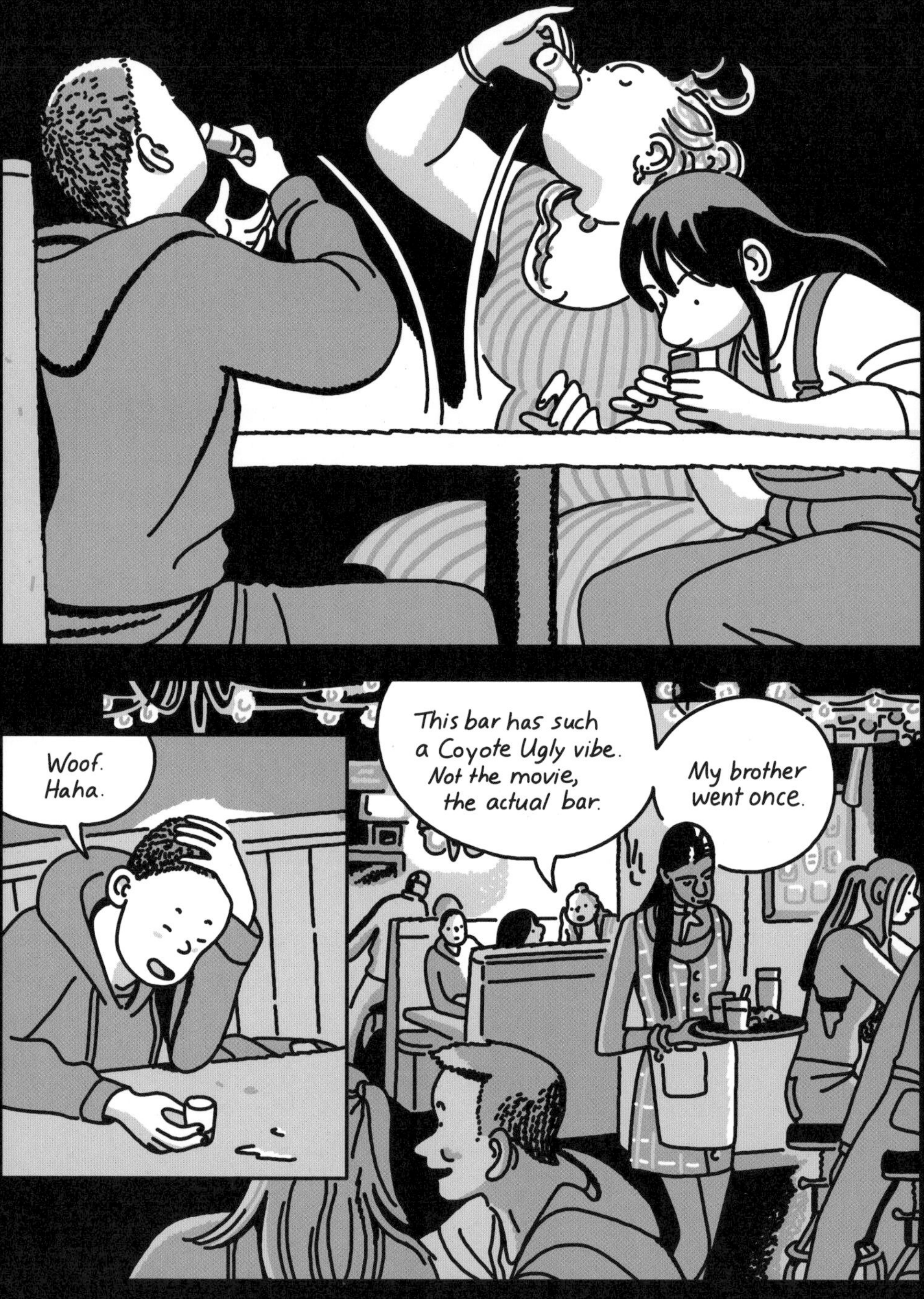
Woof. Haha.
This bar has such a Coyote Ugly vibe. Not the movie, the actual bar.
My brother went once.

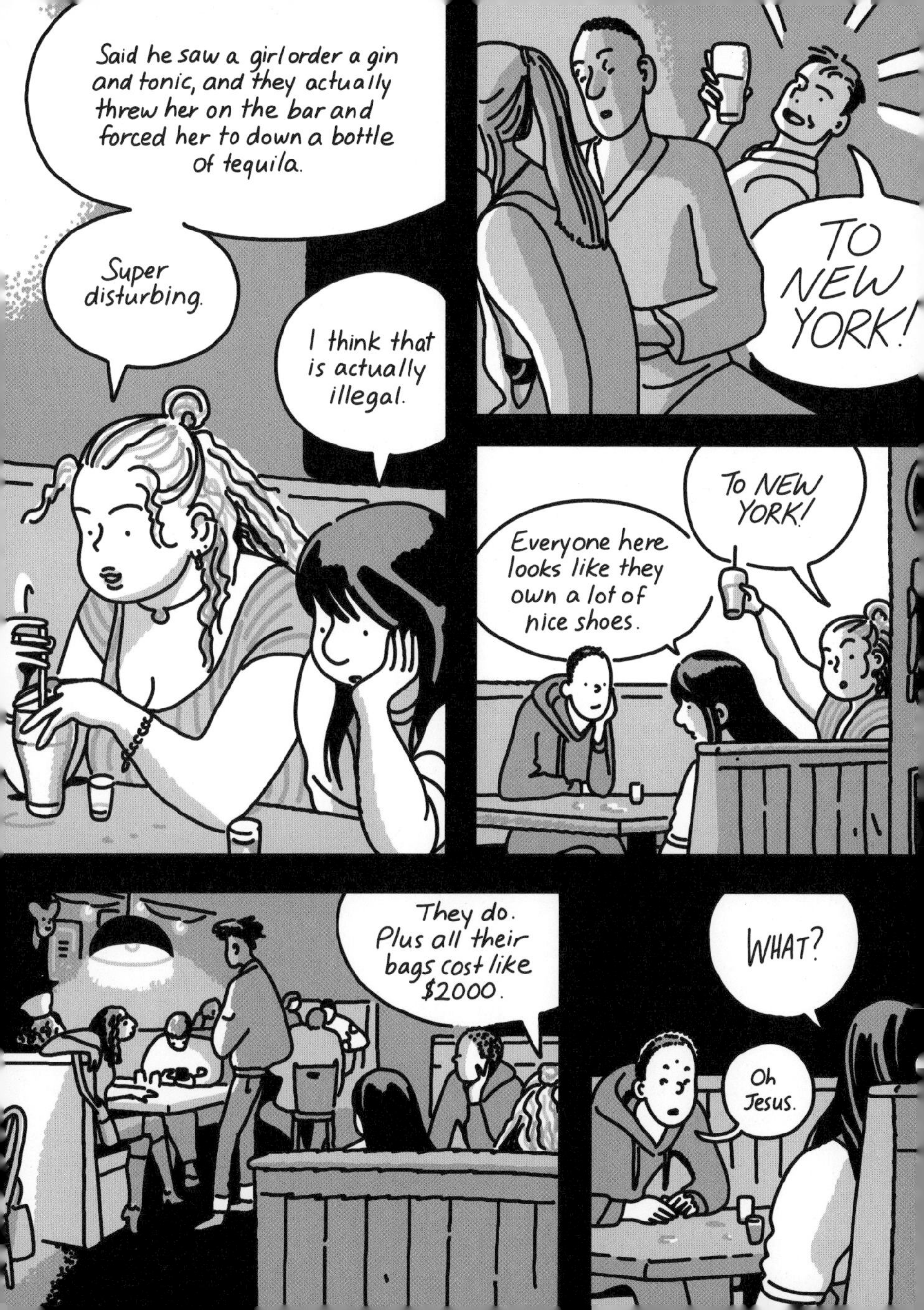
Said he saw a girl order a gin and tonic, and they actually threw her on the bar and forced her to down a bottle of tequila.
Super disturbing.
I think that is actually illegal.
TO NEW YORK!
Everyone here looks like they own a lot of nice shoes.
To NEW YORK!
They do. Plus all their bags cost like $2000.
WHAT?
Oh Jesus.

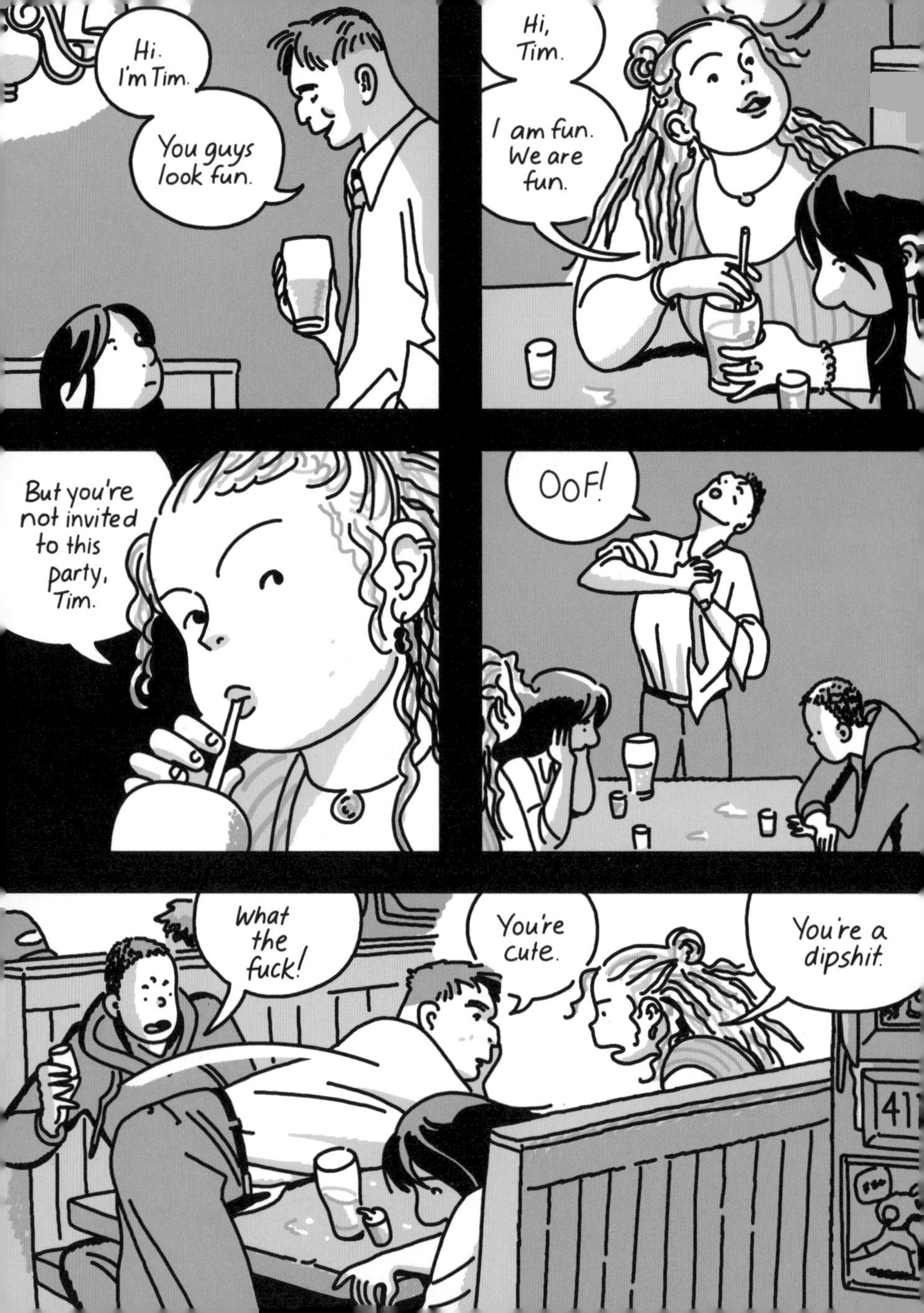
Hi. I'm Tim.
You guys look fun.
Hi, Tim.
I am fun. We are fun.
But you're not invited to this party, Tim.
OOF!
What the fuck!
You're cute.
You're a dipshit.
411

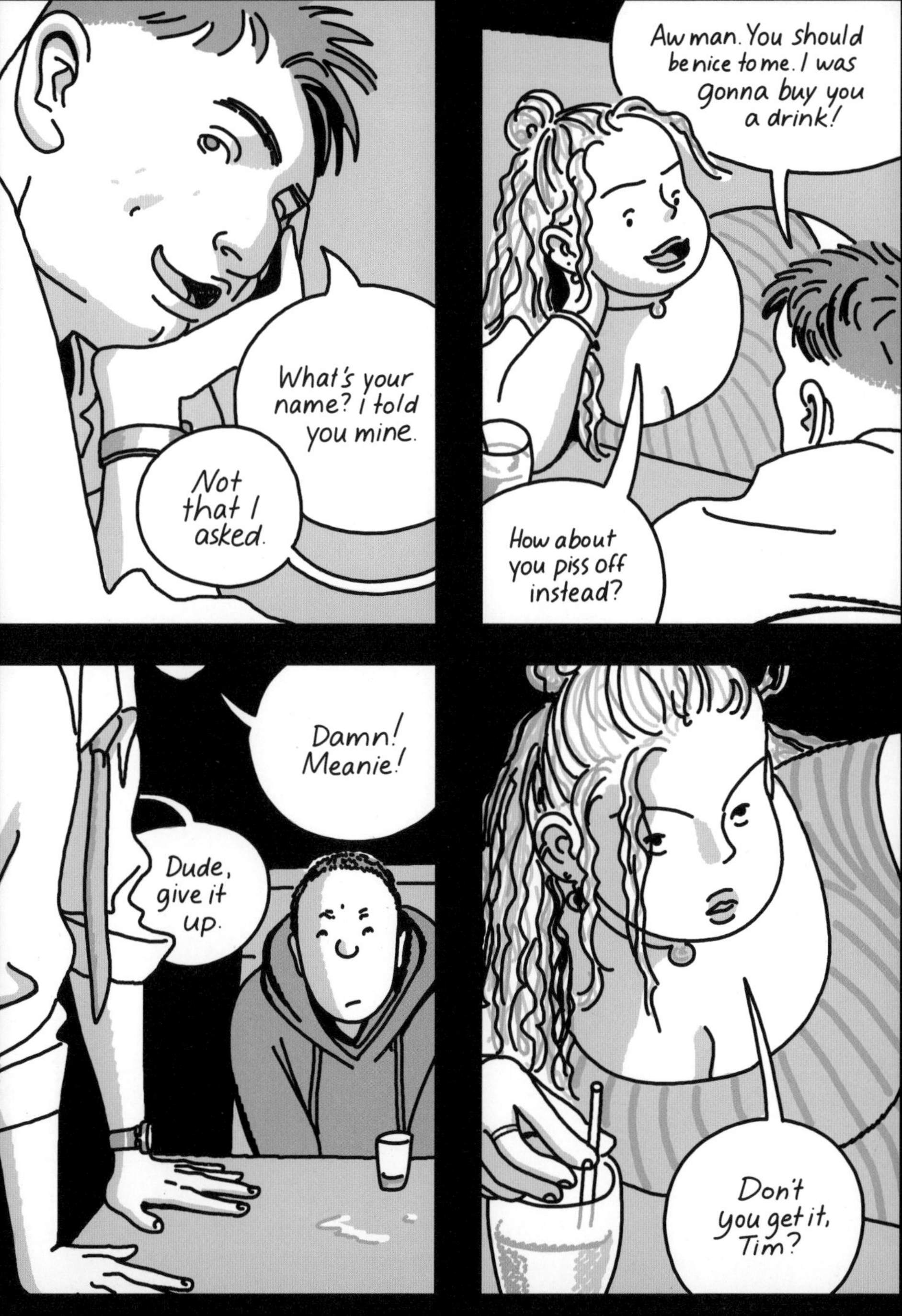
What's your name? I told you mine.
Not that I asked.
Aw man. You should be nice to me. I was gonna buy you a drink!
How about you piss off instead?
Damn! Meanie!
Dude, give it up.
Don't you get it, Tim?

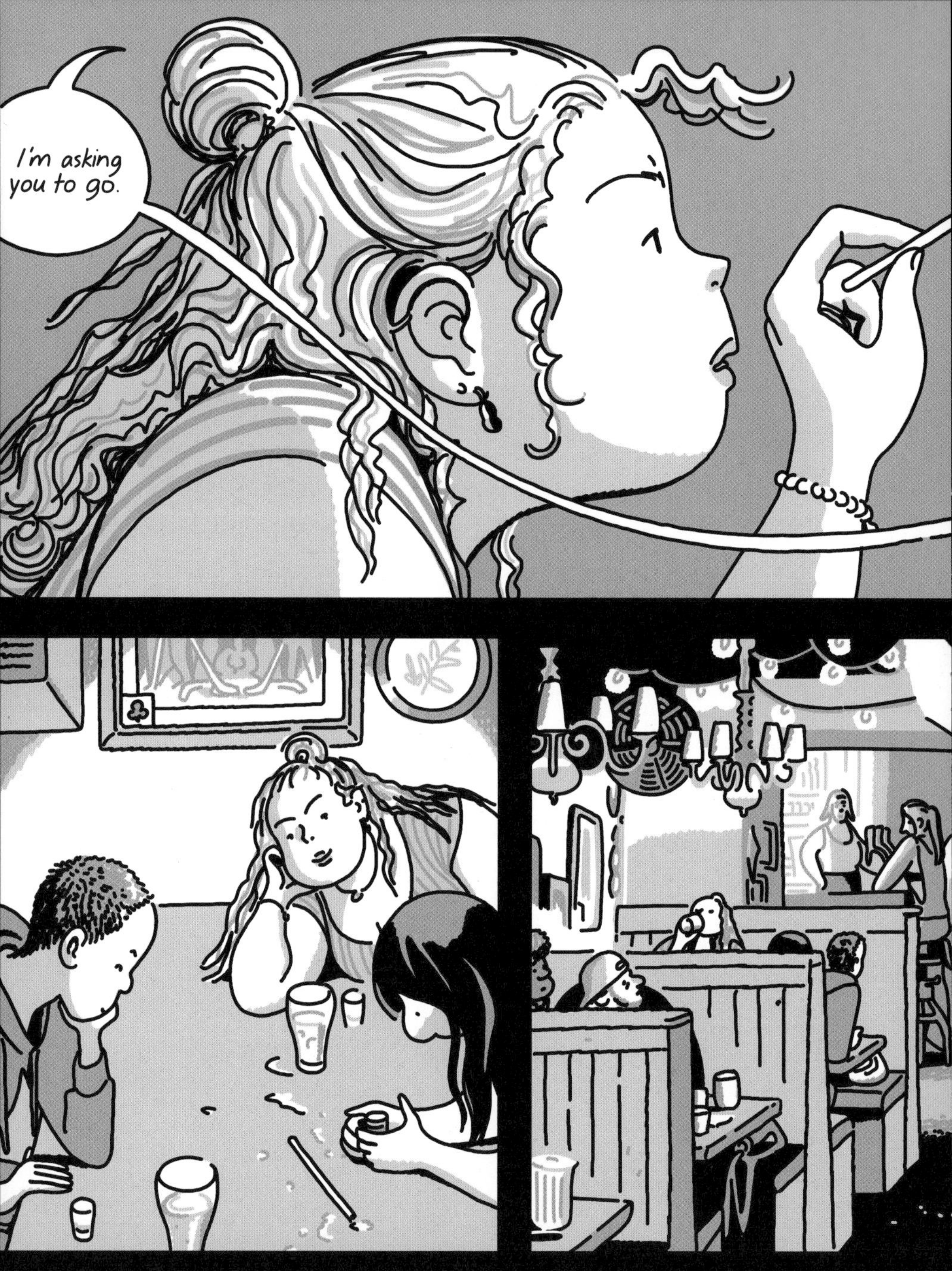
I'm asking you to go.

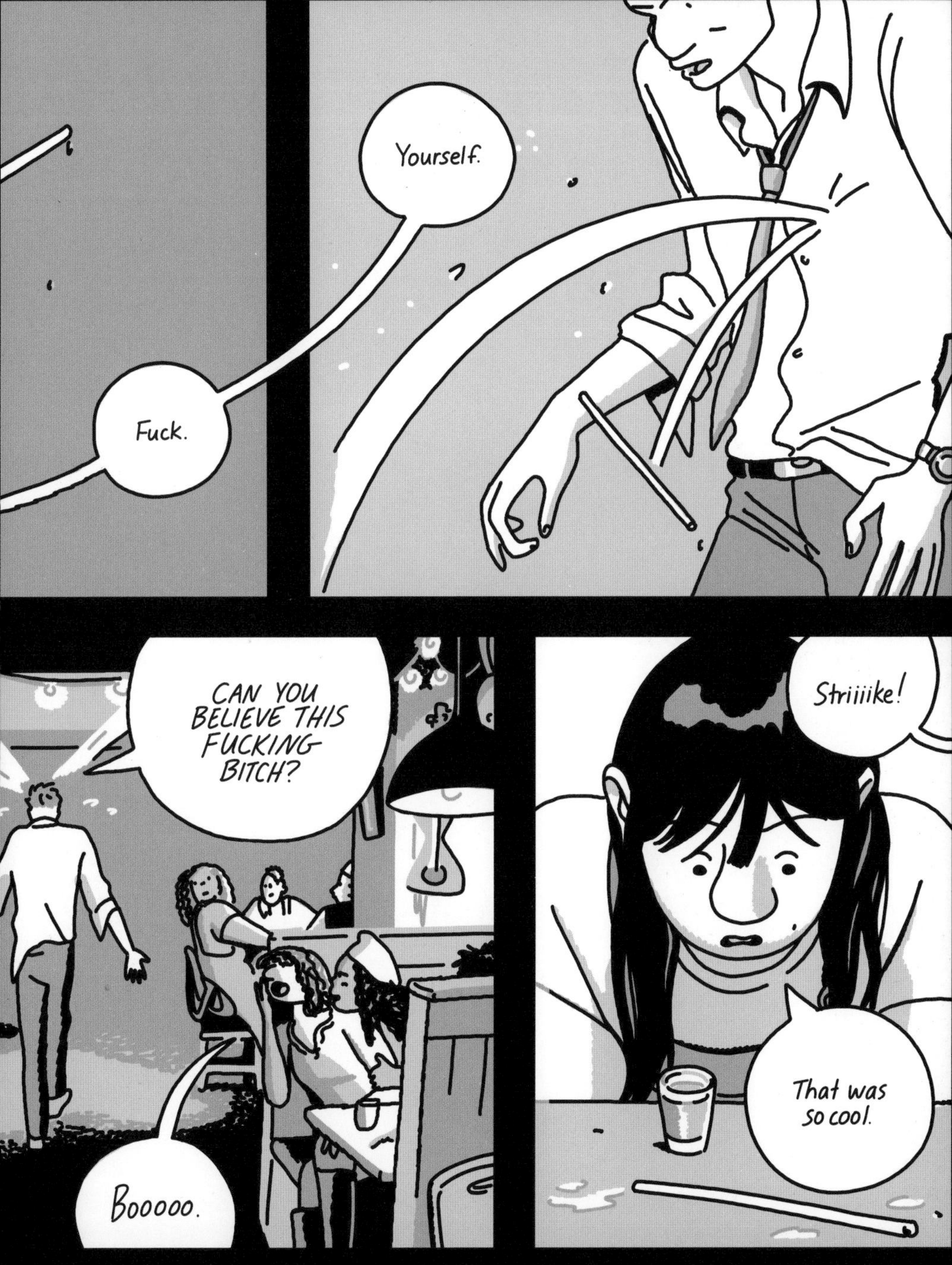
Fuck.
Yourself.
CAN YOU BELIEVE THIS FUCKING BITCH?
Booooo.
Striiiike!
That was so cool.

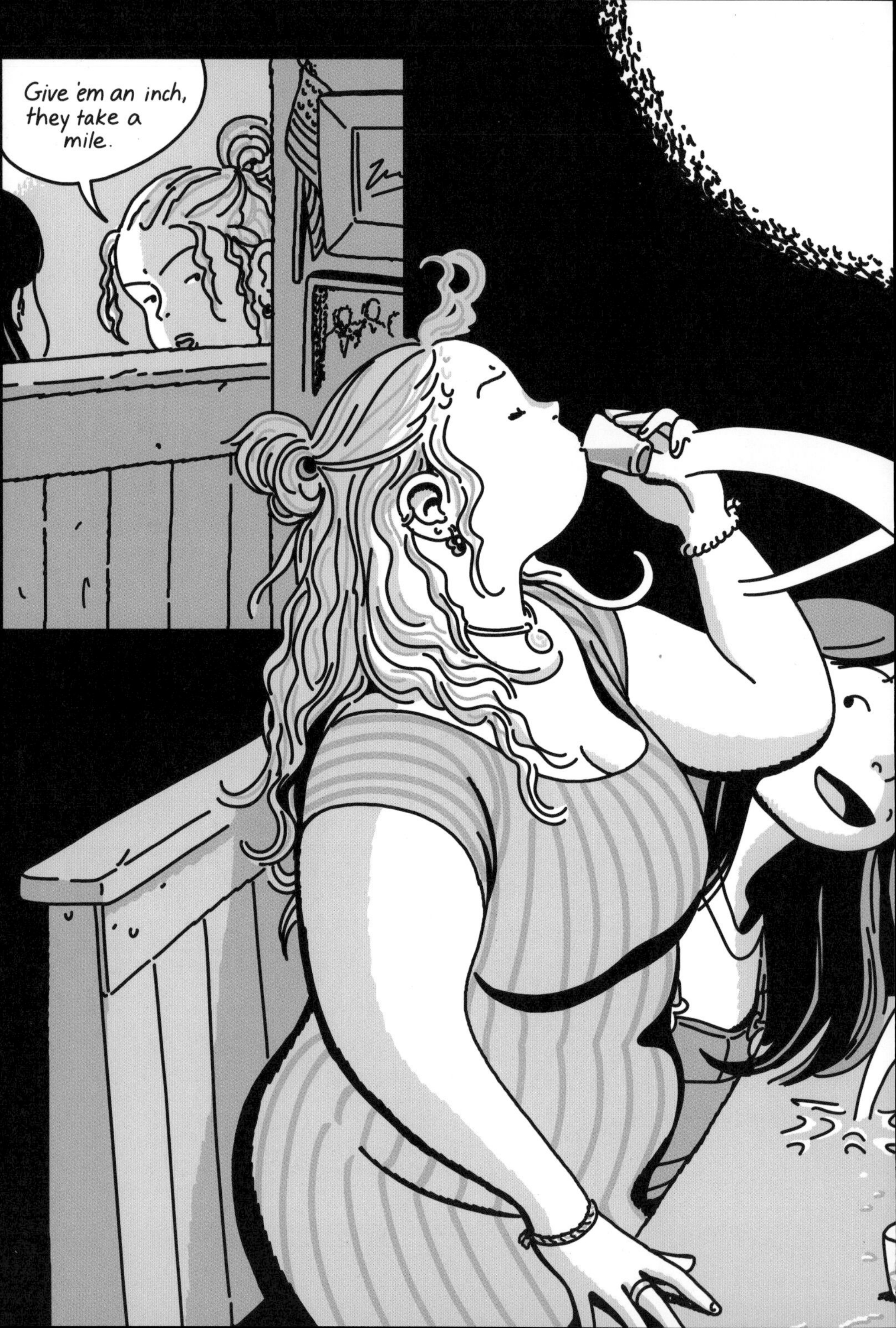
Give 'em an inch, they take a mile.

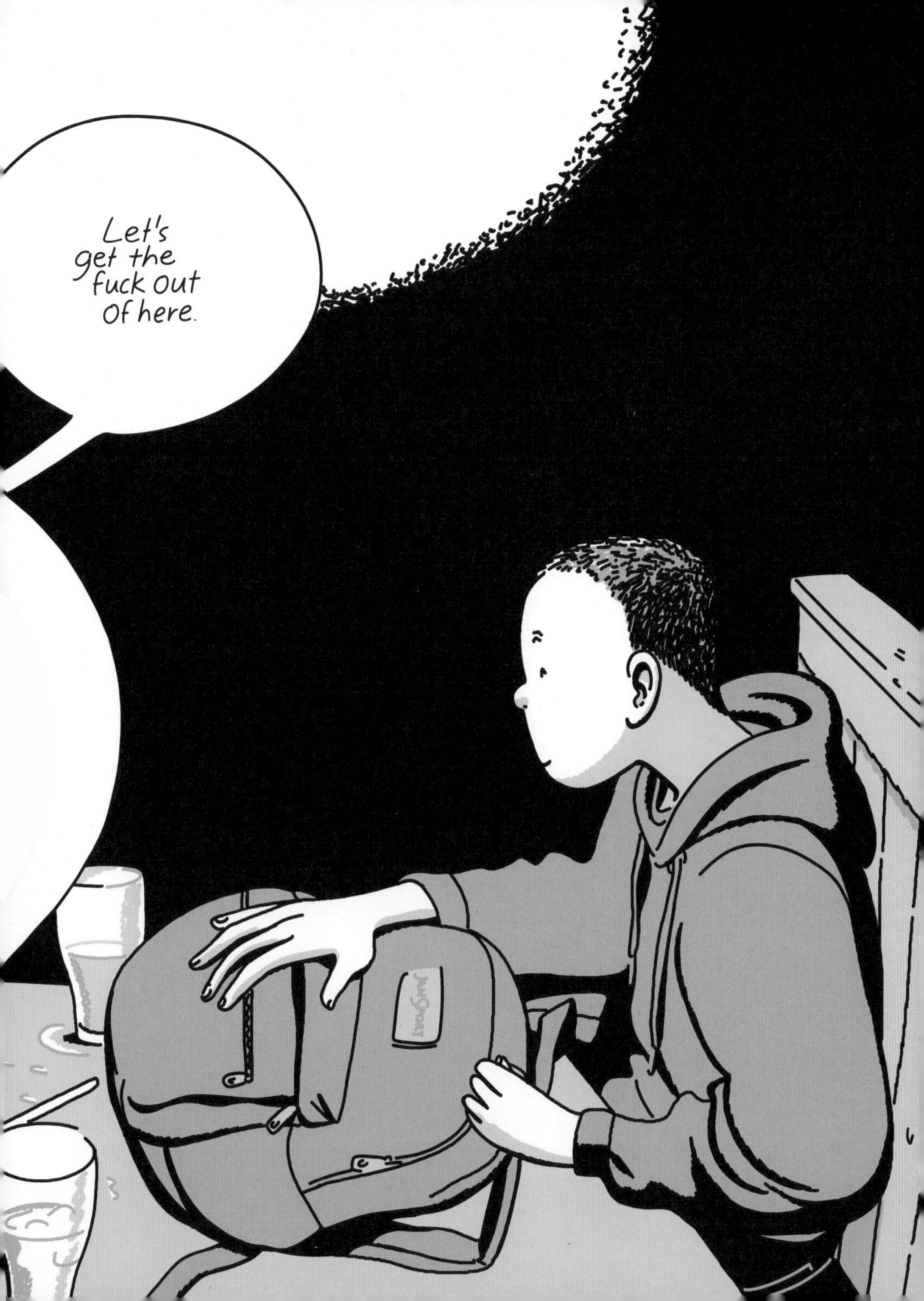
Let's get the fuck out of here.

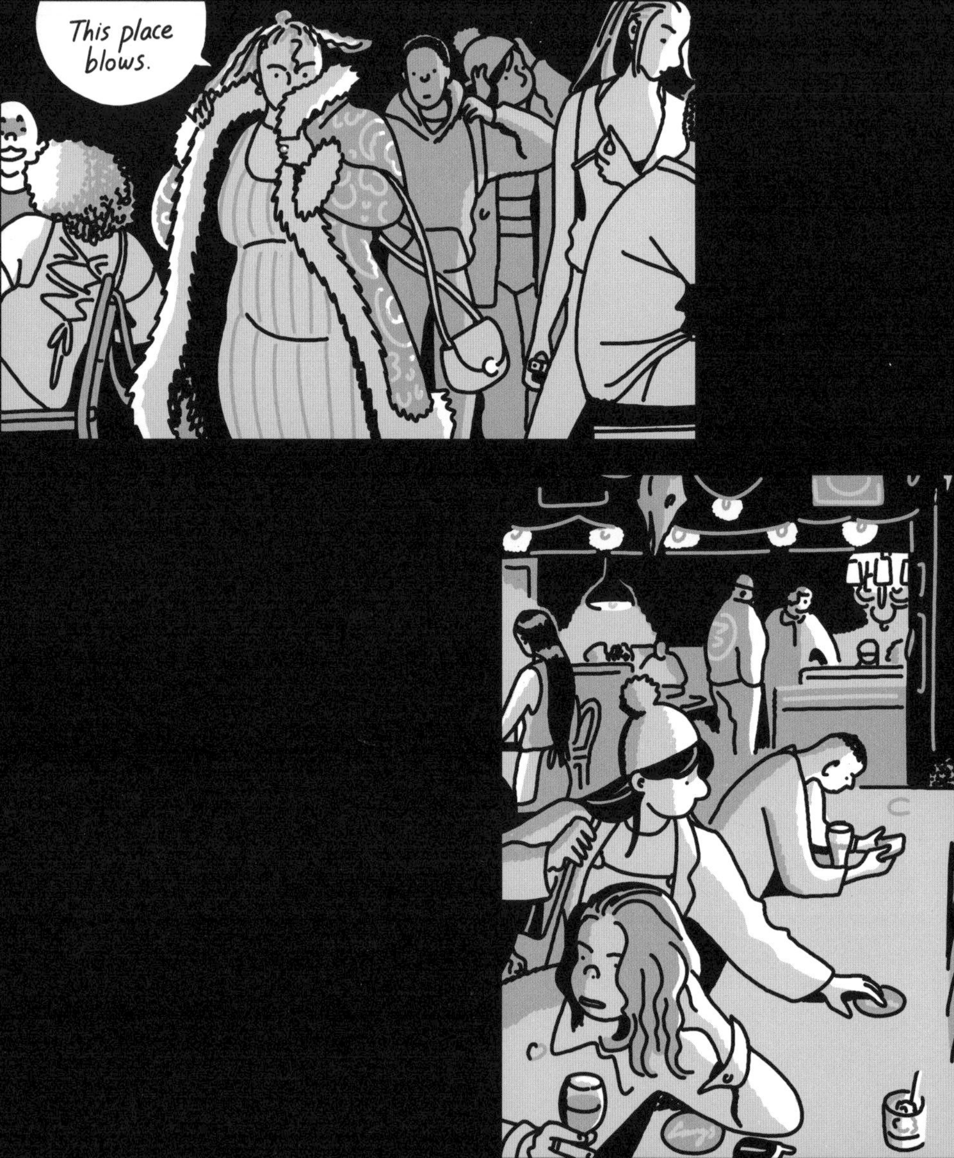
This place blows.

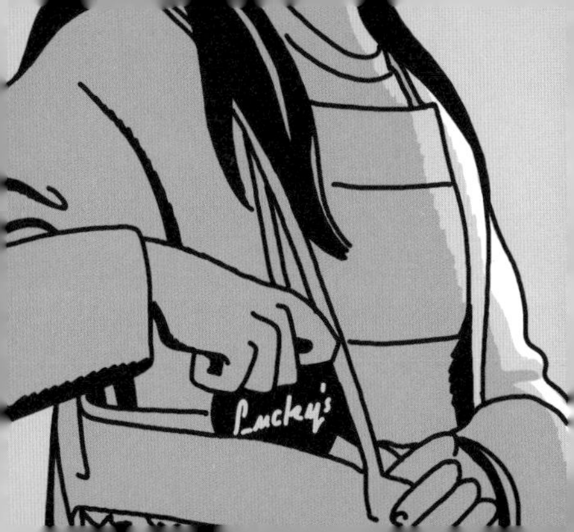
Lucky's

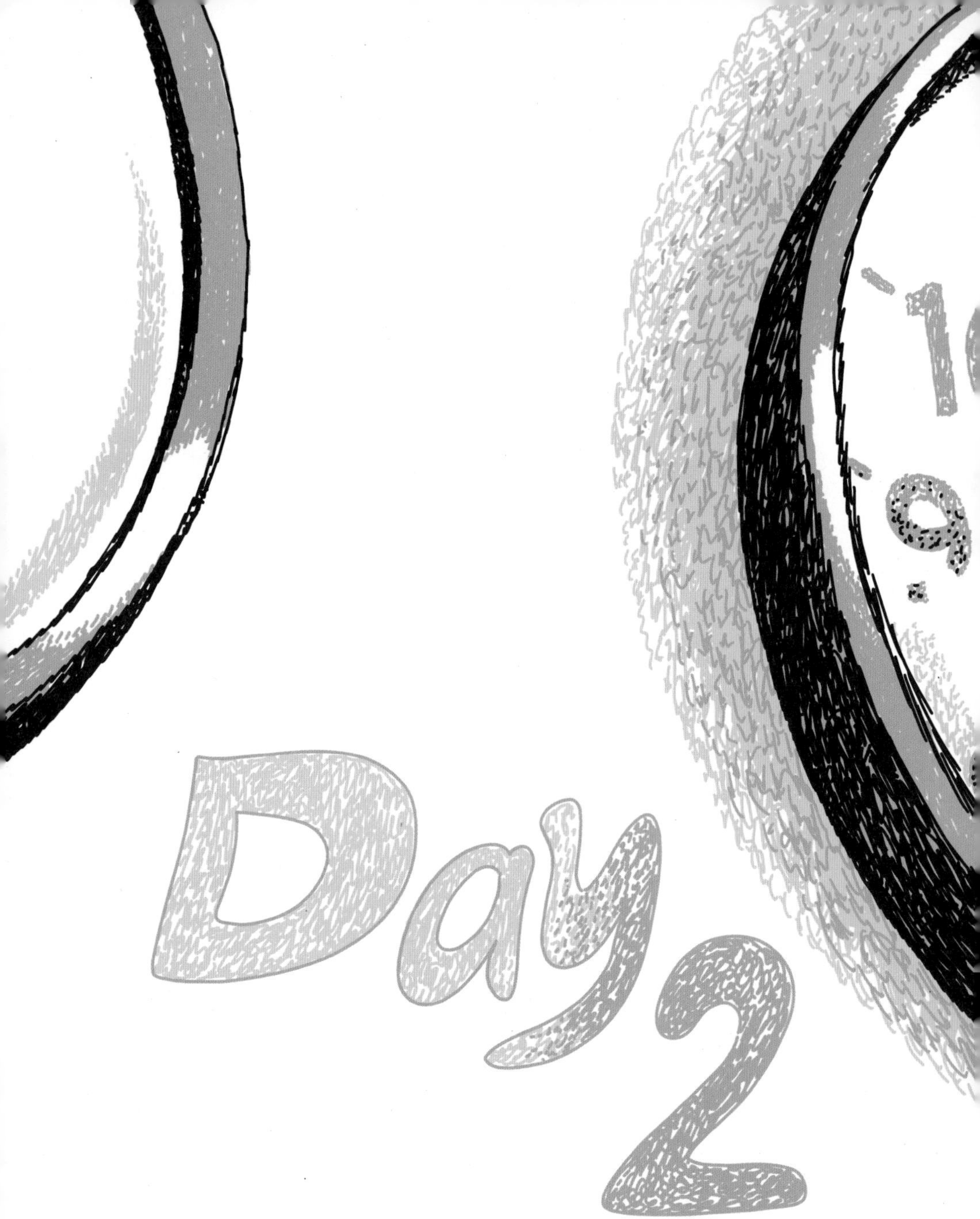
Day 2

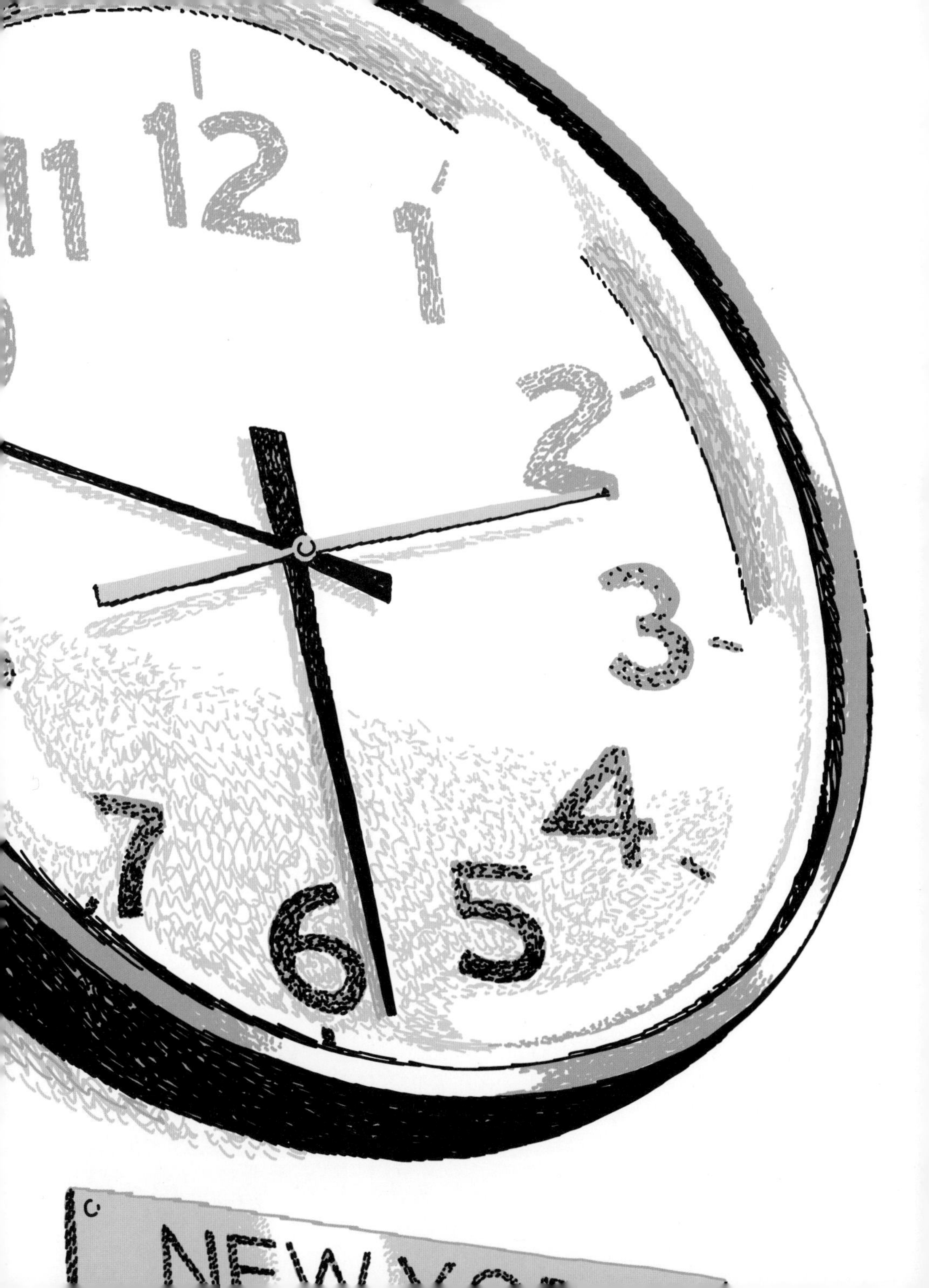
NEW

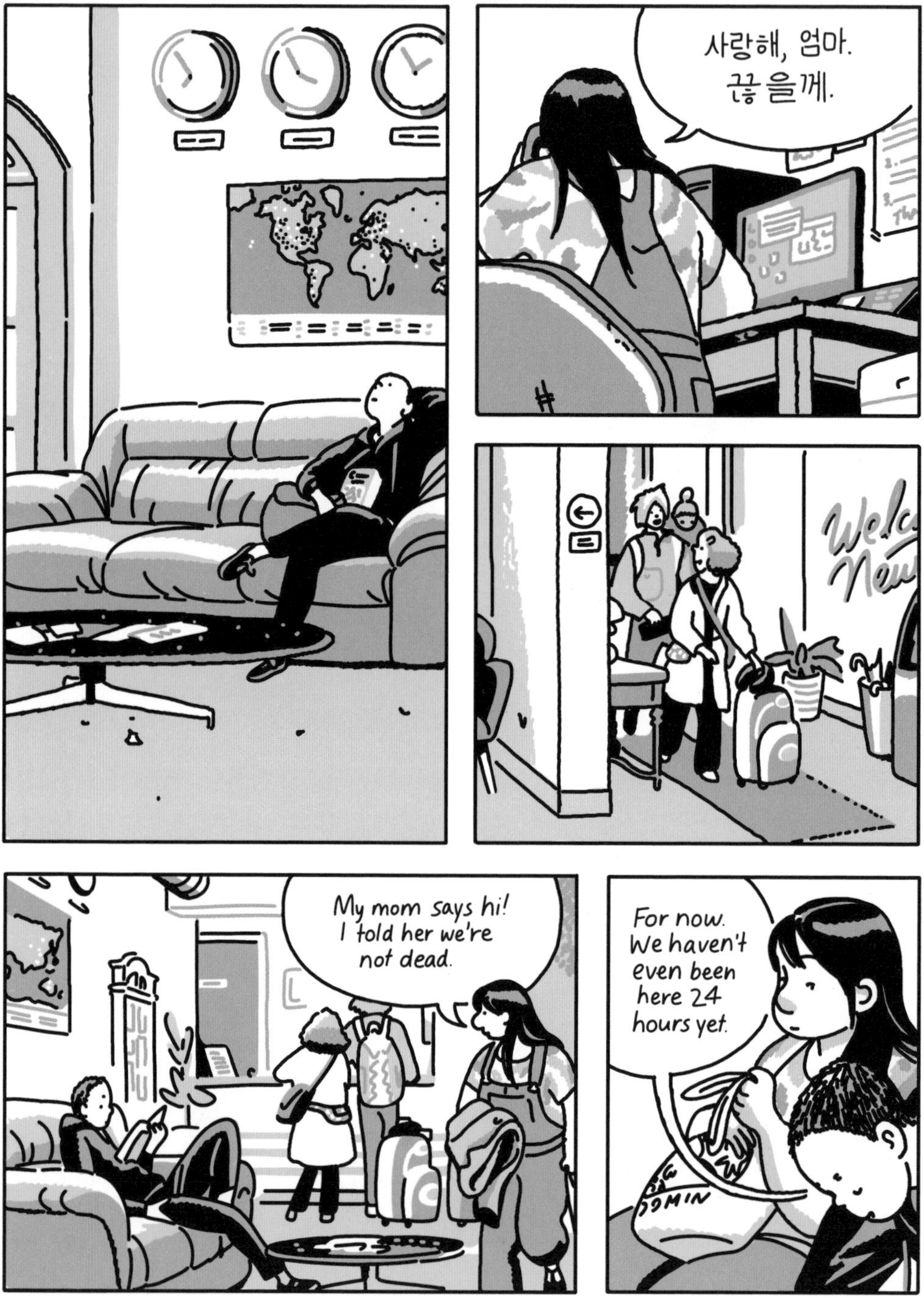

사랑해, 엄마.
끊을게.
Welc
New
My mom says hi! I told her we're not dead.
For now. We haven't even been here 24 hours yet.

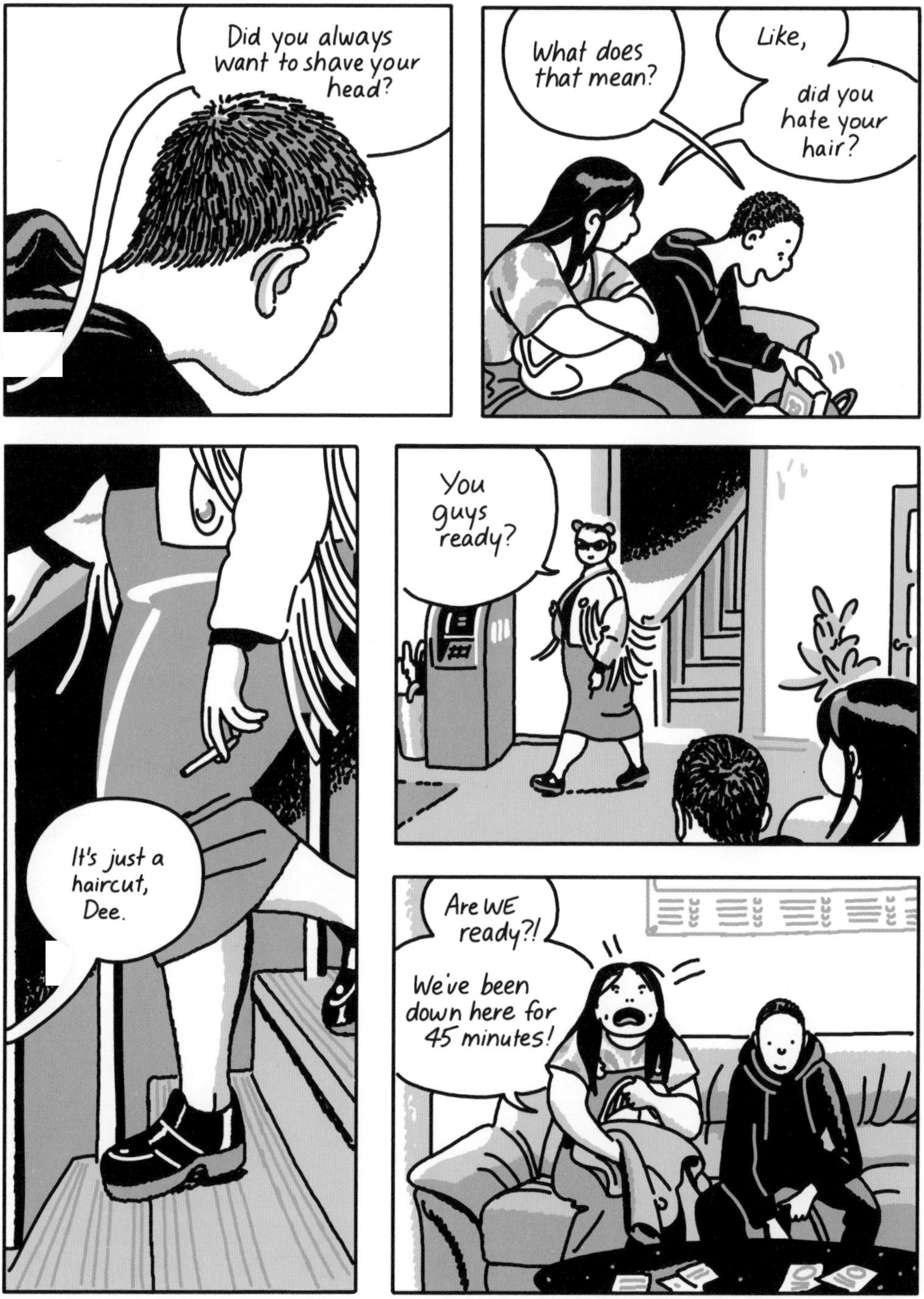

Did you always want to shave your head?
What does that mean?
Like,
did you hate your hair?
It's just a haircut, Dee.
You guys ready?
Are WE ready?!
We've been down here for 45 minutes!

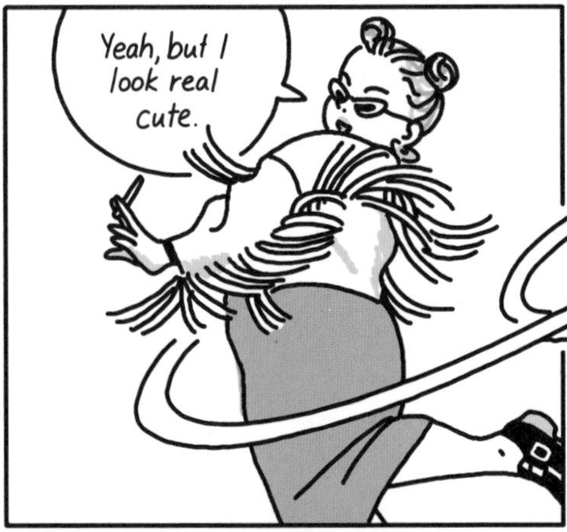
Yeah, but I look real cute.
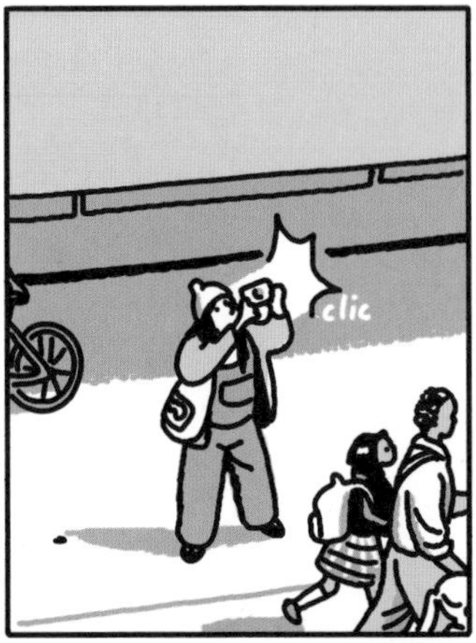
clic
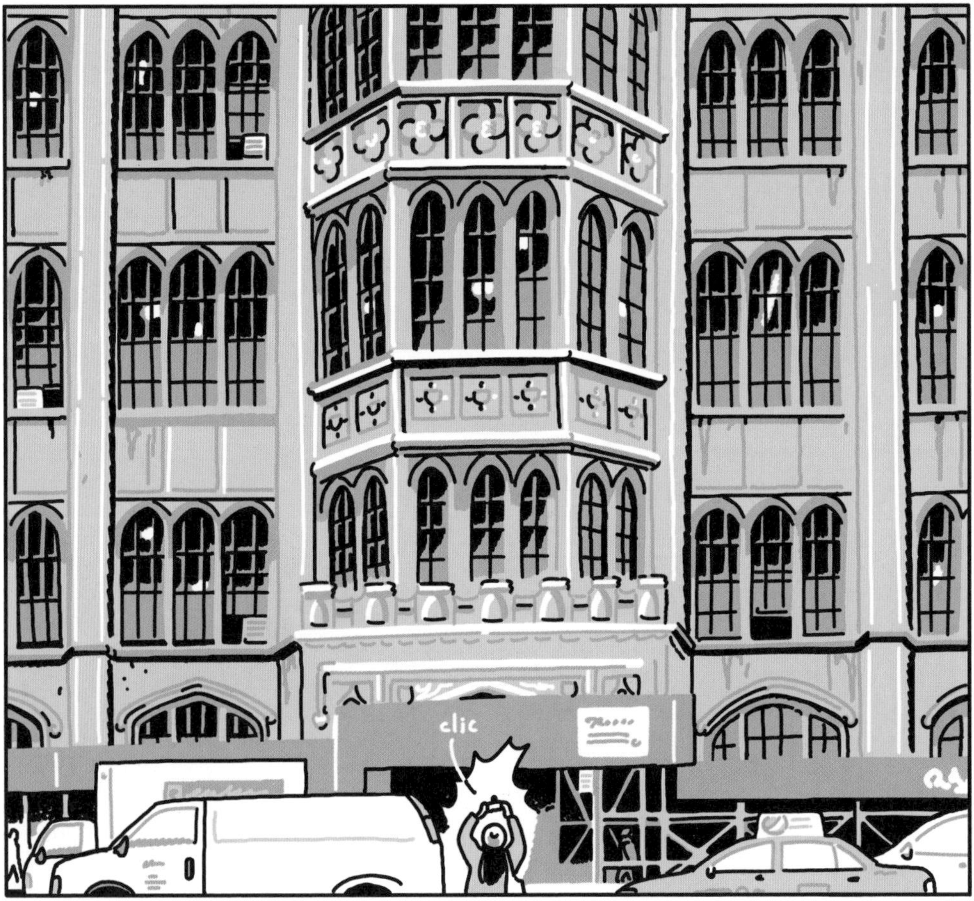
clic

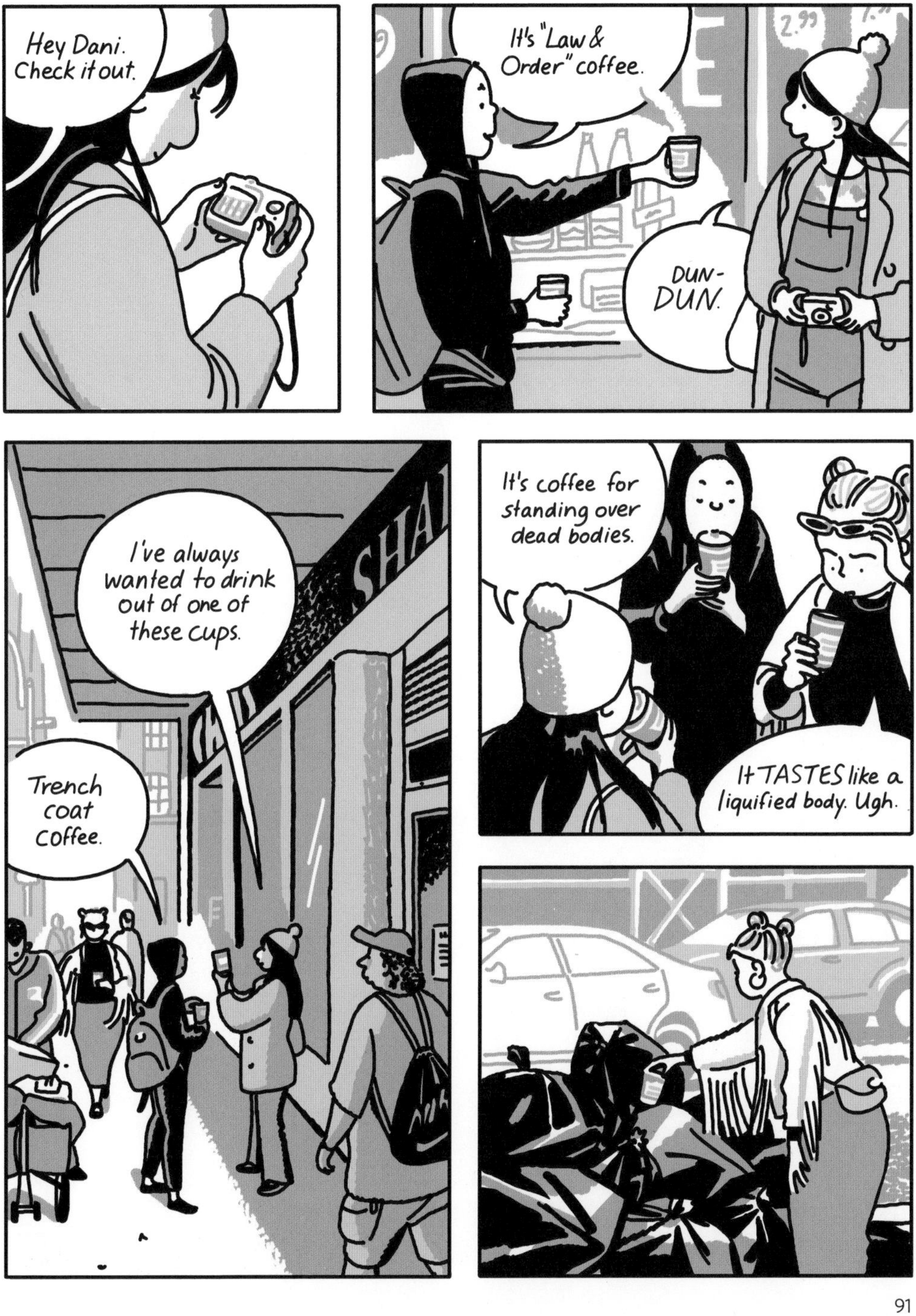
Hey Dani. Check it out.
It's "Law & Order" coffee.
DUN-DUN.
I've always wanted to drink out of one of these cups.
Trench coat coffee.
It's coffee for standing over dead bodies.
It TASTES like a liquified body. Ugh.

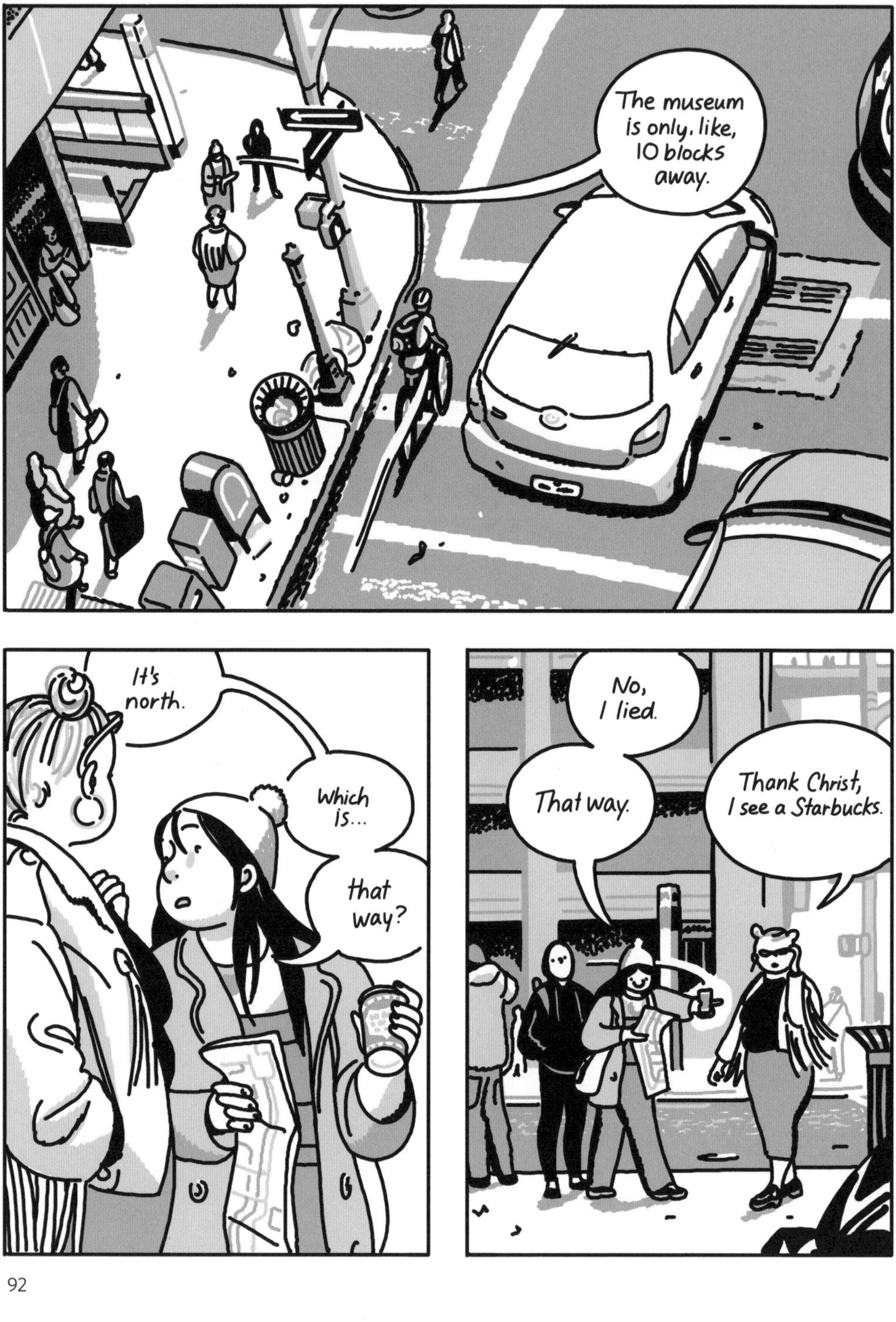
The museum is only, like, 10 blocks away.
It's north.
Which is...
that way?
No, I lied.
That way.
Thank Christ, I see a Starbucks.

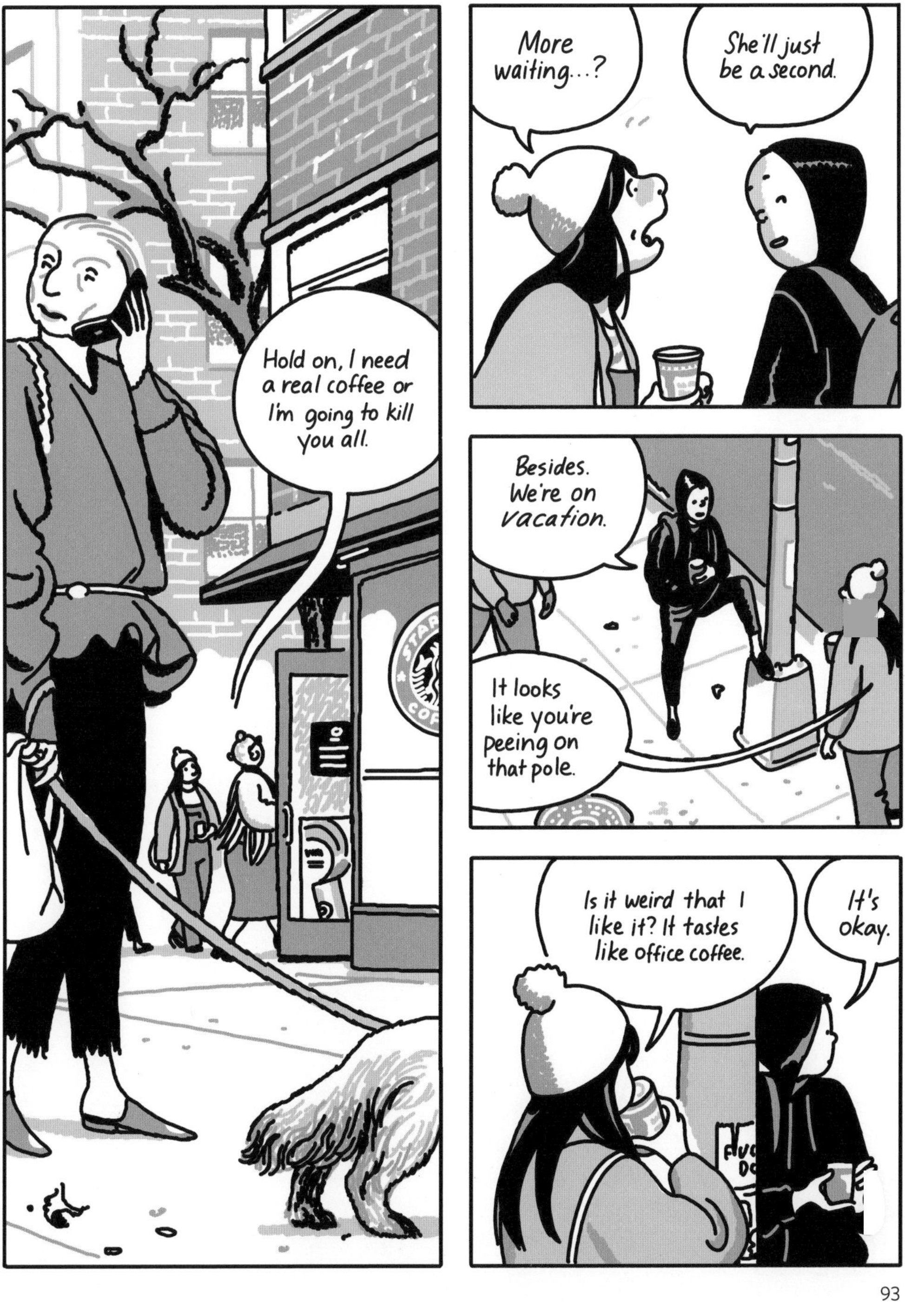
Hold on, I need a real coffee or I'm going to kill you all.
More waiting...?
She'll just be a second.
Besides. We're on vacation.
It looks like you're peeing on that pole.
Is it weird that I like it? It tastes like office coffee.
It's okay.

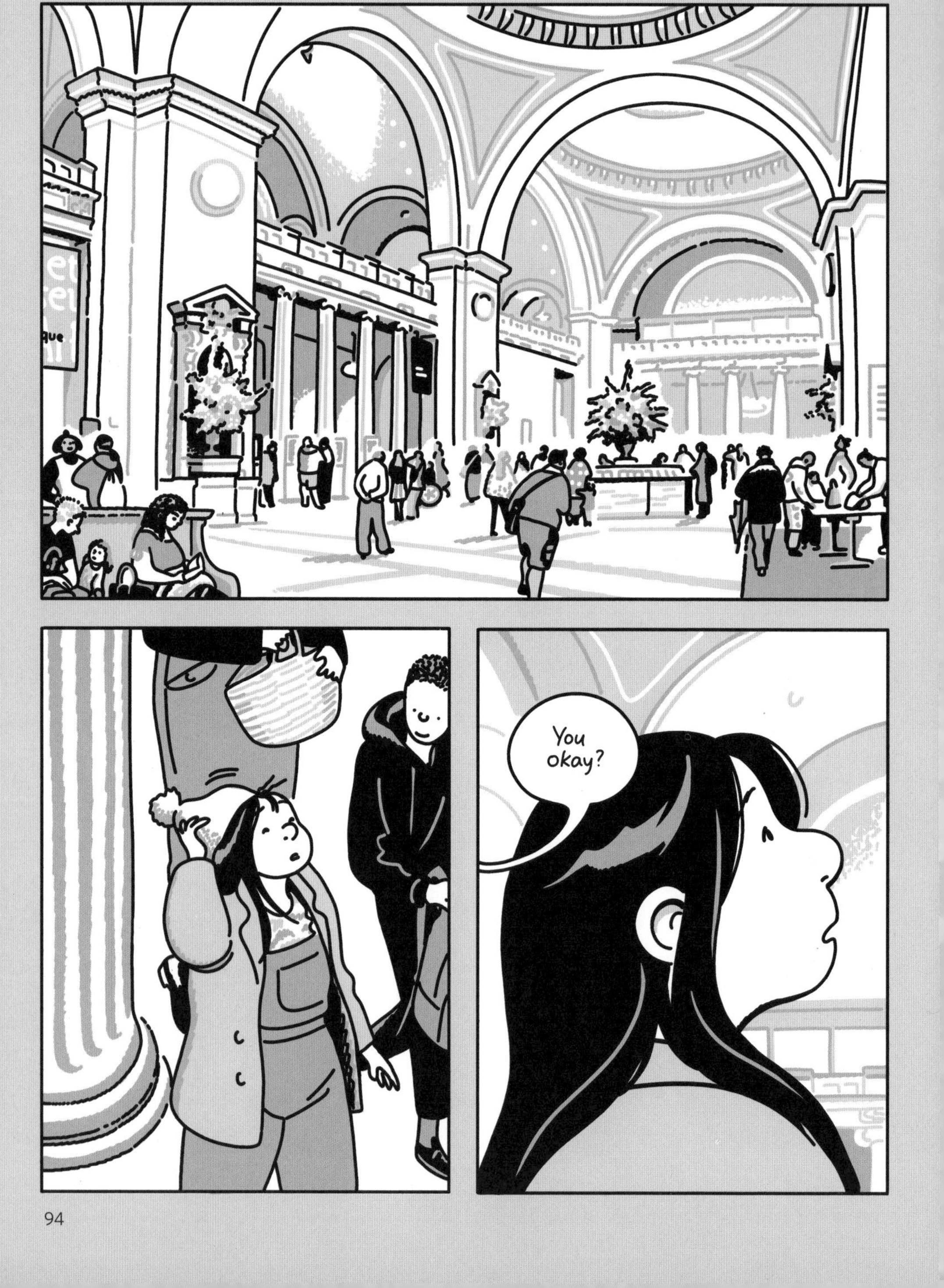
You okay?

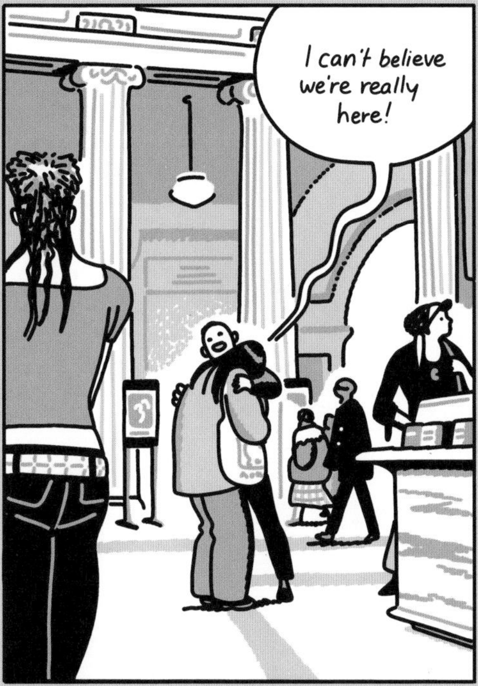
I can't believe we're really here!

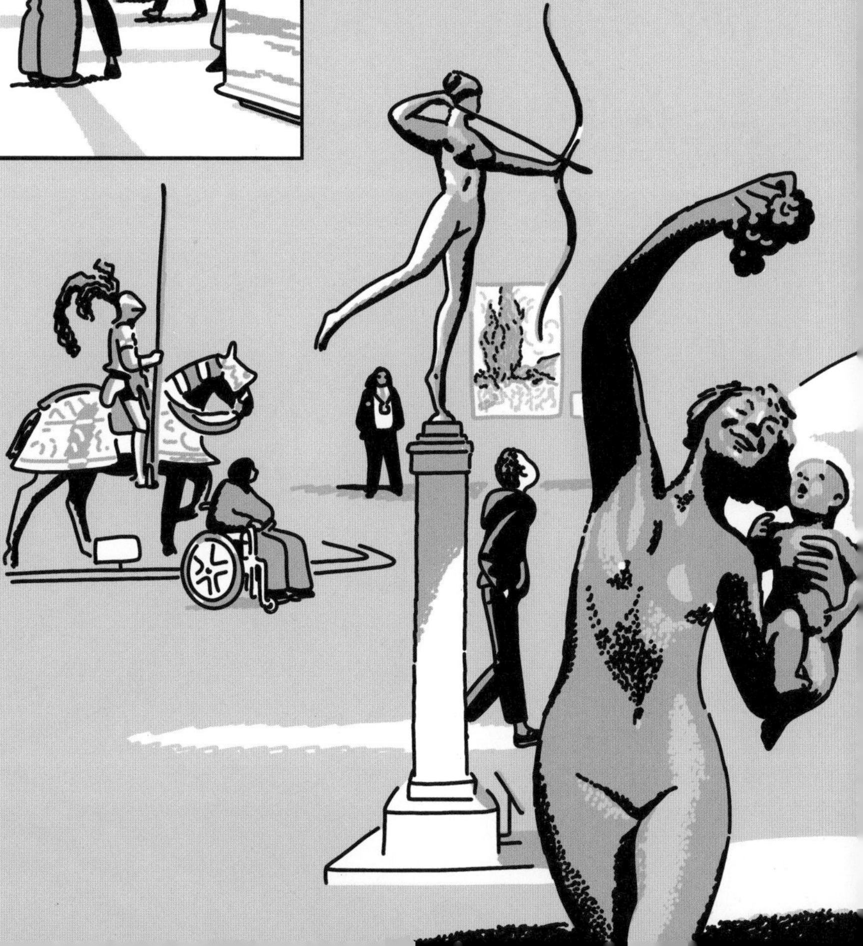

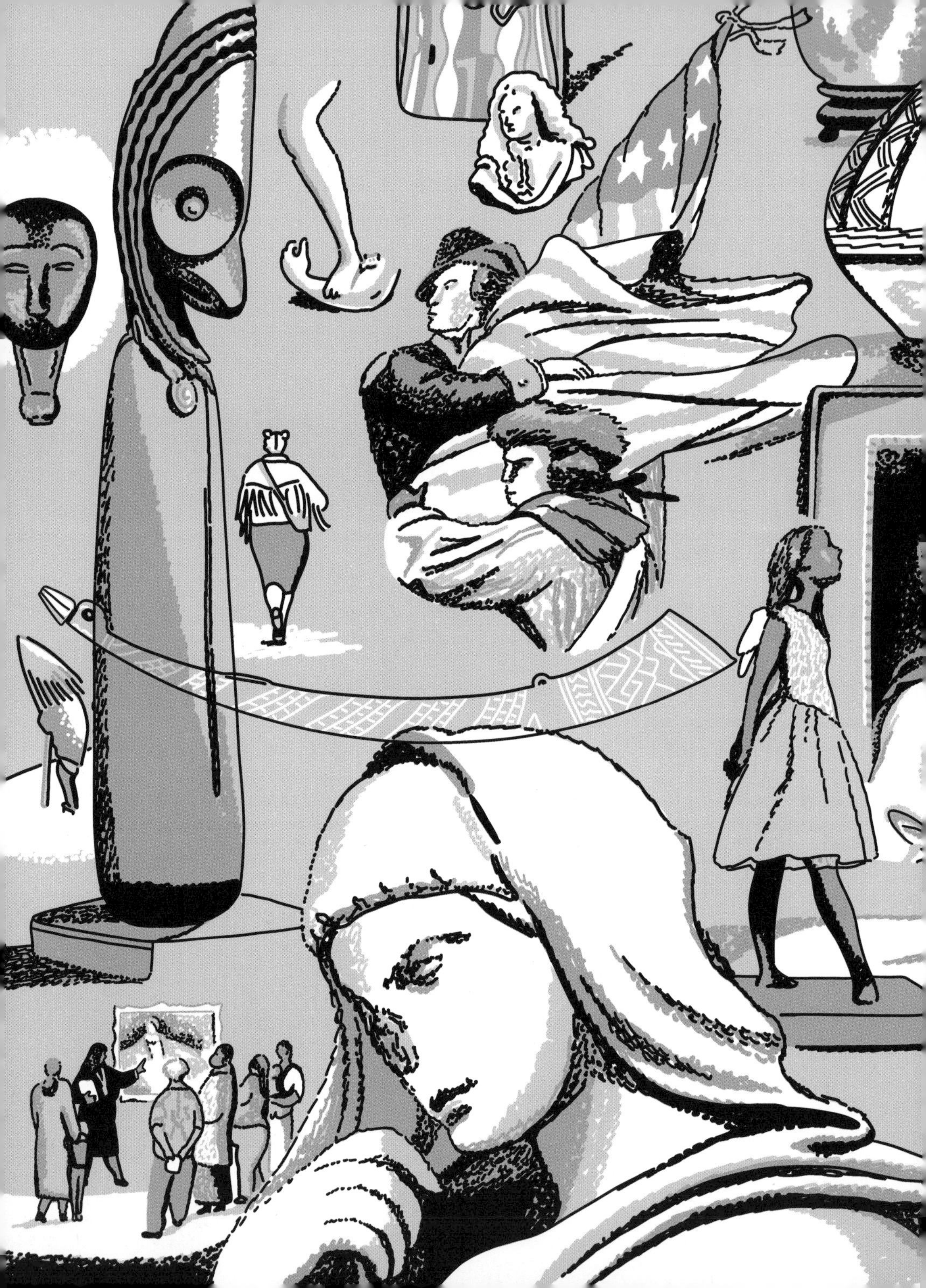

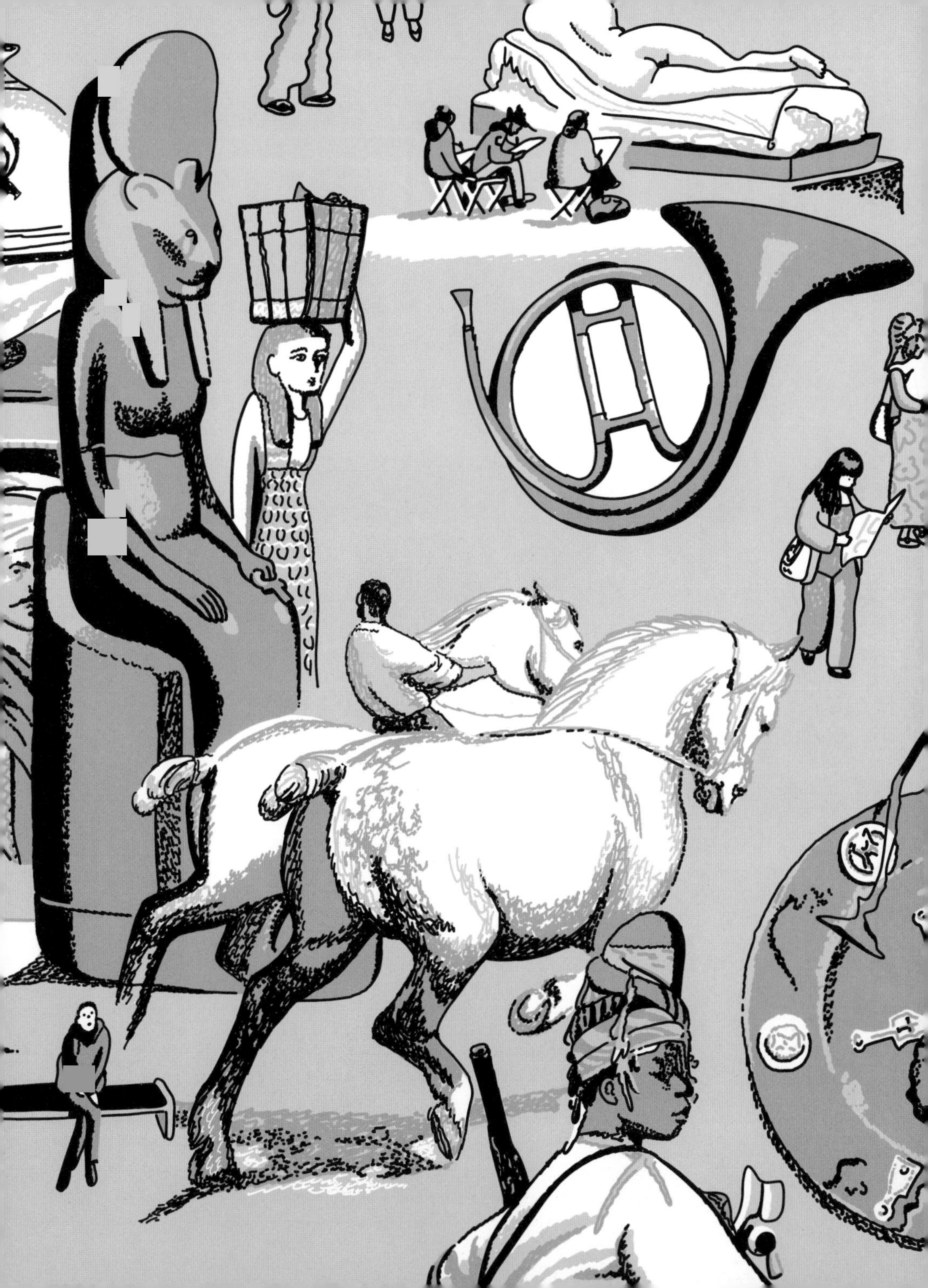

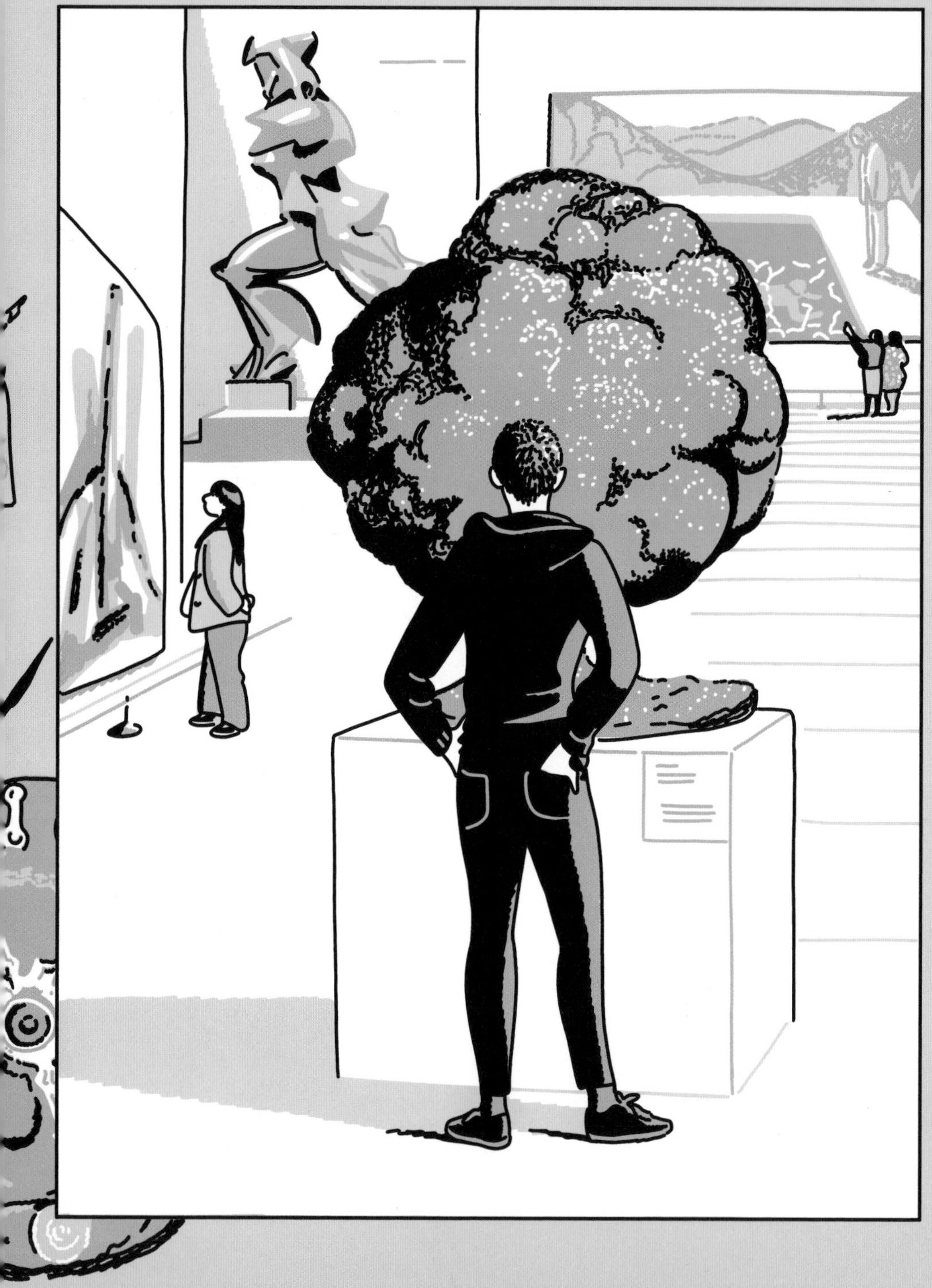

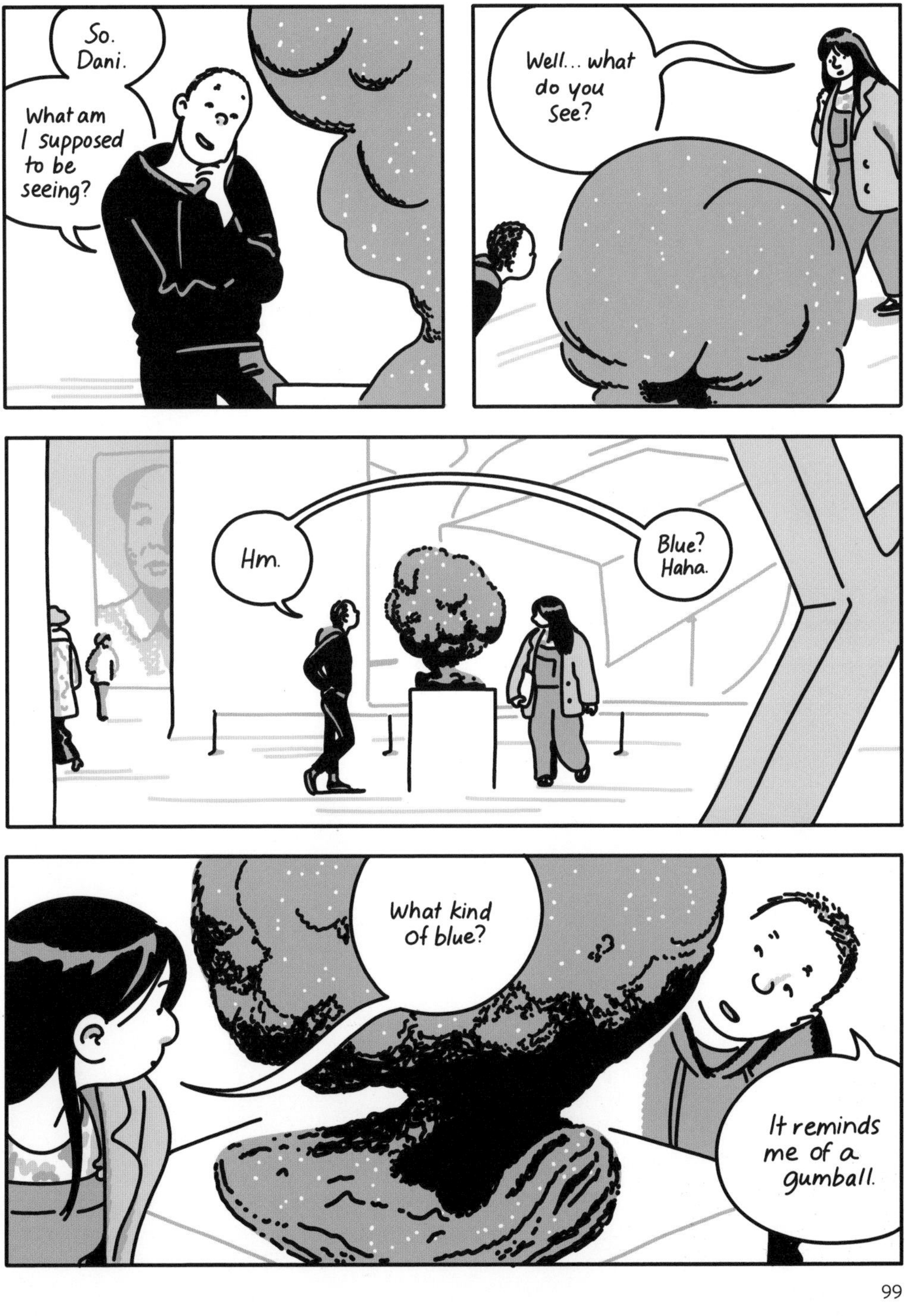

So. Dani.
What am I supposed to be seeing?
Well... what do you see?
Hm.
Blue? Haha.
What kind of blue?
It reminds me of a gumball.

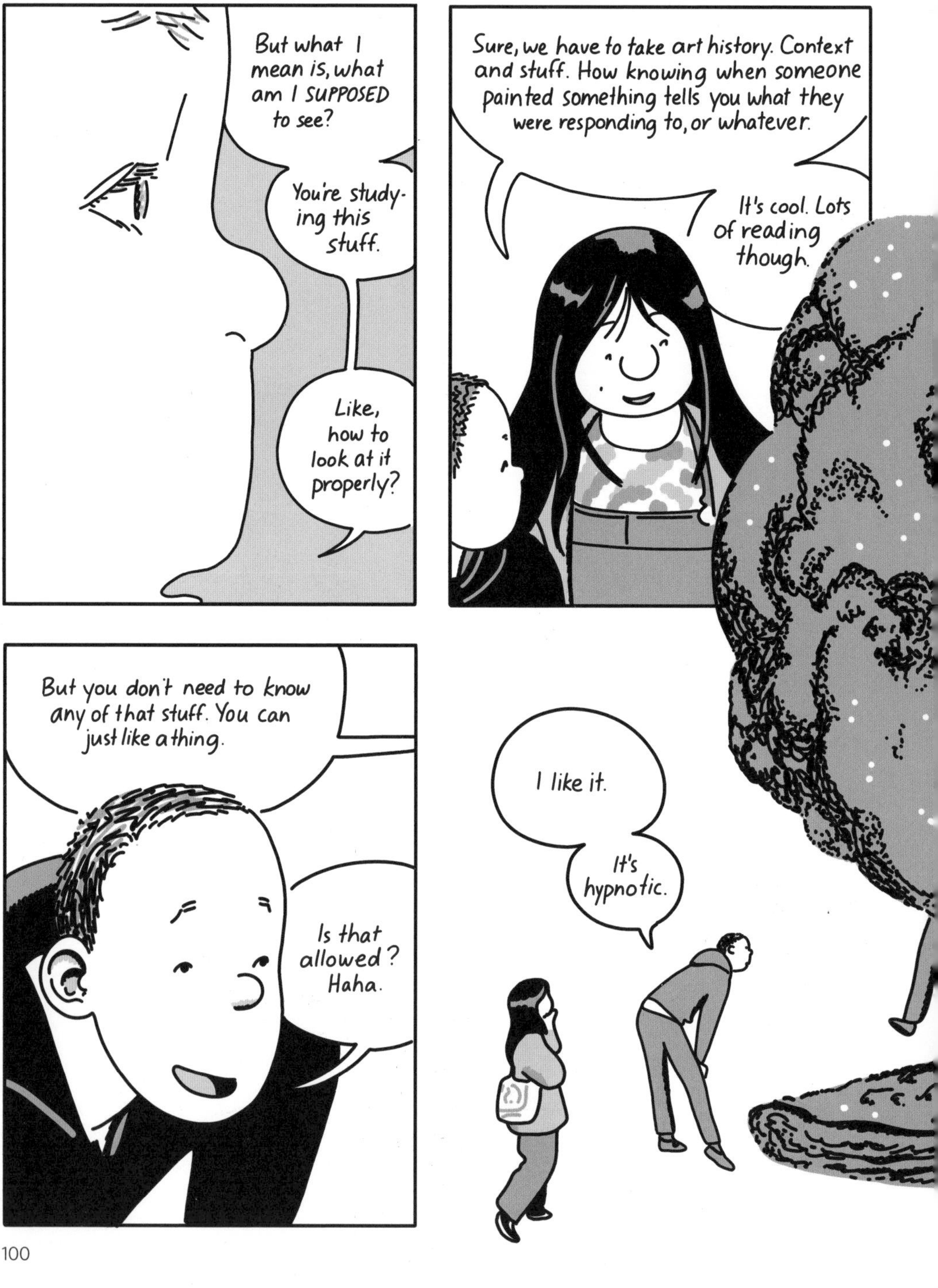
But what I mean is, what am I SUPPOSED to see?
You're studying this stuff.
Like, how to look at it properly?
Sure, we have to take art history. Context and stuff. How knowing when someone painted something tells you what they were responding to, or whatever.
It's cool. Lots of reading though.
But you don't need to know any of that stuff. You can just like a thing.
Is that allowed? Haha.
I like it.
It's hypnotic.

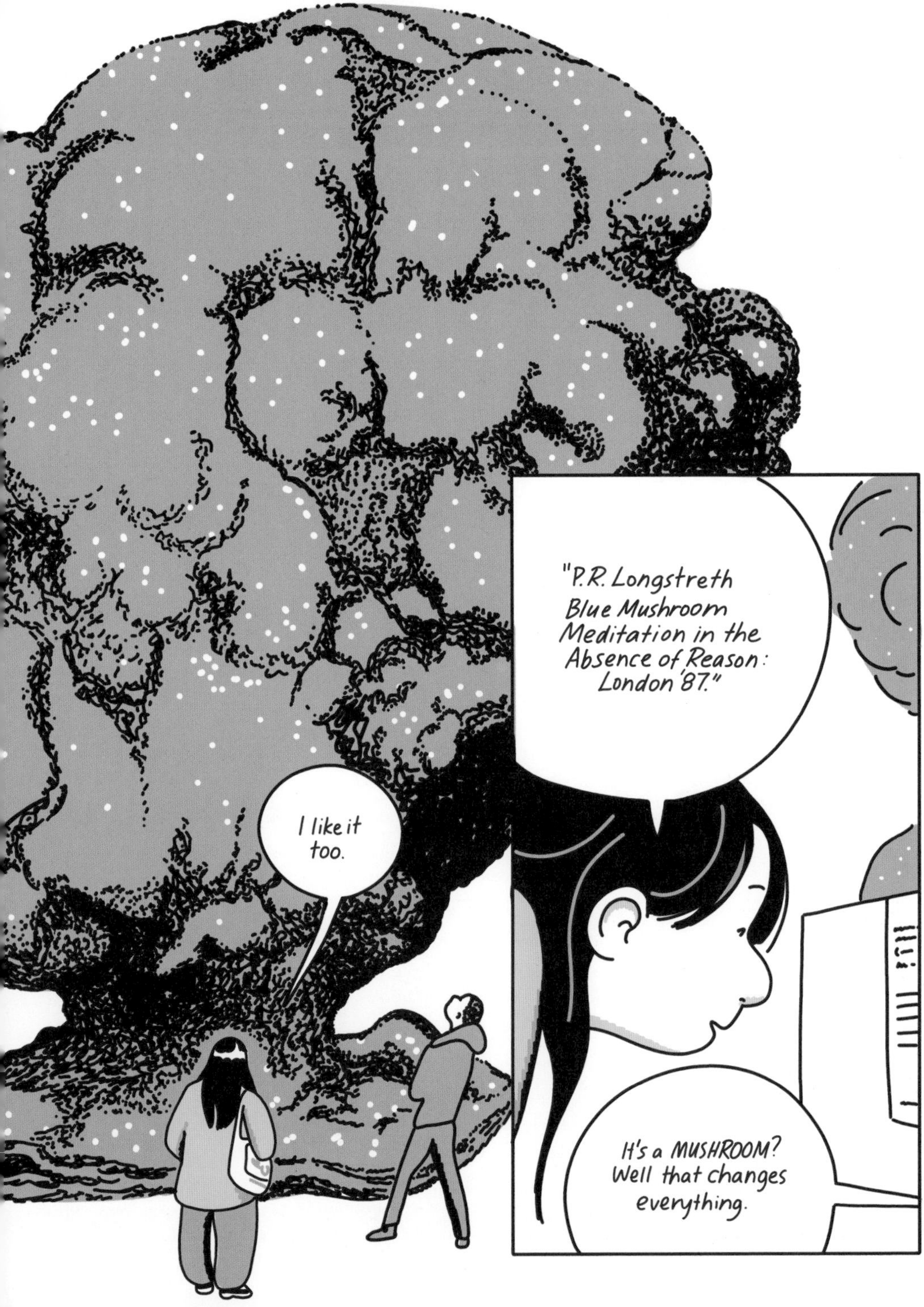
I like it too.
"P.R. Longstreth Blue Mushroom Meditation in the Absence of Reason: London '87."
It's a MUSHROOM? Well that changes everything.

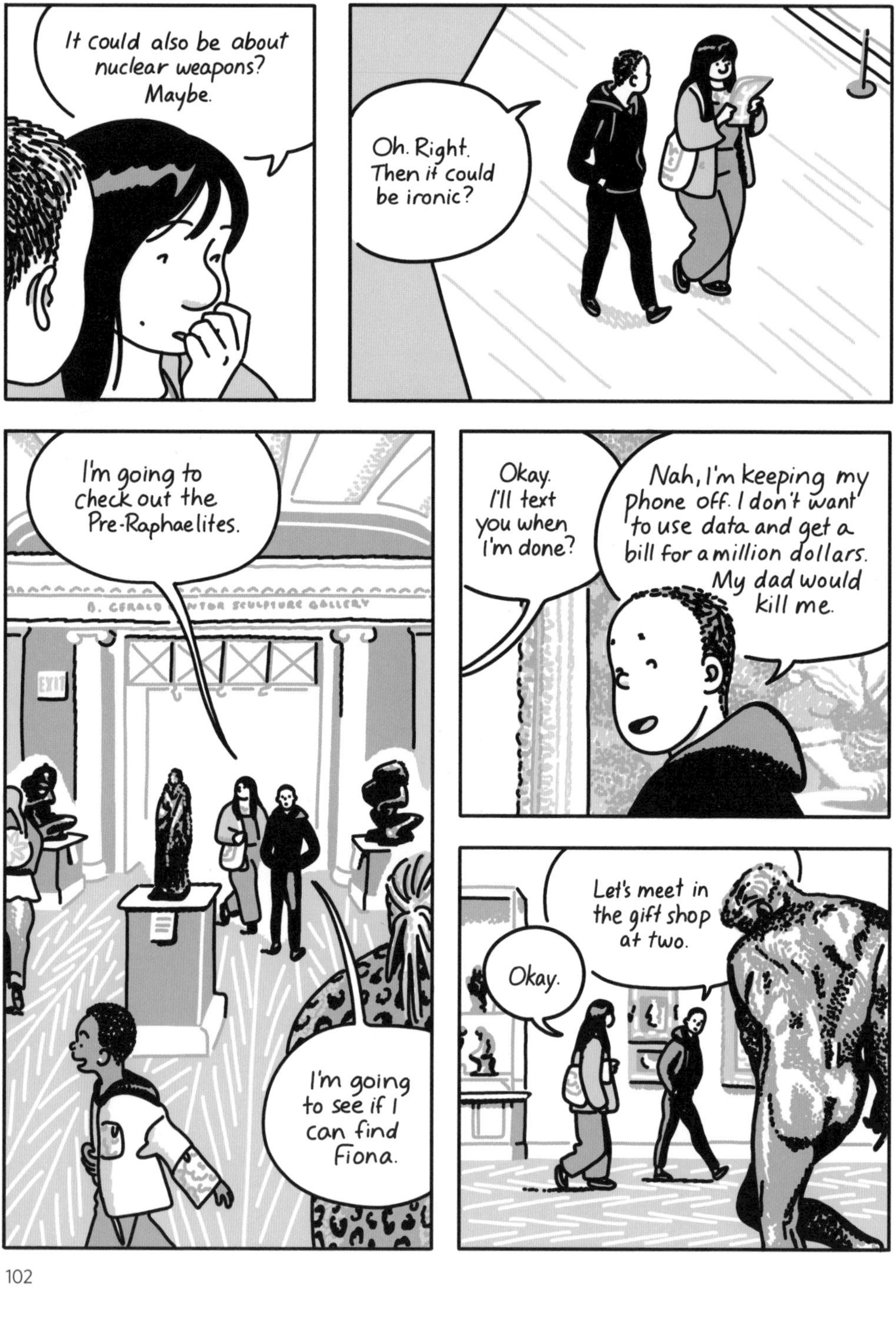
It could also be about nuclear weapons? Maybe.
Oh. Right. Then it could be ironic?
I'm going to check out the Pre-Raphaelites.
I'm going to see if I can find Fiona.
Okay. I'll text you when I'm done?
Nah, I'm keeping my phone off. I don't want to use data and get a bill for a million dollars. My dad would kill me.
Let's meet in the gift shop at two.
Okay.

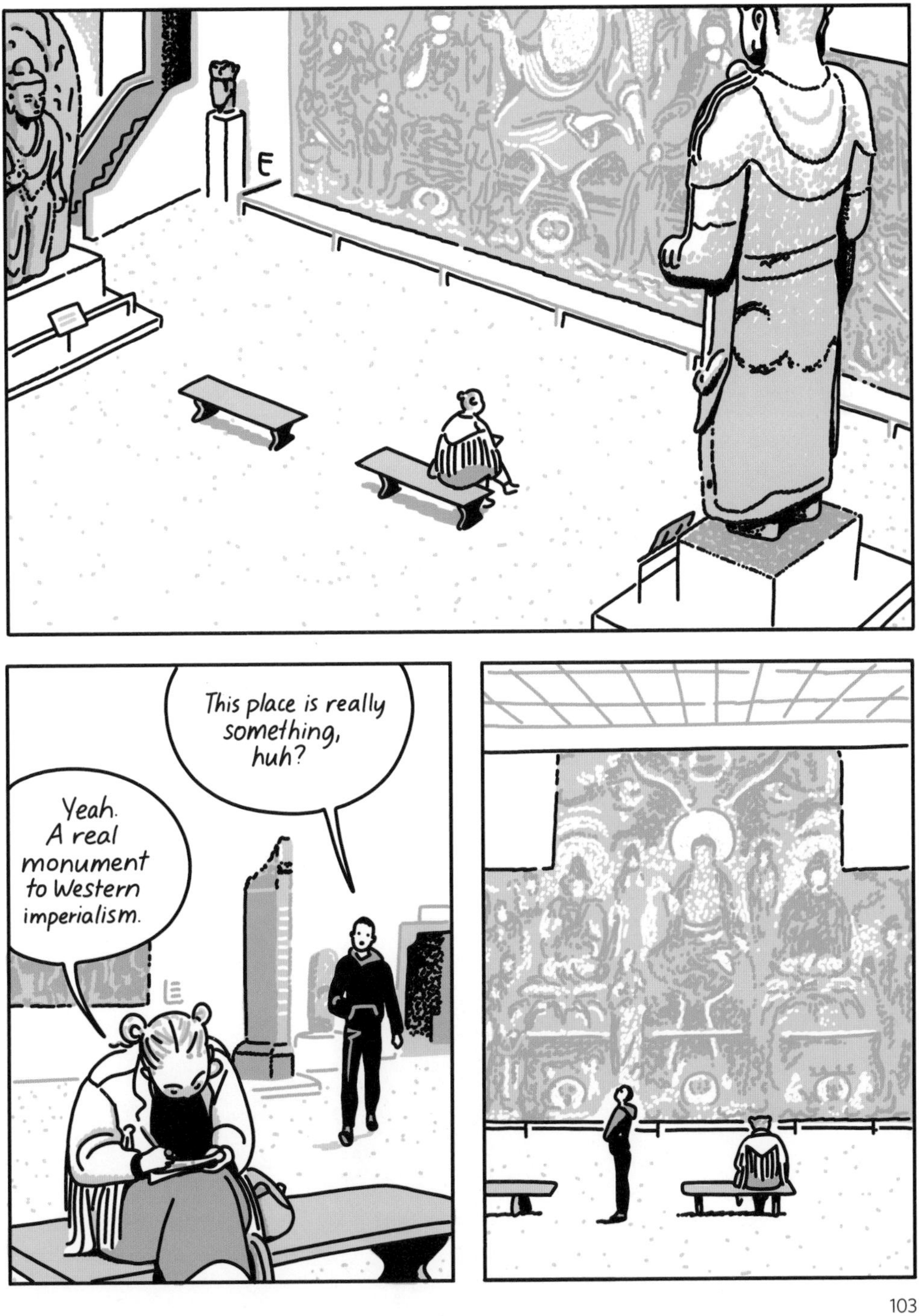
This place is really something, huh?
Yeah. A real monument to Western imperialism.

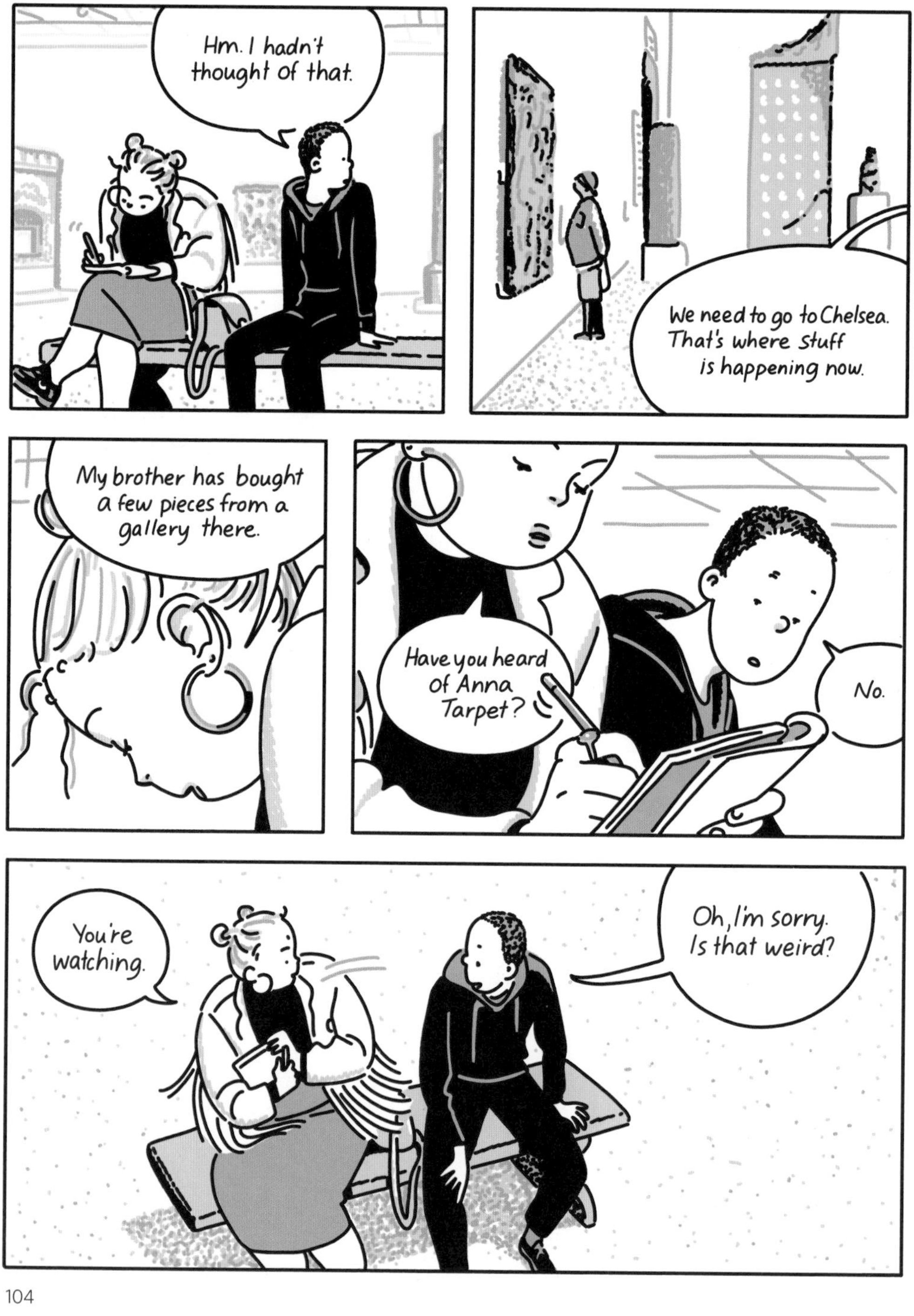
Hm. I hadn't thought of that.
We need to go to Chelsea. That's where stuff is happening now.
My brother has bought a few pieces from a gallery there.
Have you heard of Anna Tarpet?
No.
You're watching.
Oh, I'm sorry. Is that weird?

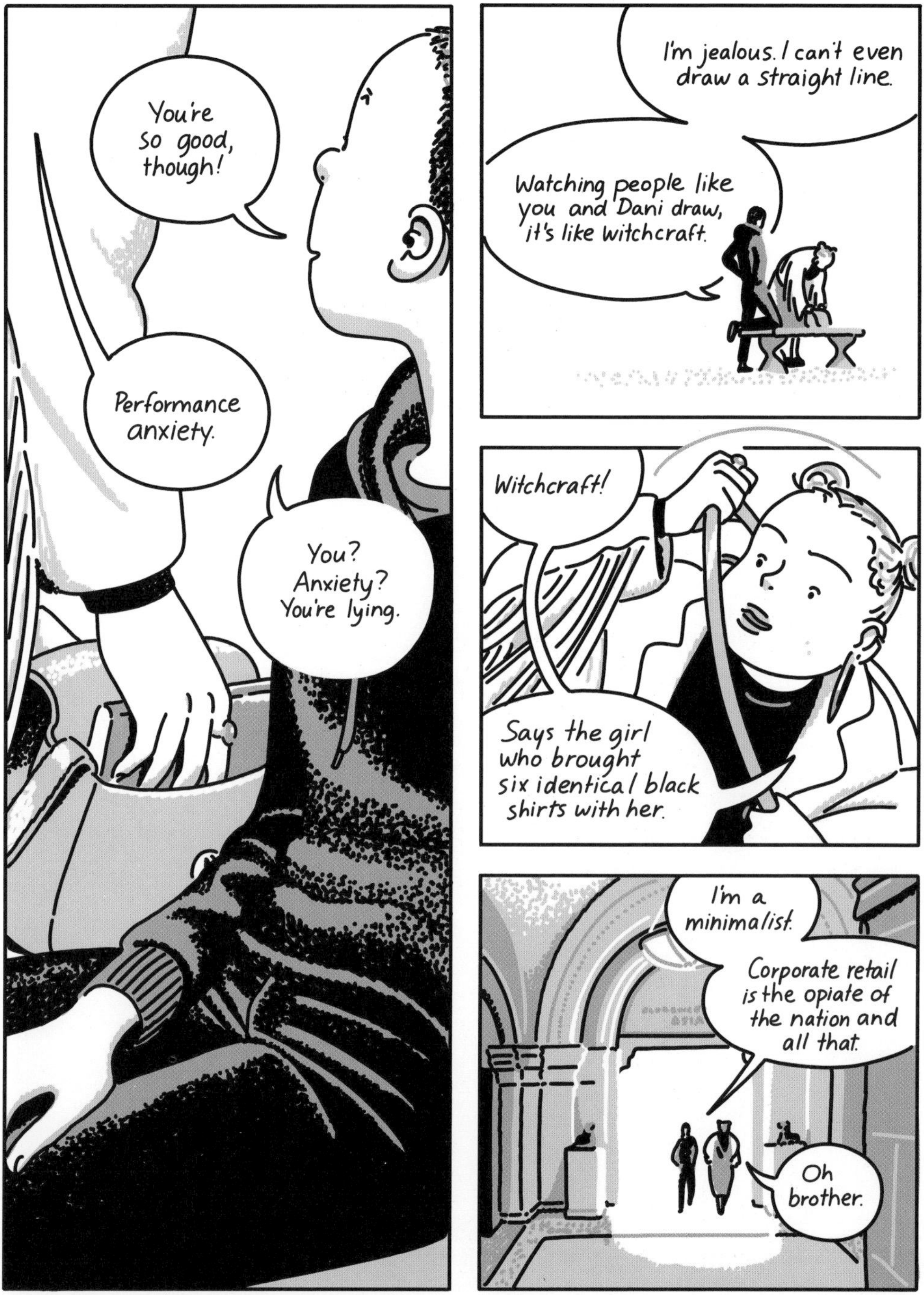
You're so good, though!
Performance anxiety.
You? Anxiety? You're lying.
I'm jealous. I can't even draw a straight line.
Watching people like you and Dani draw, it's like witchcraft.
Witchcraft!
Says the girl who brought six identical black shirts with her.
I'm a minimalist.
Corporate retail is the opiate of the nation and all that.
Oh brother.

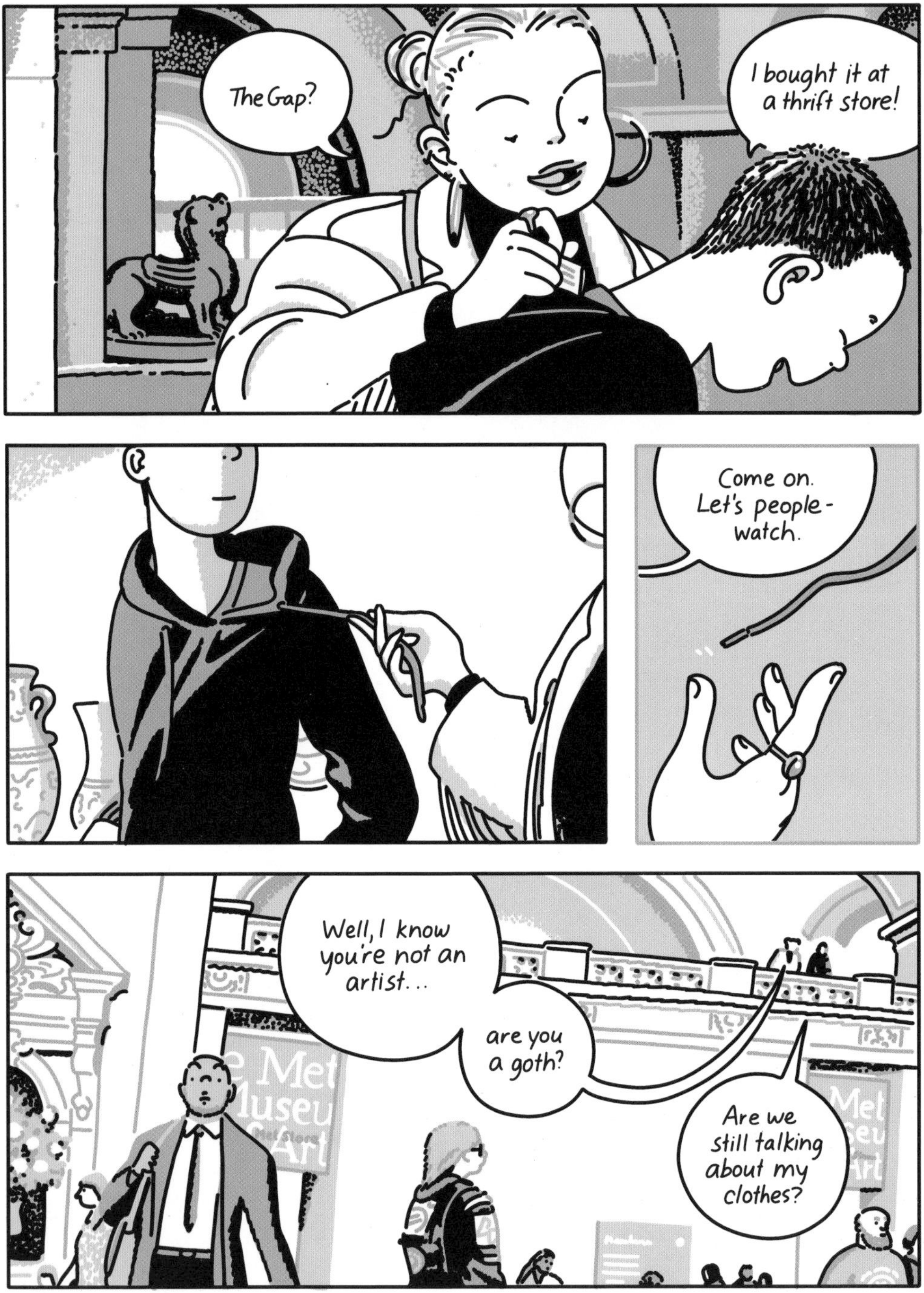
The Gap?
I bought it at a thrift store!
Come on. Let's people-watch.
Well, I know you're not an artist...
are you a goth?
Are we still talking about my clothes?
Met Museu Art
Met Museu Art

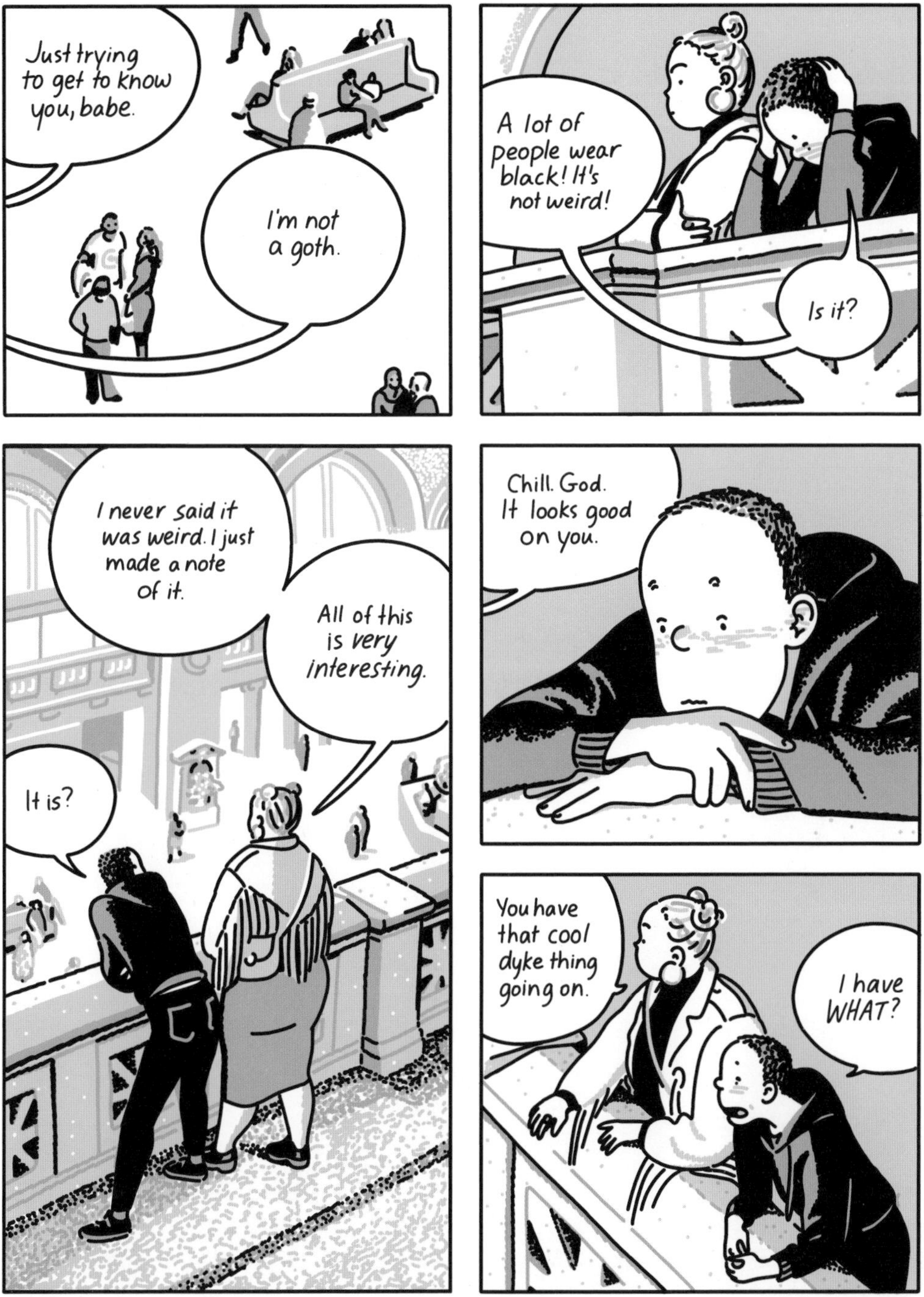
Just trying to get to know you, babe.
I'm not a goth.
A lot of people wear black! It's not weird!
Is it?
I never said it was weird. I just made a note of it.
All of this is *very interesting*.
It is?
Chill. God. It looks good on you.
You have that cool dyke thing going on.
I have *WHAT?*

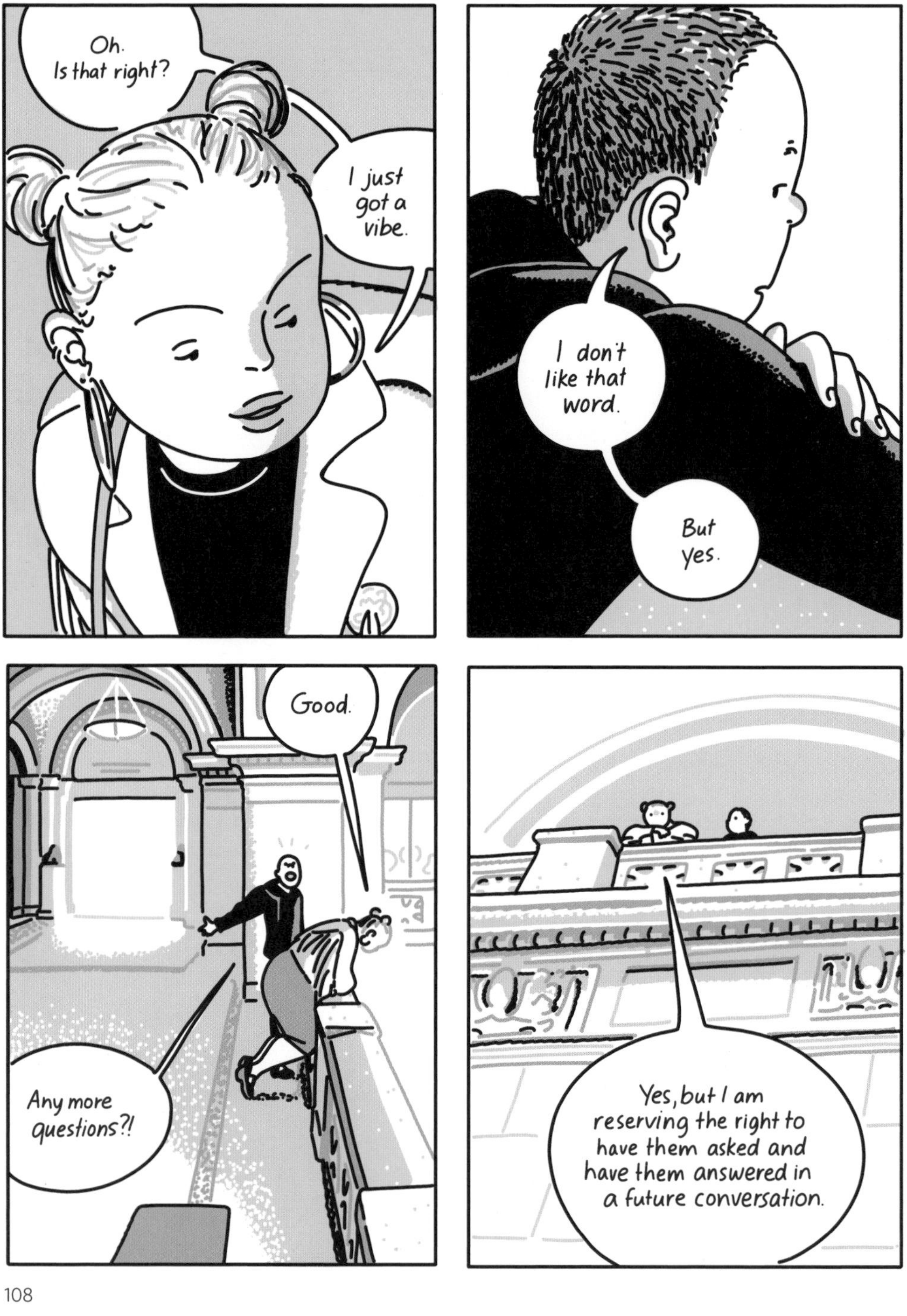

Oh. Is that right?
I just got a vibe.
I don't like that word.
But yes.
Good.
Any more questions?!
Yes, but I am reserving the right to have them asked and have them answered in a future conversation.

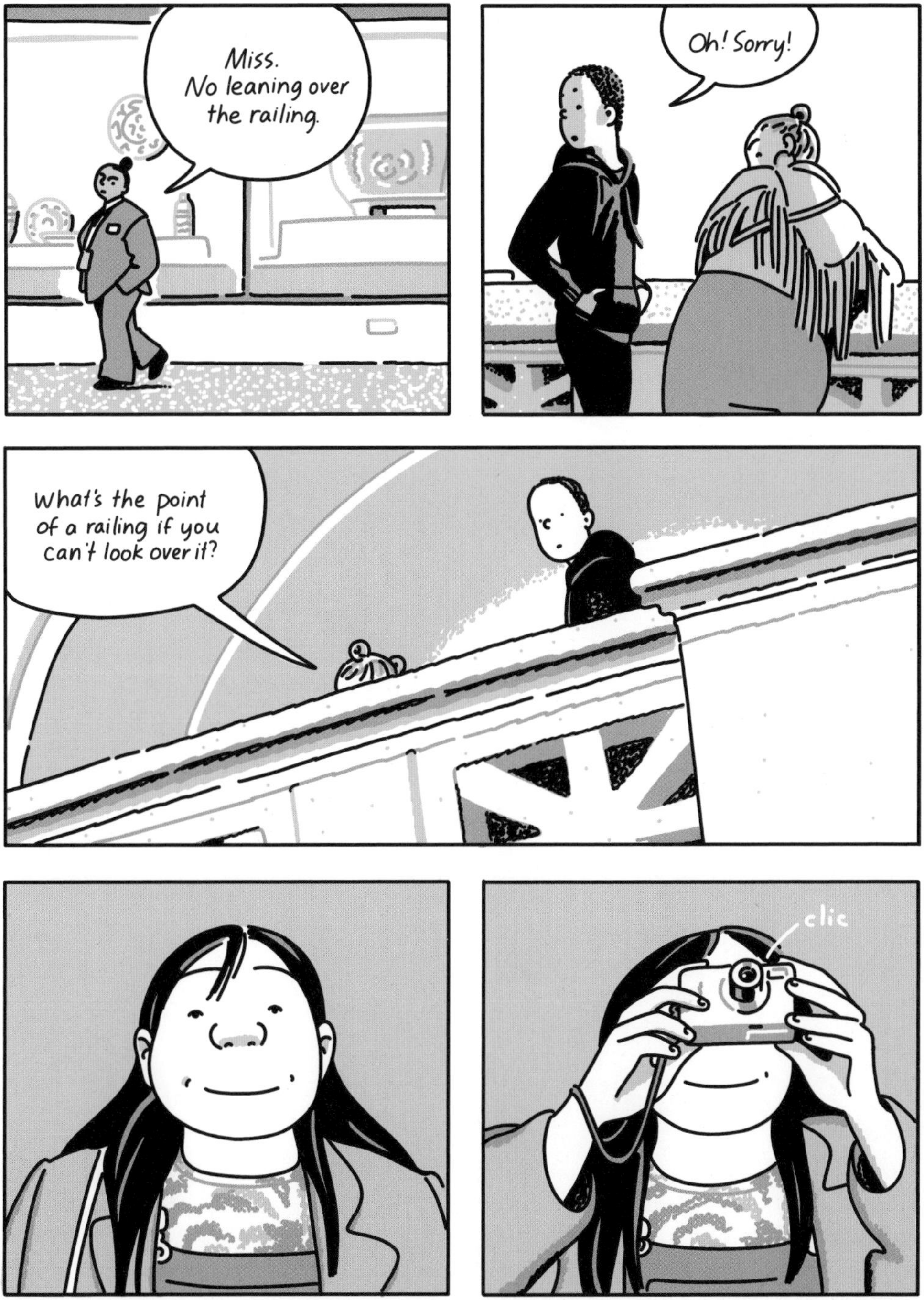
Miss. No leaning over the railing.
Oh! Sorry!
What's the point of a railing if you can't look over it?
clic

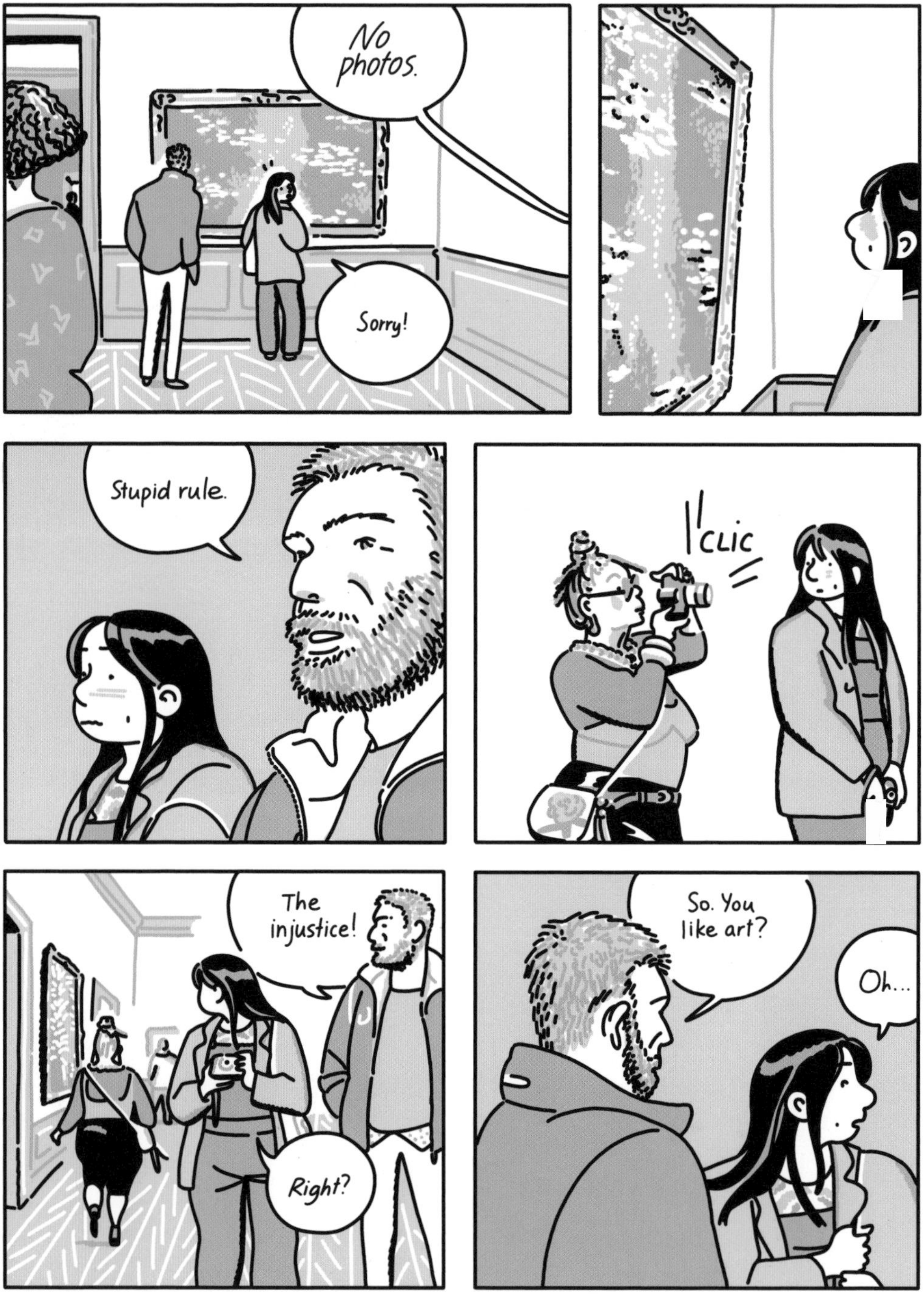
No photos.
Sorry!
Stupid rule.
CLIC
The injustice!
Right?
So. You like art?
Oh...

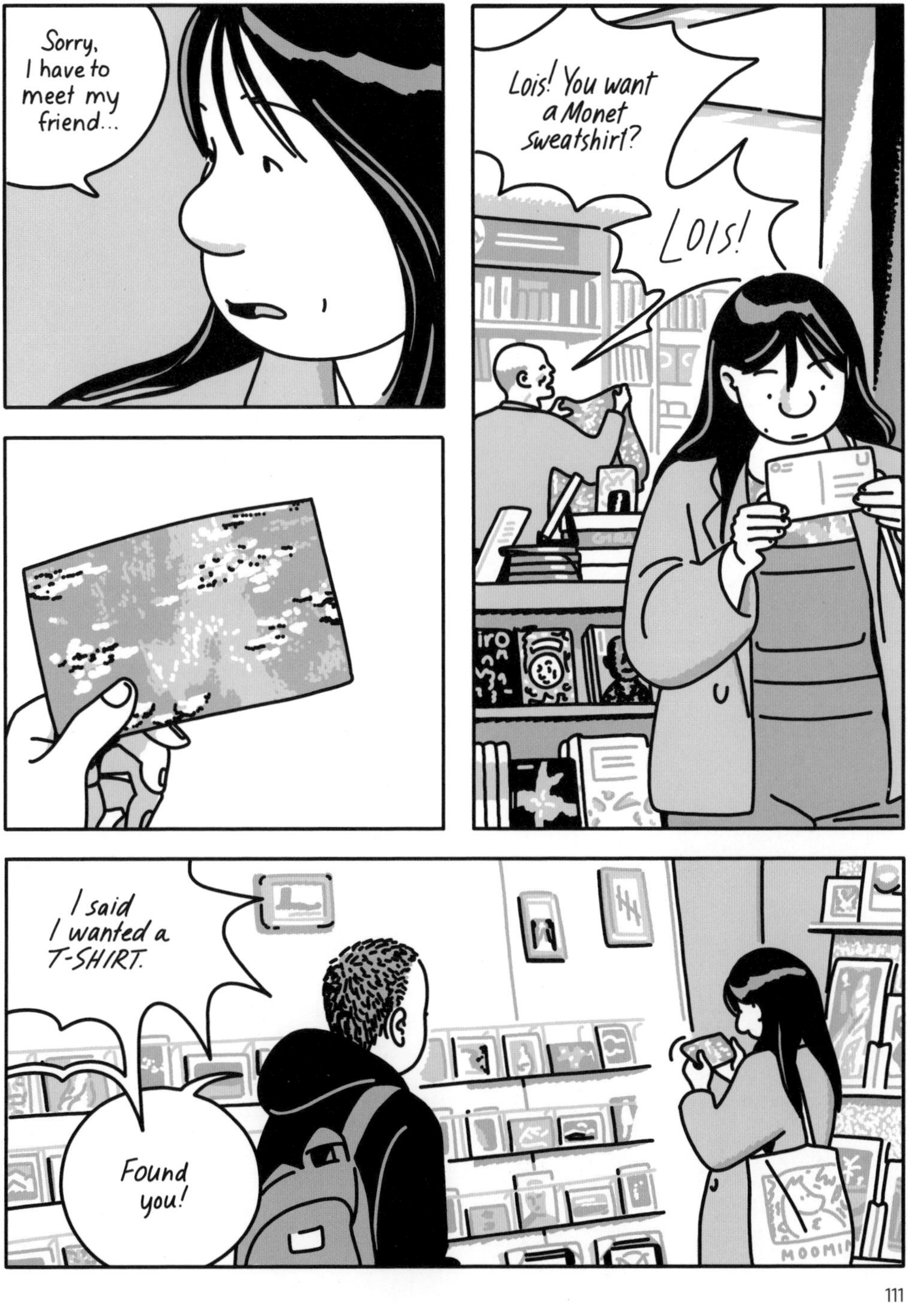
Sorry, I have to meet my friend...
Lois! You want a Monet sweatshirt?
LOIS!
I said I wanted a T-SHIRT.
Found you!
MOOMIN

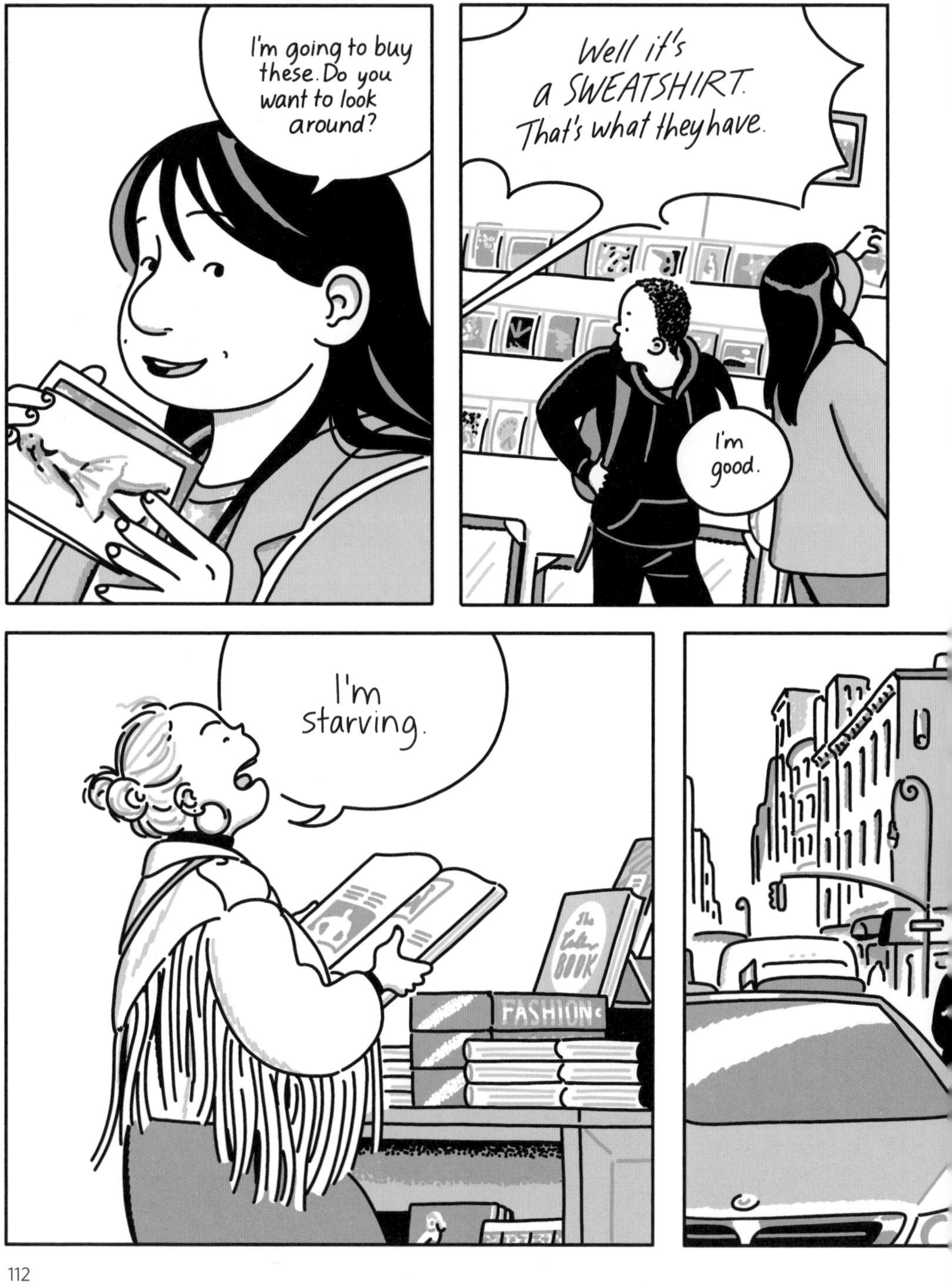
I'm going to buy these. Do you want to look around?
Well it's a SWEATSHIRT. That's what they have.
I'm good.
I'm starving.
FASHION
BOOK

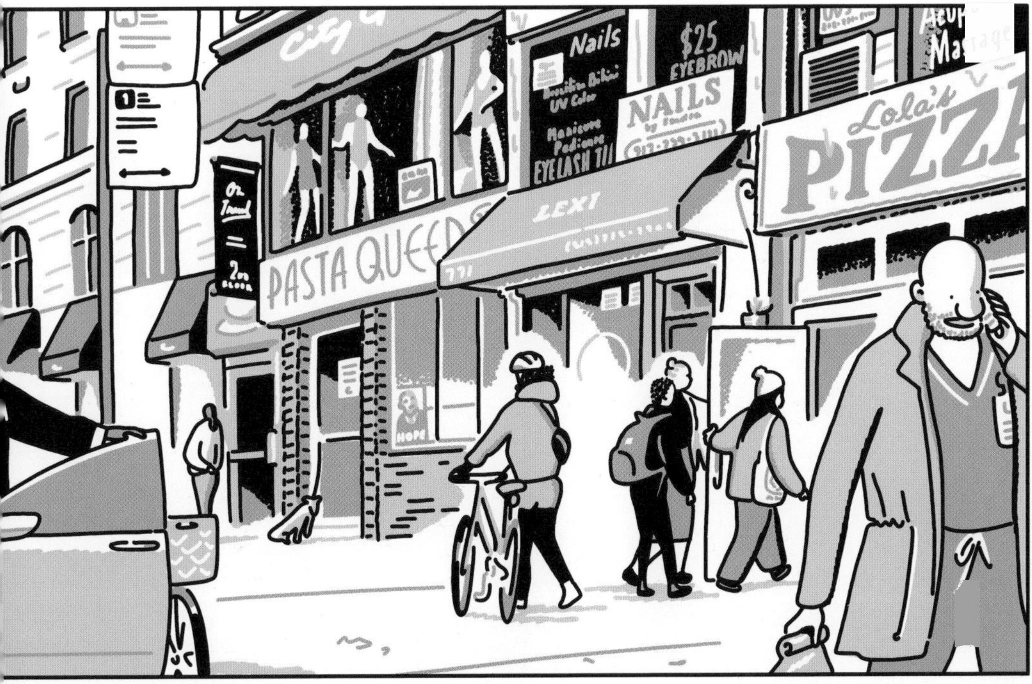
Nails
$25
EYEBROW
NAILS
Manicure
Pedicure
LEXI
PASTA QUEE
771
Lola's
PIZZ
HOPE

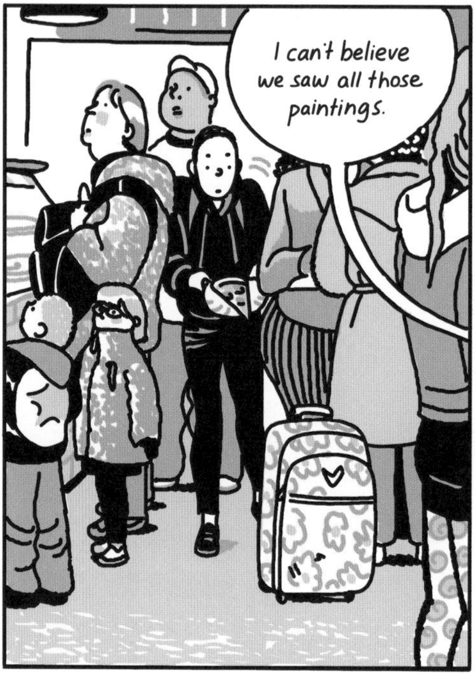
I can't believe we saw all those paintings.

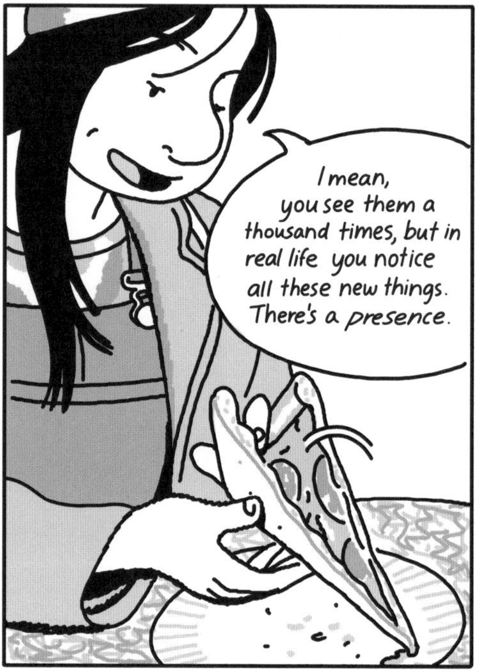
I mean, you see them a thousand times, but in real life you notice all these new things. There's a *presence*.

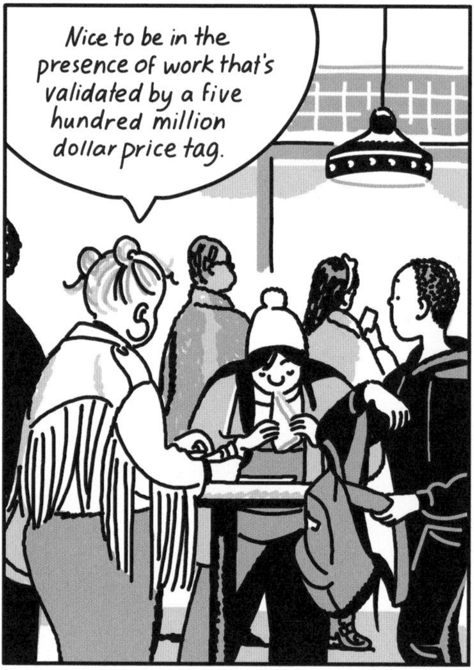
Nice to be in the presence of work that's validated by a five hundred million dollar price tag.

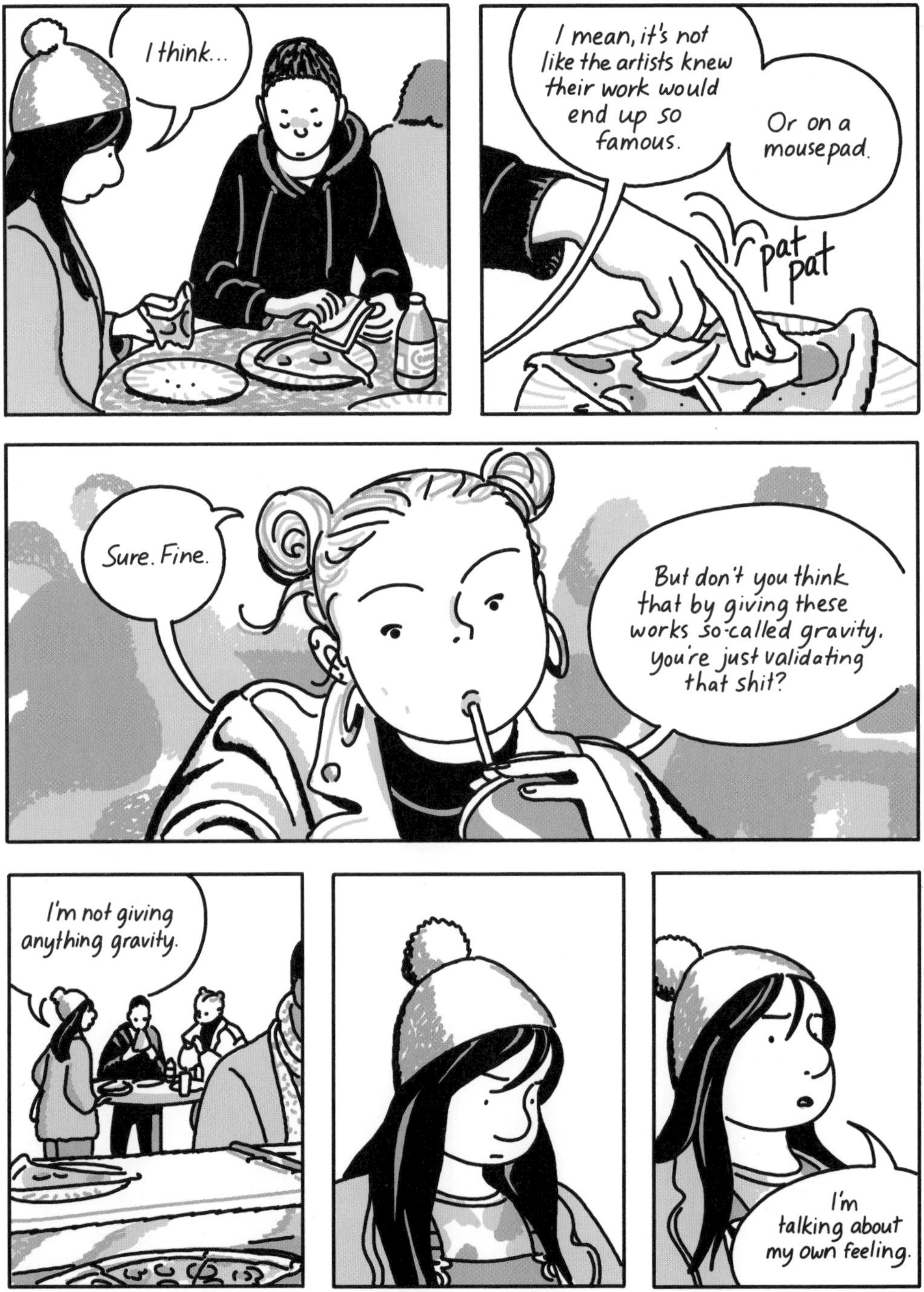

I think...
I mean, it's not like the artists knew their work would end up so famous.
Or on a mousepad.
pat pat
Sure. Fine.
But don't you think that by giving these works so-called gravity, you're just validating that shit?
I'm not giving anything gravity.
I'm talking about my own feeling.

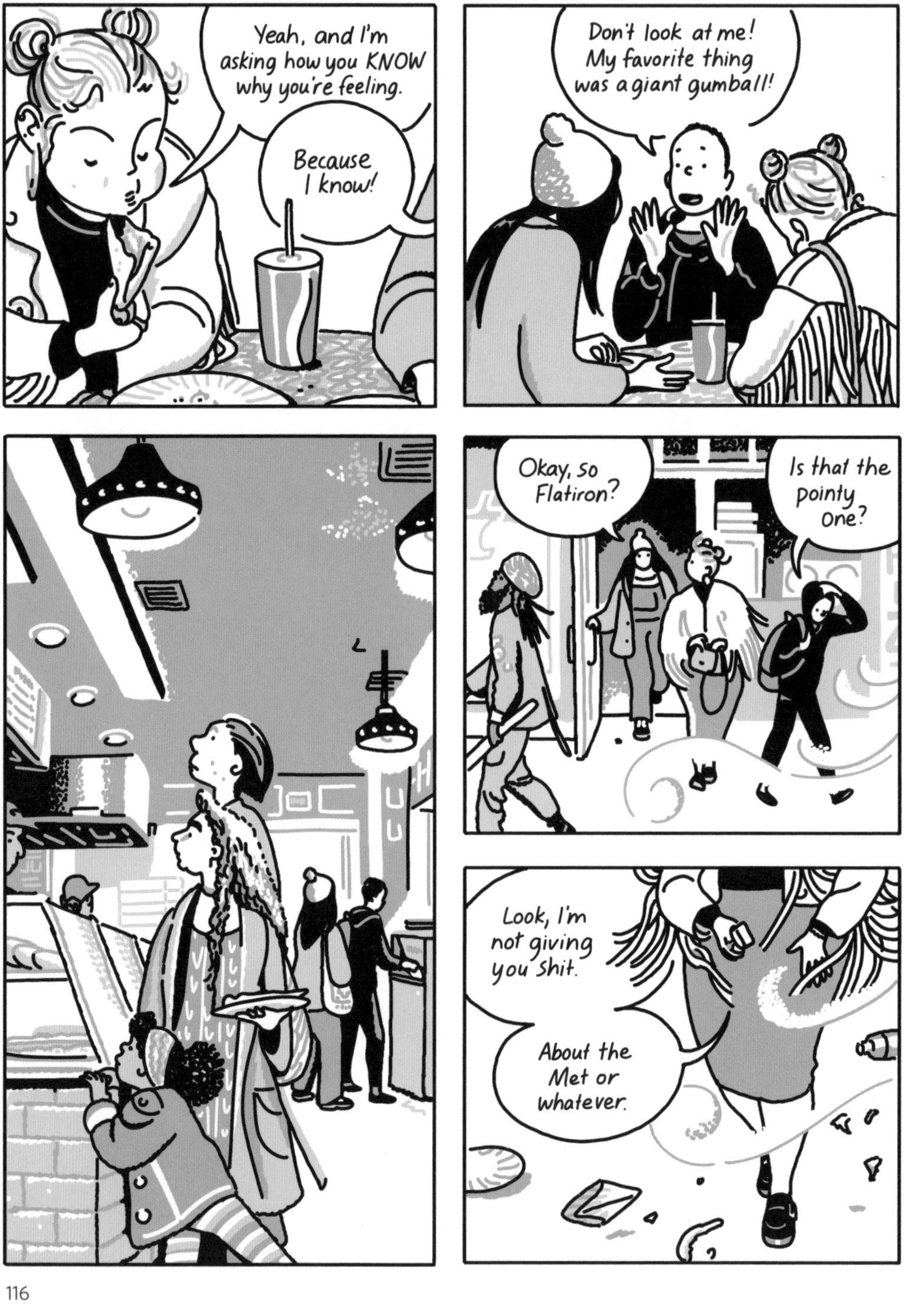
Yeah, and I'm asking how you KNOW why you're feeling.
Because I know!
Don't look at me! My favorite thing was a giant gumball!
Okay, so Flatiron?
Is that the pointy one?
Look, I'm not giving you shit.
About the Met or whatever.

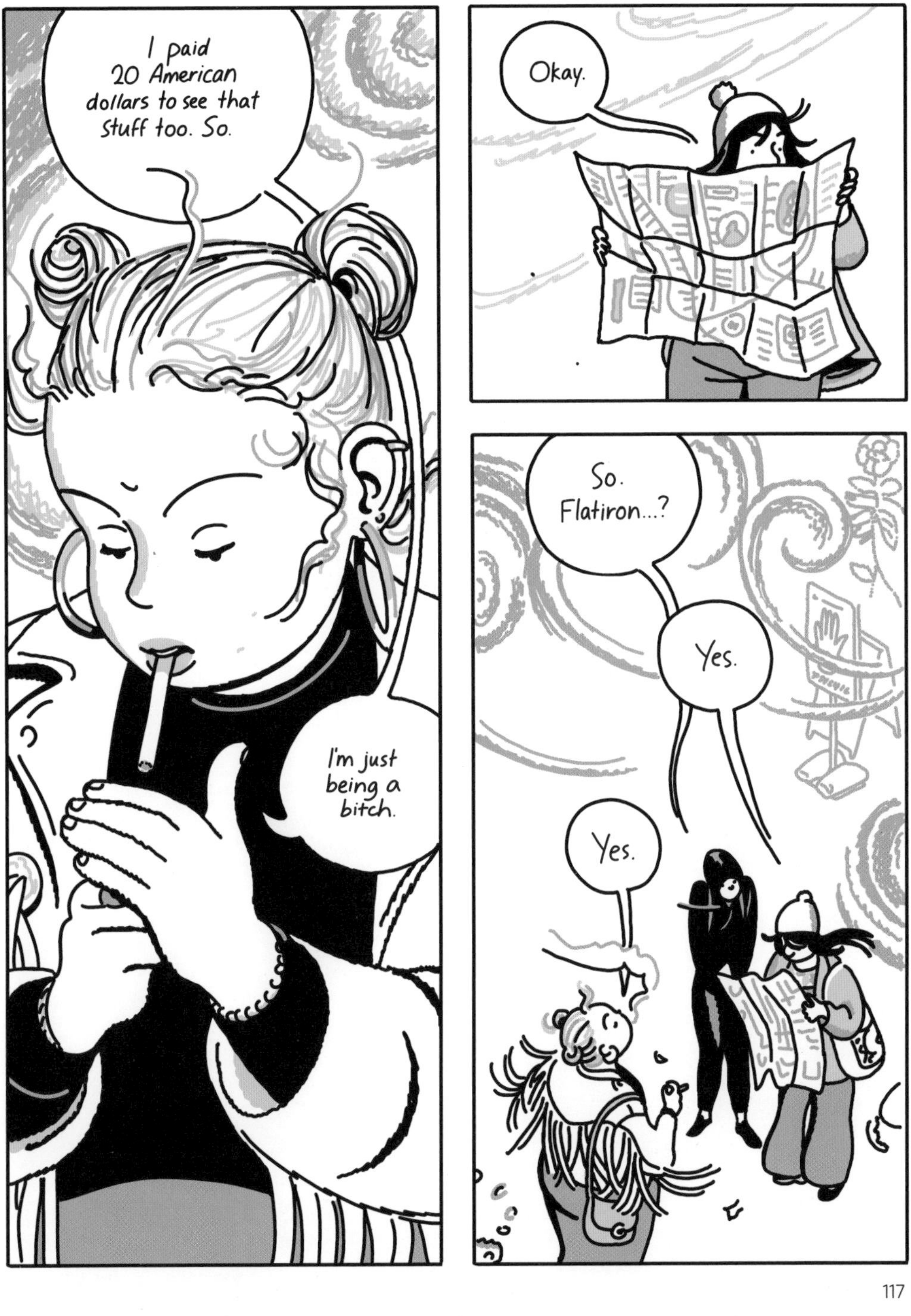
I paid 20 American dollars to see that stuff too. So.
I'm just being a bitch.
Okay.
So. Flatiron...?
Yes.
Yes.

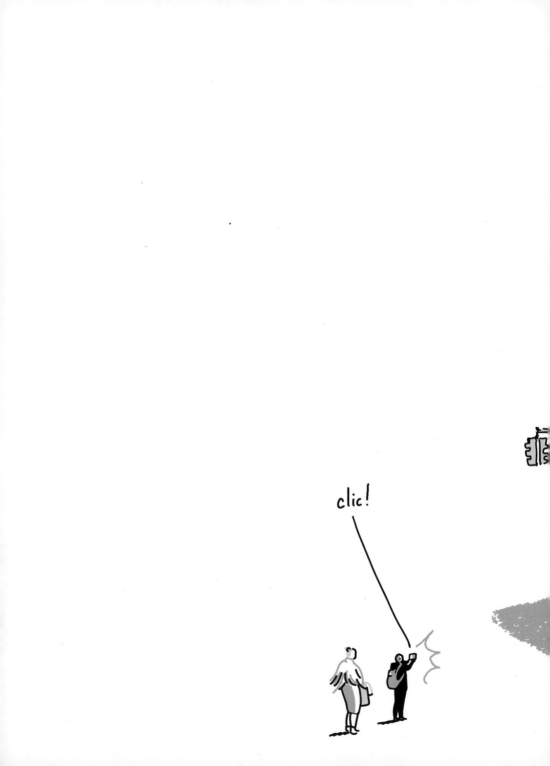

clic!

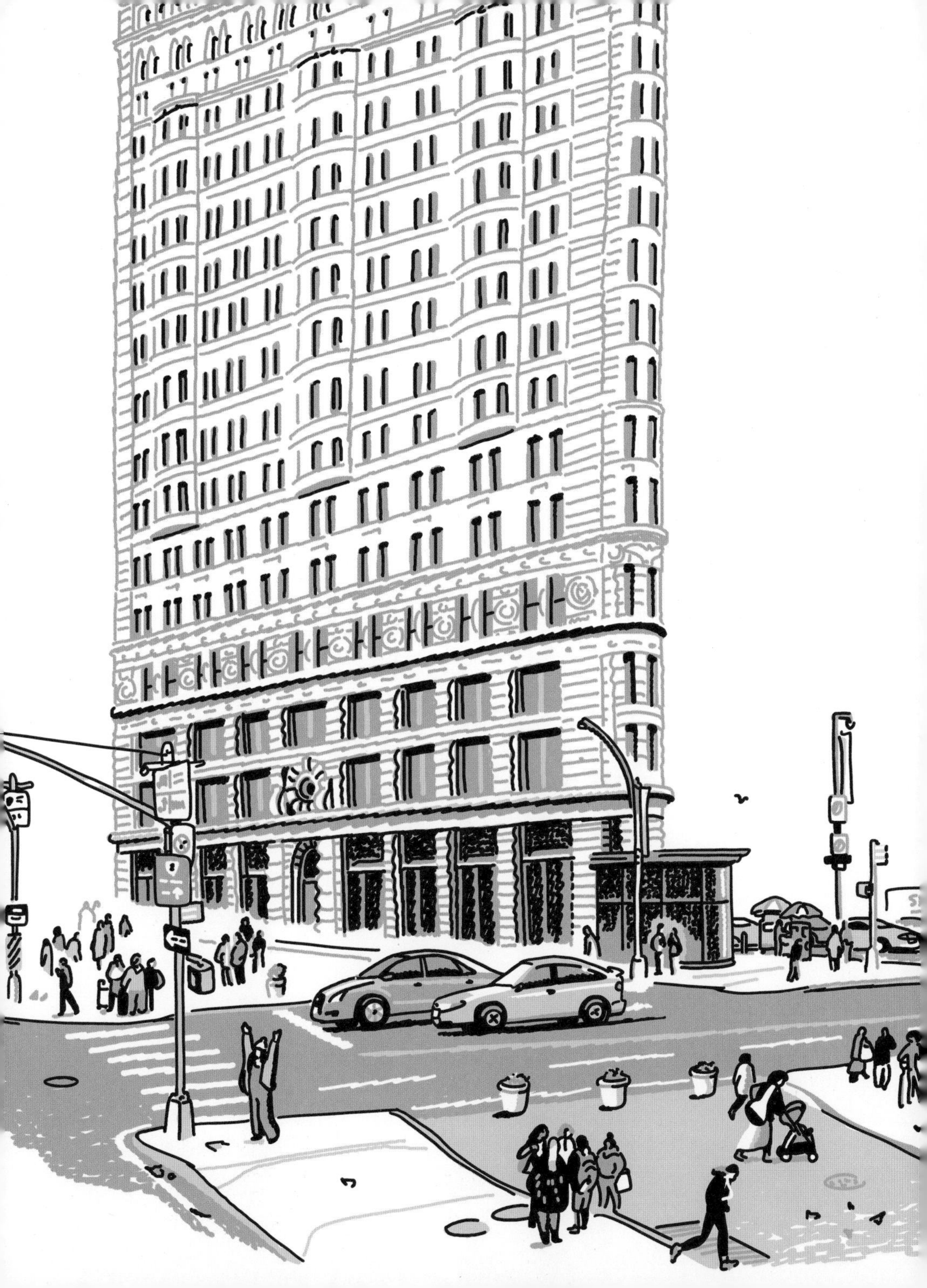

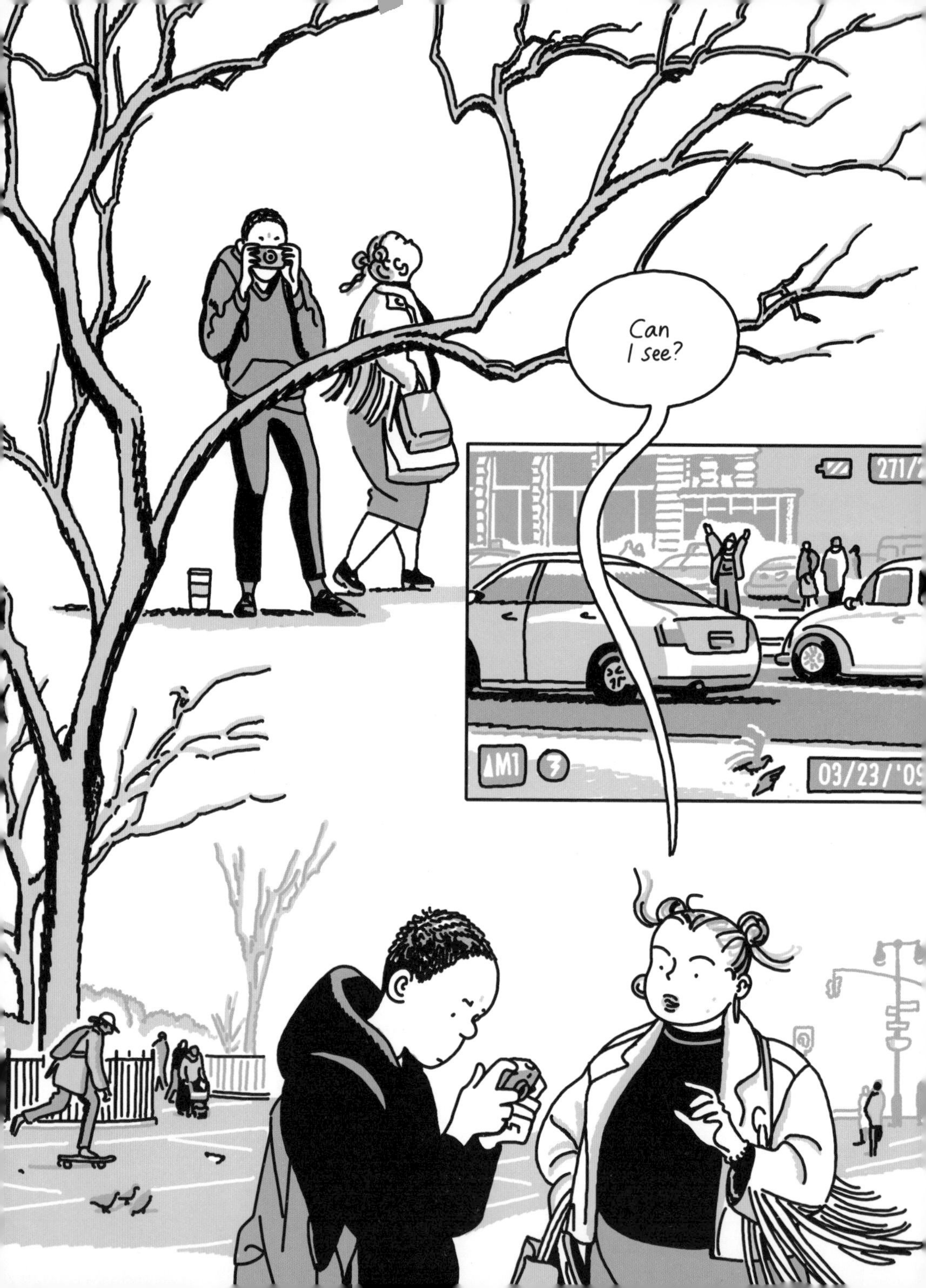
Can I see?
271/2
M1
3
03/23/'09

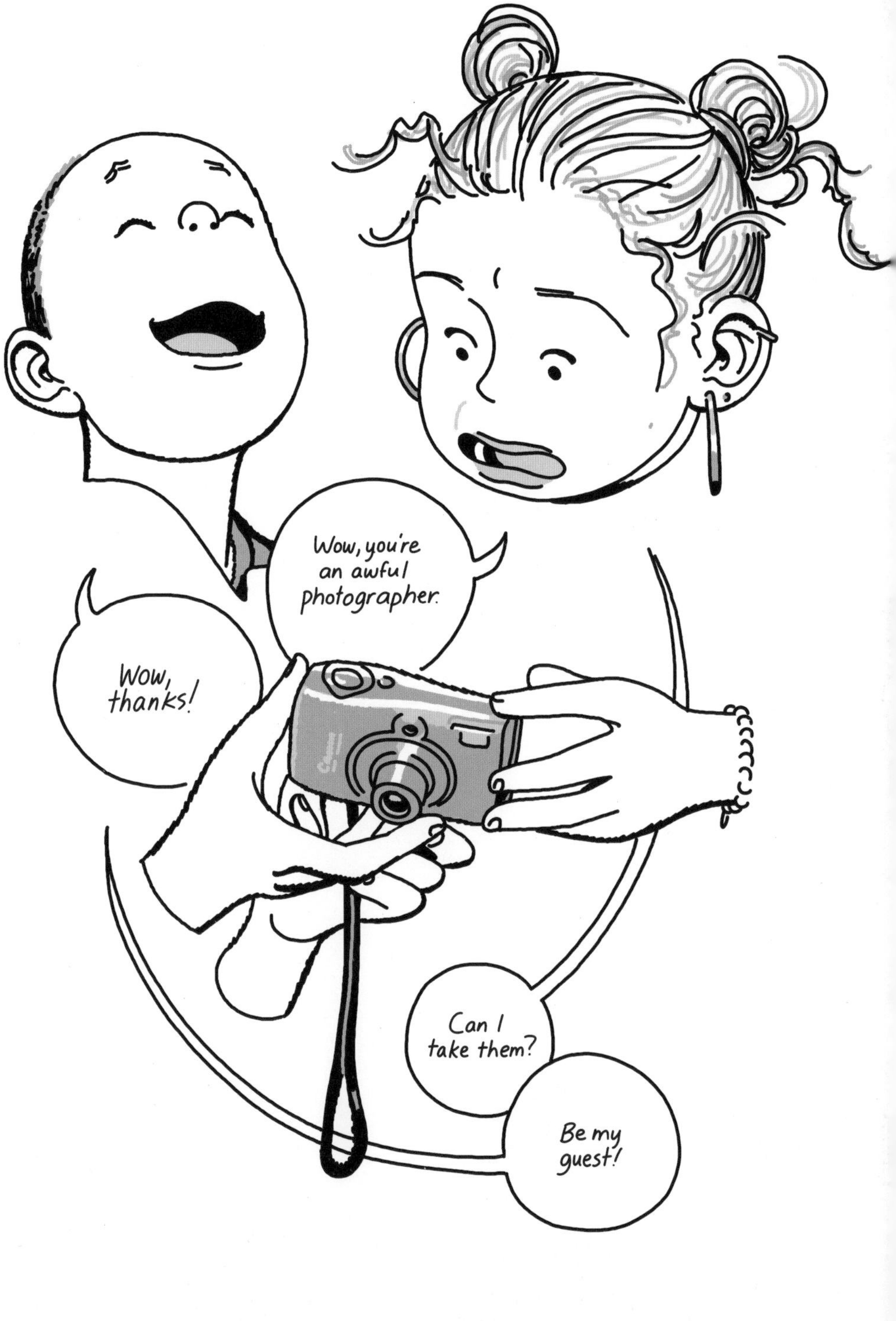
Wow, you're an awful photographer.
Wow, thanks!
Can I take them?
Be my guest!

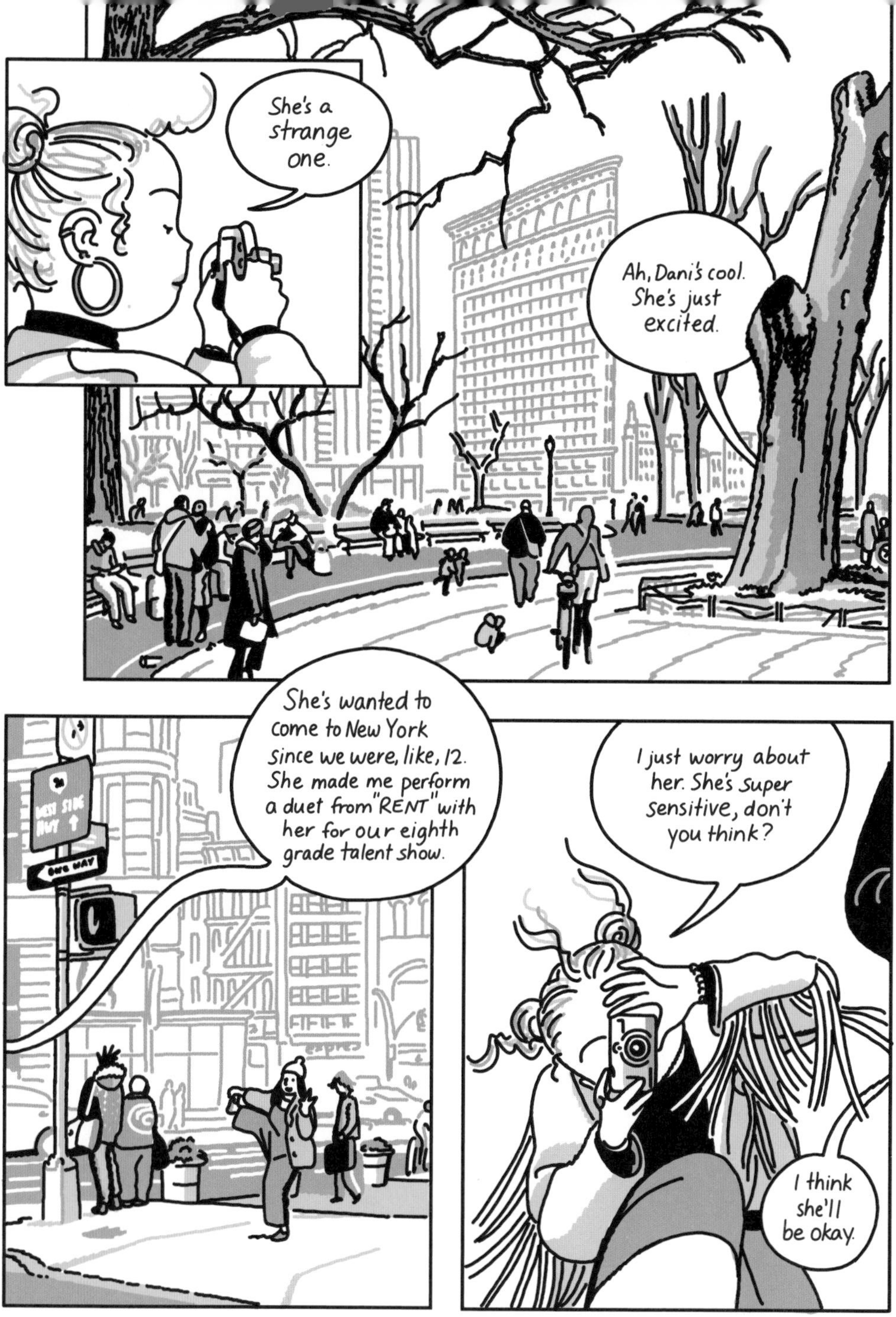
She's a strange one.
Ah, Dani's cool. She's just excited.
She's wanted to come to New York since we were, like, 12. She made me perform a duet from "RENT" with her for our eighth grade talent show.
ONE WAY
I just worry about her. She's super sensitive, don't you think?
I think she'll be okay.

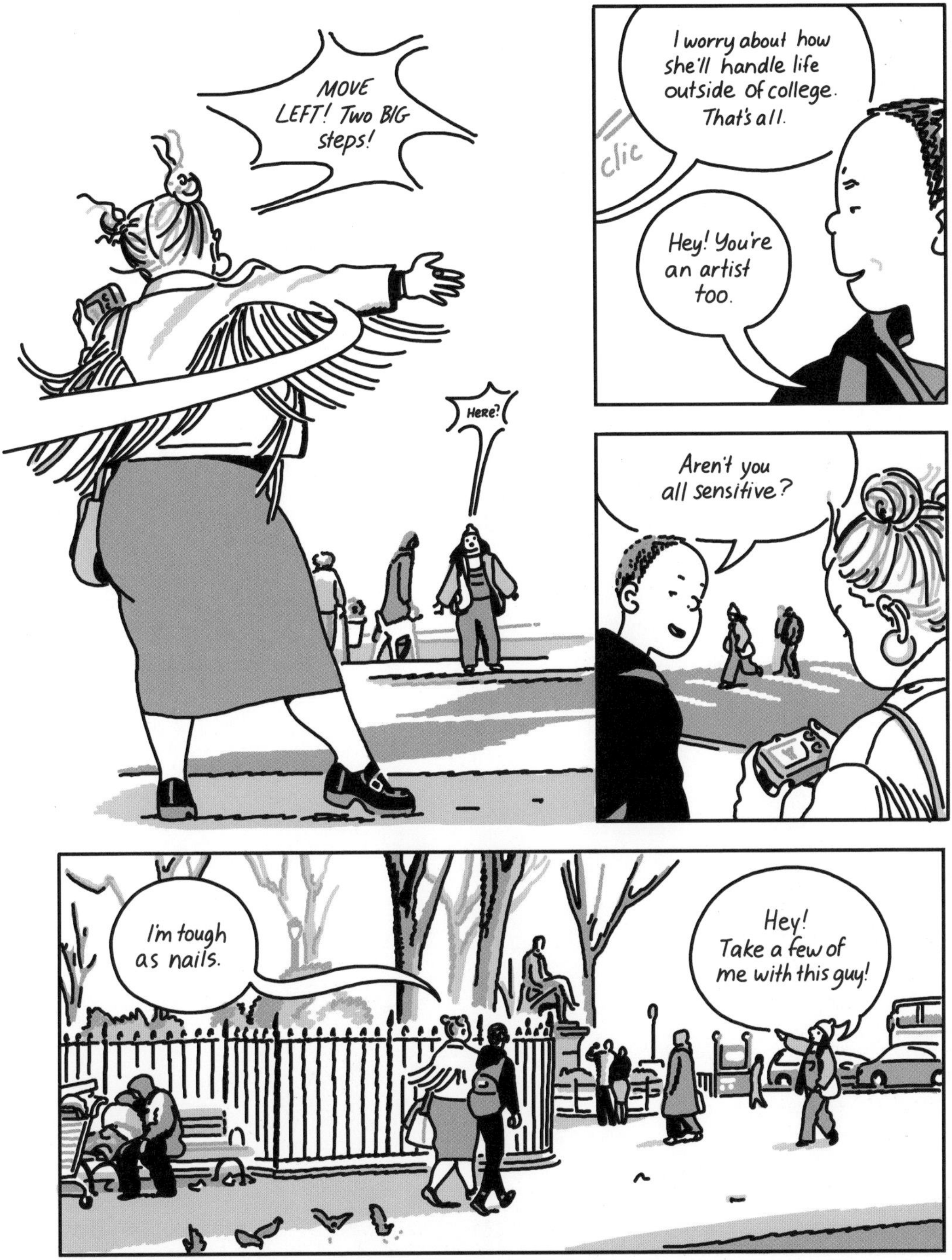
MOVE LEFT! Two BIG steps!
Here?
I worry about how she'll handle life outside of college. That's all.
clic
Hey! You're an artist too.
Aren't you all sensitive?
I'm tough as nails.
Hey! Take a few of me with this guy!

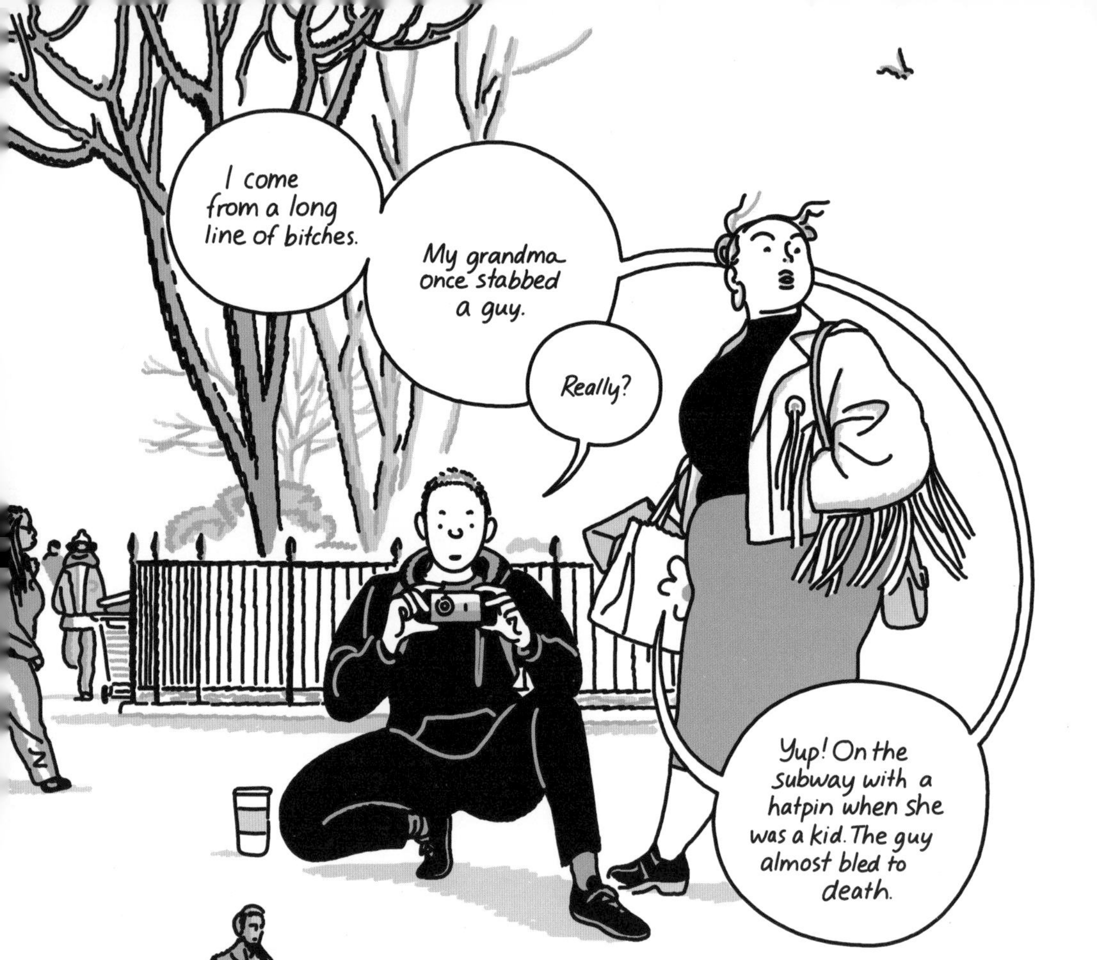
I come from a long line of bitches.
My grandma once stabbed a guy.
Really?
Yup! On the subway with a hatpin when she was a kid. The guy almost bled to death.

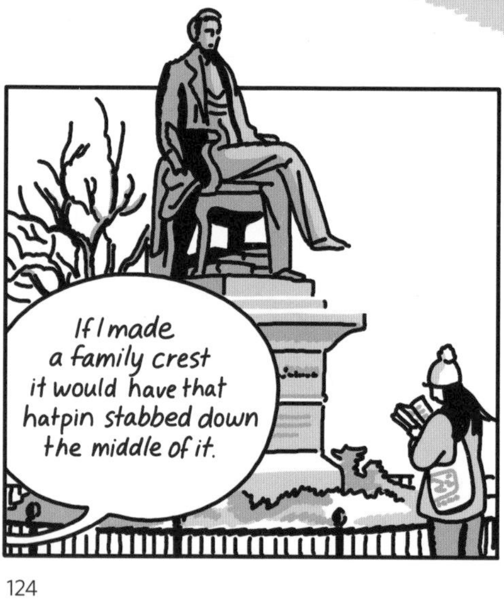
If I made a family crest it would have that hatpin stabbed down the middle of it.

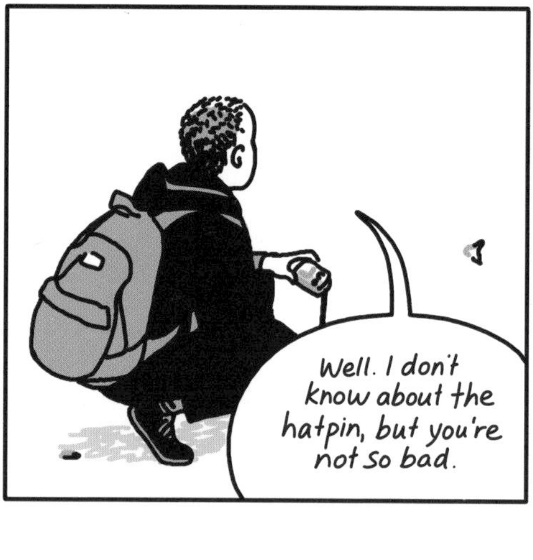
Well. I don't know about the hatpin, but you're not so bad.

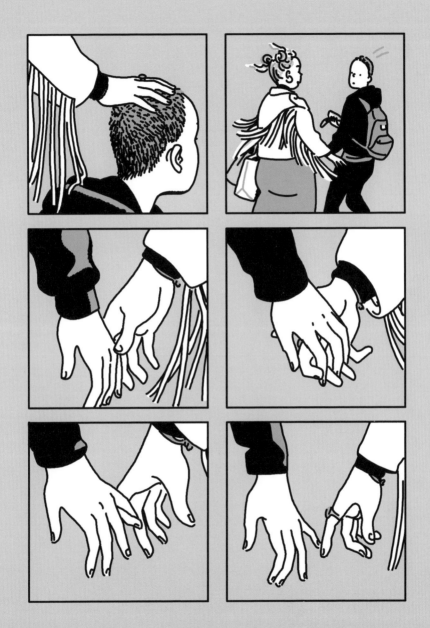

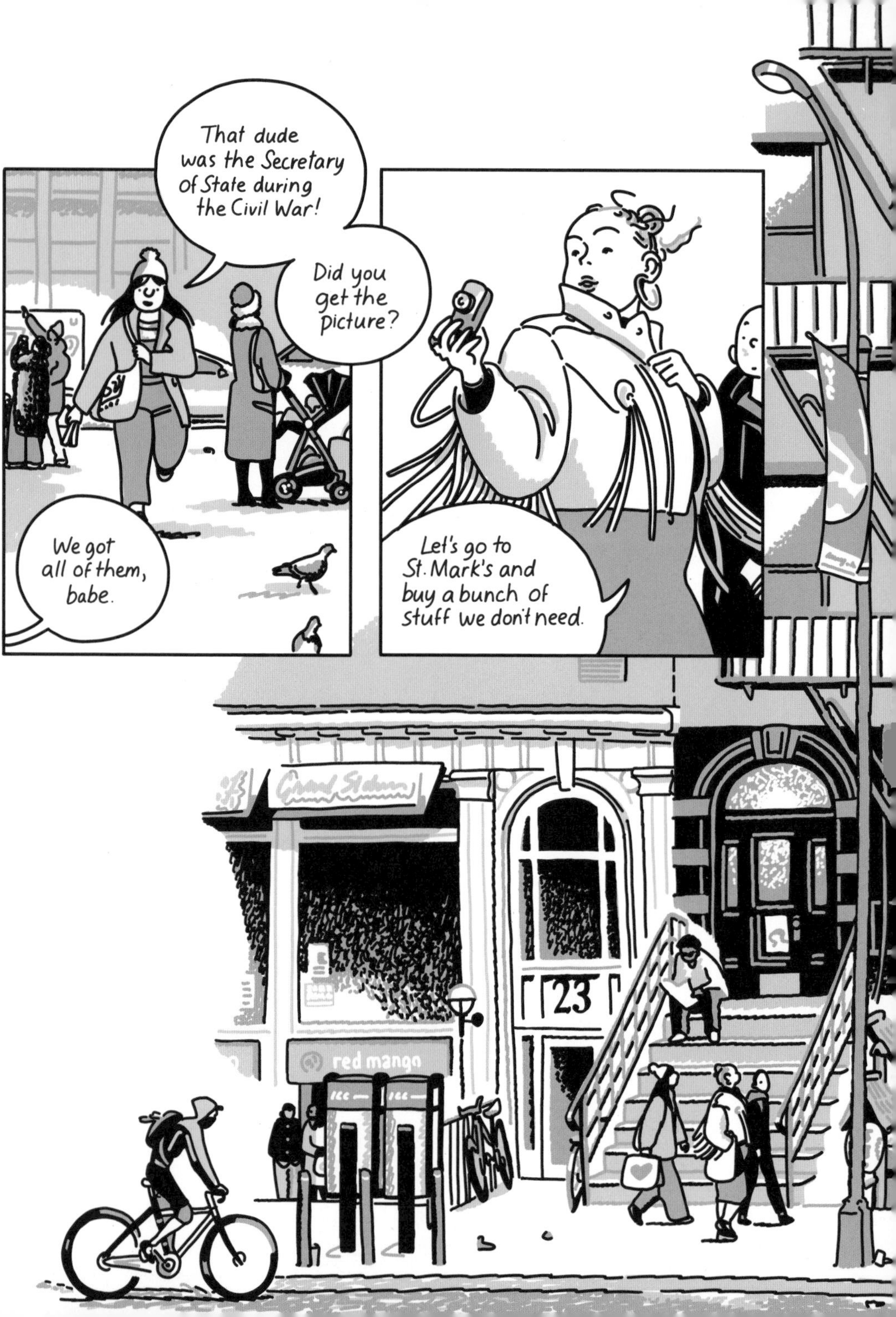
That dude was the Secretary of State during the Civil War!
Did you get the picture?
We got all of them, babe.
Let's go to St. Mark's and buy a bunch of stuff we don't need.
red mango
23

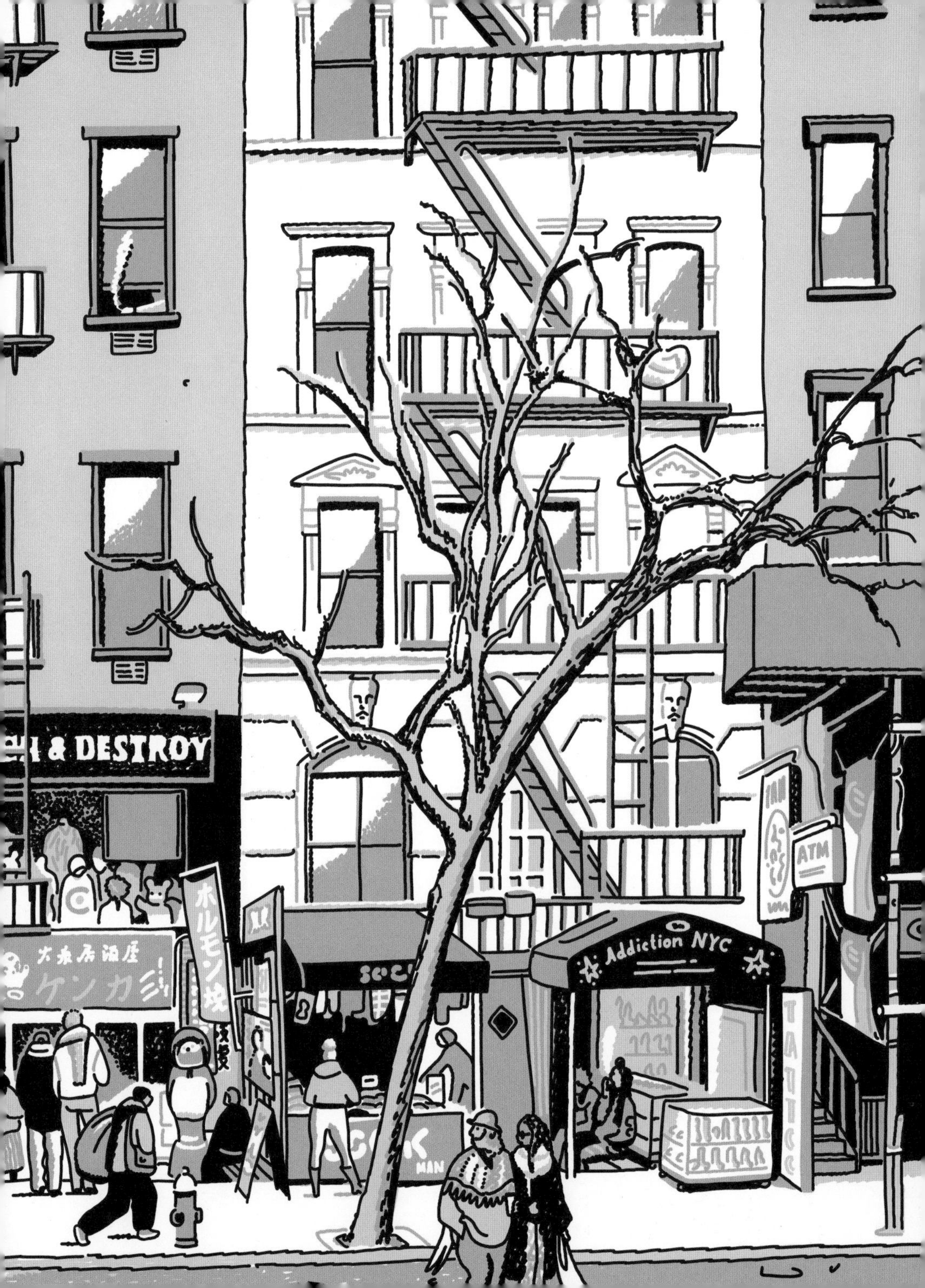
H & DESTROY
ホルモン焼
大衆居酒屋
ケンカ
Addiction NYC
ATM

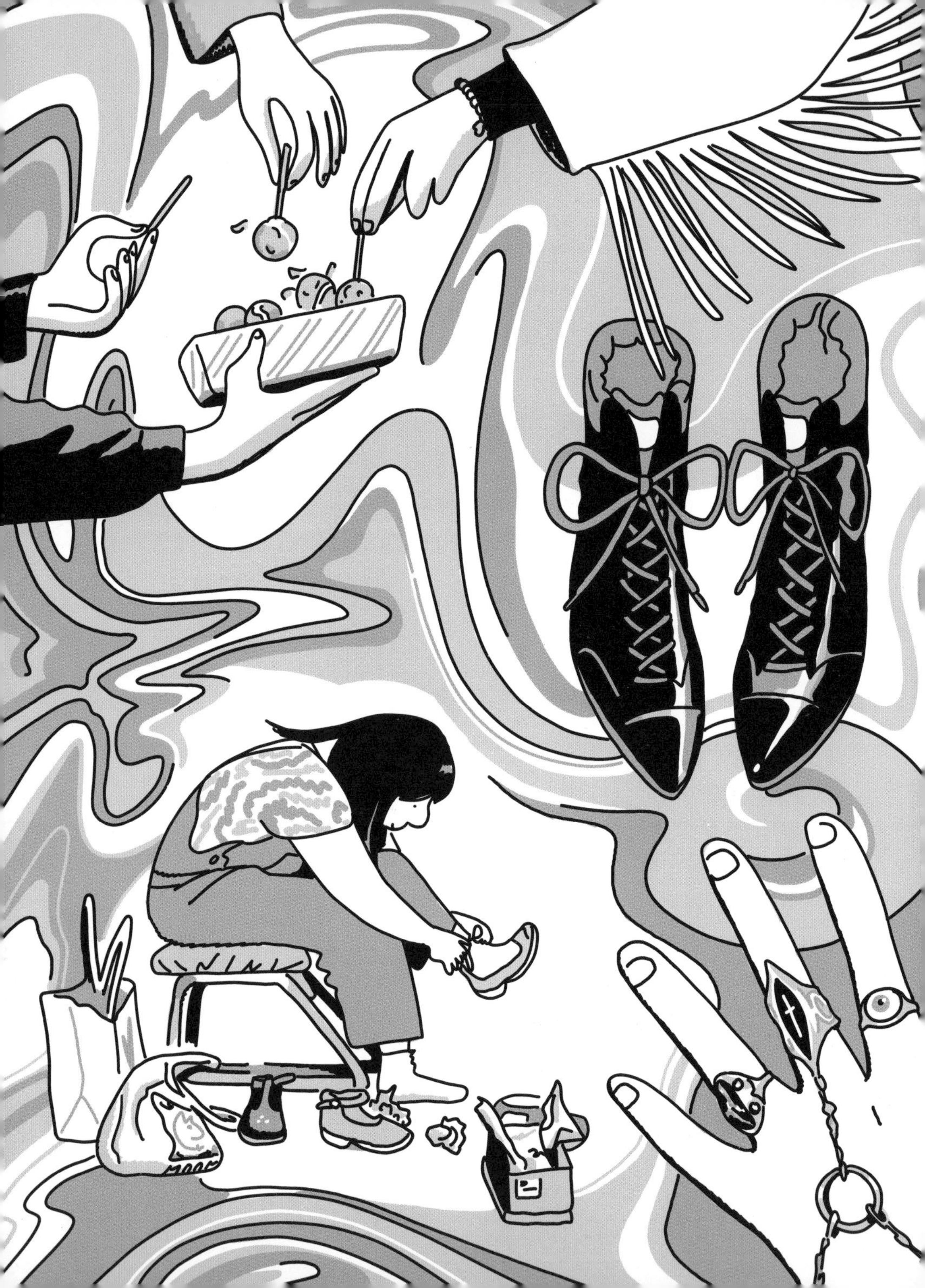

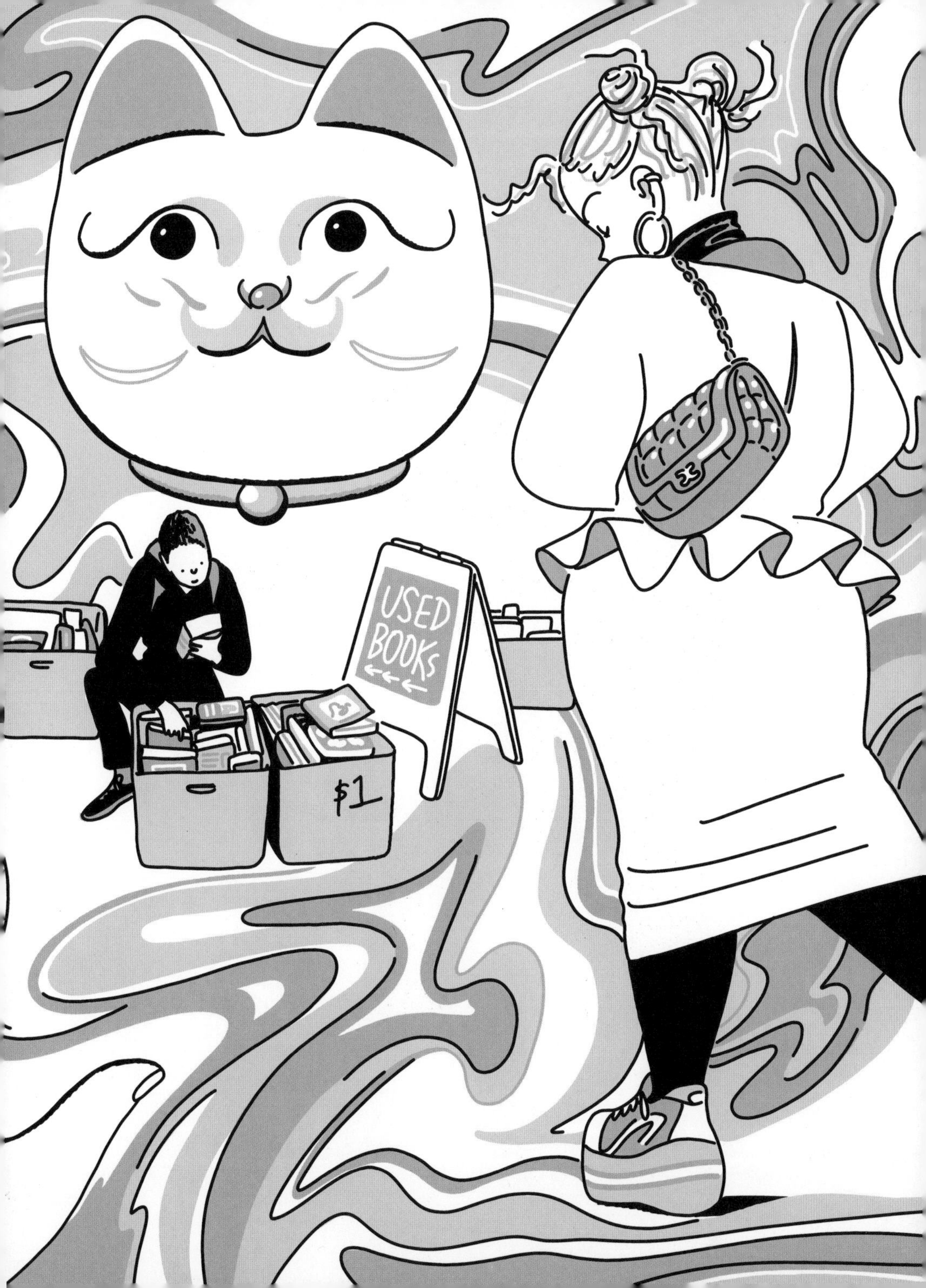
USED BOOKS
$1

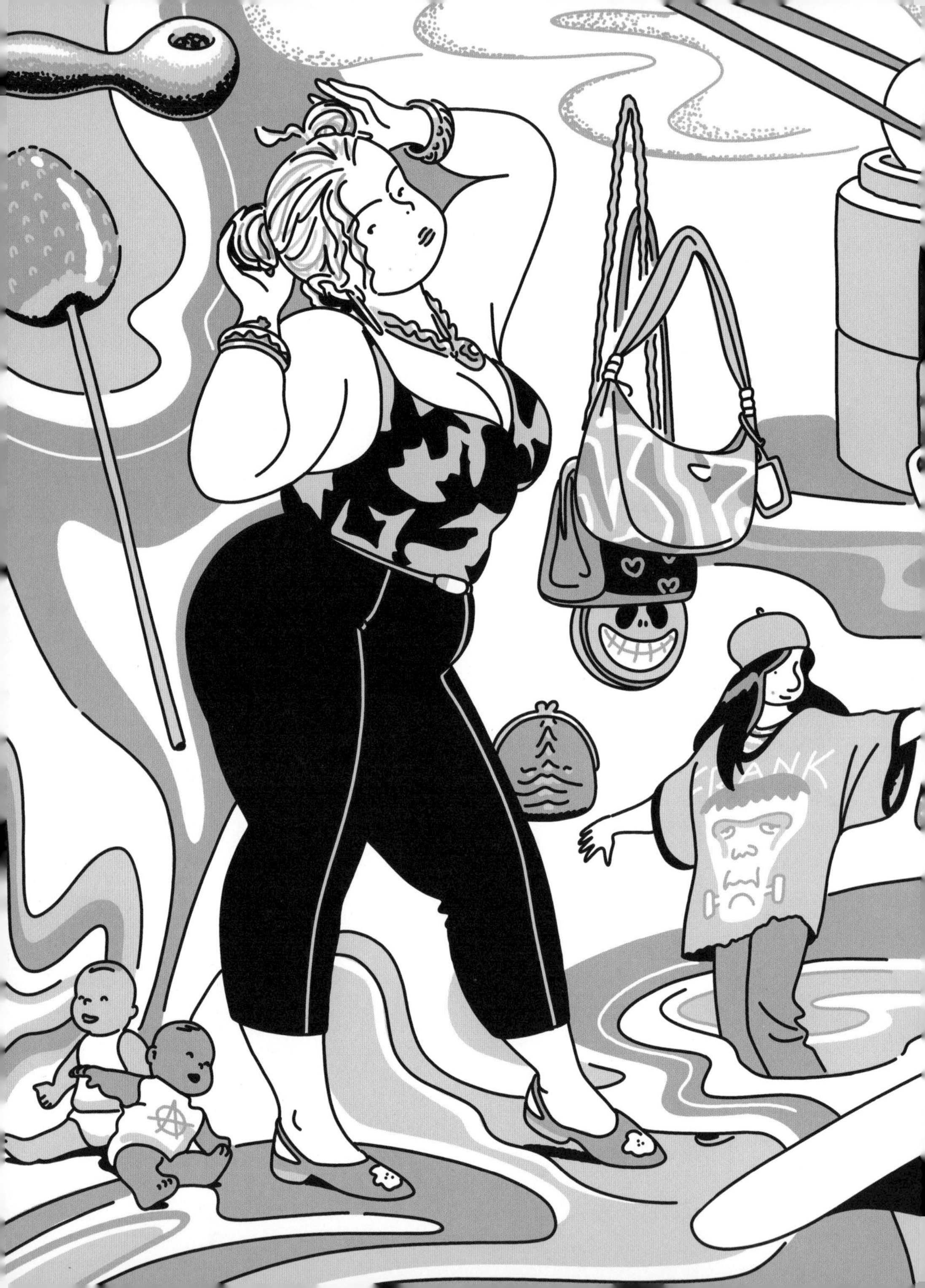

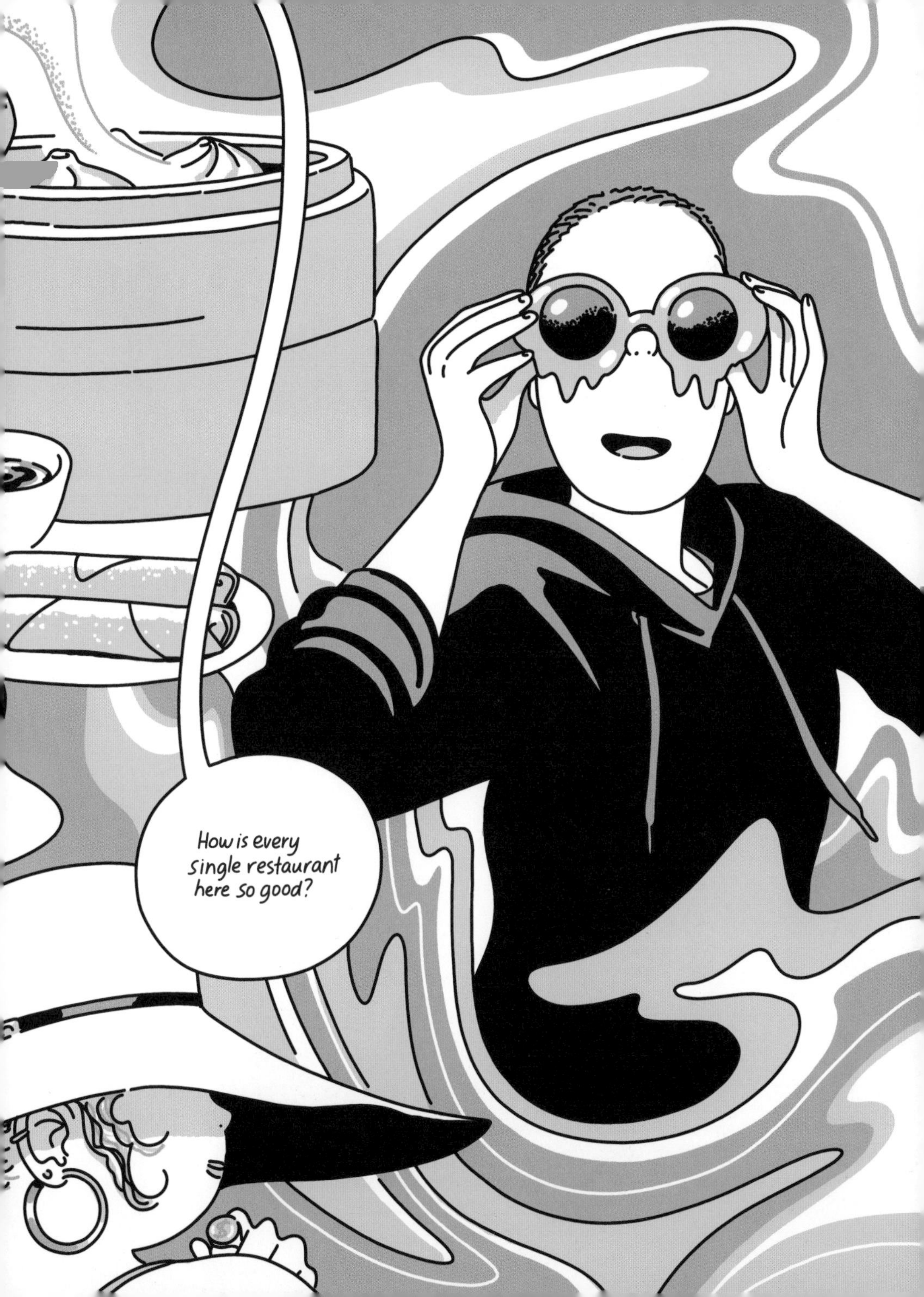
How is every single restaurant here so good?

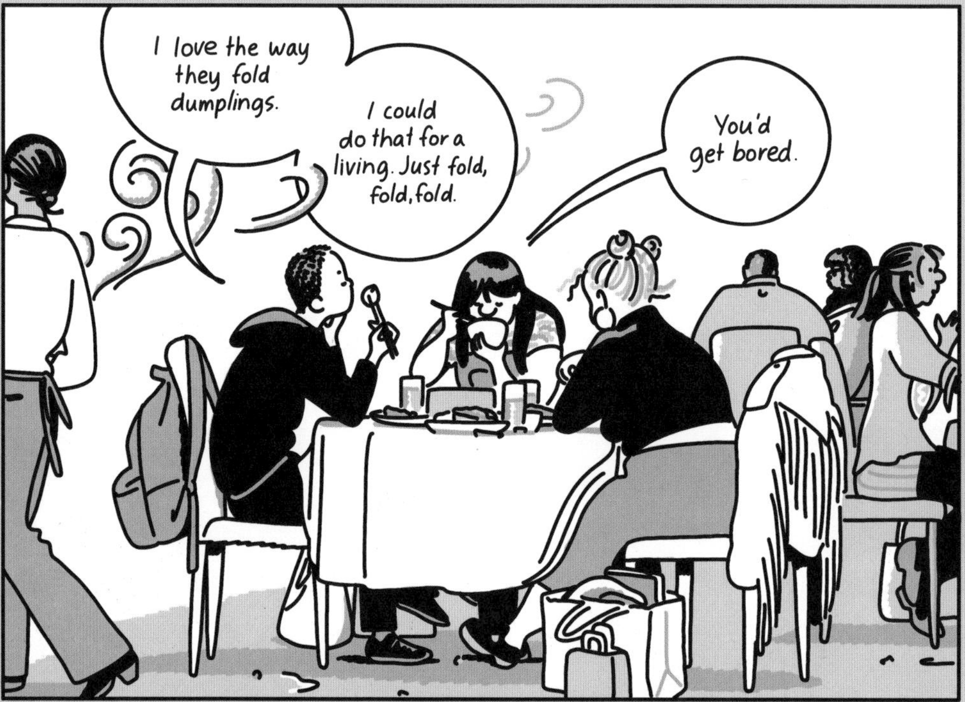
I love the way they fold dumplings.
I could do that for a living. Just fold, fold, fold.
You'd get bored.

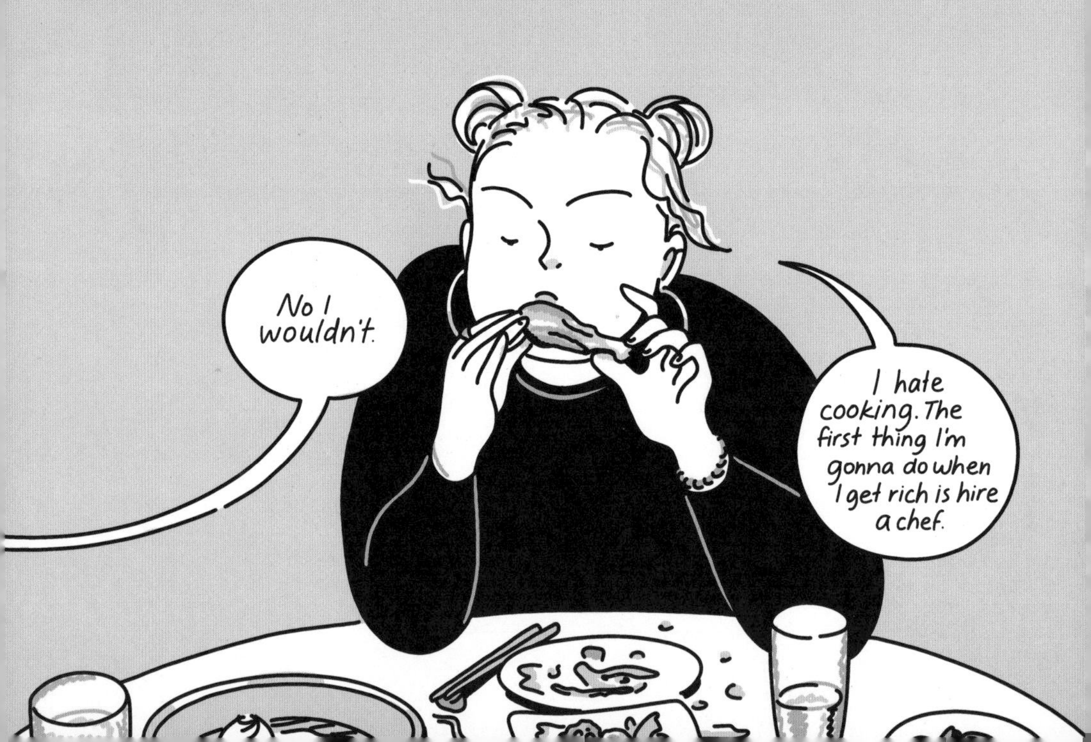
No I wouldn't.
I hate cooking. The first thing I'm gonna do when I get rich is hire a chef.

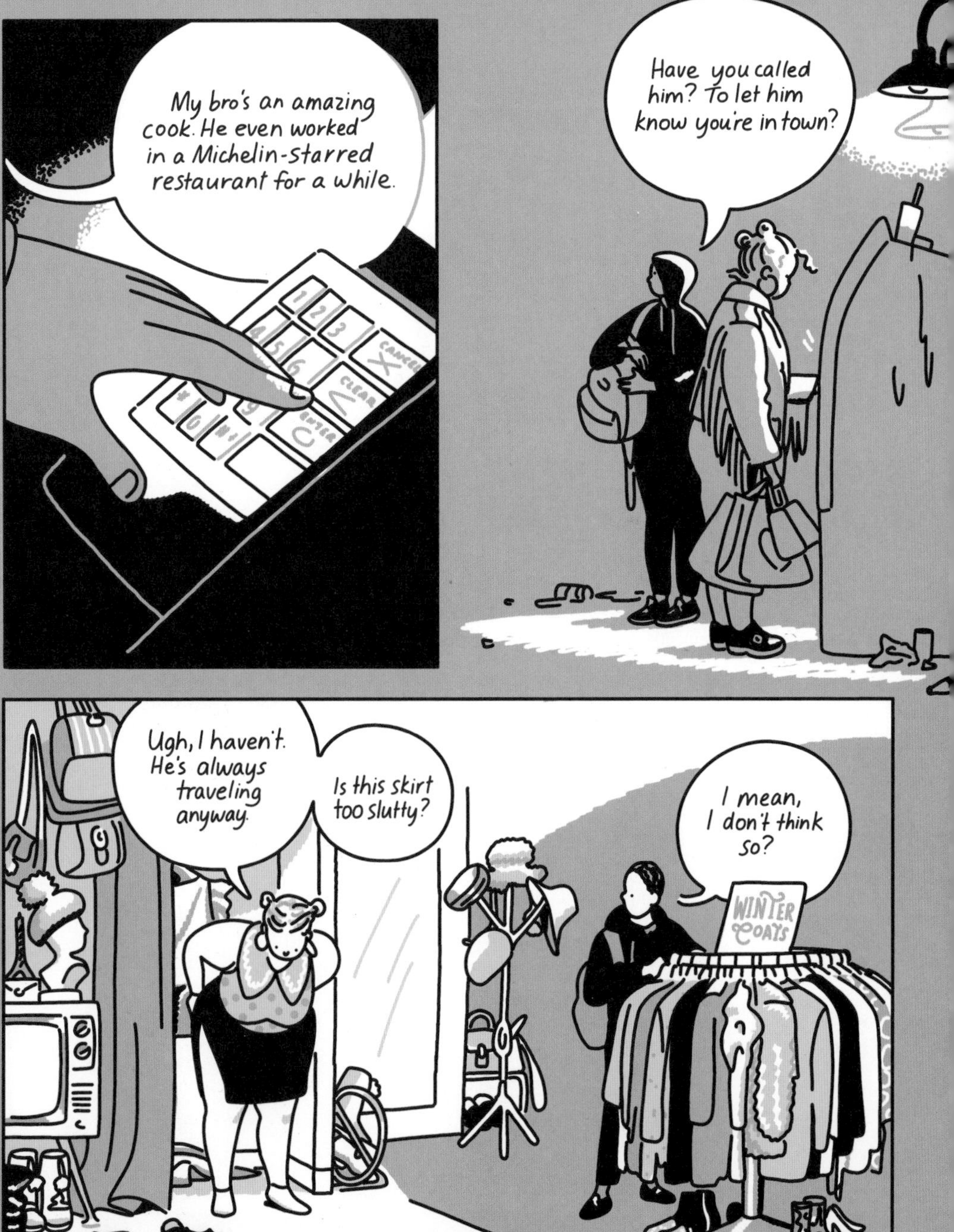
My bro's an amazing cook. He even worked in a Michelin-starred restaurant for a while.
Have you called him? To let him know you're in town?
Ugh, I haven't. He's always traveling anyway.
Is this skirt too slutty?
I mean, I don't think so?
WINTER COATS

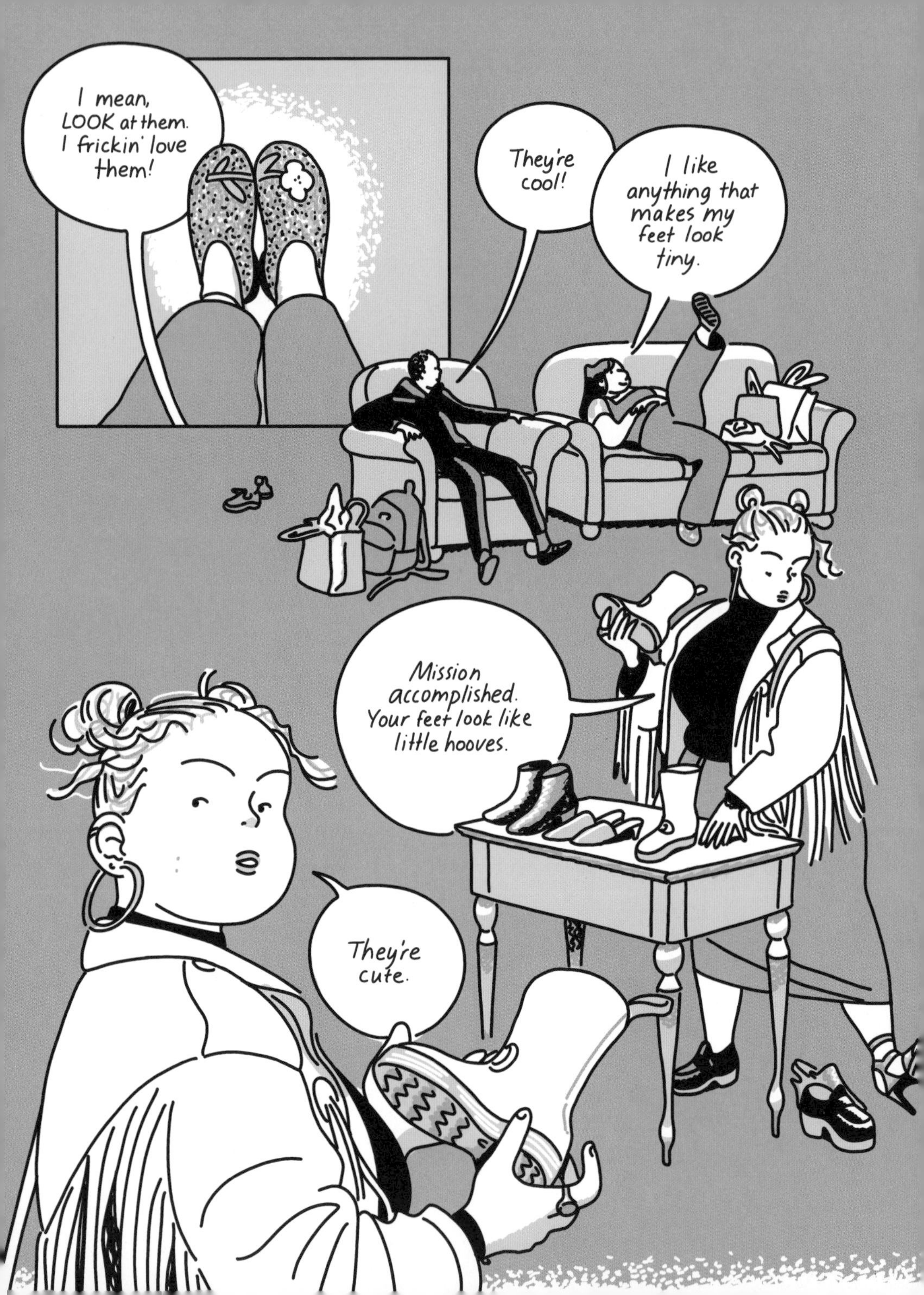
I mean, LOOK at them. I frickin' love them!
They're cool!
I like anything that makes my feet look tiny.
Mission accomplished. Your feet look like little hooves.
They're cute.

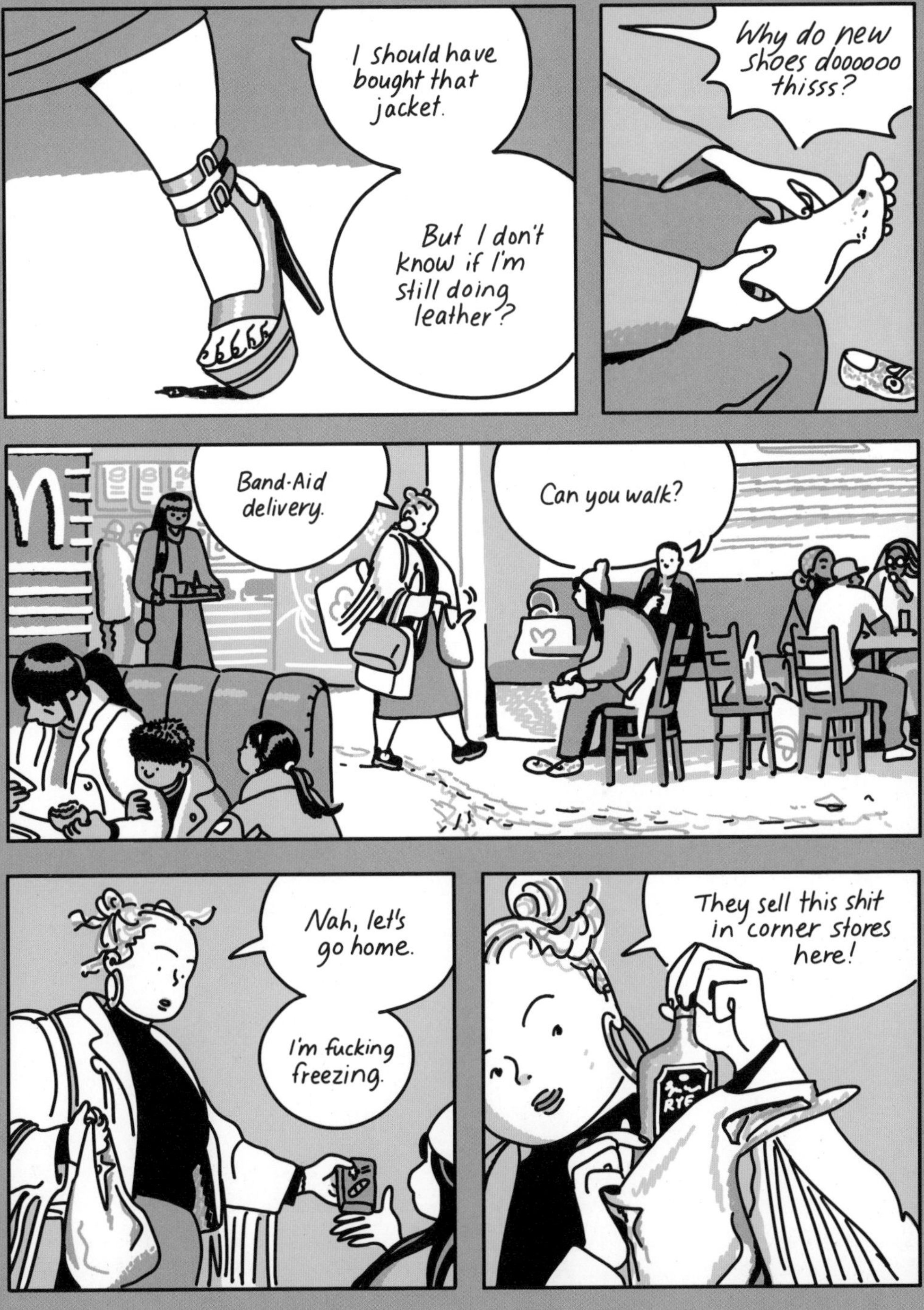
I should have bought that jacket.
But I don't know if I'm still doing leather?
Why do new shoes doooooo thisss?
Band-Aid delivery.
Can you walk?
Nah, let's go home.
I'm fucking freezing.
They sell this shit in corner stores here!
RYE

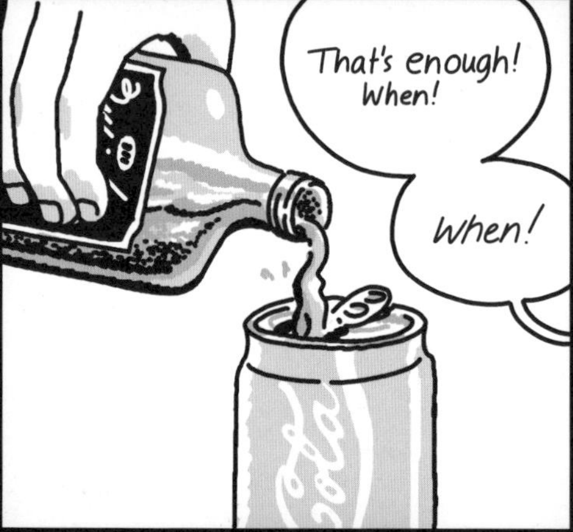
That's enough! When!
When!

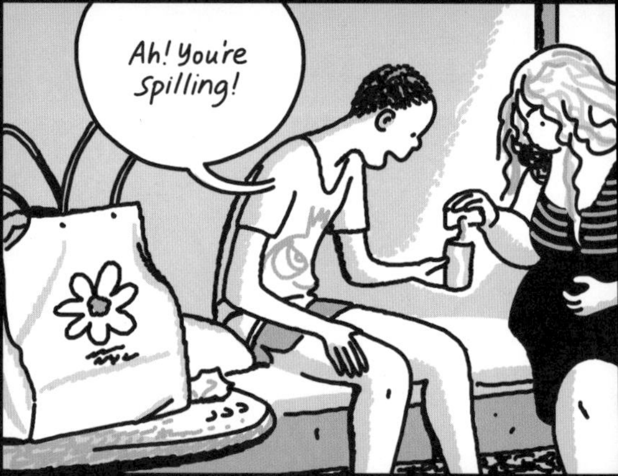
Ah! You're Spilling!

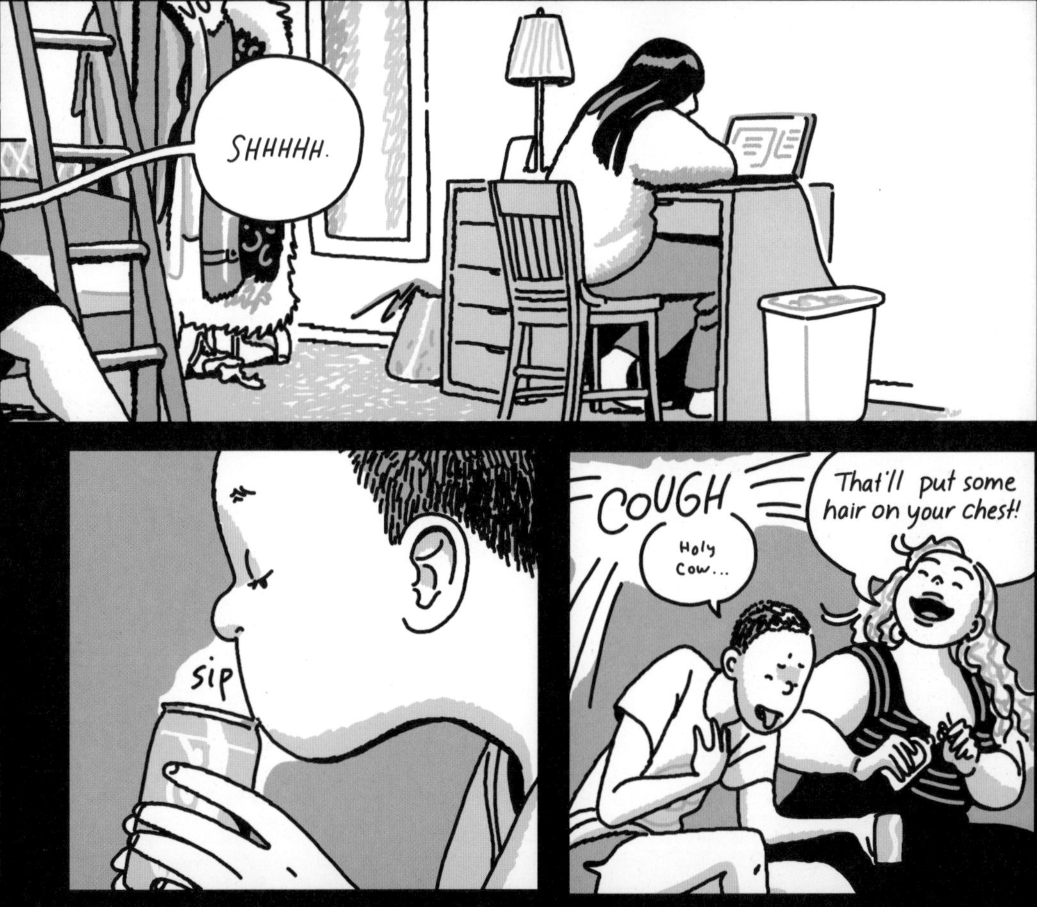
SHHHHH.
sip
COUGH
Holy cow...
That'll put some hair on your chest!

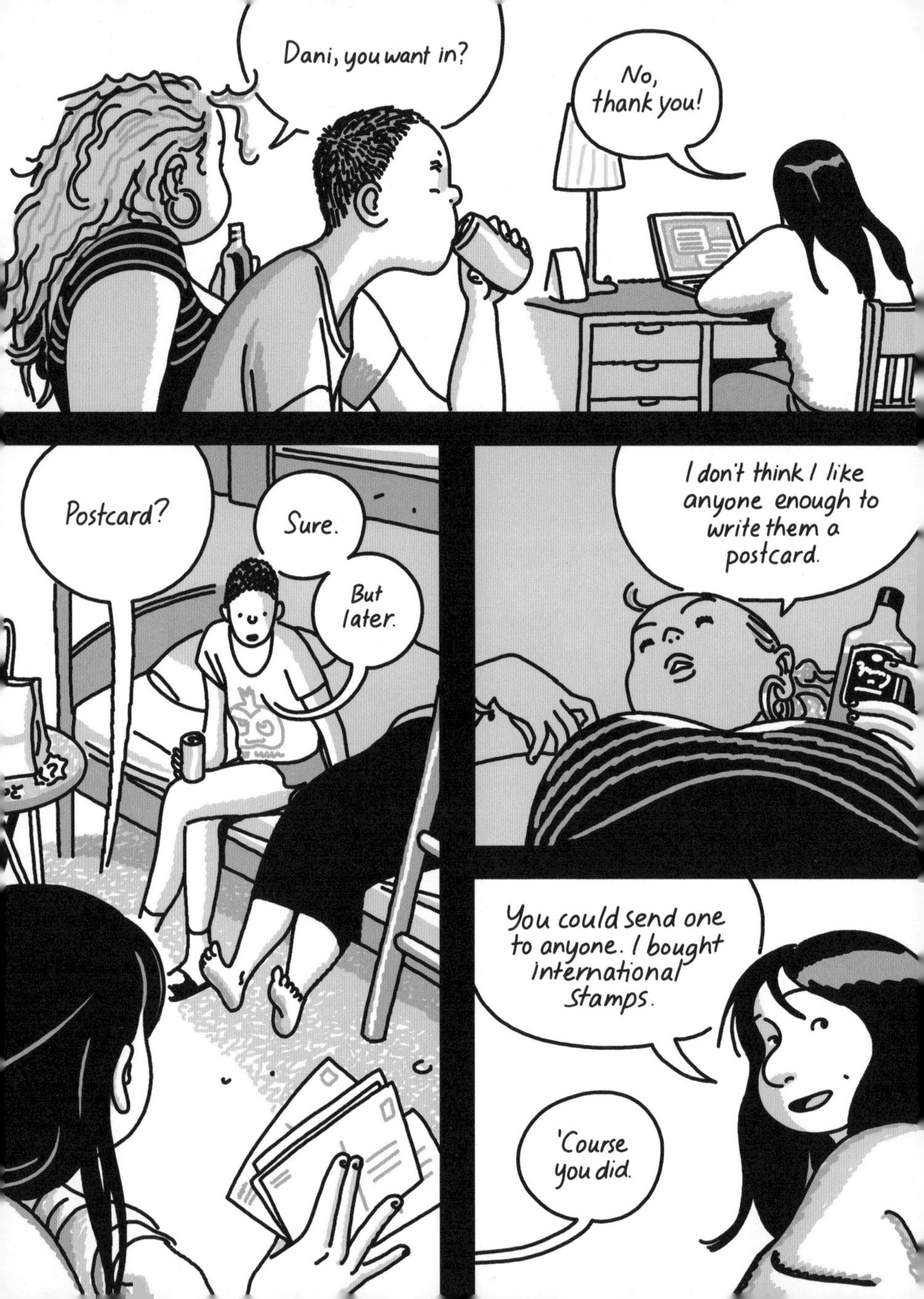

Dani, you want in?
No, thank you!
Postcard?
Sure.
But later.
I don't think I like anyone enough to write them a postcard.
You could send one to anyone. I bought international stamps.
'Course you did.

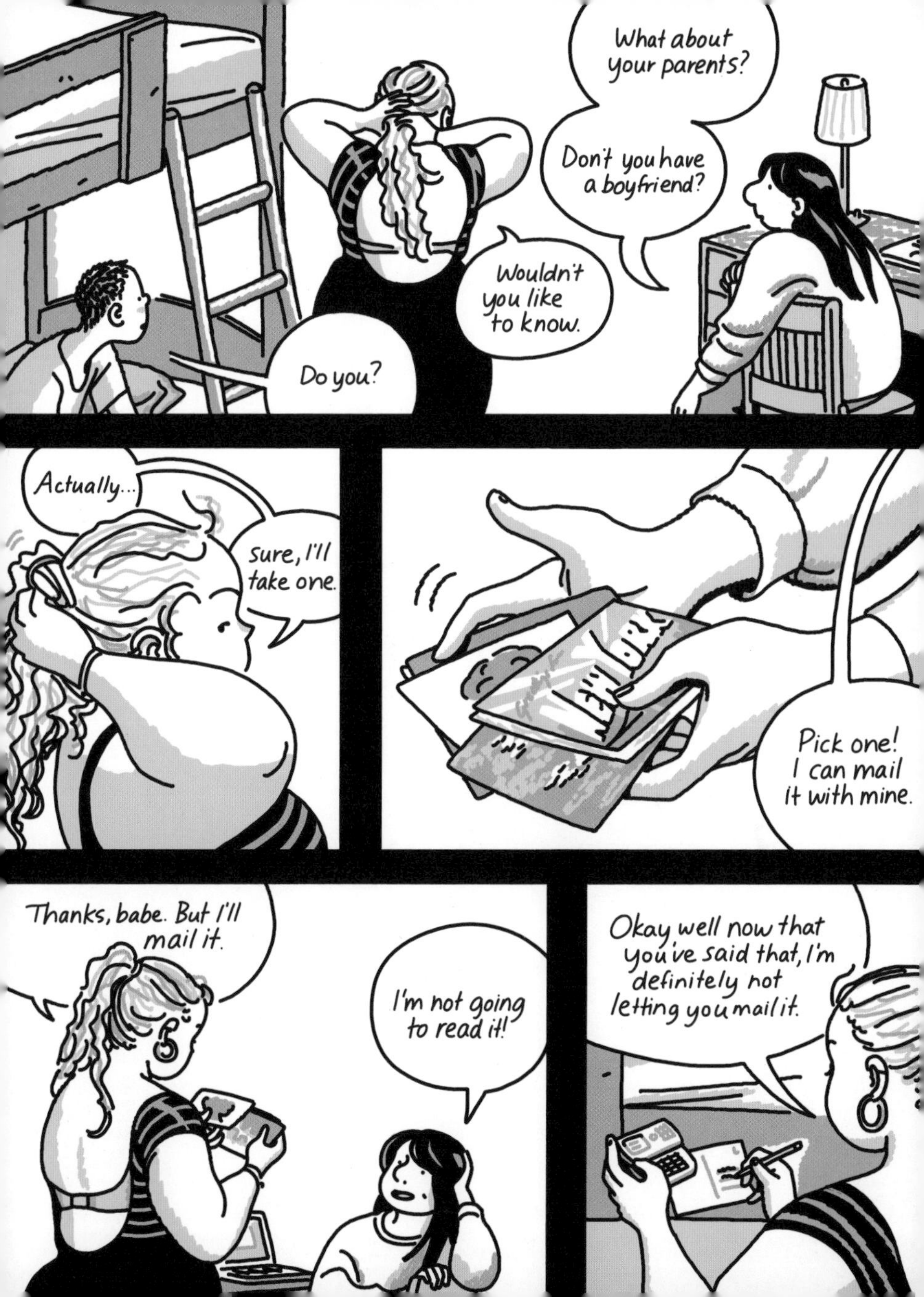
What about your parents?
Don't you have a boyfriend?
Wouldn't you like to know.
Do you?
Actually...
sure, I'll take one.
Pick one! I can mail it with mine.
Thanks, babe. But I'll mail it.
I'm not going to read it!
Okay well now that you've said that, I'm definitely not letting you mail it.

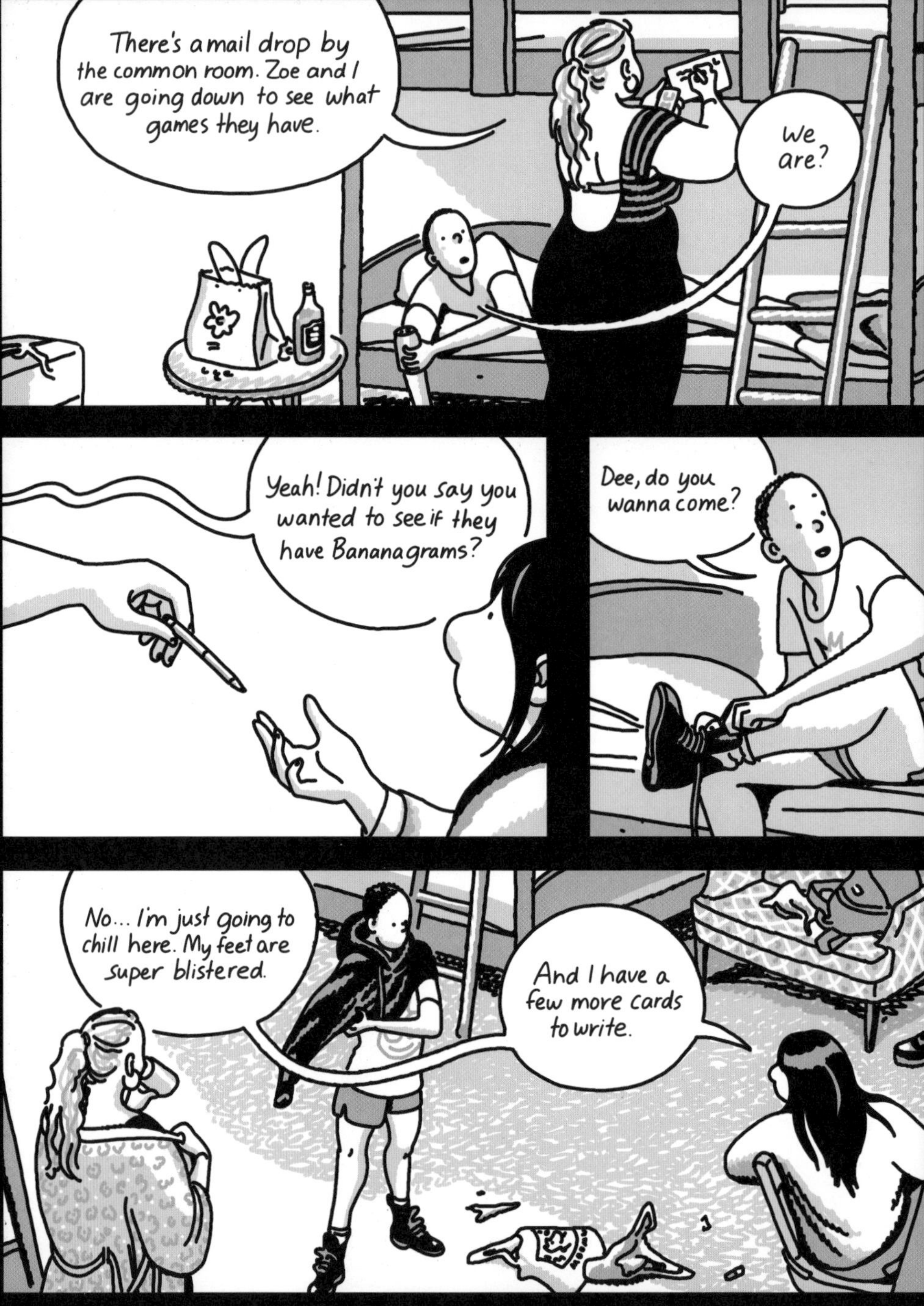
There's a mail drop by the common room. Zoe and I are going down to see what games they have.
We are?
Yeah! Didn't you say you wanted to see if they have Bananagrams?
Dee, do you wanna come?
No... I'm just going to chill here. My feet are super blistered.
And I have a few more cards to write.

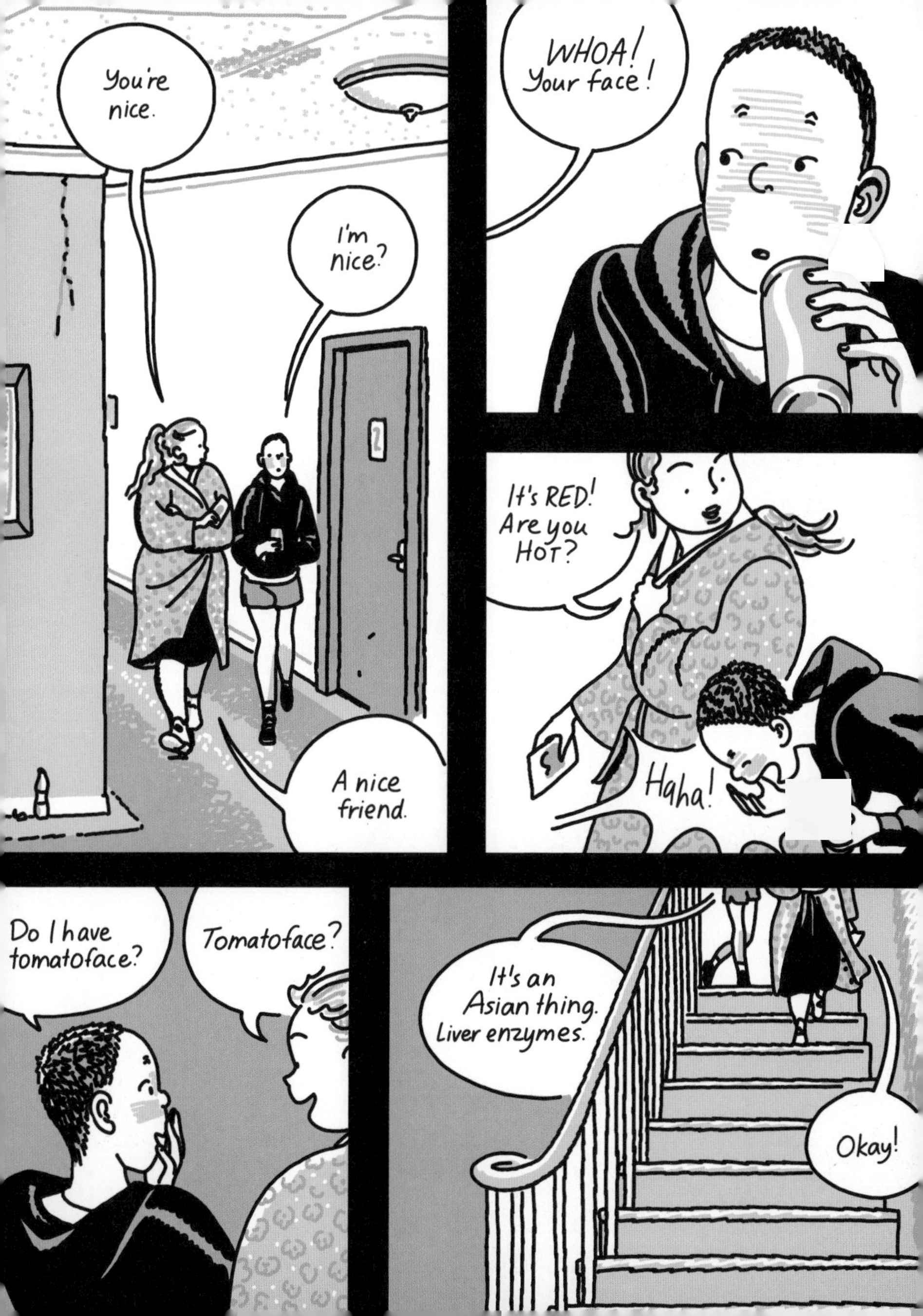
You're nice.
I'm nice?
A nice friend.
WHOA! Your face!
It's RED! Are you HOT?
Haha!
Do I have tomatoface?
Tomatoface?
It's an Asian thing. Liver enzymes.
Okay!

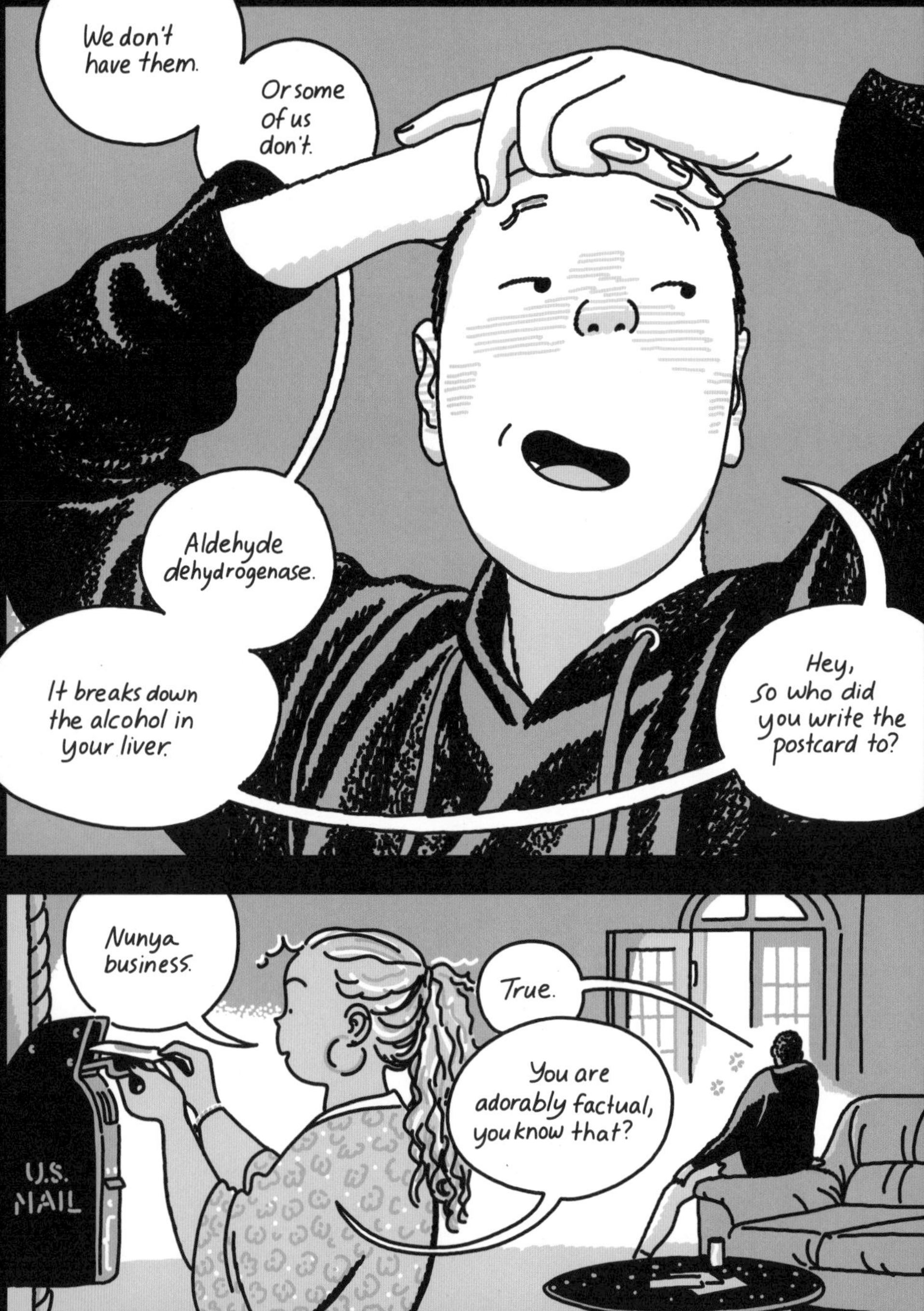
We don't have them.
Or some of us don't.
Aldehyde dehydrogenase.
It breaks down the alcohol in your liver.
Hey, so who did you write the postcard to?
Nunya business.
True.
You are adorably factual, you know that?
U.S. MAIL

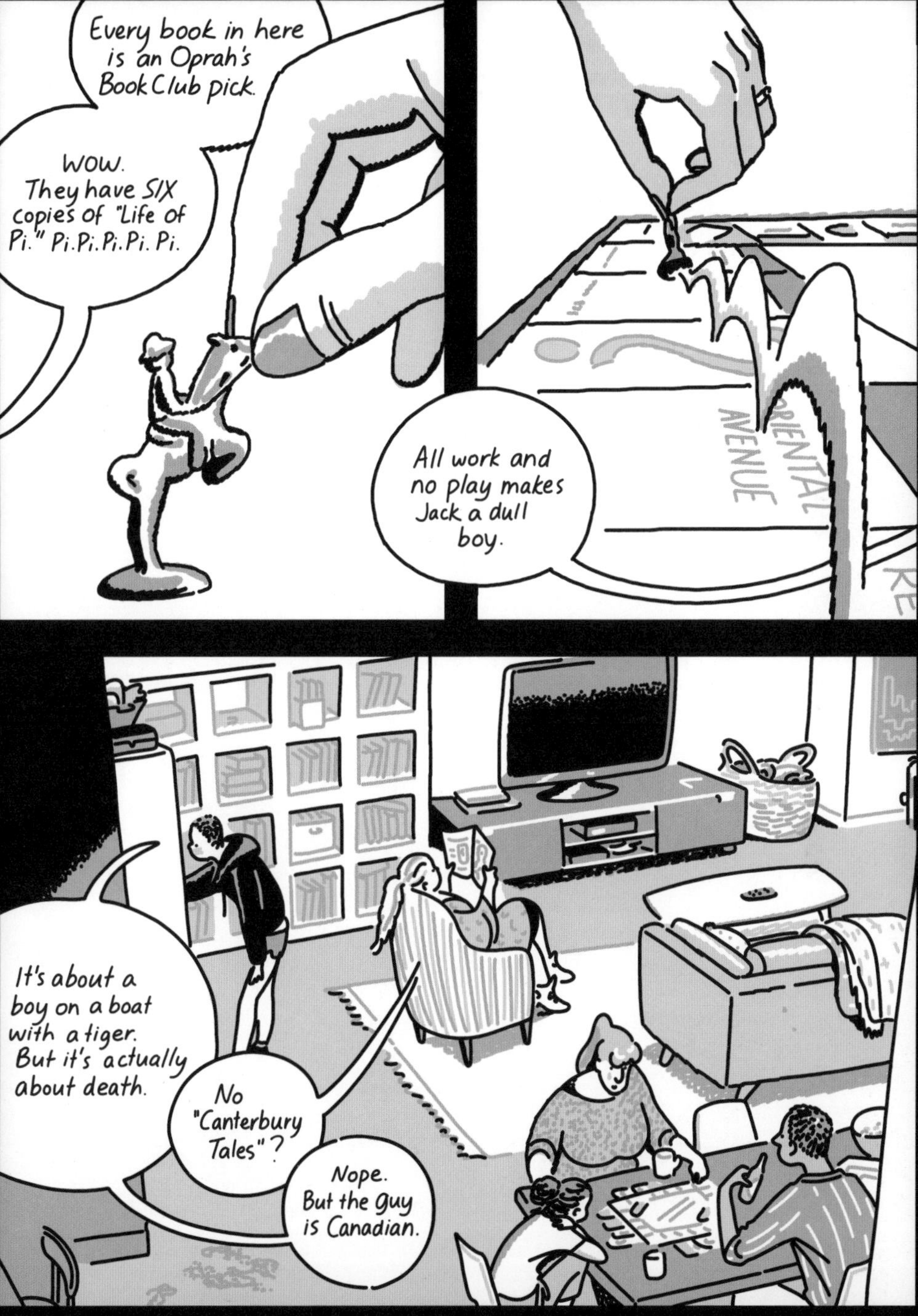
Every book in here is an Oprah's Book Club pick.
WOW. They have SIX copies of "Life of Pi." Pi. Pi. Pi. Pi. Pi.
All work and no play makes Jack a dull boy.
ORIENTAL AVENUE
It's about a boy on a boat with a tiger. But it's actually about death.
No "Canterbury Tales"?
Nope. But the guy is Canadian.

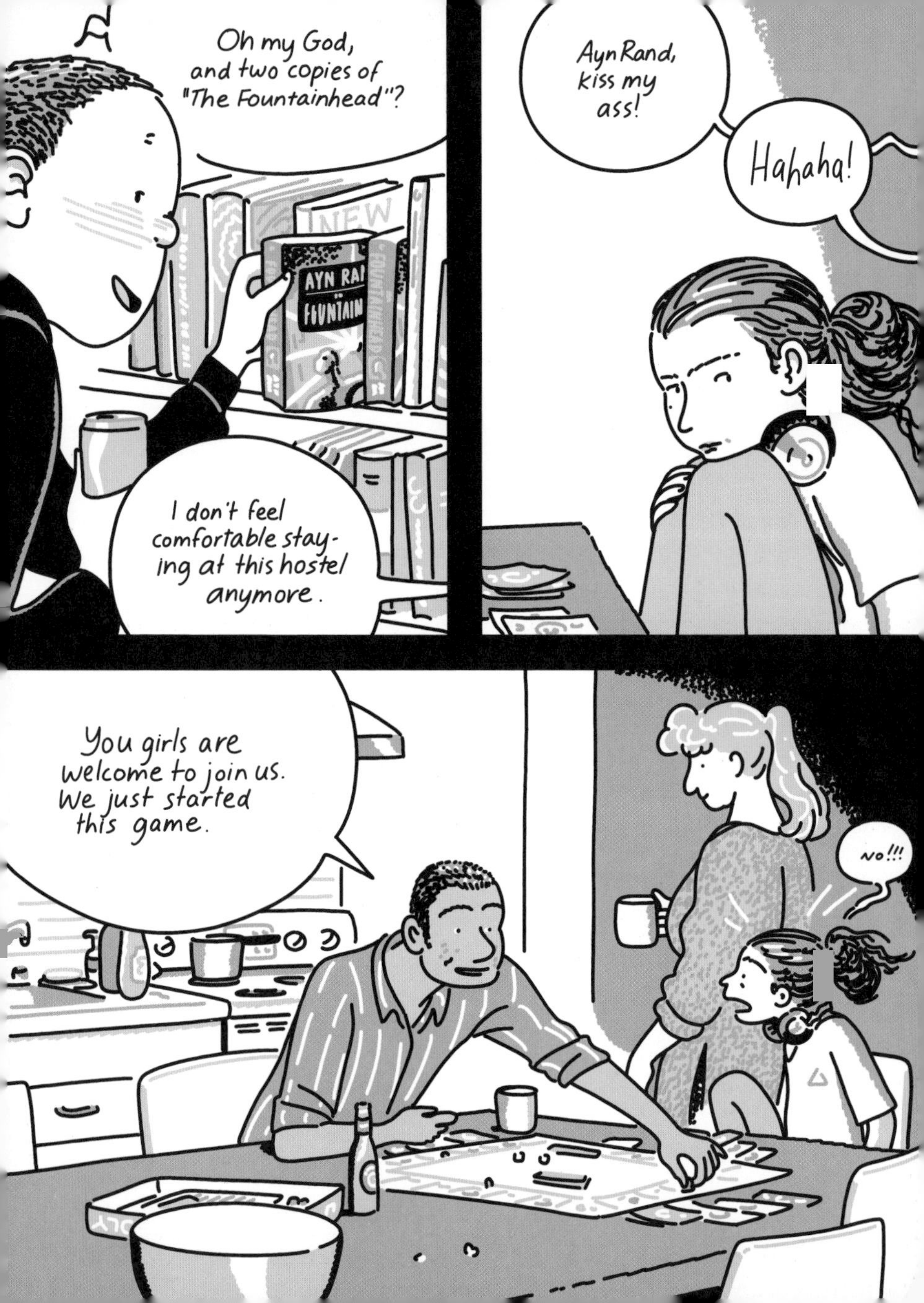
Oh my God, and two copies of "The Fountainhead"?
AYN RAND FOUNTAIN
I don't feel comfortable stay-ing at this hostel anymore.
Ayn Rand, kiss my ass!
Hahaha!
You girls are welcome to join us. We just started this game.
NO!!!

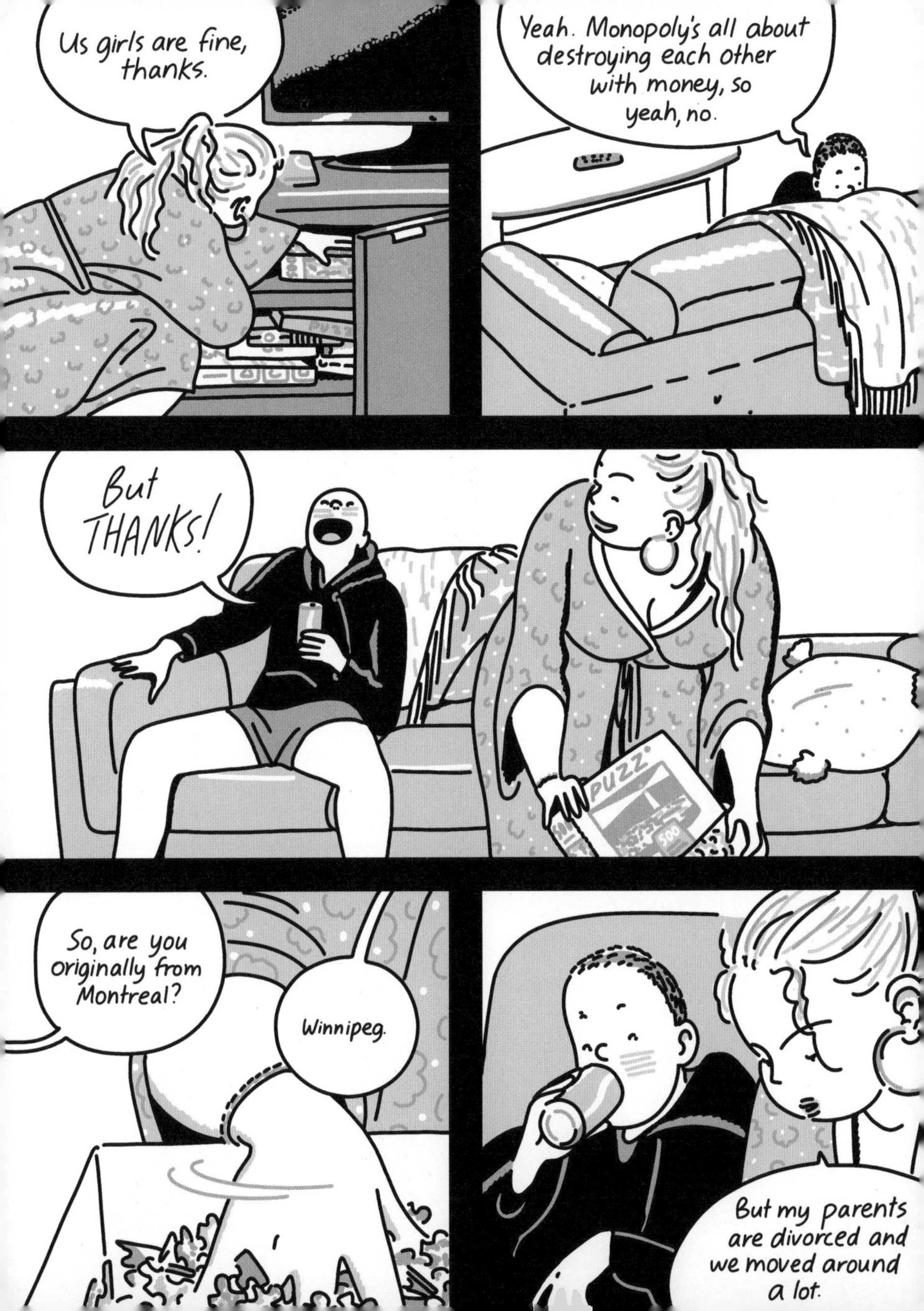
Us girls are fine, thanks.
Yeah. Monopoly's all about destroying each other with money, so yeah, no.
But THANKS!
PUZZ
So, are you originally from Montreal?
Winnipeg.
But my parents are divorced and we moved around a lot.

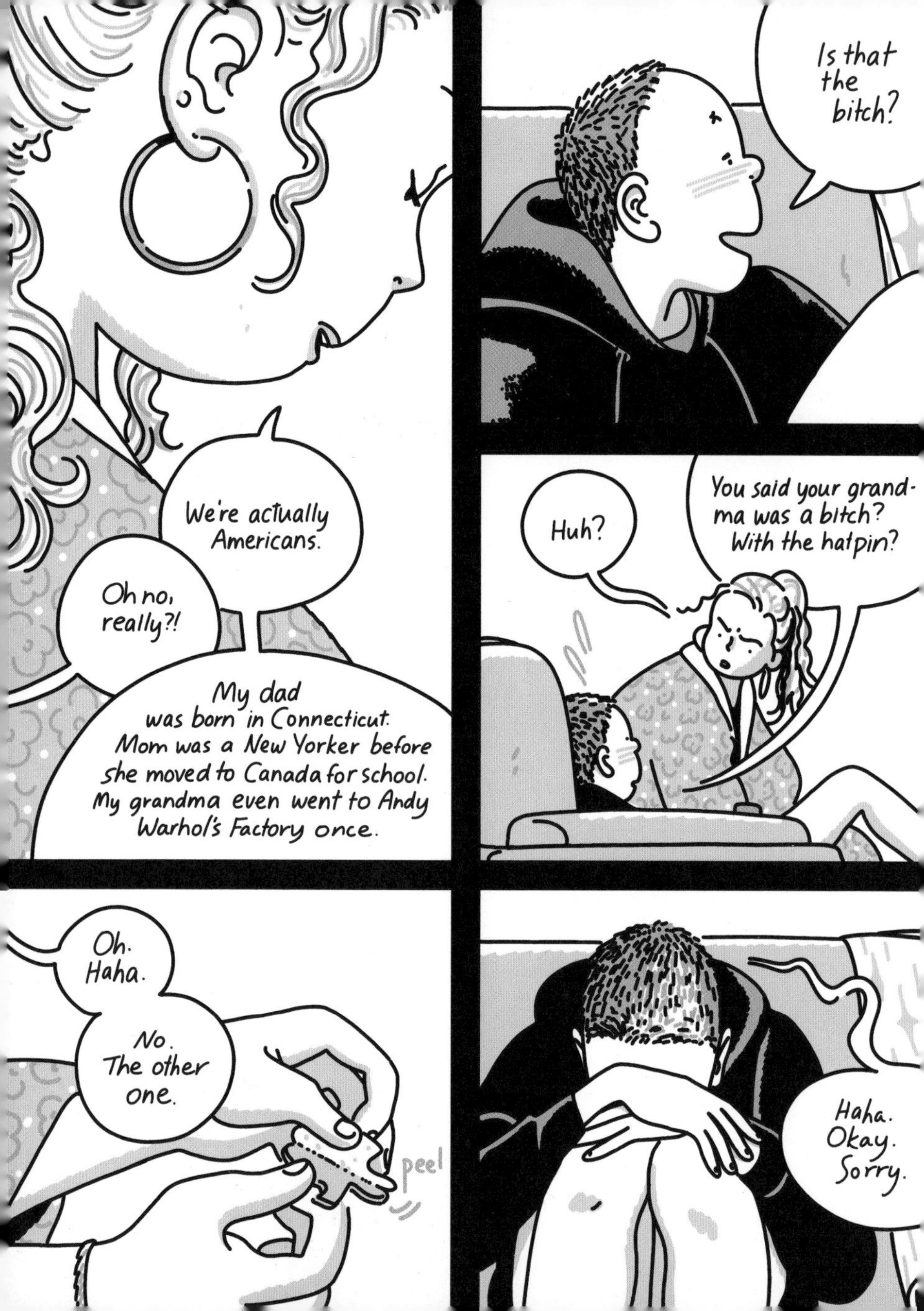
We're actually Americans.
Oh no, really?!
My dad was born in Connecticut. Mom was a New Yorker before she moved to Canada for school. My grandma even went to Andy Warhol's Factory once.
Is that the bitch?
You said your grandma was a bitch? With the hatpin?
Huh?
Oh. Haha.
No. The other one.
peel
Haha. Okay. Sorry.

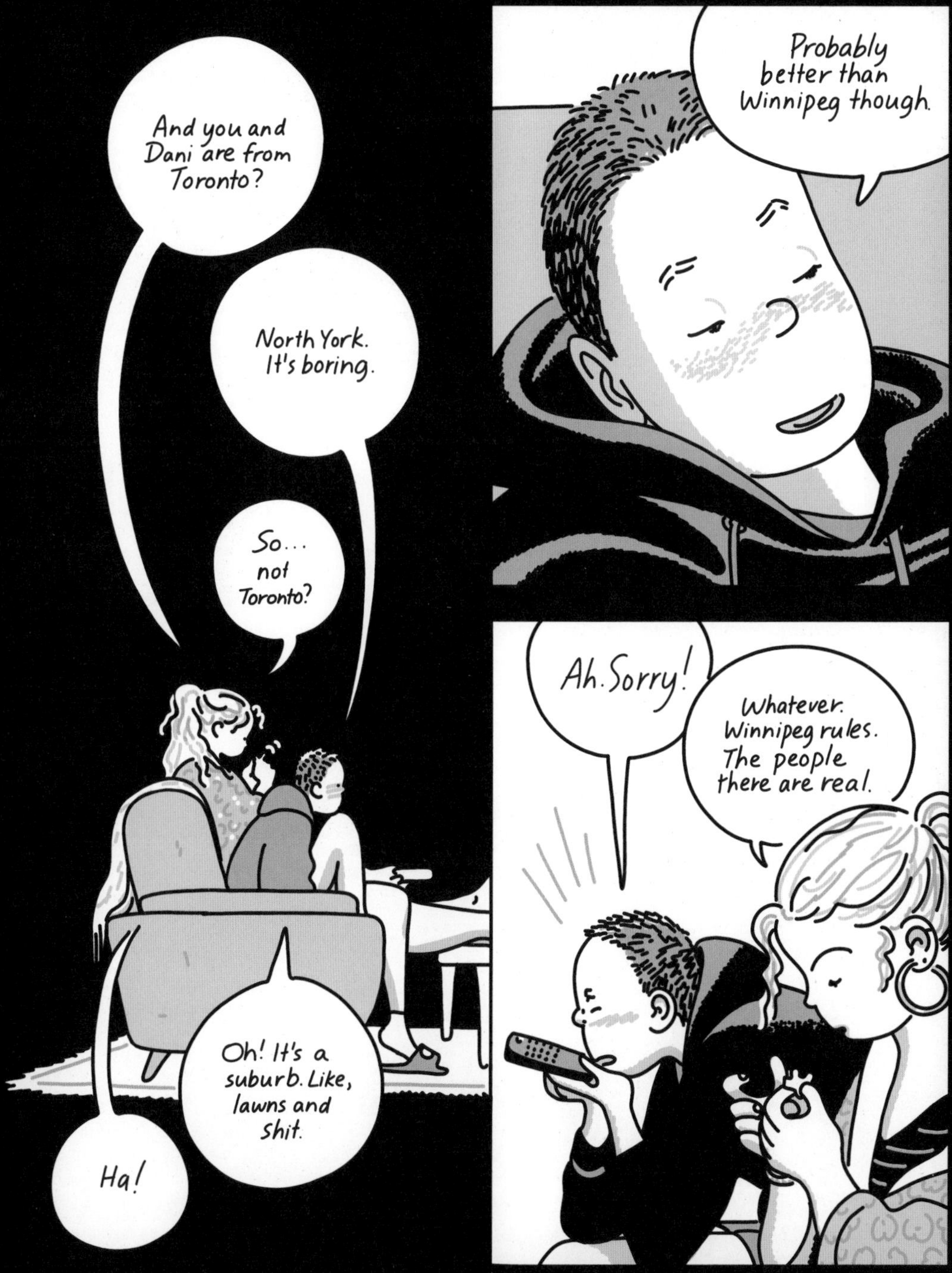
And you and Dani are from Toronto?
North York. It's boring.
So... not Toronto?
Oh! It's a suburb. Like, lawns and shit.
Ha!
Probably better than Winnipeg though.
Ah. Sorry!
Whatever. Winnipeg rules. The people there are real.

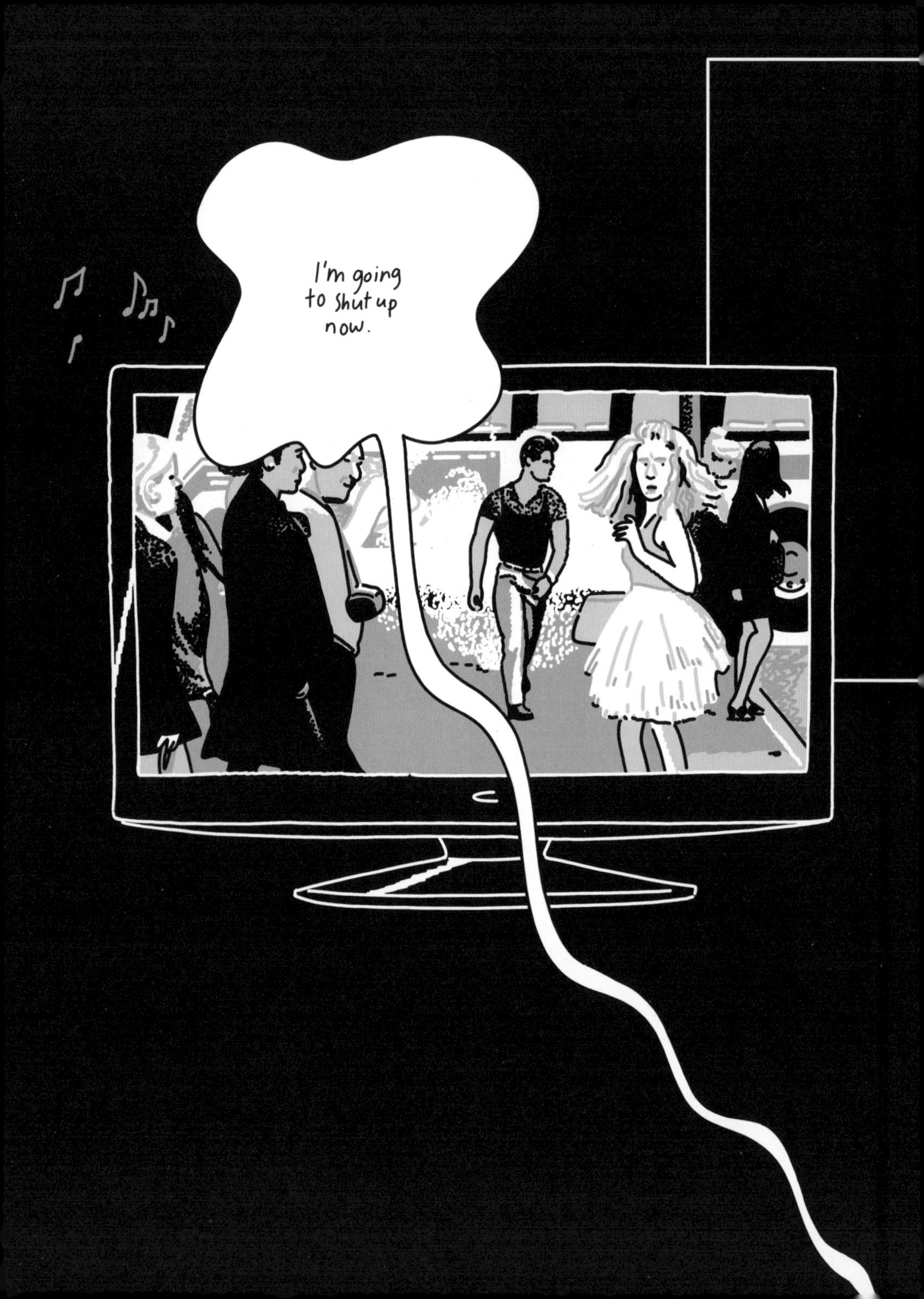
I'm going to shut up now.

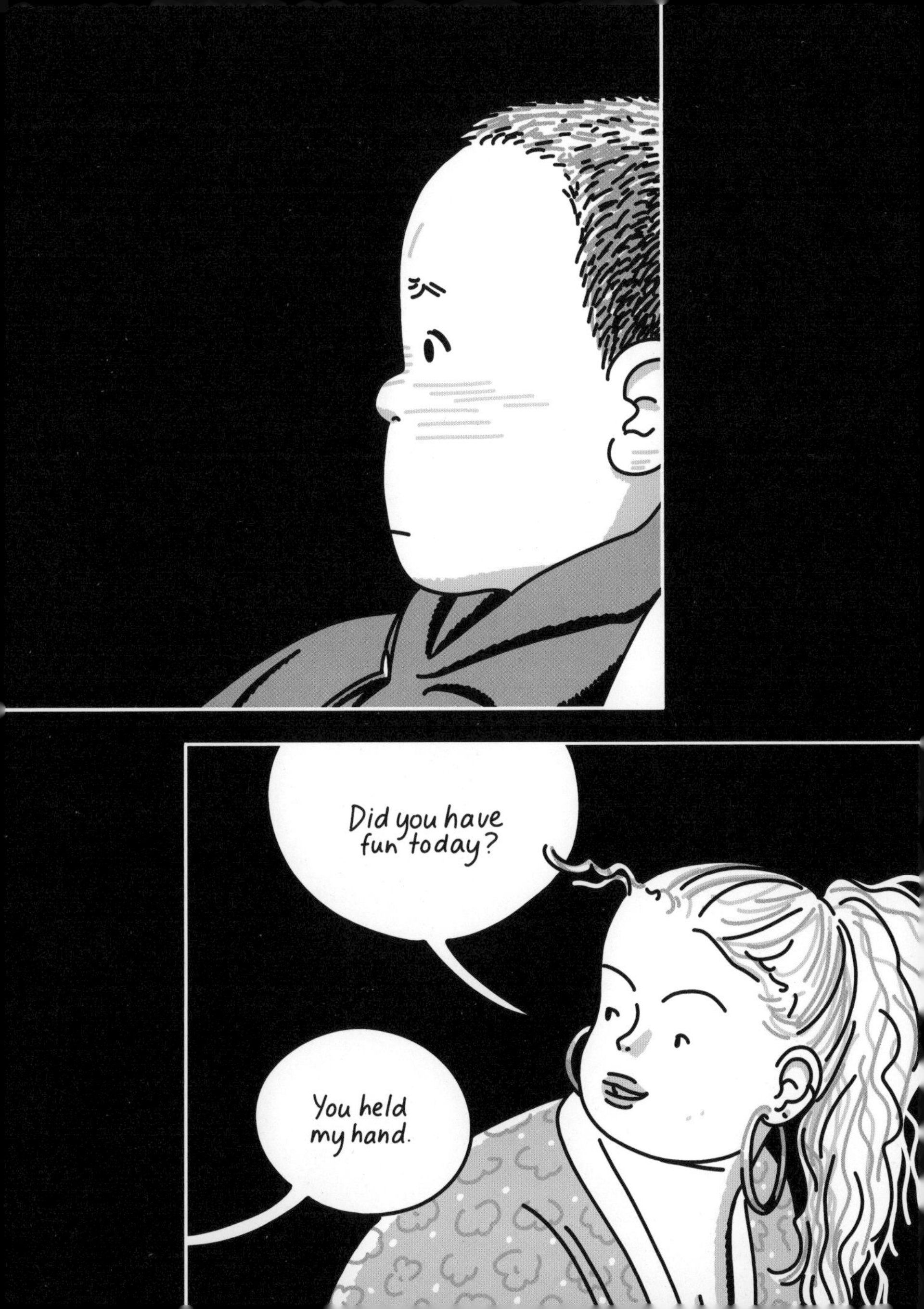
Did you have fun today?
You held my hand.

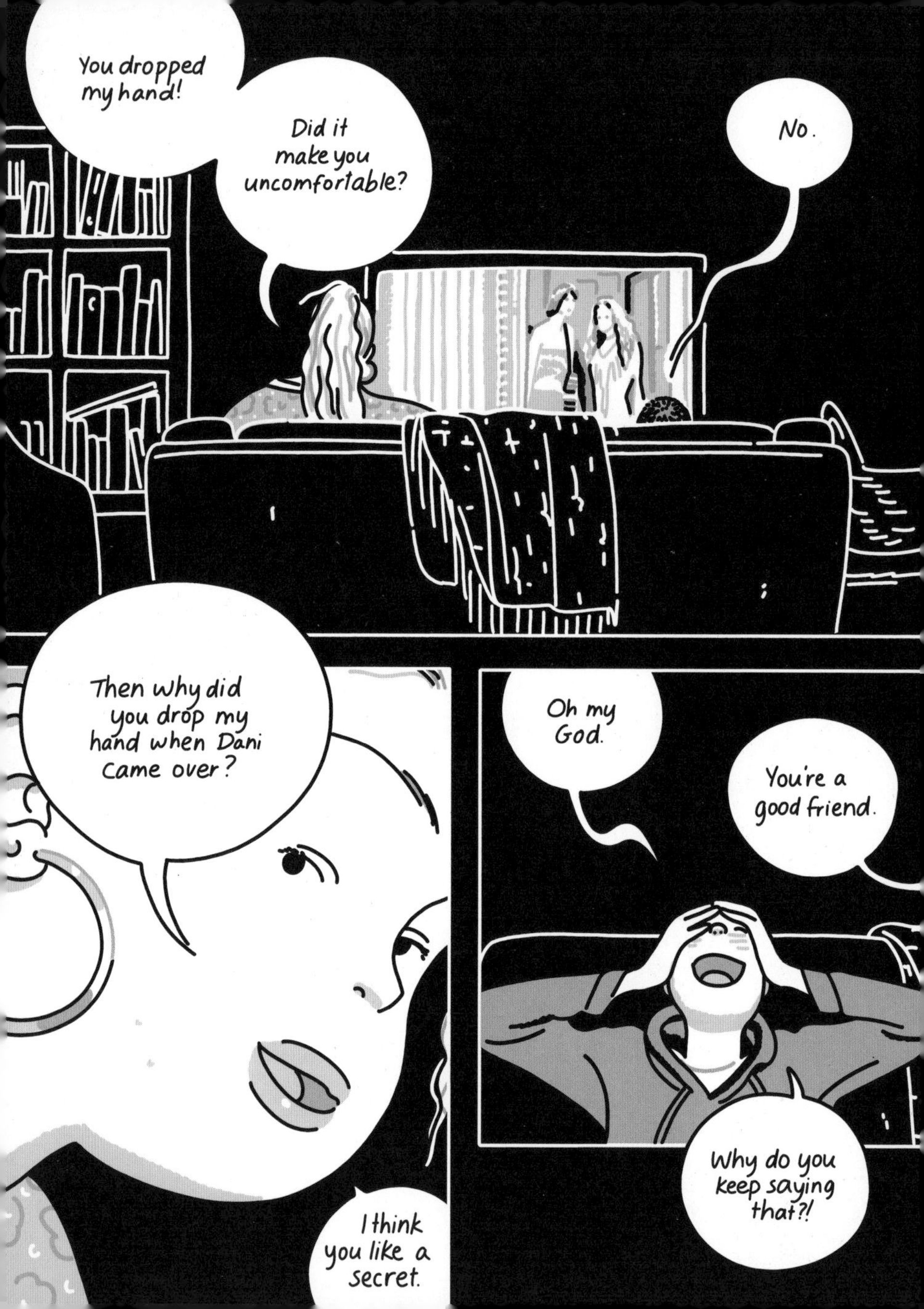
You dropped my hand!
Did it make you uncomfortable?
No.
Then why did you drop my hand when Dani came over?
Oh my God.
You're a good friend.
Why do you keep saying that?!
I think you like a secret.

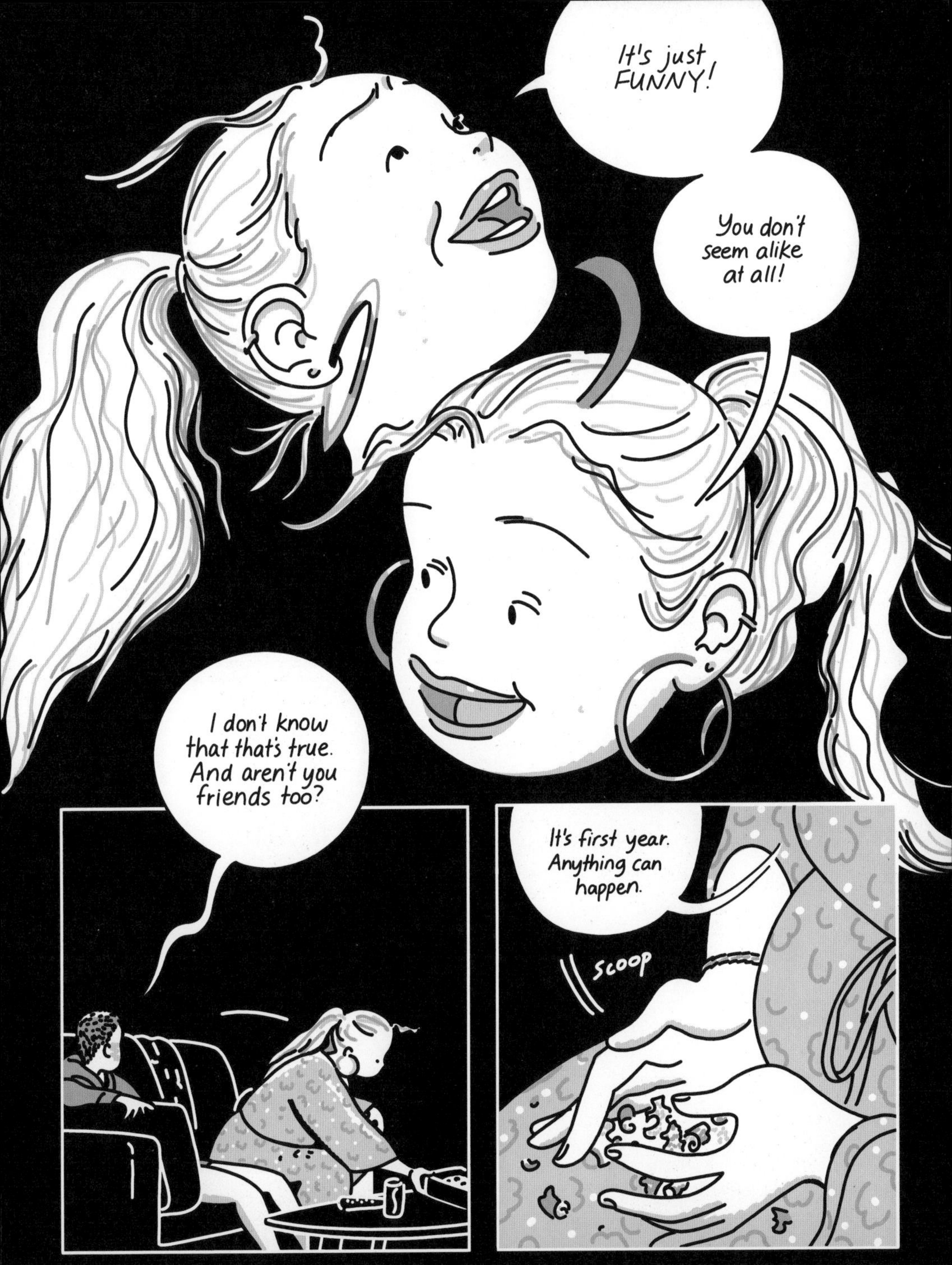
It's just FUNNY!
You don't seem alike at all!
I don't know that that's true. And aren't you friends too?
It's first year. Anything can happen.
SCOOP

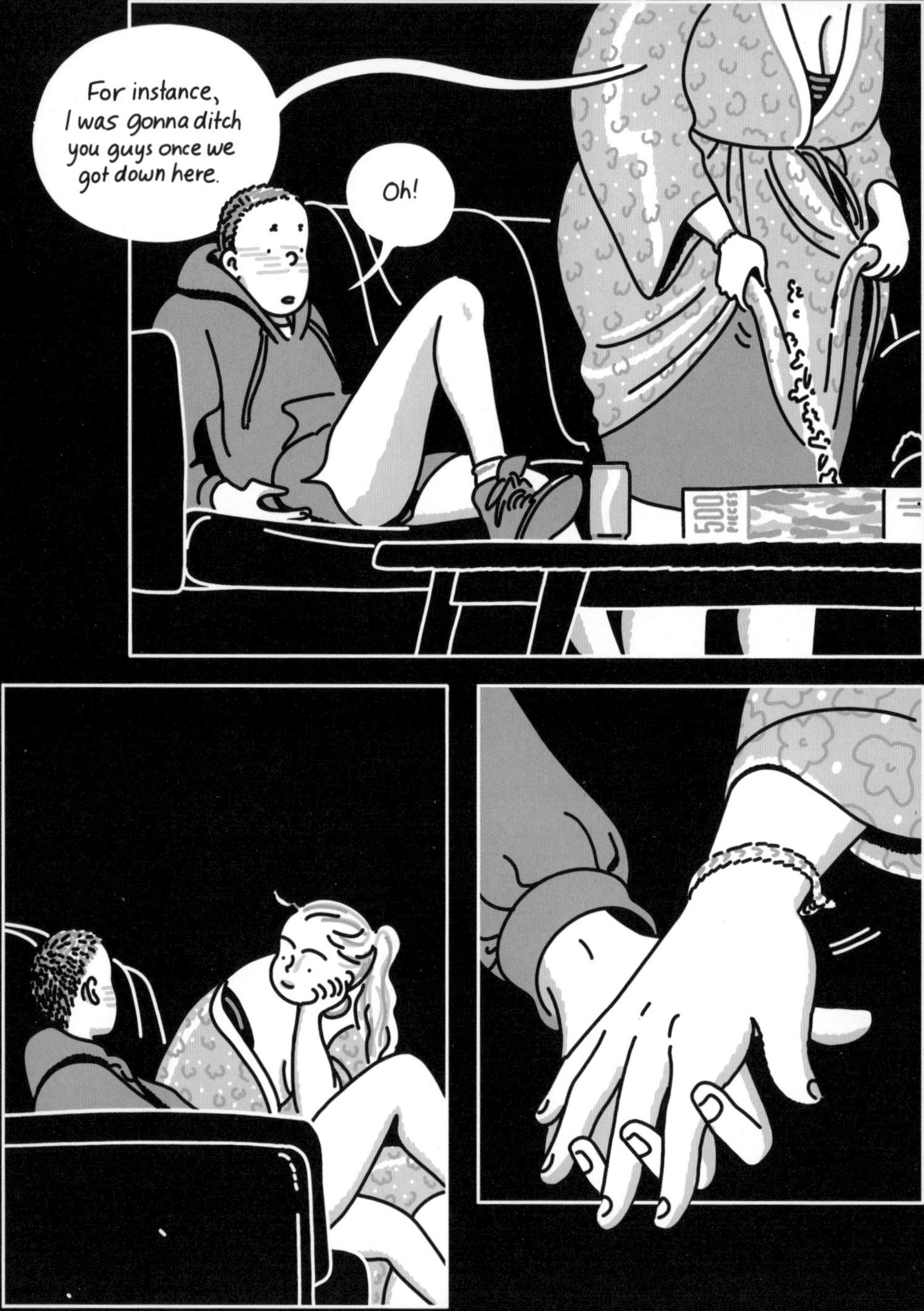
For instance, I was gonna ditch you guys once we got down here.
Oh!
500 PIECES

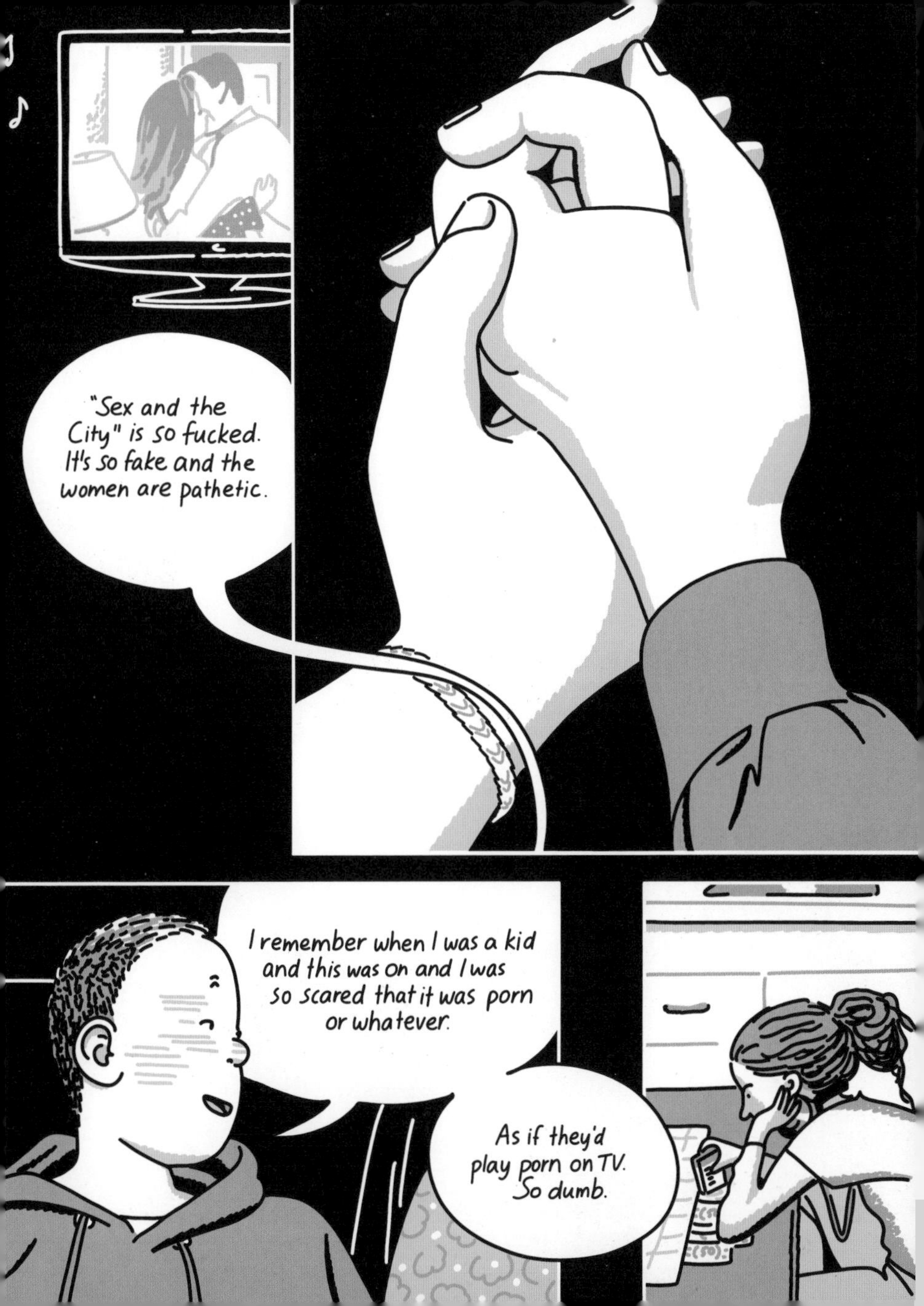
"Sex and the City" is so fucked. It's so fake and the women are pathetic.
I remember when I was a kid and this was on and I was so scared that it was porn or whatever.
As if they'd play porn on TV. So dumb.

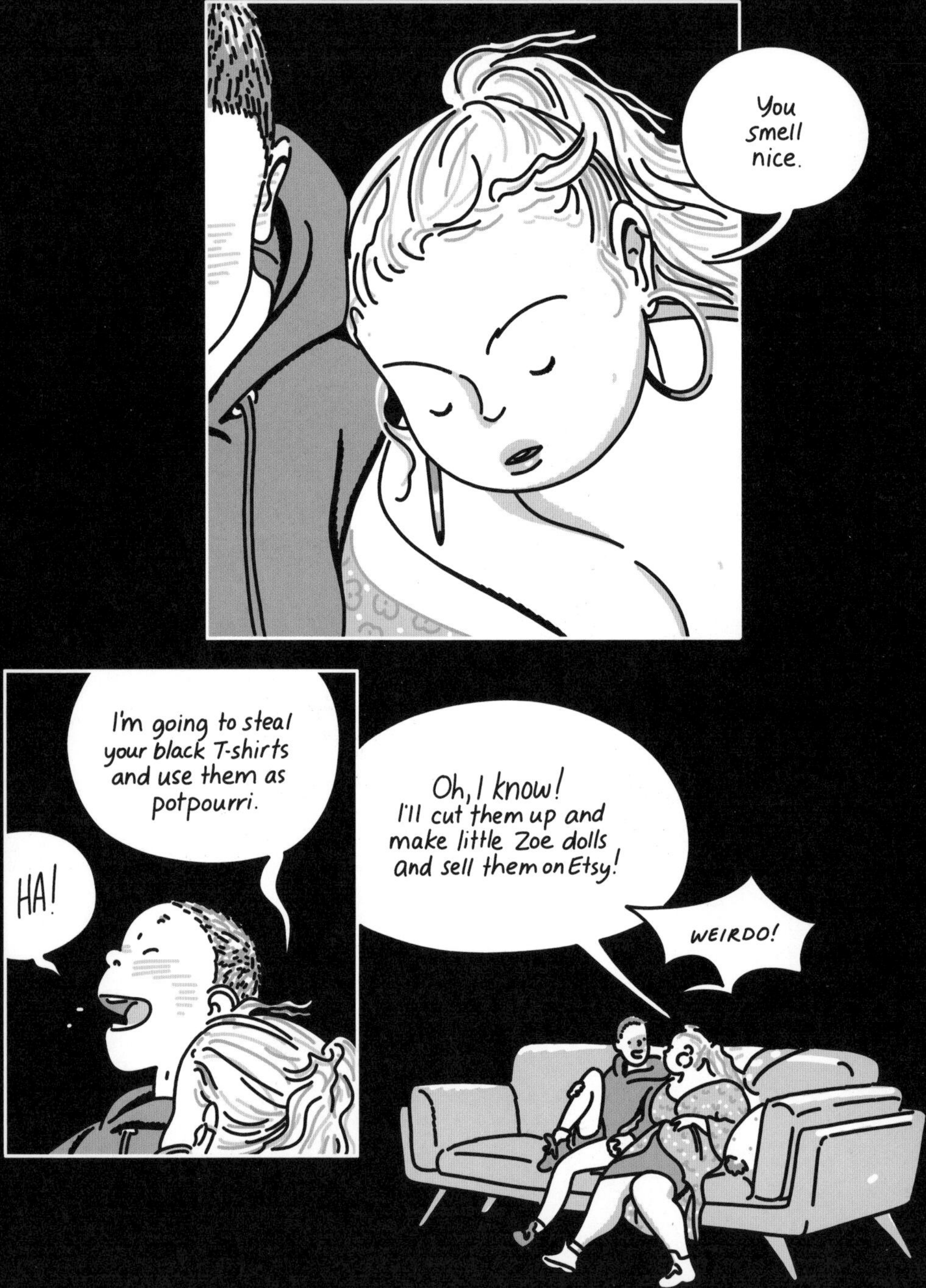
You smell nice.
I'm going to steal your black T-shirts and use them as potpourri.
HA!
Oh, I know! I'll cut them up and make little Zoe dolls and sell them on Etsy!
WEIRDO!

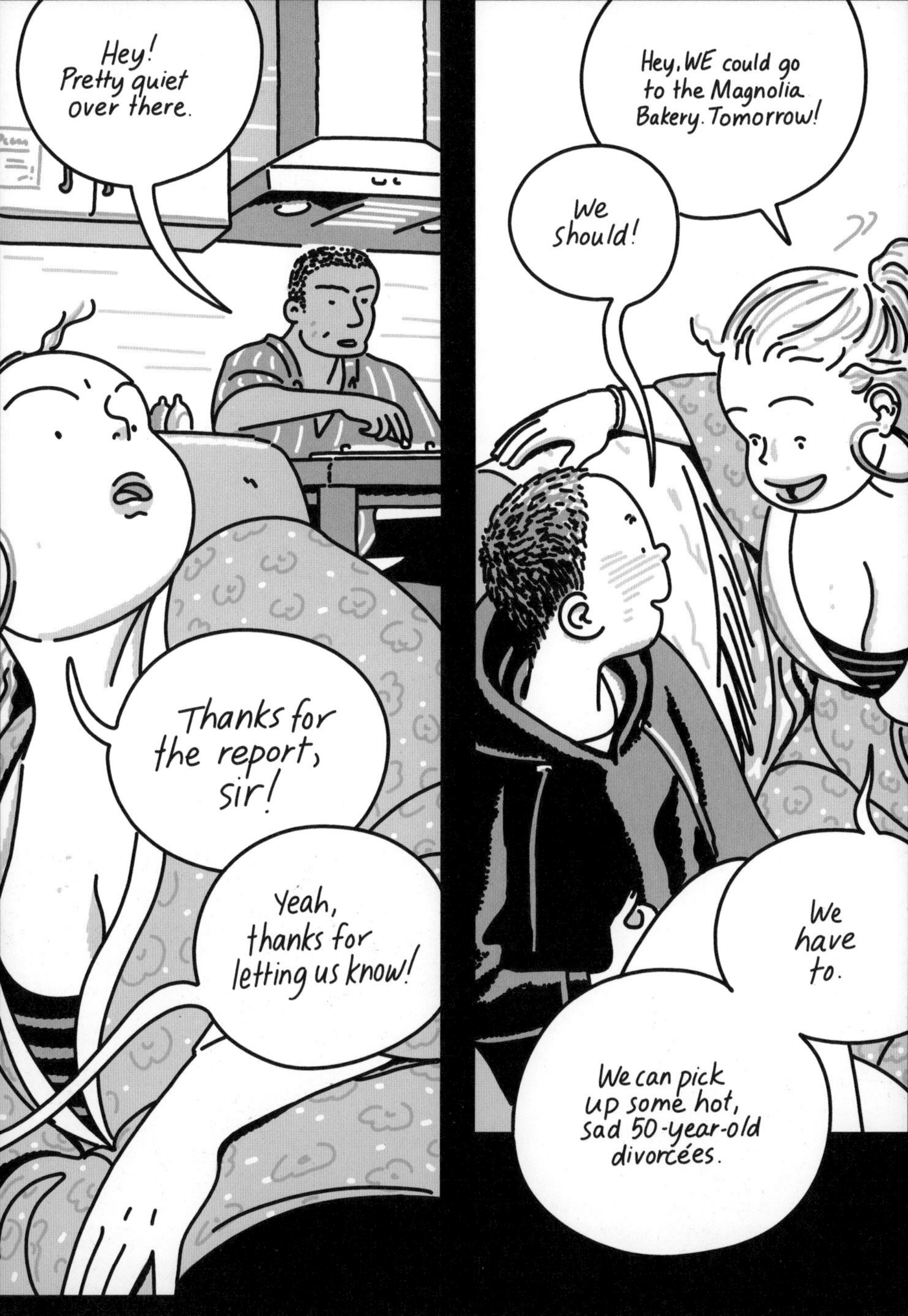
Hey! Pretty quiet over there.
Thanks for the report, sir!
Yeah, thanks for letting us know!
Hey, WE could go to the Magnolia Bakery. Tomorrow!
We should!
We have to.
We can pick up some hot, sad 50-year-old divorcées.

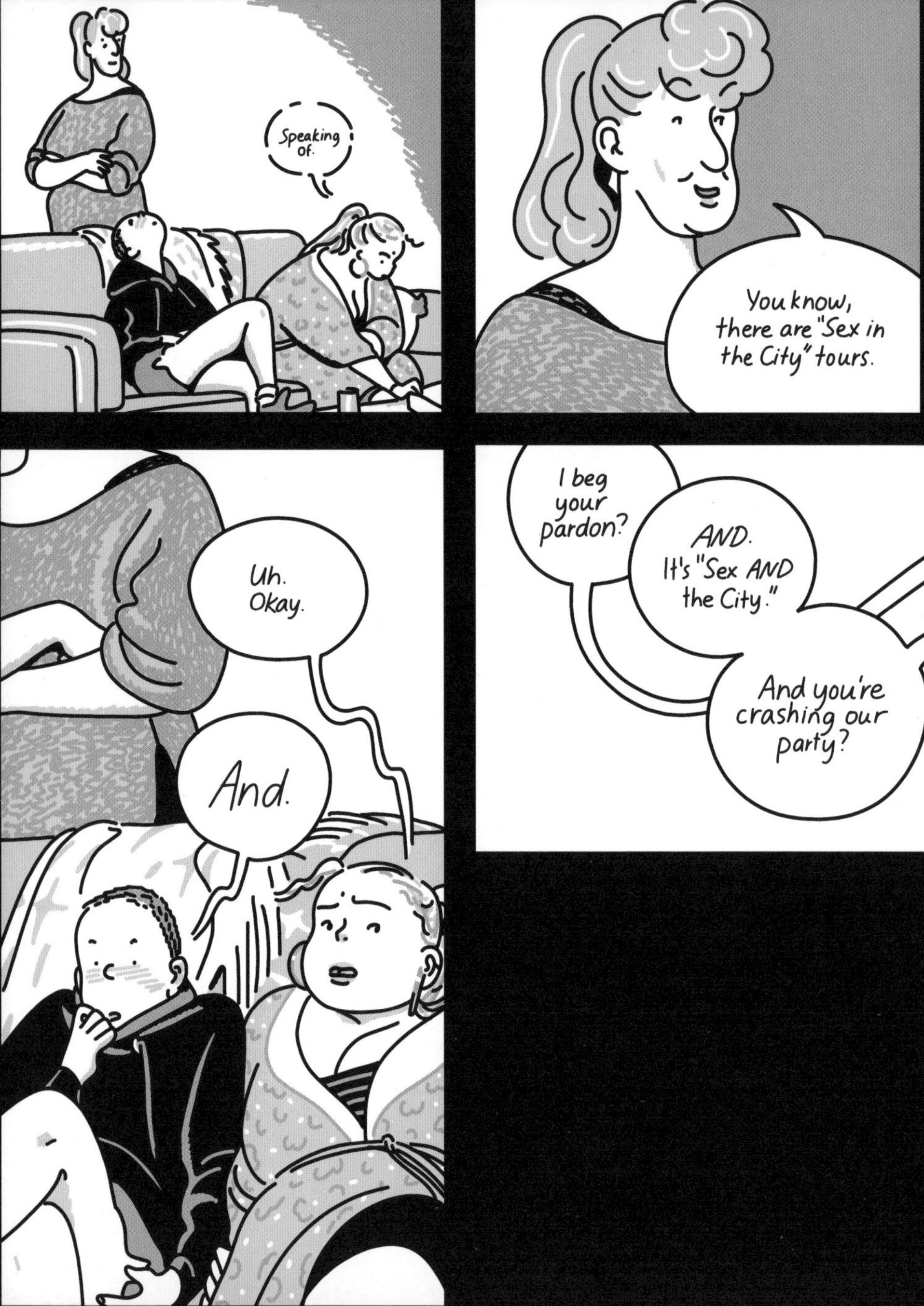
Speaking of.
You know, there are "Sex in the City" tours.
Uh. Okay.
And.
I beg your pardon?
AND. It's "Sex AND the City."
And you're crashing our party?

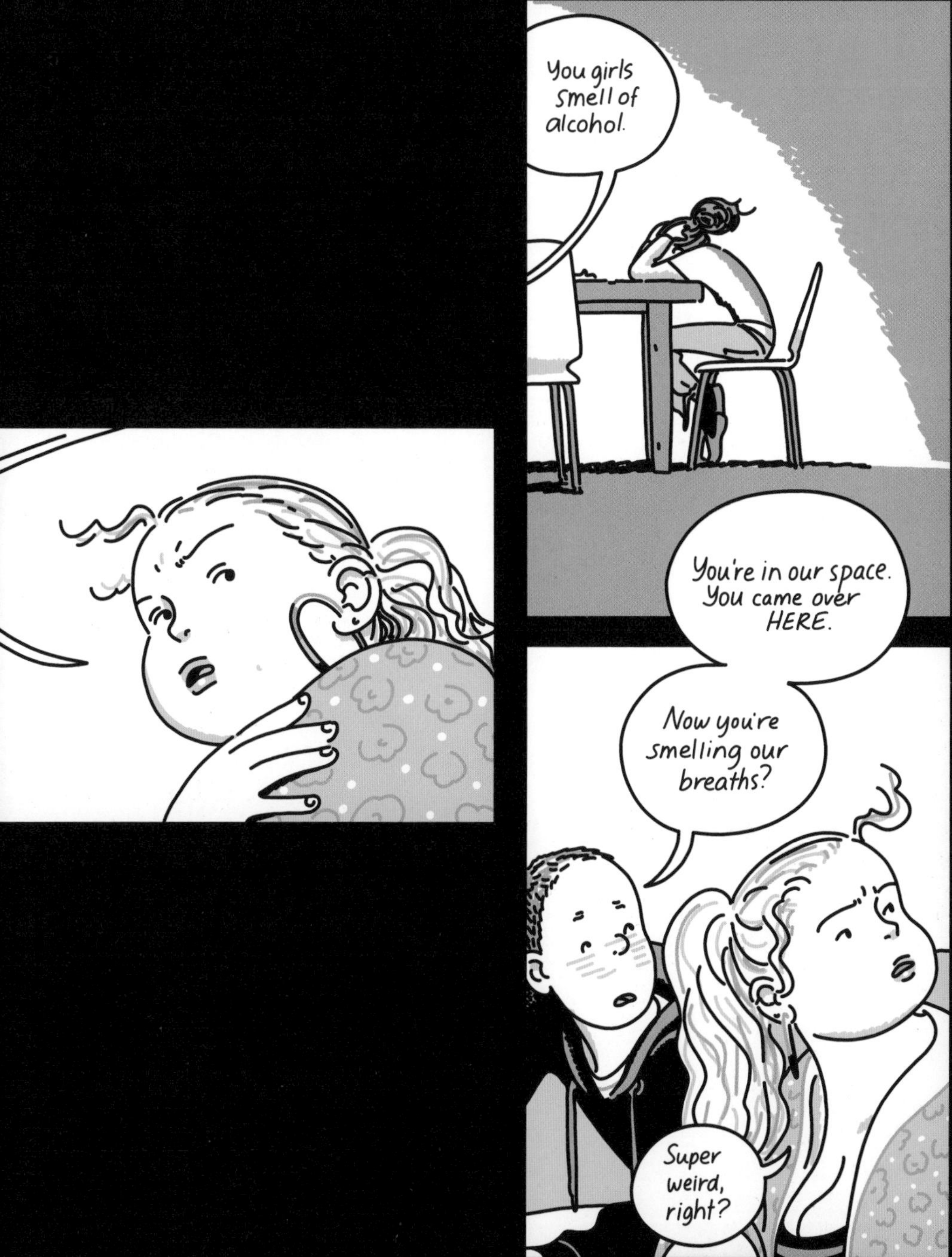
You girls smell of alcohol.
You're in our space. You came over HERE.
Now you're smelling our breaths?
Super weird, right?

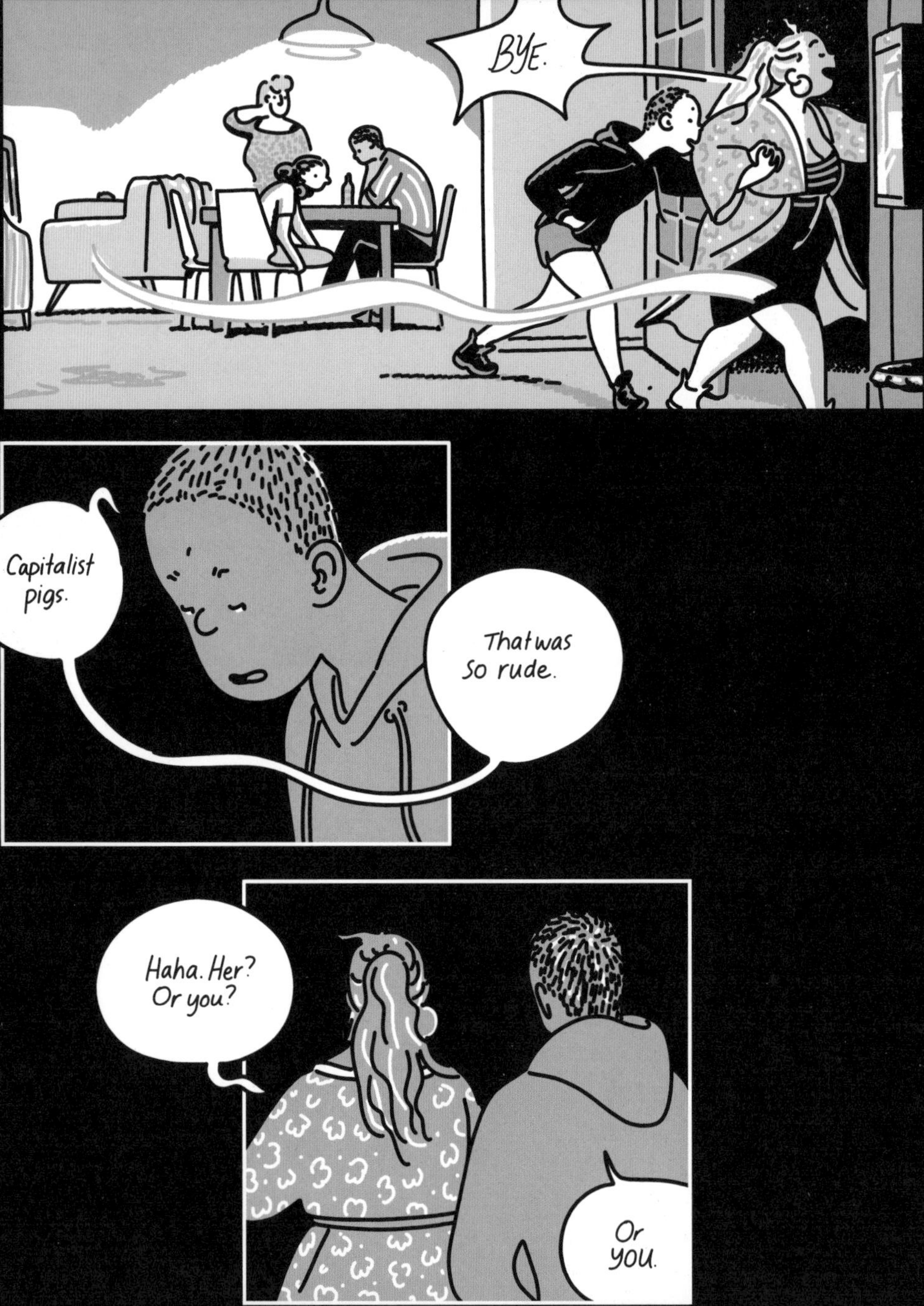
BYE.
Capitalist pigs.
That was so rude.
Haha. Her? Or you?
Or you.

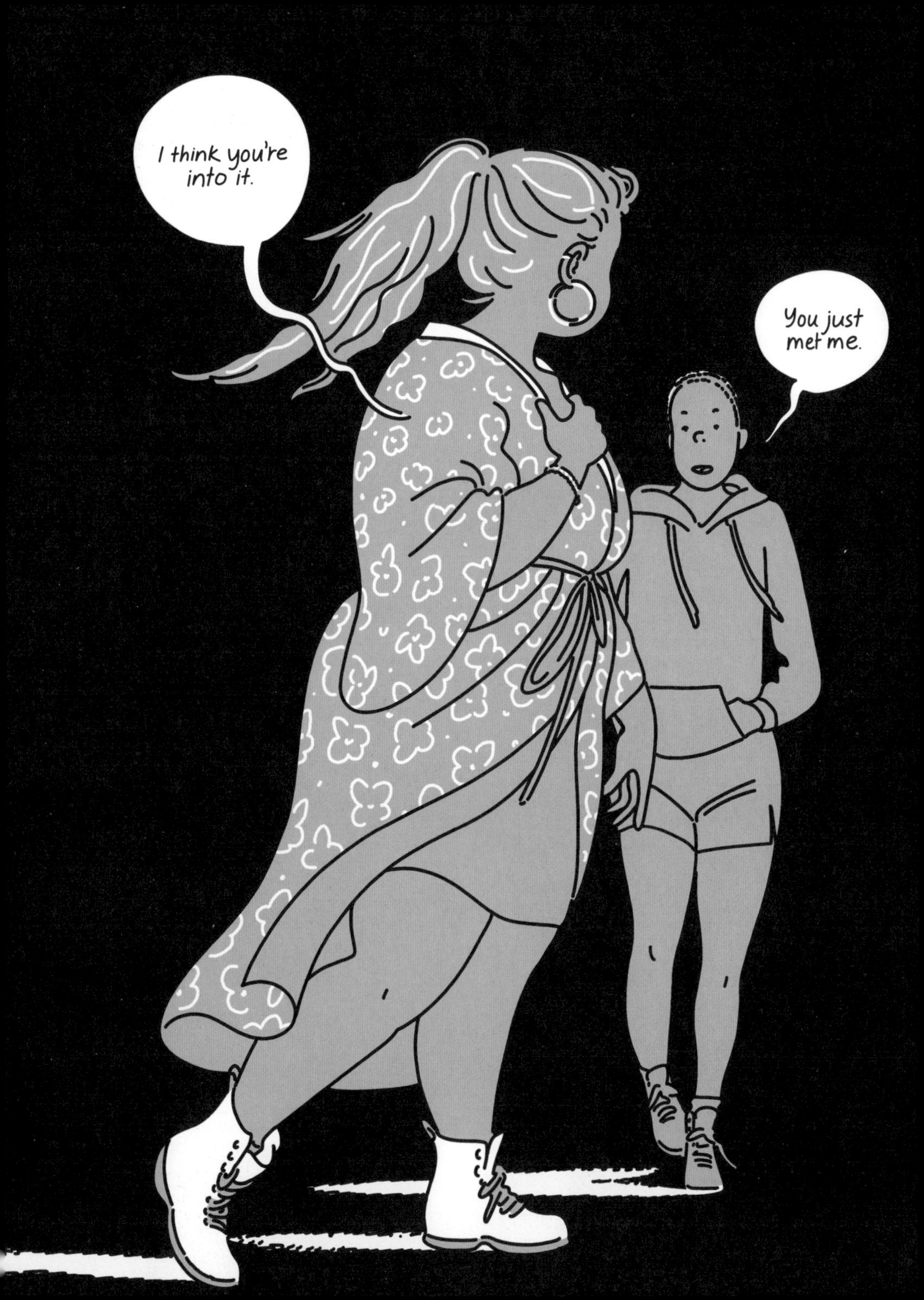
I think you're into it.
You just met me.

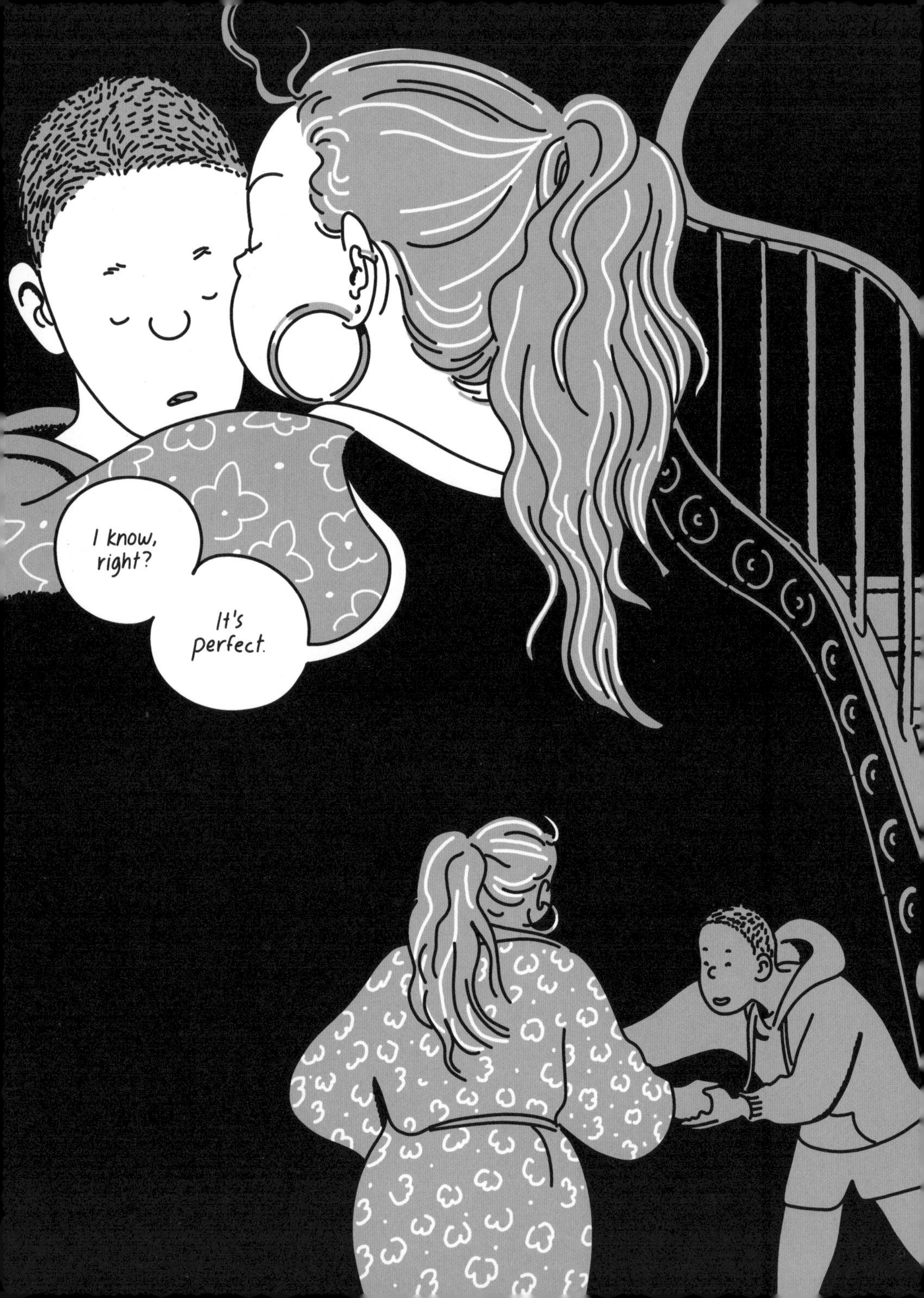
I know, right?
It's perfect.

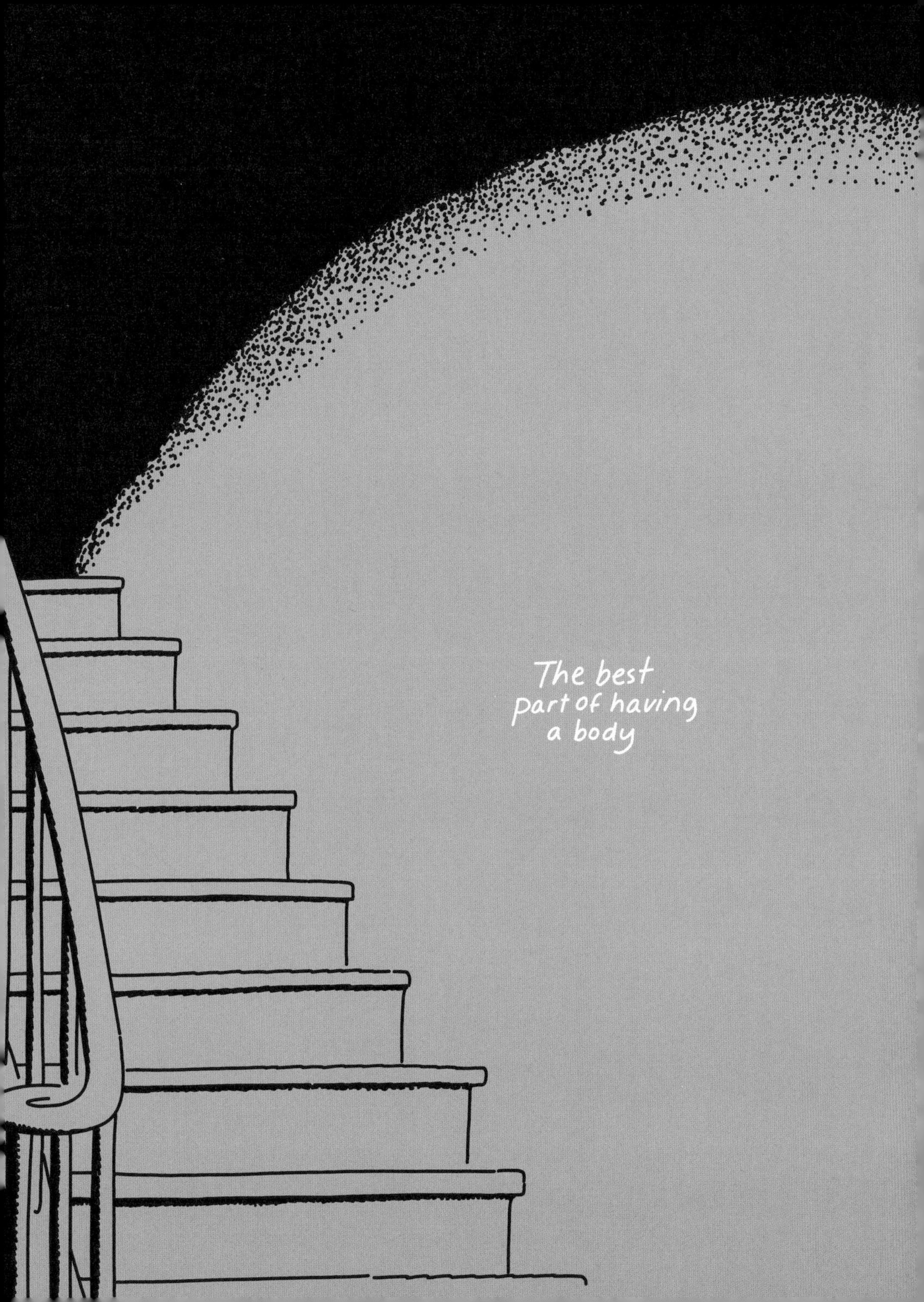
The best part of having a body

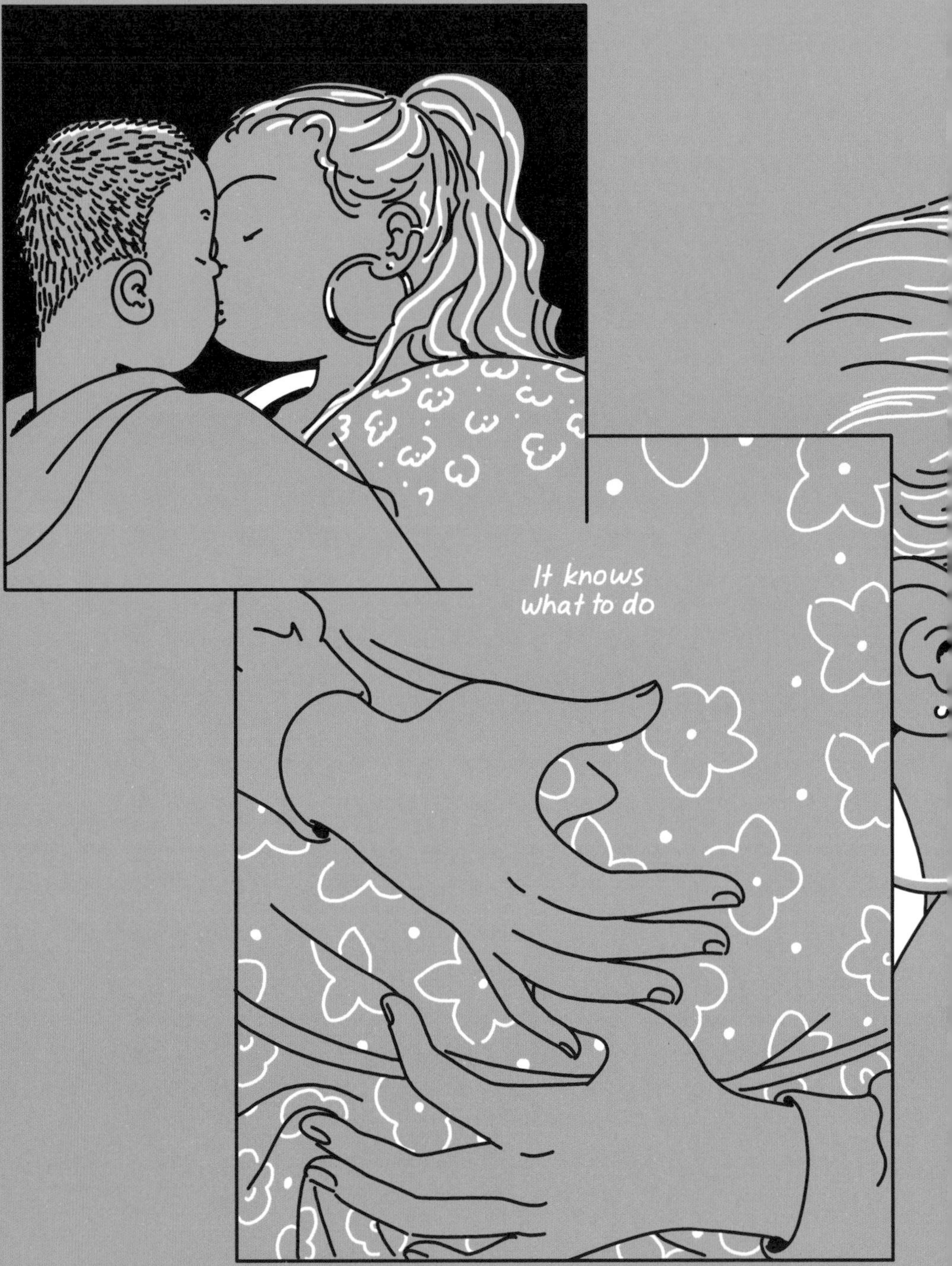
It knows what to do

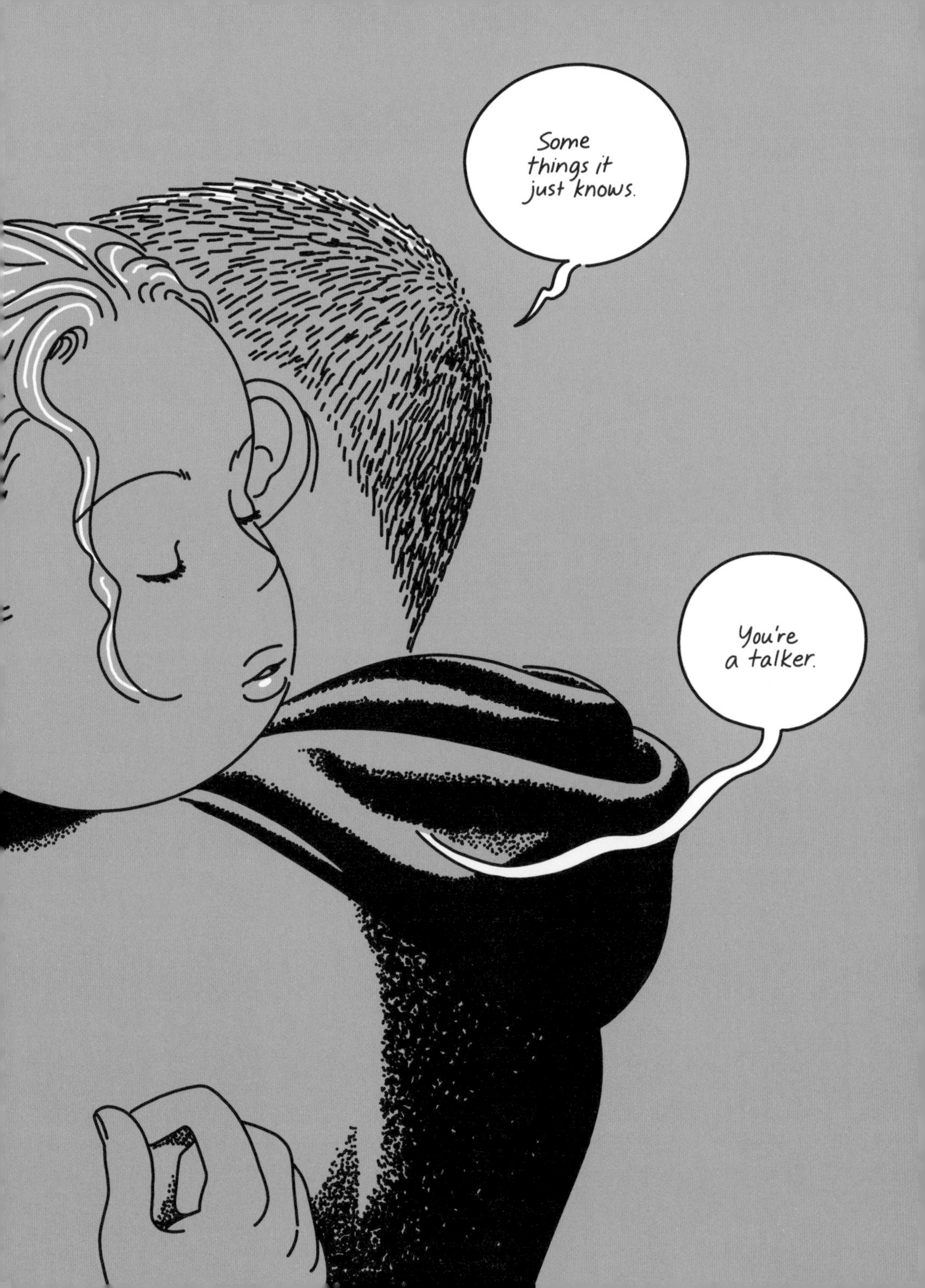
Some things it just knows.
You're a talker.

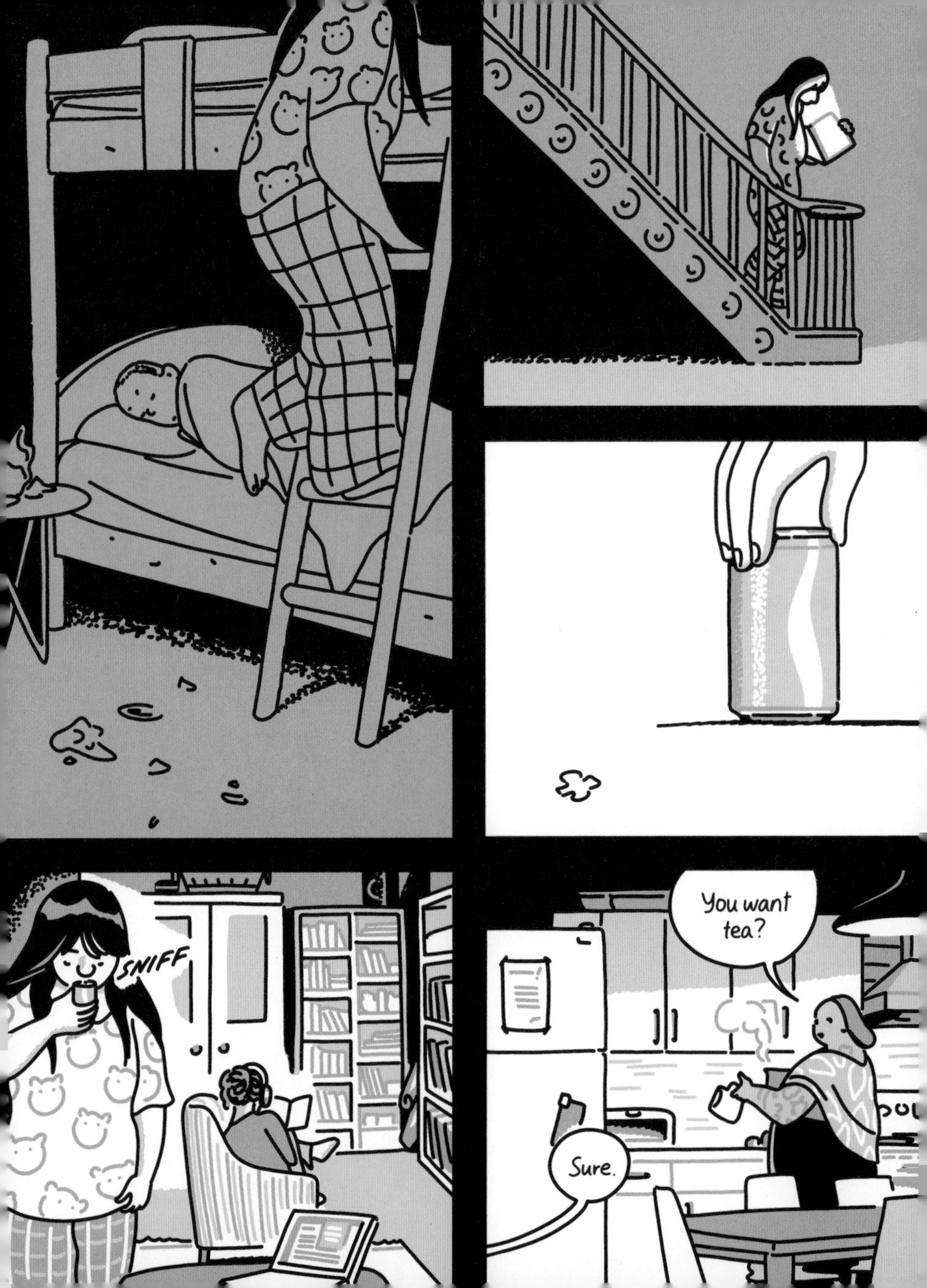
SNIFF
You want tea?
Sure.

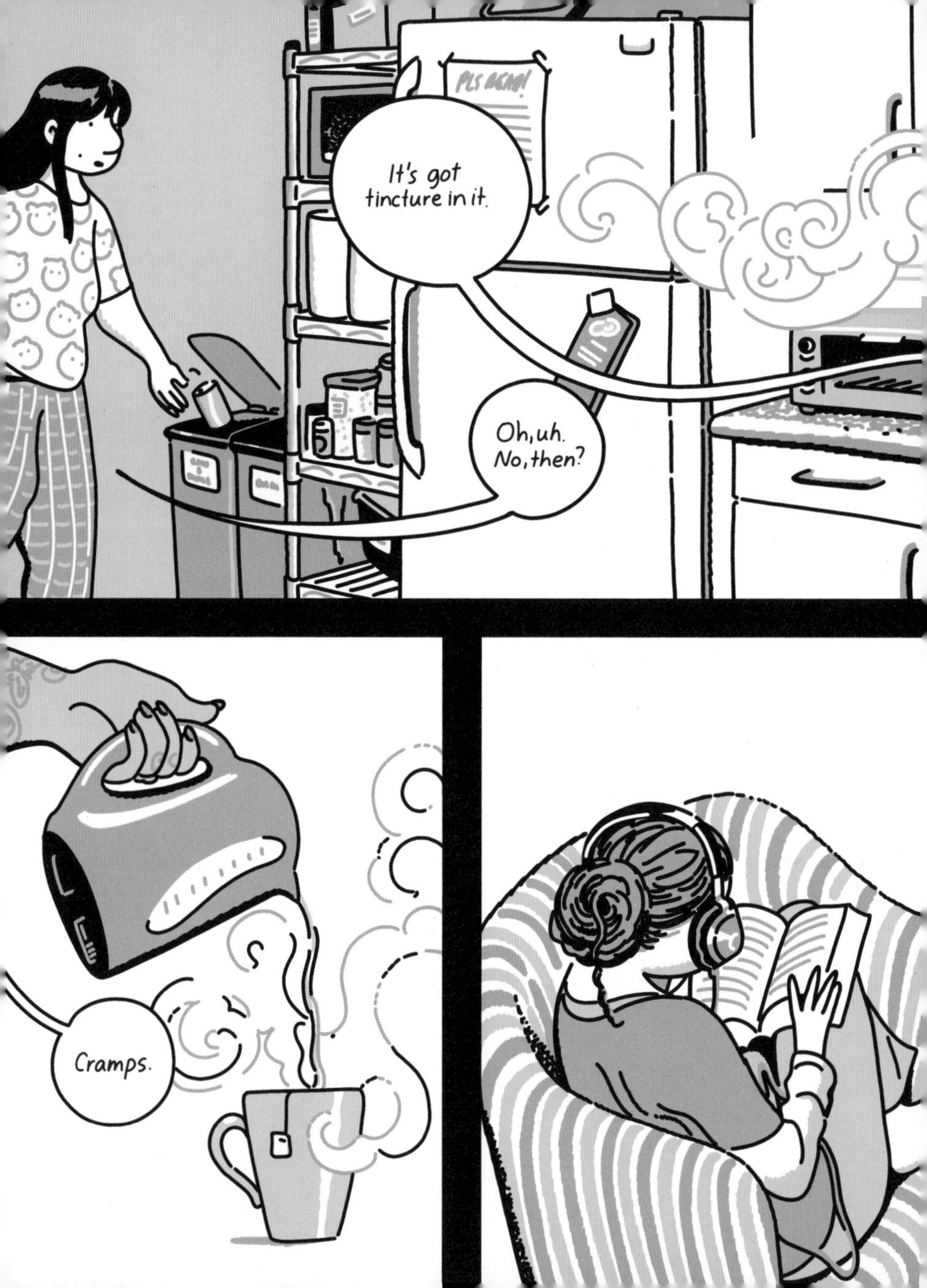
It's got tincture in it.
Oh, uh. No, then?
Cramps.

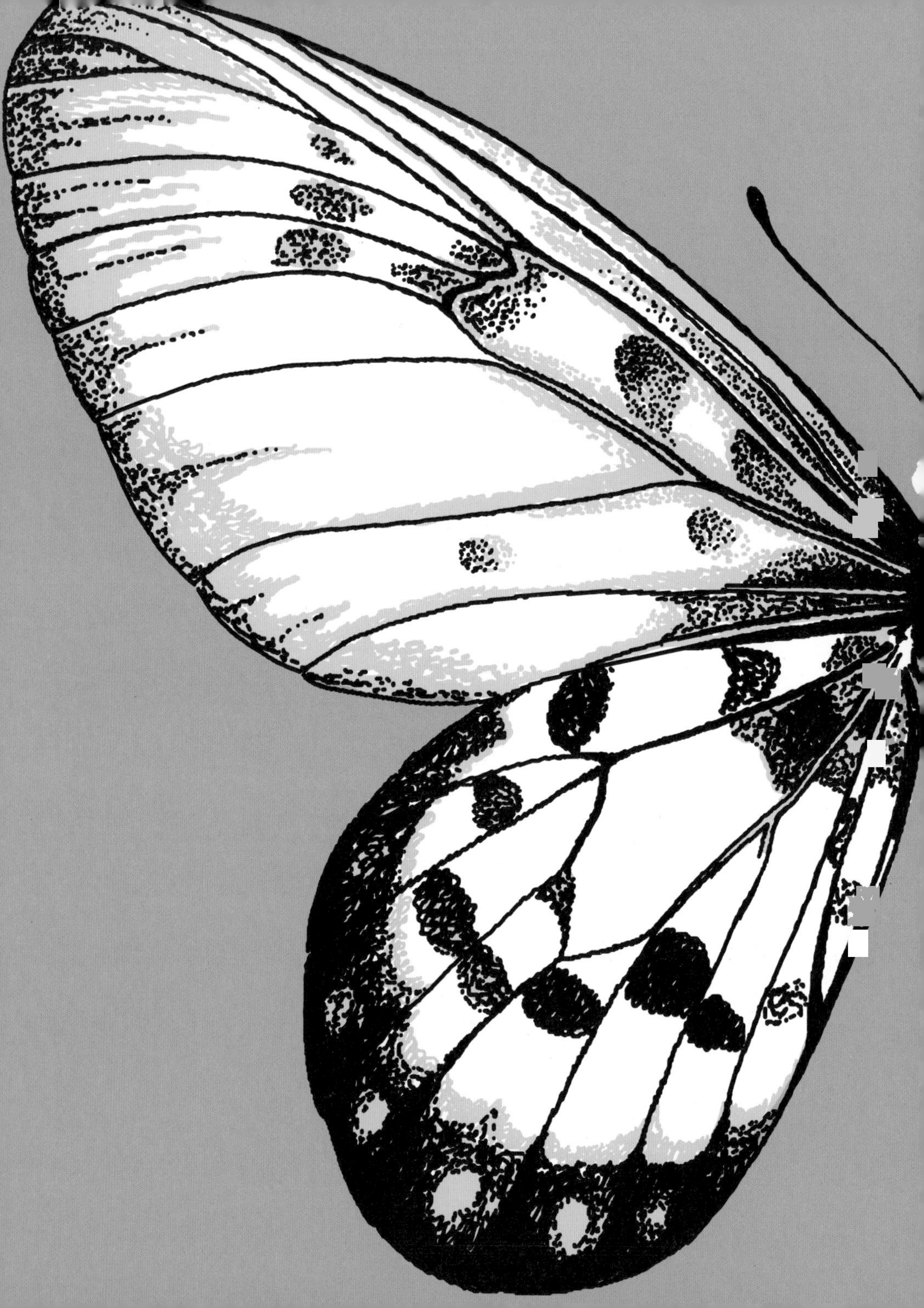

Day 3

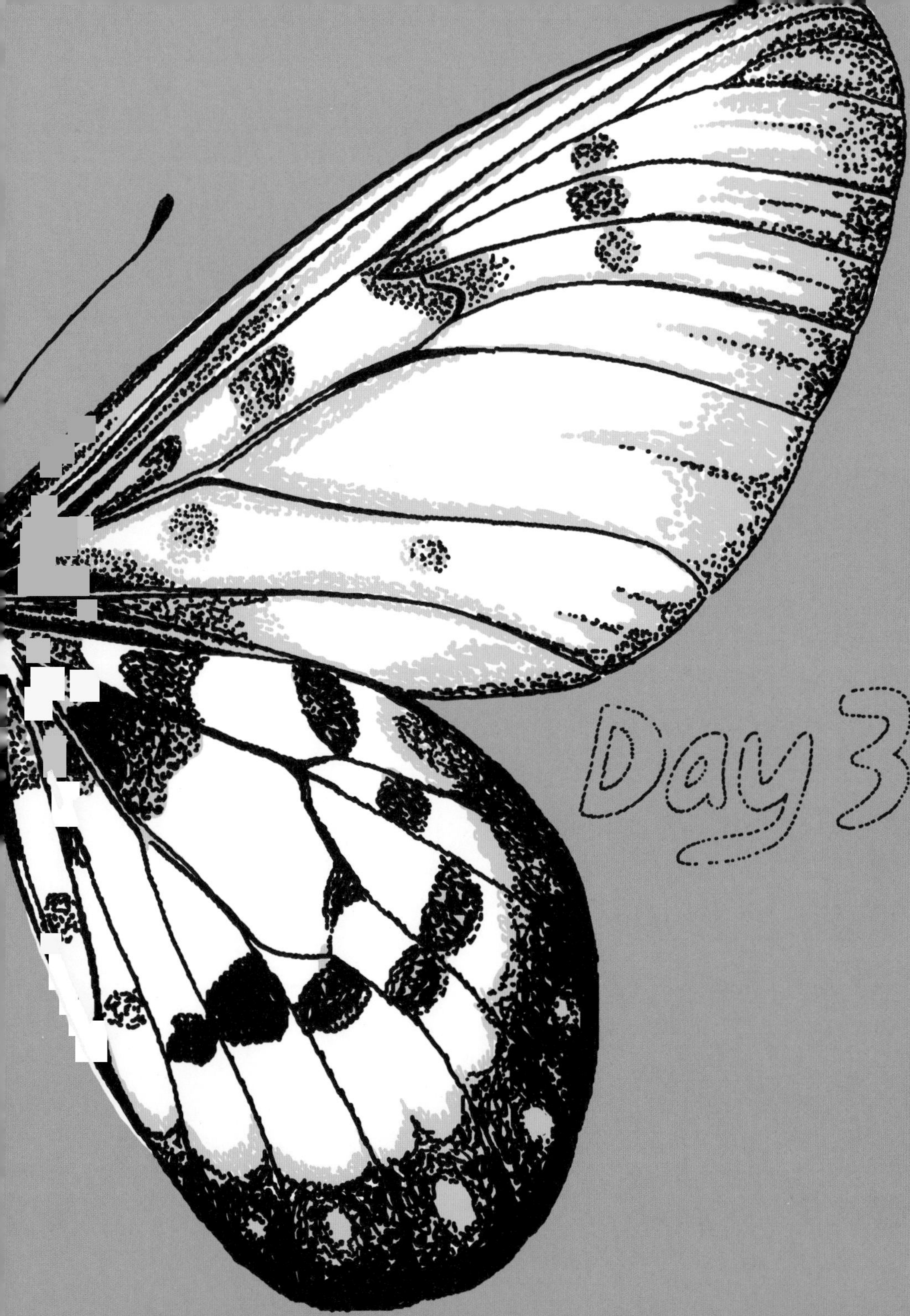

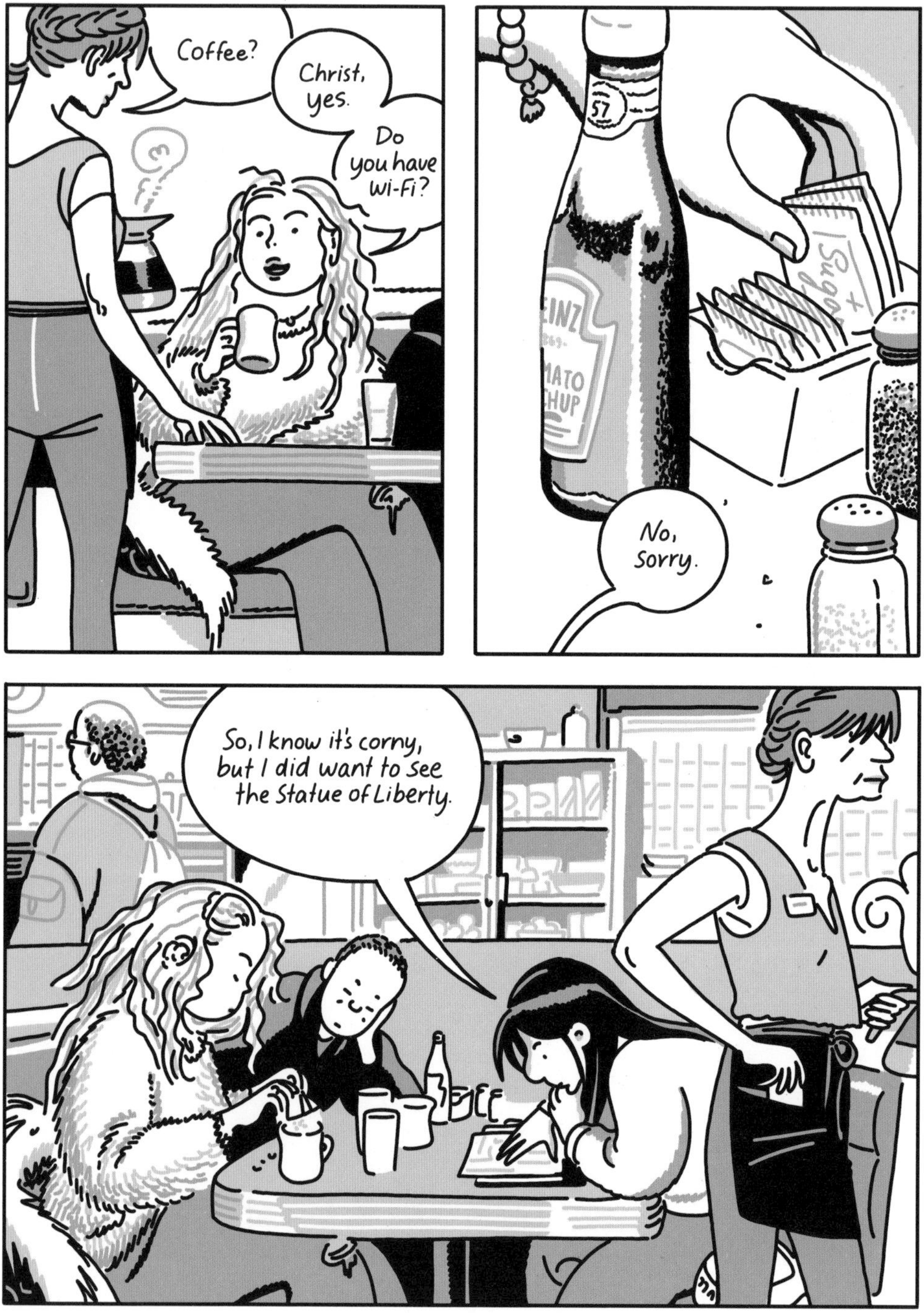
Coffee?
Christ, yes.
Do you have wi-fi?
57
EINZ
MATO
CHUP
Sugar
No, sorry.
So, I know it's corny, but I did want to see the Statue of Liberty.

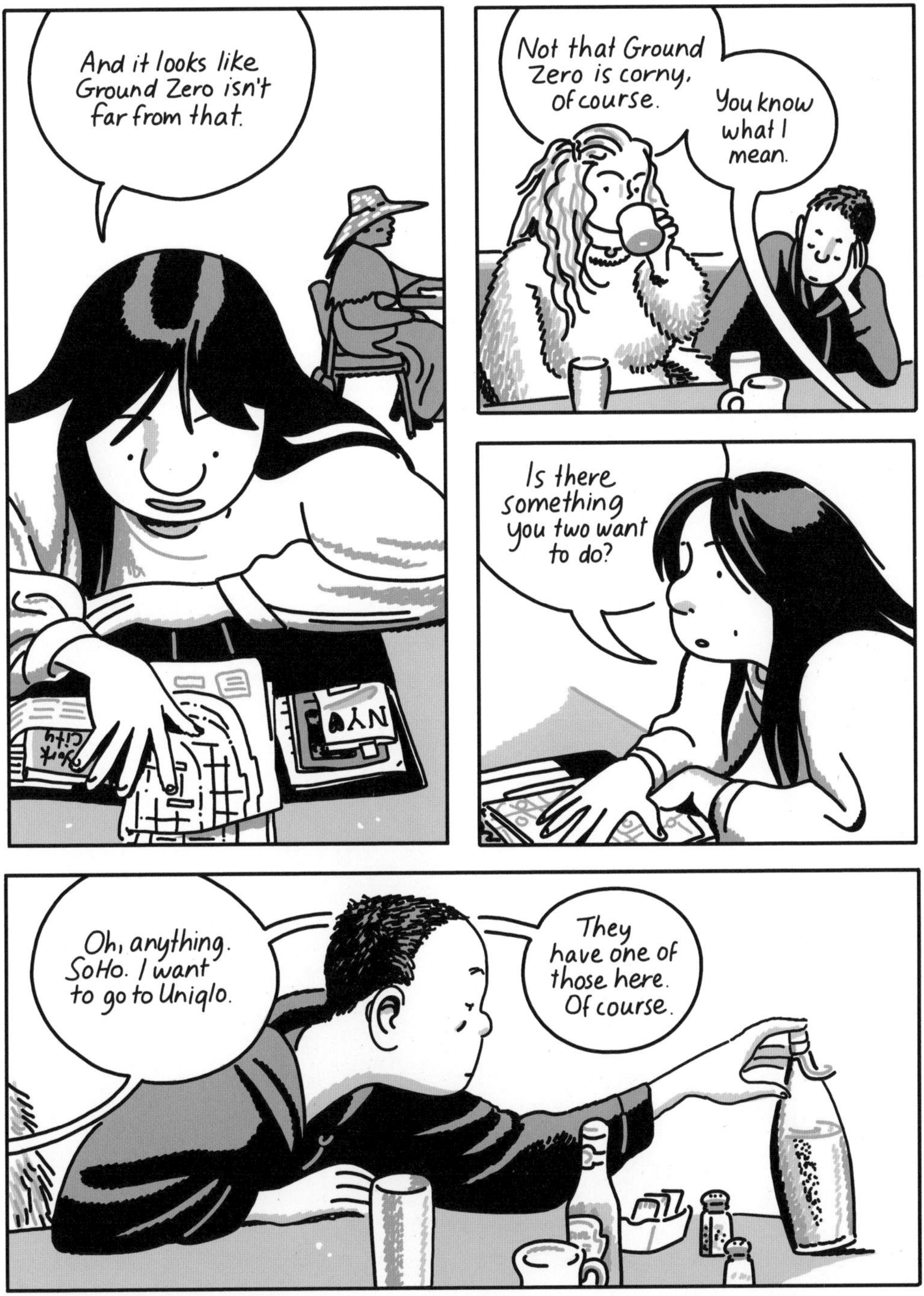
And it looks like Ground Zero isn't far from that.
Not that Ground Zero is corny, of course.
You know what I mean.
Is there something you two want to do?
Oh, anything. SoHo. I want to go to Uniqlo.
They have one of those here. Of course.

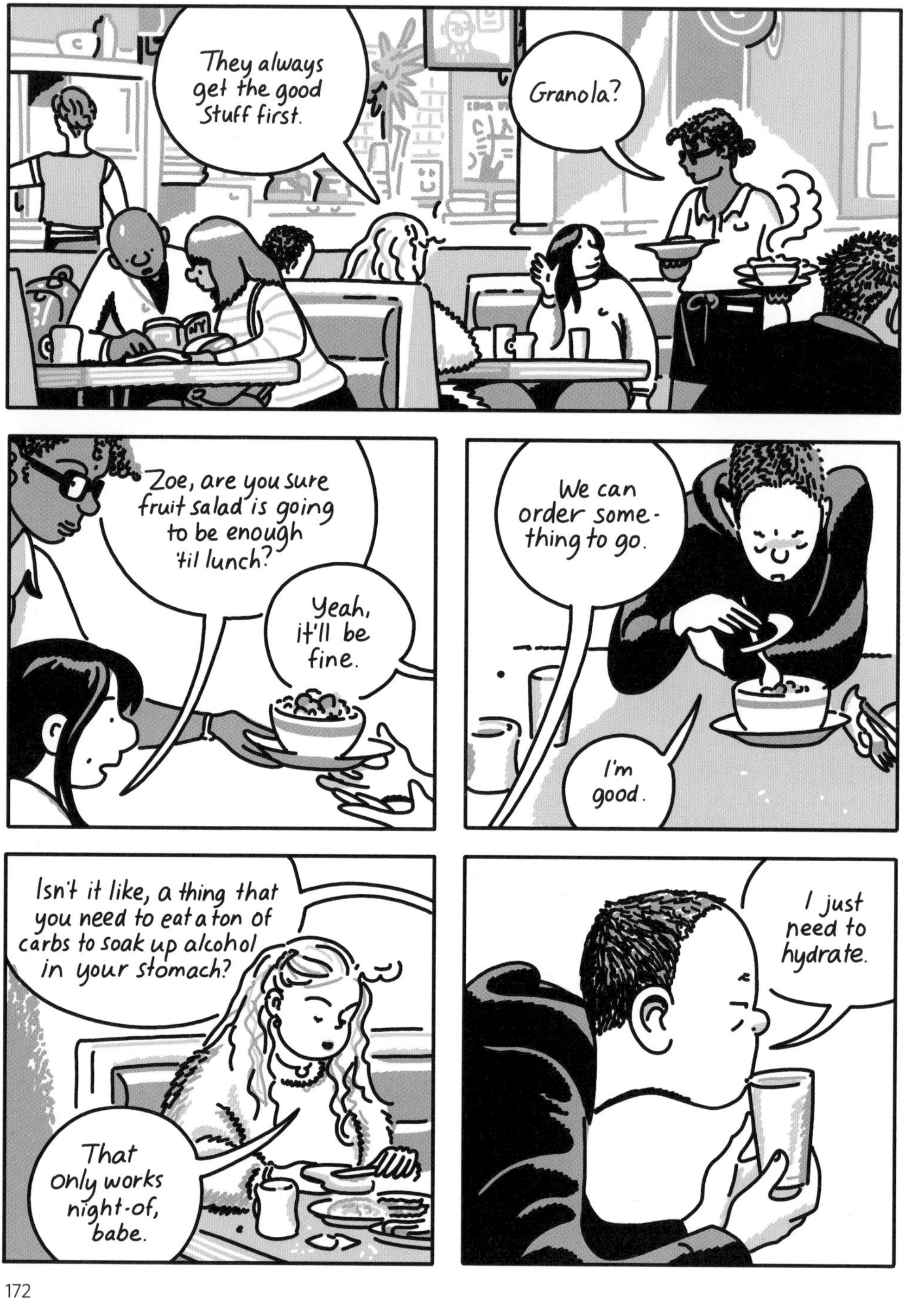
They always get the good stuff first.
Granola?
Zoe, are you sure fruit salad is going to be enough 'til lunch?
Yeah, it'll be fine.
We can order some-thing to go.
I'm good.
Isn't it like, a thing that you need to eat a ton of carbs to soak up alcohol in your stomach?
That only works night-of, babe.
I just need to hydrate.

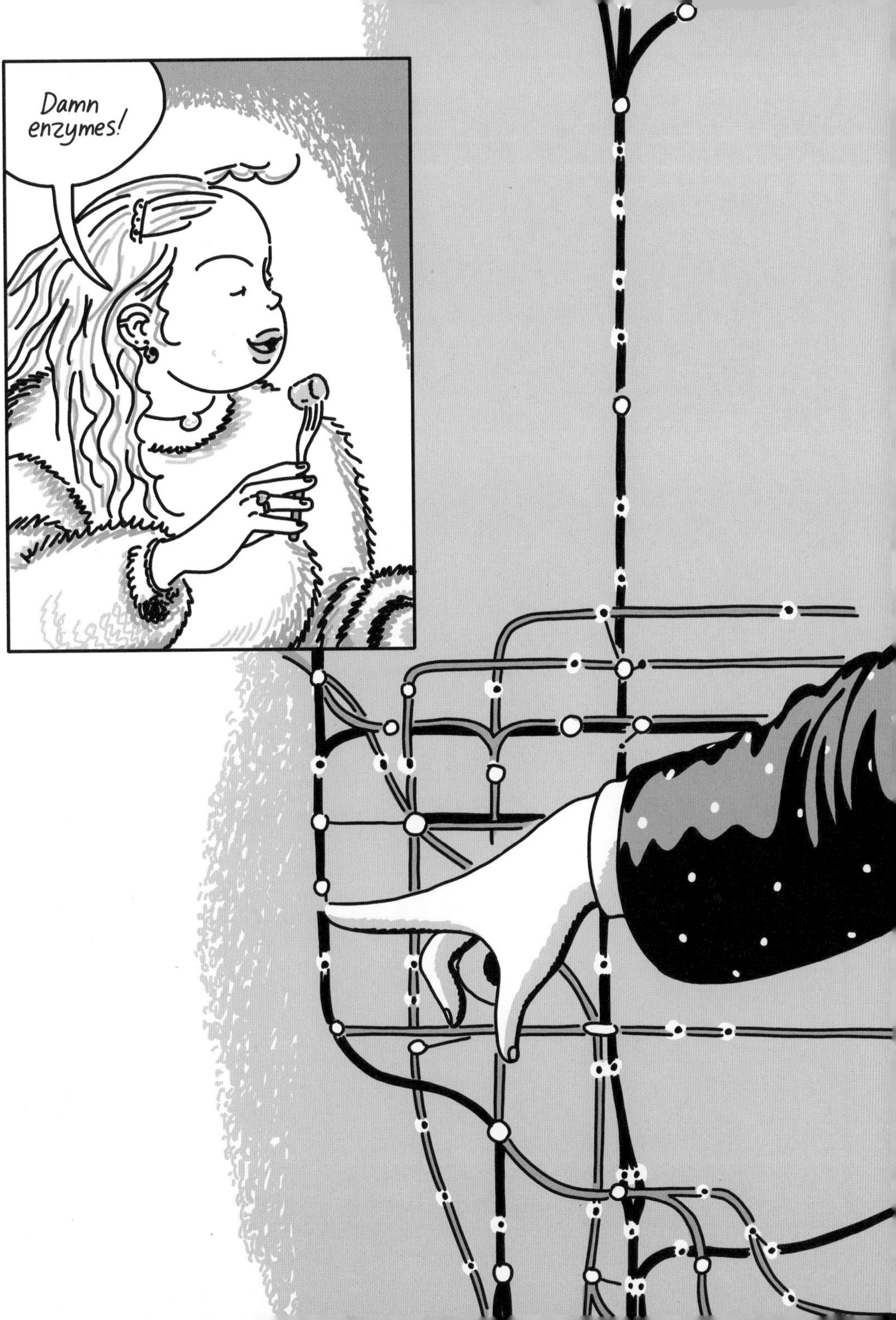
Damn enzymes!

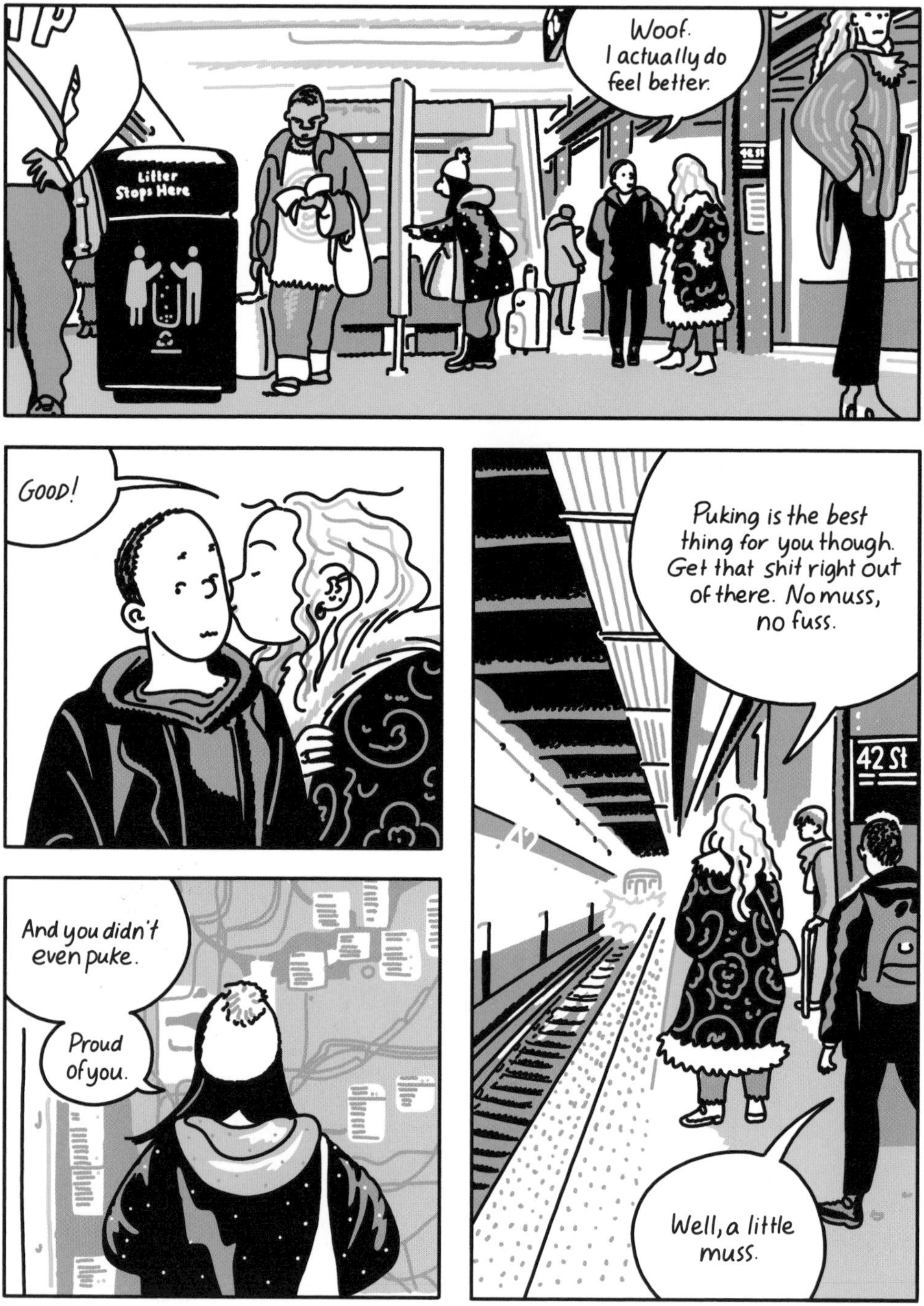

Litter Stops Here
42 St
Woof. I actually do feel better.
GOOD!
And you didn't even puke.
Proud of you.
Puking is the best thing for you though. Get that shit right out of there. No muss, no fuss.
42 St
Well, a little muss.

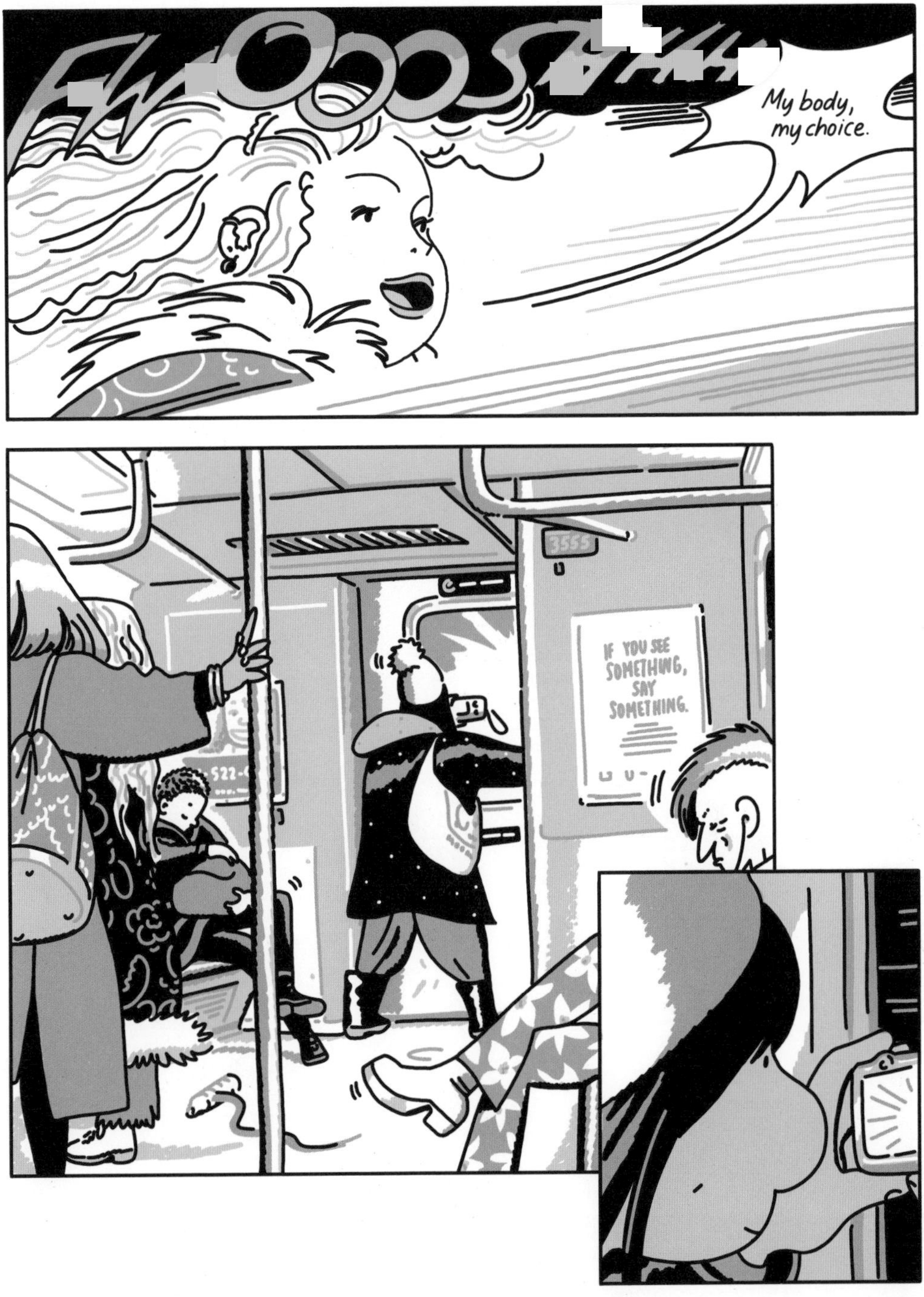
My body, my choice.
IF YOU SEE SOMETHING, SAY SOMETHING.
3555

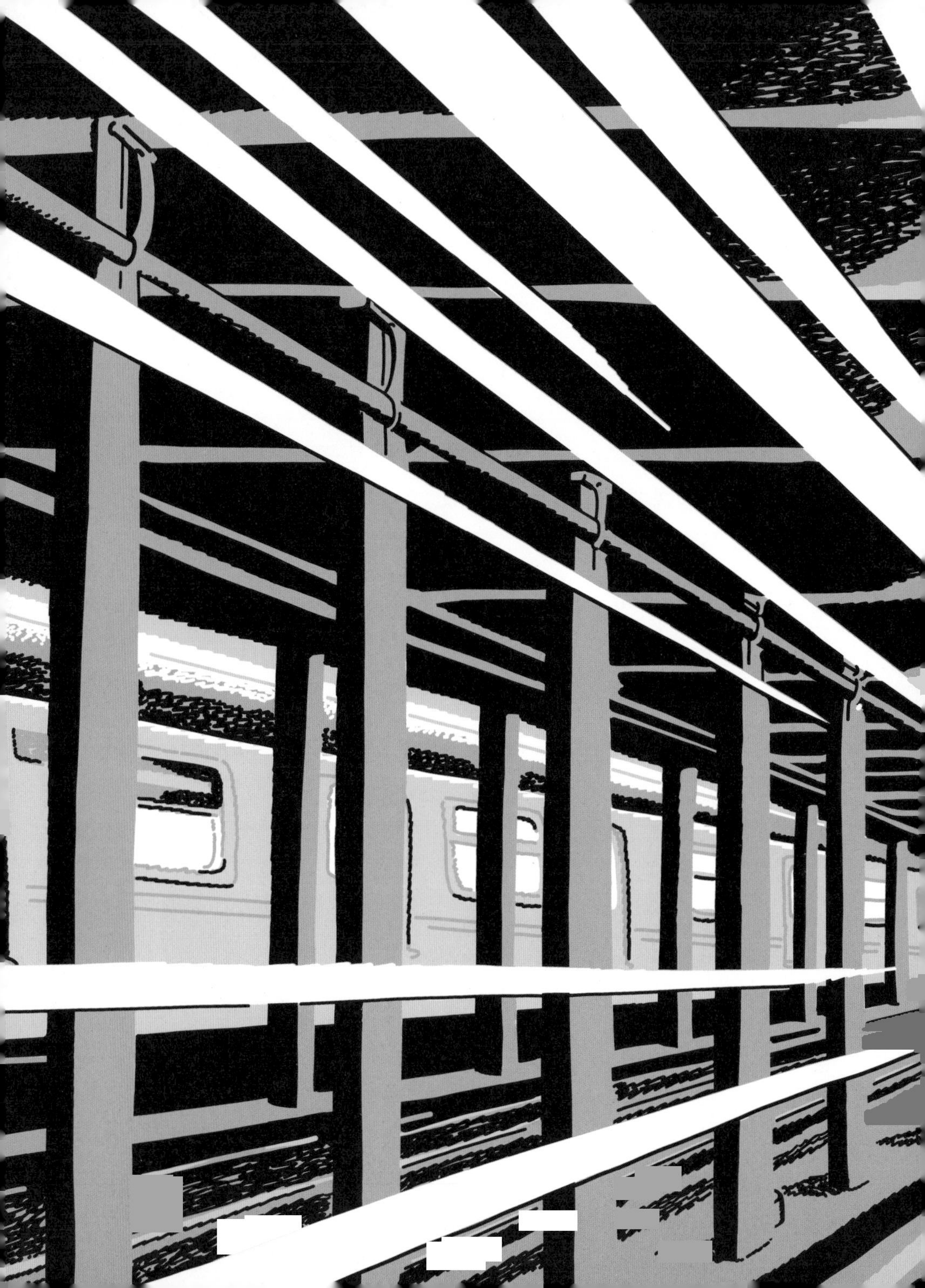

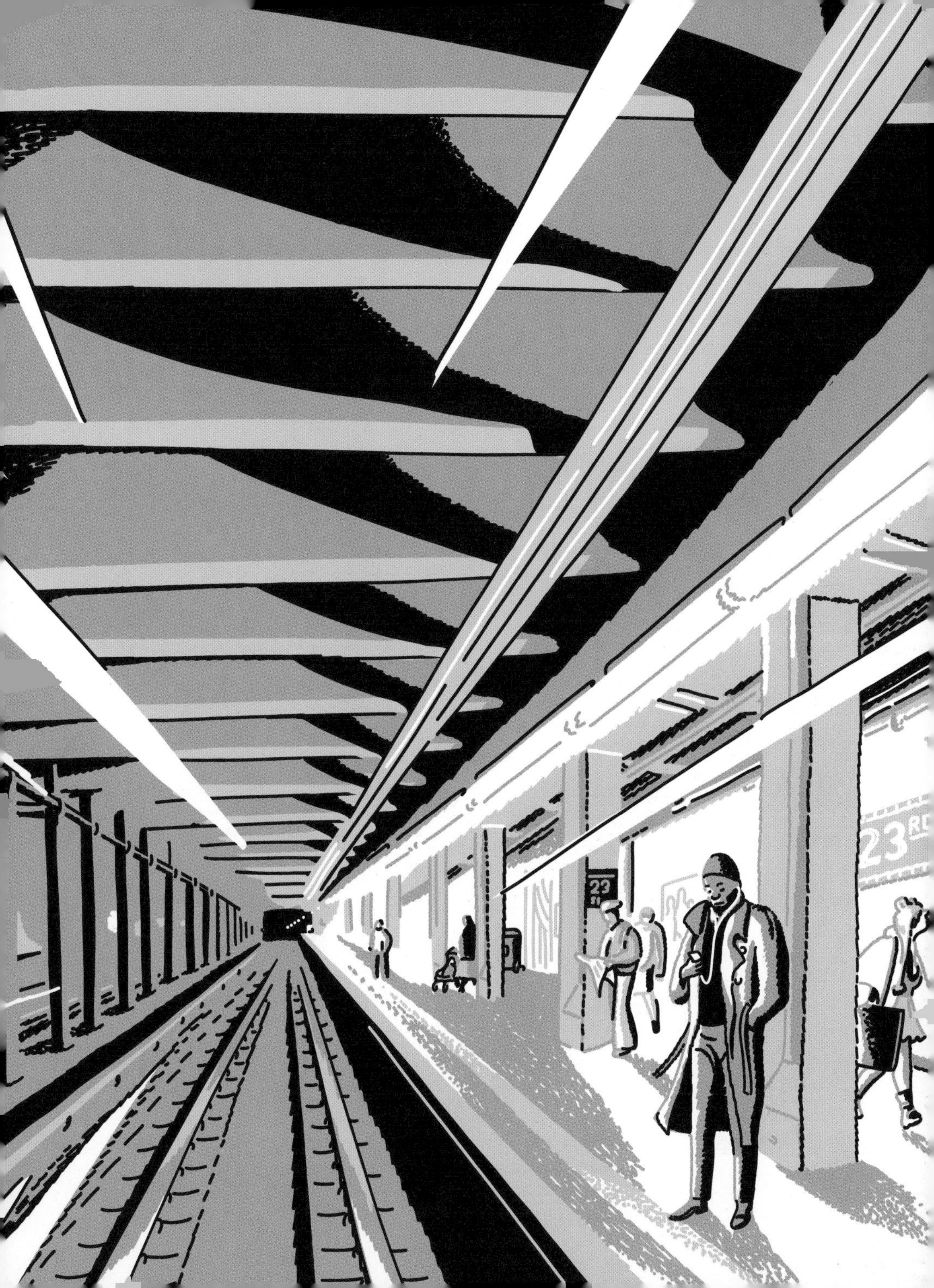
23
23RD

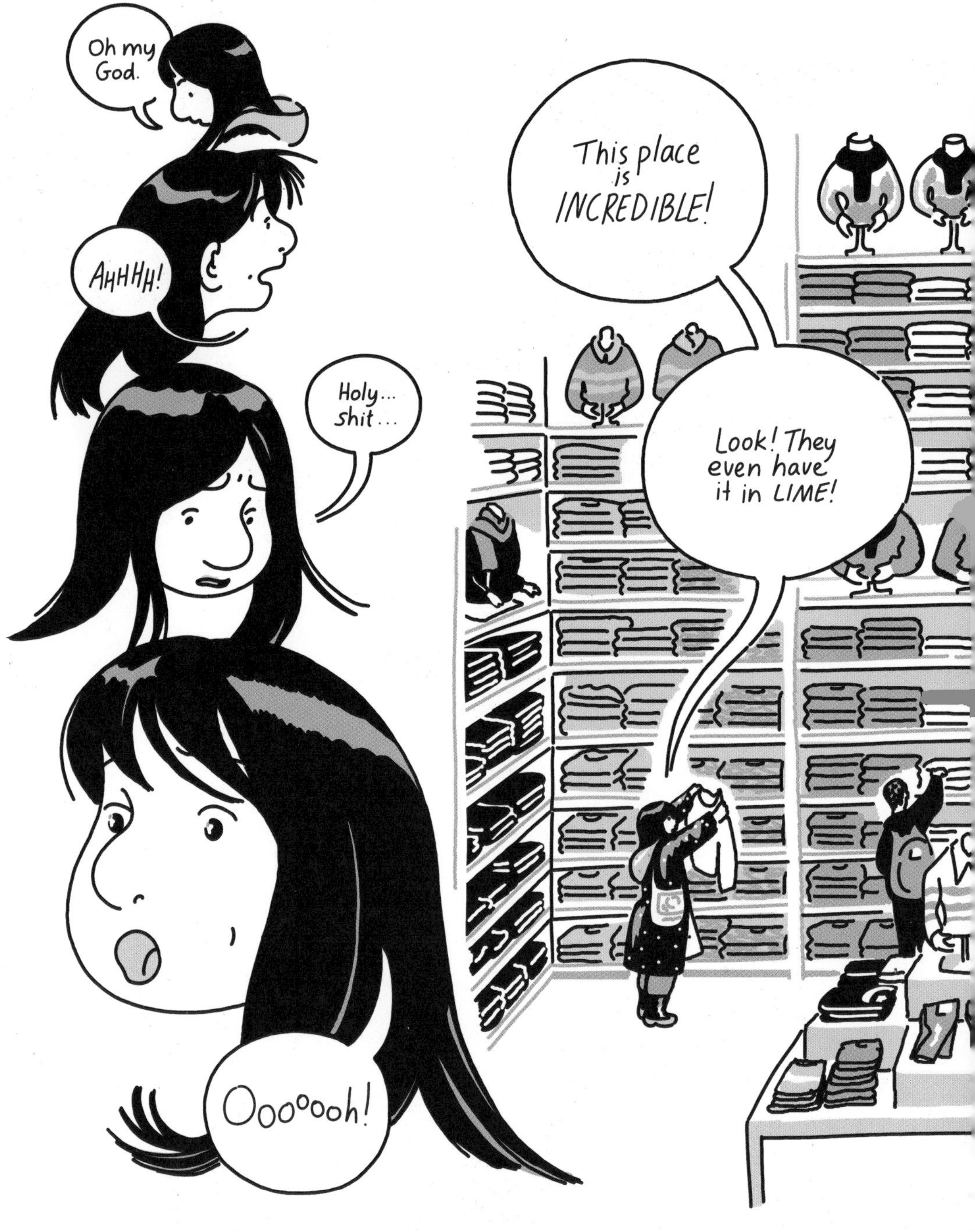
Oh my God.
AHHHH!
Holy... shit...
Oooooh!
This place is INCREDIBLE!
Look! They even have it in LIME!

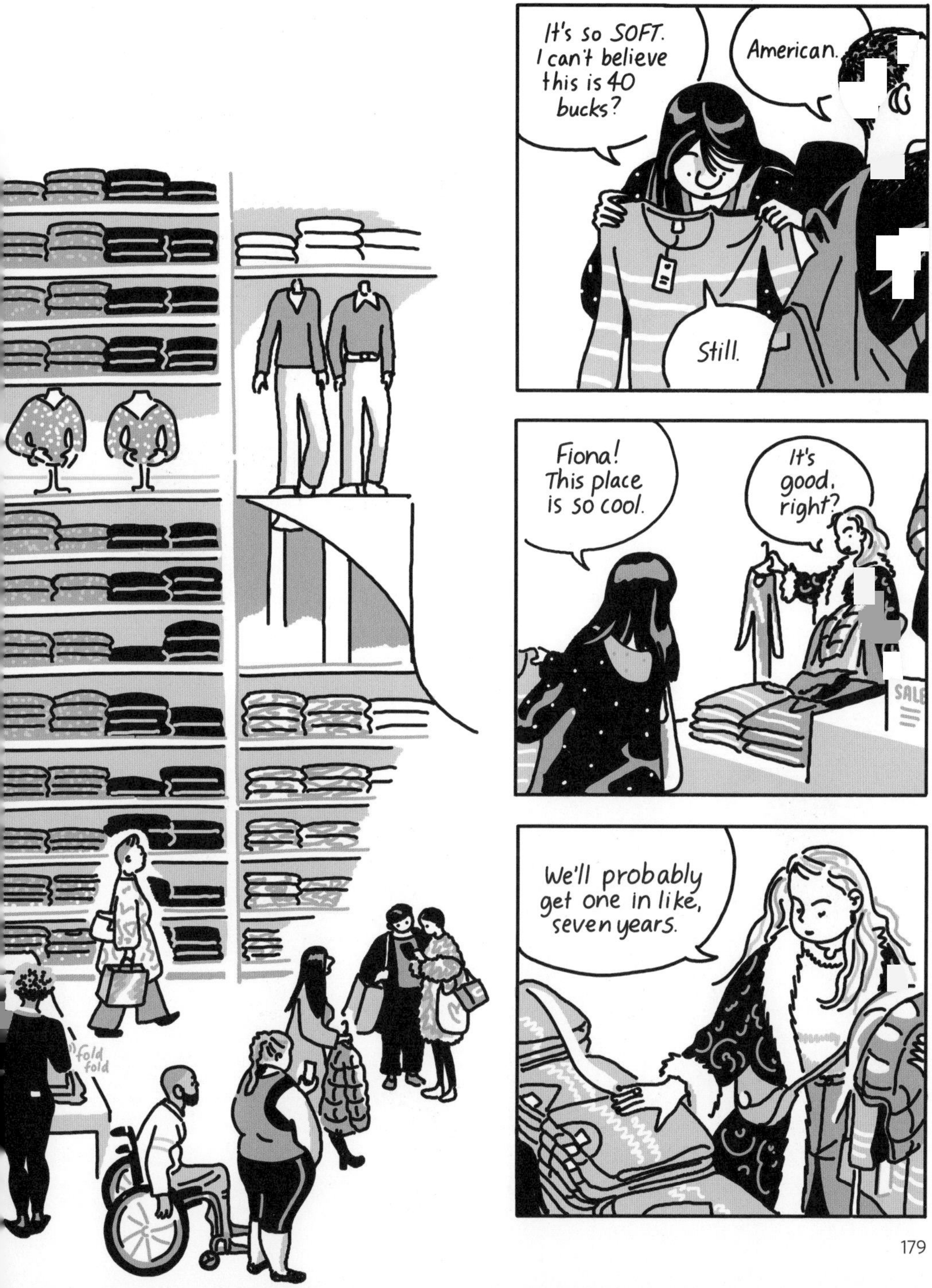
fold
fold
It's so SOFT. I can't believe this is 40 bucks?
American.
Still.
Fiona! This place is so cool.
It's good, right?
SALE
We'll probably get one in like, seven years.

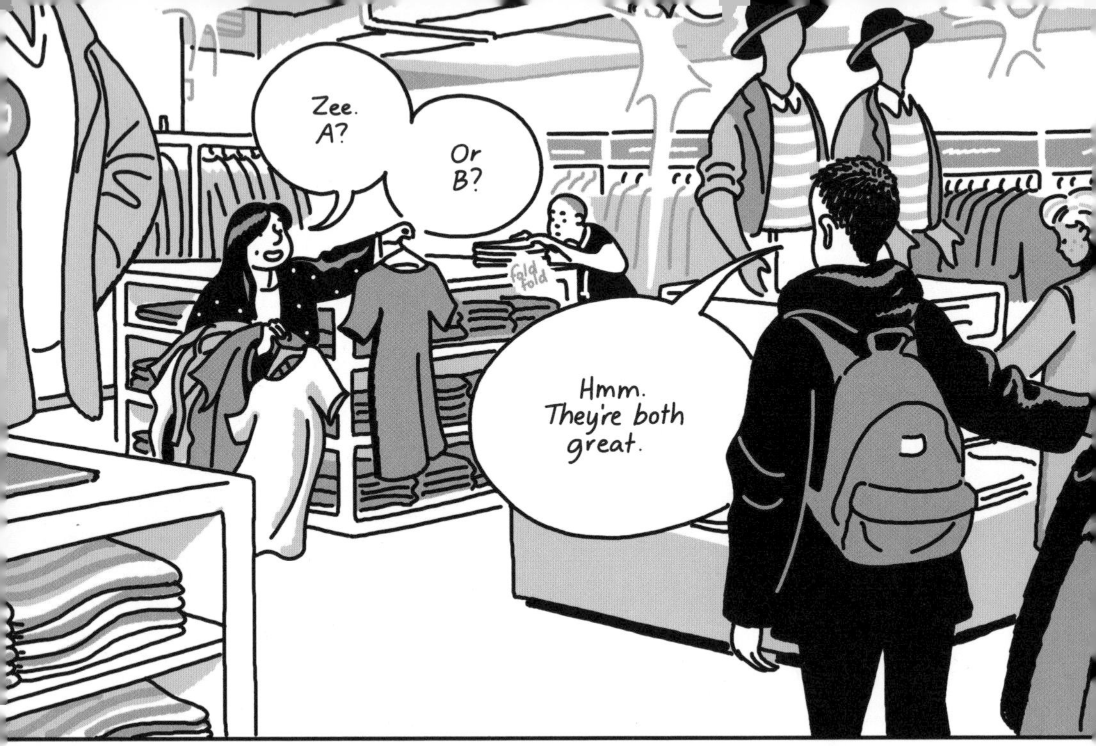
Zee. A?
Or B?
fold fold
Hmm. They're both great.

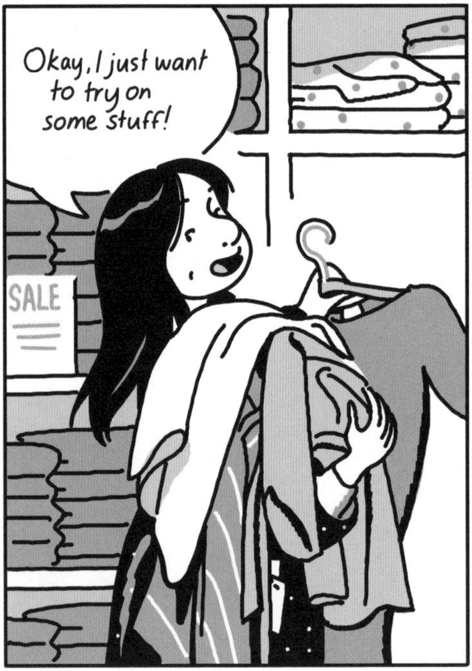
Okay, I just want to try on some stuff!
SALE

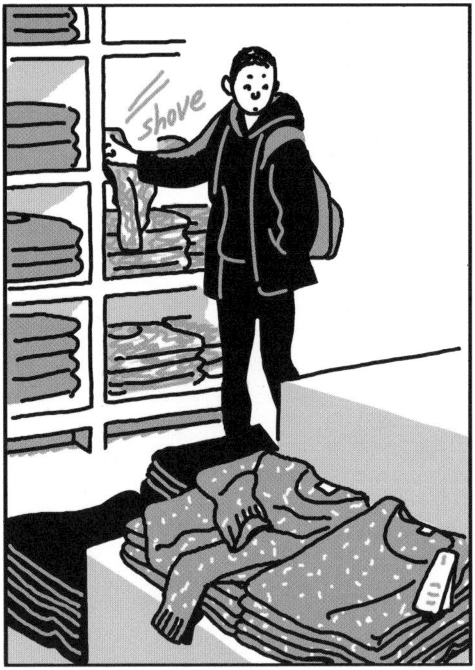
shove

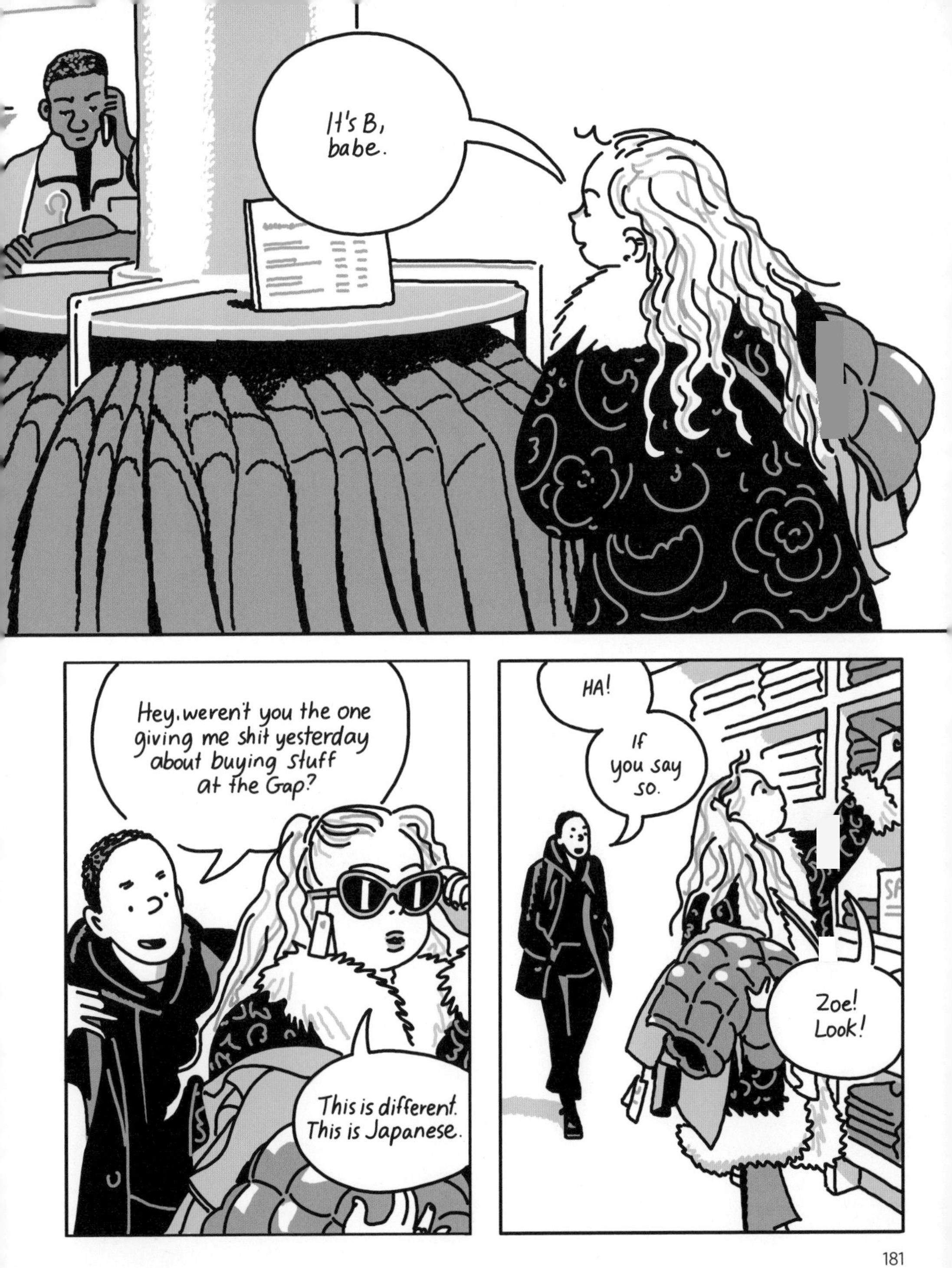
It's B, babe.
Hey, weren't you the one giving me shit yesterday about buying stuff at the Gap?
This is different. This is Japanese.
HA!
If you say so.
Zoe! Look!

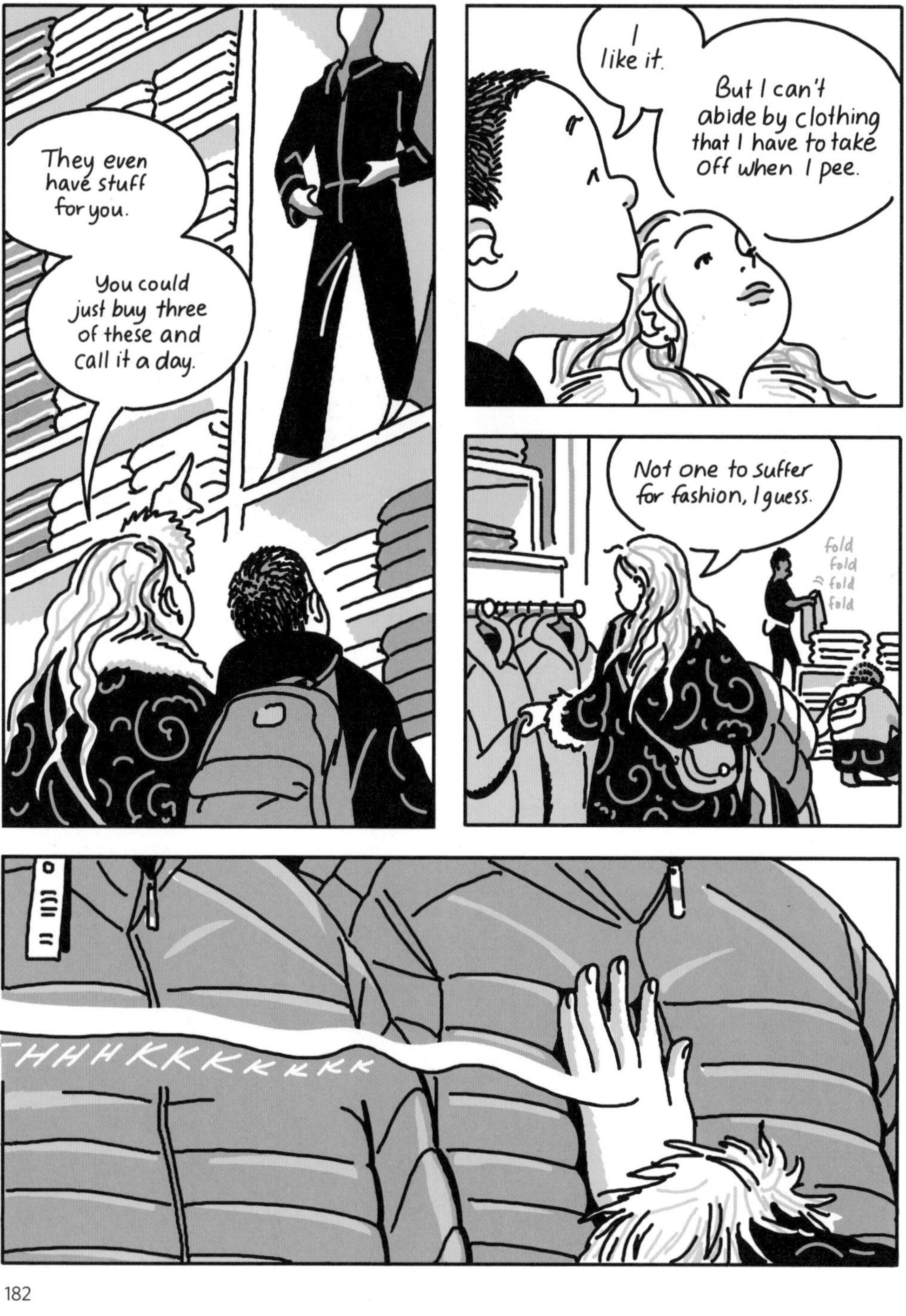
They even have stuff for you.
You could just buy three of these and call it a day.
I like it.
But I can't abide by clothing that I have to take off when I pee.
Not one to suffer for fashion, I guess.
fold fold fold fold
SHHHKKKKKKKK

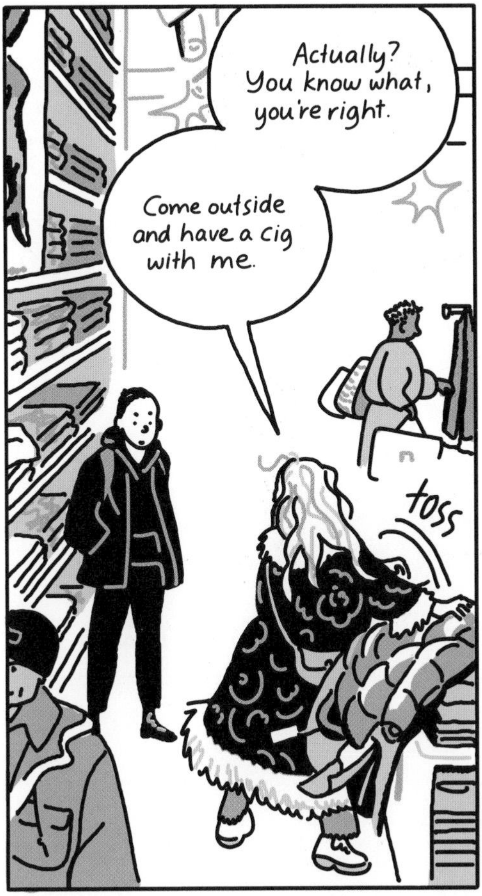
Actually? You know what, you're right.
Come outside and have a cig with me.
toss

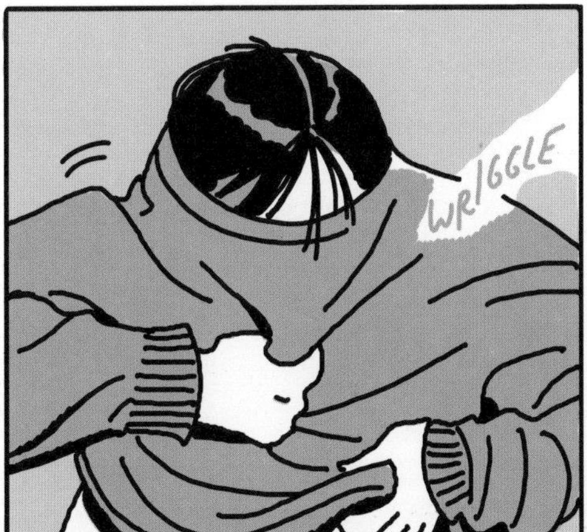
WRIGGLE

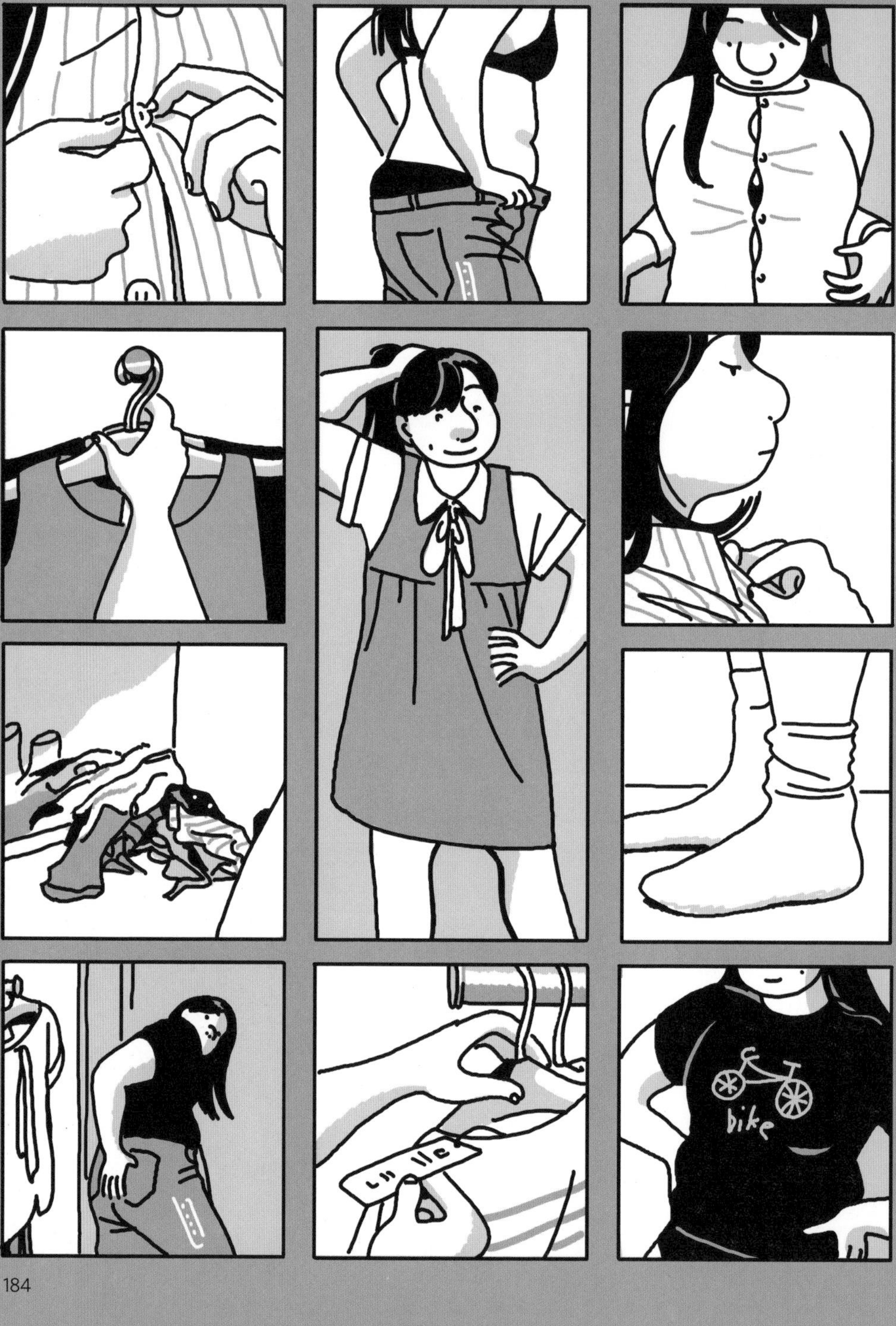
bike

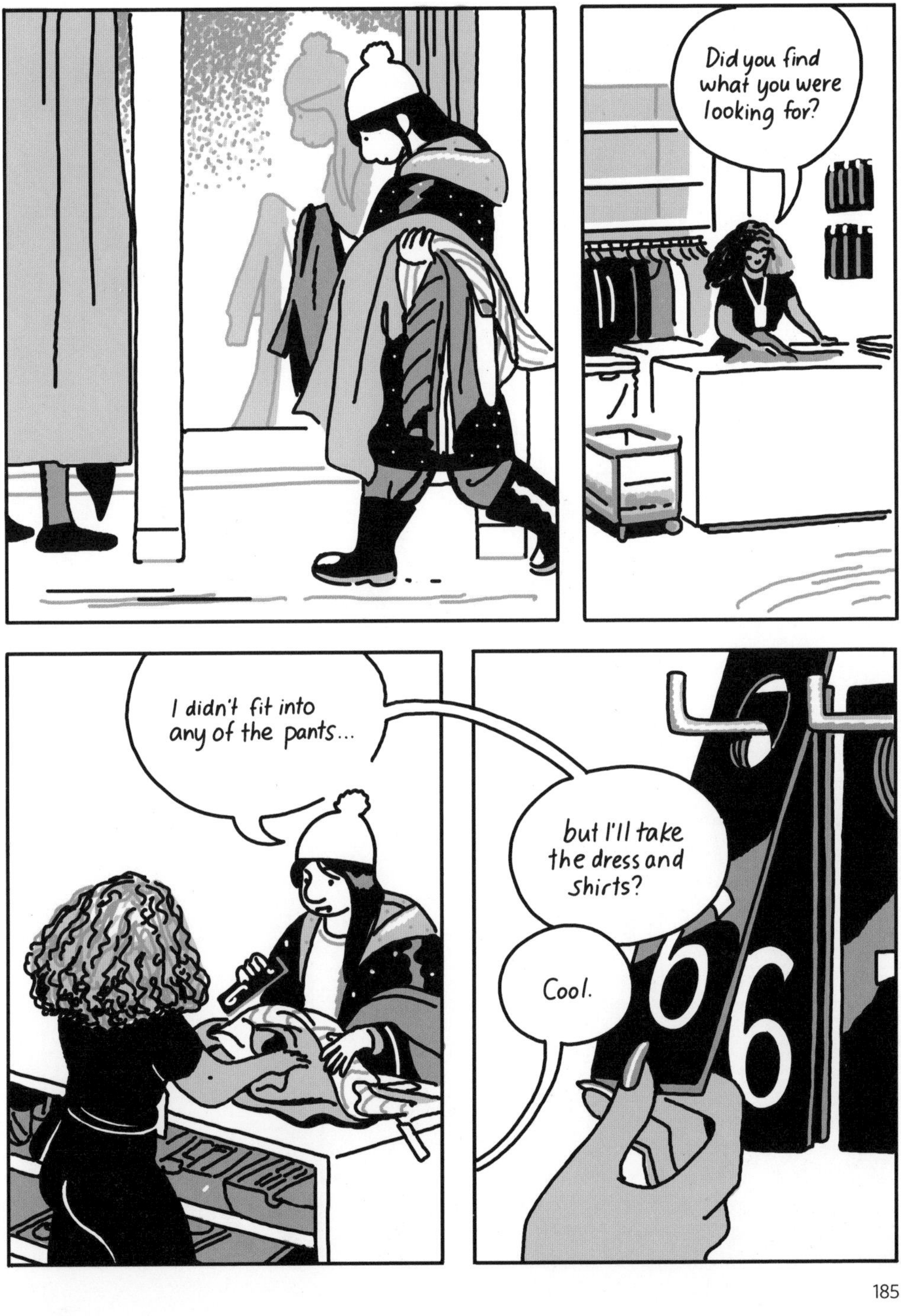
Did you find what you were looking for?
I didn't fit into any of the pants...
but I'll take the dress and shirts?
Cool.
66

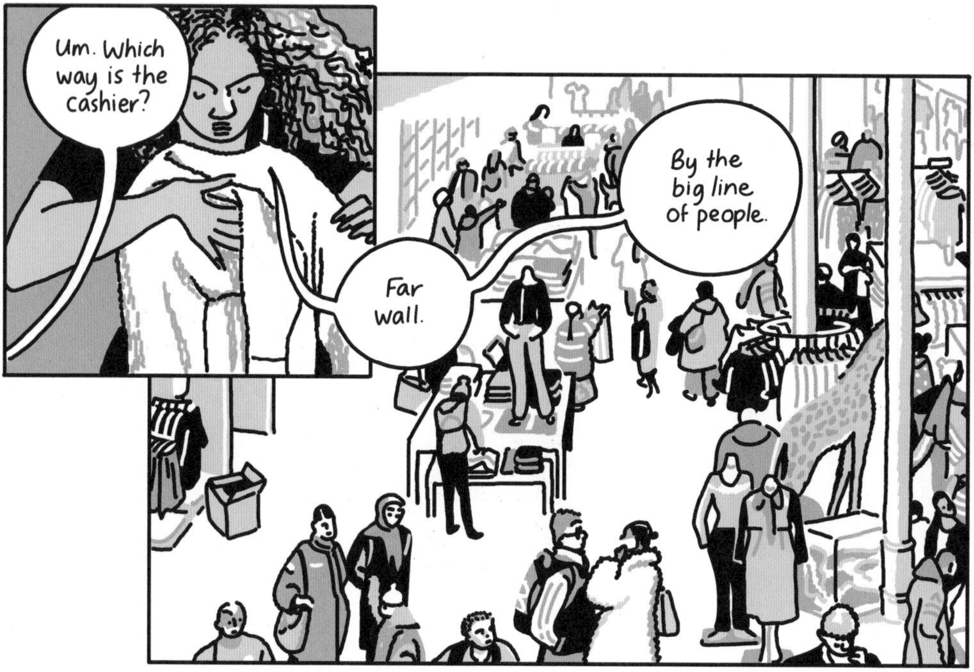
Um. Which way is the cashier?
Far wall.
By the big line of people.

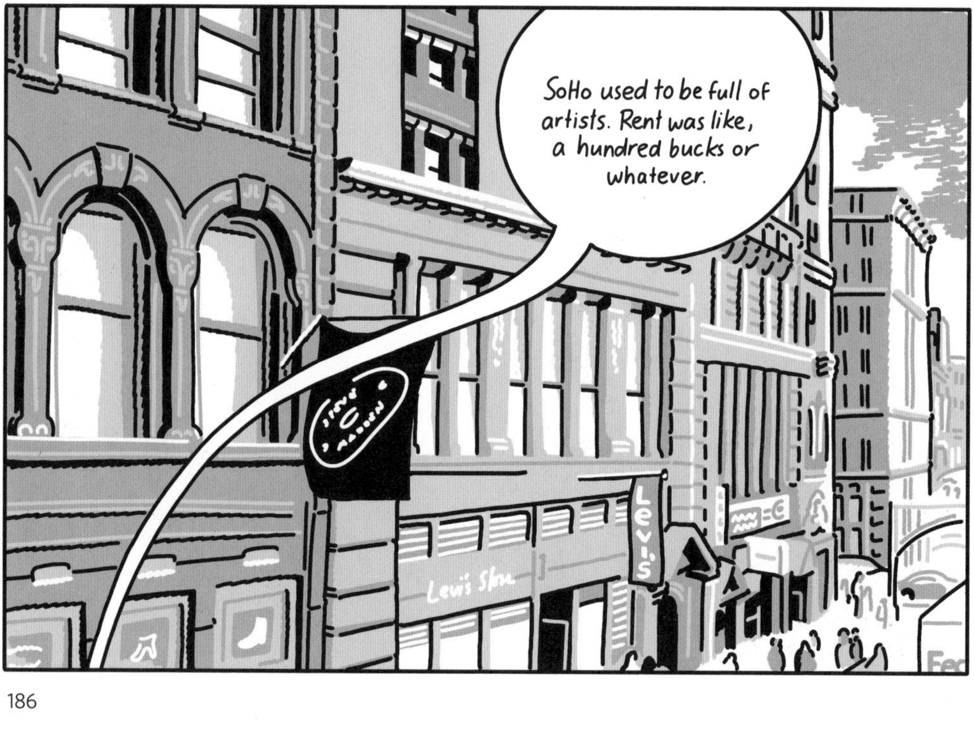
SoHo used to be full of artists. Rent was like, a hundred bucks or whatever.
Levi's

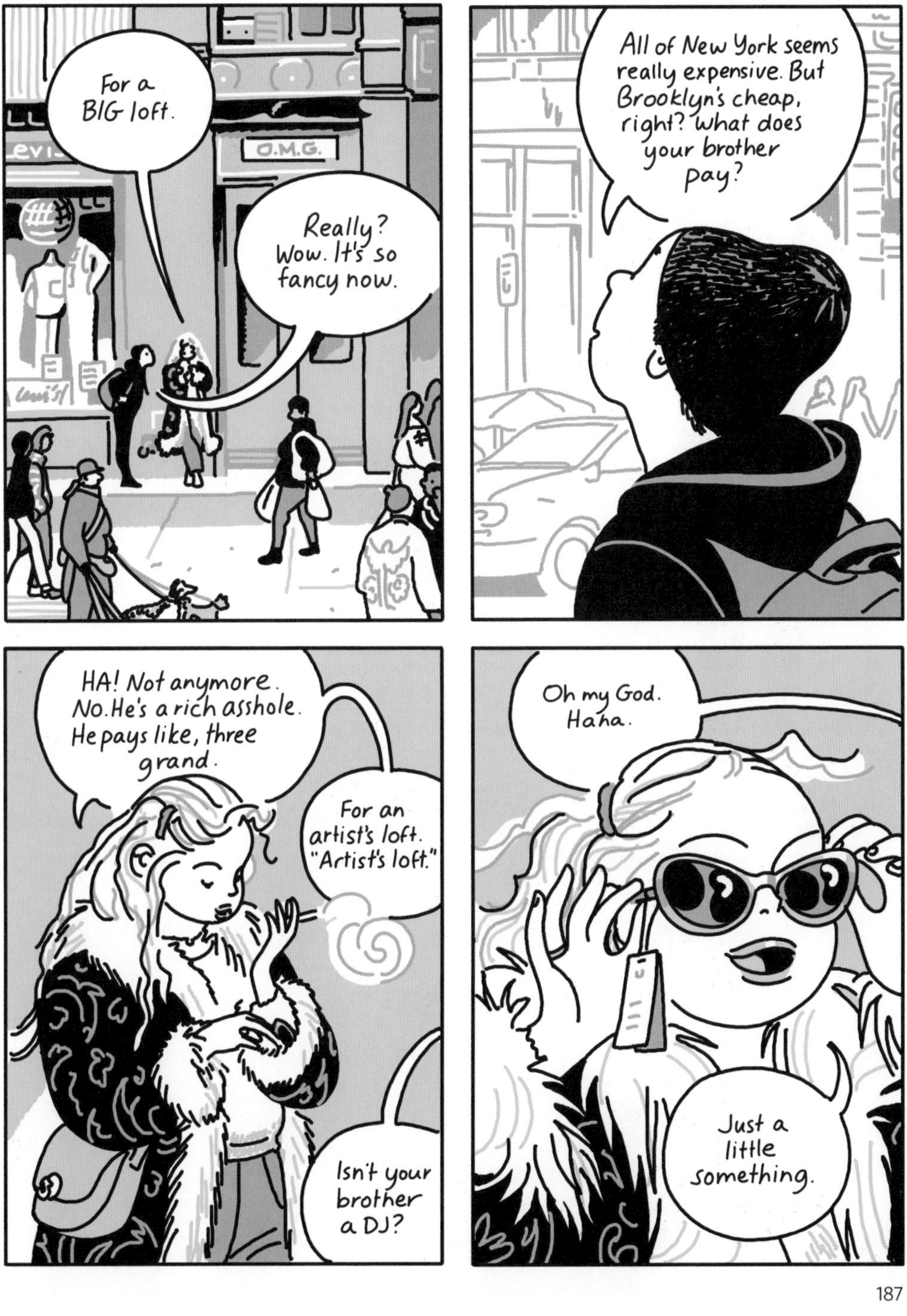
For a BIG loft.
Really? Wow. It's so fancy now.
O.M.G.
All of New York seems really expensive. But Brooklyn's cheap, right? what does your brother pay?
HA! Not anymore. No. He's a rich asshole. He pays like, three grand.
For an artist's loft. "Artist's loft."
Isn't your brother a DJ?
Oh my God. Haha.
Just a little something.

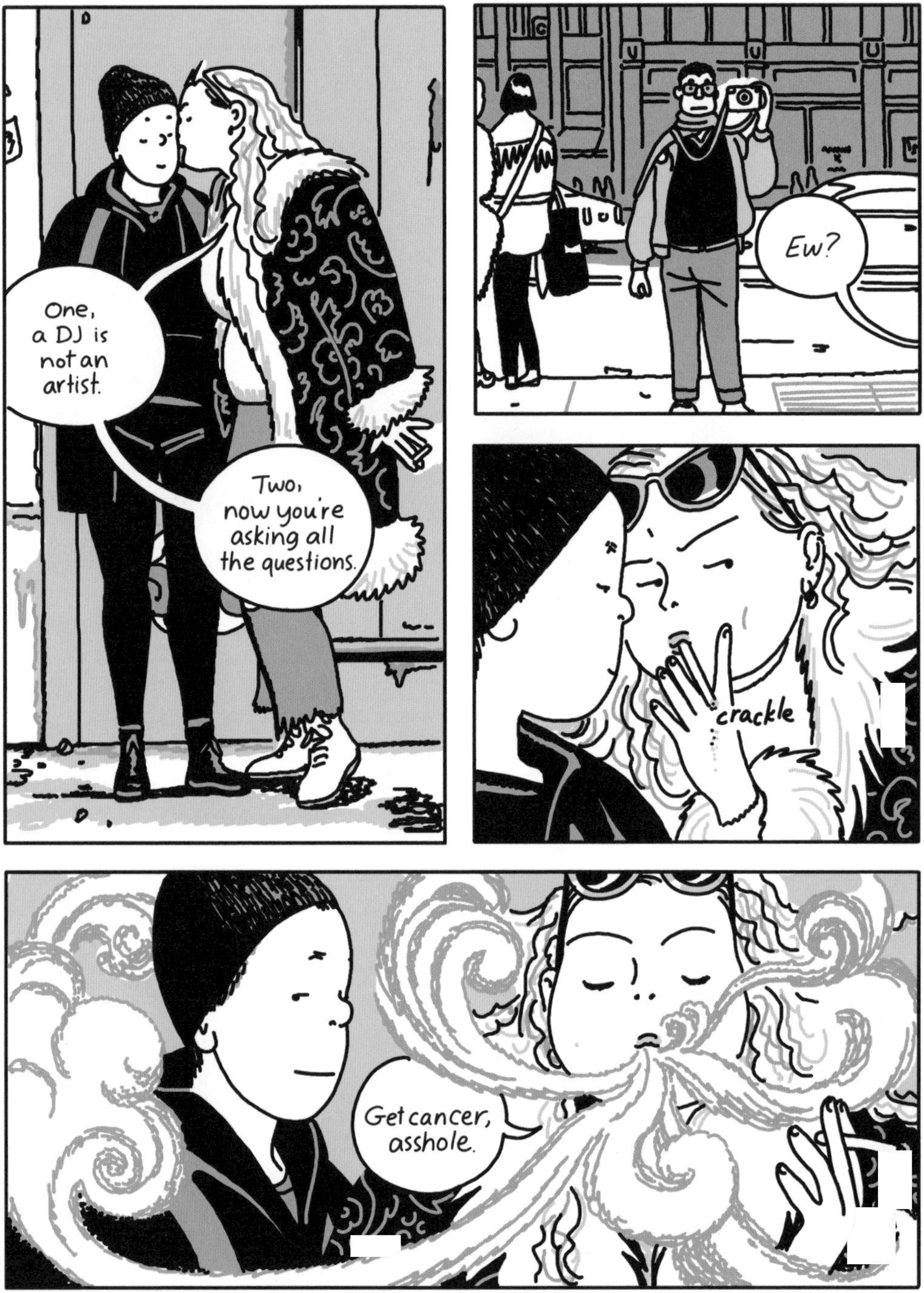
One, a DJ is not an artist.
Two, now you're asking all the questions.
Ew?
crackle
Get cancer, asshole.

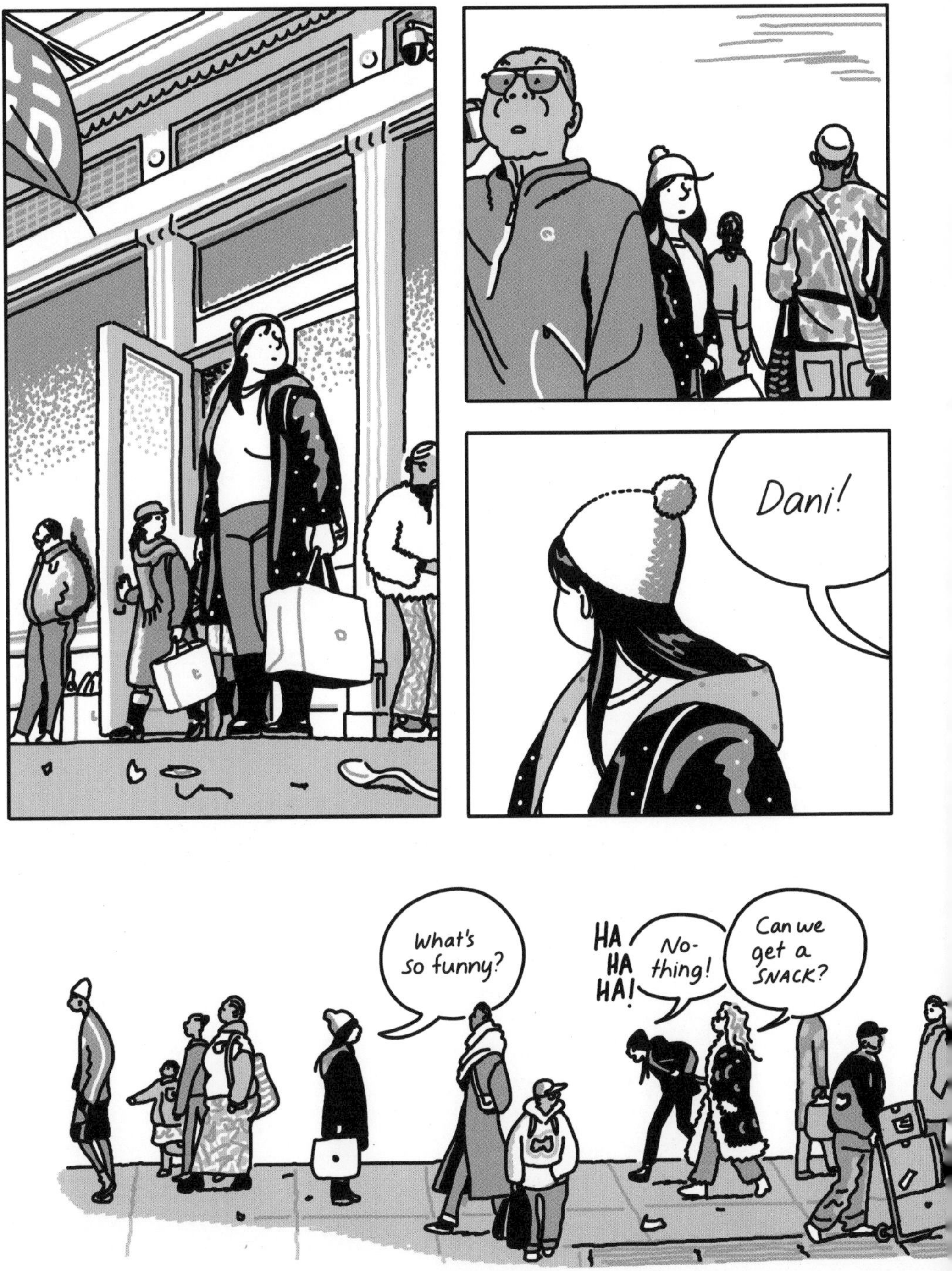
Dani!
What's so funny?
HA HA HA!
No-thing!
Can we get a SNACK?

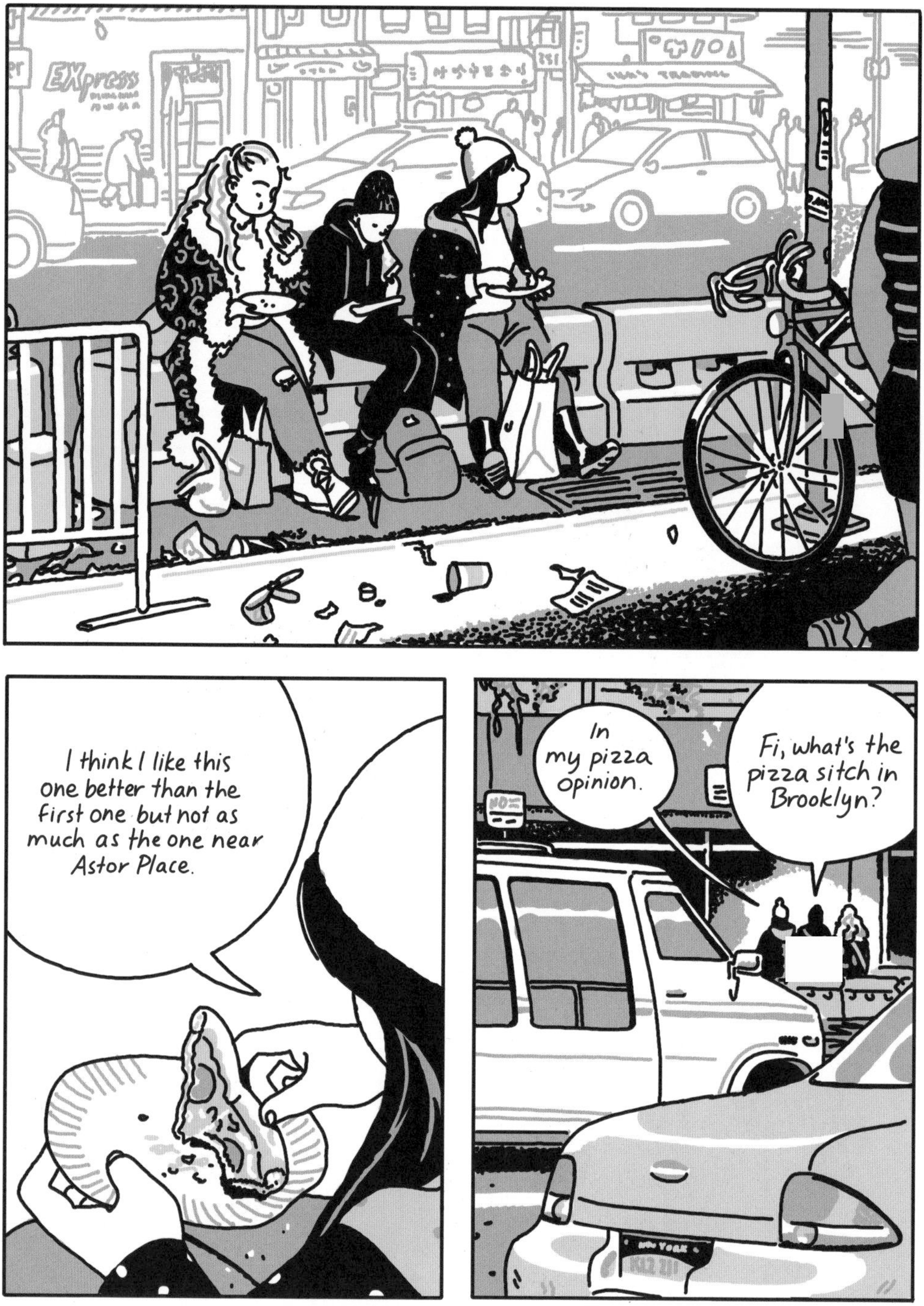
I think I like this one better than the first one but not as much as the one near Astor Place.
In my pizza opinion.
Fi, what's the pizza sitch in Brooklyn?

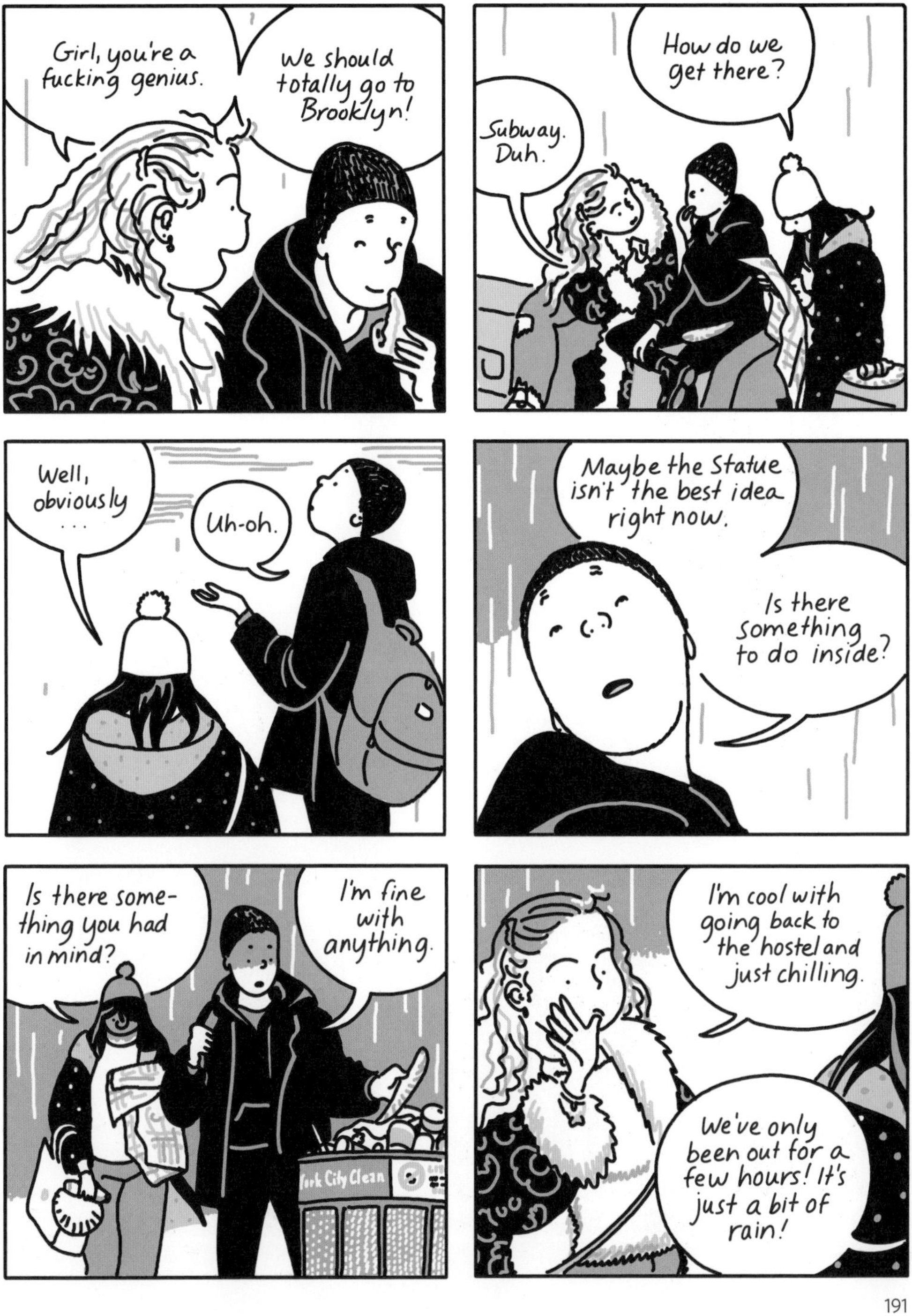
Girl, you're a fucking genius.
We should totally go to Brooklyn!
How do we get there?
Subway. Duh.
Well, obviously . . .
Uh-oh.
Maybe the Statue isn't the best idea right now.
Is there something to do inside?
Is there some-thing you had in mind?
I'm fine with anything.
York City Clean
I'm cool with going back to the hostel and just chilling.
We've only been out for a few hours! It's just a bit of rain!

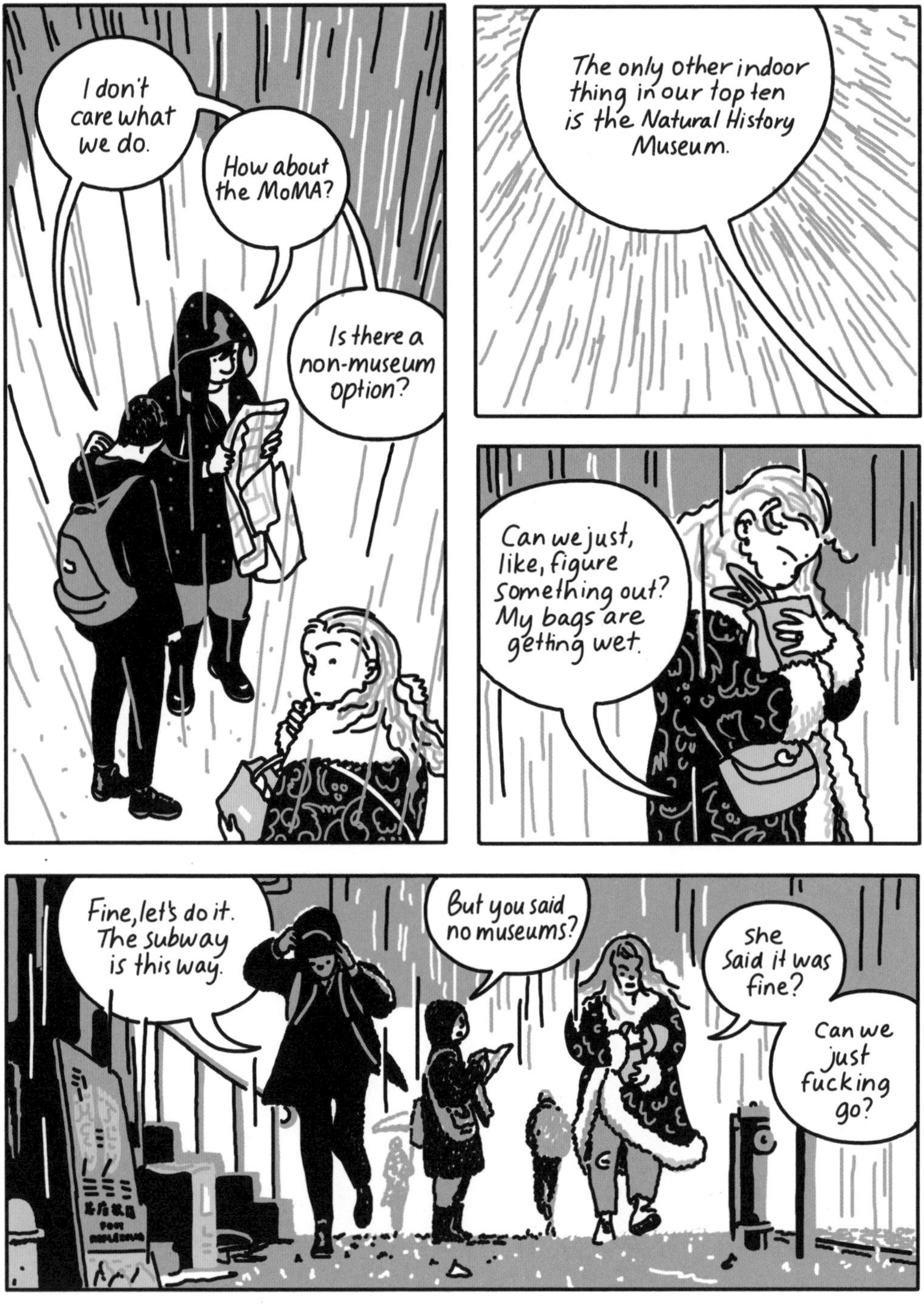
I don't care what we do.
How about the MoMA?
Is there a non-museum option?
The only other indoor thing in our top ten is the Natural History Museum.
Can we just, like, figure something out? My bags are getting wet.
Fine, let's do it. The subway is this way.
But you said no museums?
She said it was fine?
Can we just fucking go?

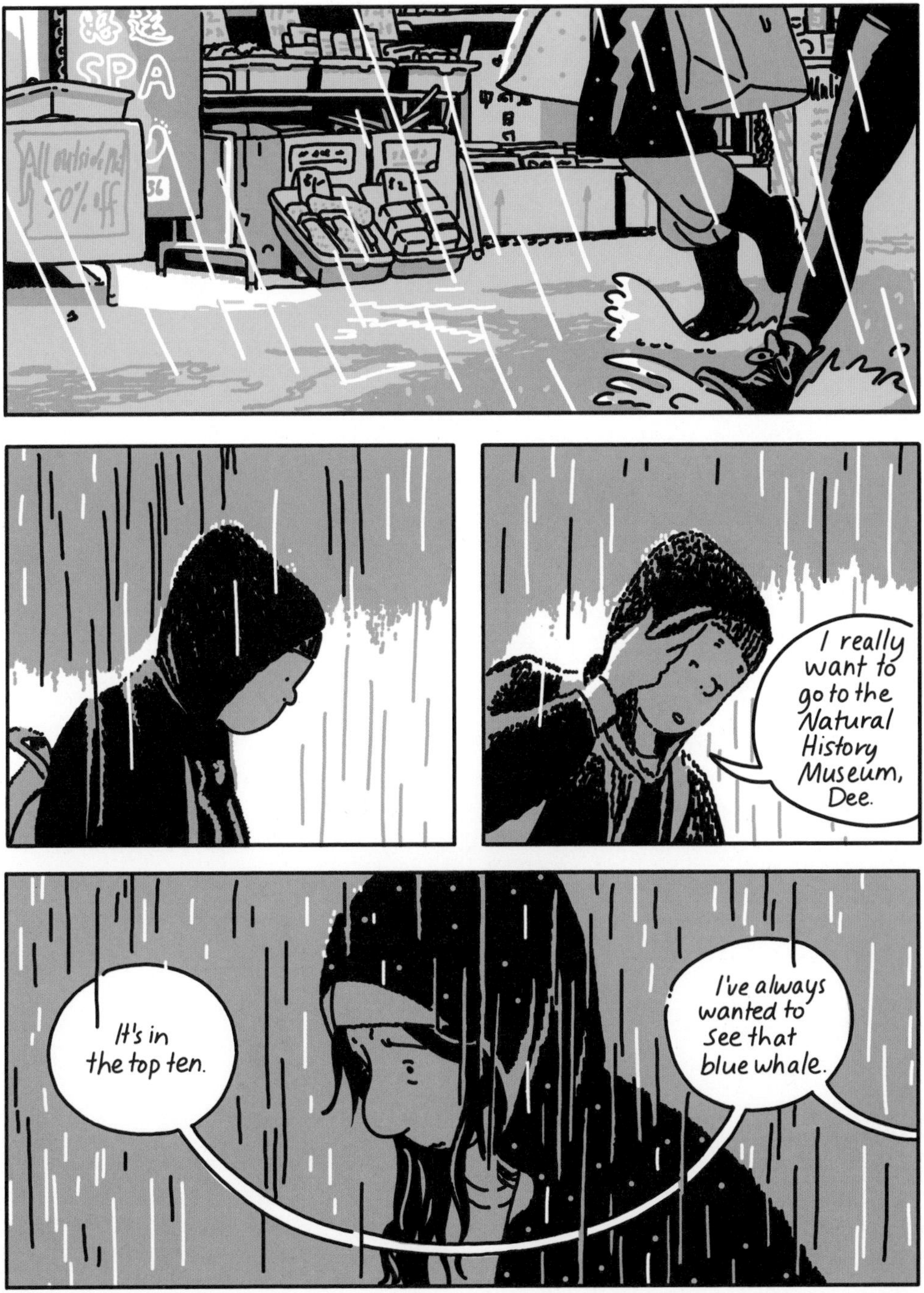
SPA
All outside plants 50% off
I really want to go to the Natural History Museum, Dee.
It's in the top ten.
I've always wanted to see that blue whale.

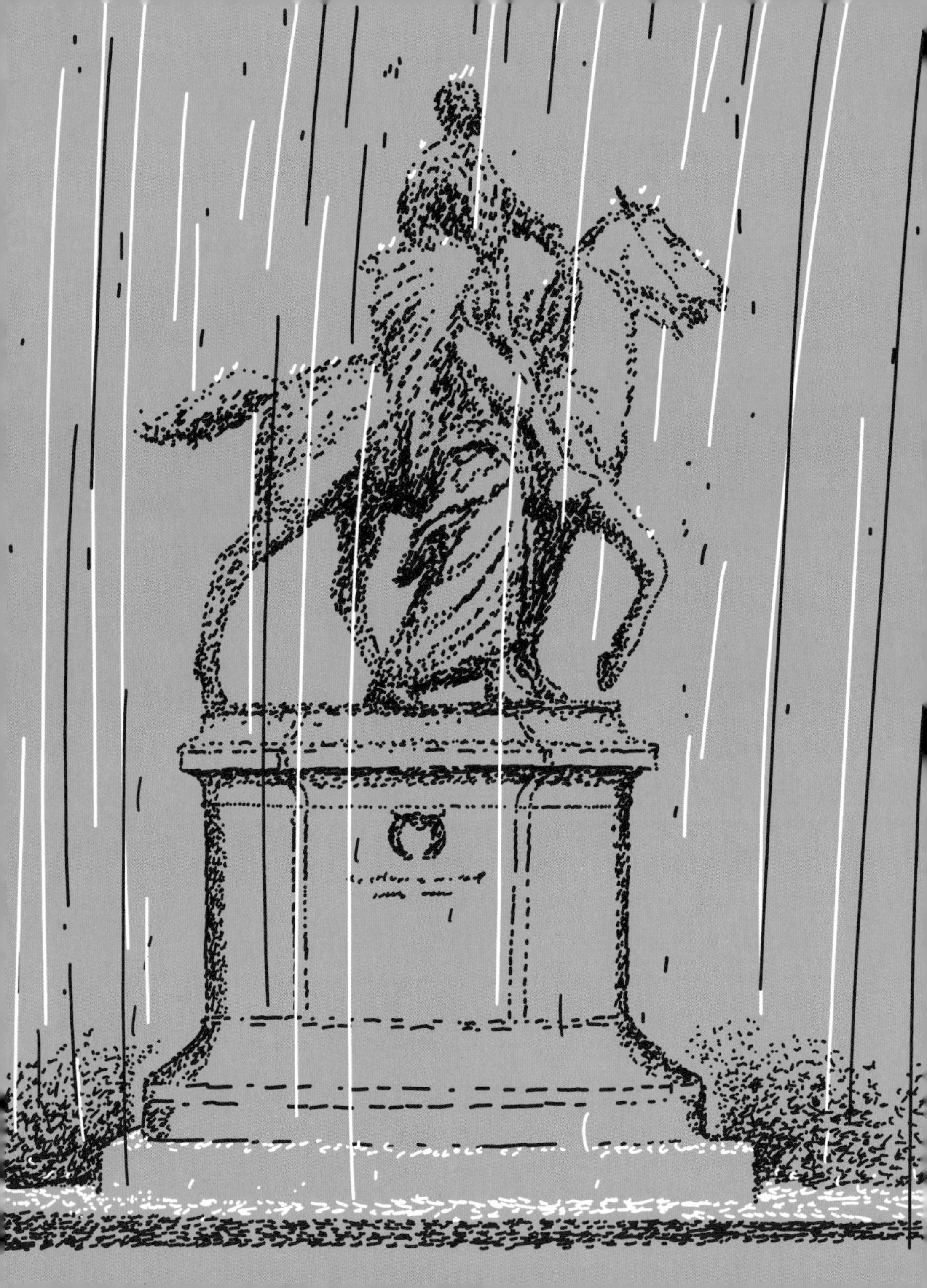

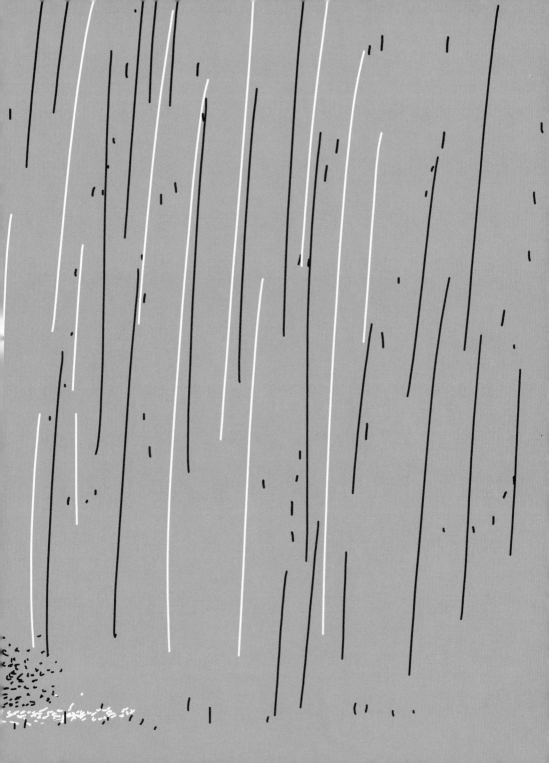

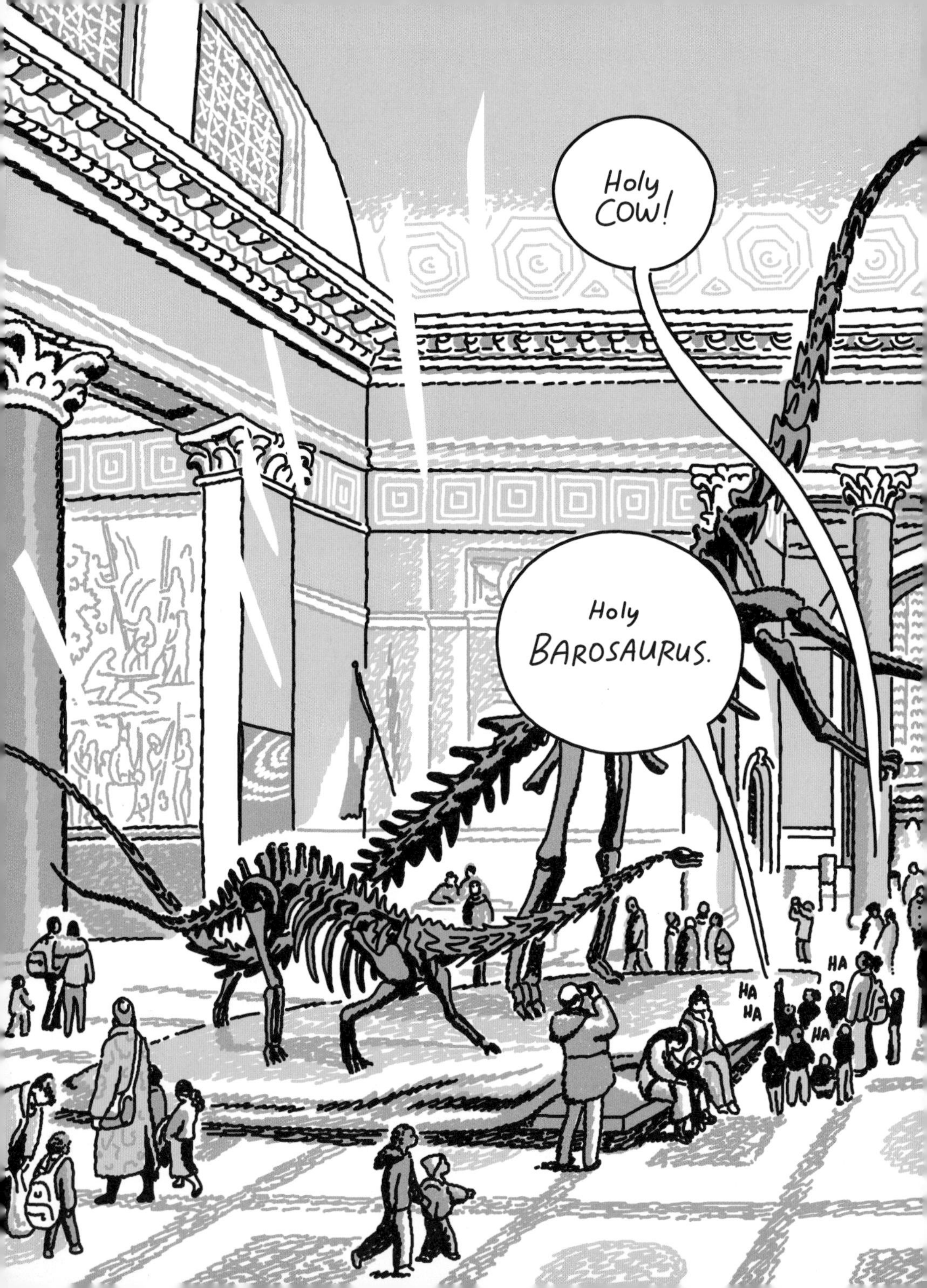
Holy COW!
Holy BAROSAURUS.
HA HA
HA
HA

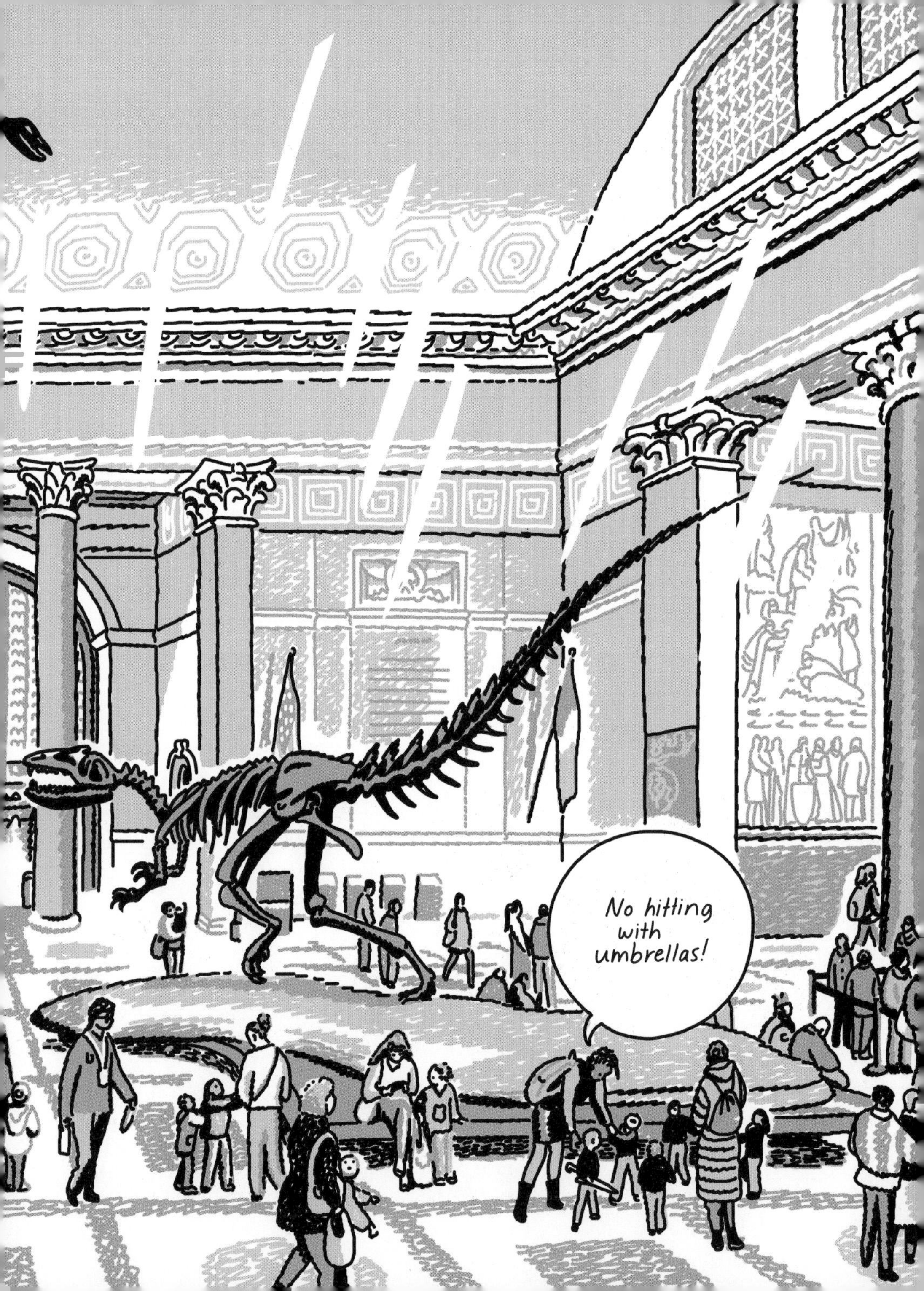
No hitting with umbrellas!

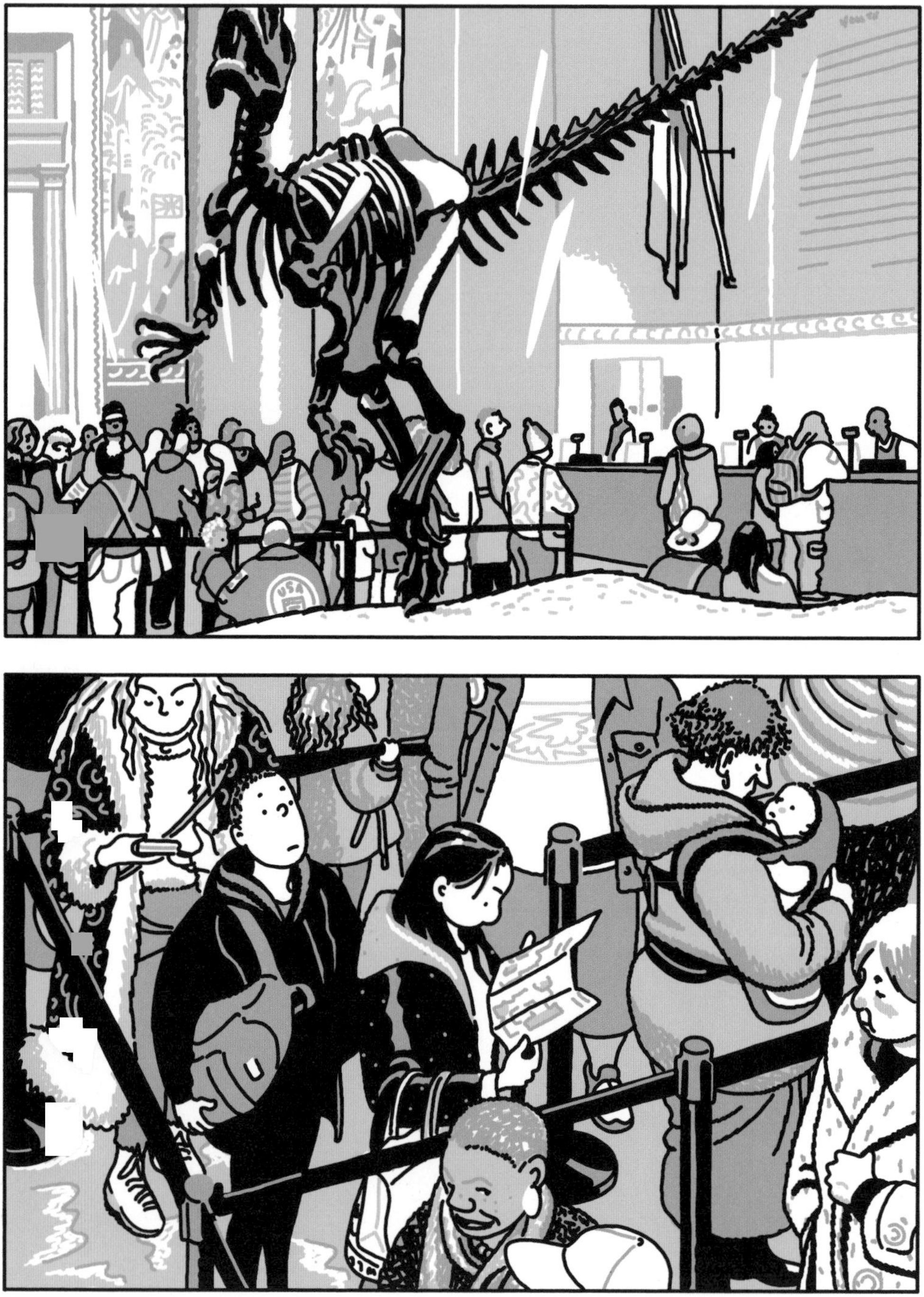

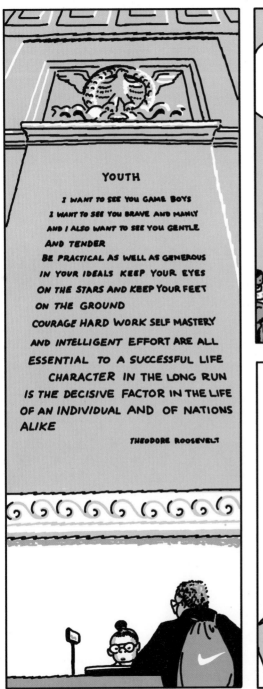

YOUTH

I want to see you game boys
I want to see you brave and manly
and I also want to see you gentle
and tender
Be practical as well as generous
in your ideals keep your eyes
on the stars and keep your feet
on the ground
Courage hard work self mastery
and intelligent effort are all
essential to a successful life
character in the long run
is the decisive factor in the life
of an individual and of nations
alike

THEODORE ROOSEVELT

I'm going to check these. It's only two bucks.

We'll meet you in the taxidermy hall.

It'll only be five minutes!

We'll wait in there!

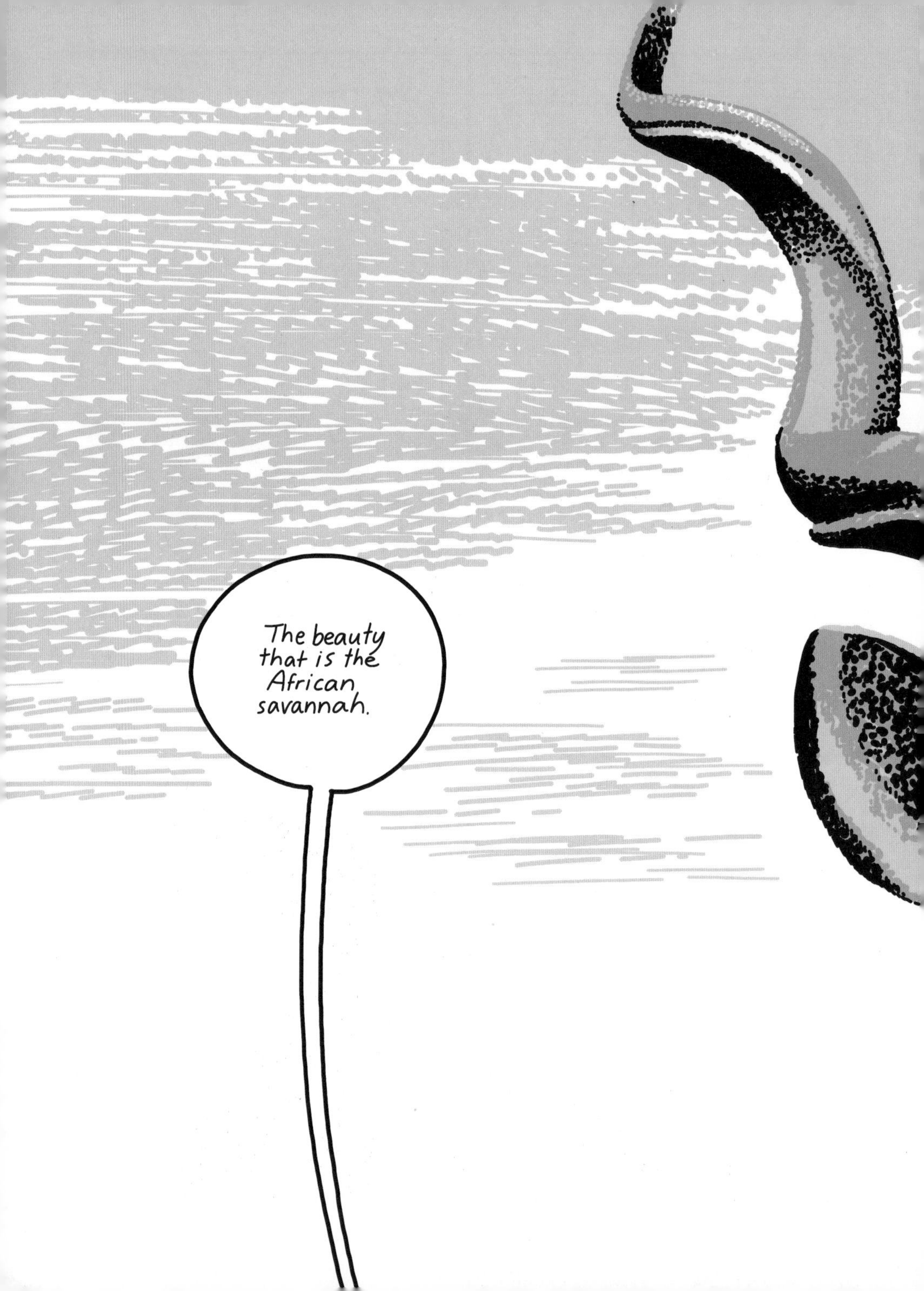
The beauty that is the African savannah.

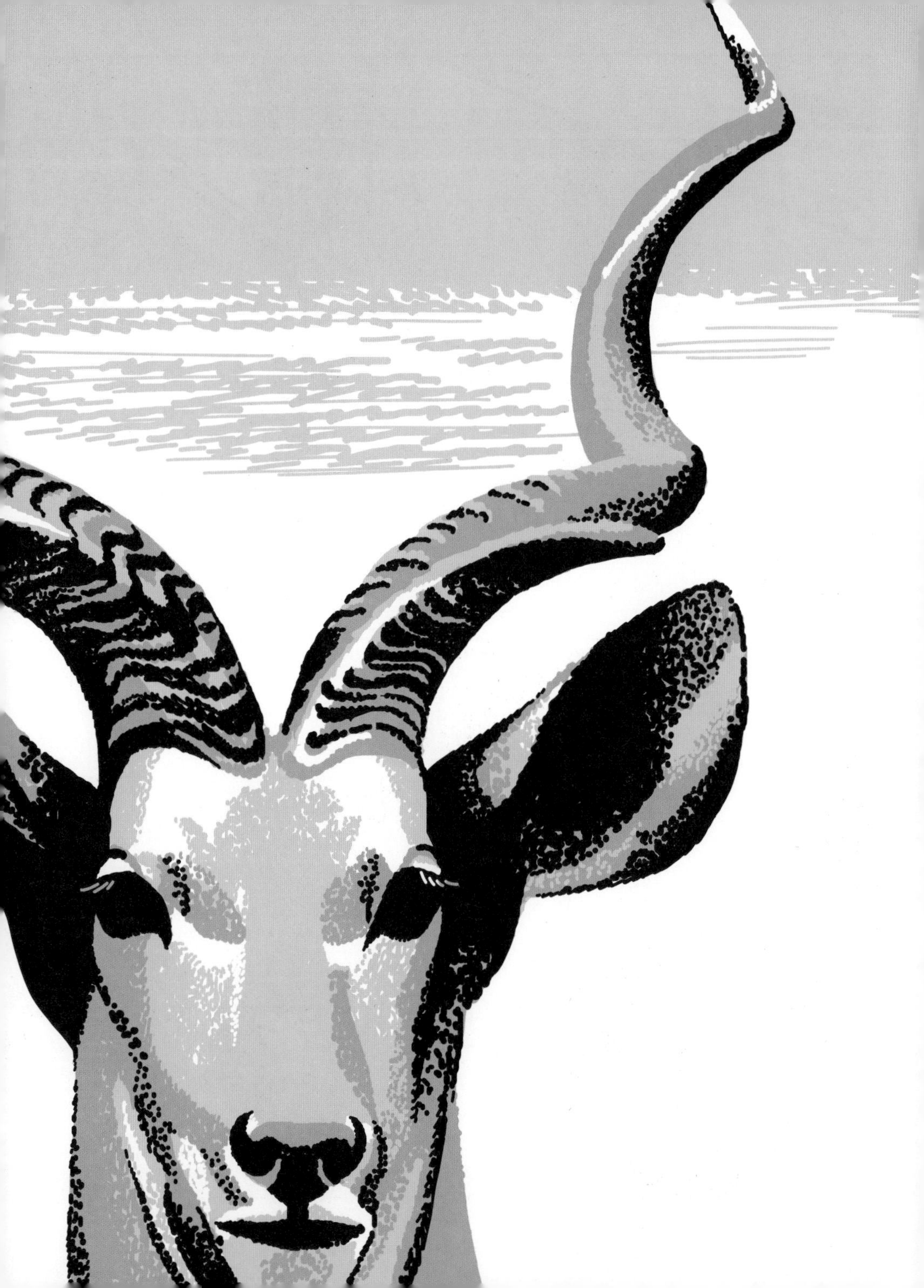

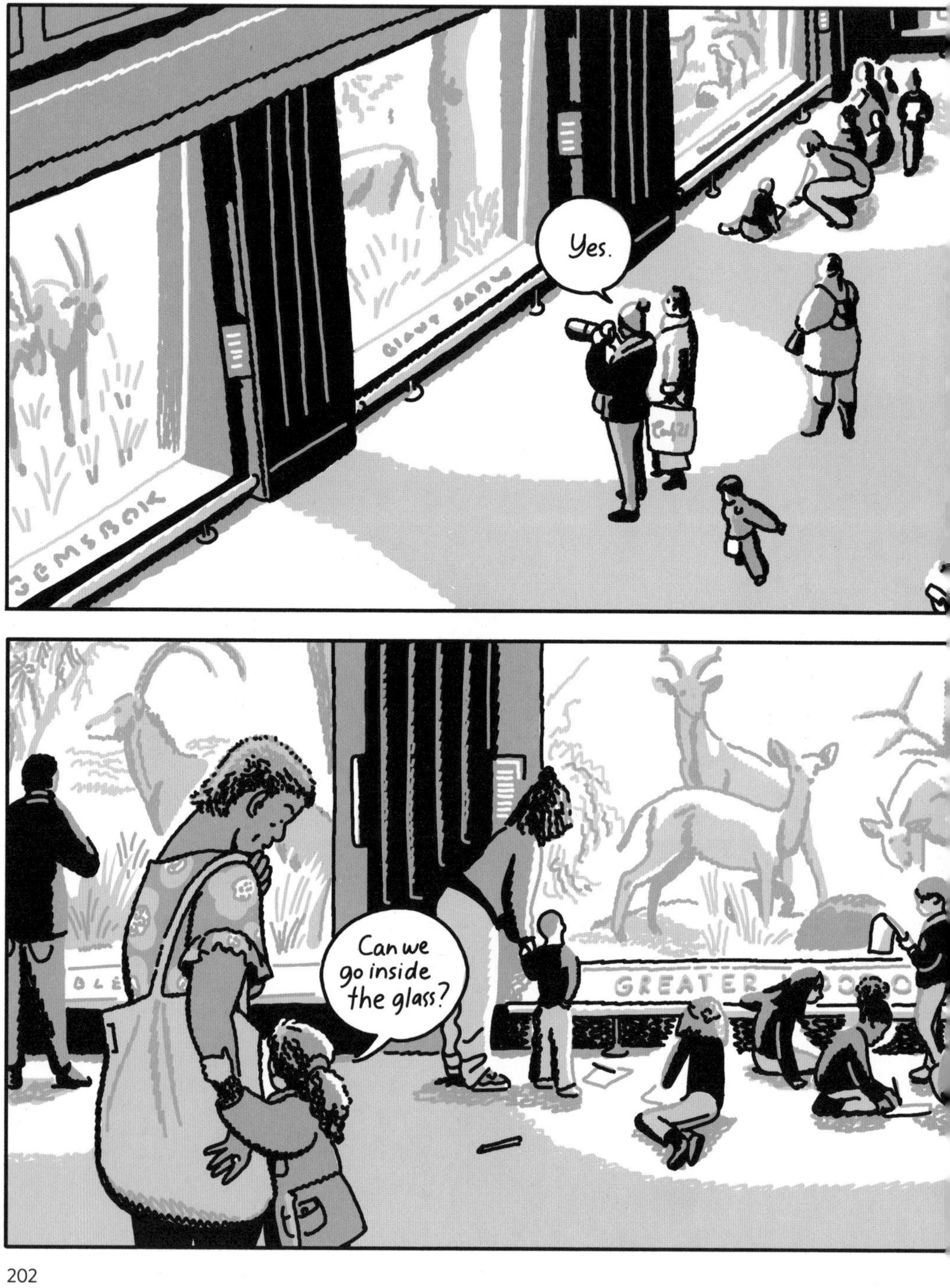
GEMSBOK
Yes.
Can we go inside the glass?
GREATER

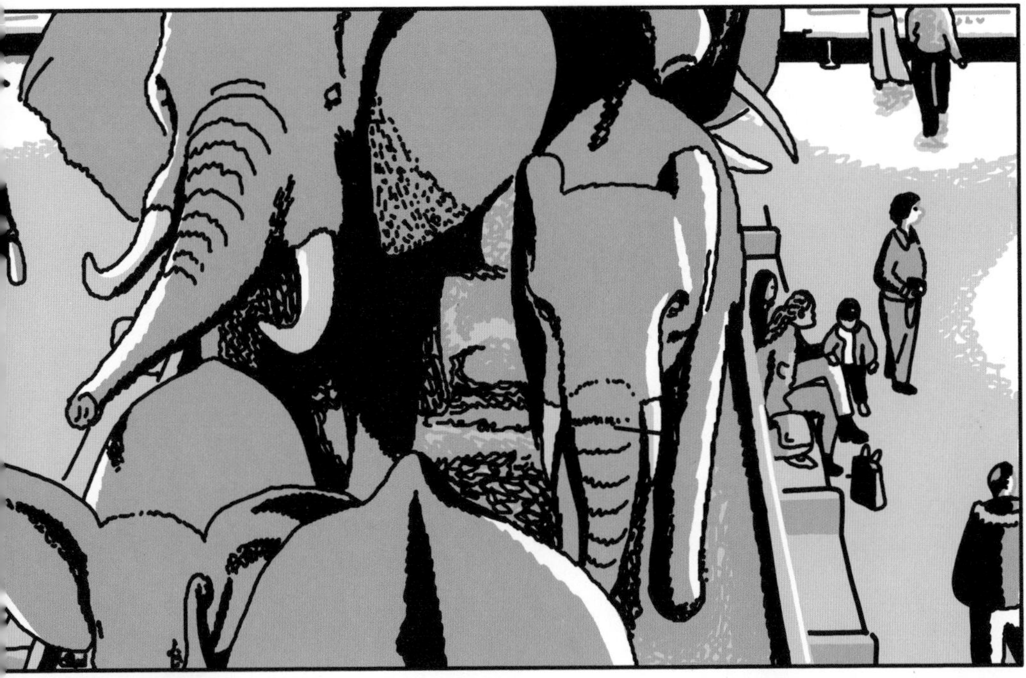

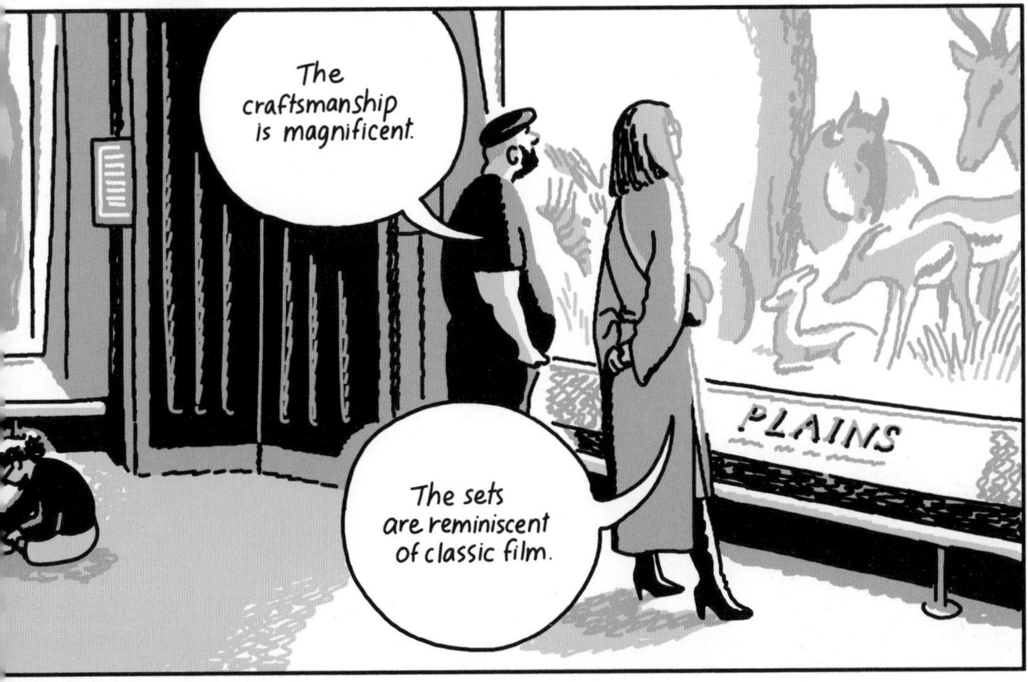
The craftsmanship is magnificent.
PLAINS
The sets are reminiscent of classic film.

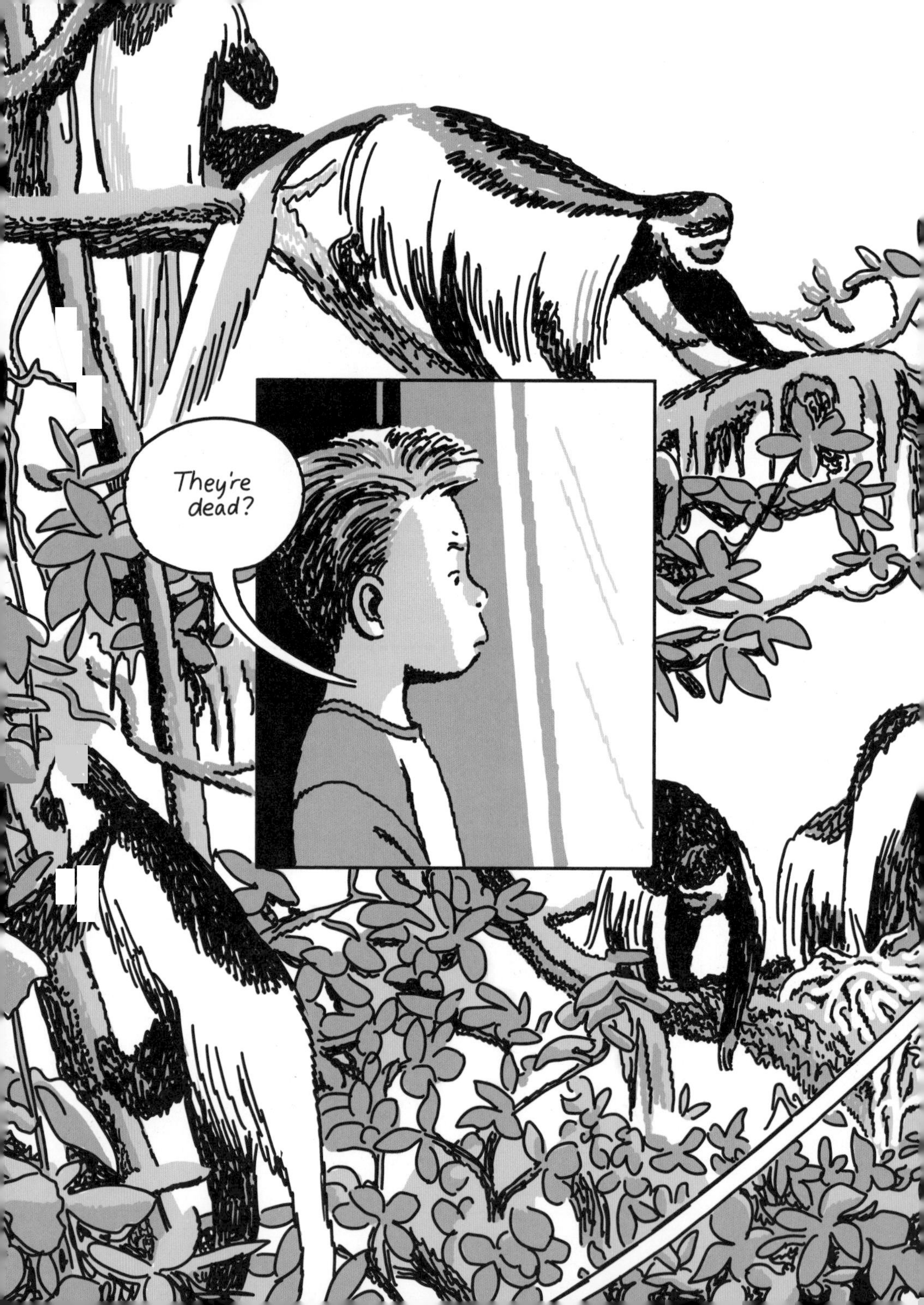
They're dead?

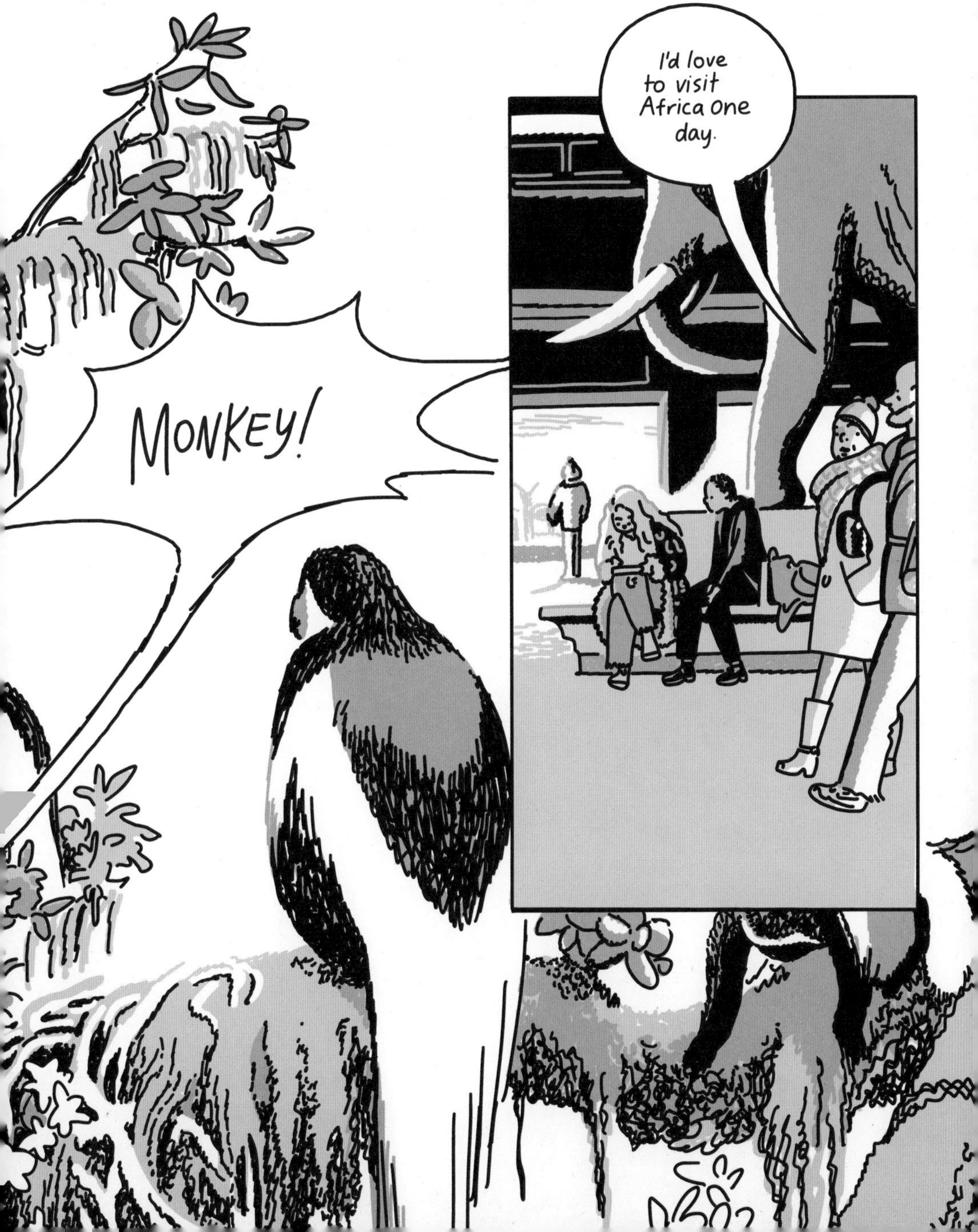
MONKEY!
I'd love to visit Africa one day.

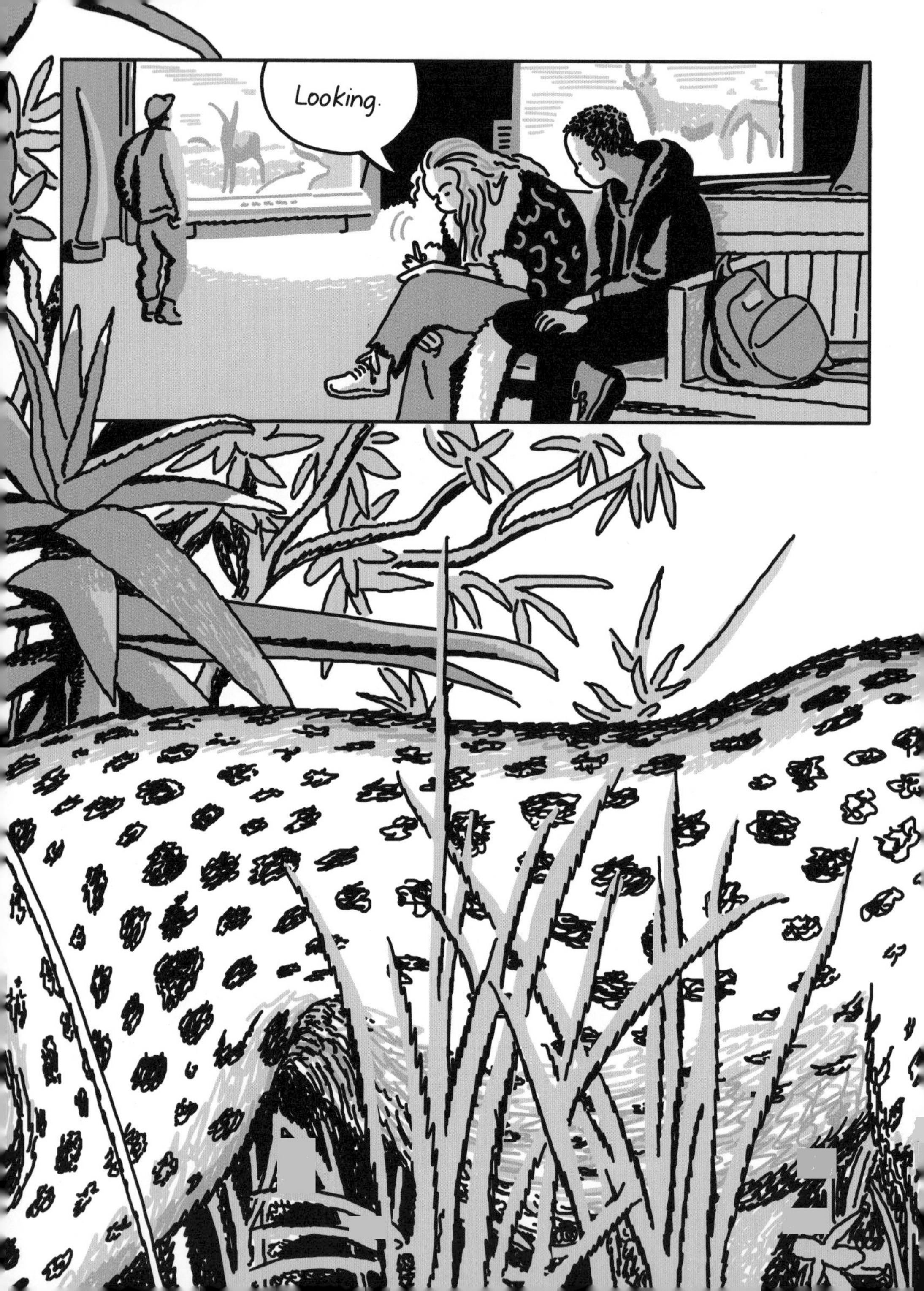
Looking.

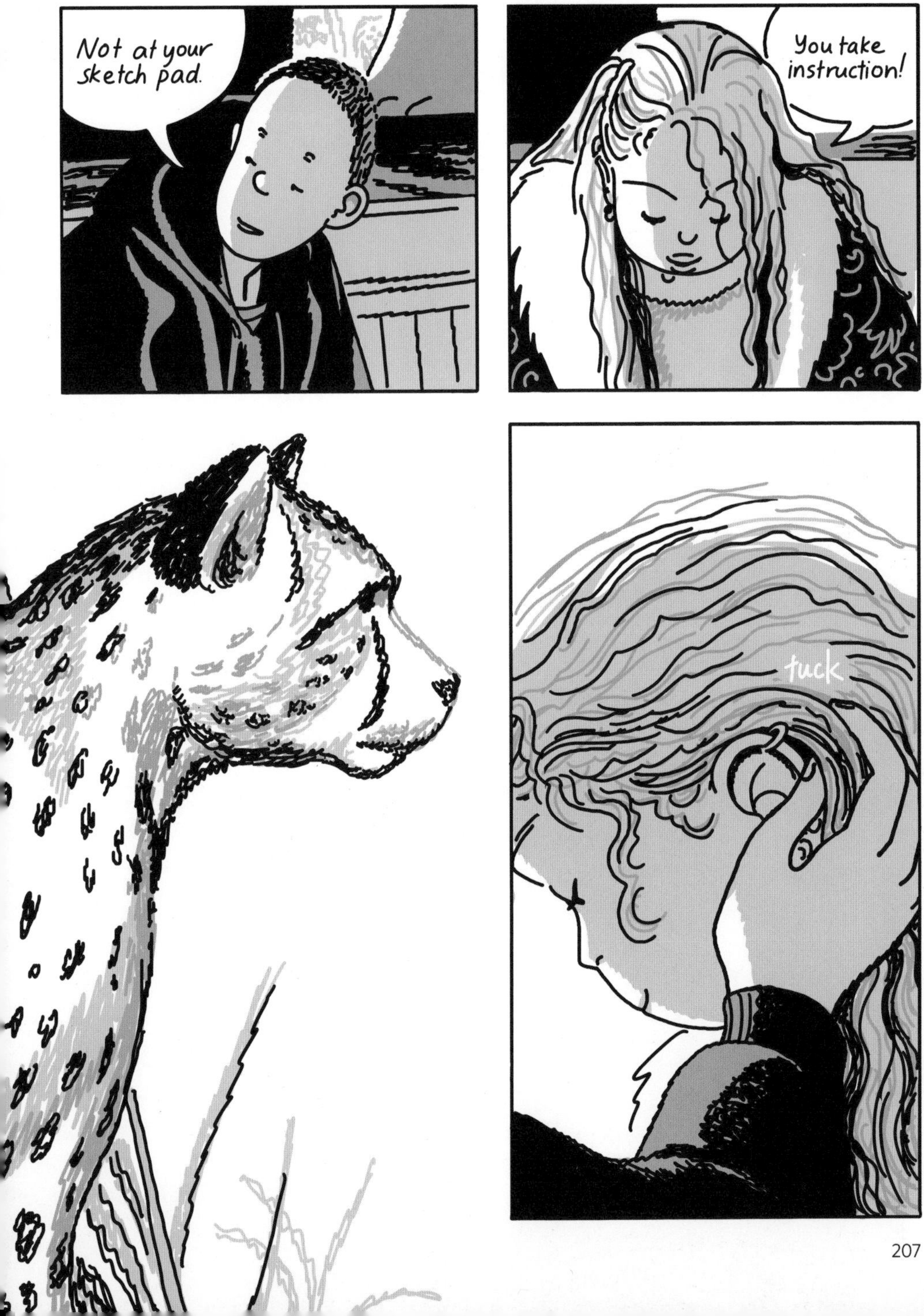
Not at your sketch pad.
You take instruction!
tuck

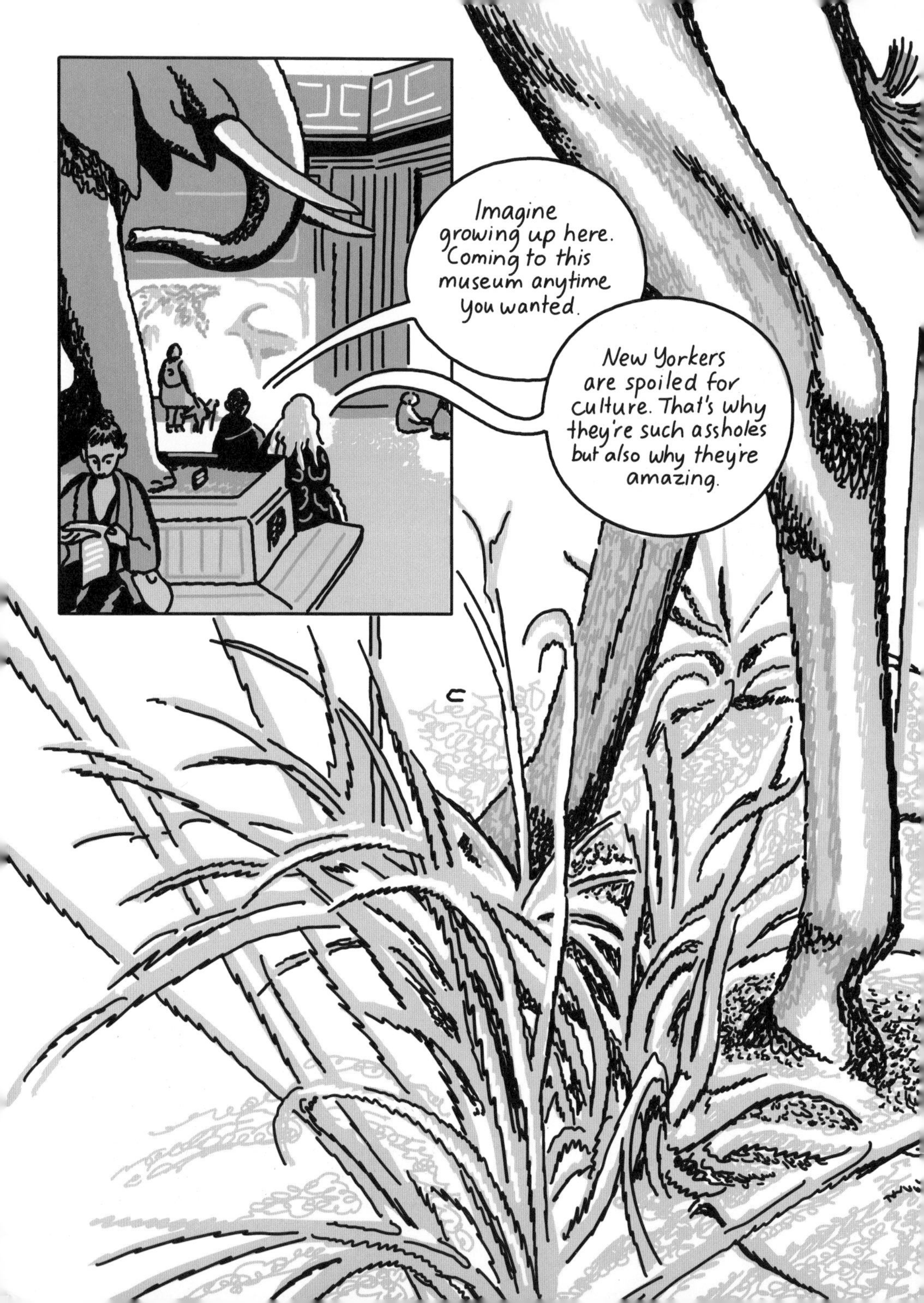
Imagine growing up here. Coming to this museum anytime you wanted.
New Yorkers are spoiled for culture. That's why they're such assholes but also why they're amazing.

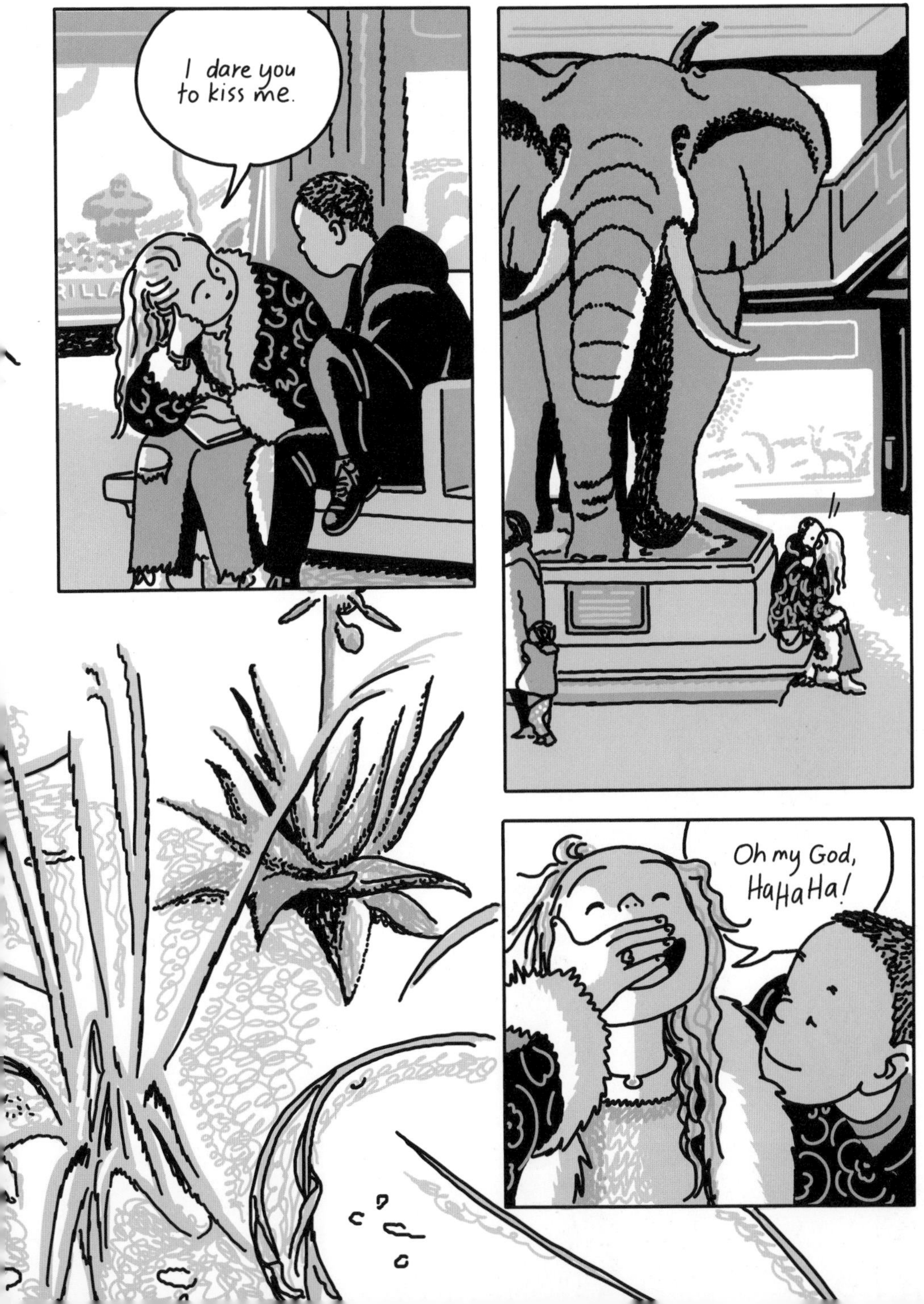
I dare you to kiss me.
Oh my God, HaHaHa!

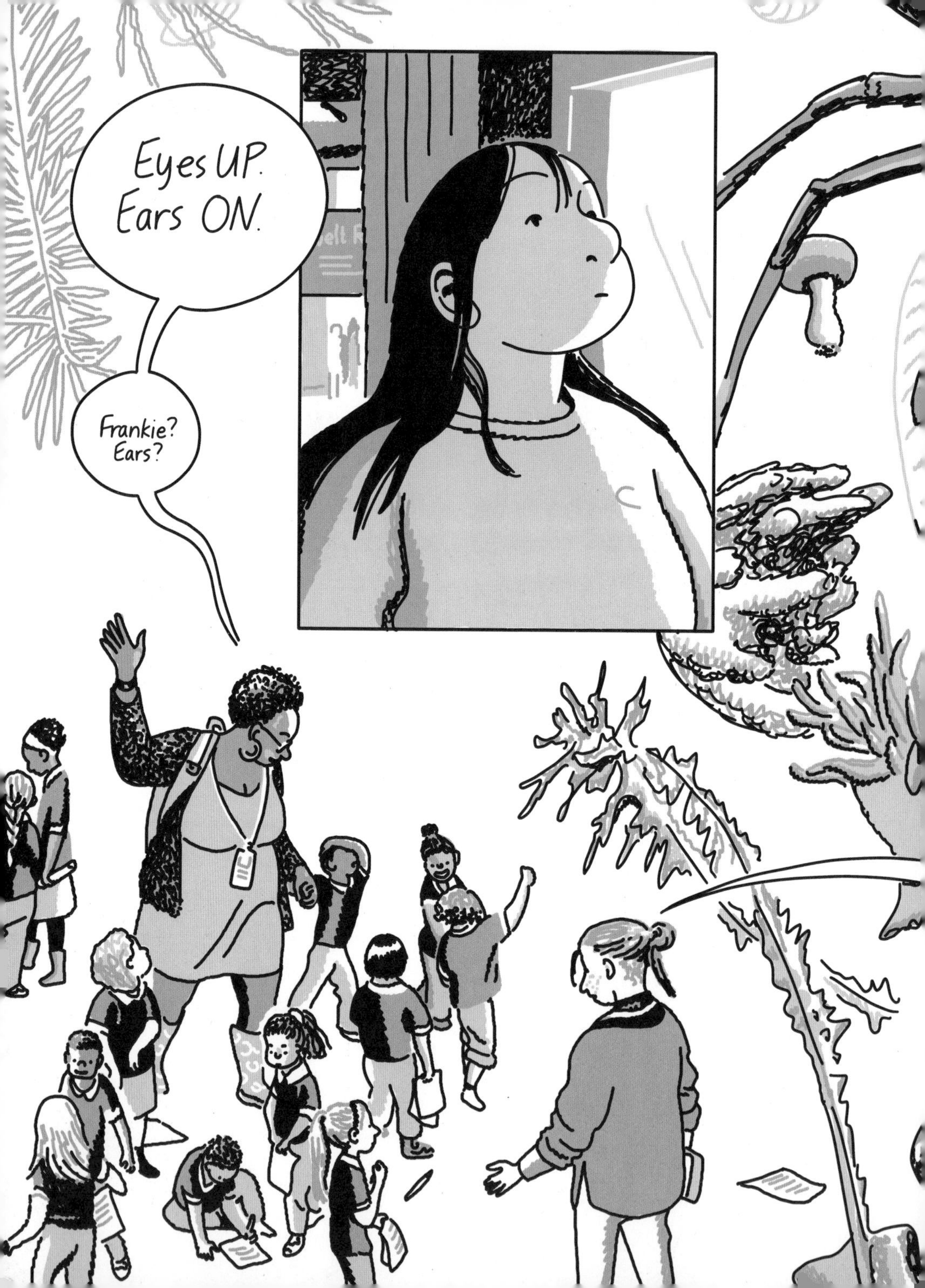
Eyes UP. Ears ON.
Frankie? Ears?

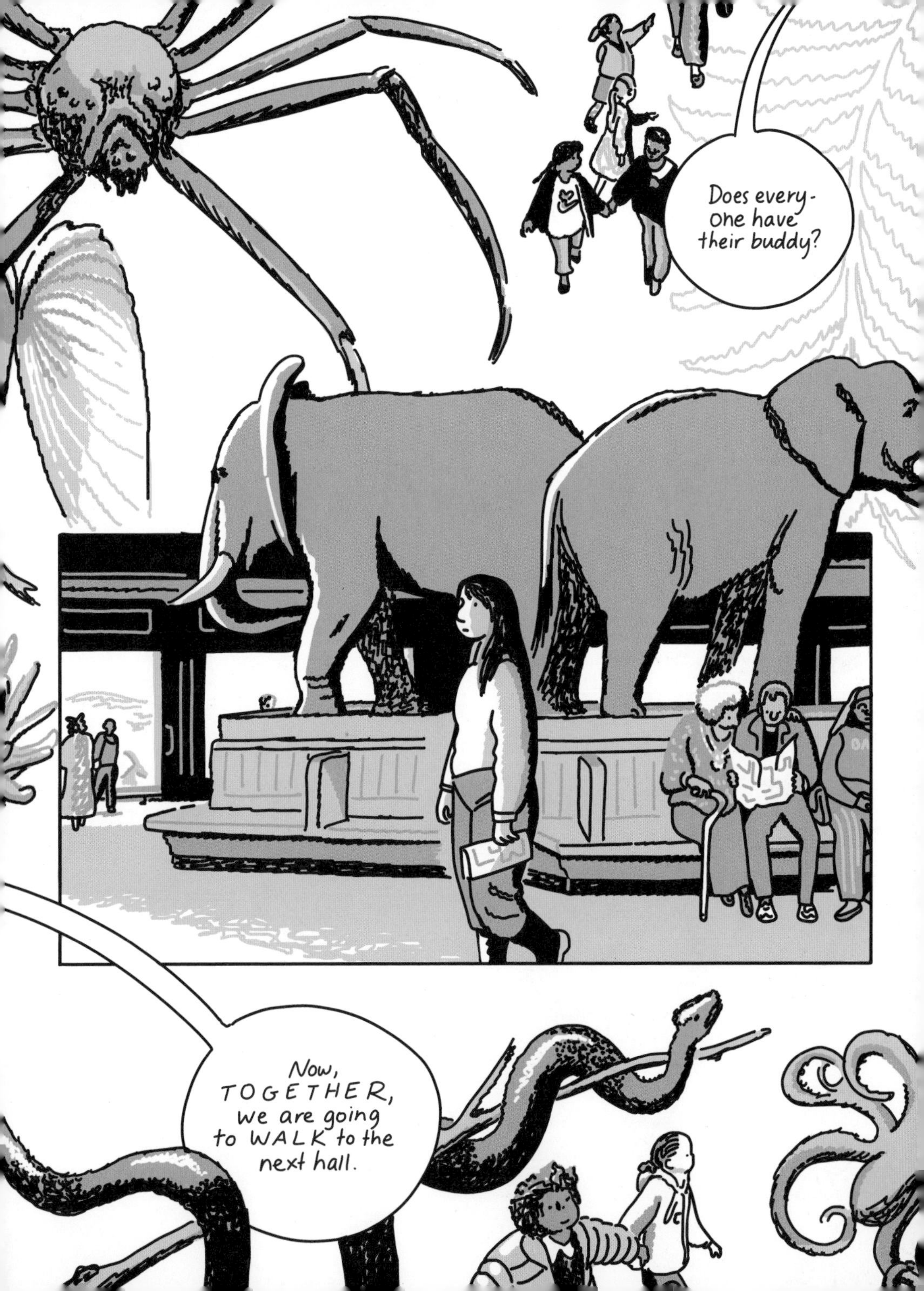
Does every-one have their buddy?
Now, TOGETHER, we are going to WALK to the next hall.

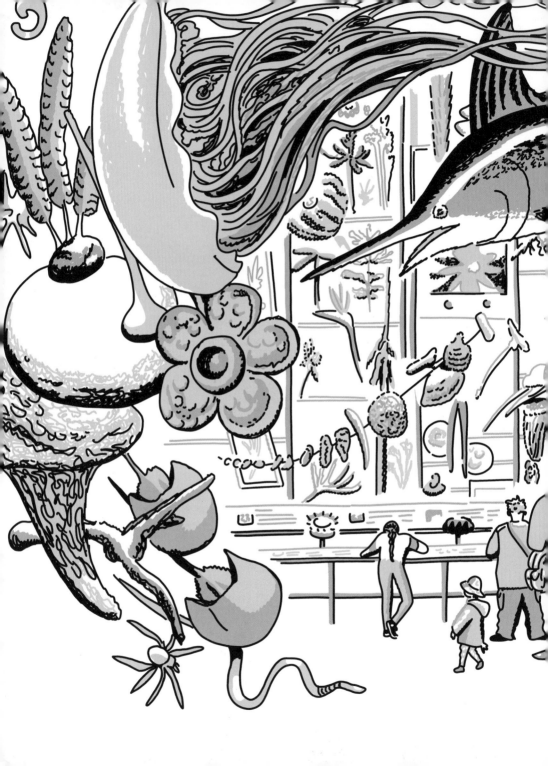

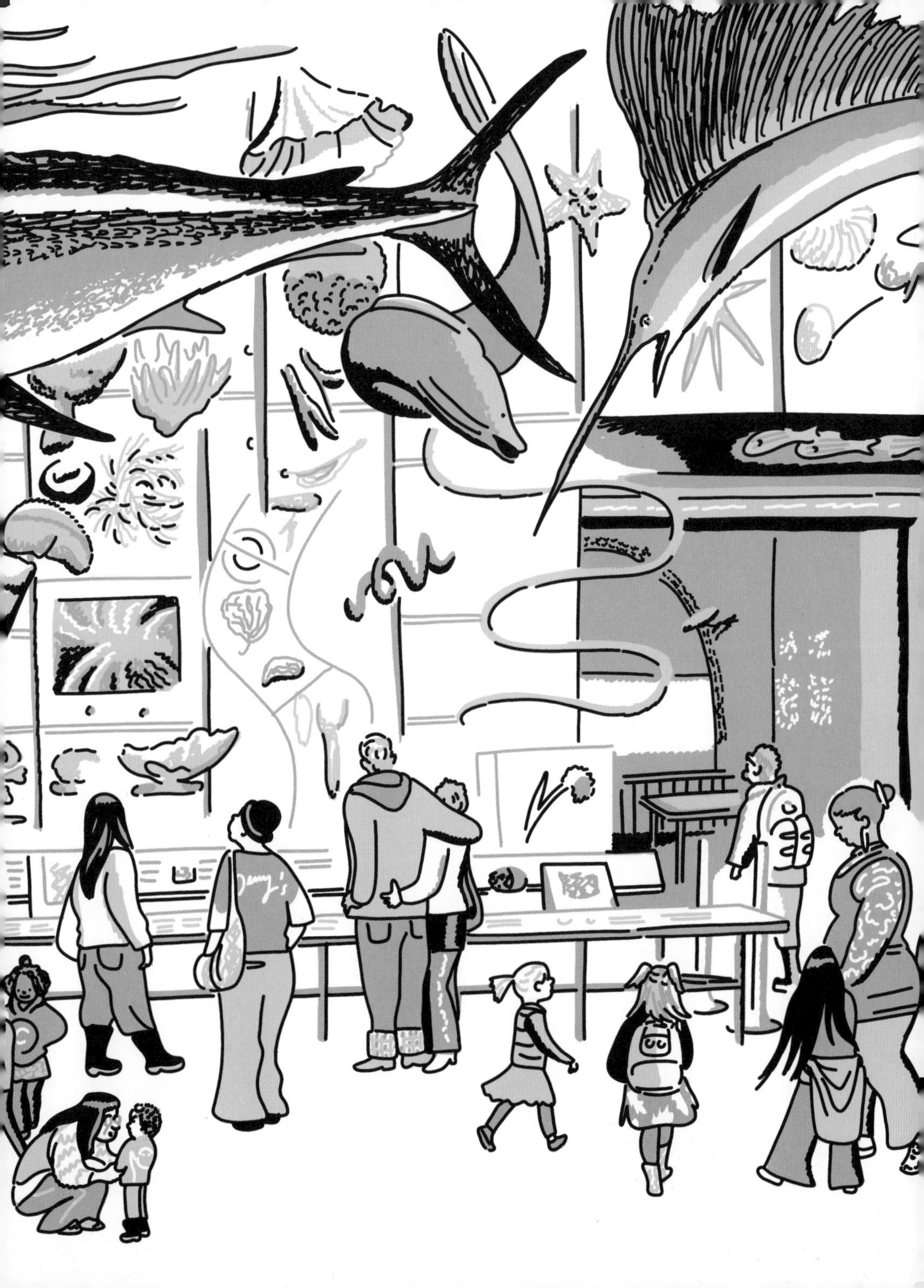

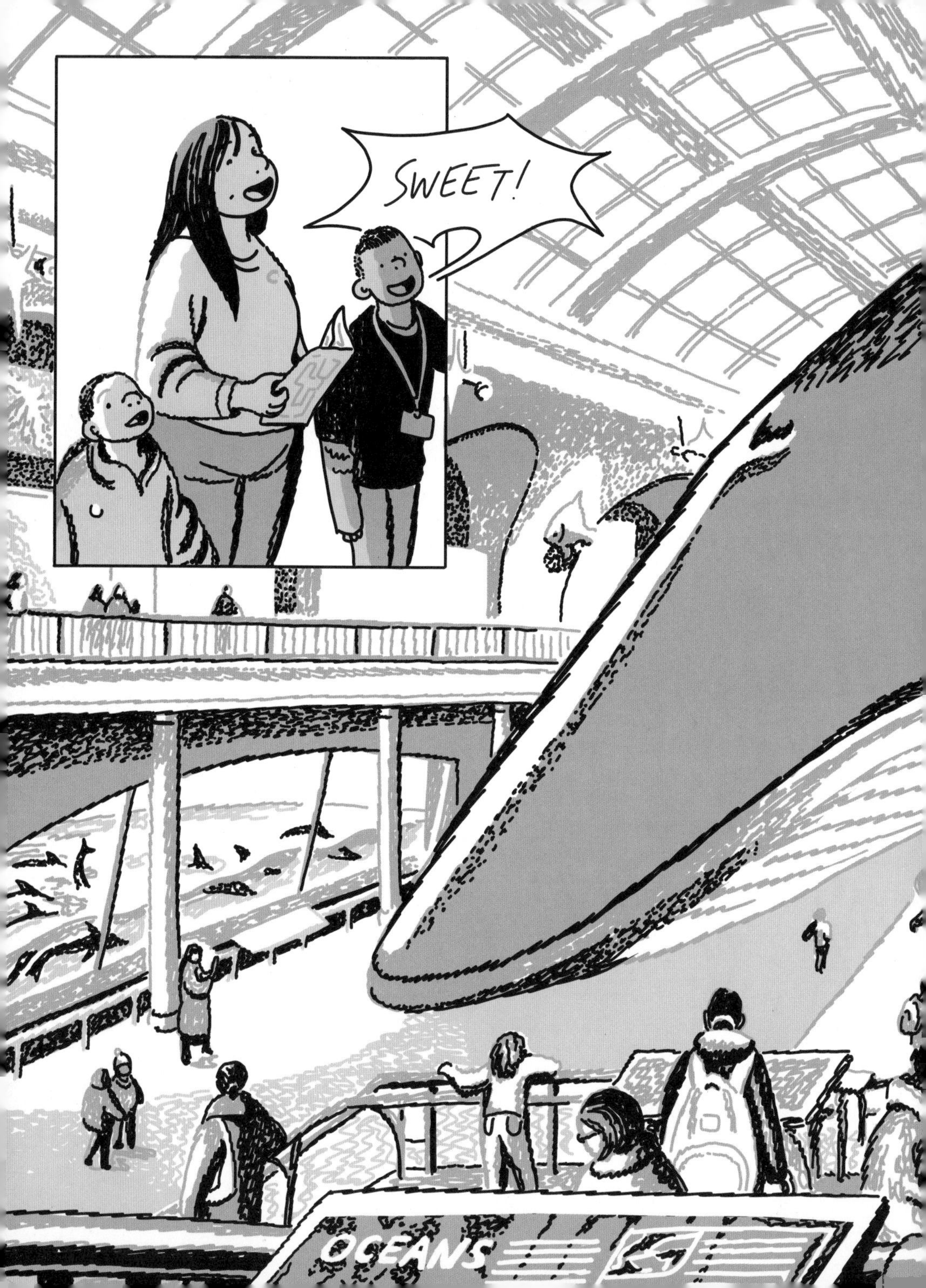
SWEET!
OCEANS

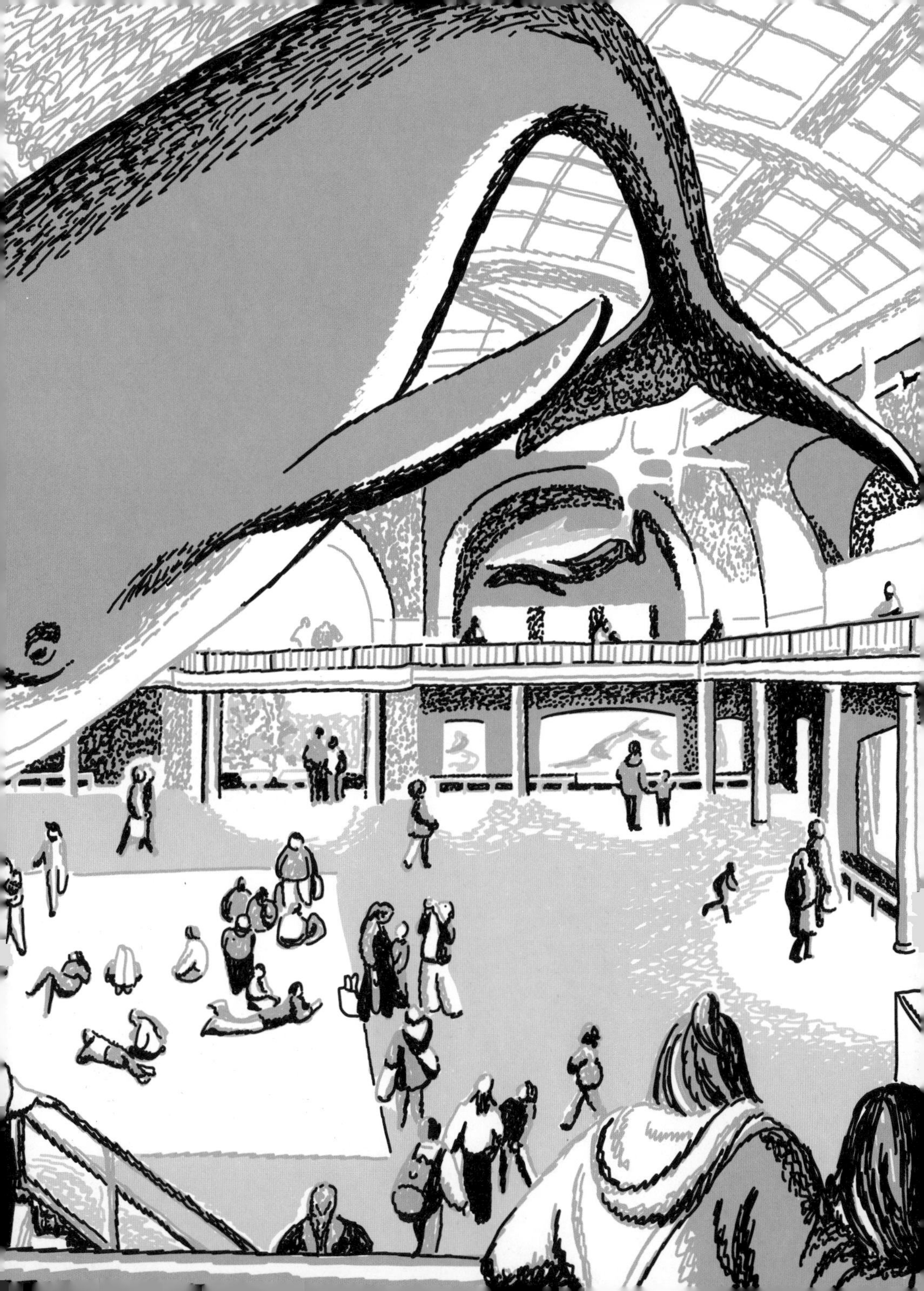

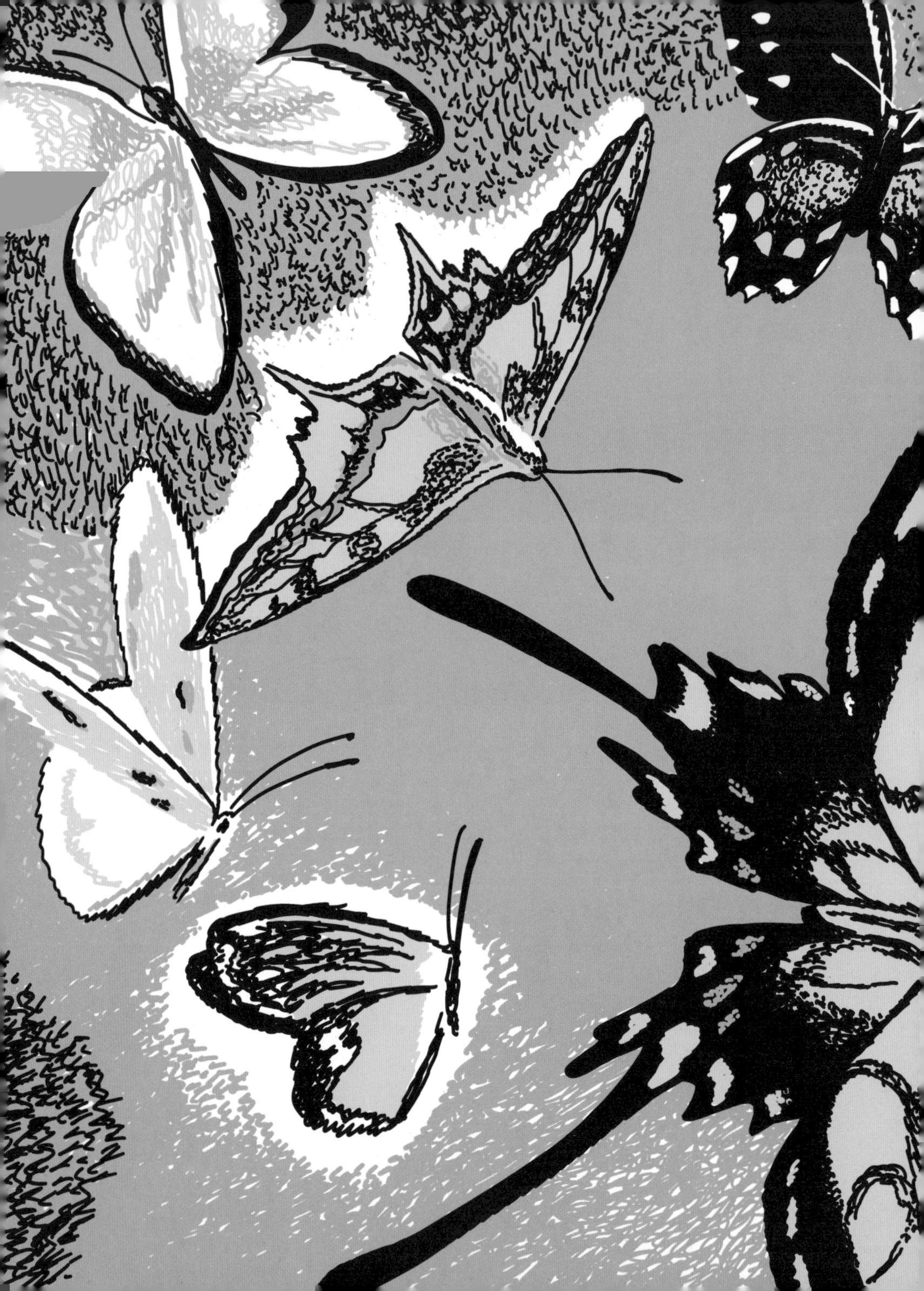

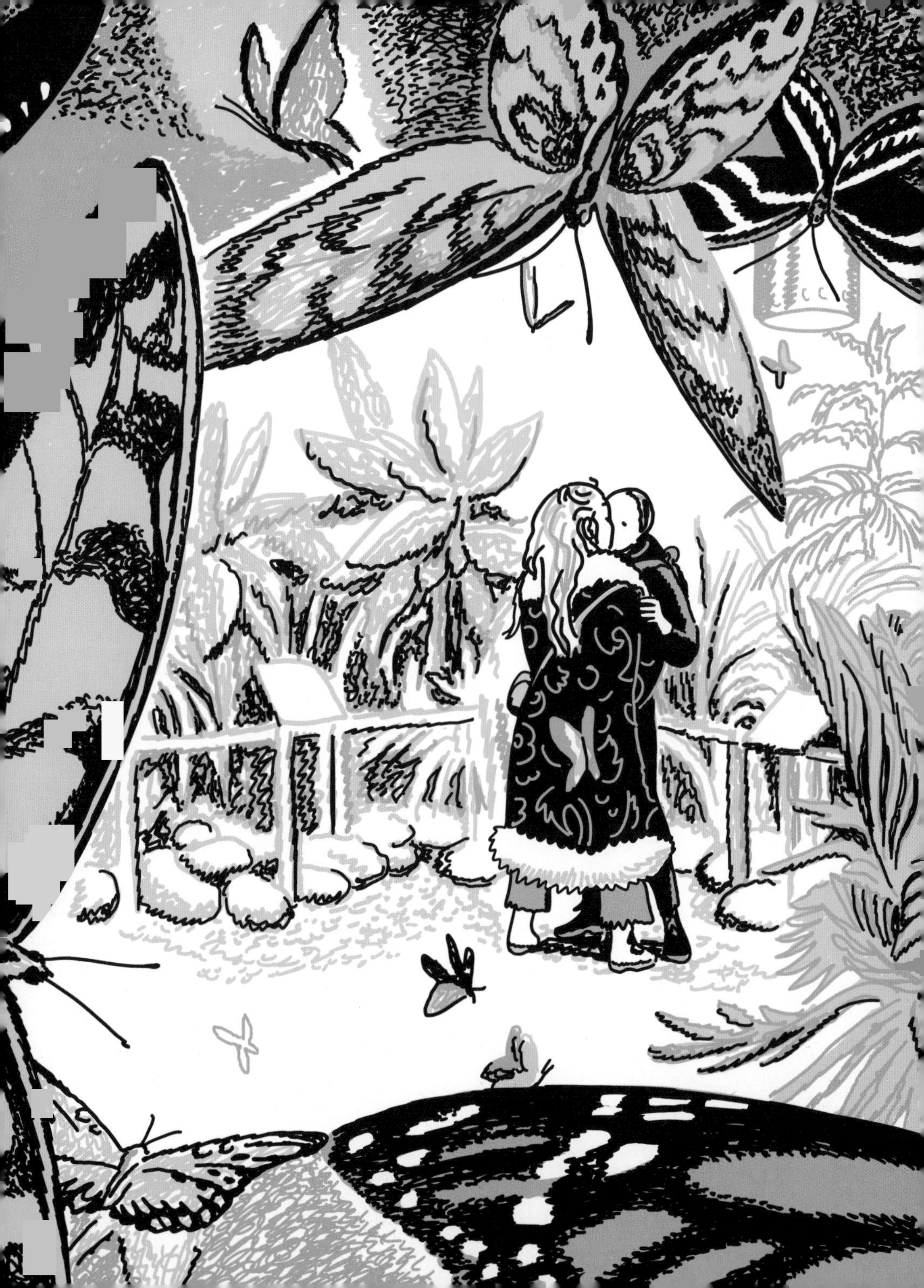

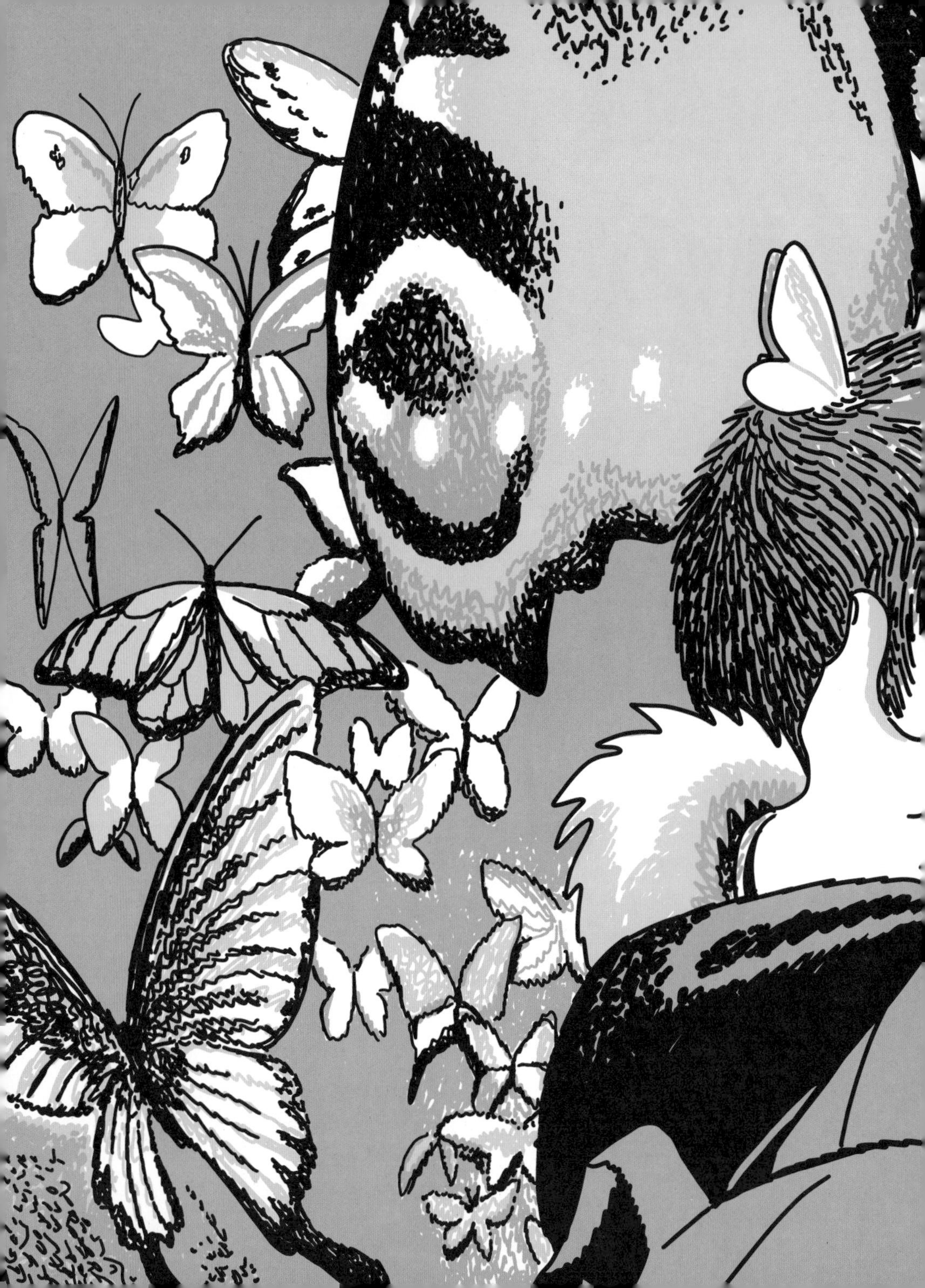

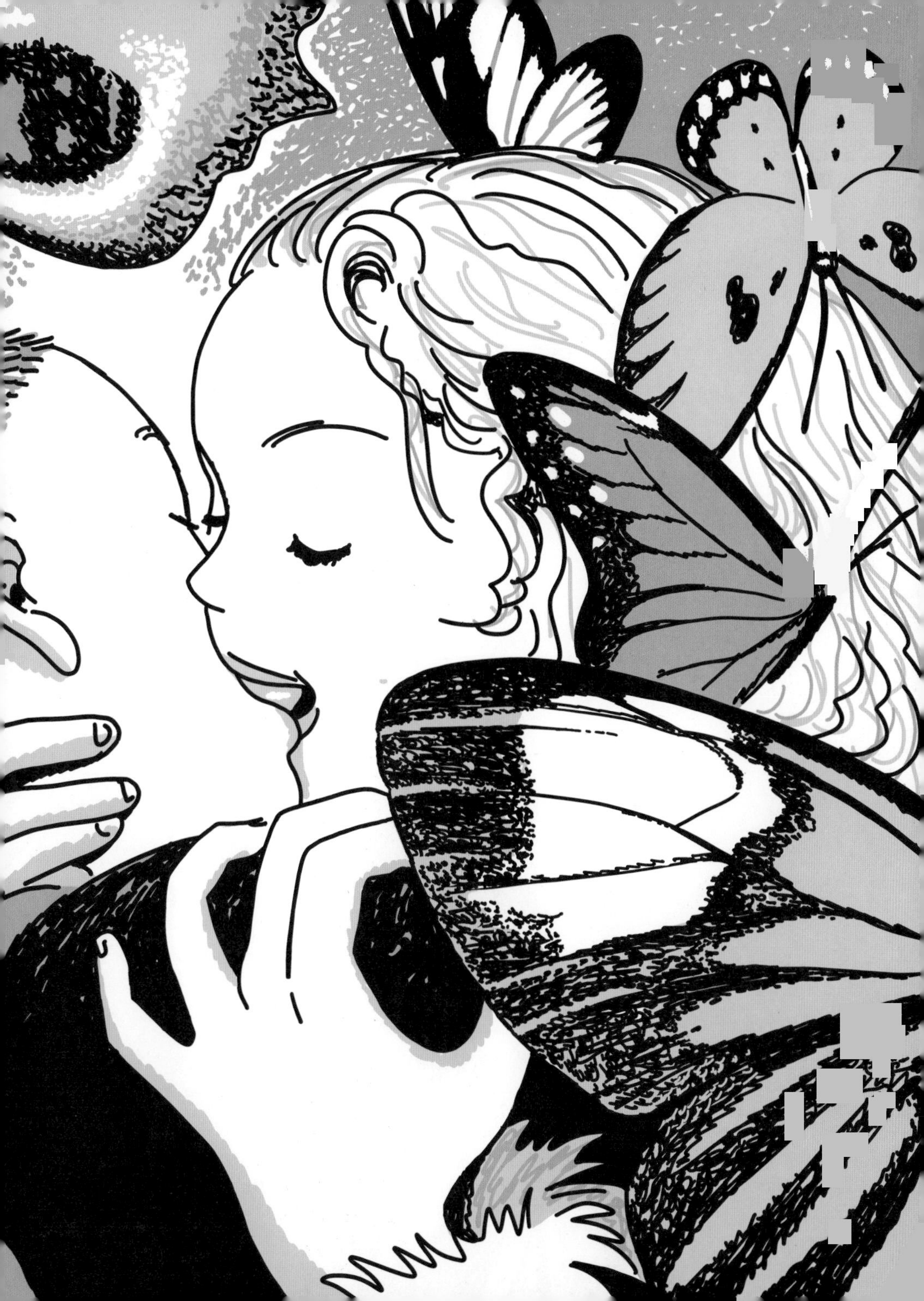

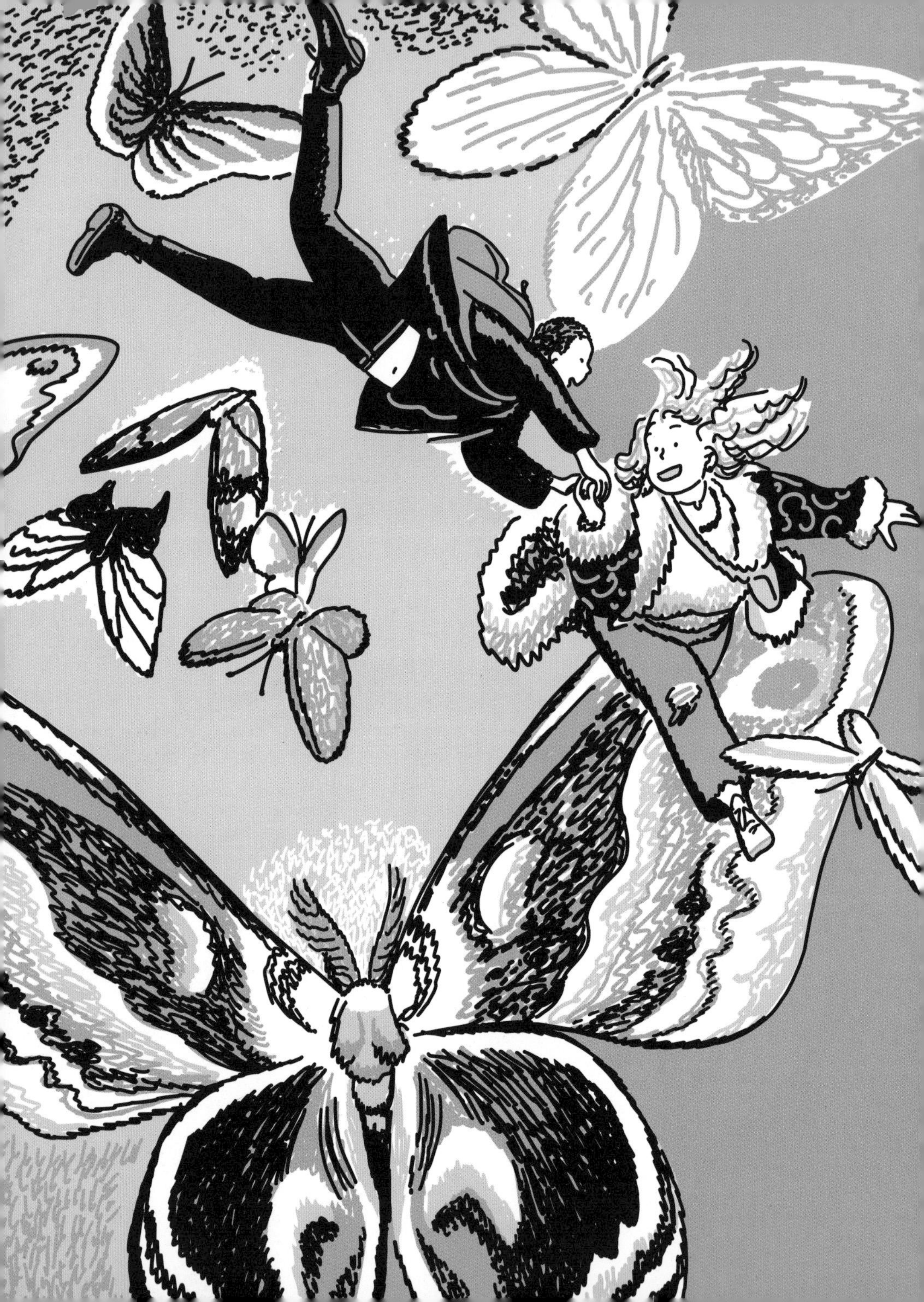

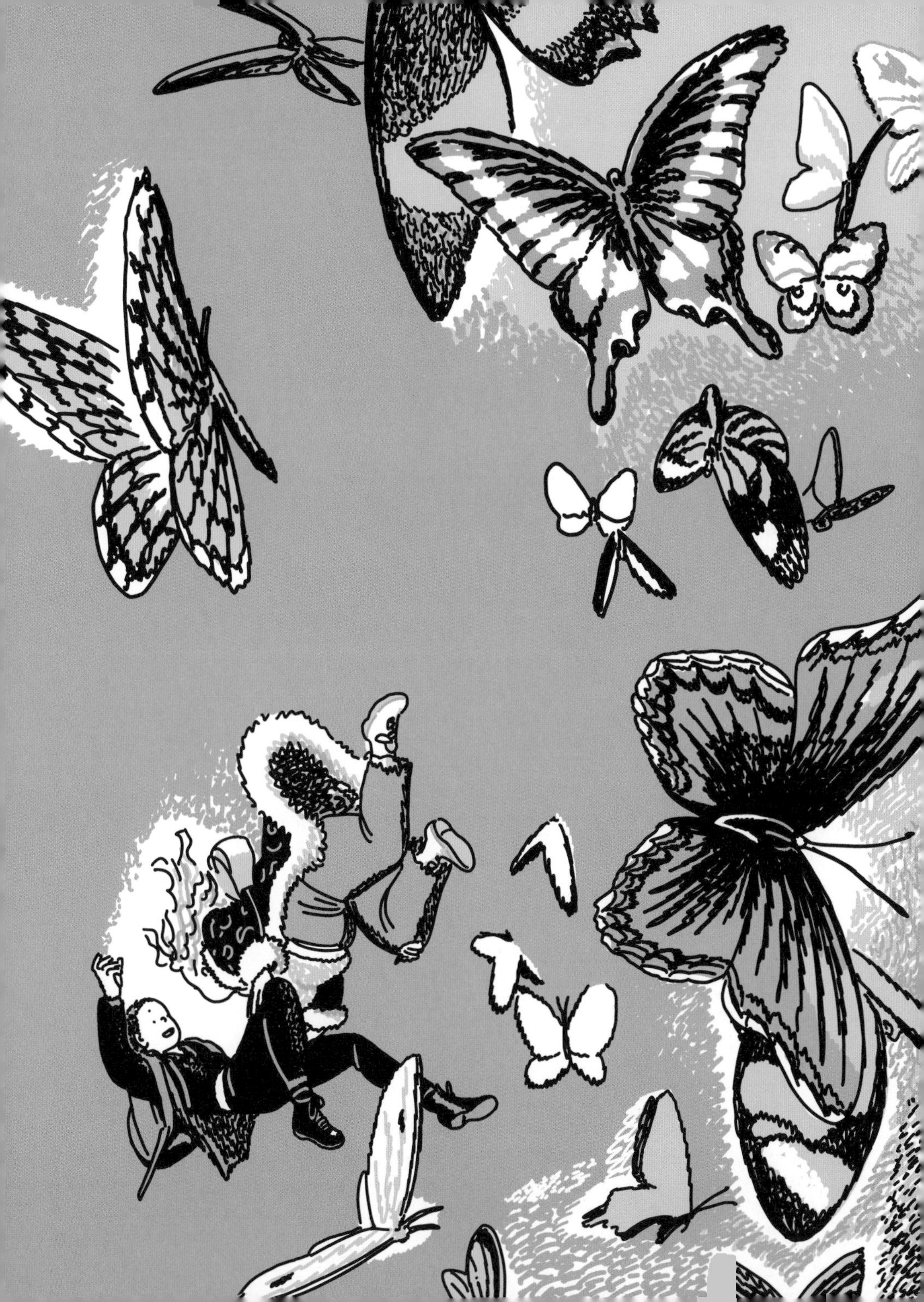

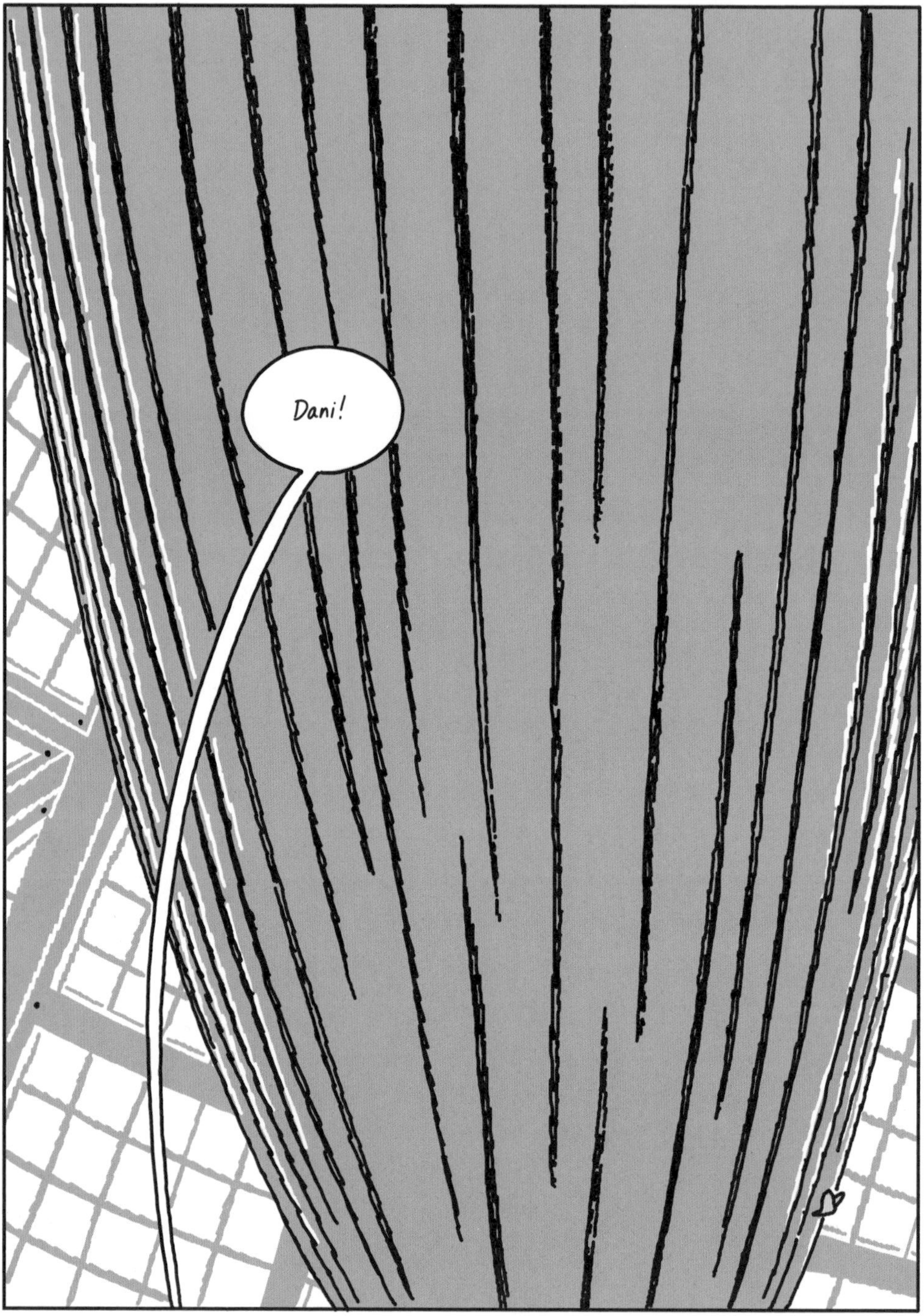
Dani!

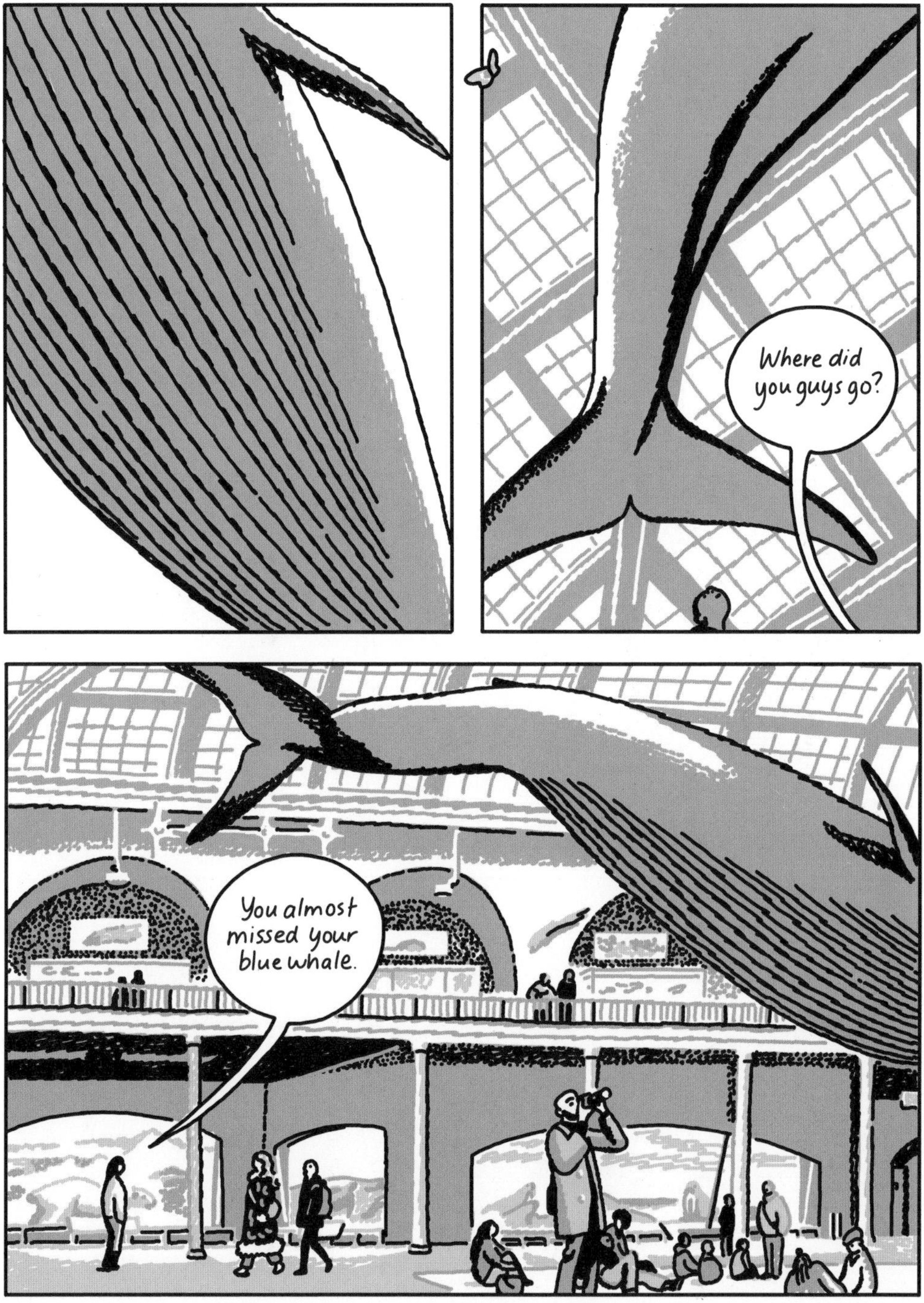
Where did you guys go?
You almost missed your blue whale.

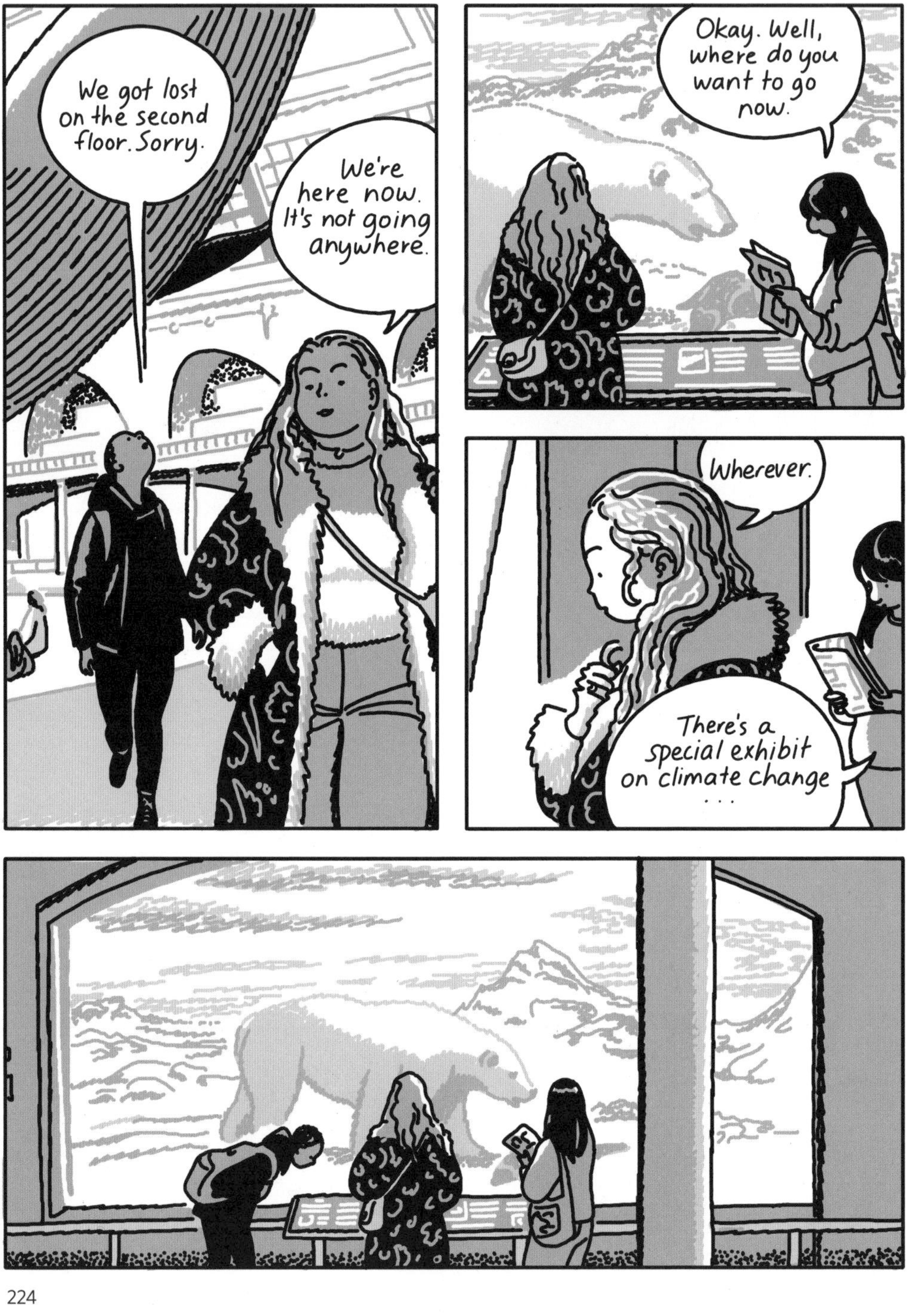
We got lost on the second floor. Sorry.
We're here now. It's not going anywhere.
Okay. Well, where do you want to go now.
Wherever.
There's a special exhibit on climate change . . .

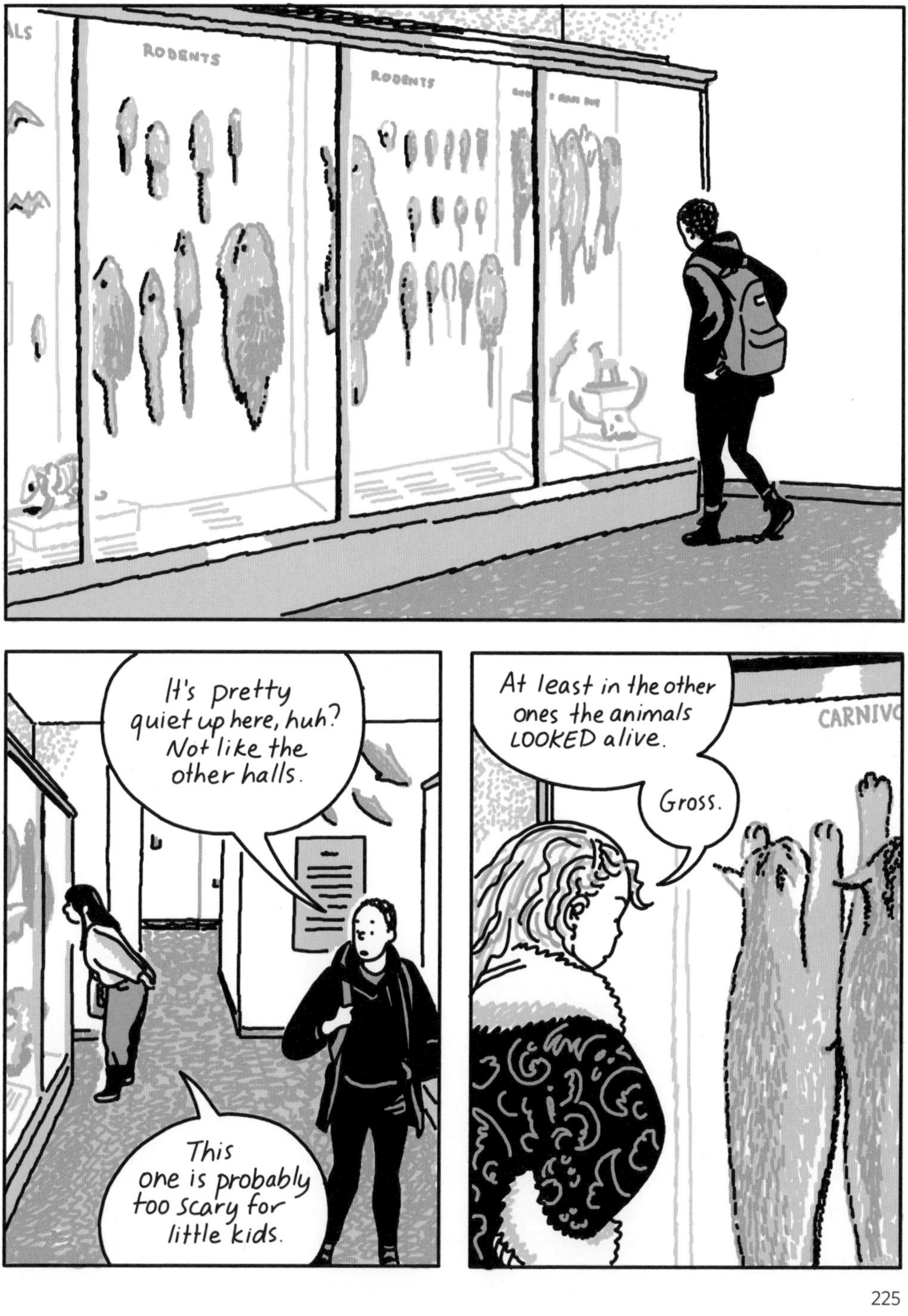
RODENTS
RODENTS
It's pretty quiet up here, huh? Not like the other halls.
This one is probably too scary for little kids.
At least in the other ones the animals LOOKED alive.
Gross.

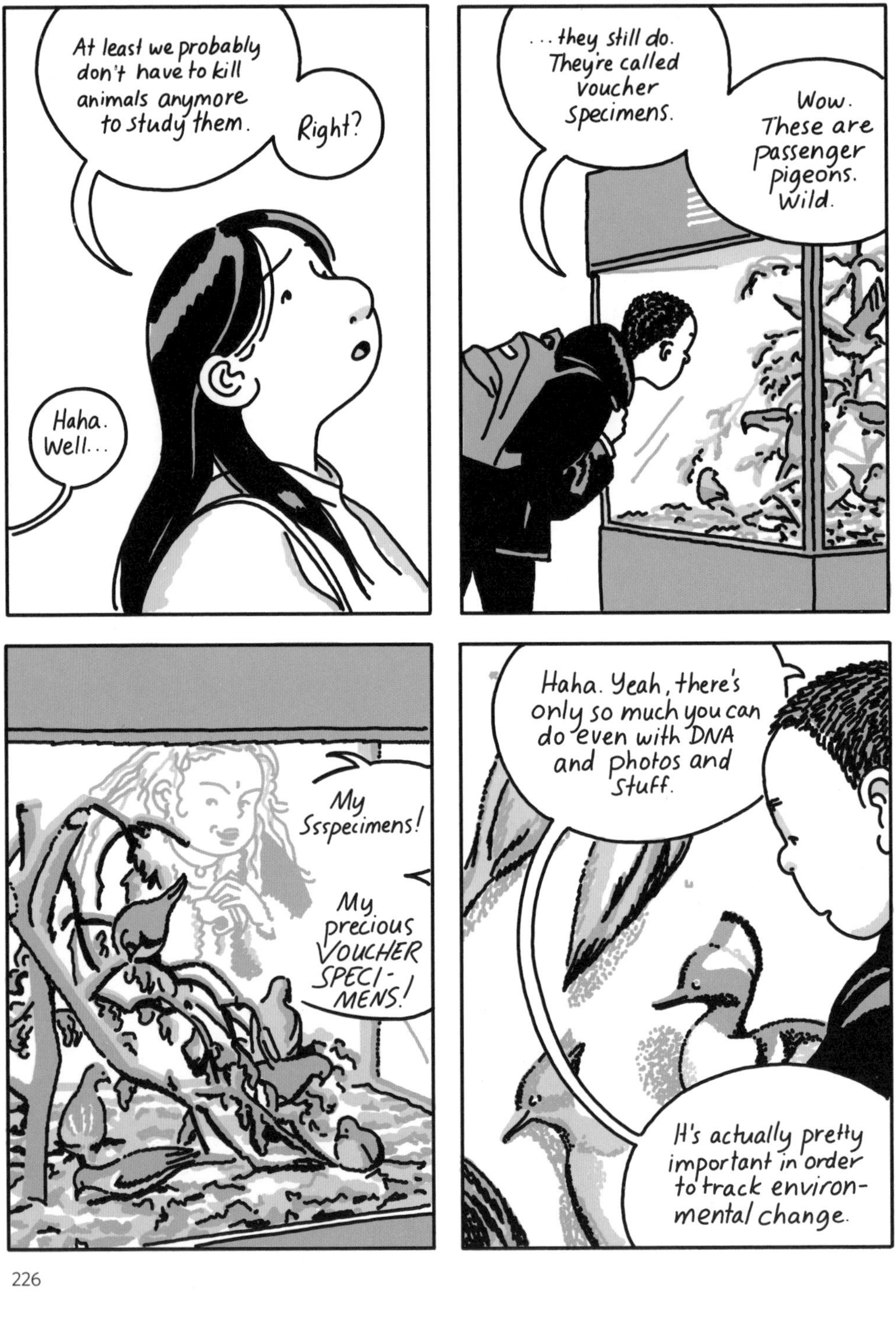
At least we probably don't have to kill animals anymore to study them.
Right?
Haha. Well...
...they still do. They're called voucher specimens.
Wow. These are passenger pigeons. Wild.
My Ssspecimens!
My precious VOUCHER SPECI-MENS!
Haha. Yeah, there's only so much you can do even with DNA and photos and stuff.
It's actually pretty important in order to track environ-mental change.

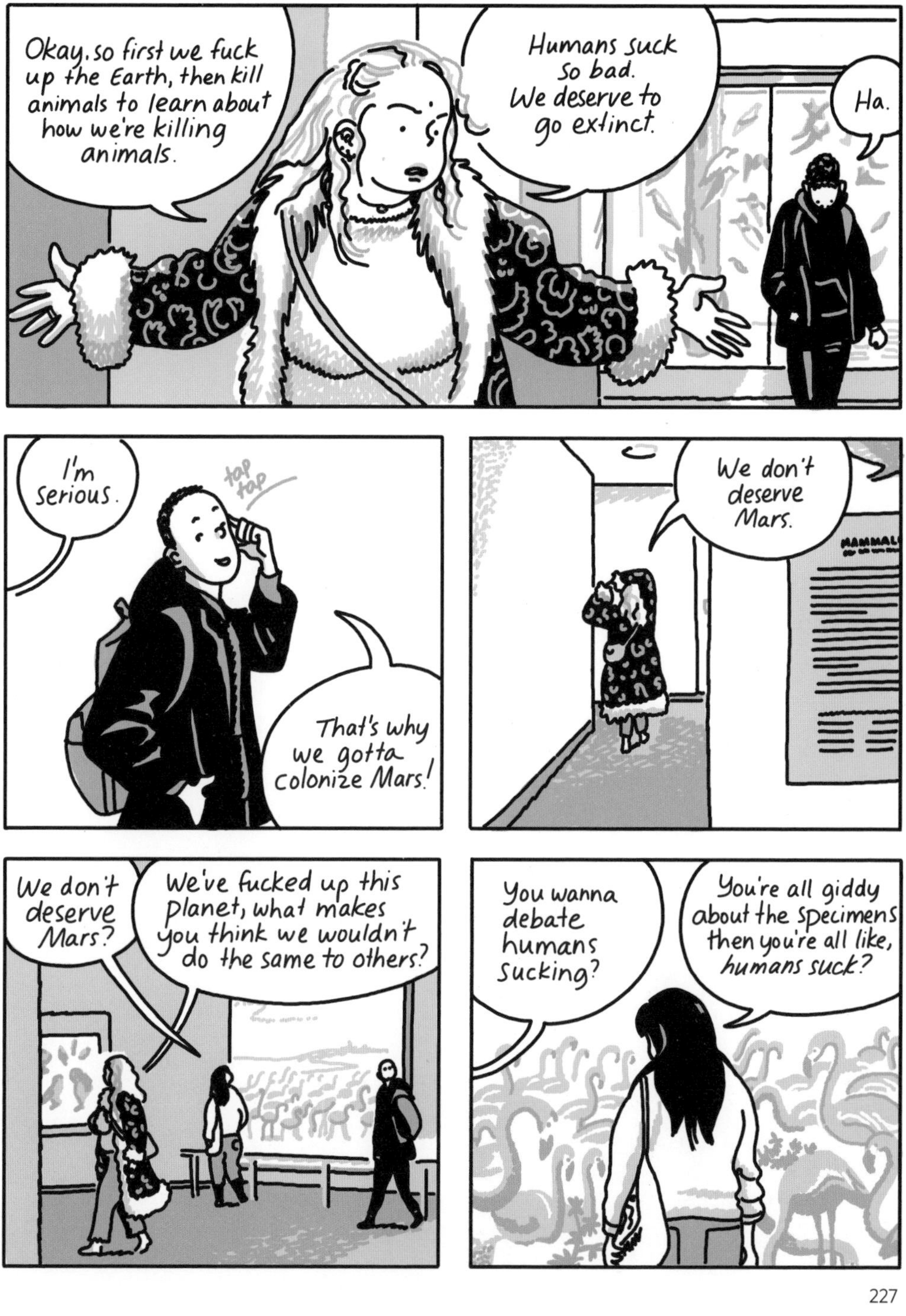
Okay, so first we fuck up the Earth, then kill animals to learn about how we're killing animals.
Humans suck so bad. We deserve to go extinct.
Ha.
I'm serious.
tap tap
That's why we gotta colonize Mars!
We don't deserve Mars.
We don't deserve Mars?
We've fucked up this planet, what makes you think we wouldn't do the same to others?
You wanna debate humans sucking?
You're all giddy about the specimens then you're all like, humans suck?

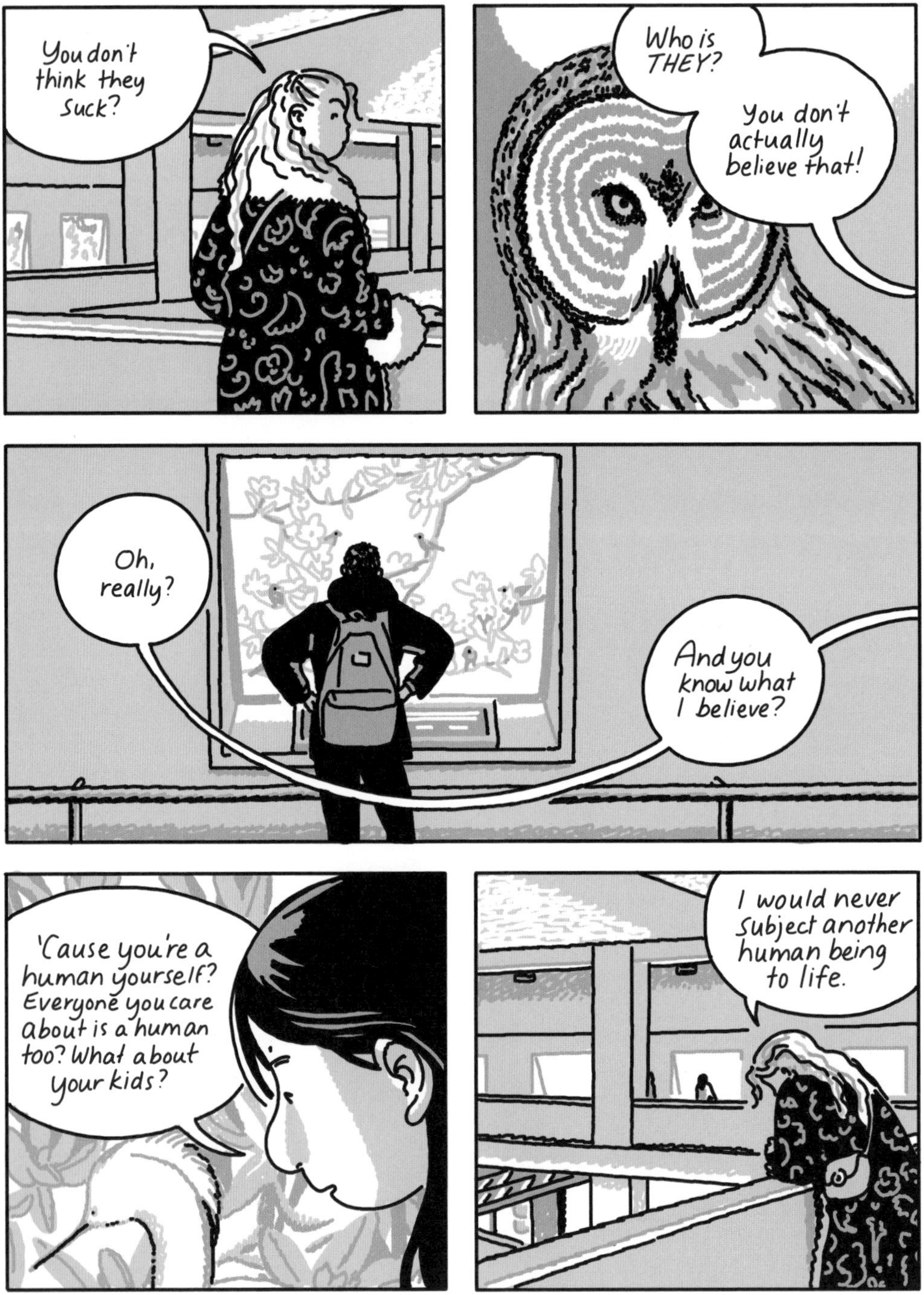
You don't think they suck?
Who is THEY?
You don't actually believe that!
Oh, really?
And you know what I believe?
'Cause you're a human yourself? Everyone you care about is a human too? What about your kids?
I would never subject another human being to life.

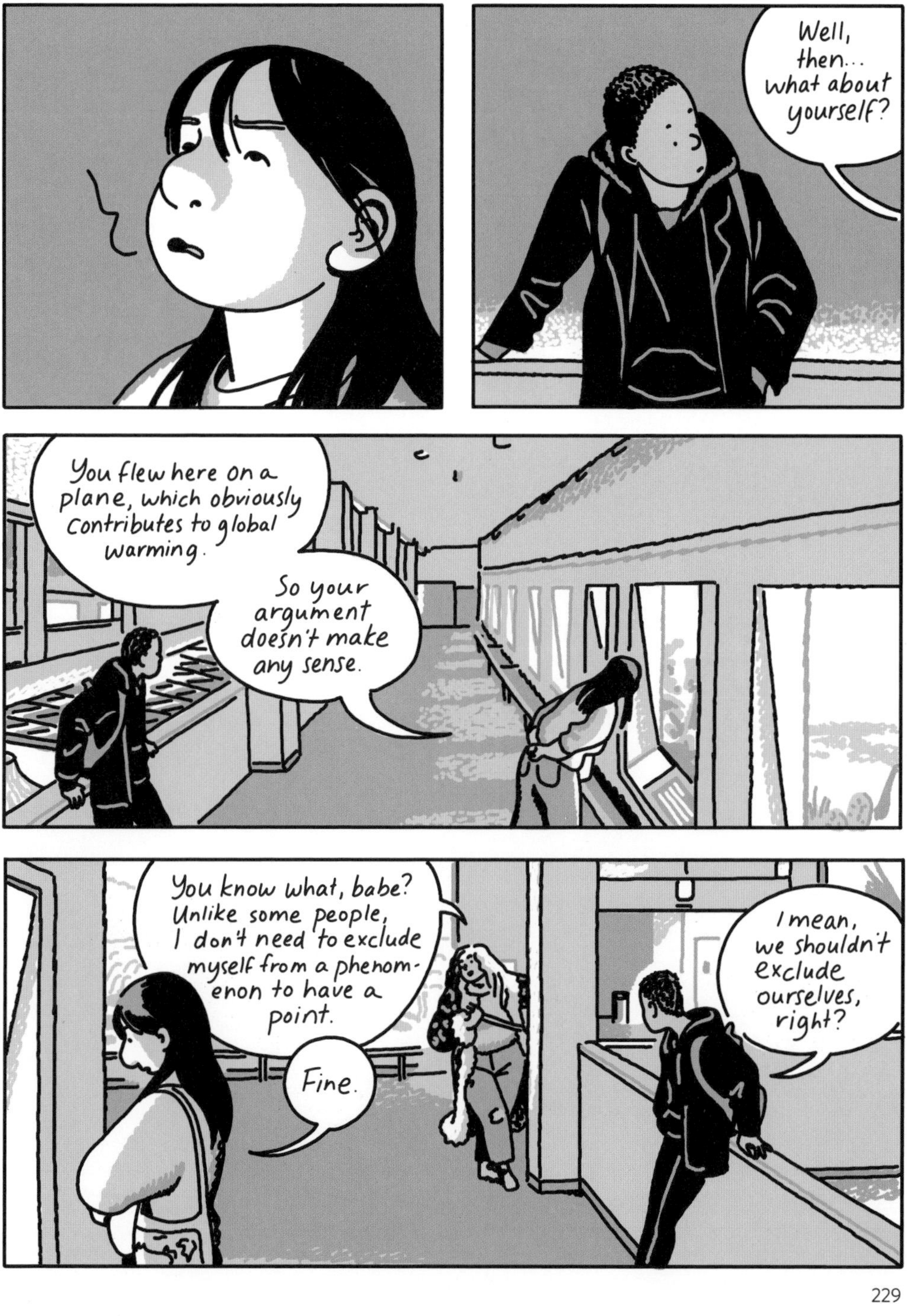

Well, then... what about yourself?
You flew here on a plane, which obviously contributes to global warming.
So your argument doesn't make any sense.
You know what, babe? Unlike some people, I don't need to exclude myself from a phenom-enon to have a point.
Fine.
I mean, we shouldn't exclude ourselves, right?

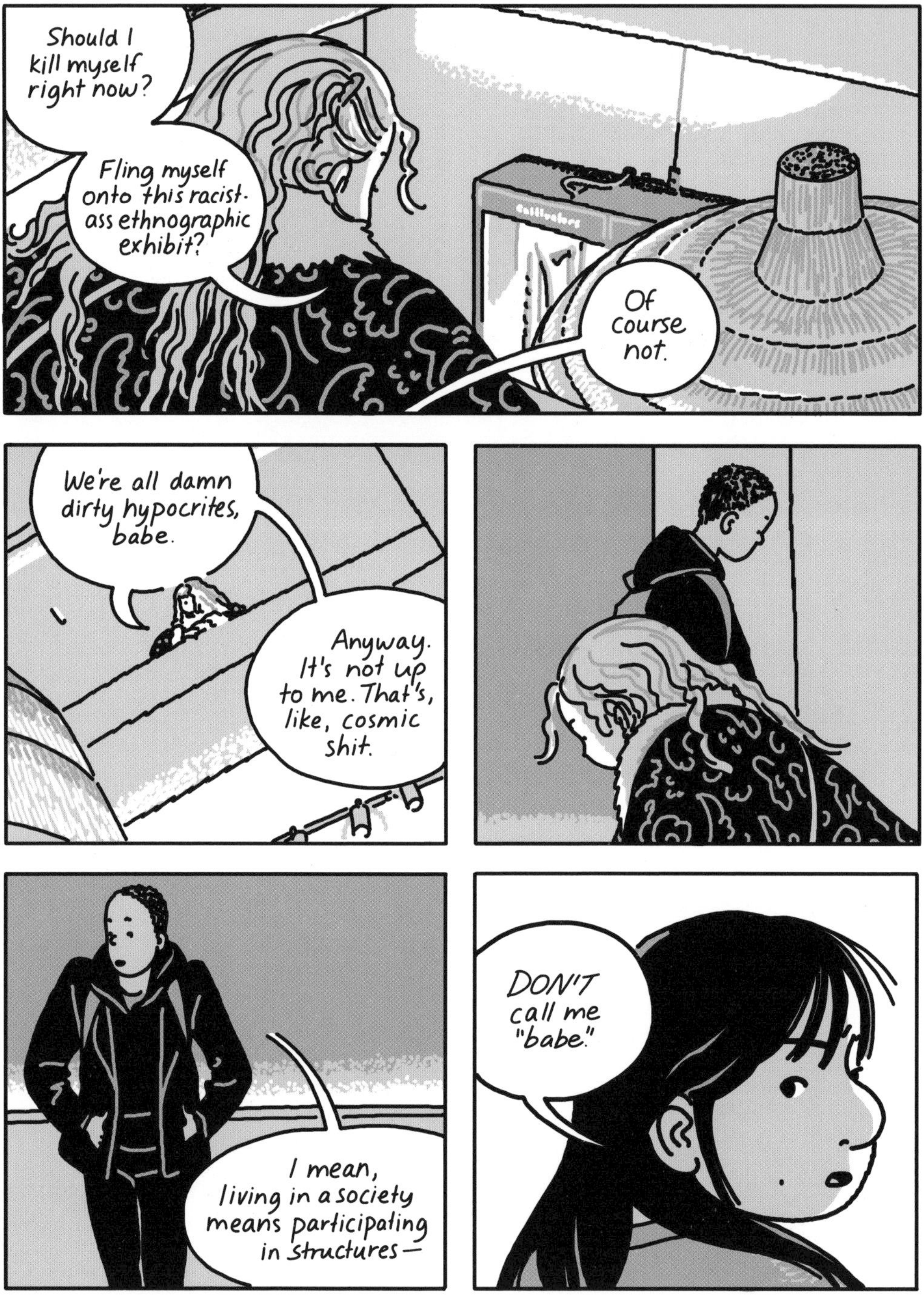
Should I kill myself right now?
Fling myself onto this racist-ass ethnographic exhibit?
Of course not.
We're all damn dirty hypocrites, babe.
Anyway. It's not up to me. That's, like, cosmic shit.
I mean, living in a society means participating in structures—
DON'T call me "babe."

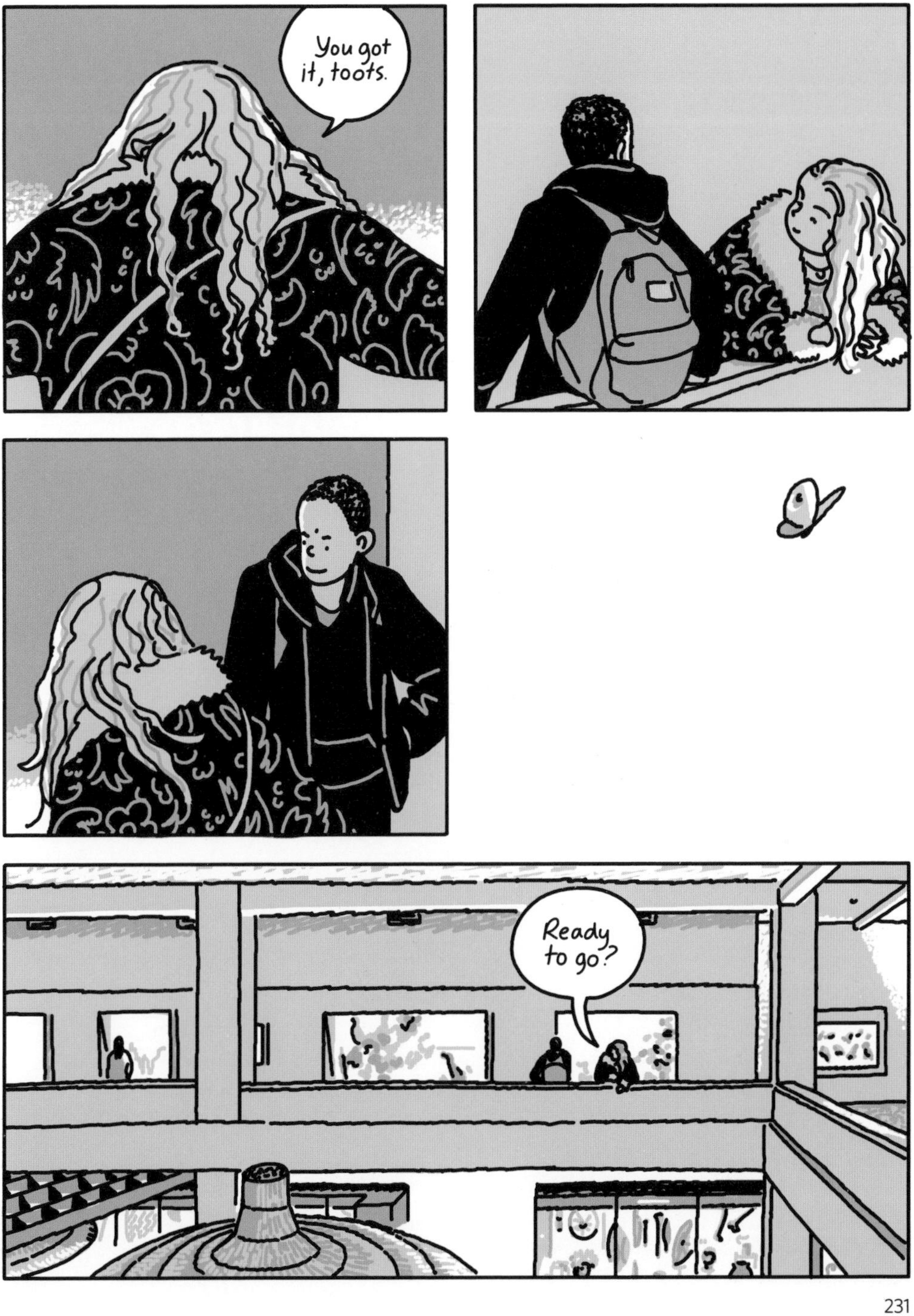
You got it, toots.
Ready to go?

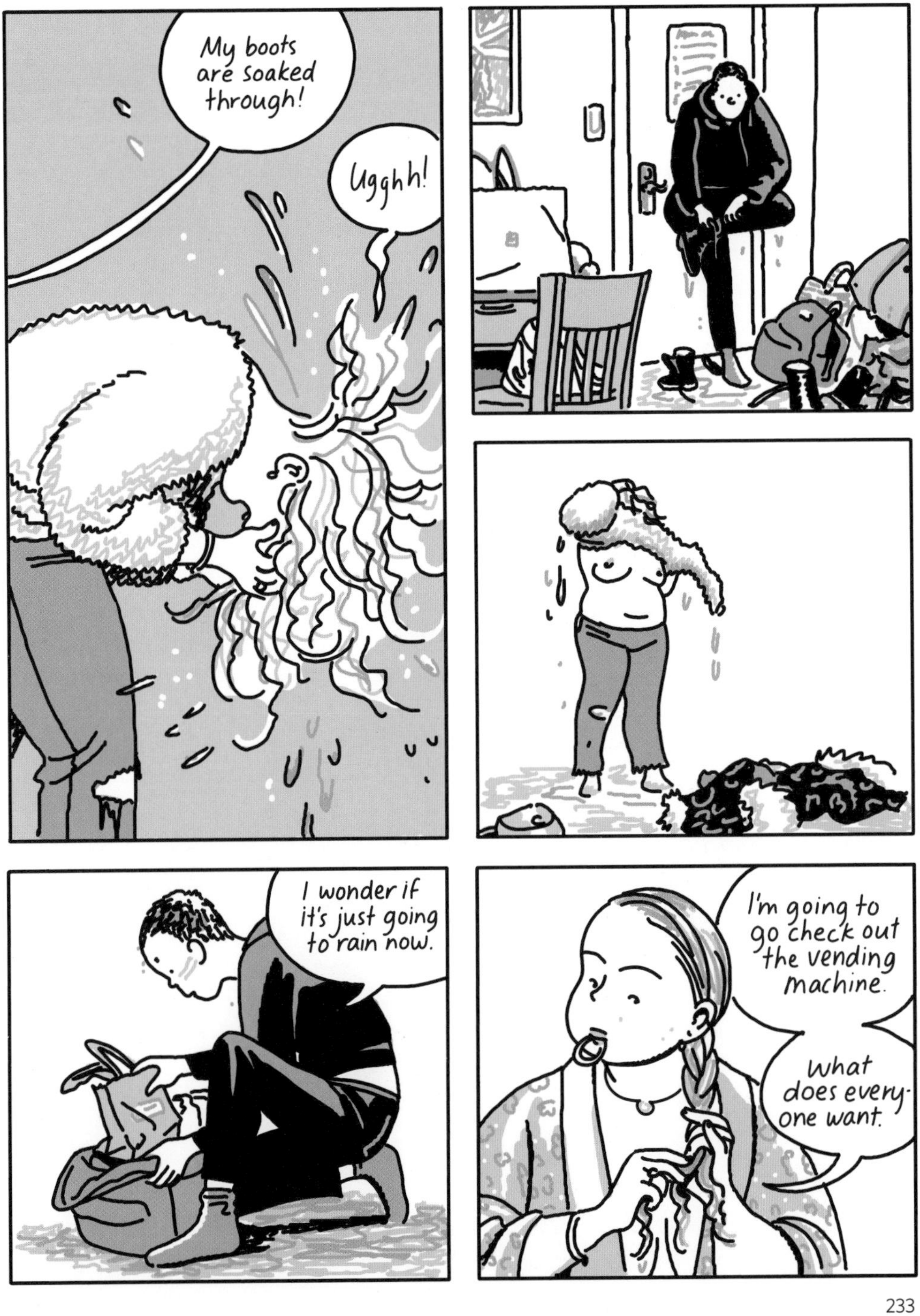
My boots are soaked through!
Ugghh!
I wonder if it's just going to rain now.
I'm going to go check out the vending machine.
What does every-one want.

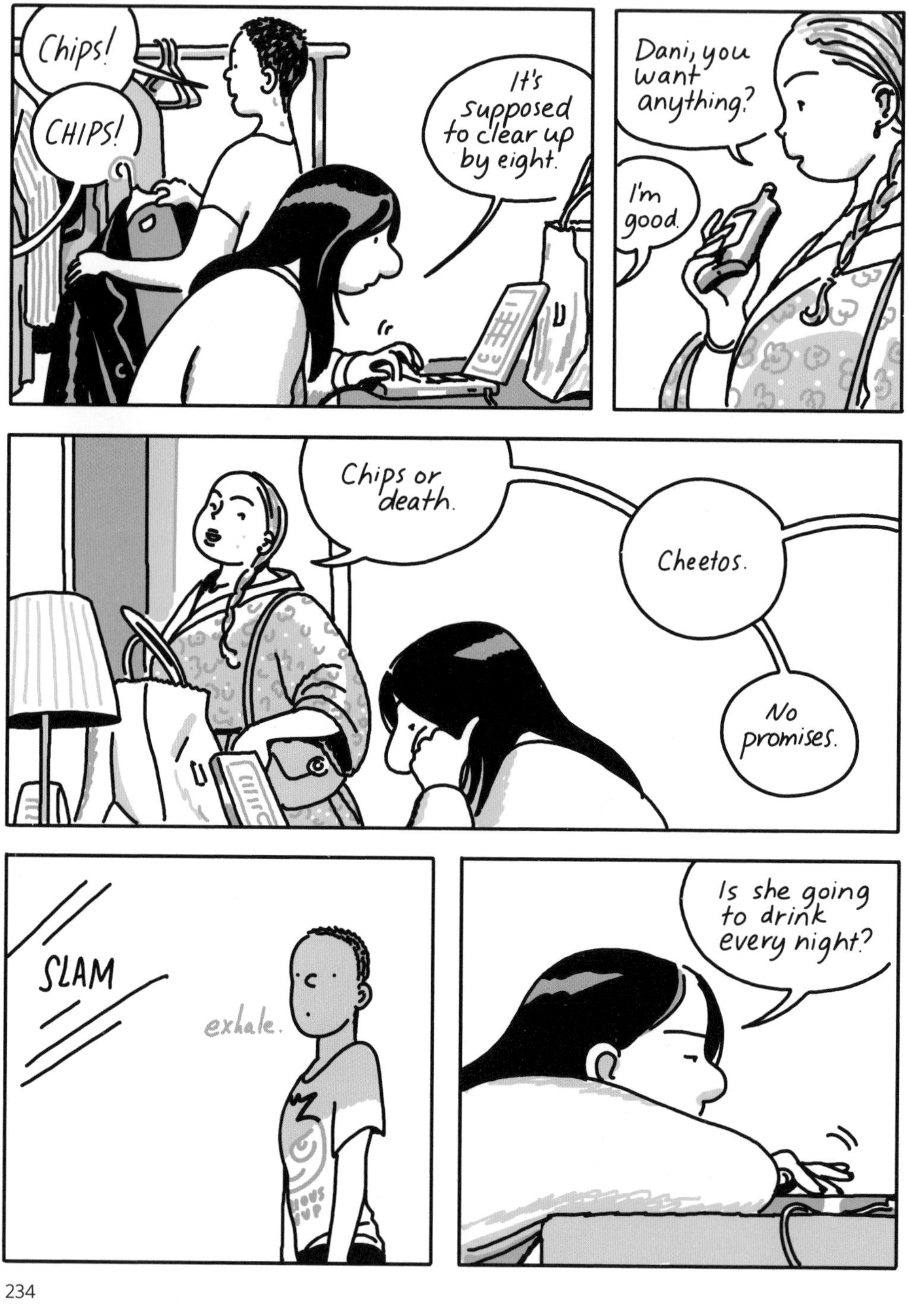
Chips!
CHIPS!
It's supposed to clear up by eight.
Dani, you want anything?
I'm good.
Chips or death.
Cheetos.
No promises.
SLAM
exhale.
Is she going to drink every night?

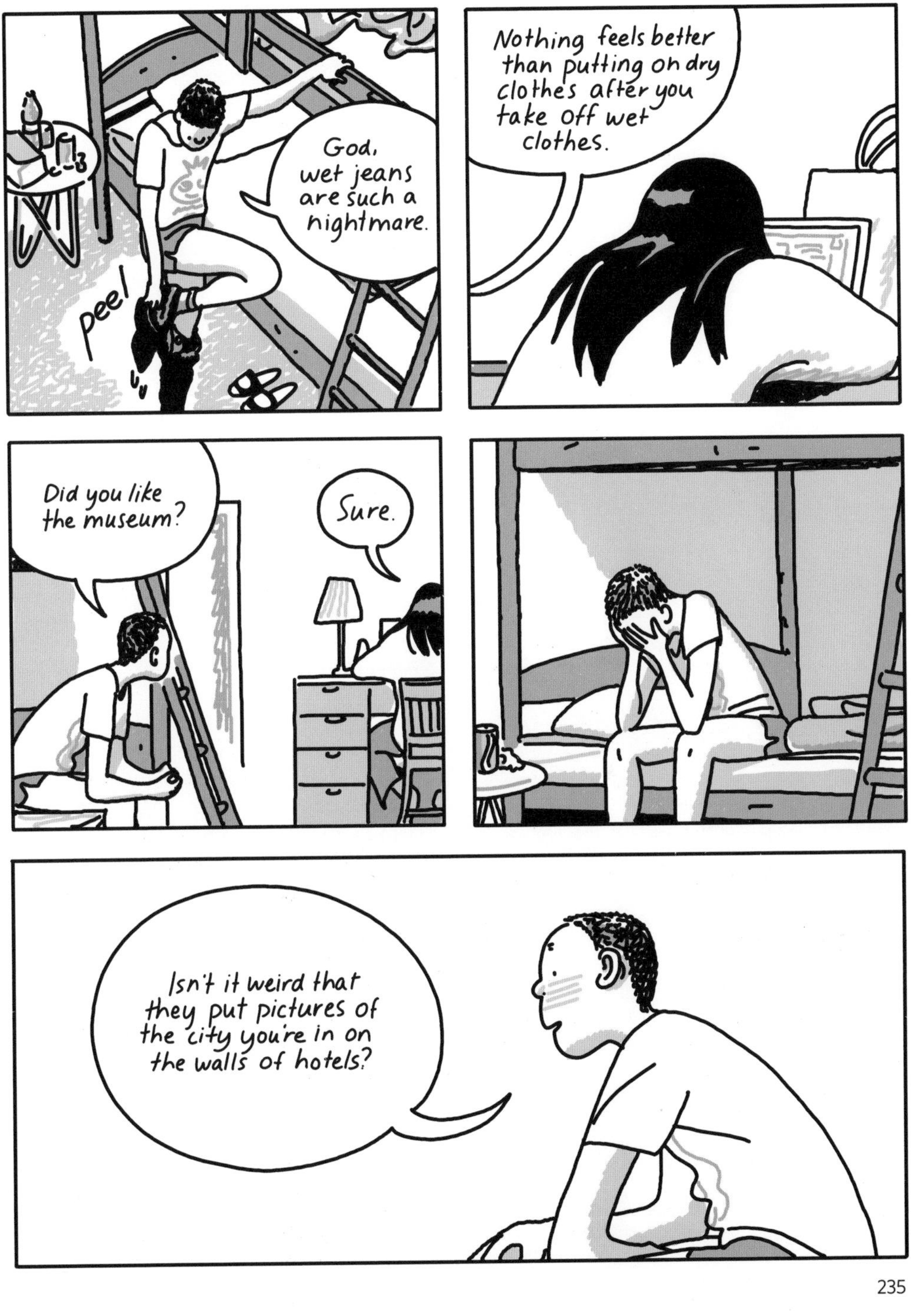

God, wet jeans are such a nightmare.
peel
Nothing feels better than putting on dry clothes after you take off wet clothes.
Did you like the museum?
Sure.
Isn't it weird that they put pictures of the city you're in on the walls of hotels?

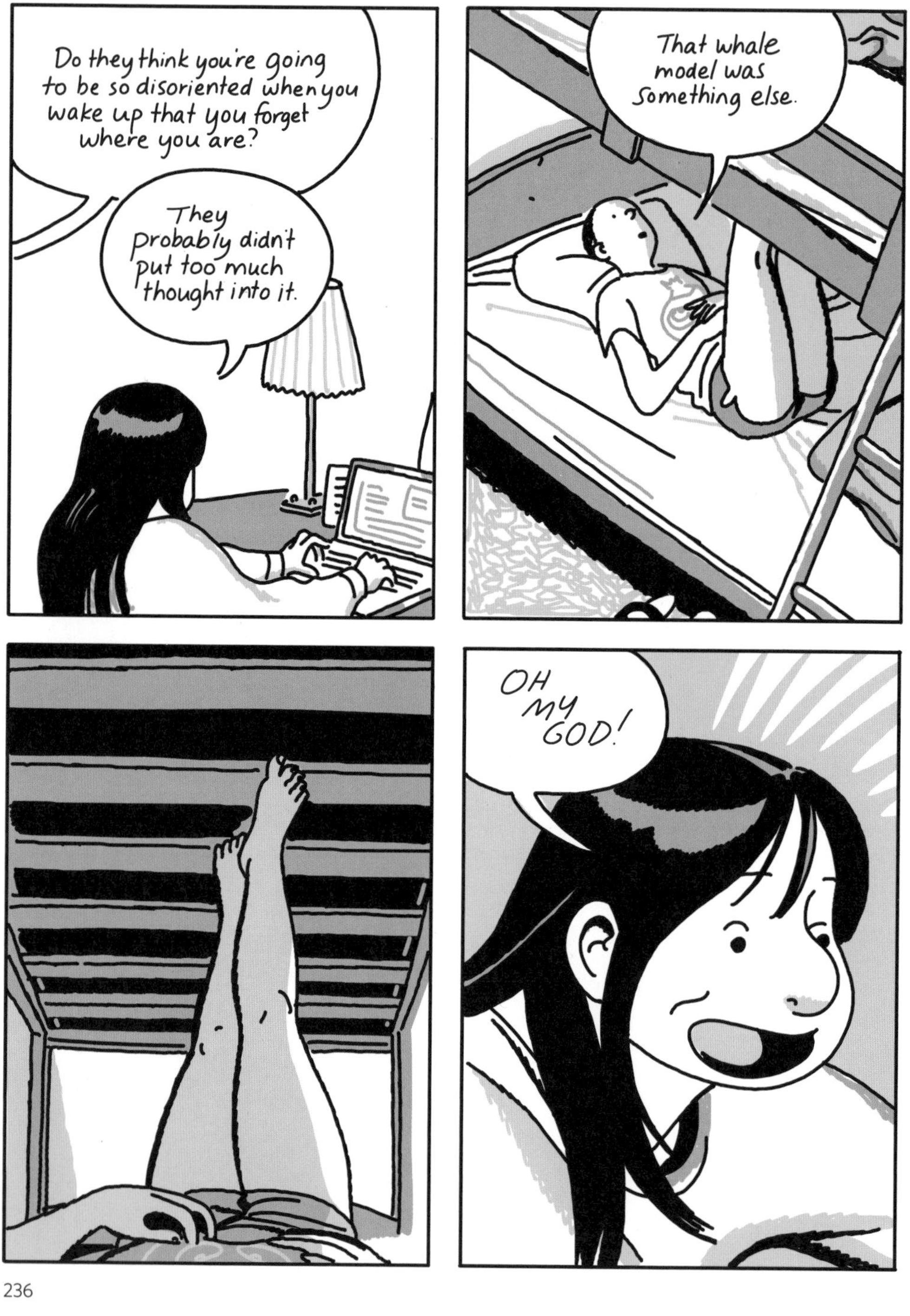
Do they think you're going to be so disoriented when you wake up that you forget where you are?
They probably didn't put too much thought into it.
That whale model was something else.
OH MY GOD!

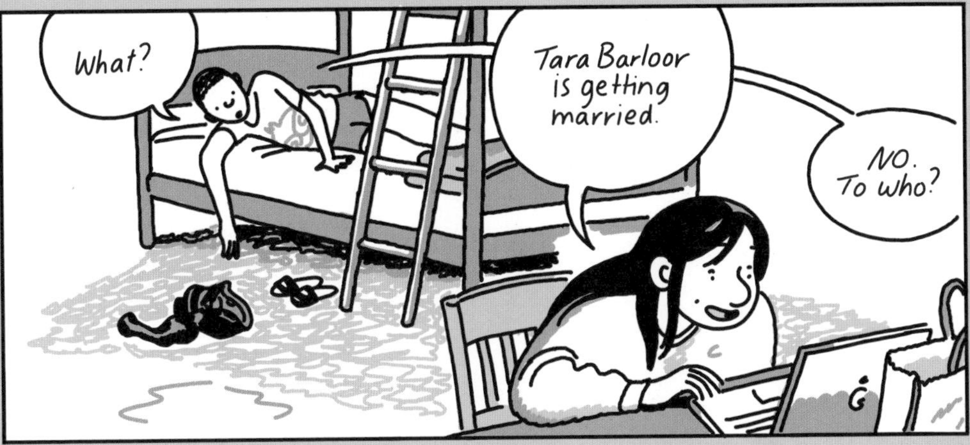
What?
Tara Barloor is getting married.
NO. To who?

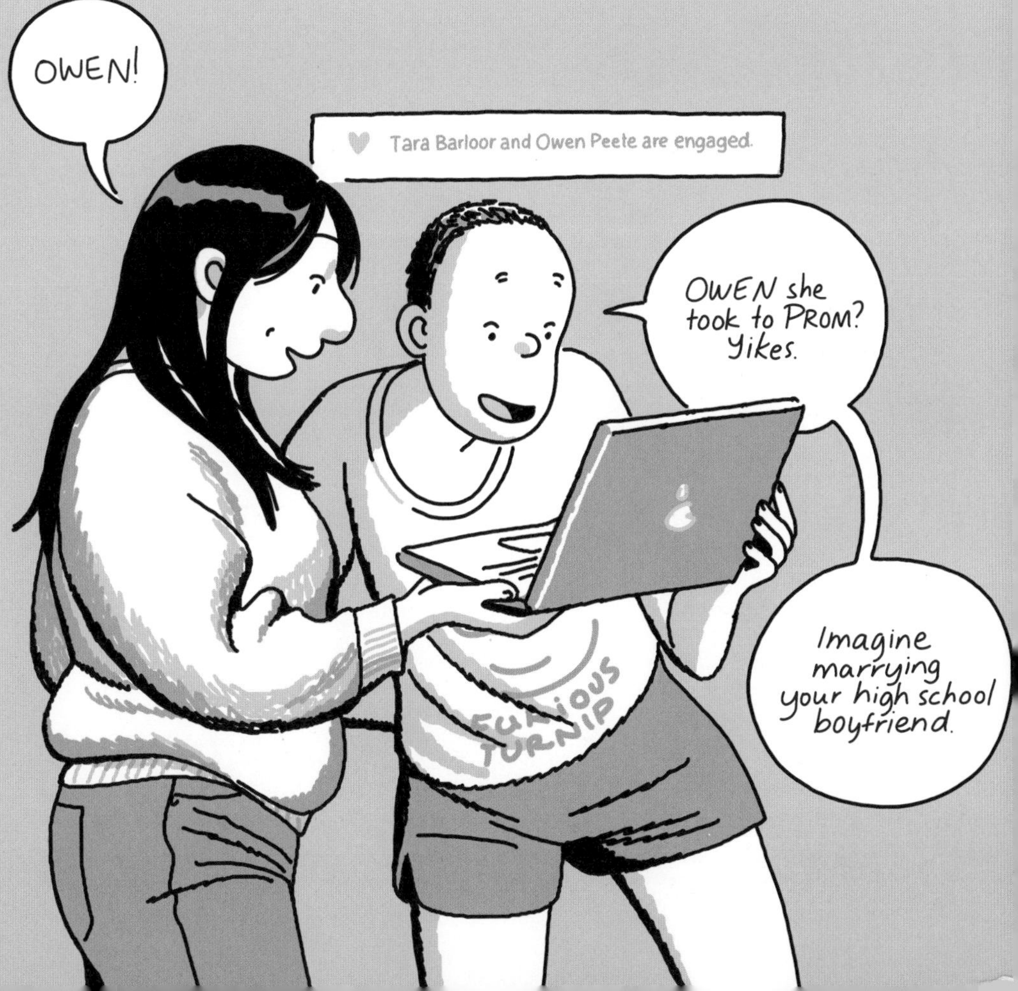
OWEN!
Tara Barloor and Owen Peete are engaged.
OWEN she took to PROM? Yikes.
Imagine marrying your high school boyfriend.
FURIOUS TURNIP

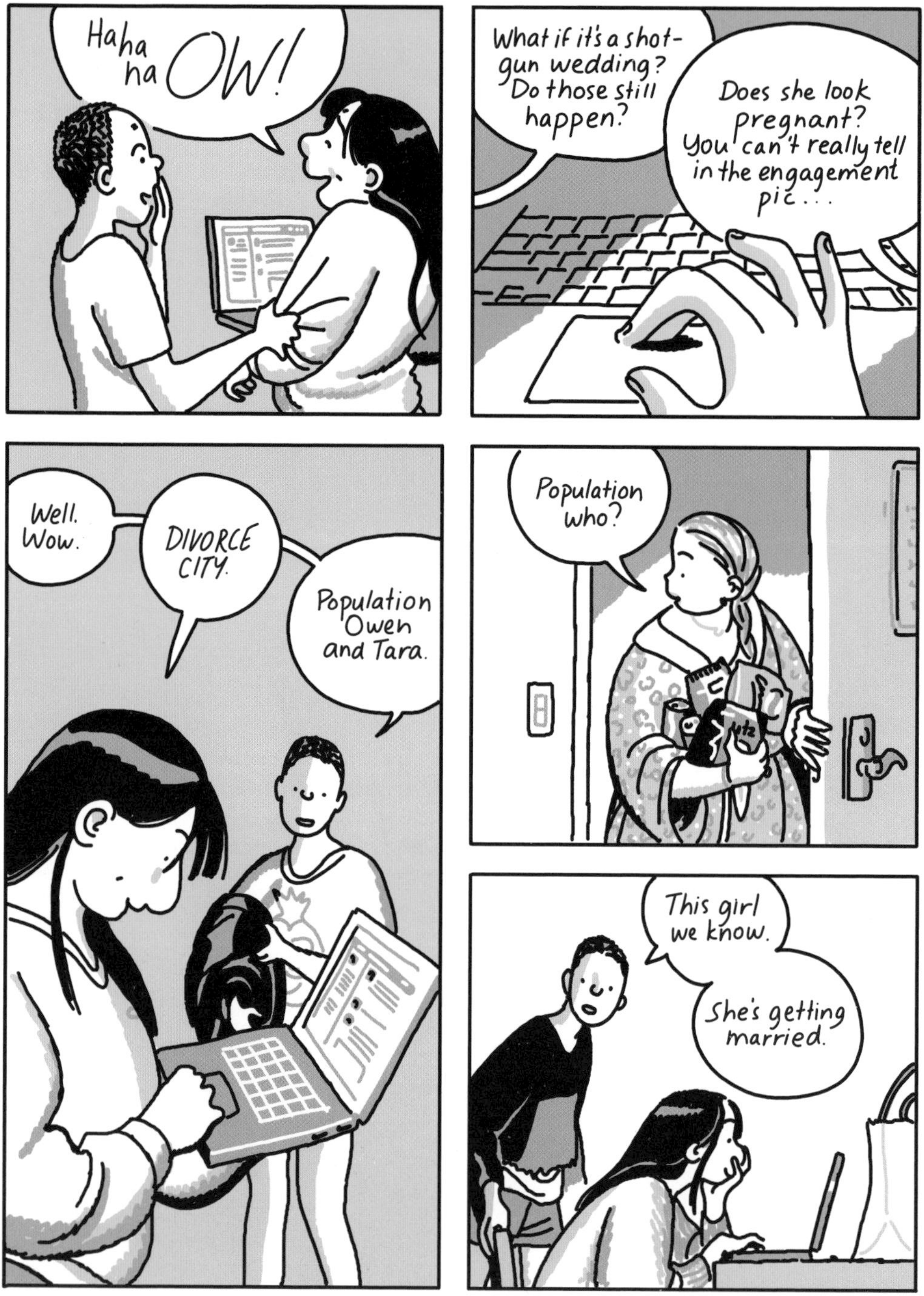
Hahaha ha OW!
What if it's a shot-gun wedding? Do those still happen?
Does she look pregnant? You can't really tell in the engagement pic...
Well. Wow.
DIVORCE CITY.
Population Owen and Tara.
Population who?
This girl we know.
She's getting married.

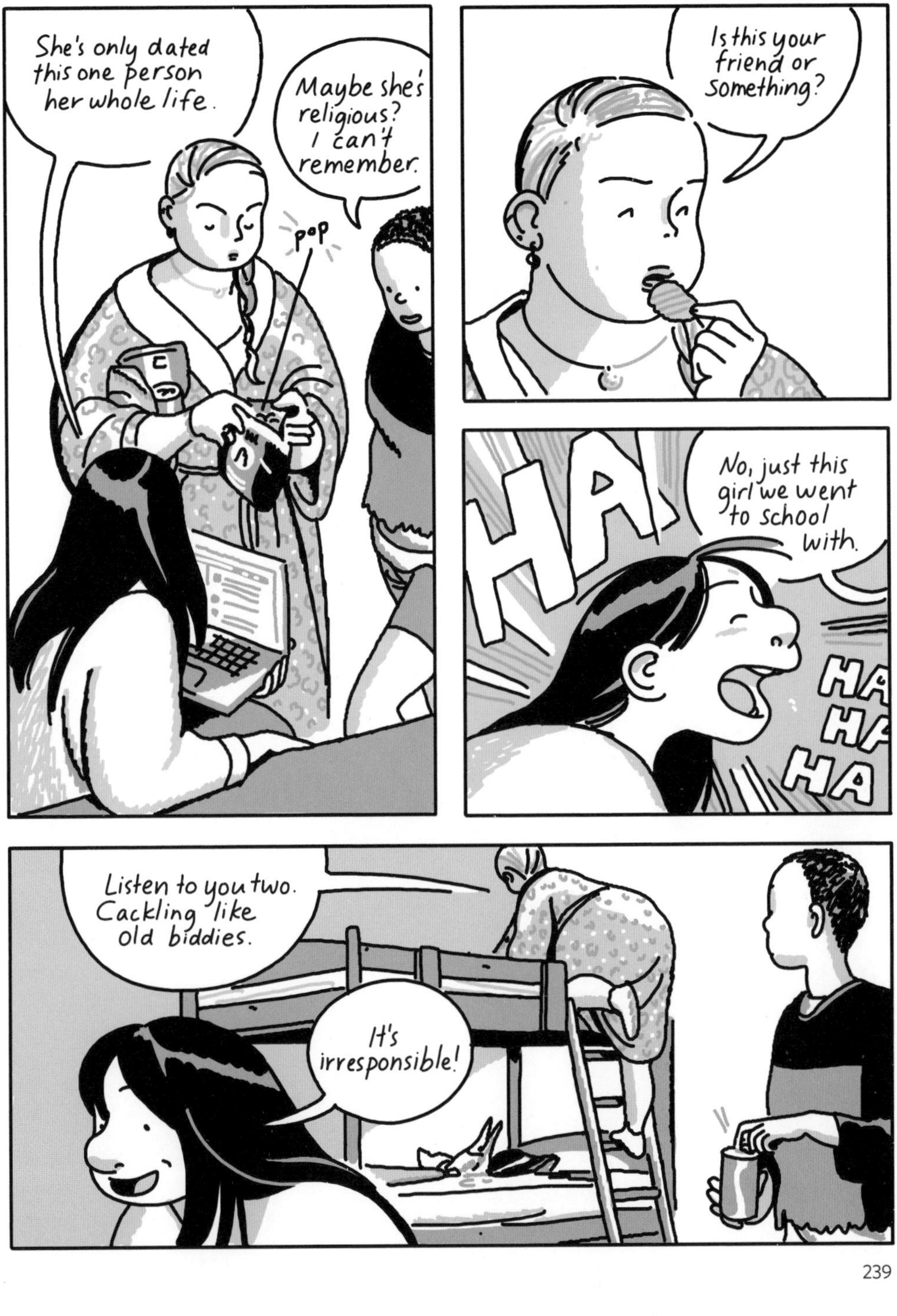
She's only dated this one person her whole life.
Maybe she's religious? I can't remember.
pop
Is this your friend or something?
HA
No, just this girl we went to school with.
HA HA HA
Listen to you two. Cackling like old biddies.
It's irresponsible!

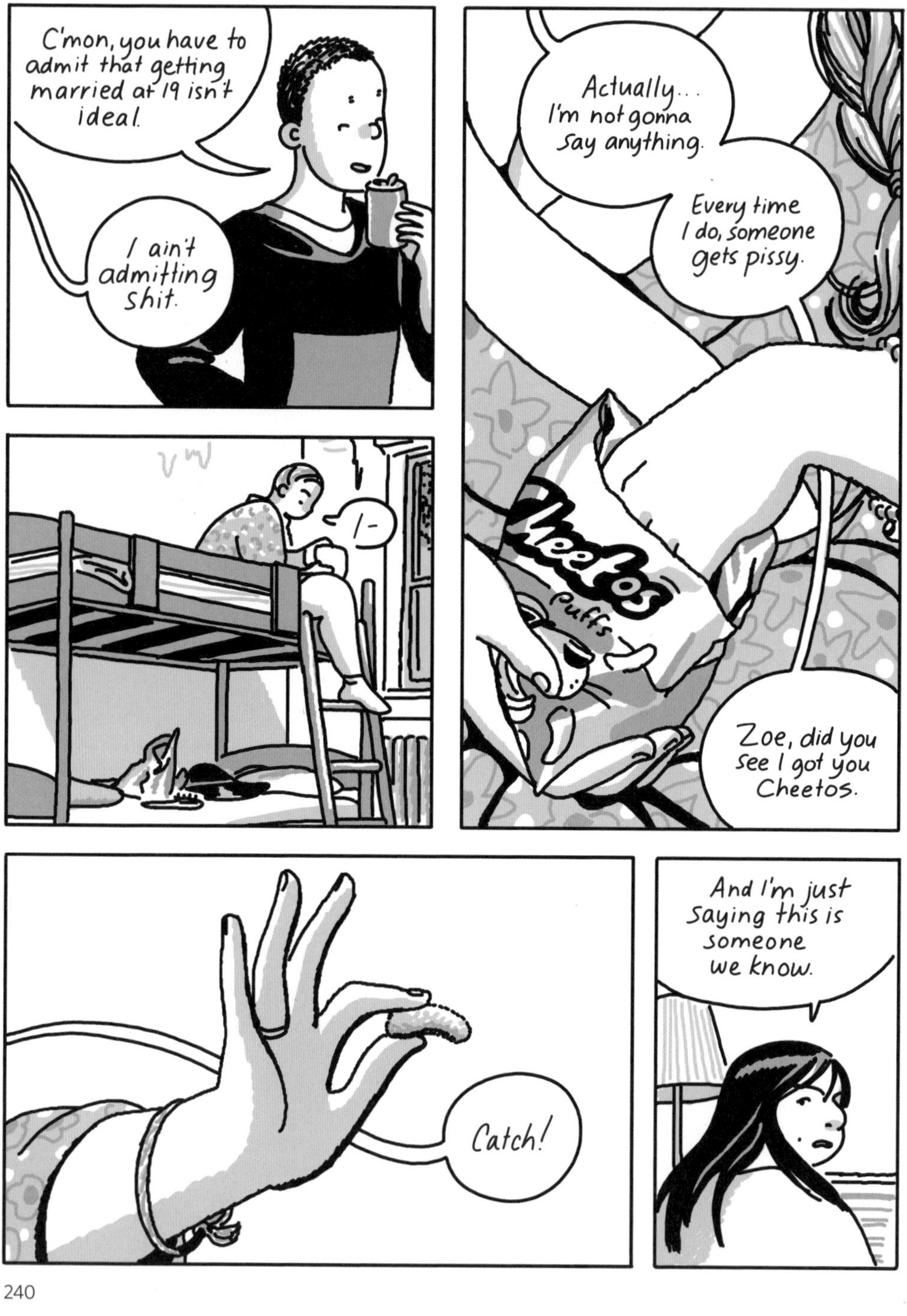
C'mon, you have to admit that getting married at 19 isn't ideal.
I ain't admitting shit.
Actually... I'm not gonna say anything.
Every time I do, someone gets pissy.
Zoe, did you see I got you Cheetos.
Cheetos
Puffs
Catch!
And I'm just saying this is someone we know.

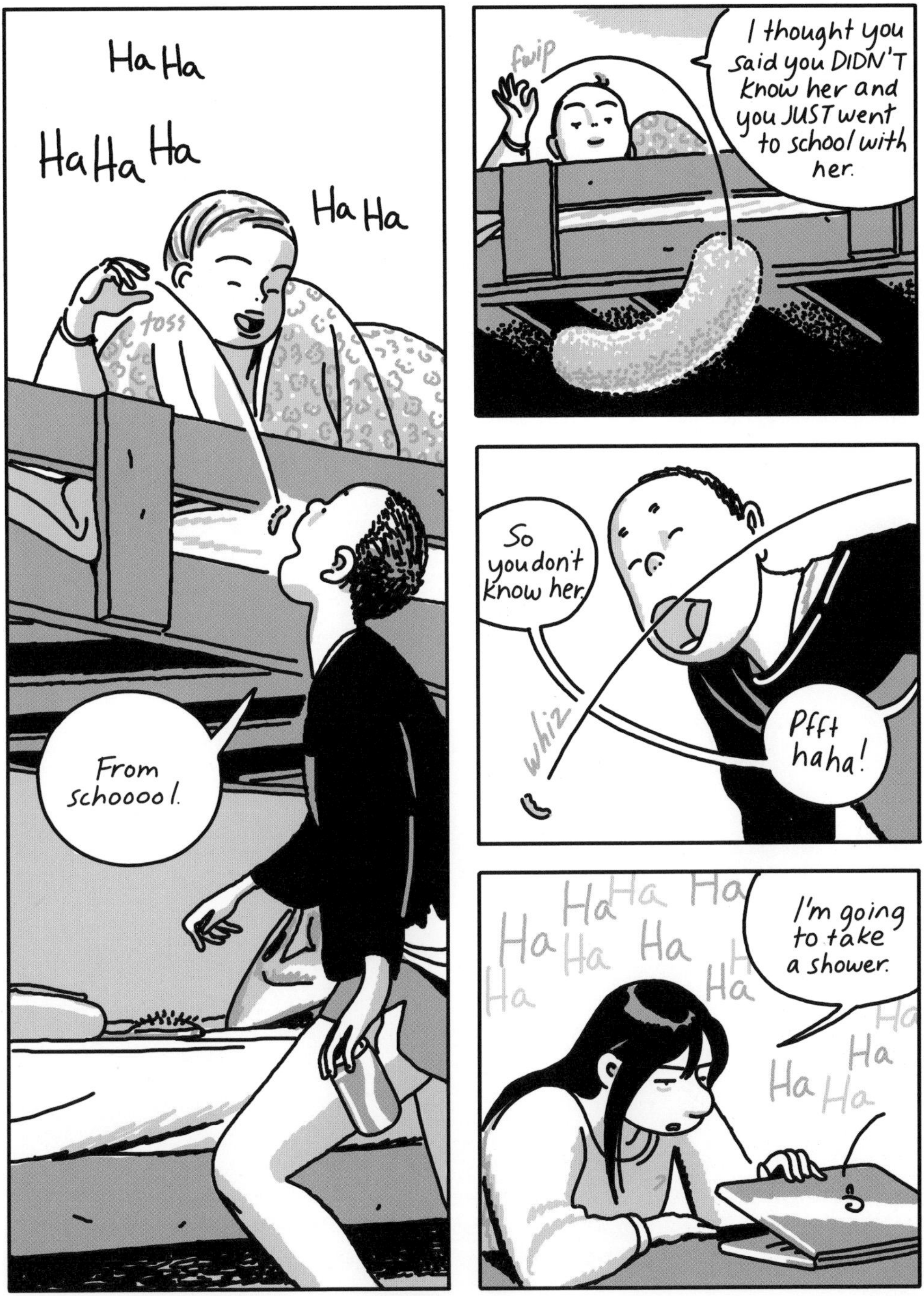
Ha Ha
Ha Ha Ha
Ha Ha
toss
From schooool.
fwip
I thought you said you DIDN'T know her and you JUST went to school with her.
So you don't know her.
whiz
Pfft haha!
Ha Ha Ha Ha Ha Ha Ha Ha
I'm going to take a shower.
Ha Ha Ha Ha

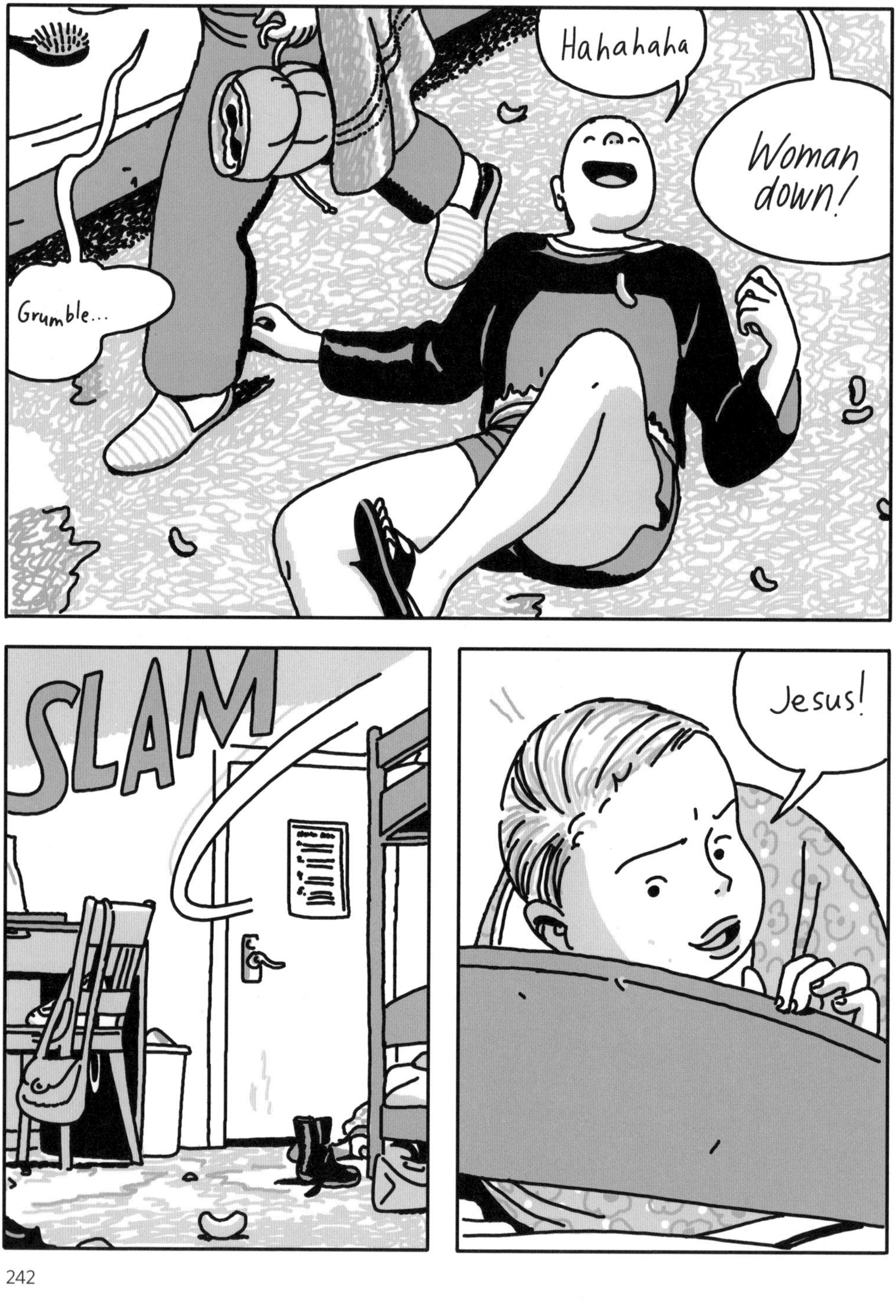
Hahahaha
Woman down!
Grumble...
SLAM
Jesus!

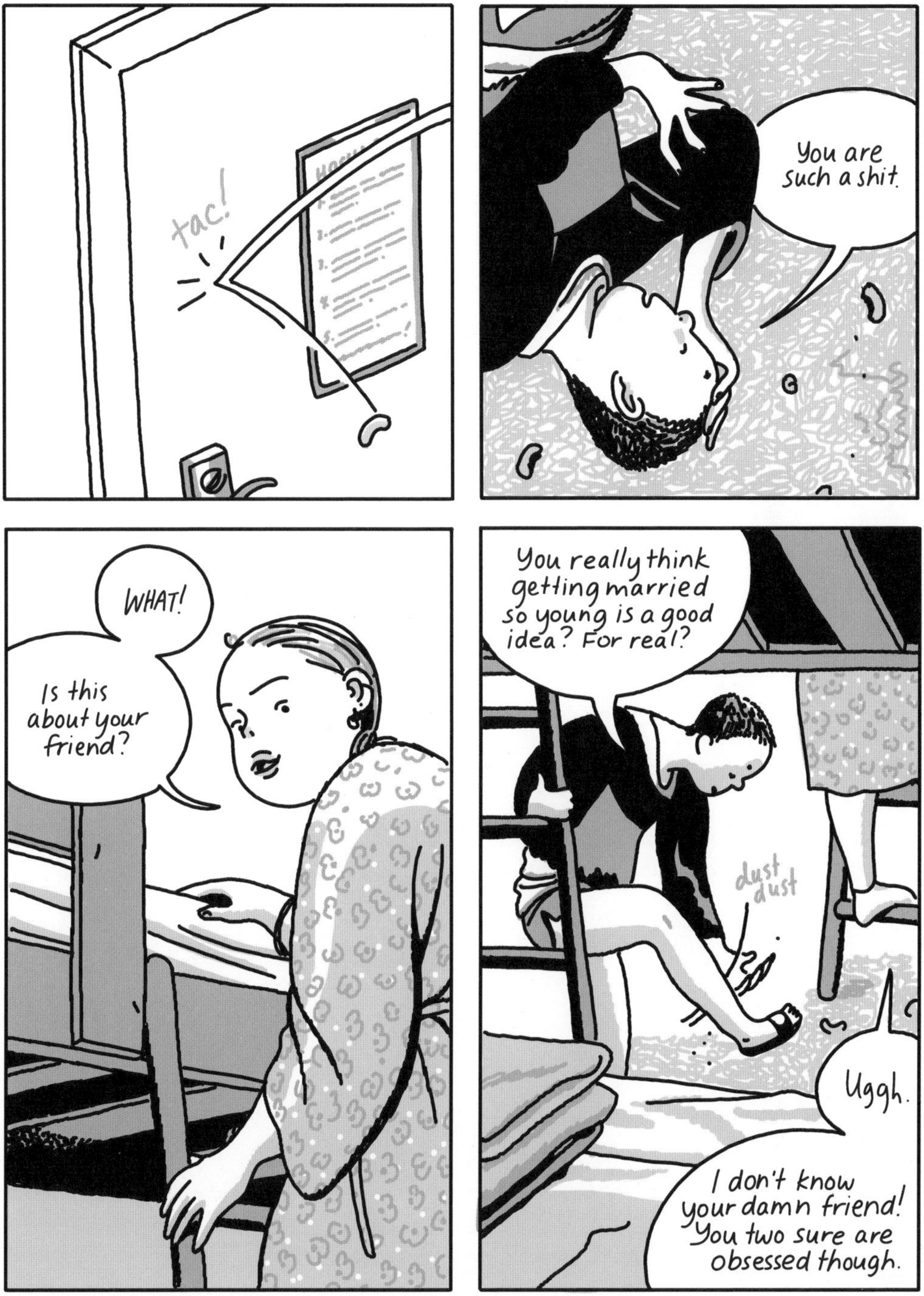

tac!
You are such a shit.
WHAT!
Is this about your friend?
You really think getting married so young is a good idea? For real?
dust dust
Uggh.
I don't know your damn friend! You two sure are obsessed though.

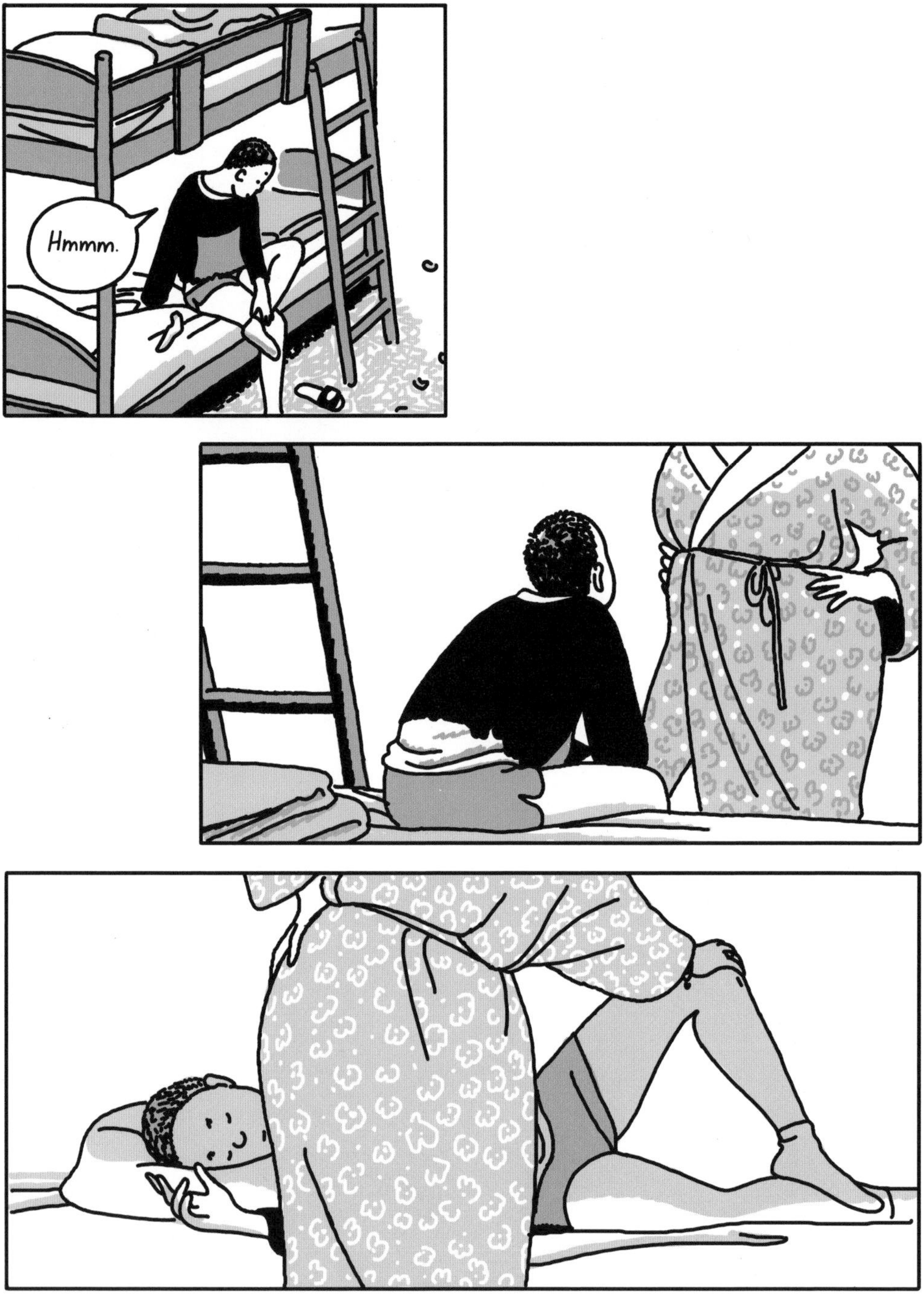
Hmmm.

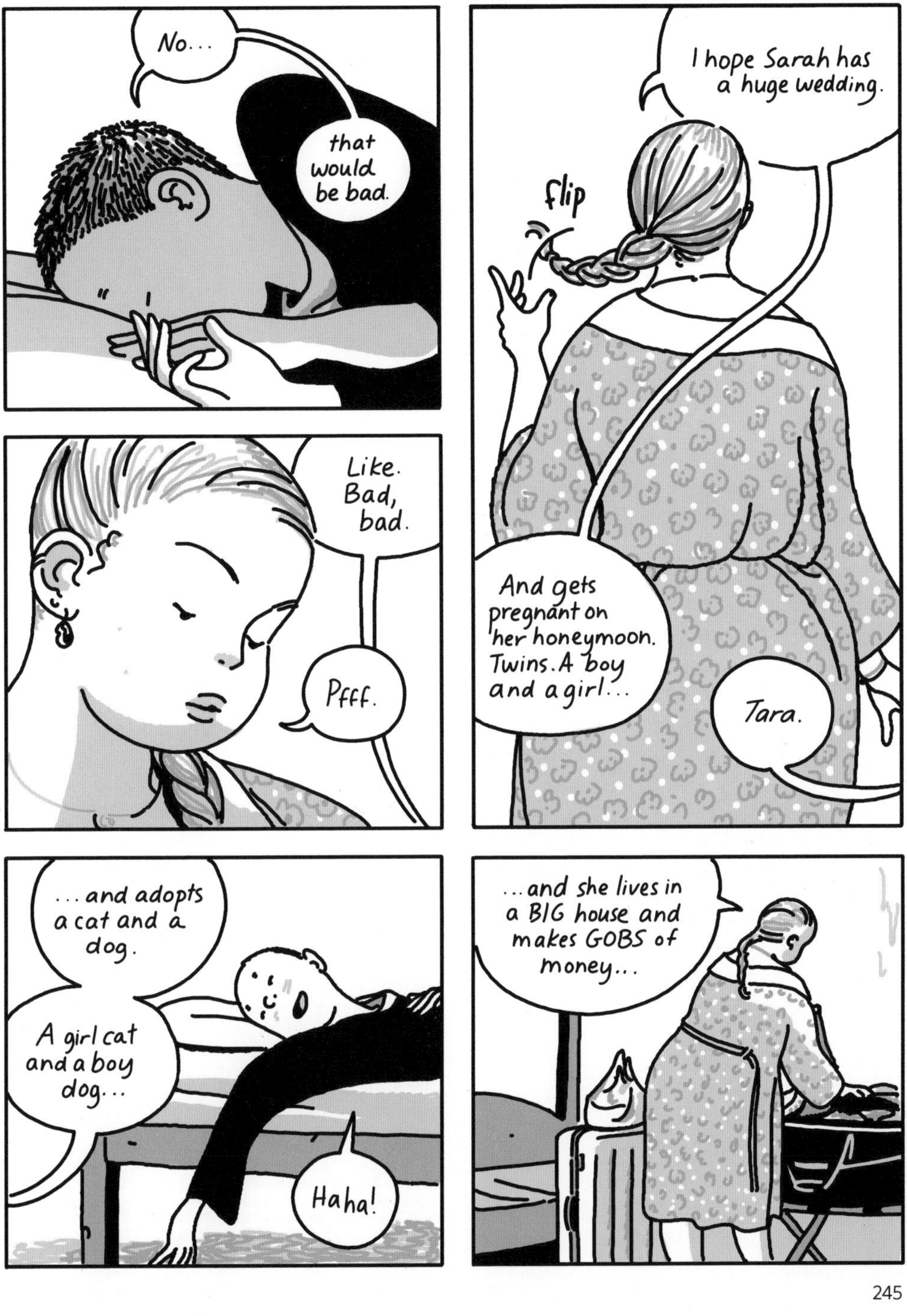
No...
that would be bad.
I hope Sarah has a huge wedding.
flip
Like. Bad, bad.
Pfff.
And gets pregnant on her honeymoon. Twins. A boy and a girl...
Tara.
...and adopts a cat and a dog.
A girl cat and a boy dog...
Haha!
...and she lives in a BIG house and makes GOBS of money...

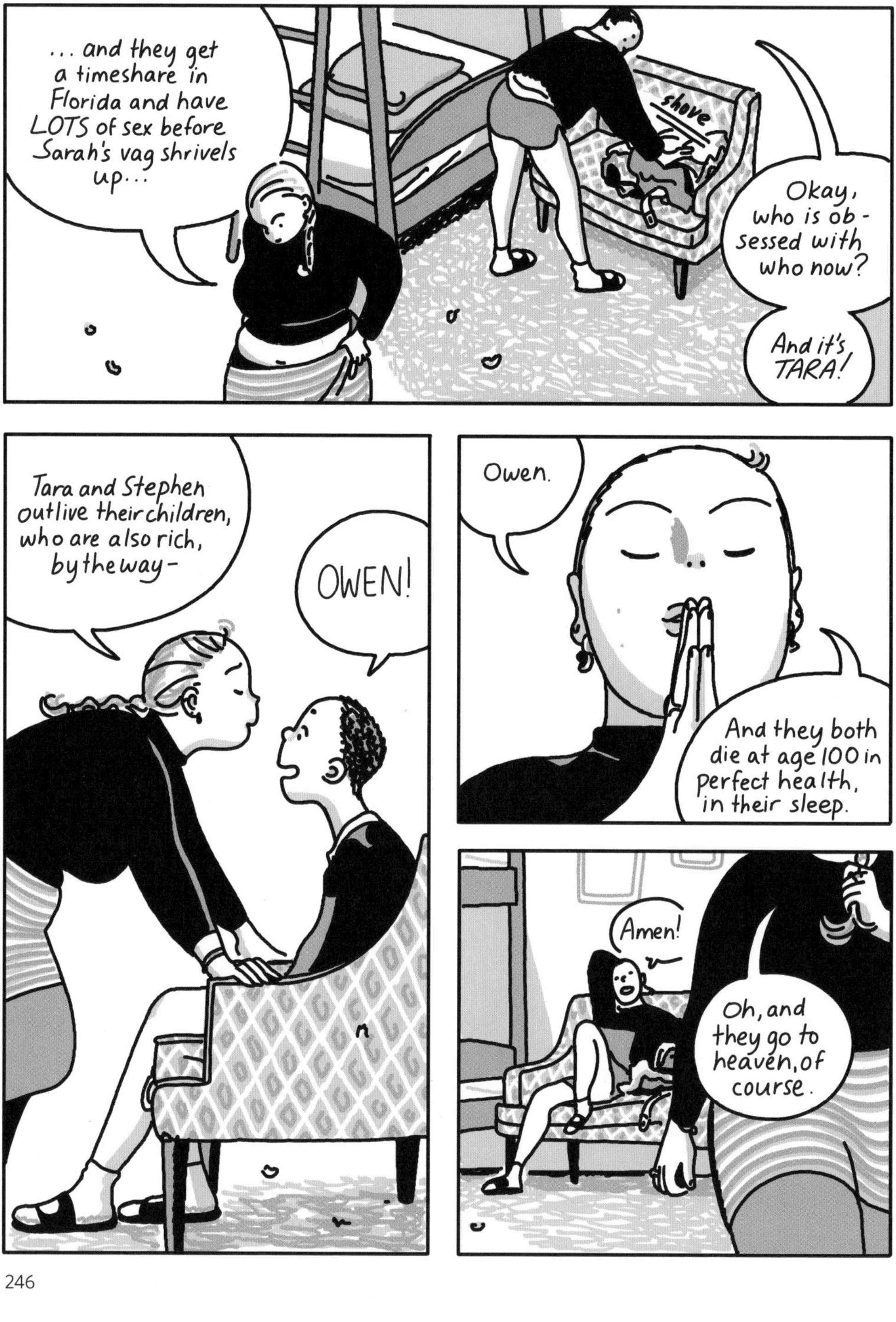
... and they get a timeshare in Florida and have LOTS of sex before Sarah's vag shrivels up...
shove
Okay, who is ob-sessed with who now?
And it's TARA!
Tara and Stephen outlive their children, who are also rich, by the way-
OWEN!
Owen.
And they both die at age 100 in perfect health, in their sleep.
Amen!
Oh, and they go to heaven, of course.

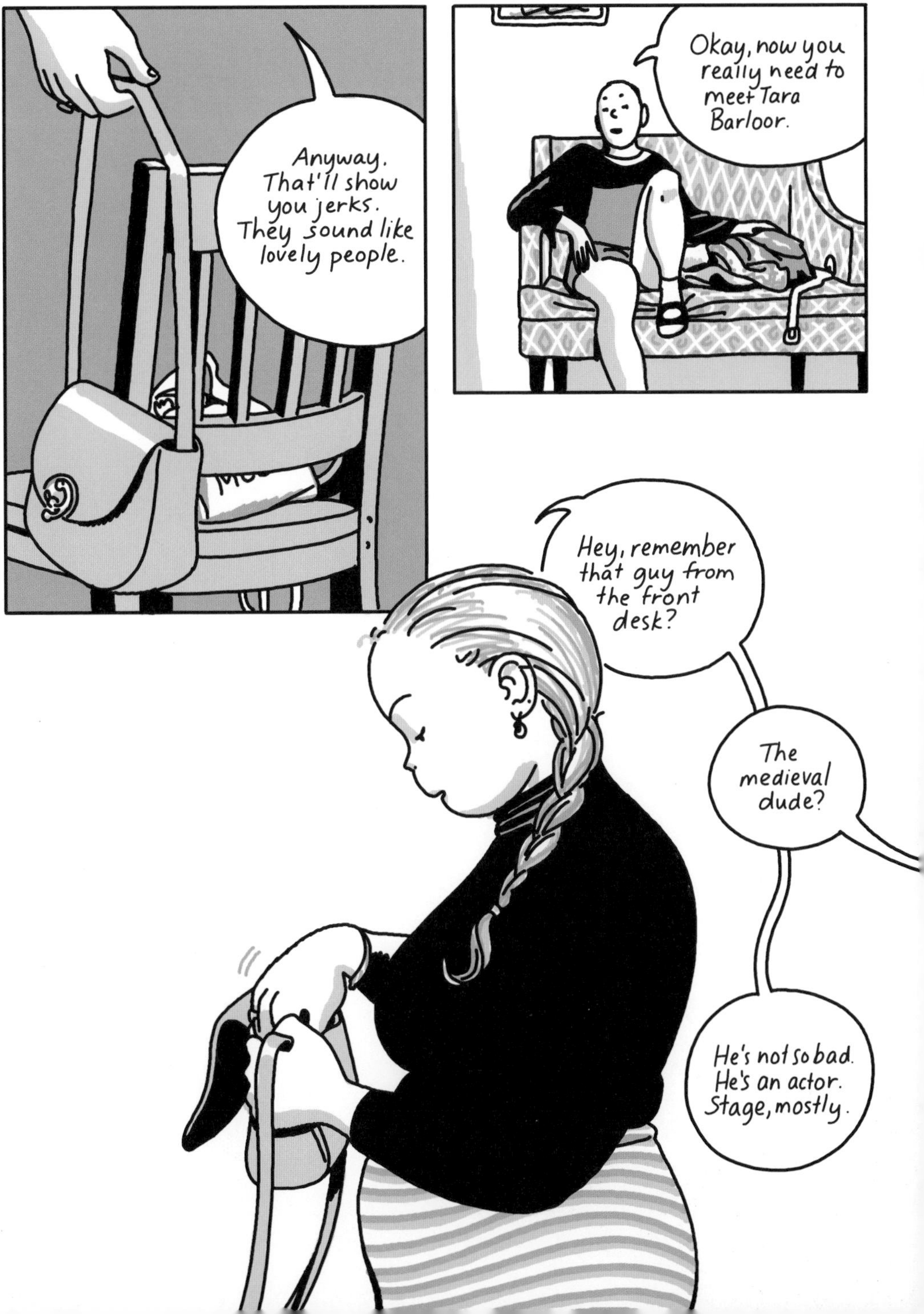
Anyway. That'll show you jerks. They sound like lovely people.
Okay, now you really need to meet Tara Barloor.
Hey, remember that guy from the front desk?
The medieval dude?
He's not so bad. He's an actor. Stage, mostly.

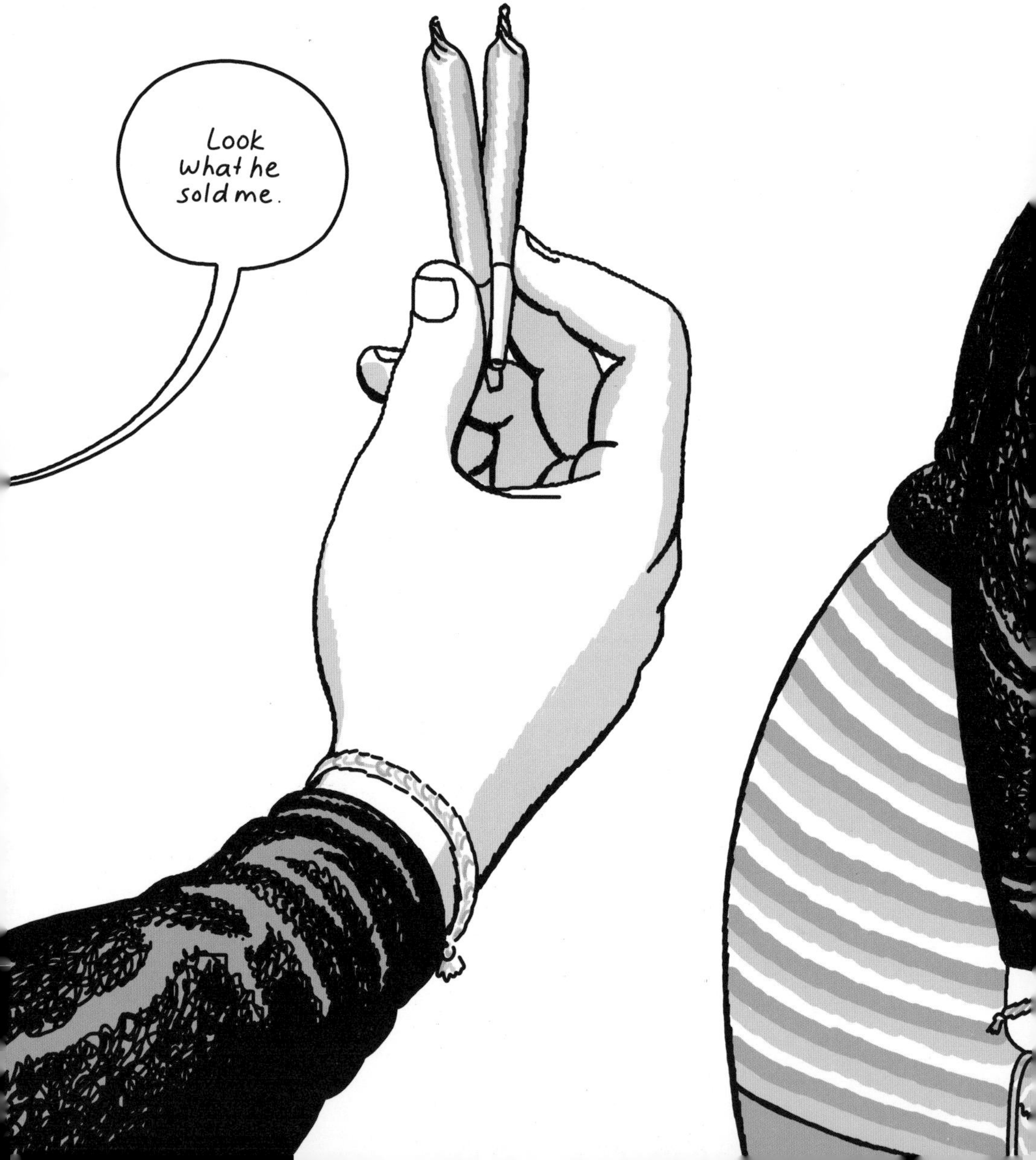
Look what he sold me.

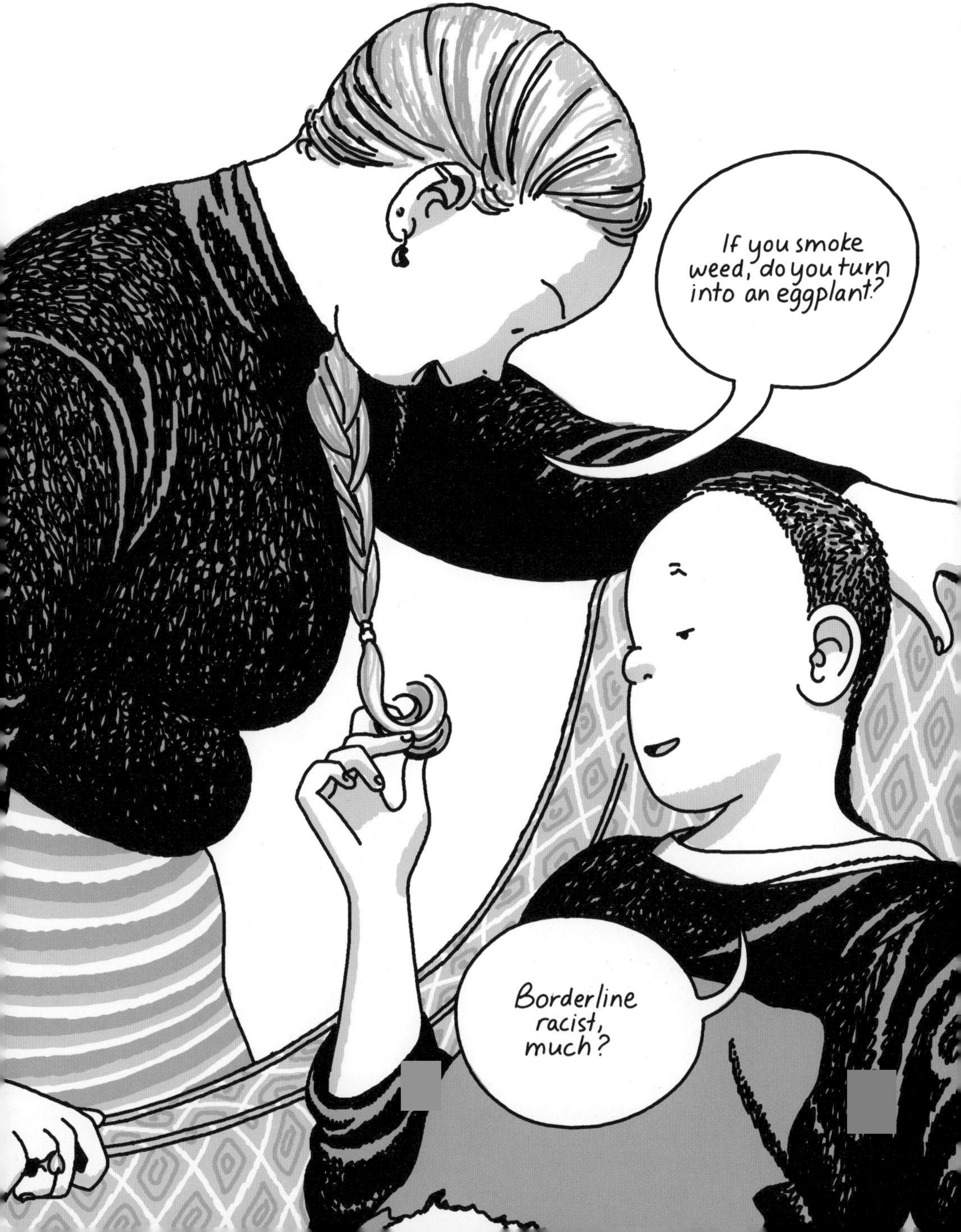
If you smoke weed, do you turn into an eggplant?
Borderline racist, much?

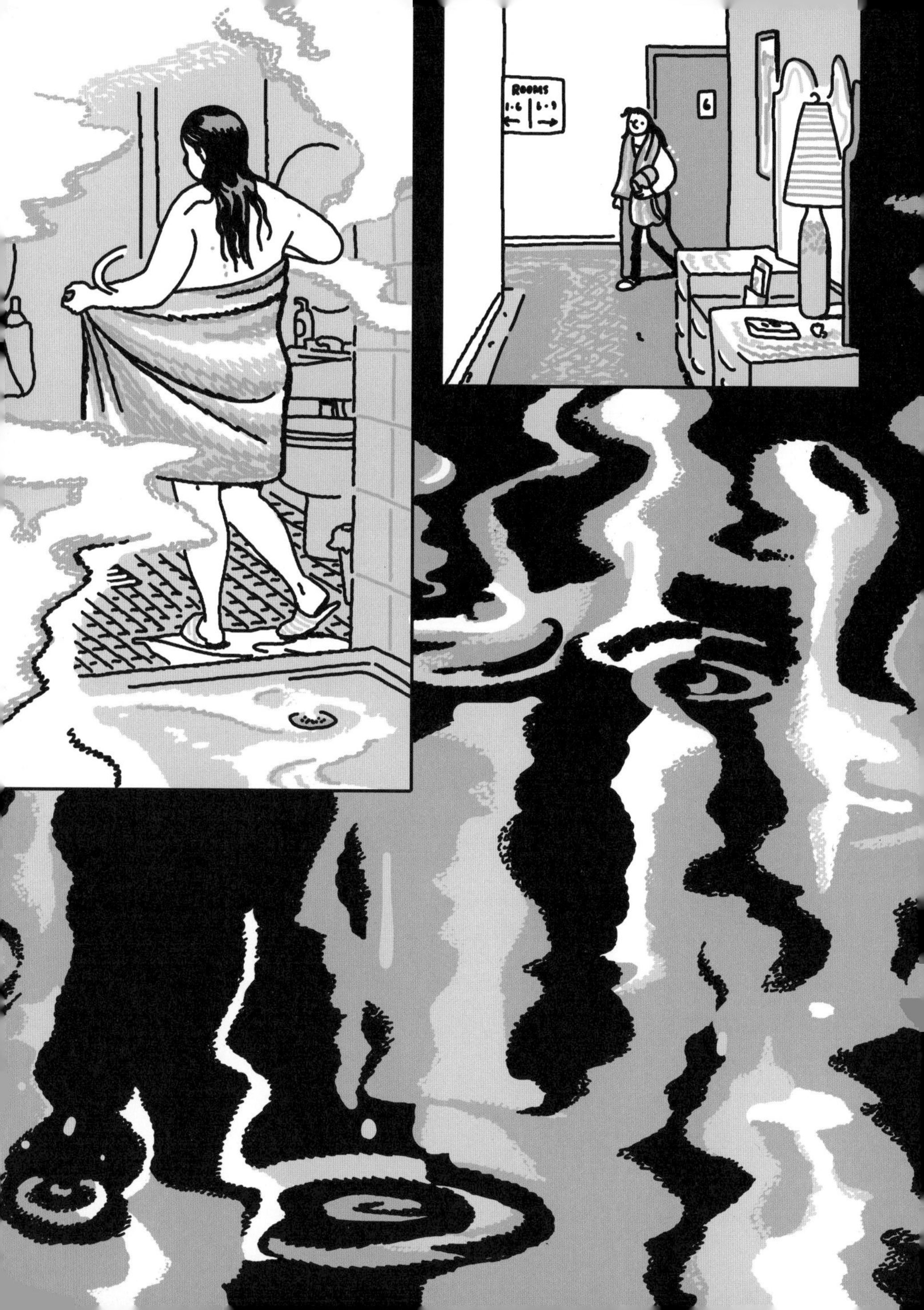
ROOMS
1-6 ←
6-9 →
6

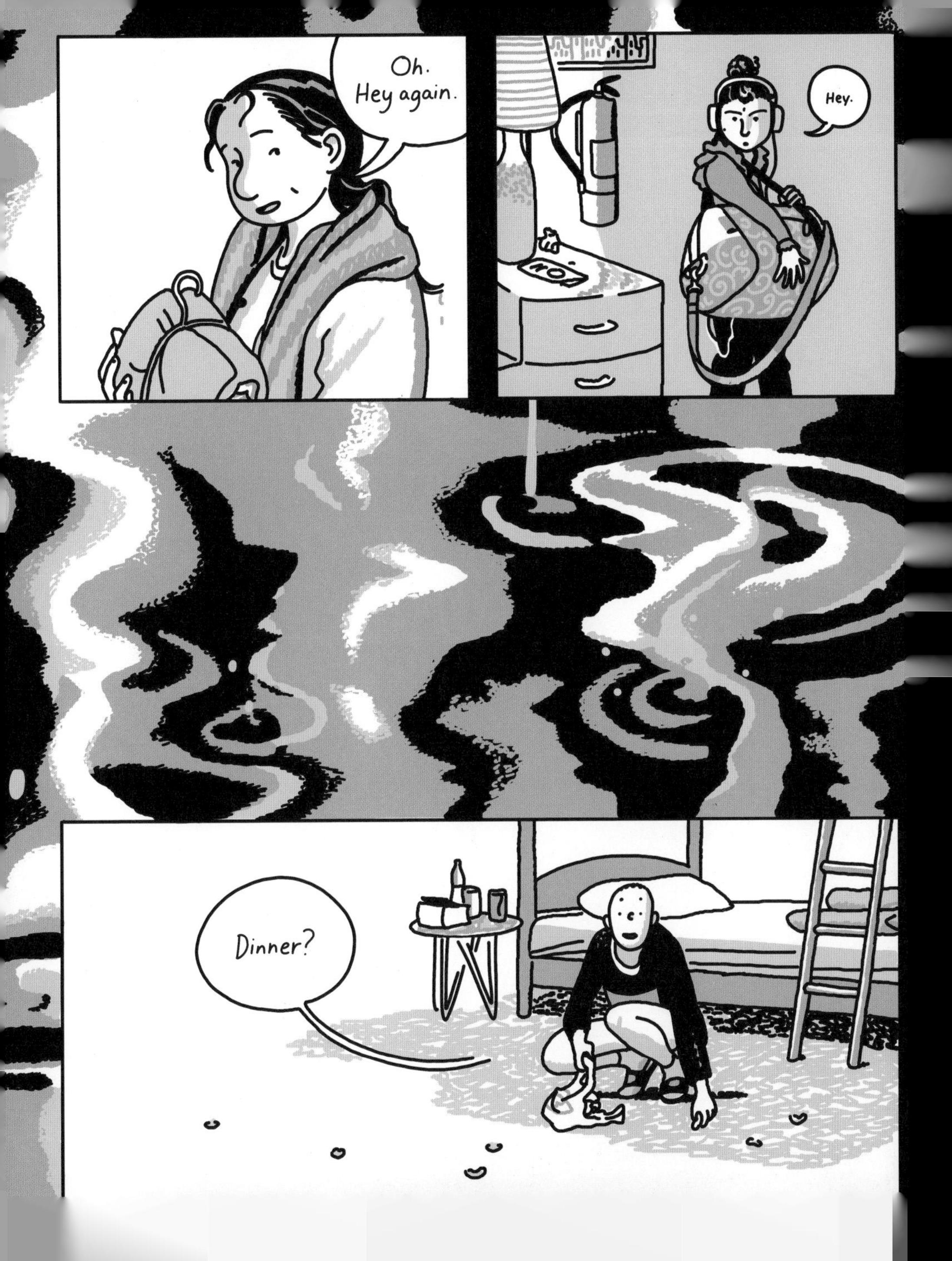
Oh. Hey again.
Hey.
Dinner?

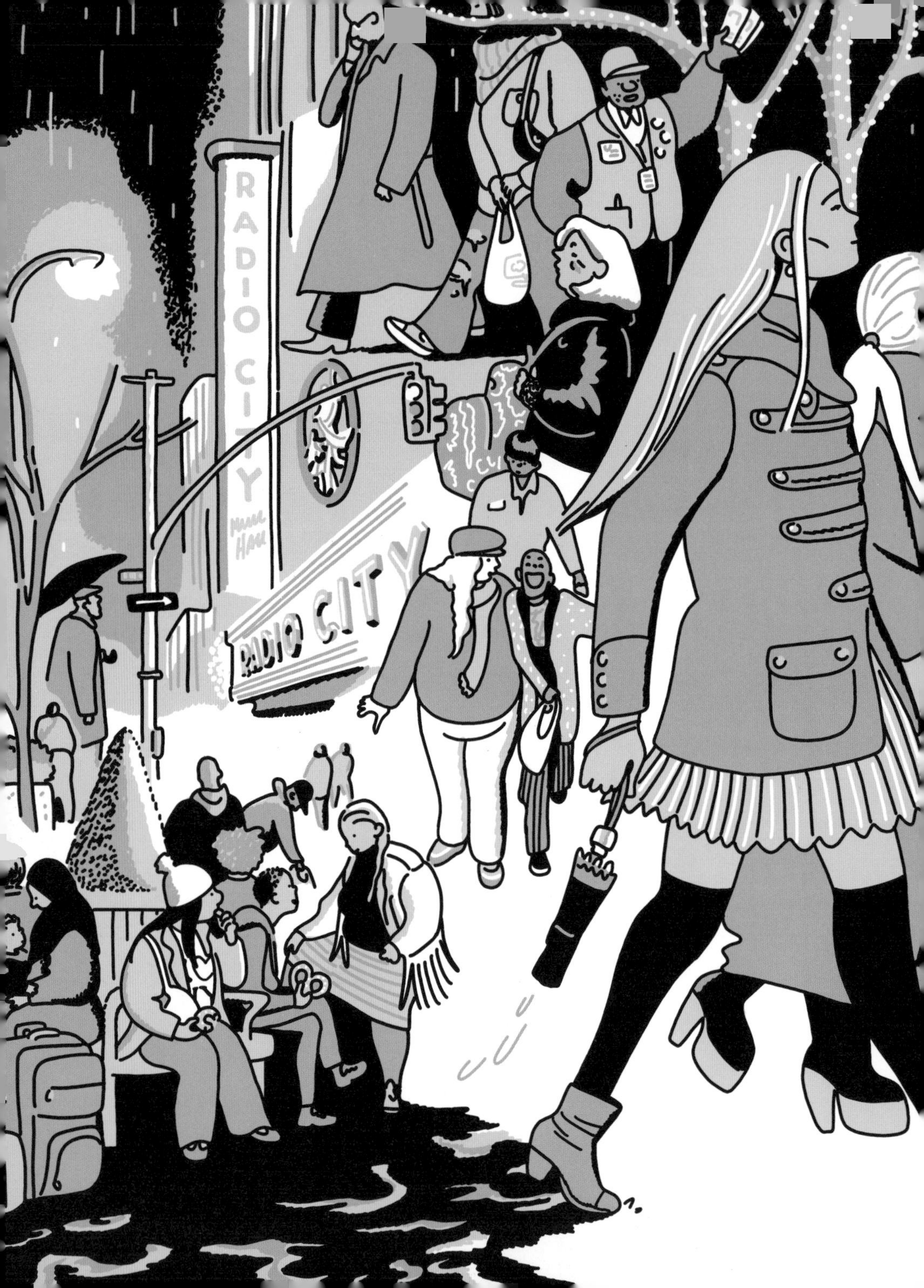
RADIO CITY
RADIO CITY

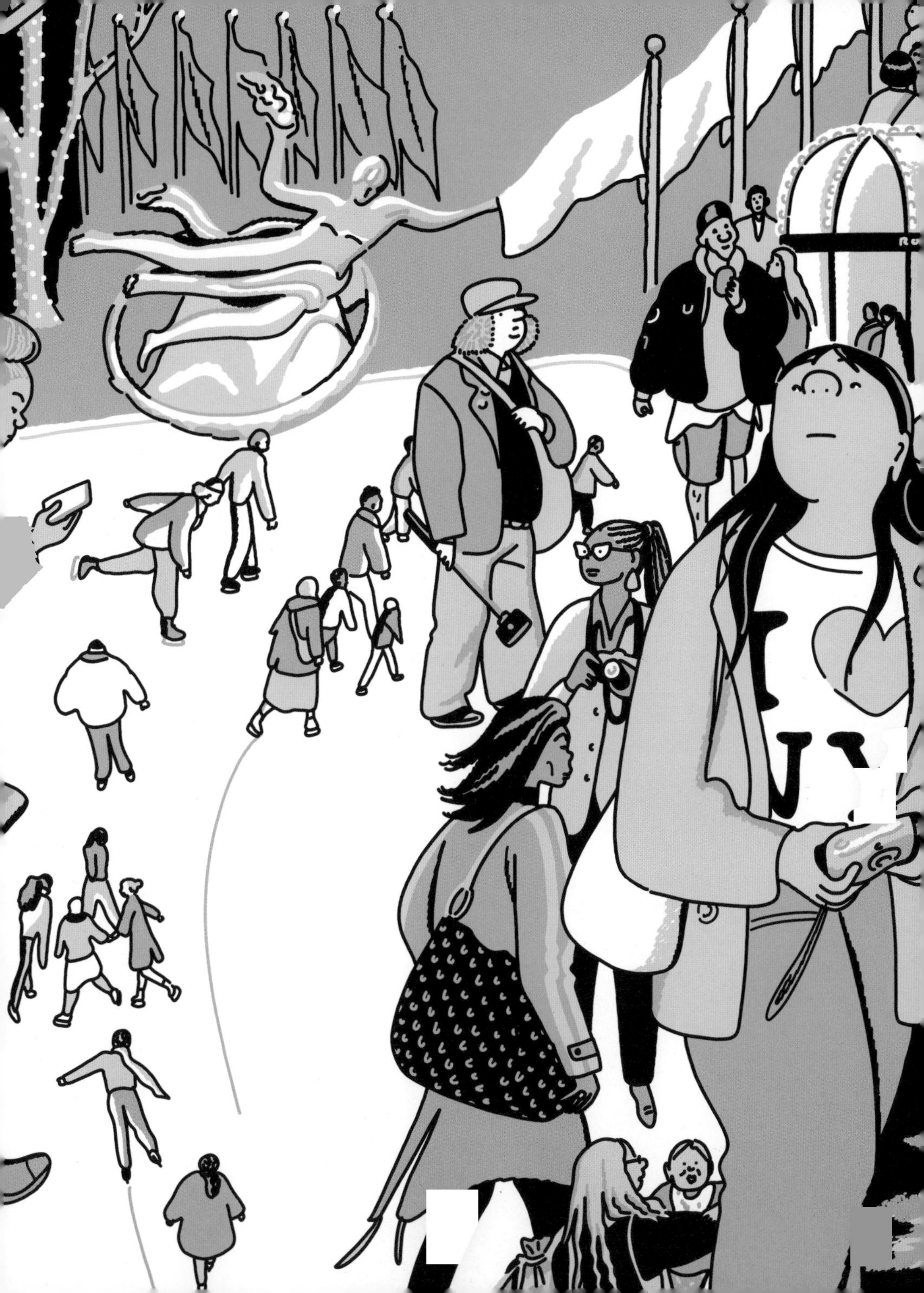

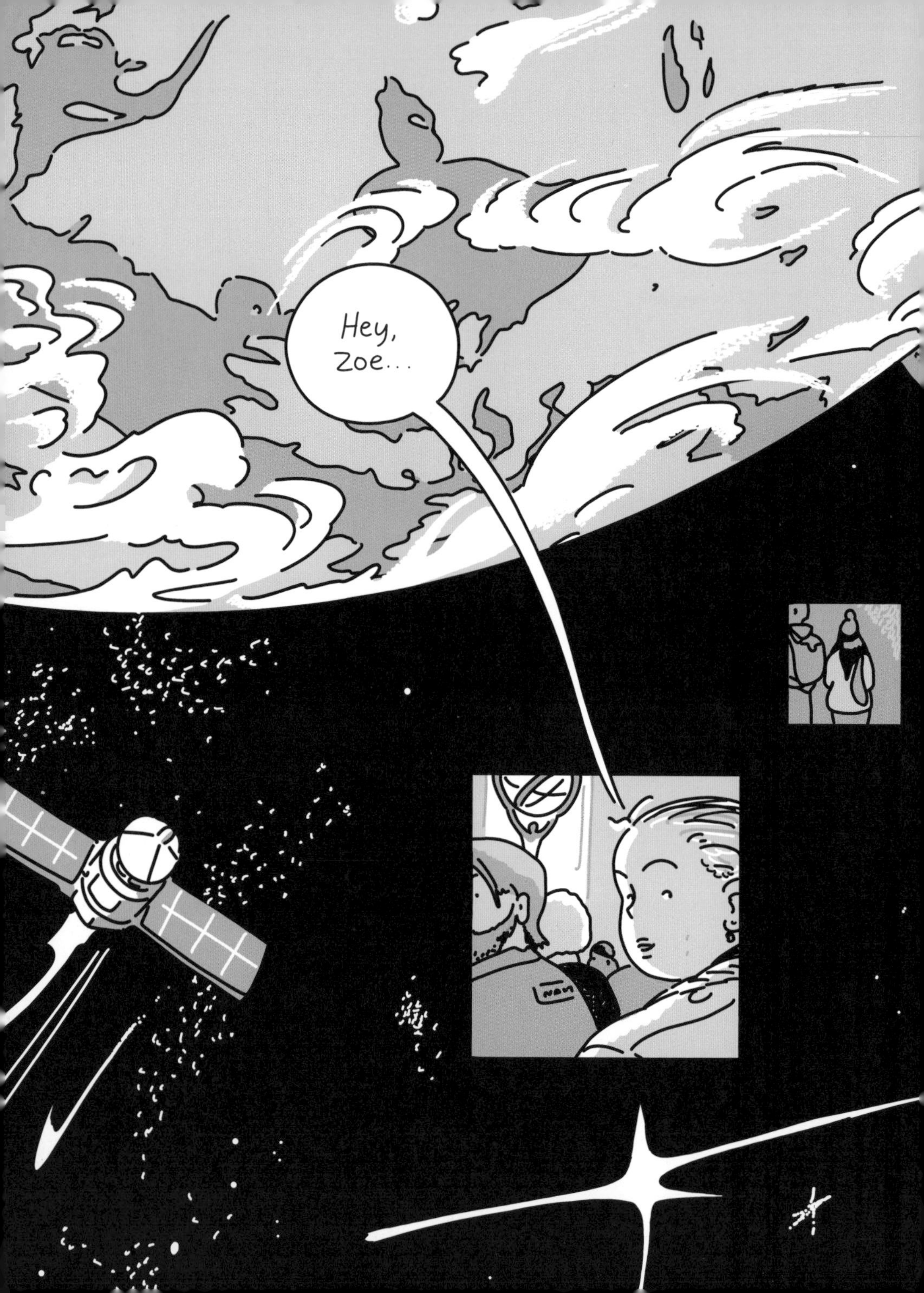
Hey, Zoe...

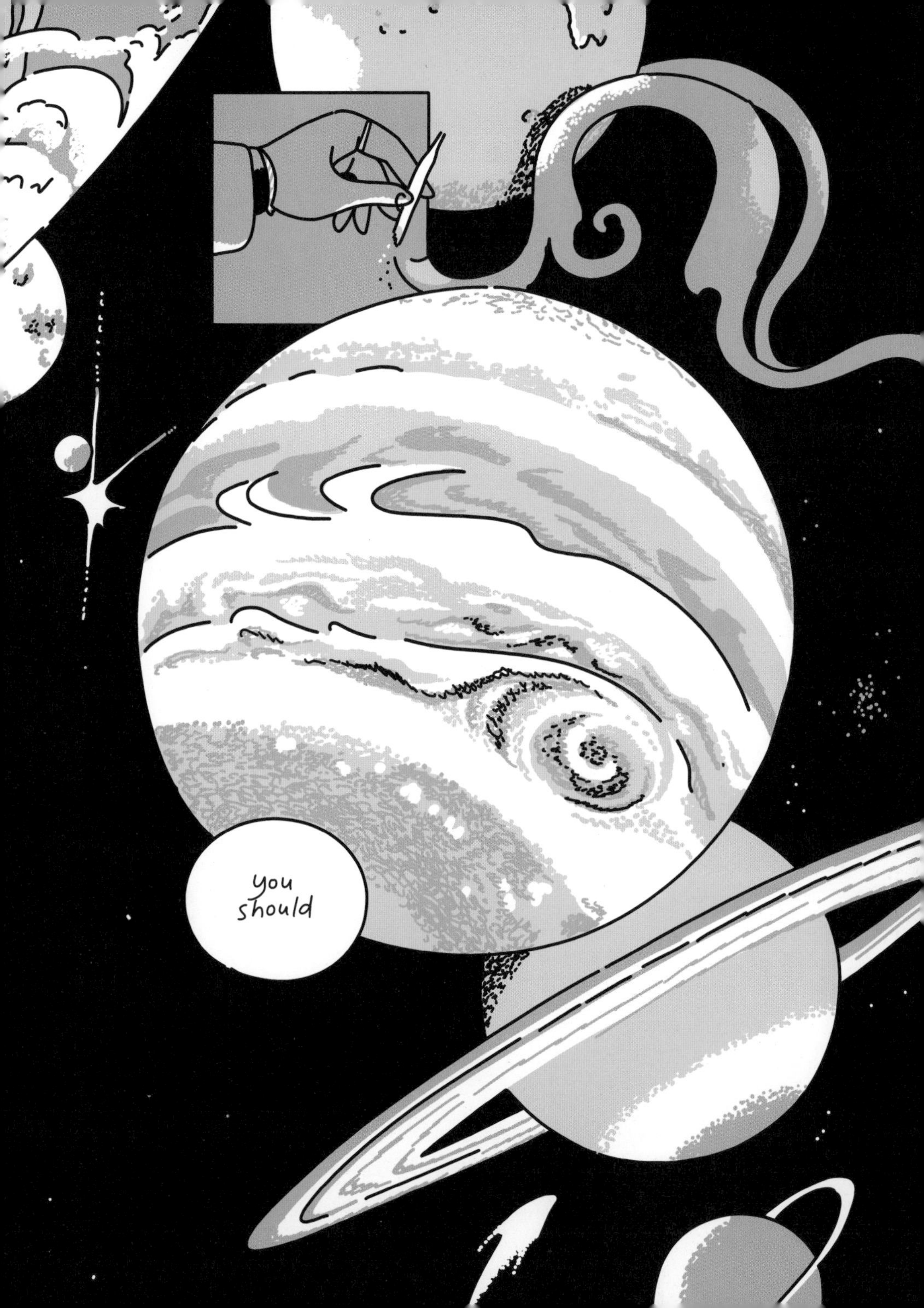
you should

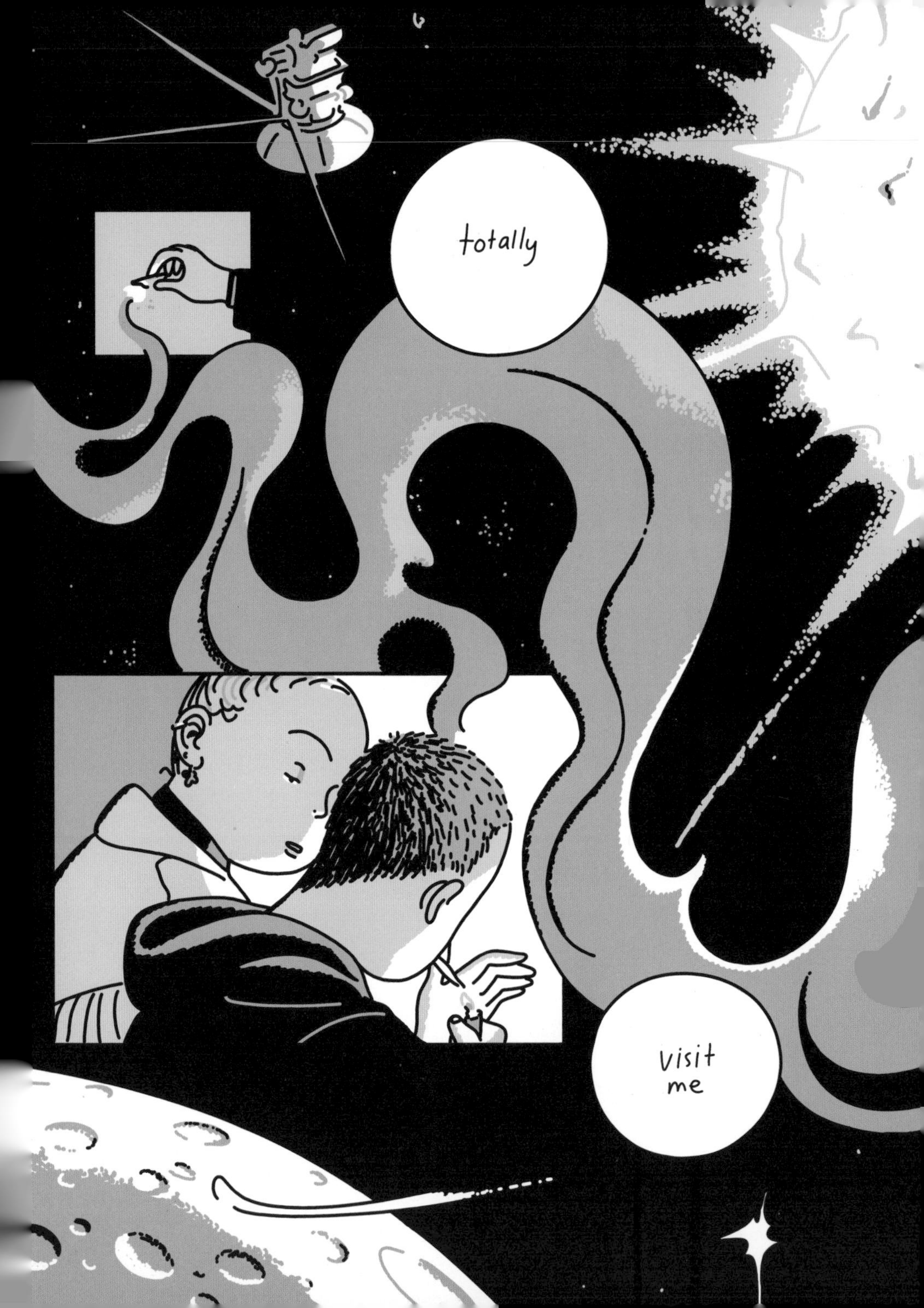
totally
visit me

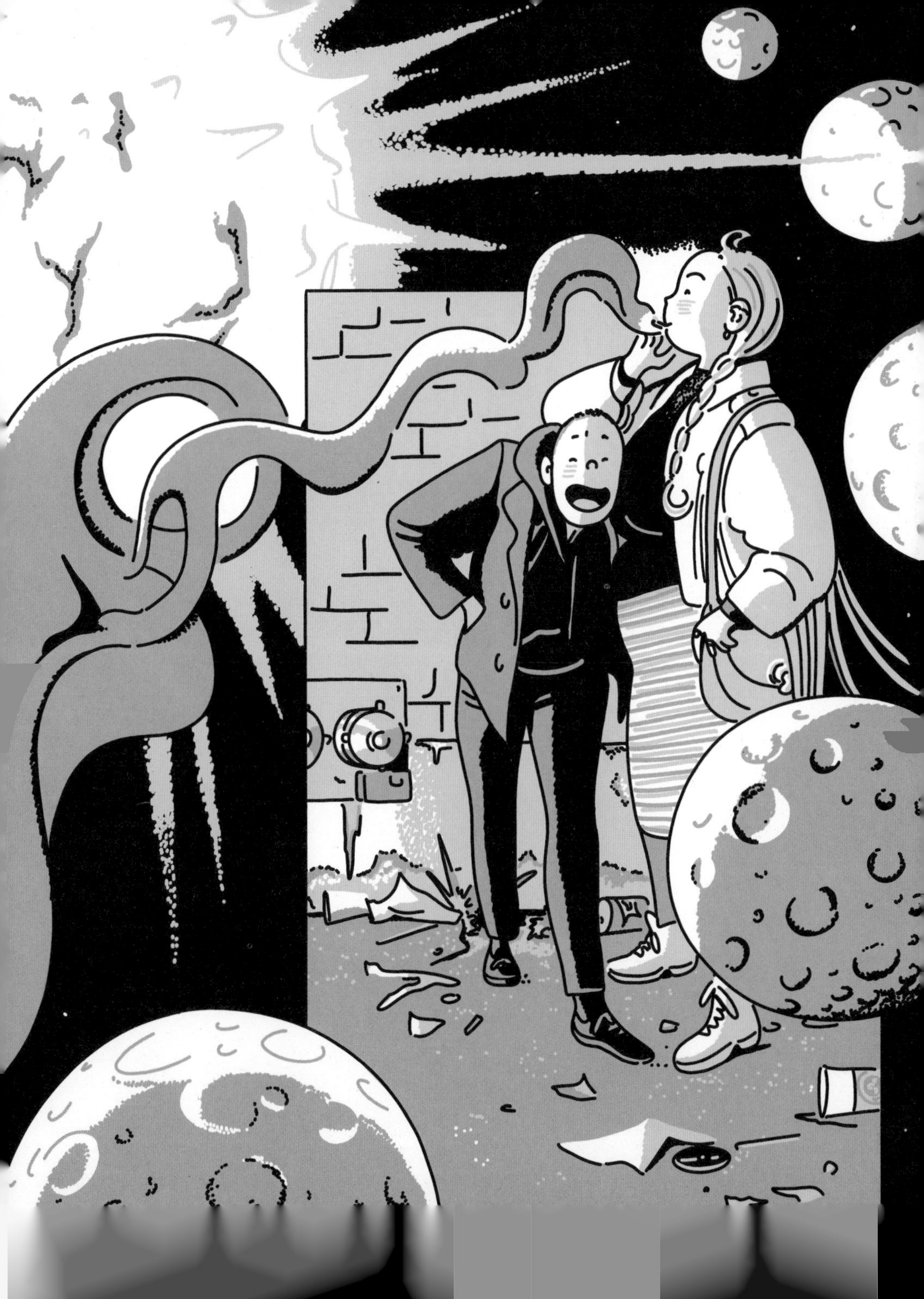

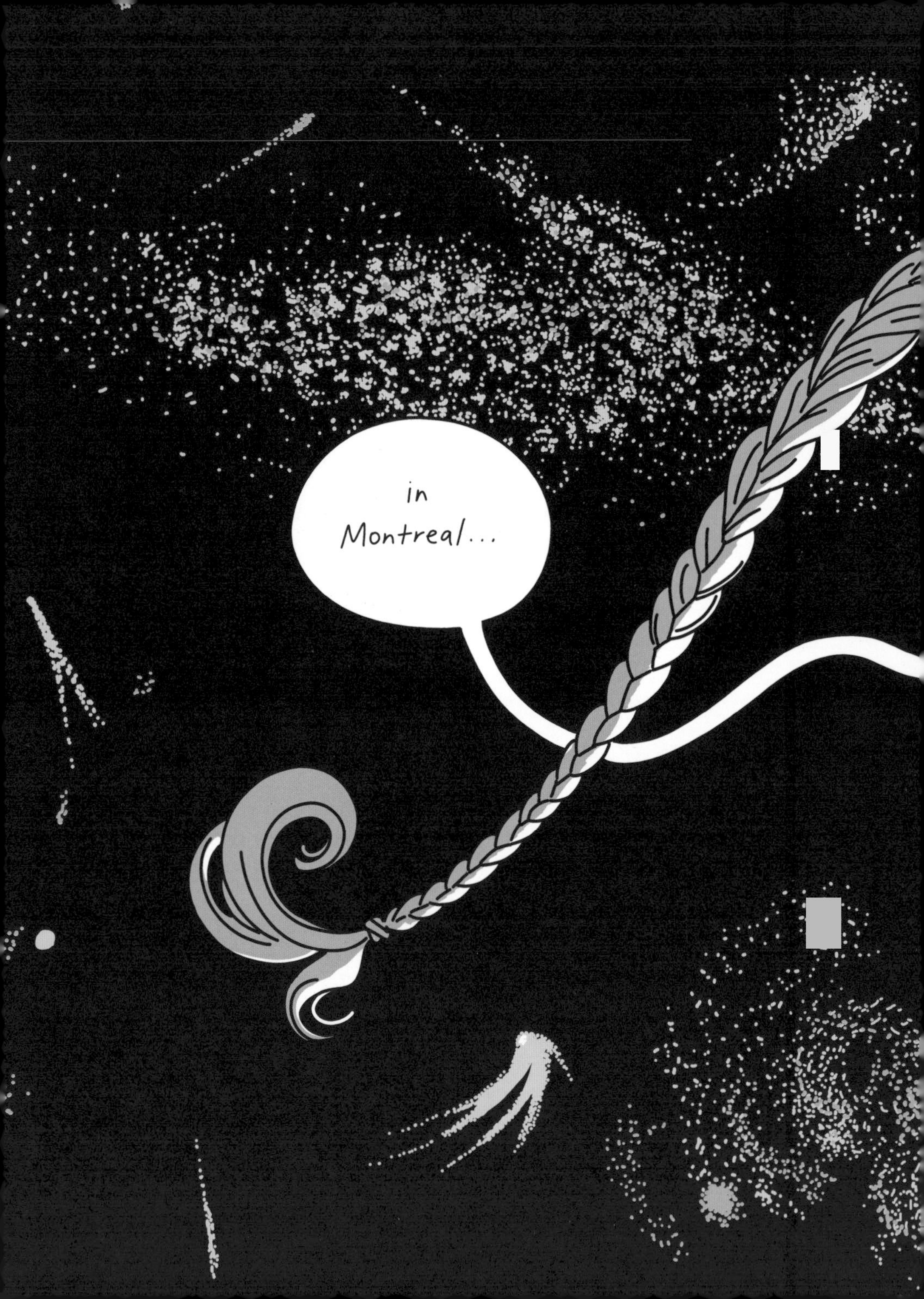
in Montreal...

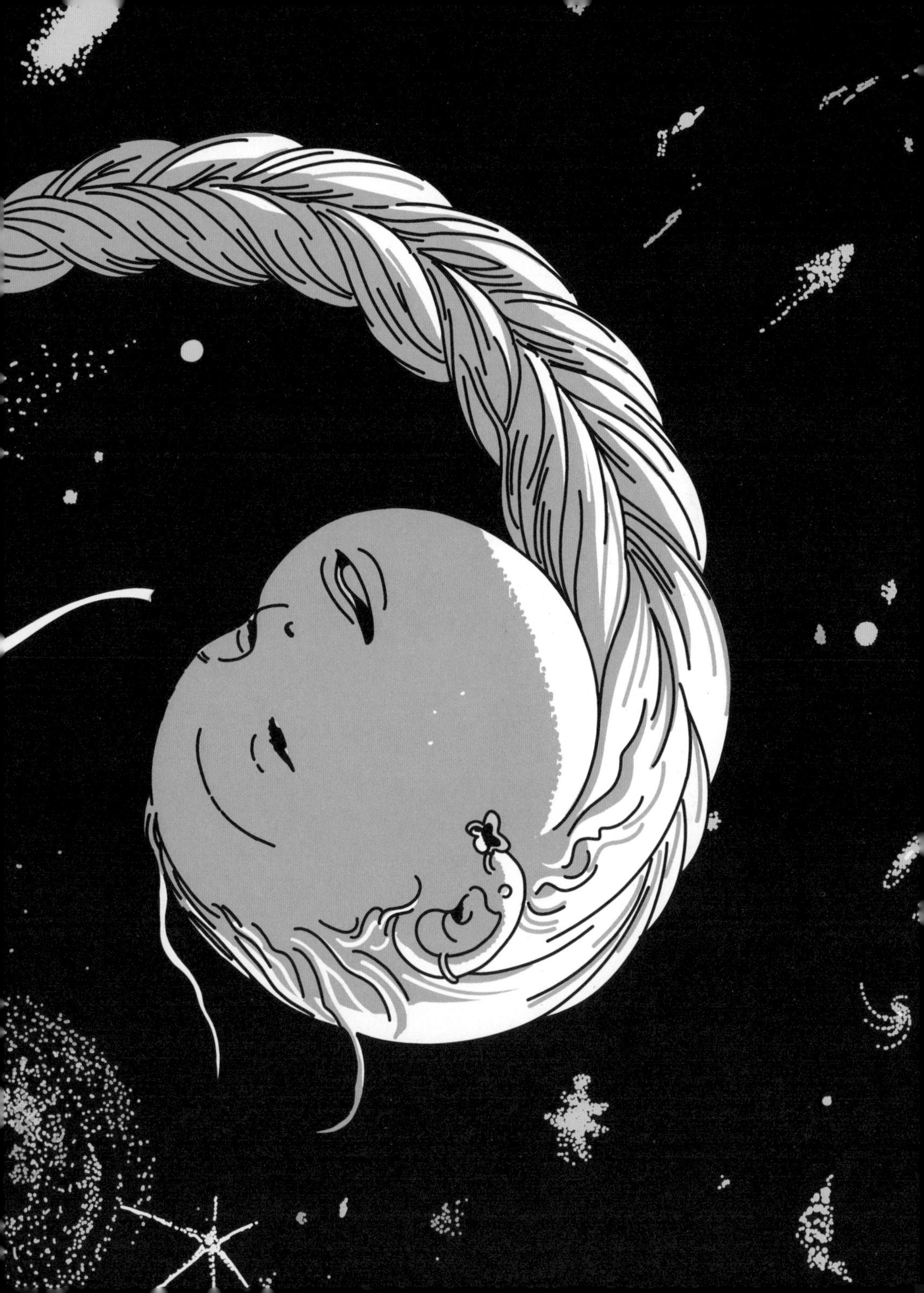

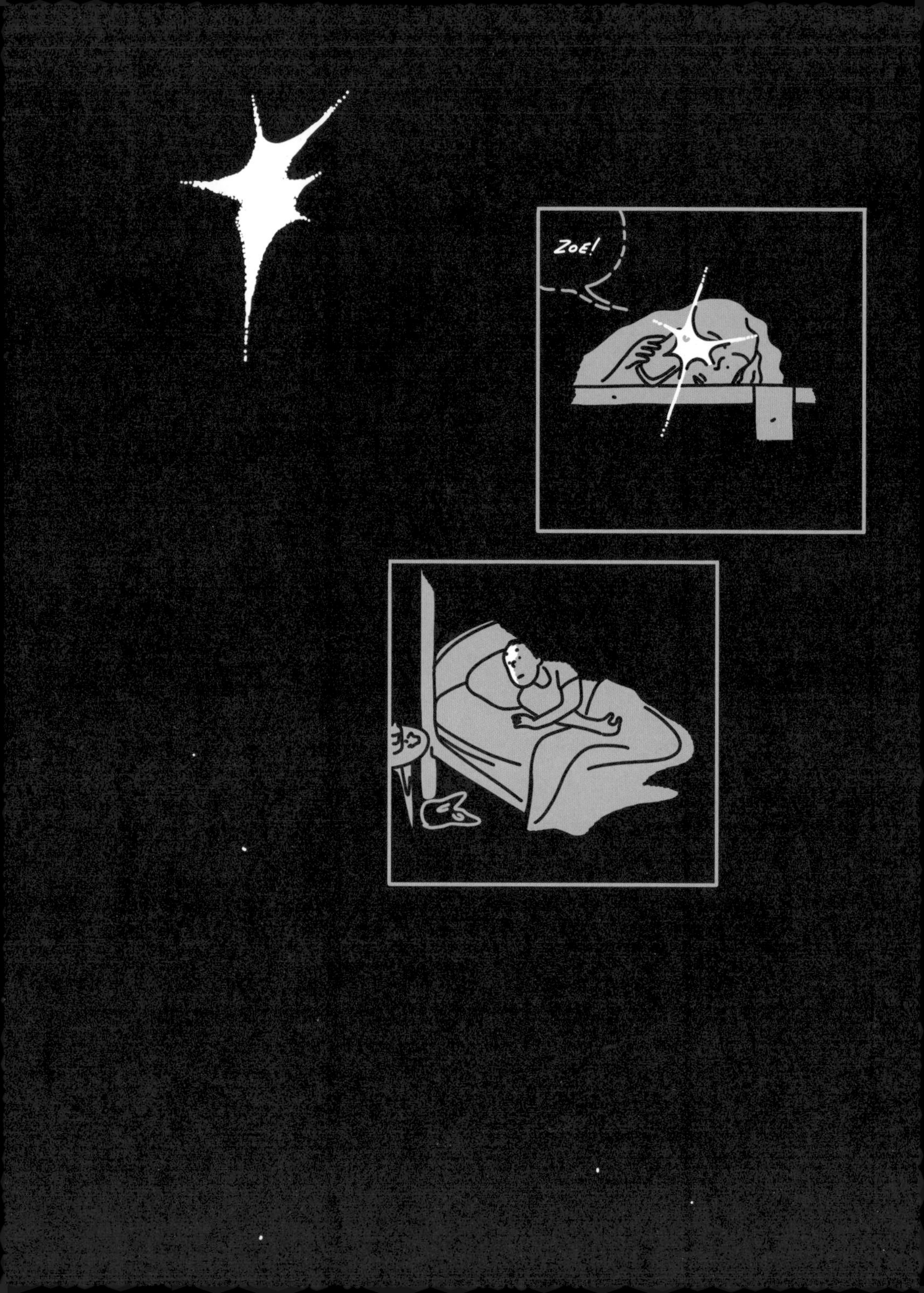
ZOE!

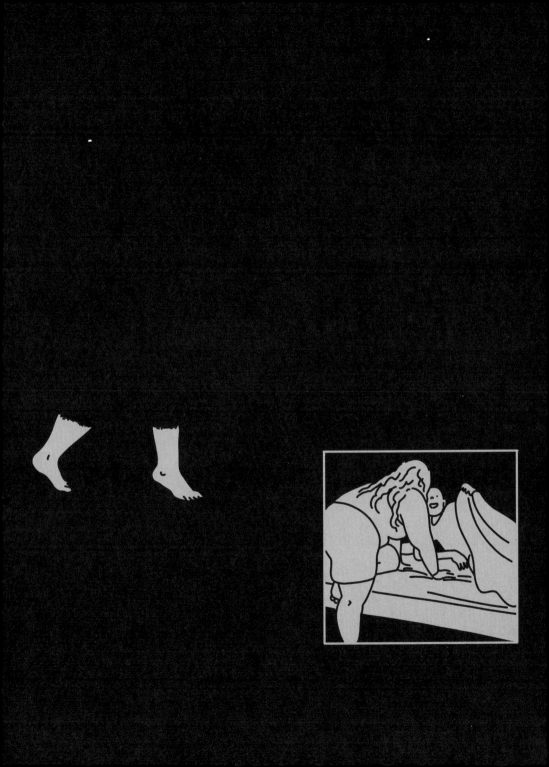

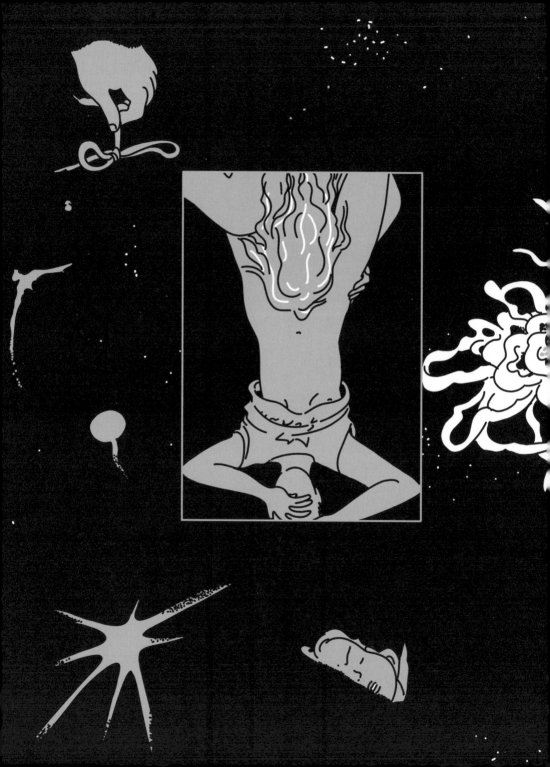

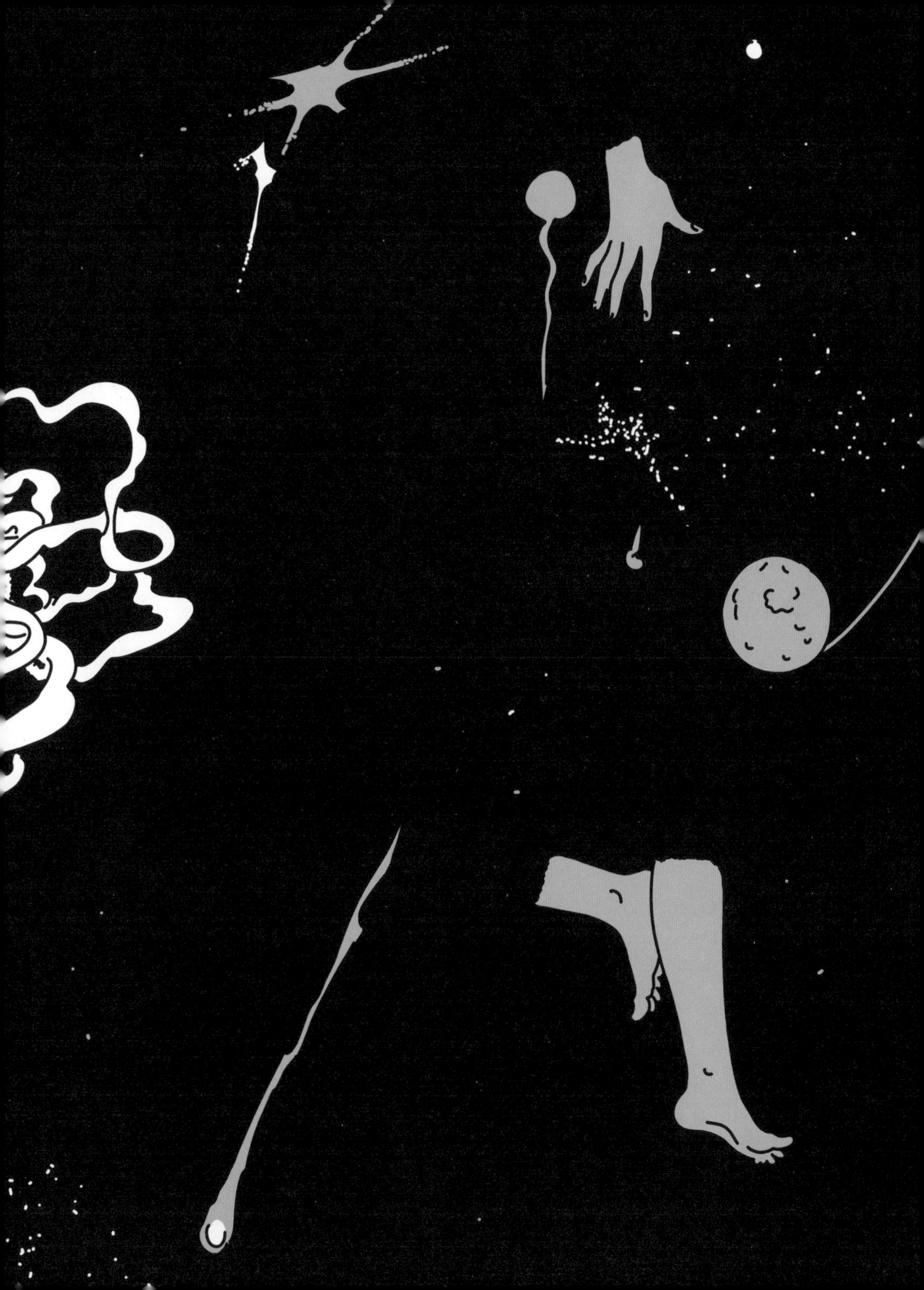

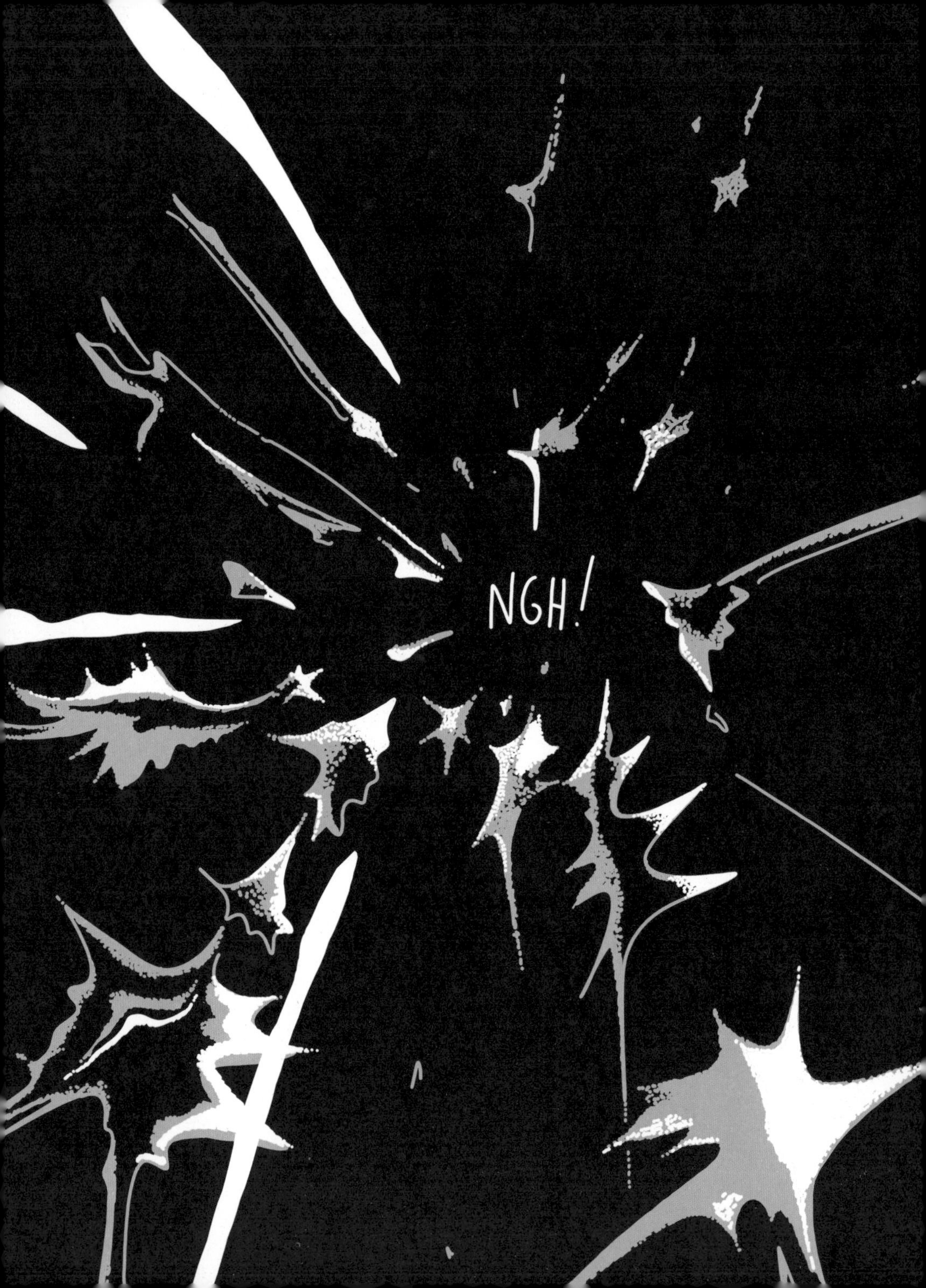
NGH!

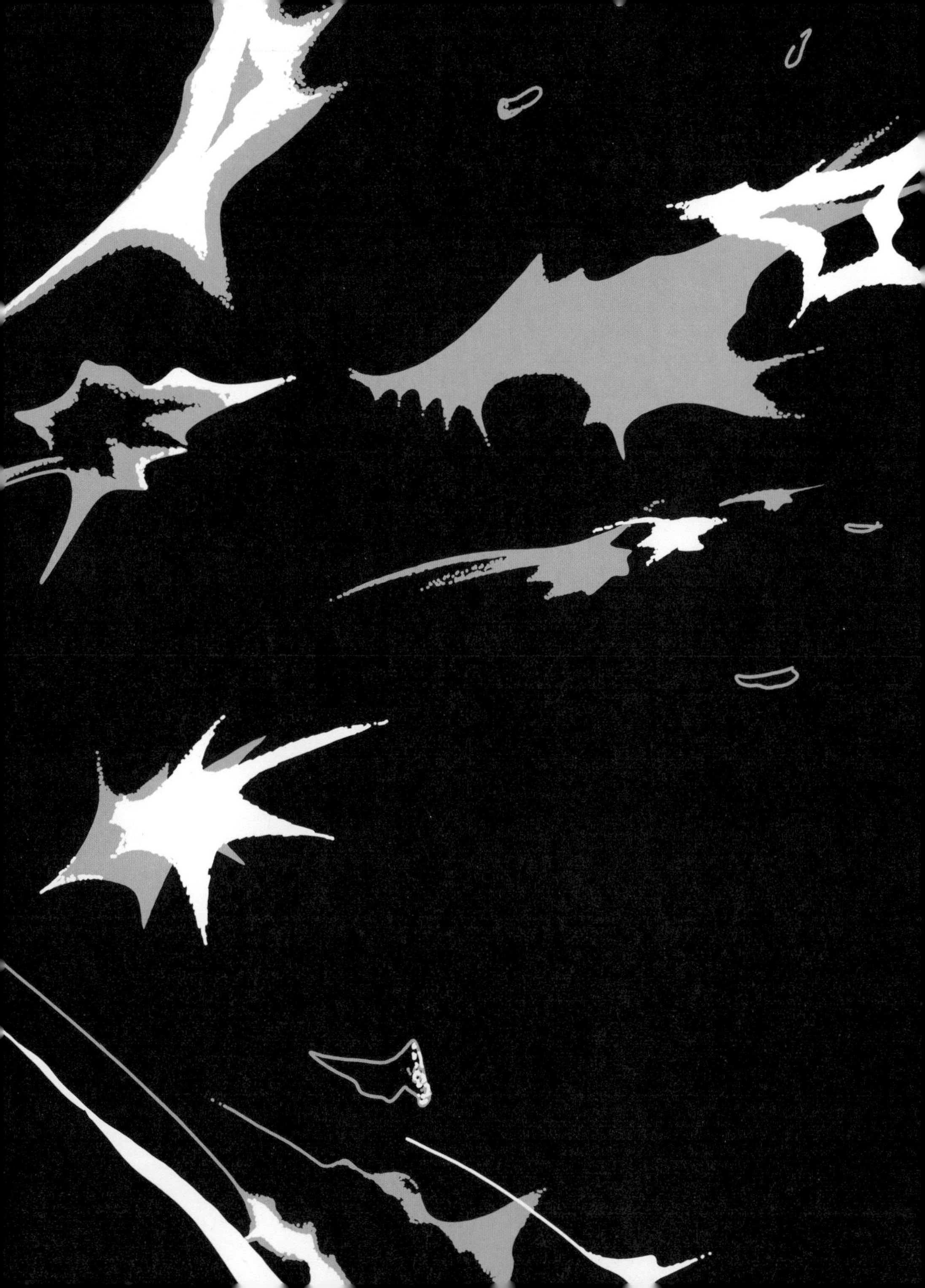

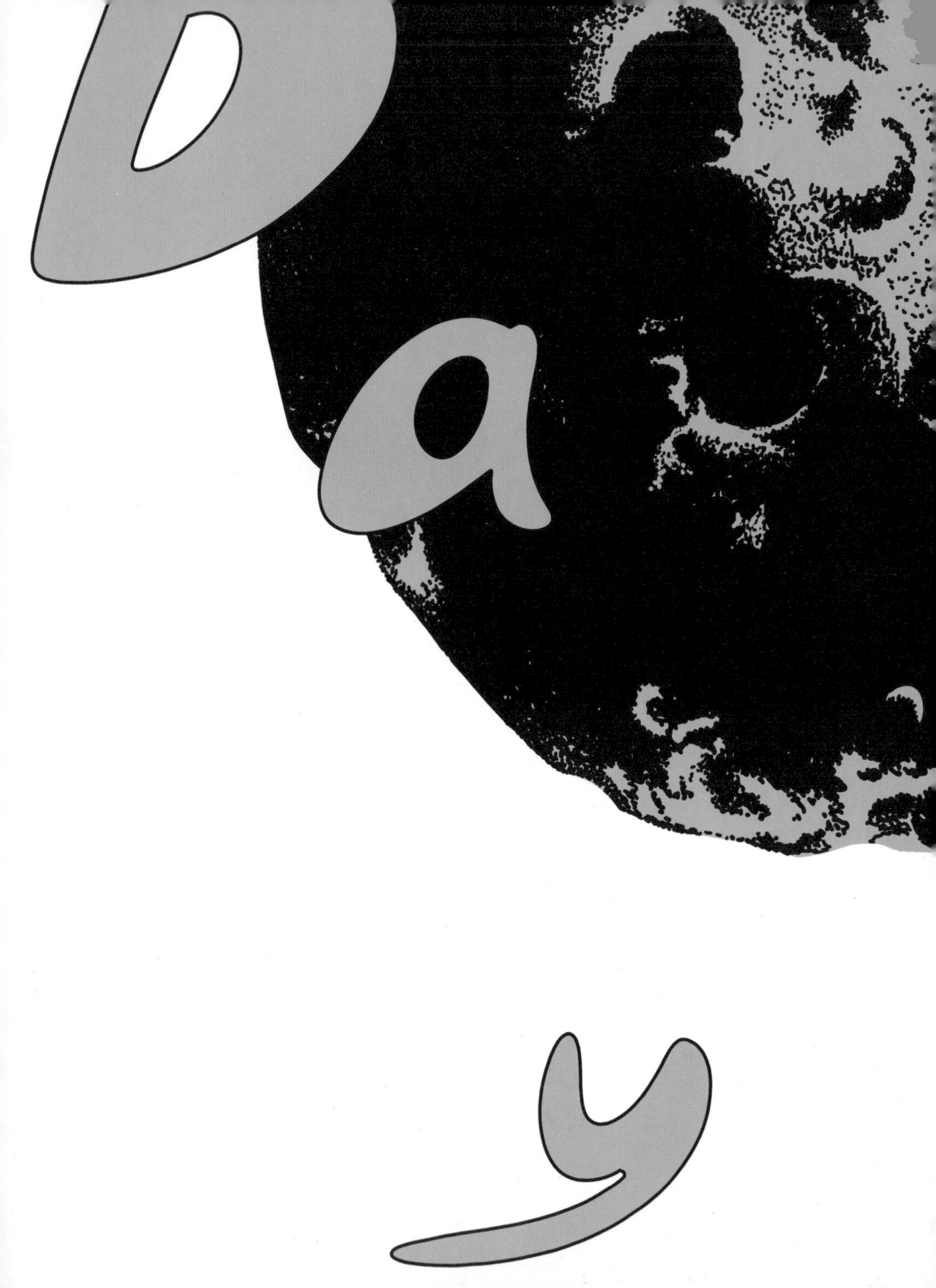
Day

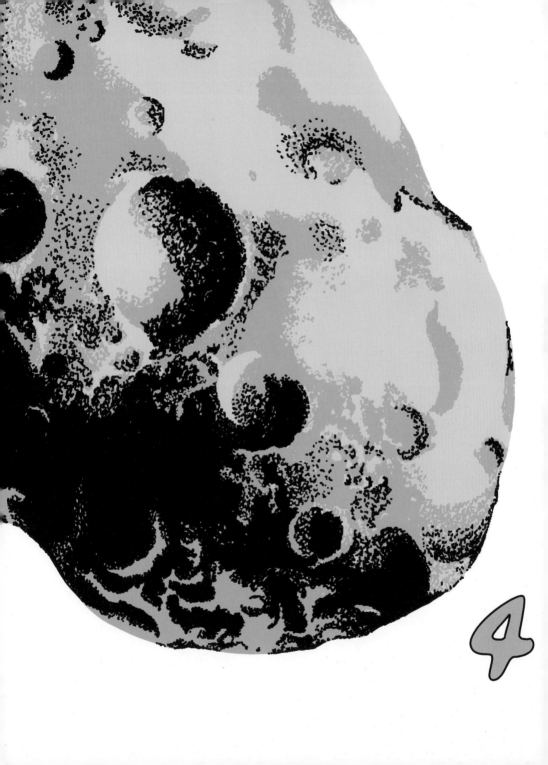

4

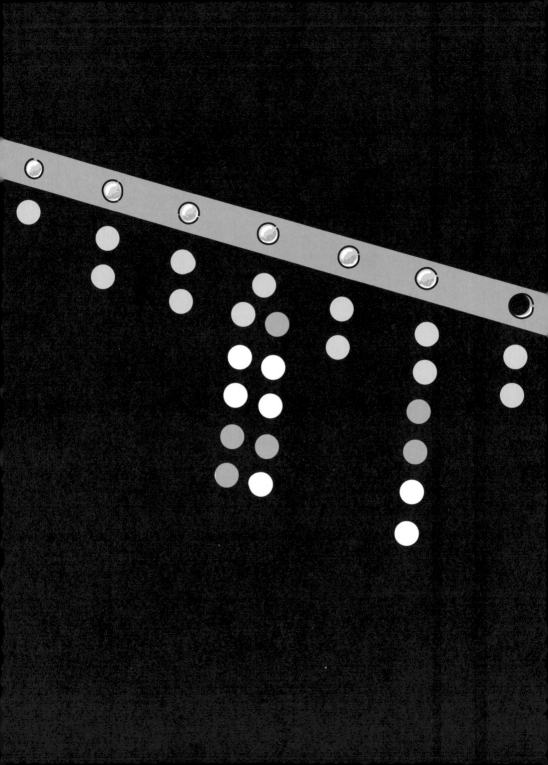

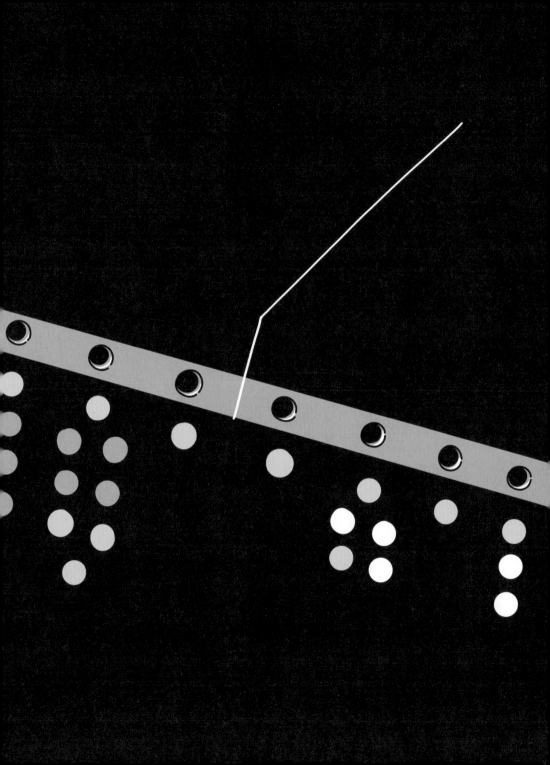

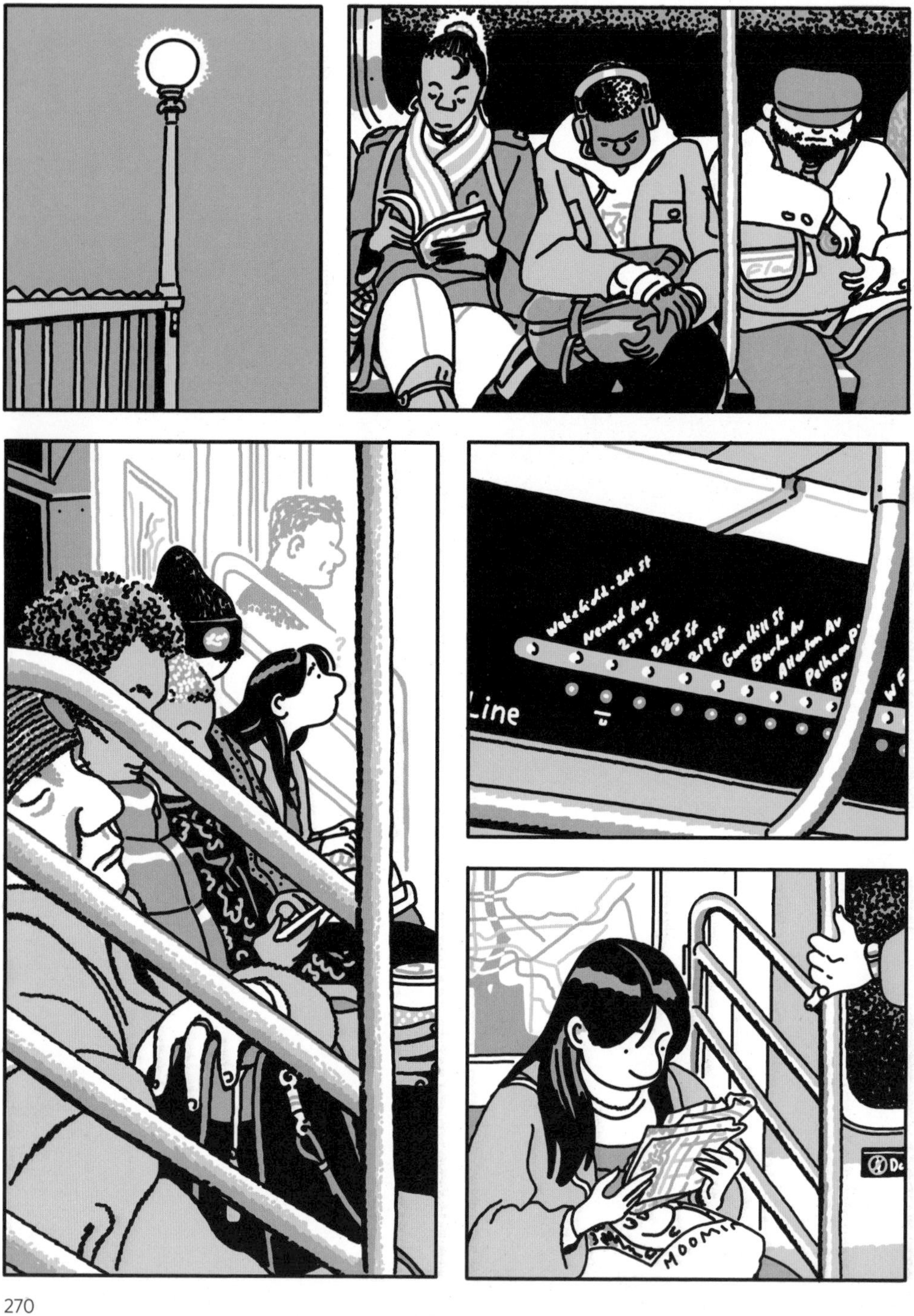
233 St
225 St
219 St
Burke Av
Allerton Av
Line

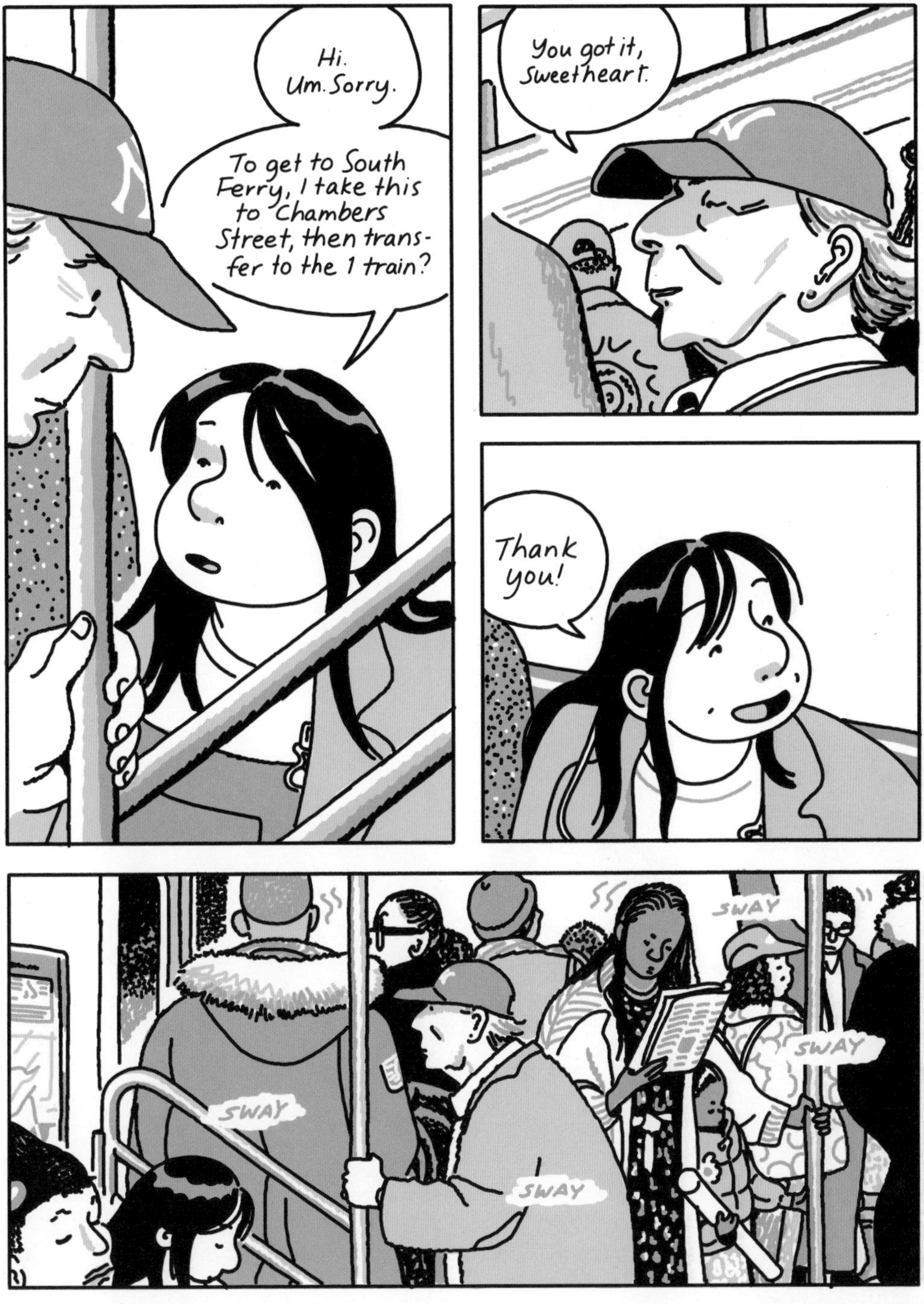
Hi. Um. Sorry.
To get to South Ferry, I take this to Chambers Street, then transfer to the 1 train?
You got it, Sweetheart.
Thank you!
SWAY
SWAY
SWAY
SWAY

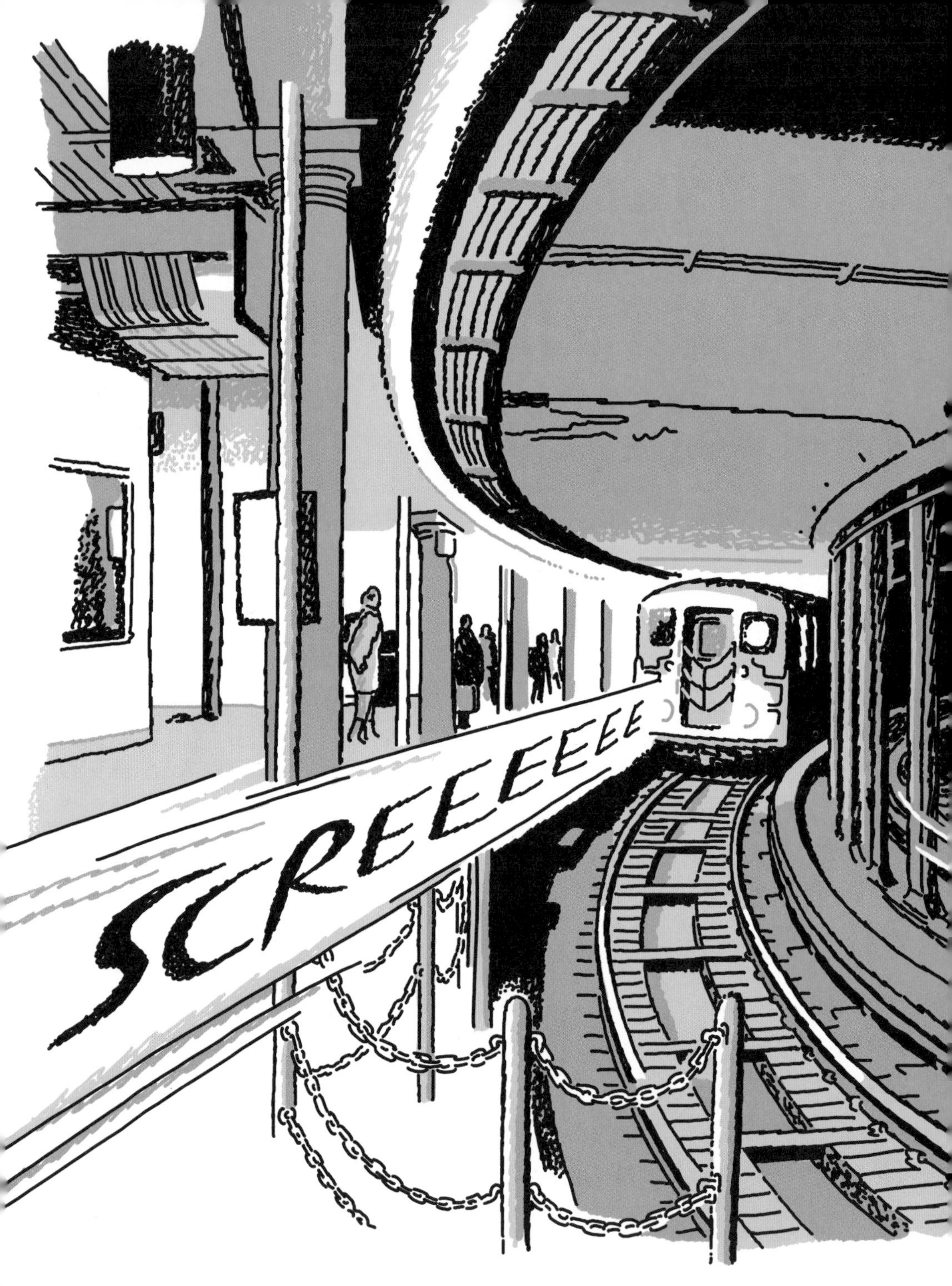
SCREEEEEE

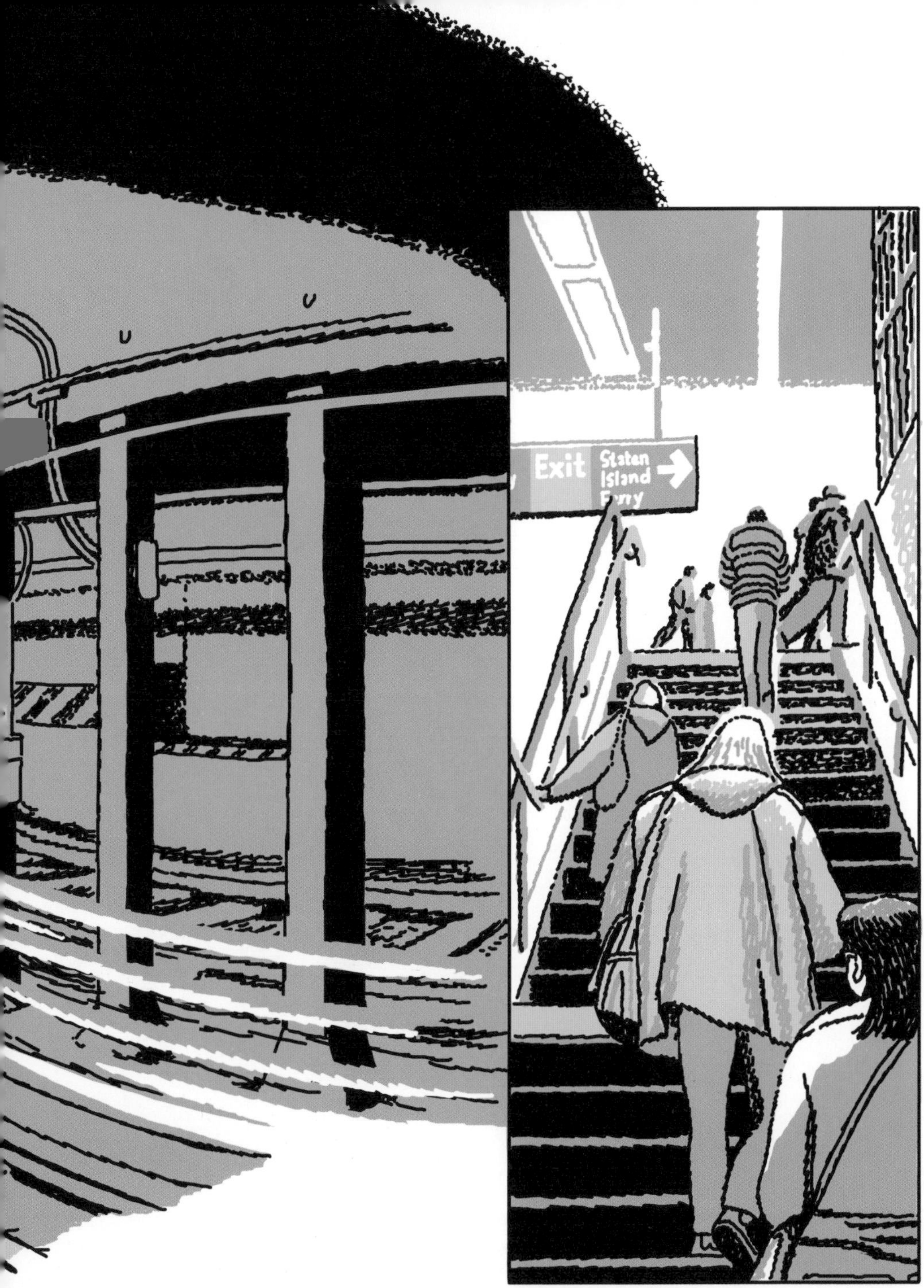
Exit
Staten Island Ferry

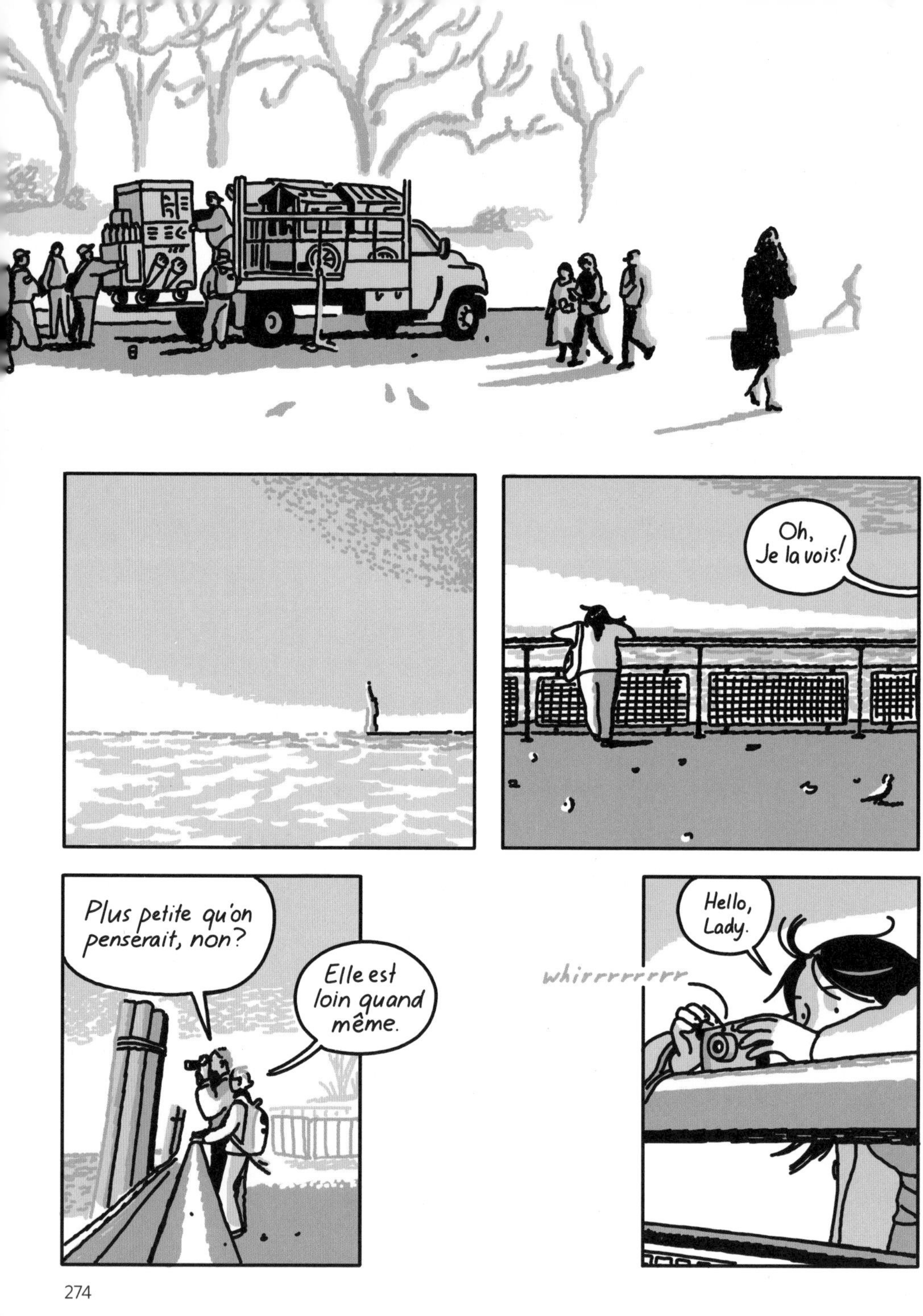
Oh, Je la vois!
Plus petite qu'on penserait, non?
Elle est loin quand même.
whirrrrrrrr
Hello, Lady.

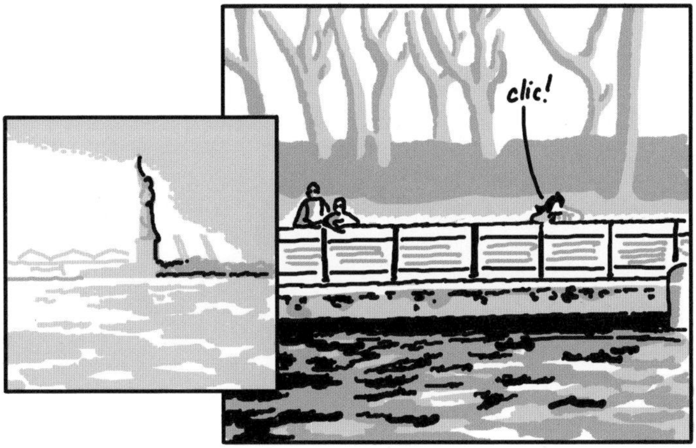
clic!

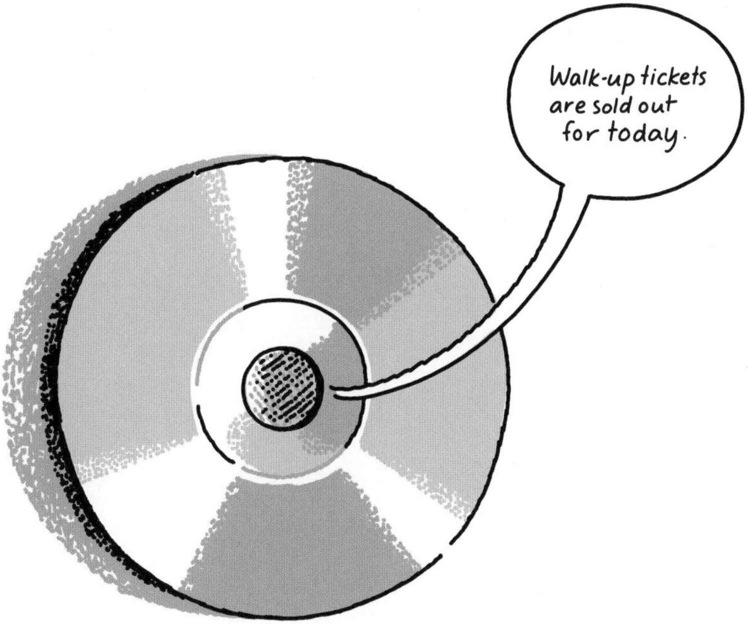
Walk-up tickets are sold out for today.

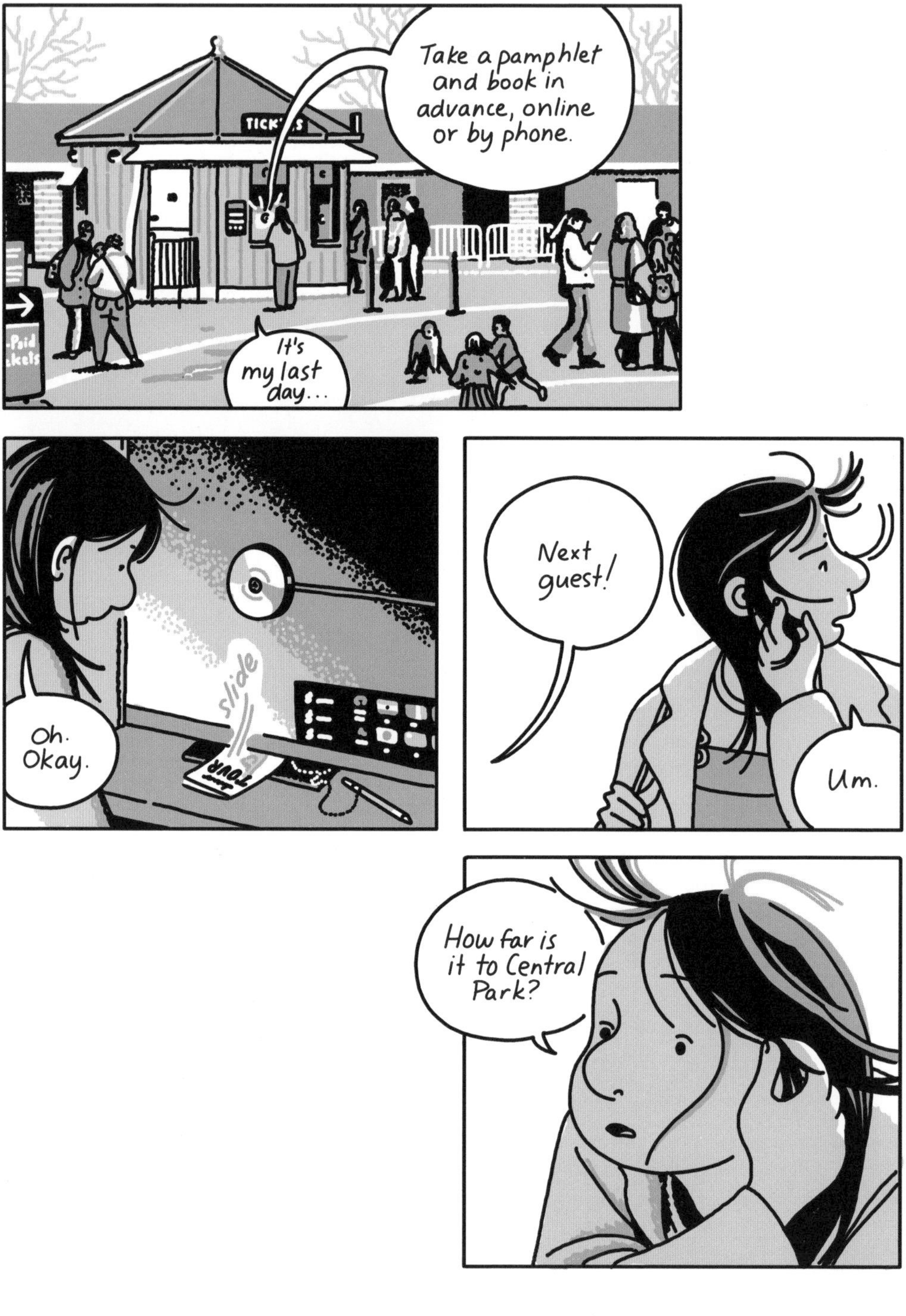
TICKETS
Take a pamphlet and book in advance, online or by phone.
It's my last day...
Oh. Okay.
slide
Next guest!
Um.
How far is it to Central Park?

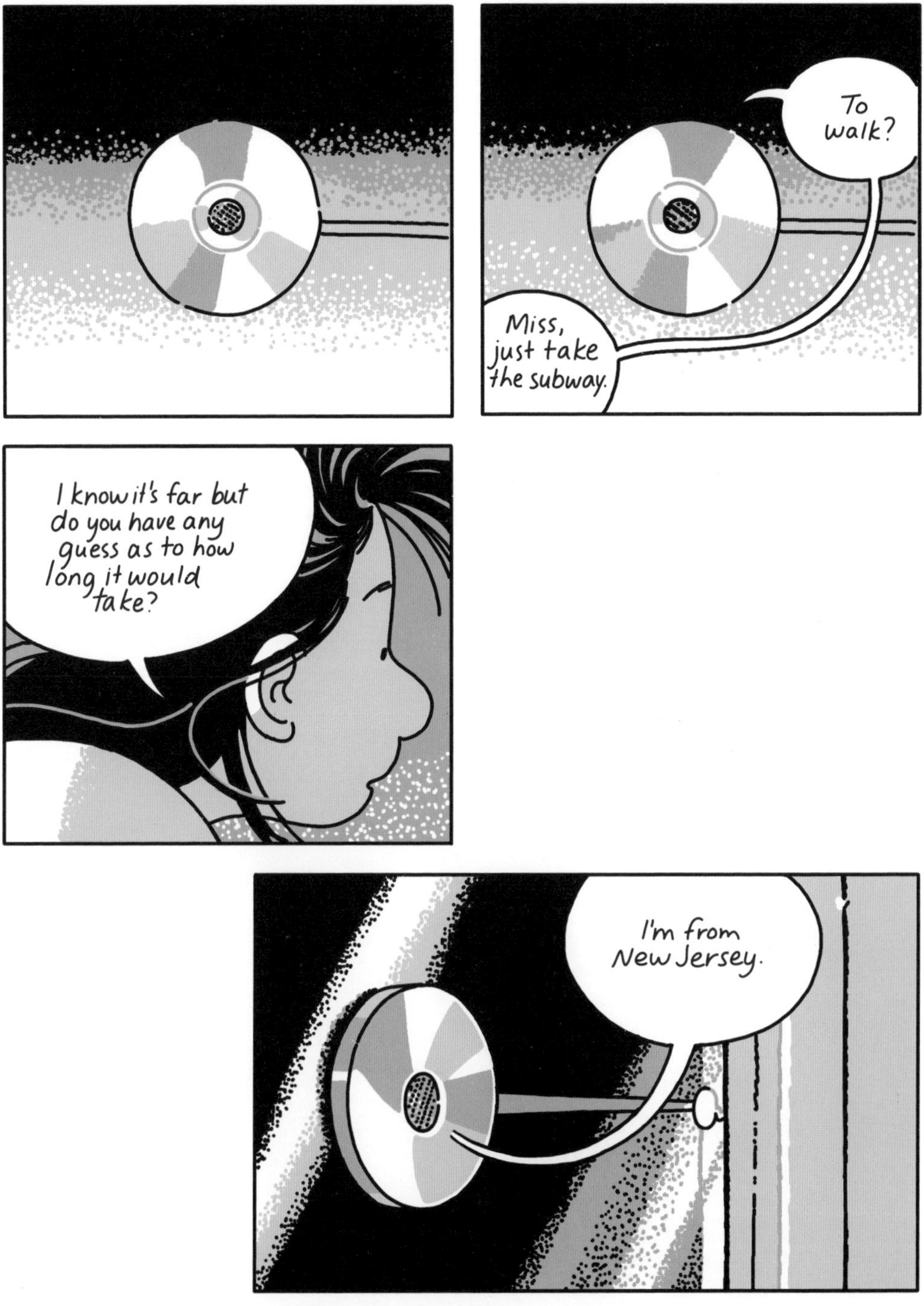
To walk?
Miss, just take the subway.
I know it's far but do you have any guess as to how long it would take?
I'm from New Jersey.

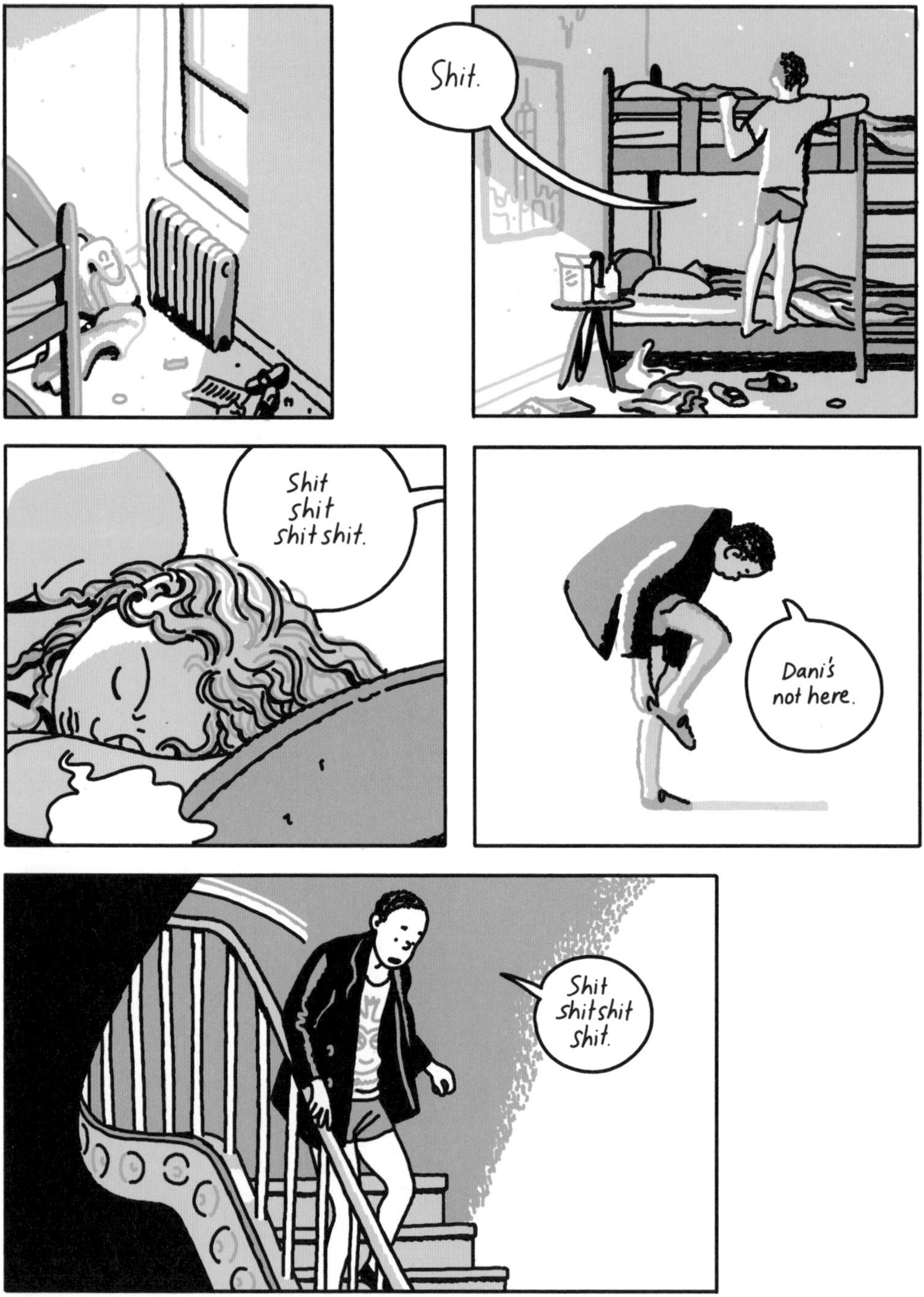
Shit.
Shit shit shit shit.
Dani's not here.
Shit shit shit shit.

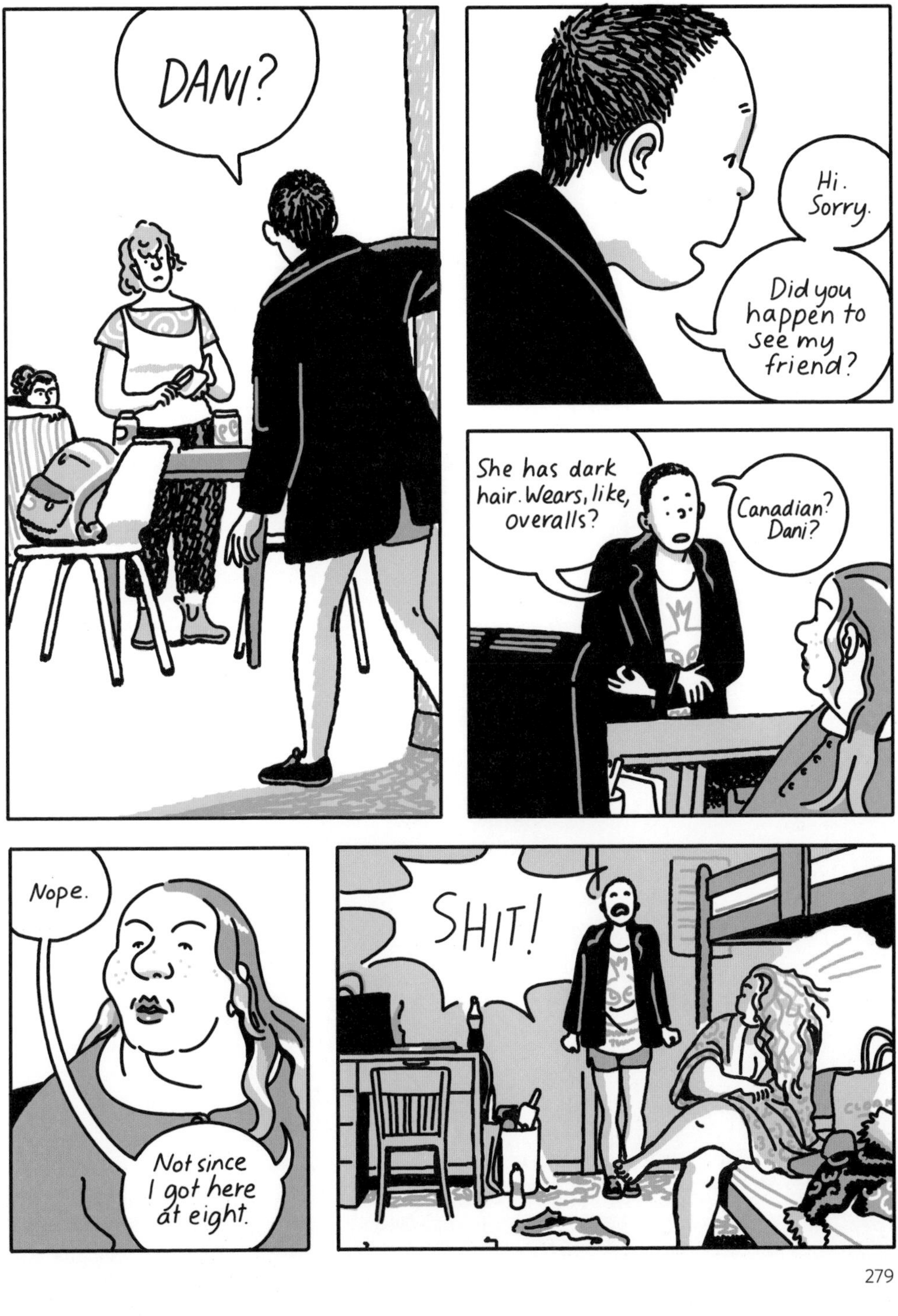
DANI?
Hi. Sorry.
Did you happen to see my friend?
She has dark hair. Wears, like, overalls?
Canadian? Dani?
Nope.
Not since I got here at eight.
SHIT!

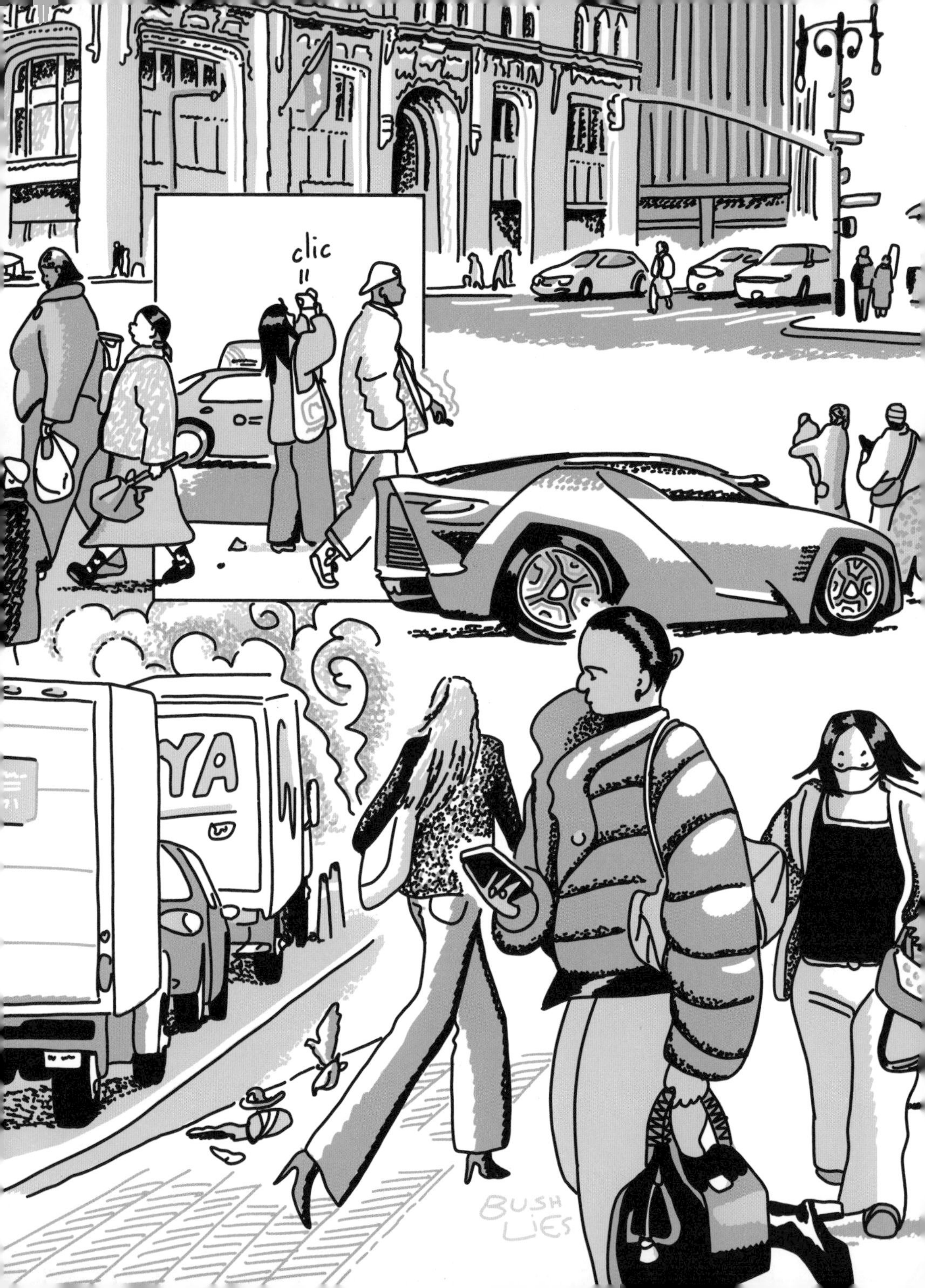
clic
YA
BUSH LIES

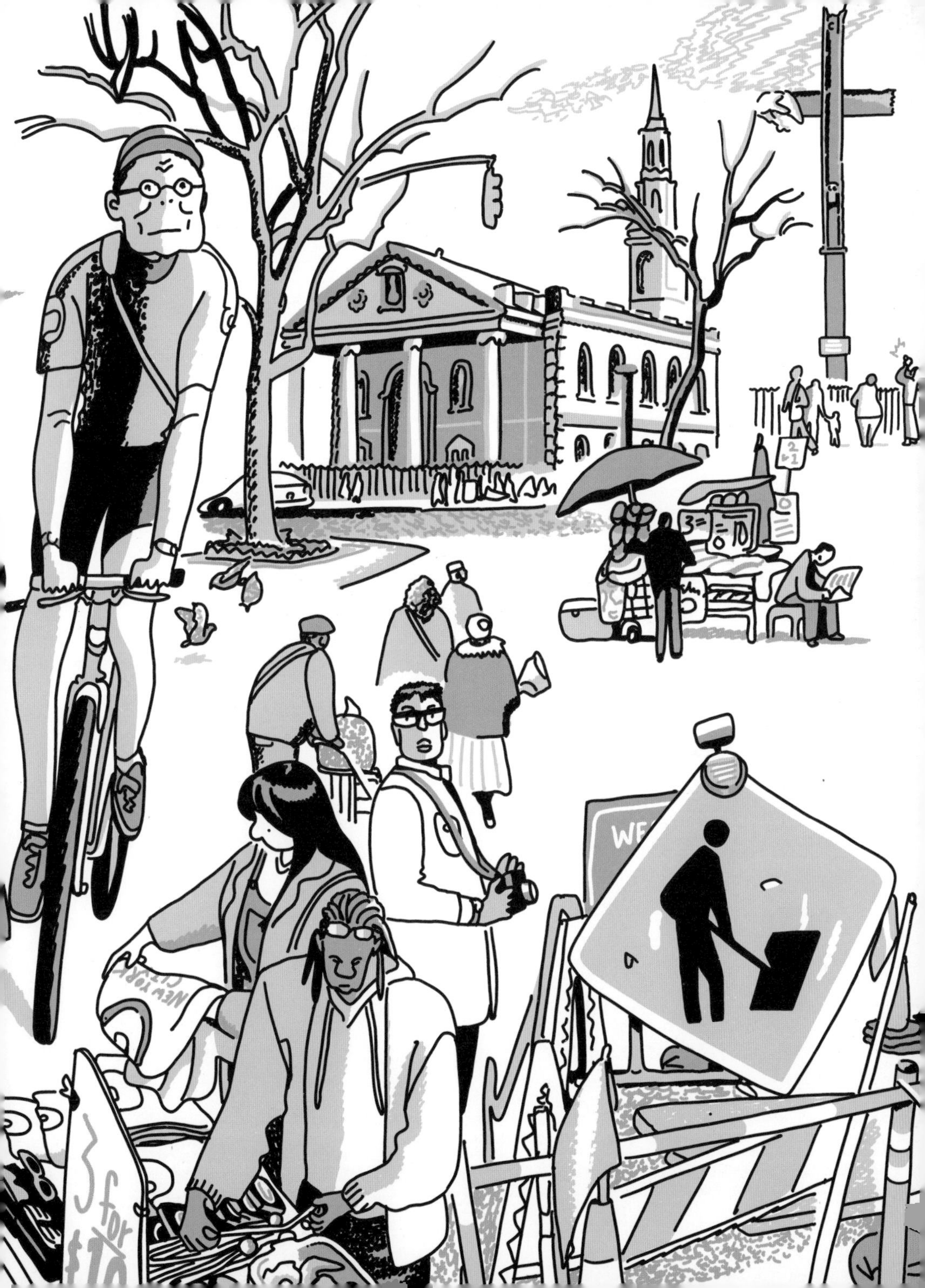
NEW YORK
3 for

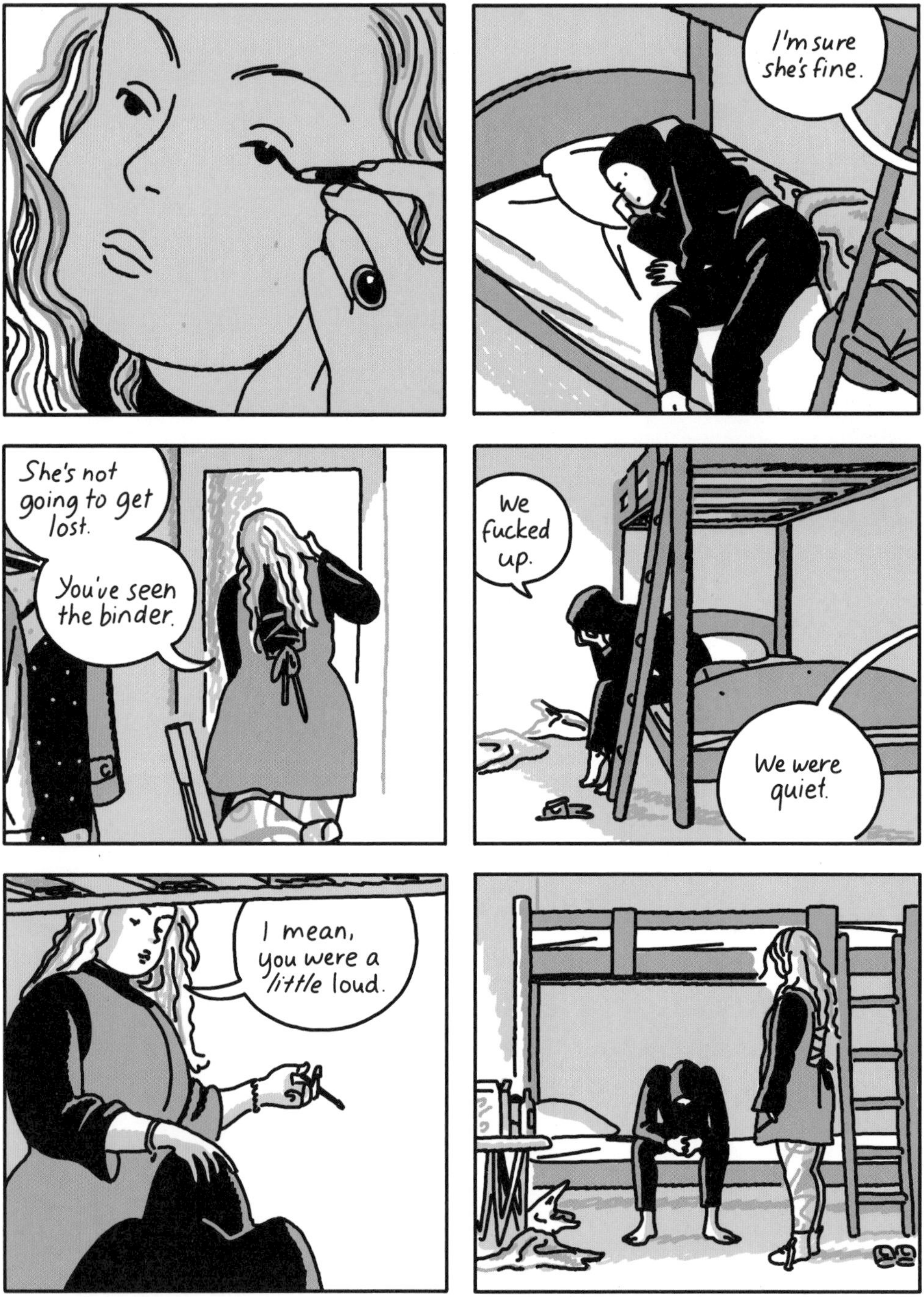
I'm sure she's fine.
She's not going to get lost.
You've seen the binder.
We fucked up.
We were quiet.
I mean, you were a *little* loud.

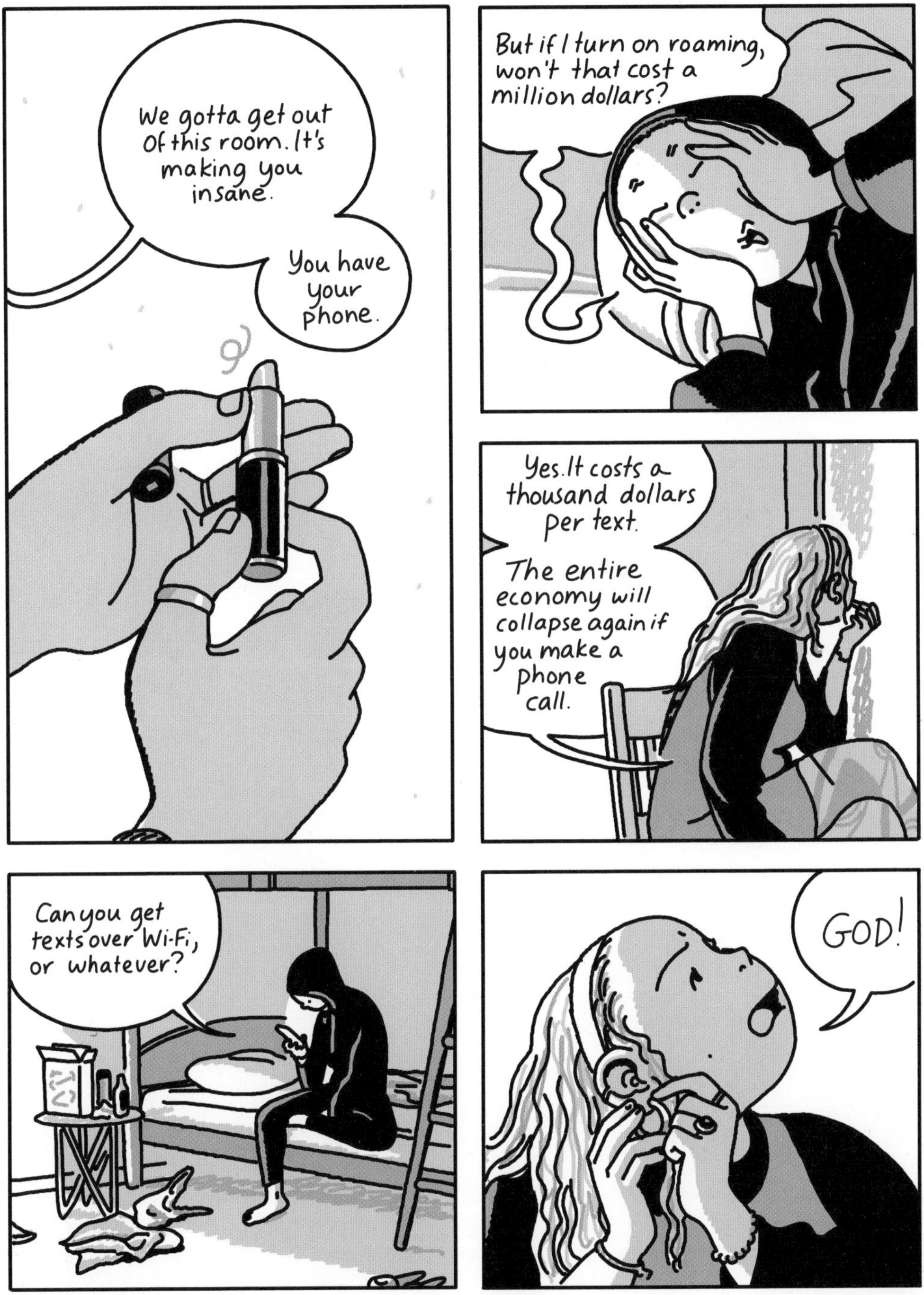
We gotta get out Of this room. It's making you insane.
You have your phone.
But if I turn on roaming, won't that cost a million dollars?
Yes. It costs a thousand dollars per text.
The entire economy will collapse again if you make a phone call.
Can you get texts over Wi-Fi, or whatever?
GOD!

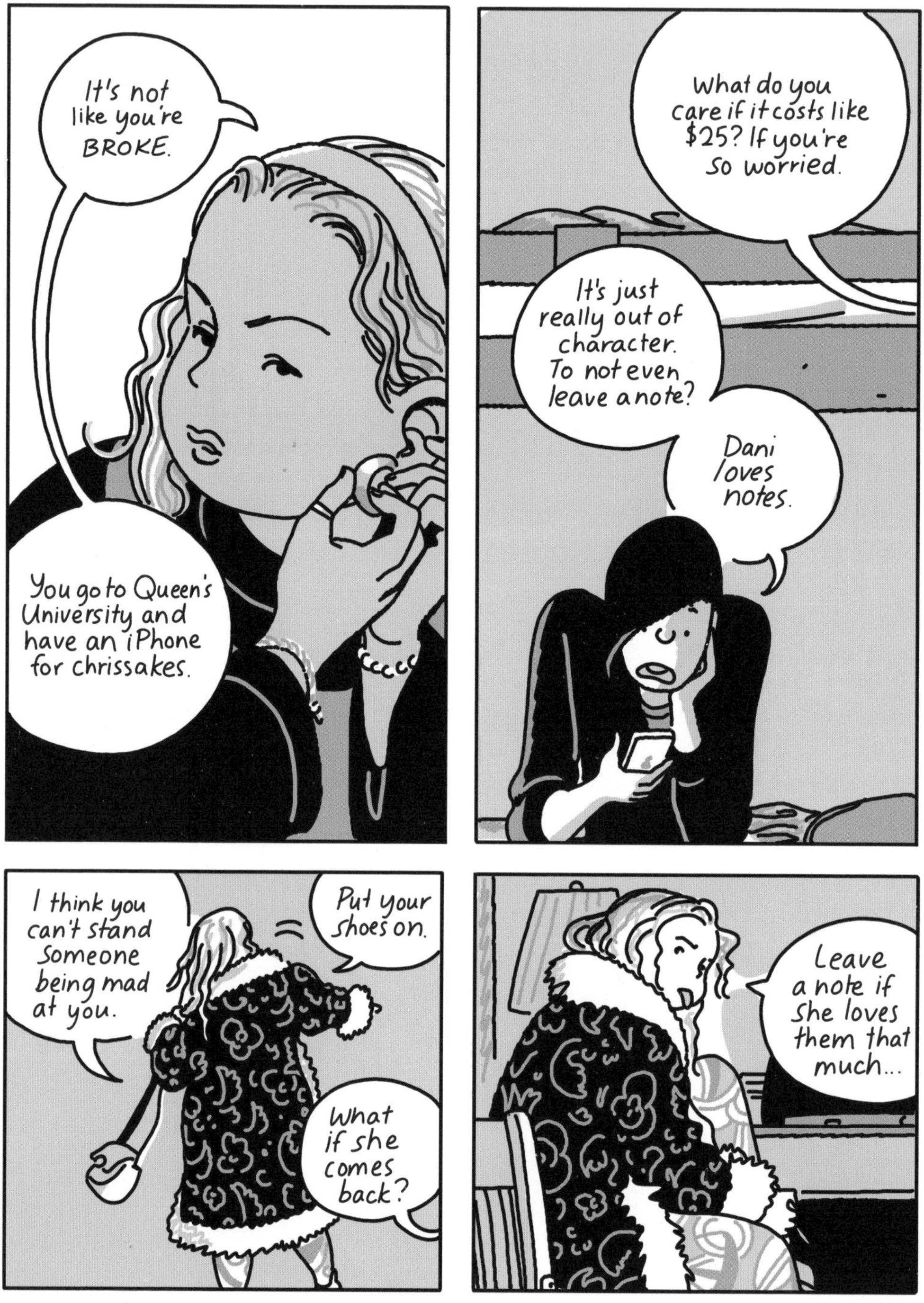

It's not like you're BROKE.
You go to Queen's University and have an iPhone for chrissakes.
What do you care if it costs like $25? If you're so worried.
It's just really out of character. To not even leave a note?
Dani loves notes.
I think you can't stand someone being mad at you.
Put your shoes on.
What if she comes back?
Leave a note if she loves them that much...

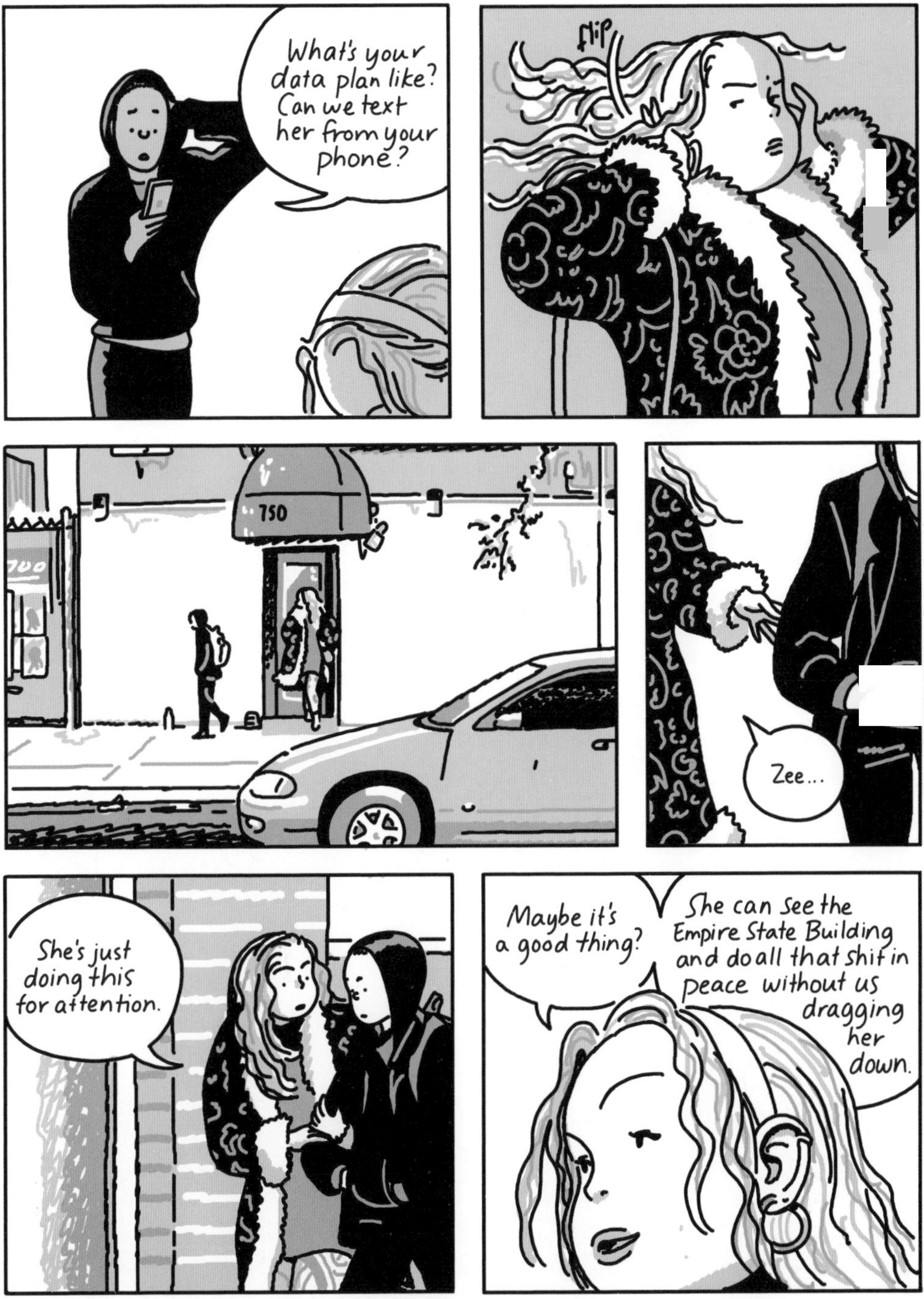
What's your data plan like? Can we text her from your phone?
flip
Zee...
She's just doing this for attention.
Maybe it's a good thing?
She can see the Empire State Building and do all that shit in peace without us dragging her down.

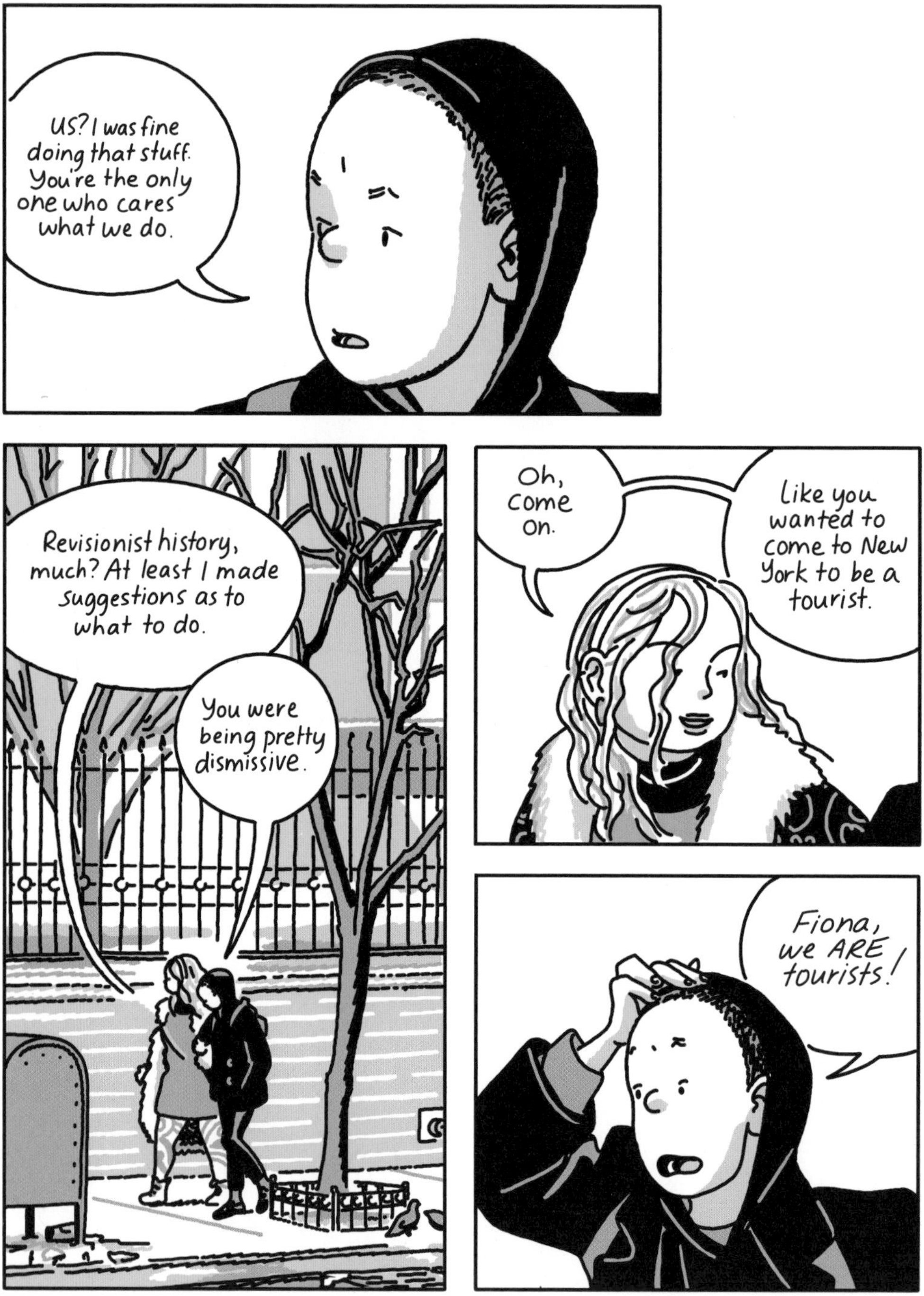
US? I was fine doing that stuff. You're the only one who cares what we do.
Revisionist history, much? At least I made suggestions as to what to do.
You were being pretty dismissive.
Oh, come on.
Like you wanted to come to New York to be a tourist.
Fiona, we ARE tourists!

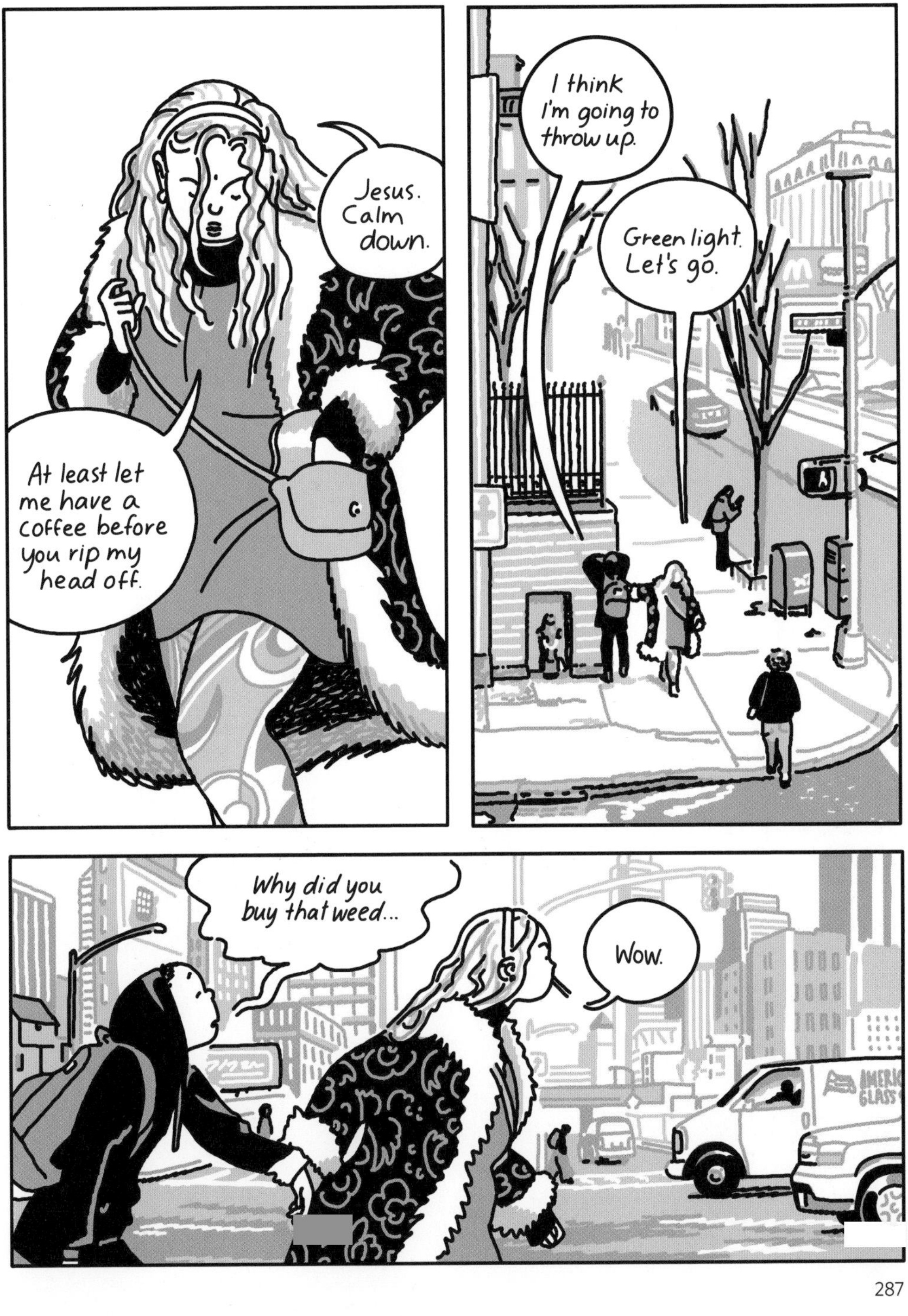
Jesus. Calm down.
At least let me have a coffee before you rip my head off.
I think I'm going to throw up.
Green light. Let's go.
Why did you buy that weed...
Wow.

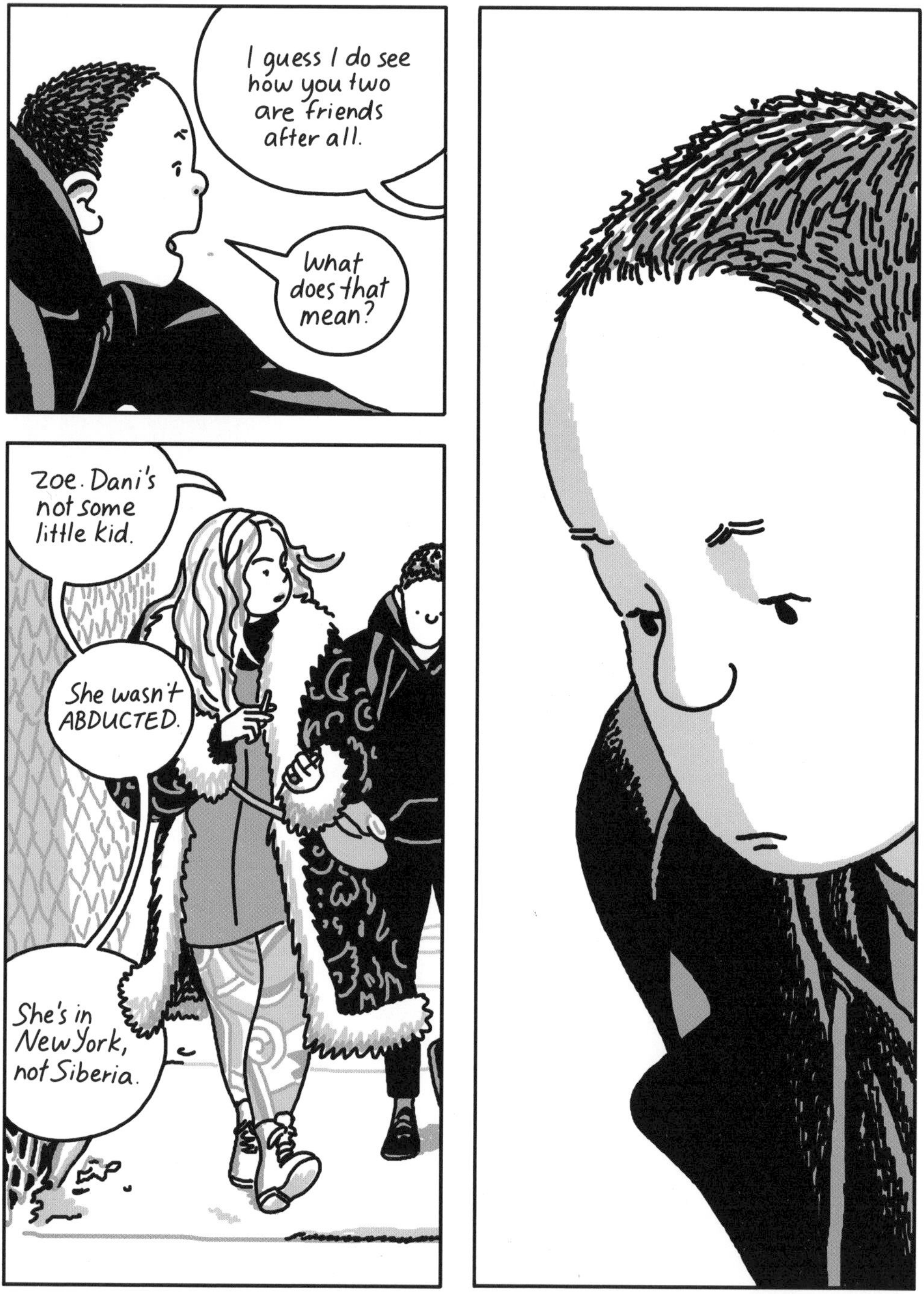
I guess I do see how you two are friends after all.
What does that mean?
Zoe. Dani's not some little kid.
She wasn't ABDUCTED.
She's in New York, not Siberia.

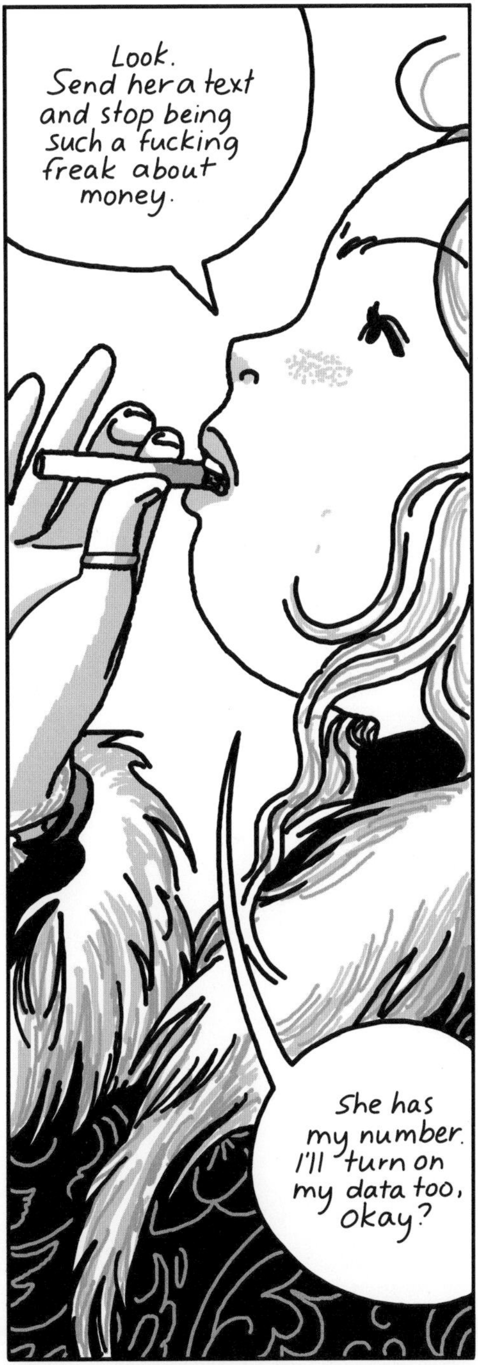
Look. Send her a text and stop being such a fucking freak about money.
She has my number. I'll turn on my data too, okay?
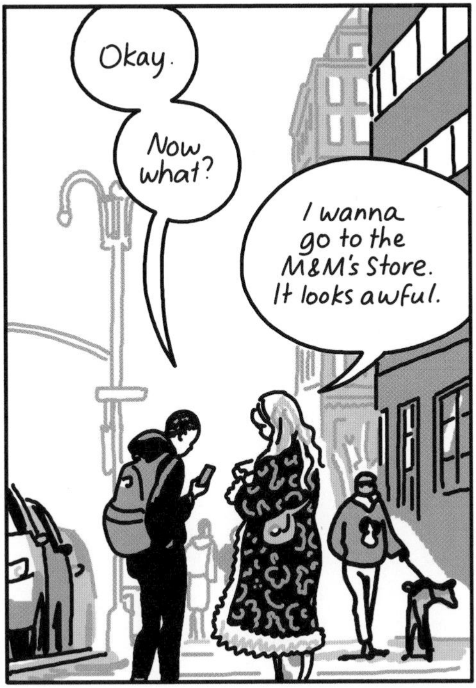
Okay.
Now what?
I wanna go to the M&M's Store. It looks awful.

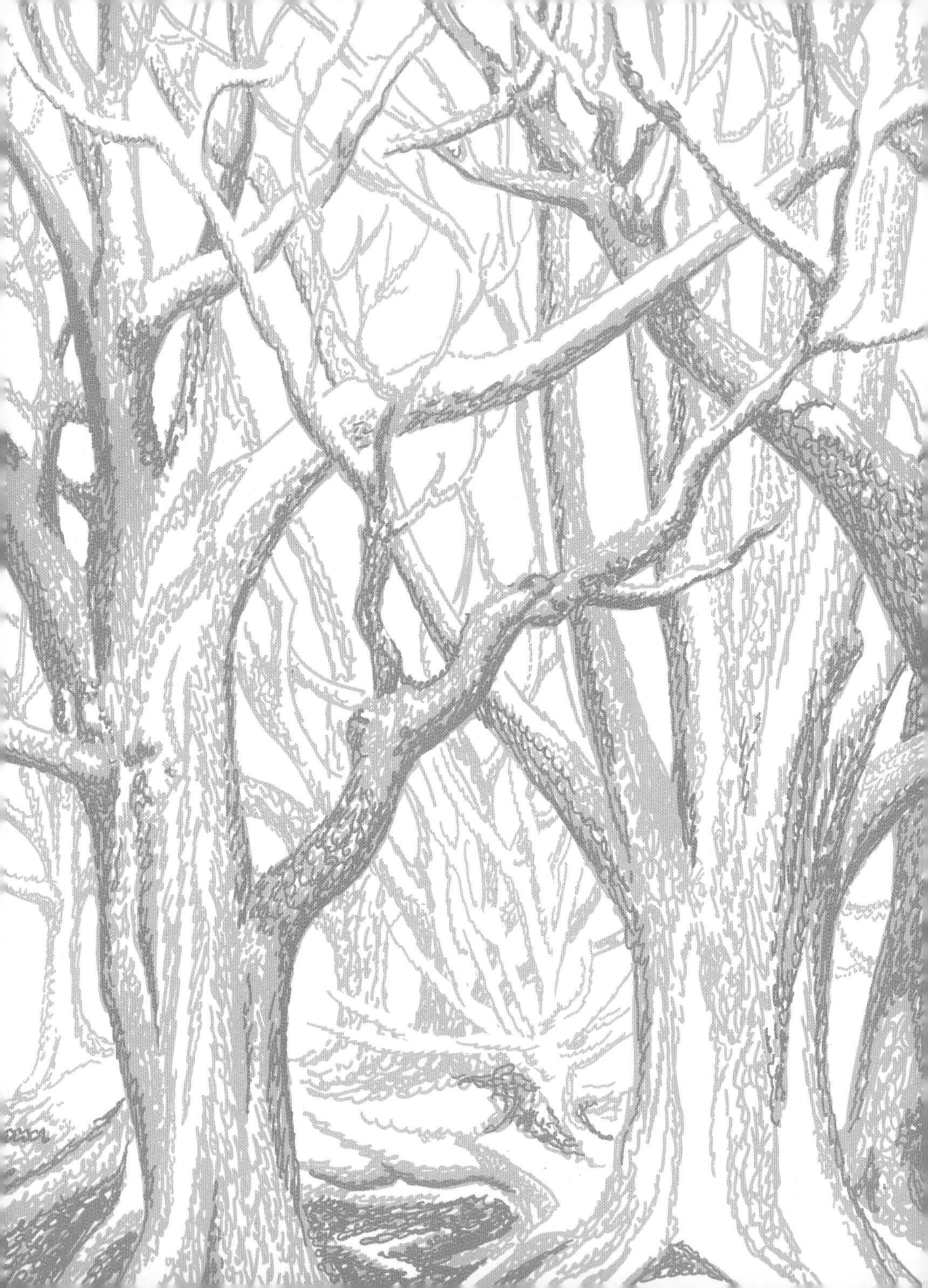

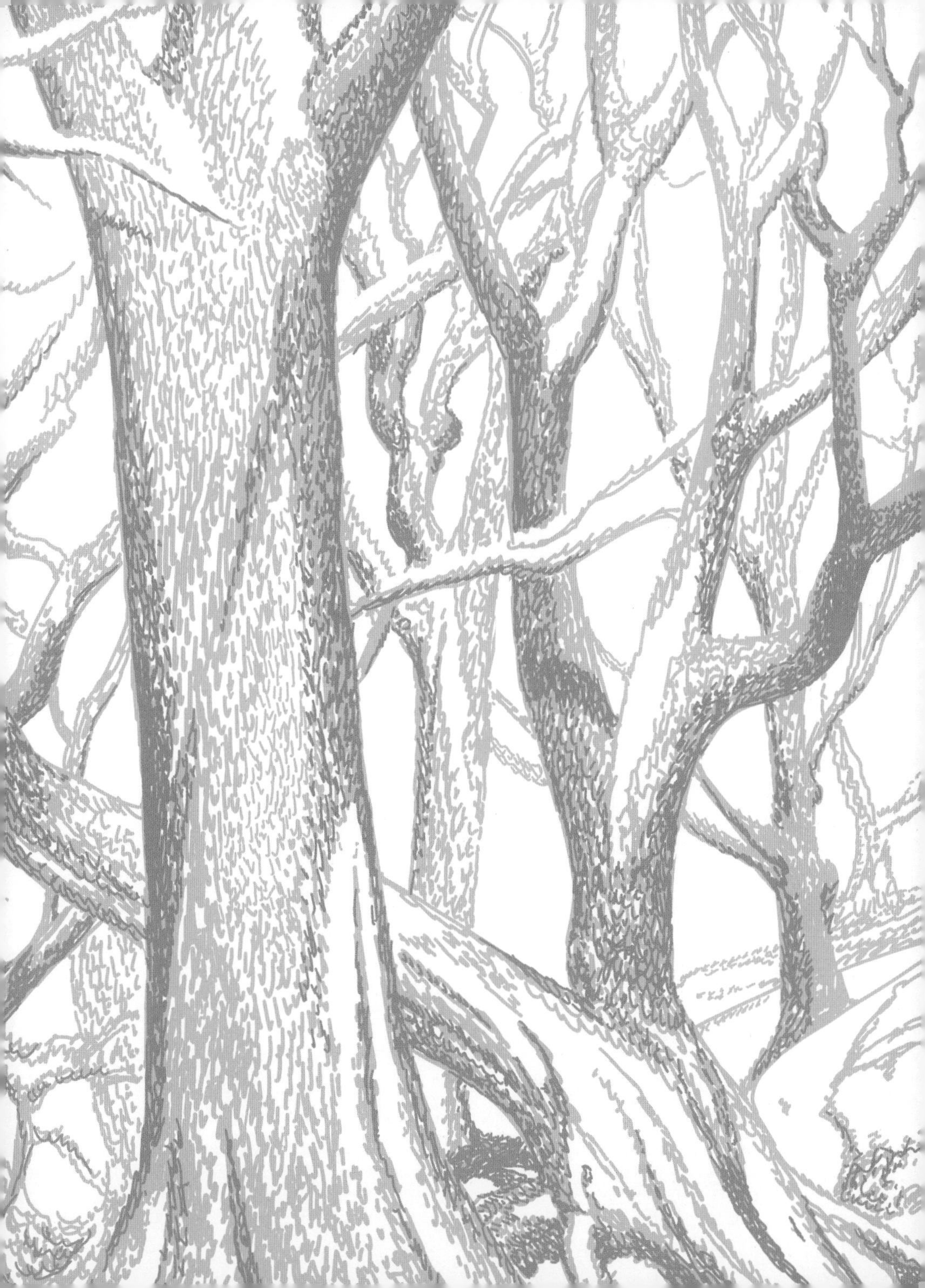

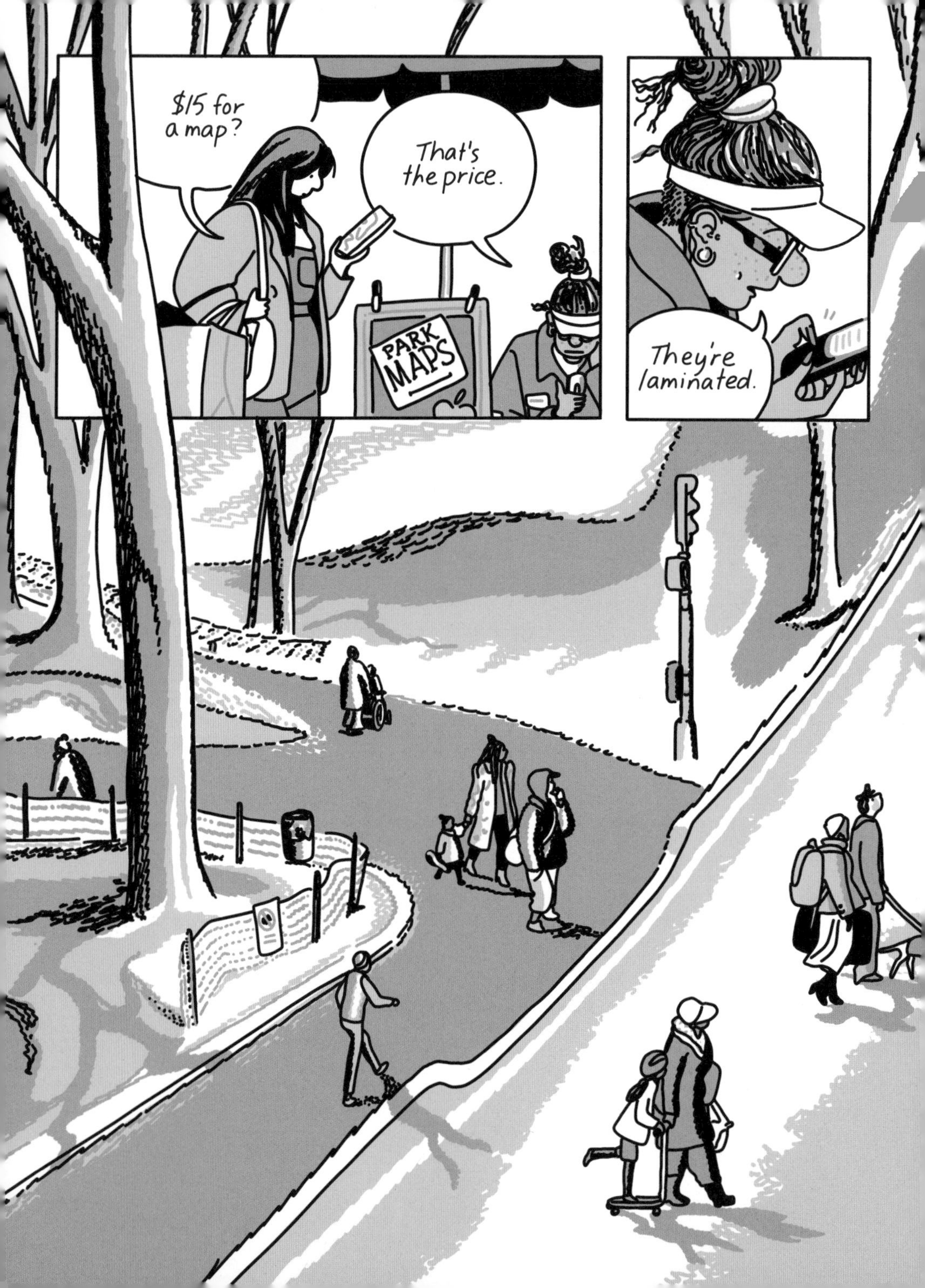
$15 for a map?
That's the price.
PARK MAPS
They're laminated.

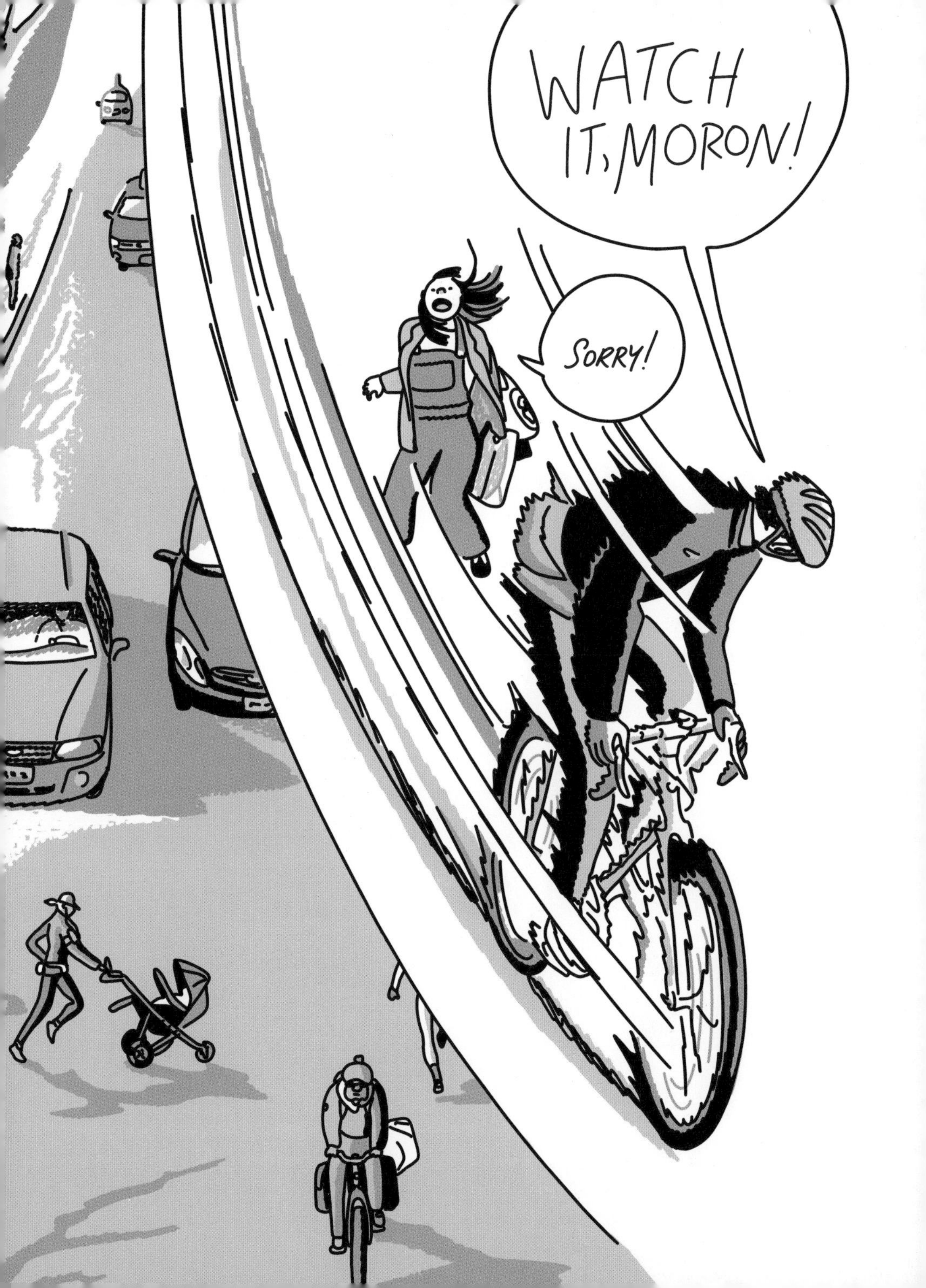
SORRY!
WATCH IT, MORON!

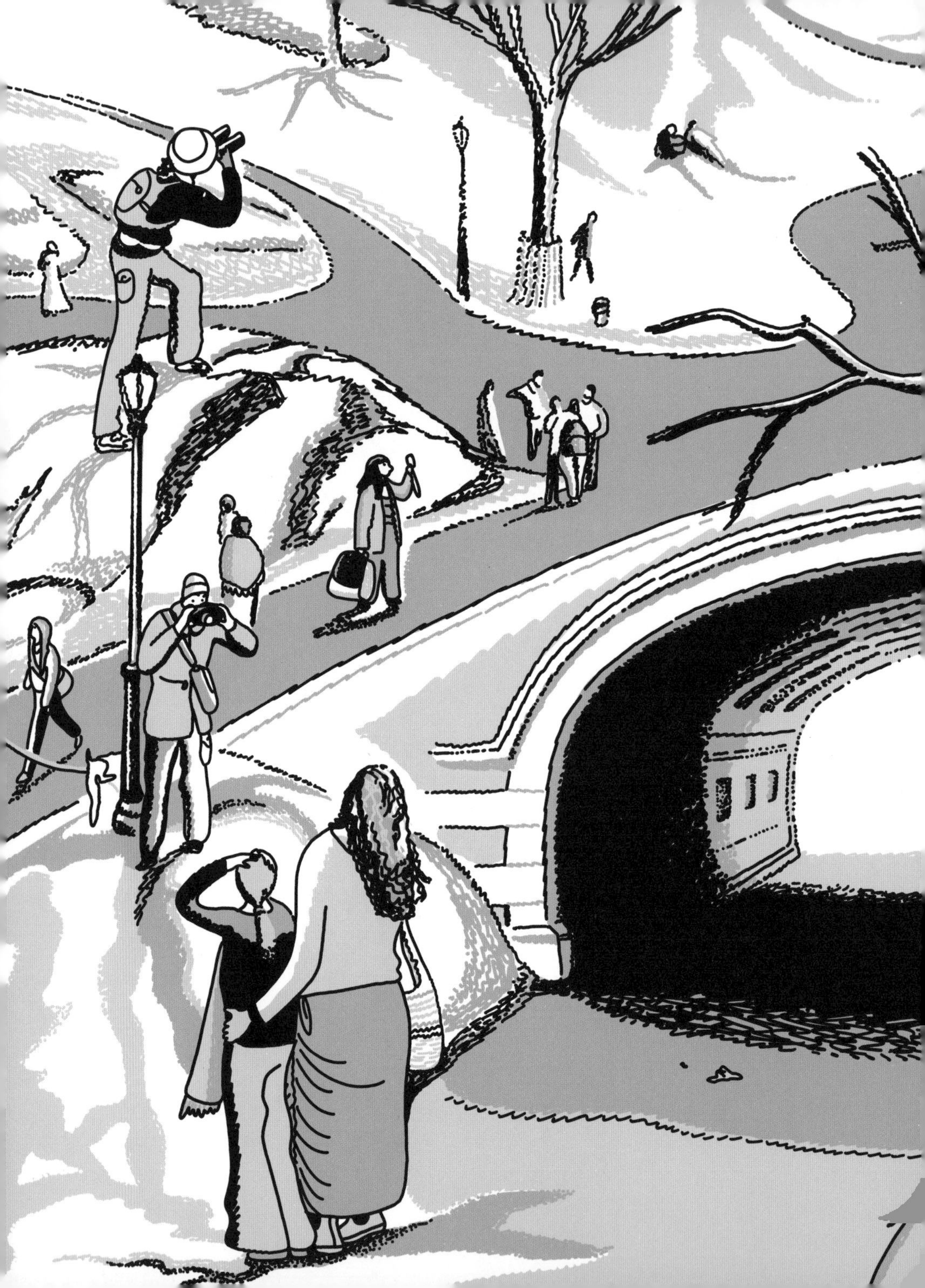

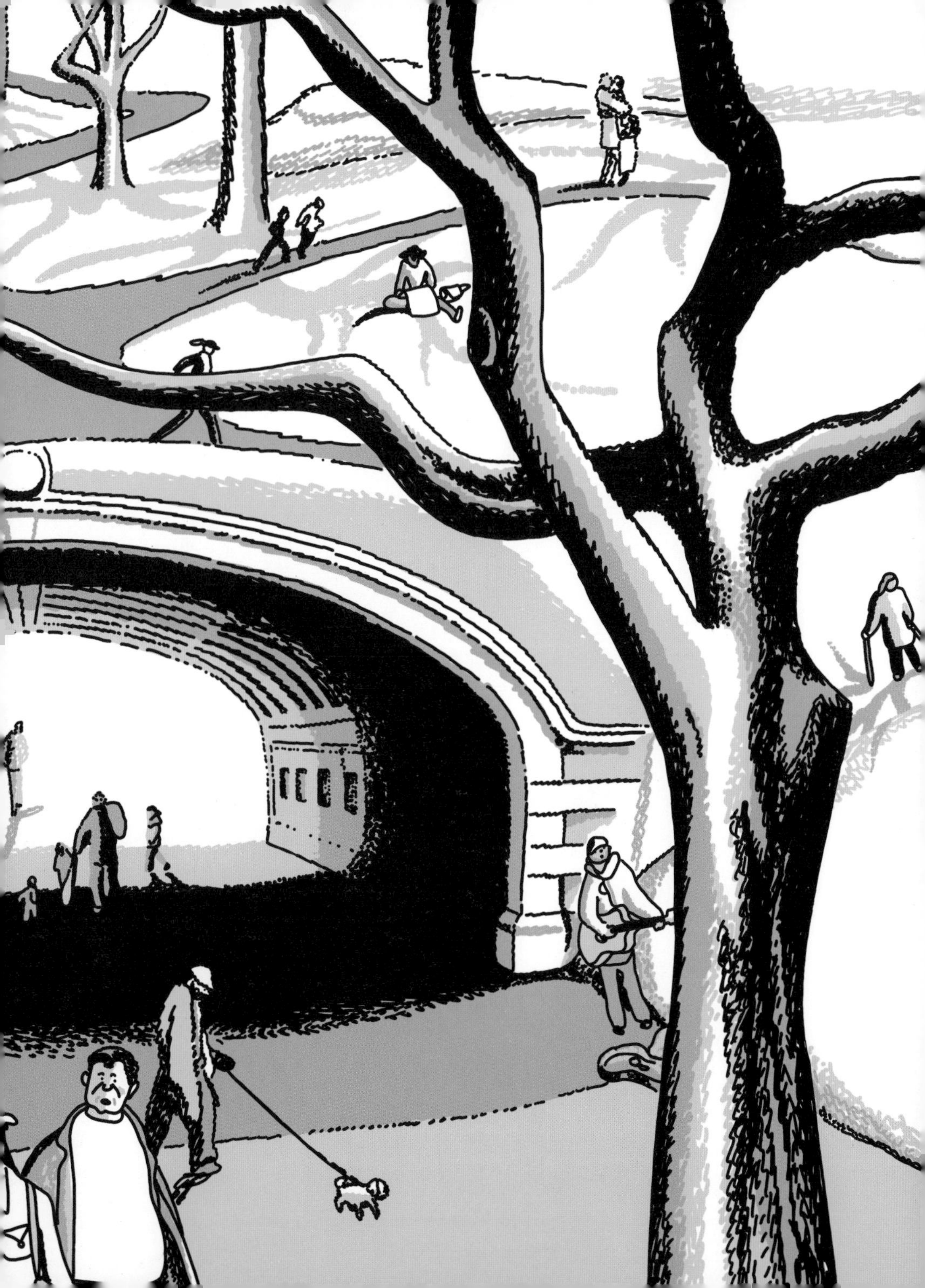

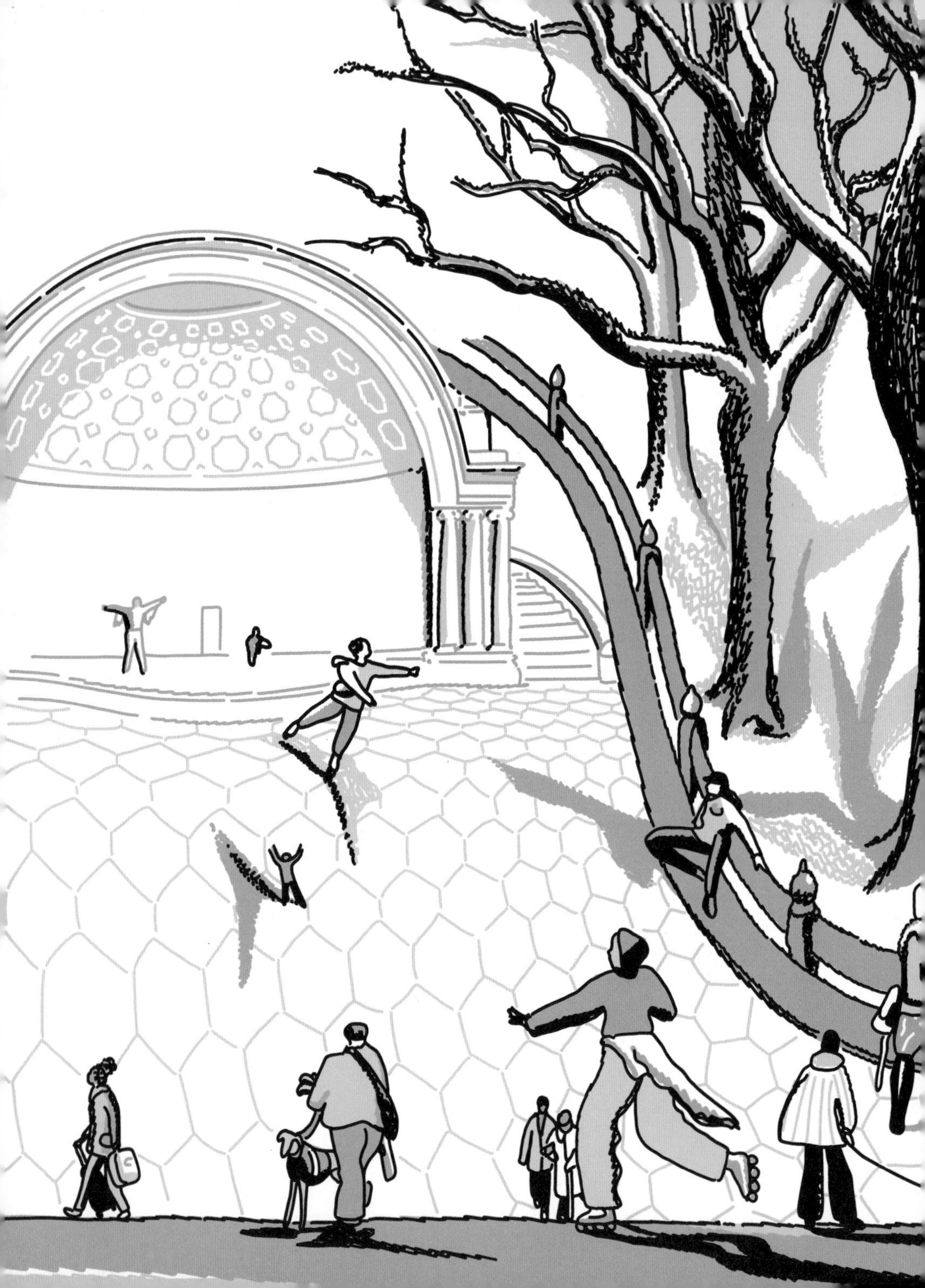

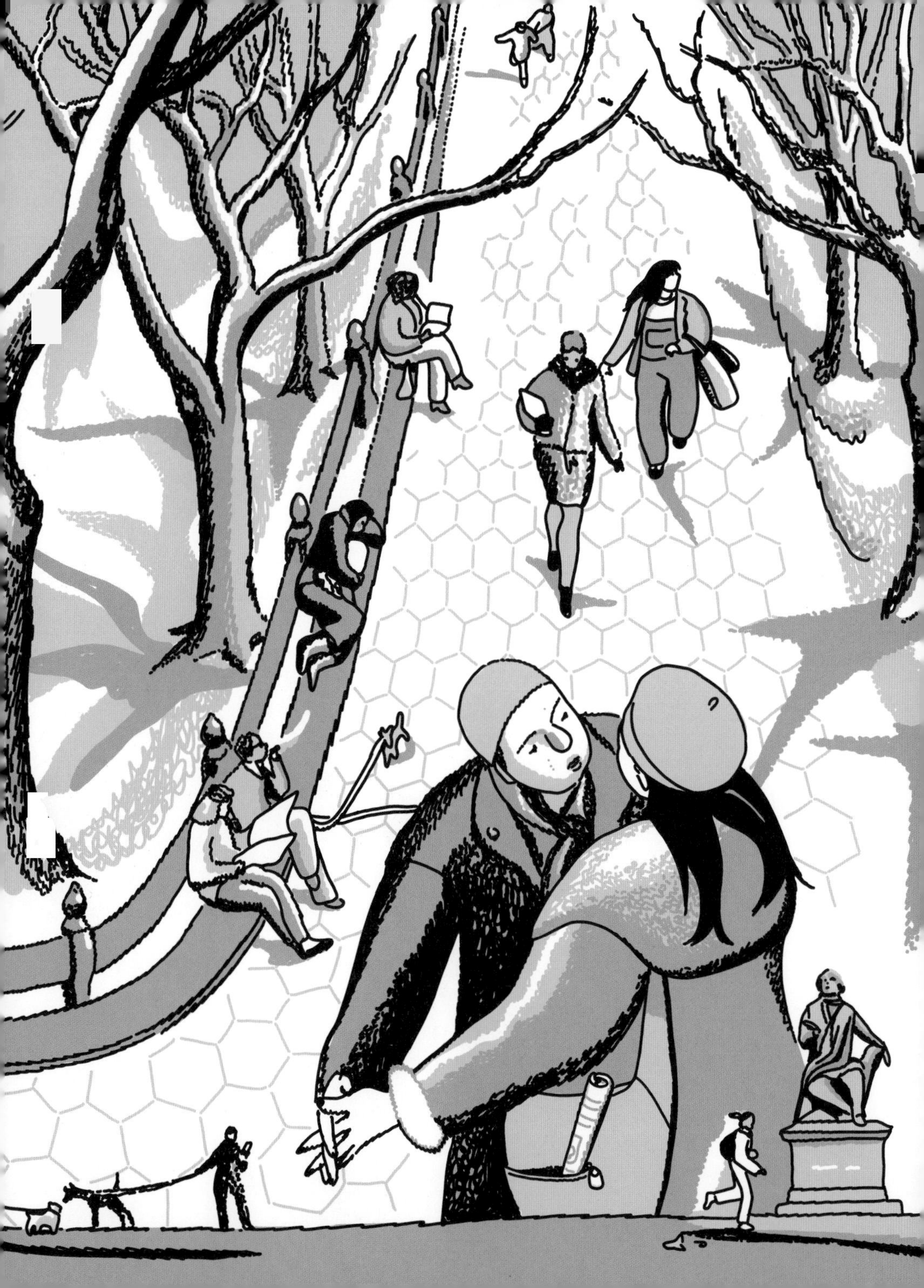

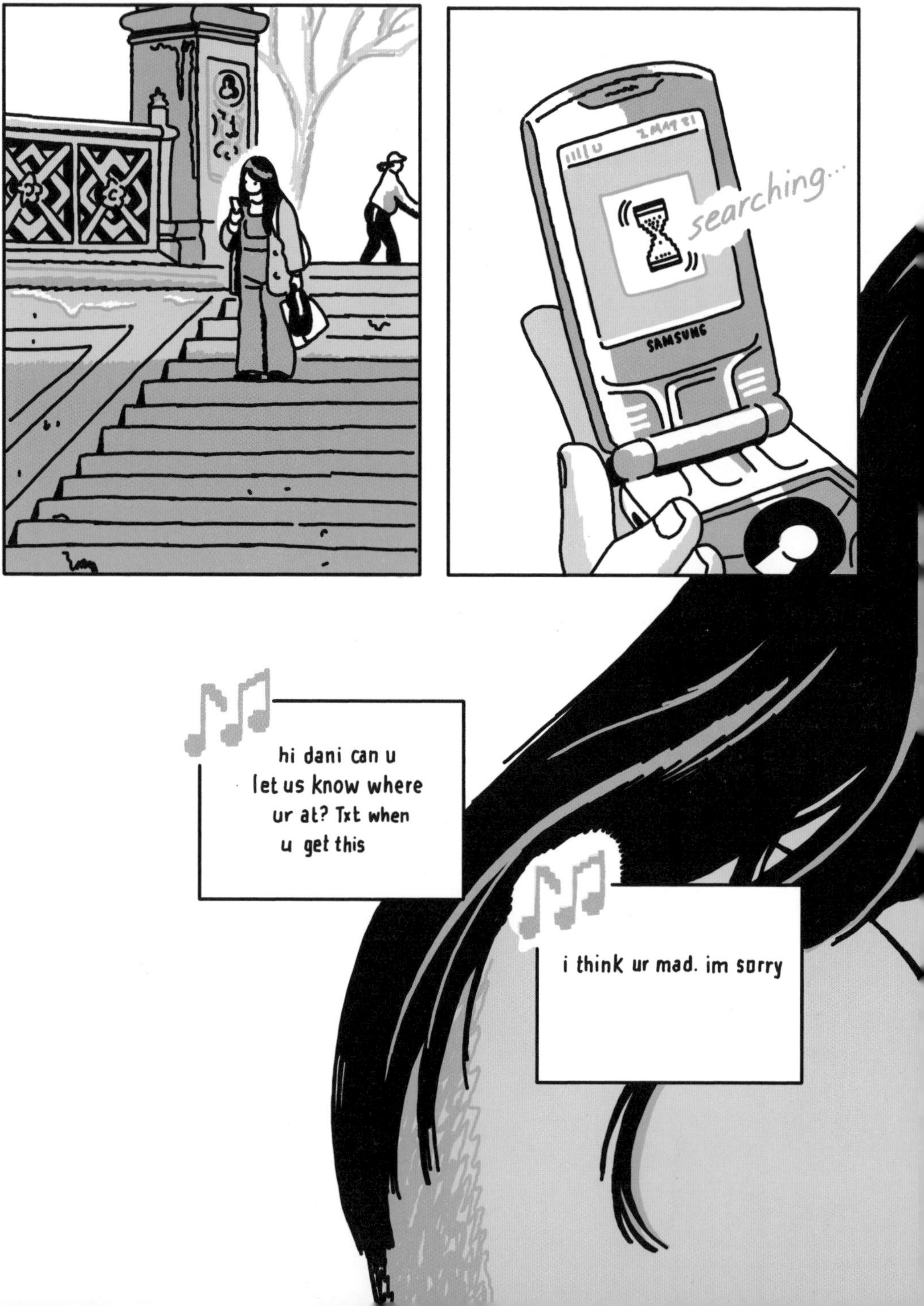
SAMSUNG
searching...
hi dani can u let us know where ur at? Txt when u get this
i think ur mad. im sorry

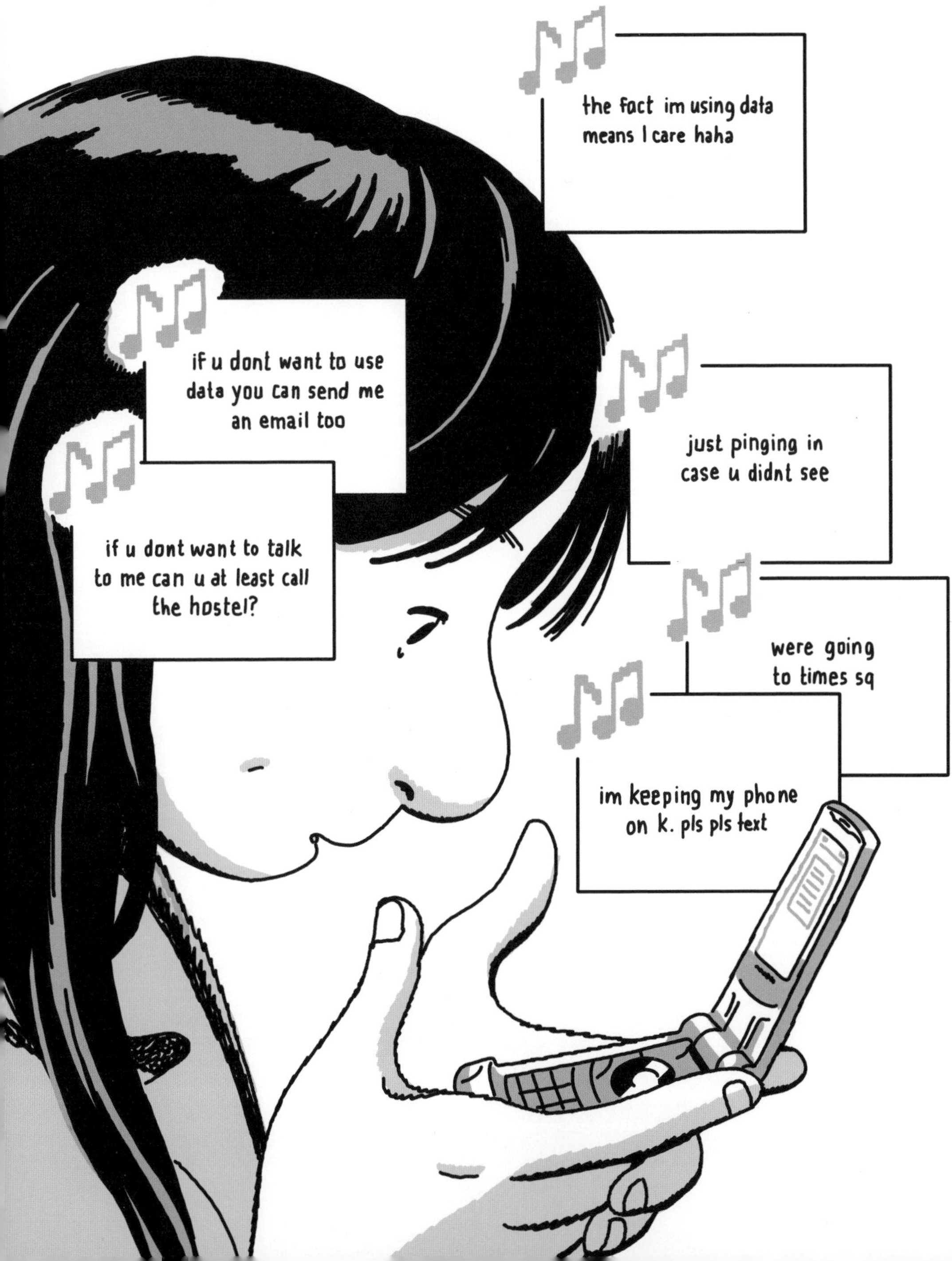
the fact im using data means I care haha
if u dont want to use data you can send me an email too
if u dont want to talk to me can u at least call the hostel?
just pinging in case u didnt see
were going to times sq
im keeping my phone on k. pls pls text

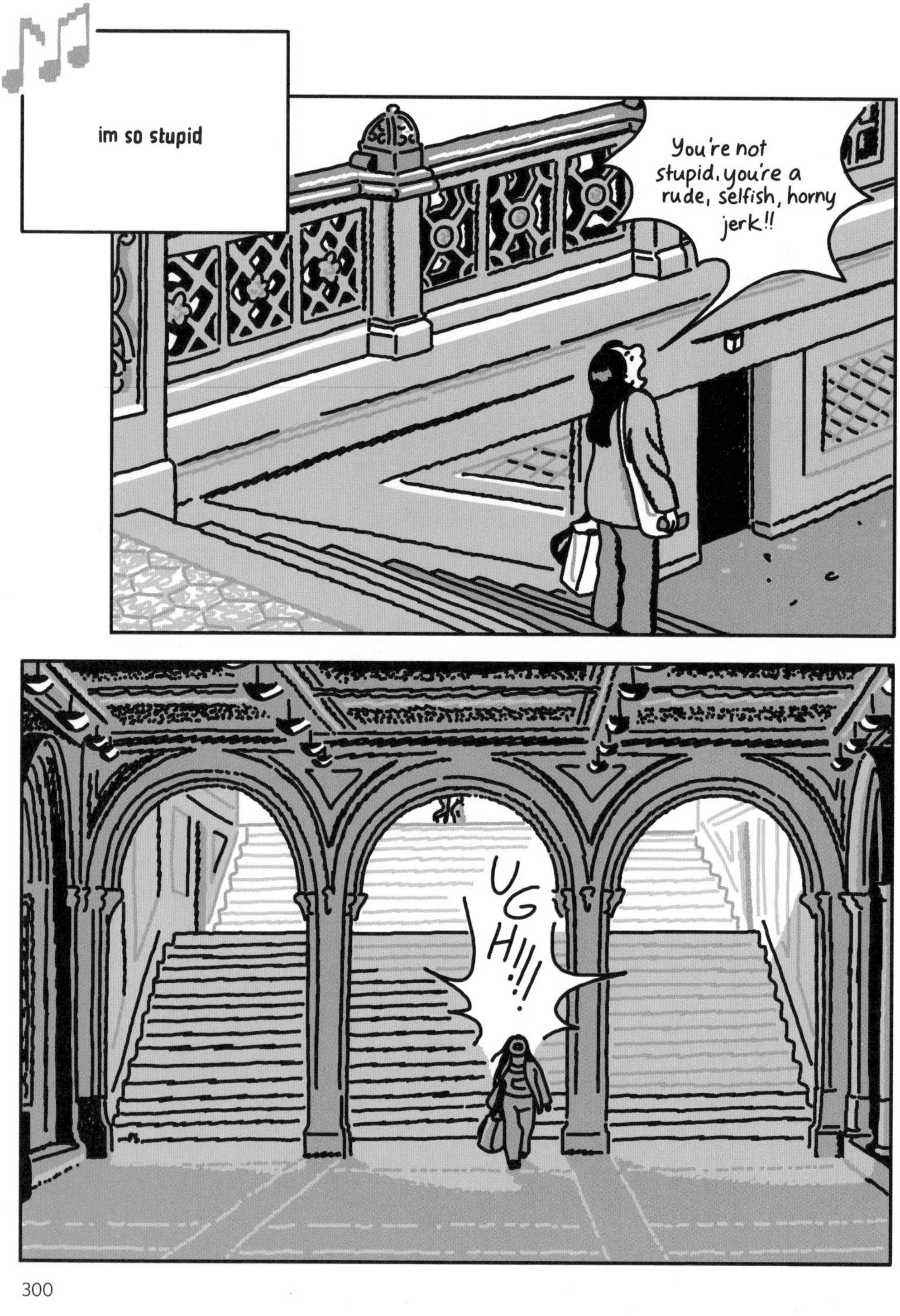
im so stupid
You're not stupid, you're a rude, selfish, horny jerk!!
UGH!!!

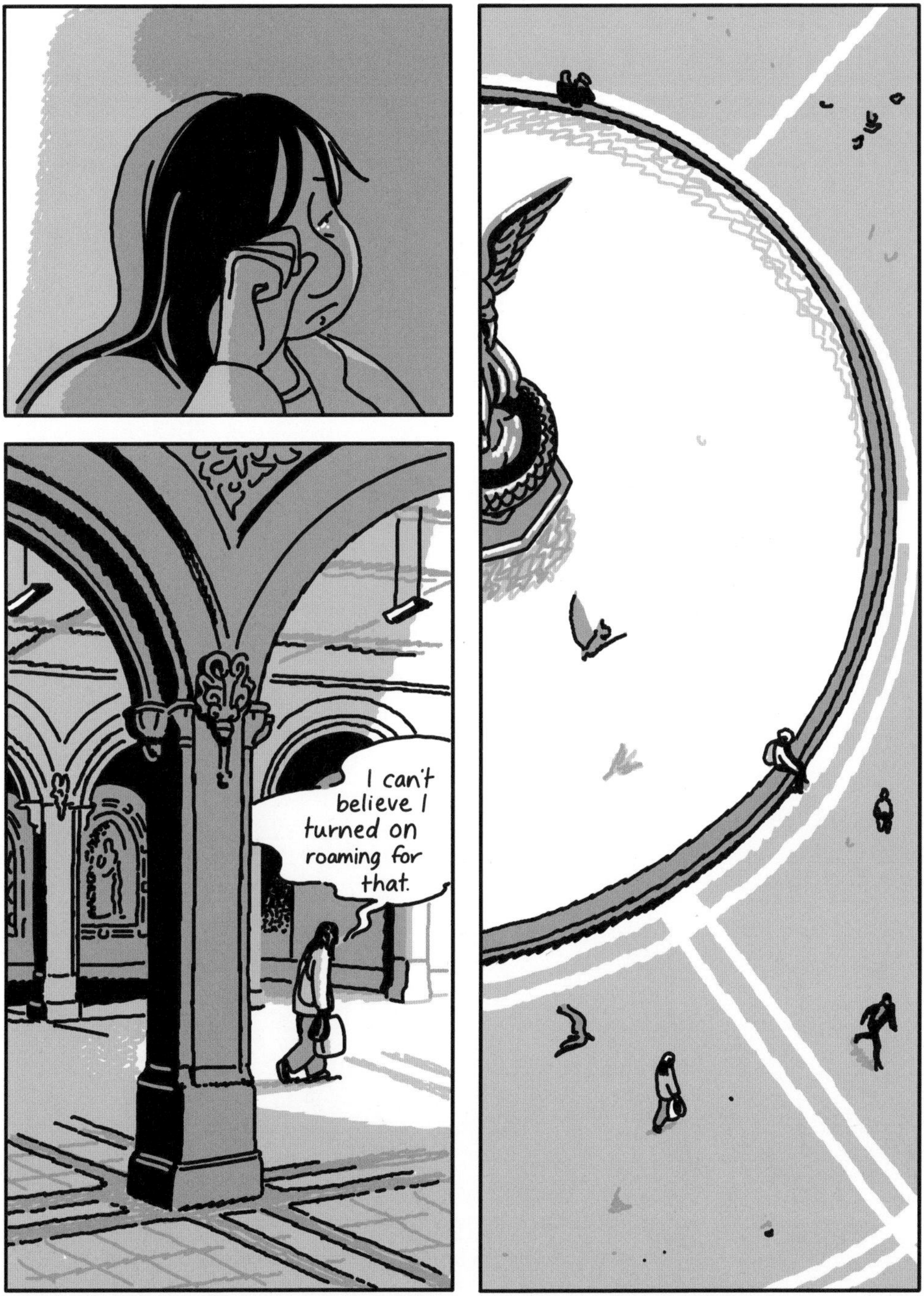
I can't believe I turned on roaming for that.

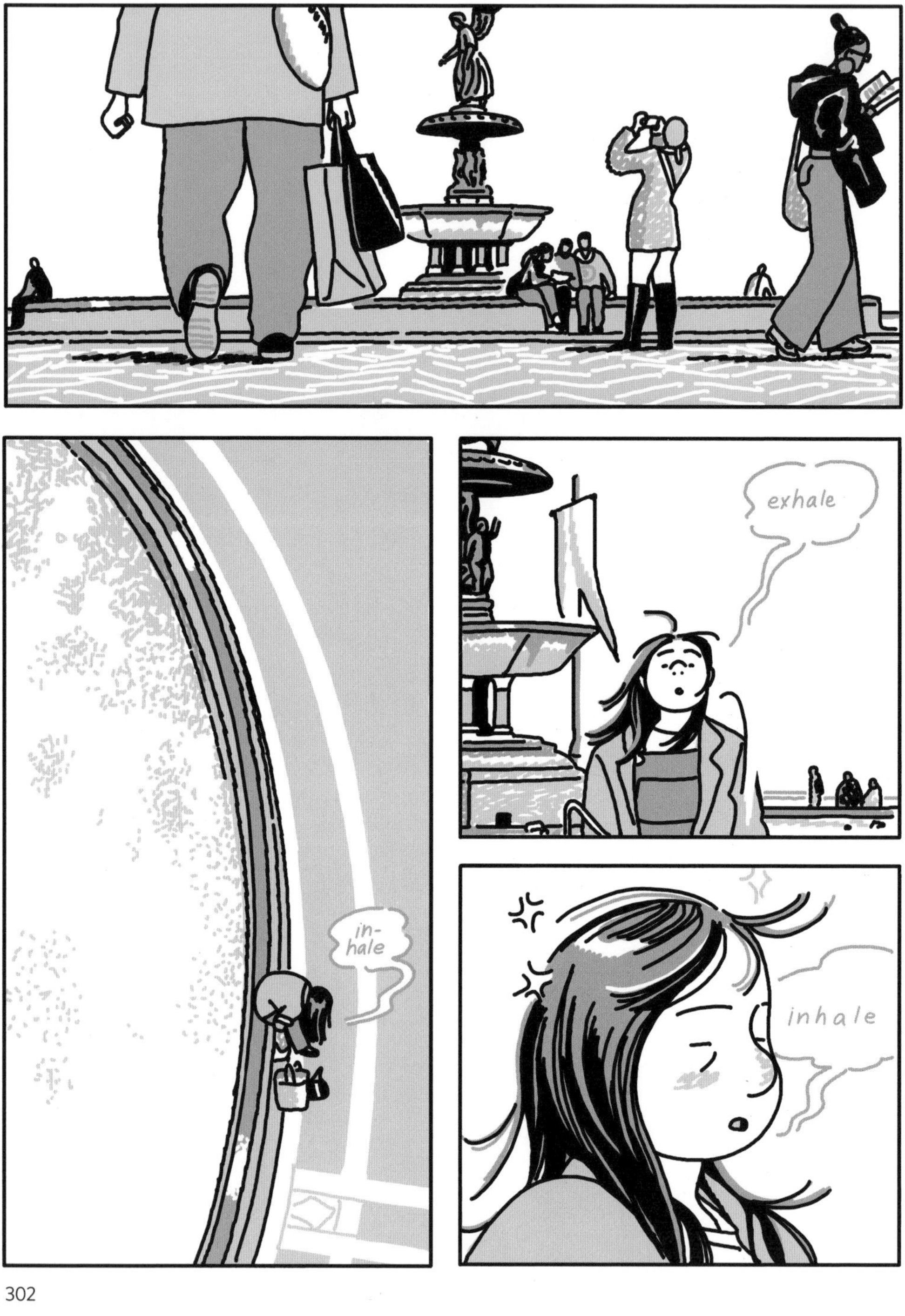
in-
hale
exhale
inhale

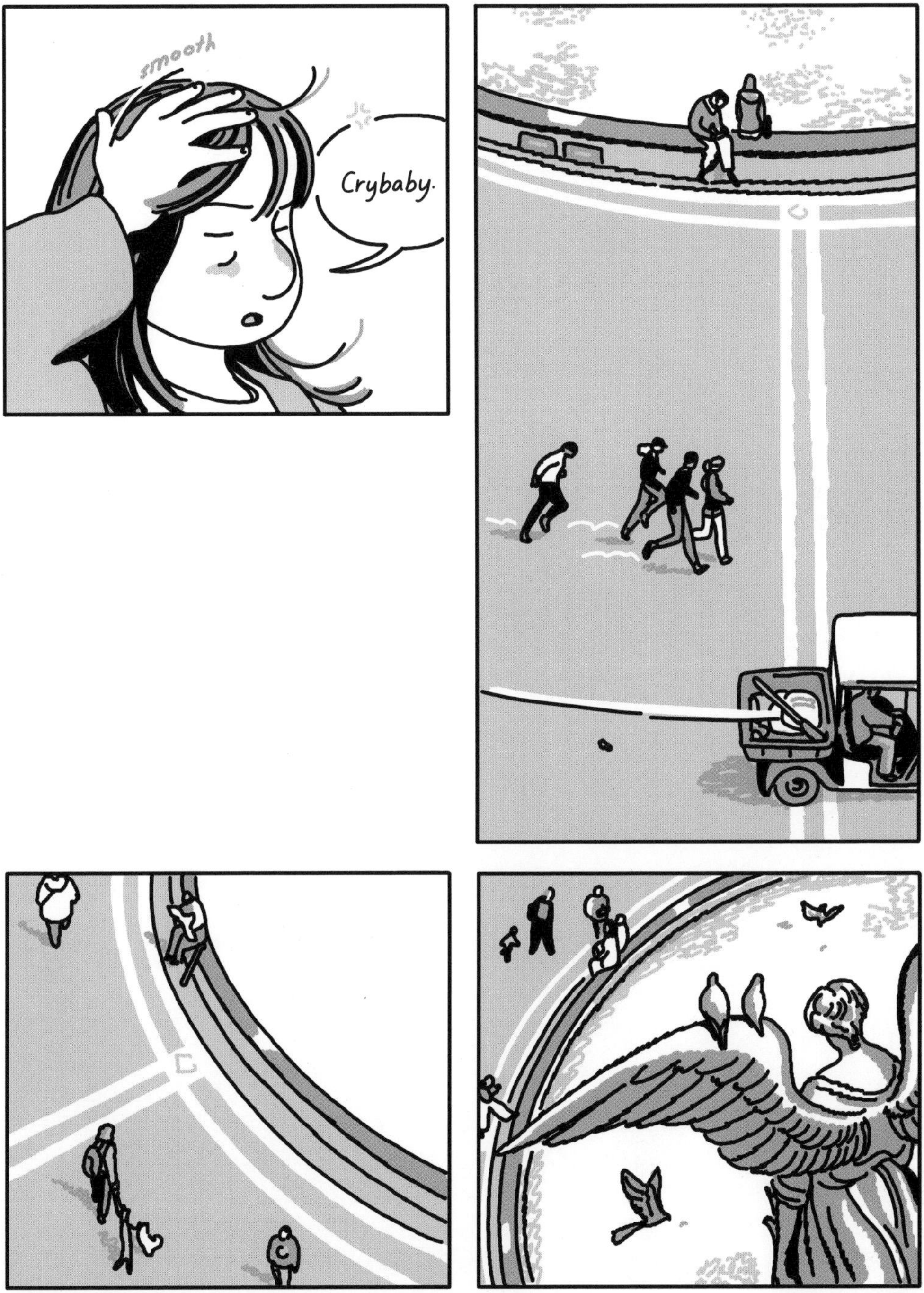
smooth
Crybaby.

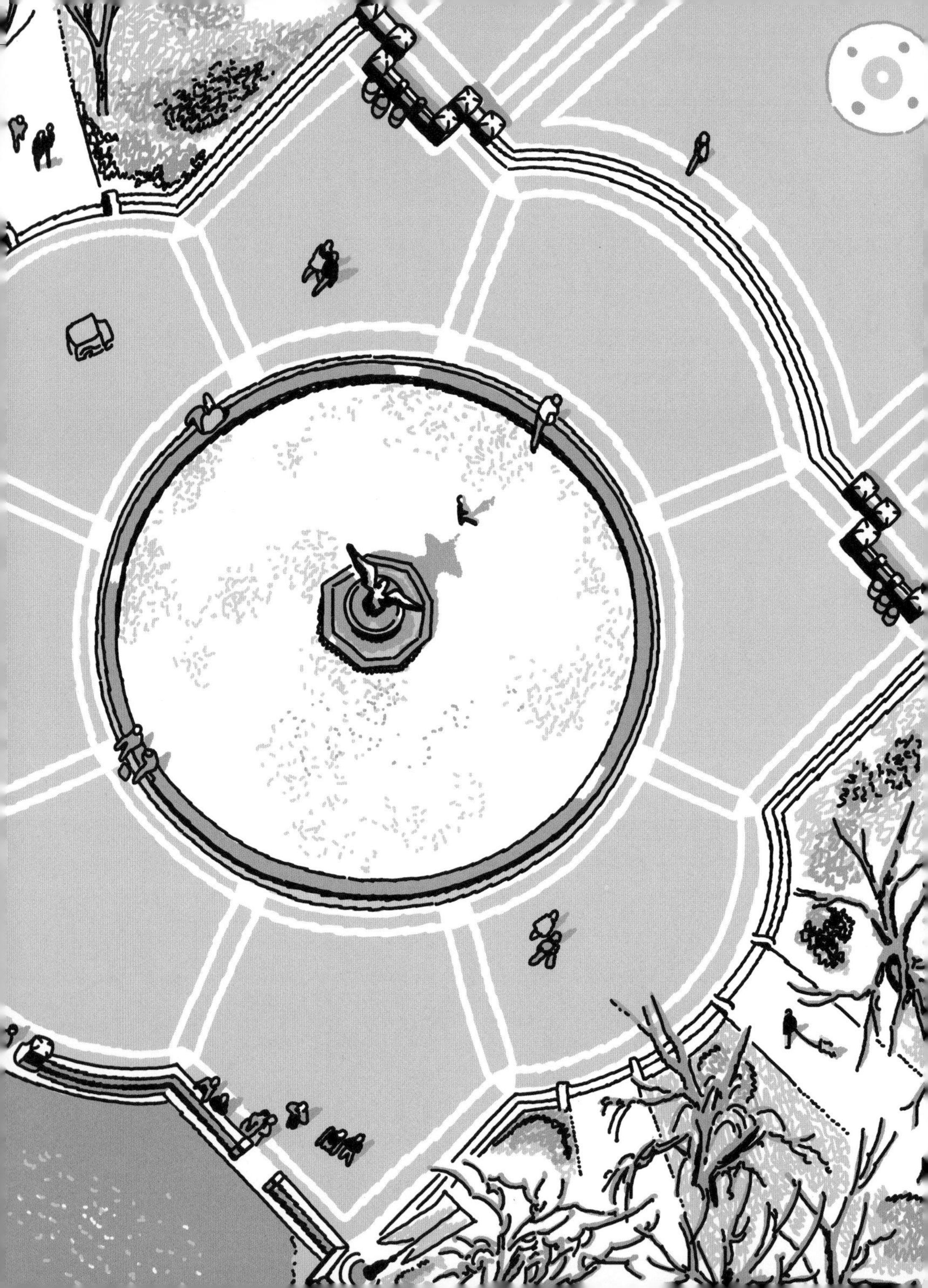

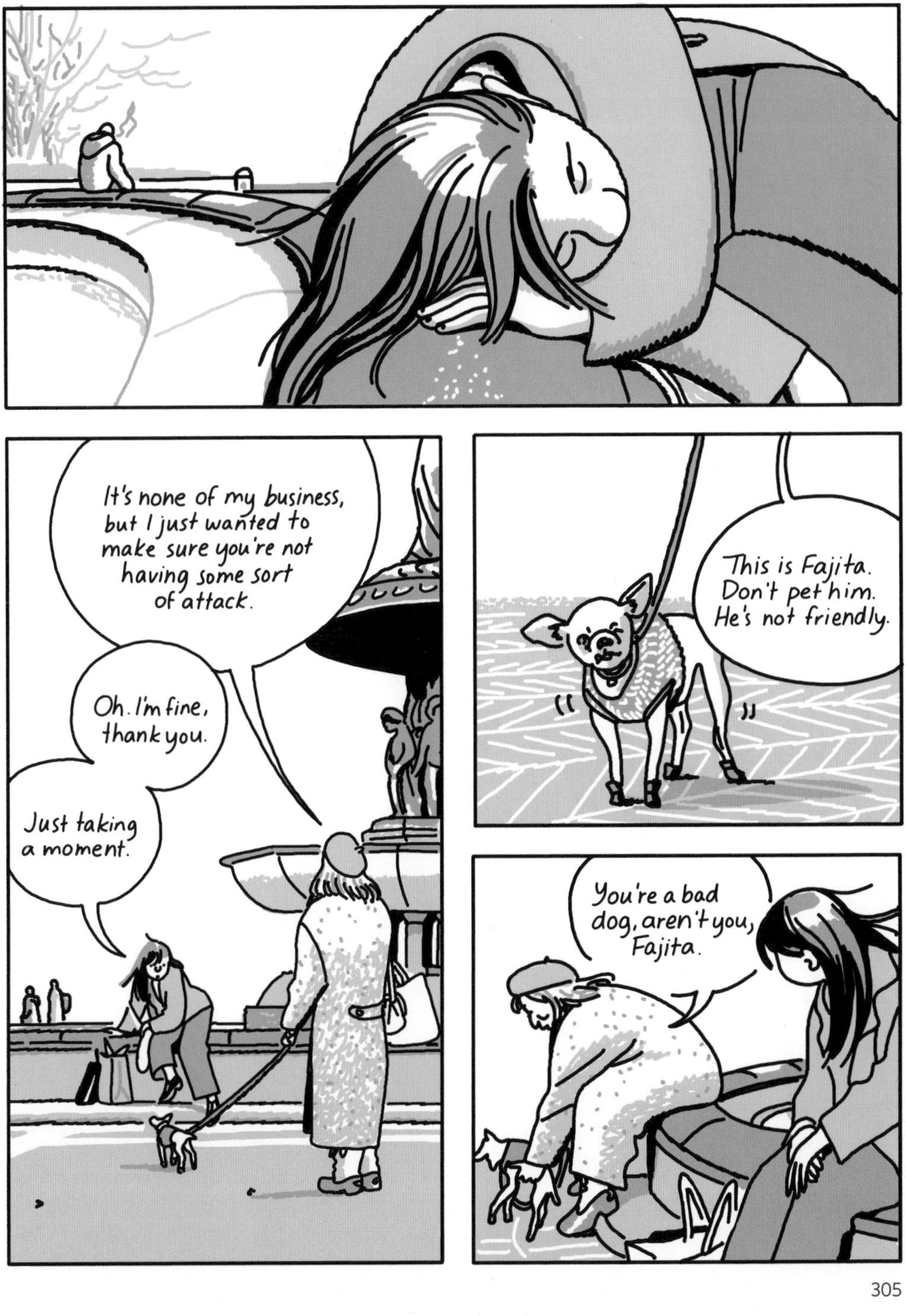
It's none of my business, but I just wanted to make sure you're not having some sort of attack.
Oh. I'm fine, thank you.
Just taking a moment.
This is Fajita. Don't pet him. He's not friendly.
You're a bad dog, aren't you, Fajita.

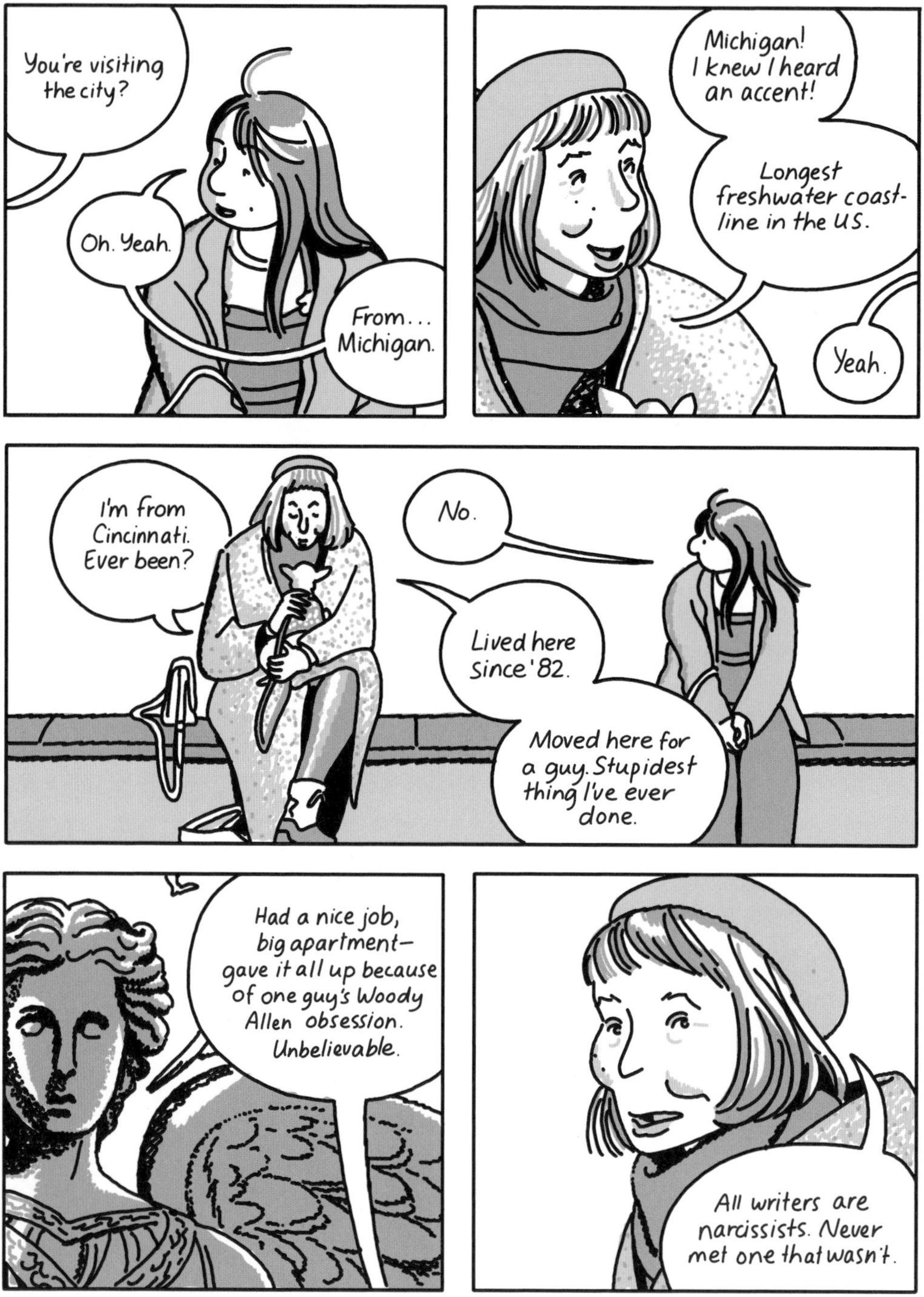
You're visiting the city?
Oh. Yeah.
From... Michigan.
Michigan! I knew I heard an accent!
Longest freshwater coast-line in the US.
Yeah.
I'm from Cincinnati. Ever been?
No.
Lived here since '82.
Moved here for a guy. Stupidest thing I've ever done.
Had a nice job, big apartment—gave it all up because of one guy's Woody Allen obsession. Unbelievable.
All writers are narcissists. Never met one that wasn't.

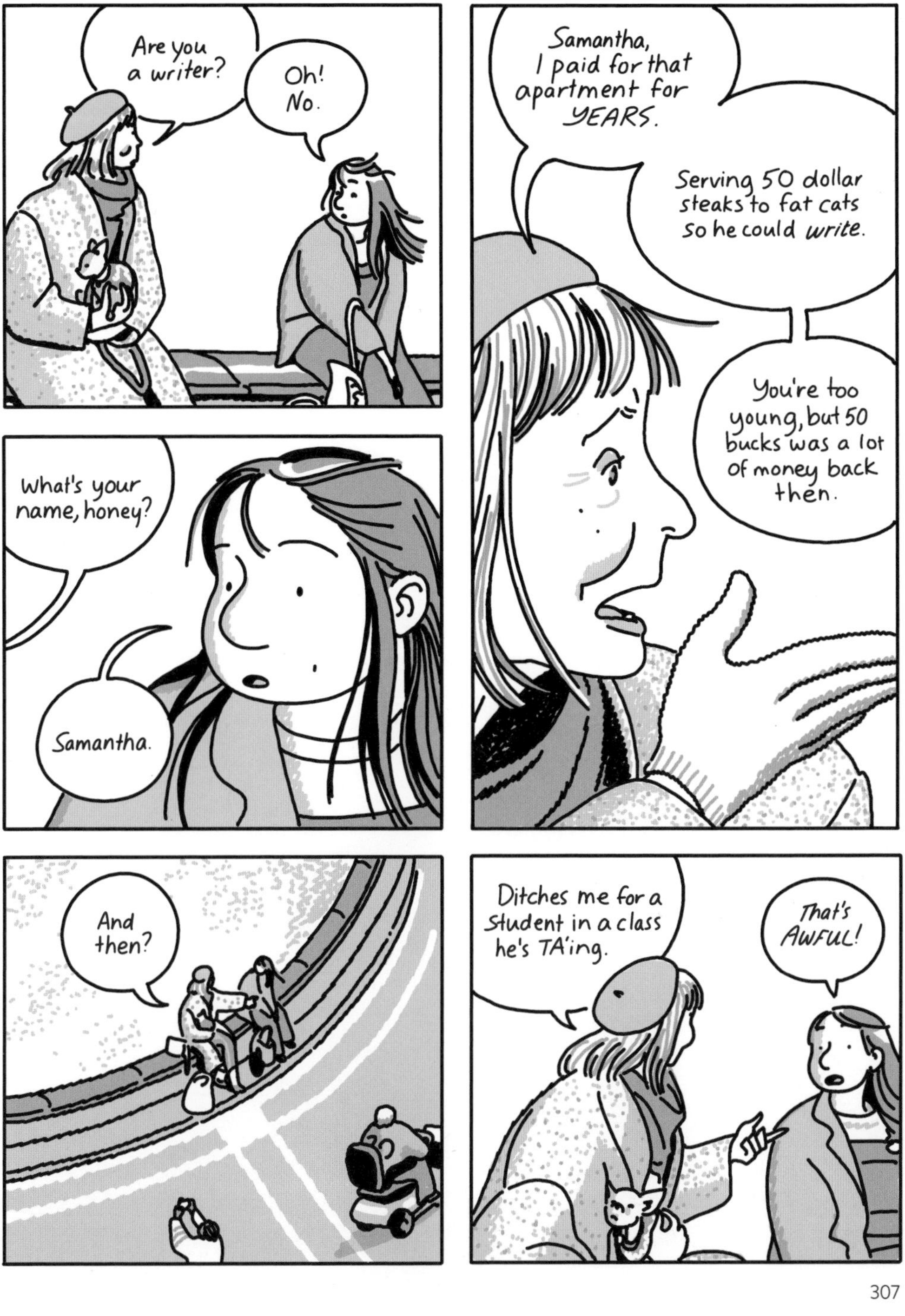

Are you a writer?
Oh! No.
What's your name, honey?
Samantha.
Samantha, I paid for that apartment for YEARS.
Serving 50 dollar steaks to fat cats so he could *write*.
You're too young, but 50 bucks was a lot of money back then.
And then?
Ditches me for a student in a class he's TA'ing.
That's AWFUL!

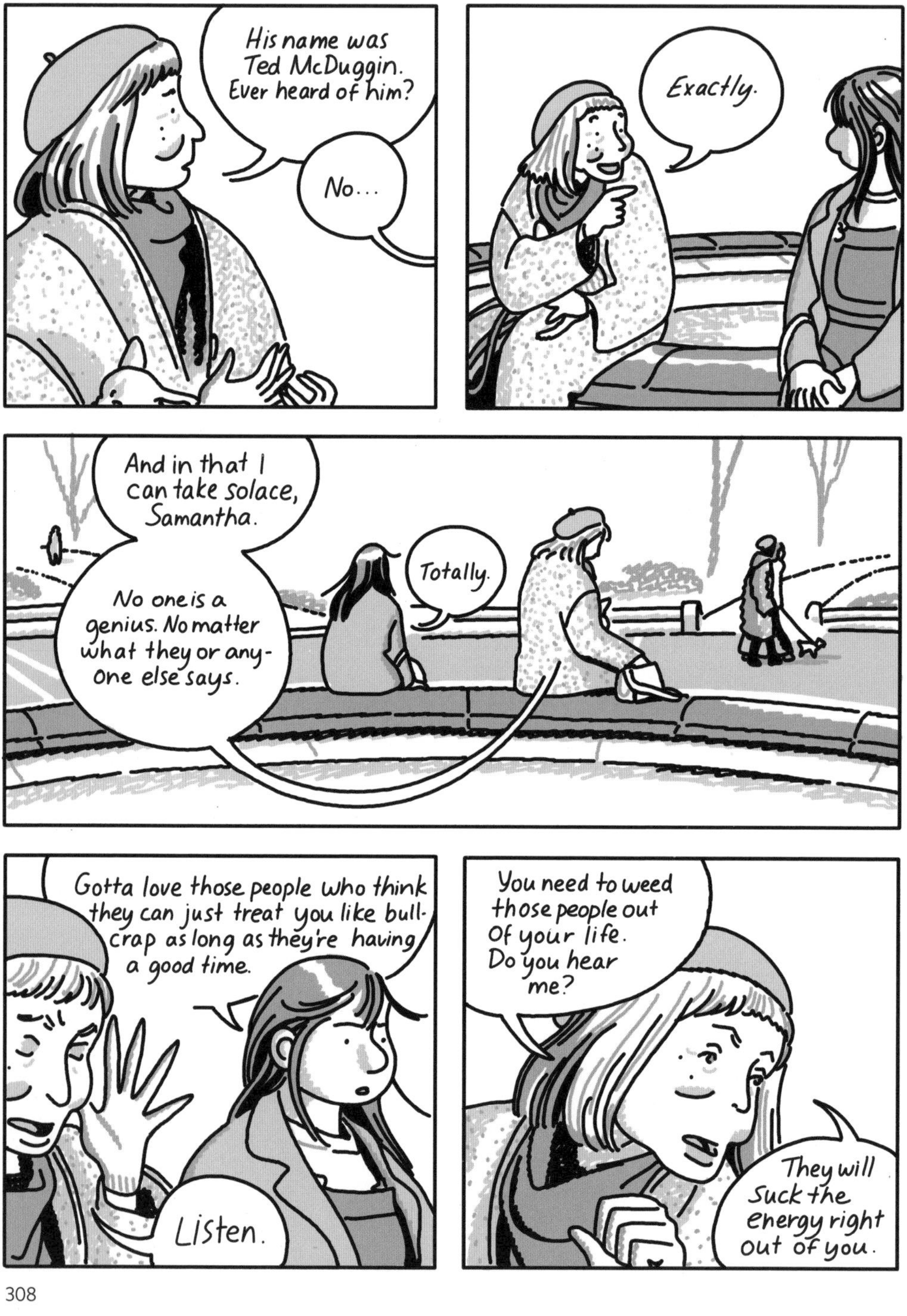

His name was Ted McDuggin. Ever heard of him?
No...
Exactly.
And in that I can take solace, Samantha.
No one is a genius. No matter what they or any-one else says.
Totally.
Gotta love those people who think they can just treat you like bull-crap as long as they're having a good time.
Listen.
You need to weed those people out of your life. Do you hear me?
They will suck the energy right out of you.

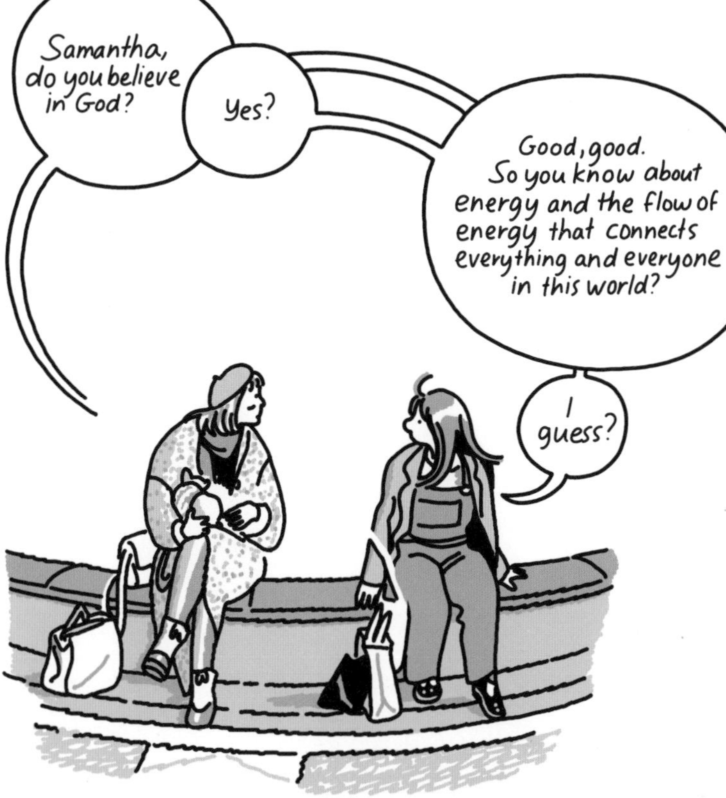
Samantha, do you believe in God?
Yes?
Good, good. So you know about energy and the flow of energy that connects everything and everyone in this world?
I guess?

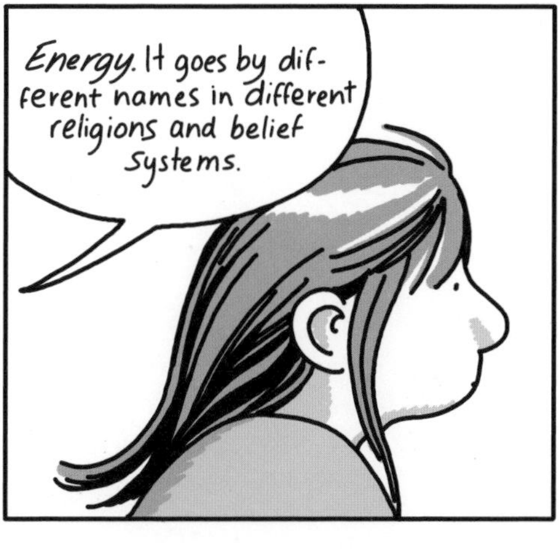
Energy. It goes by different names in different religions and belief systems.

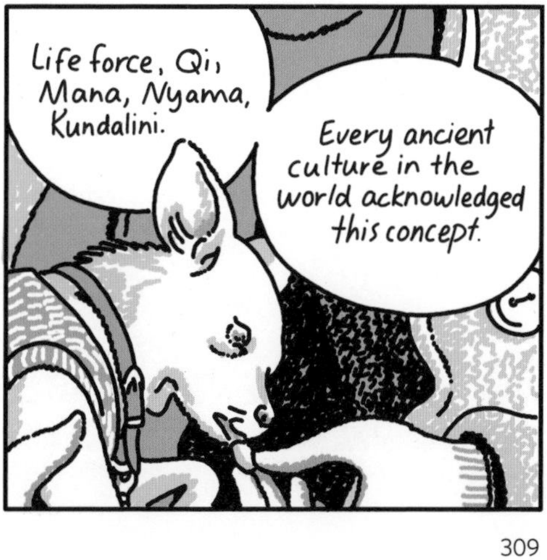
Life force, Qi, Mana, Nyama, Kundalini.
Every ancient culture in the world acknowledged this concept.

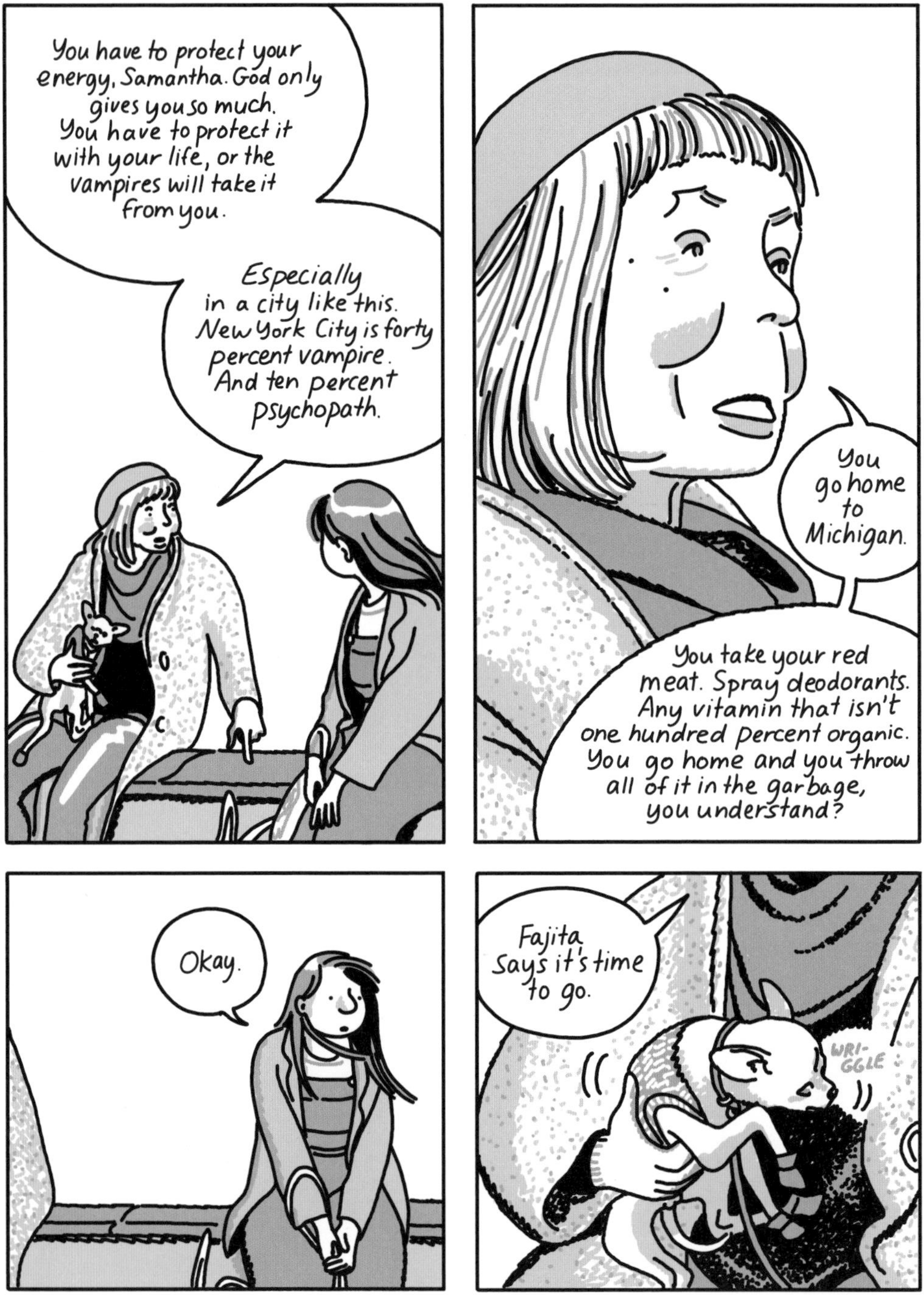
You have to protect your energy, Samantha. God only gives you so much. You have to protect it with your life, or the vampires will take it from you.
Especially in a city like this. New York City is forty percent vampire. And ten percent psychopath.
You go home to Michigan.
You take your red meat. Spray deodorants. Any vitamin that isn't one hundred percent organic. You go home and you throw all of it in the garbage, you understand?
Okay.
Fajita says it's time to go.
WRIGGLE

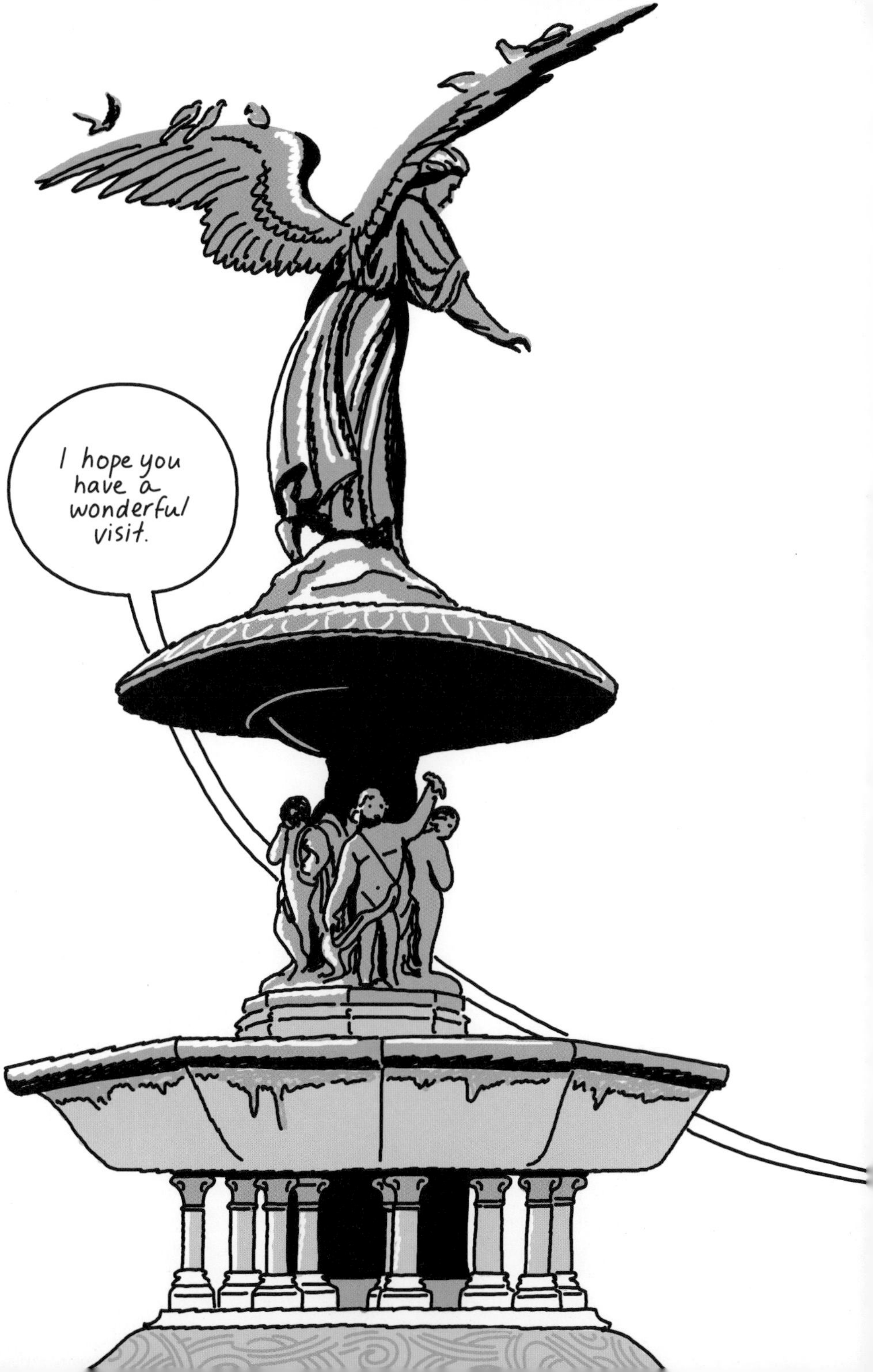
I hope you have a wonderful visit.

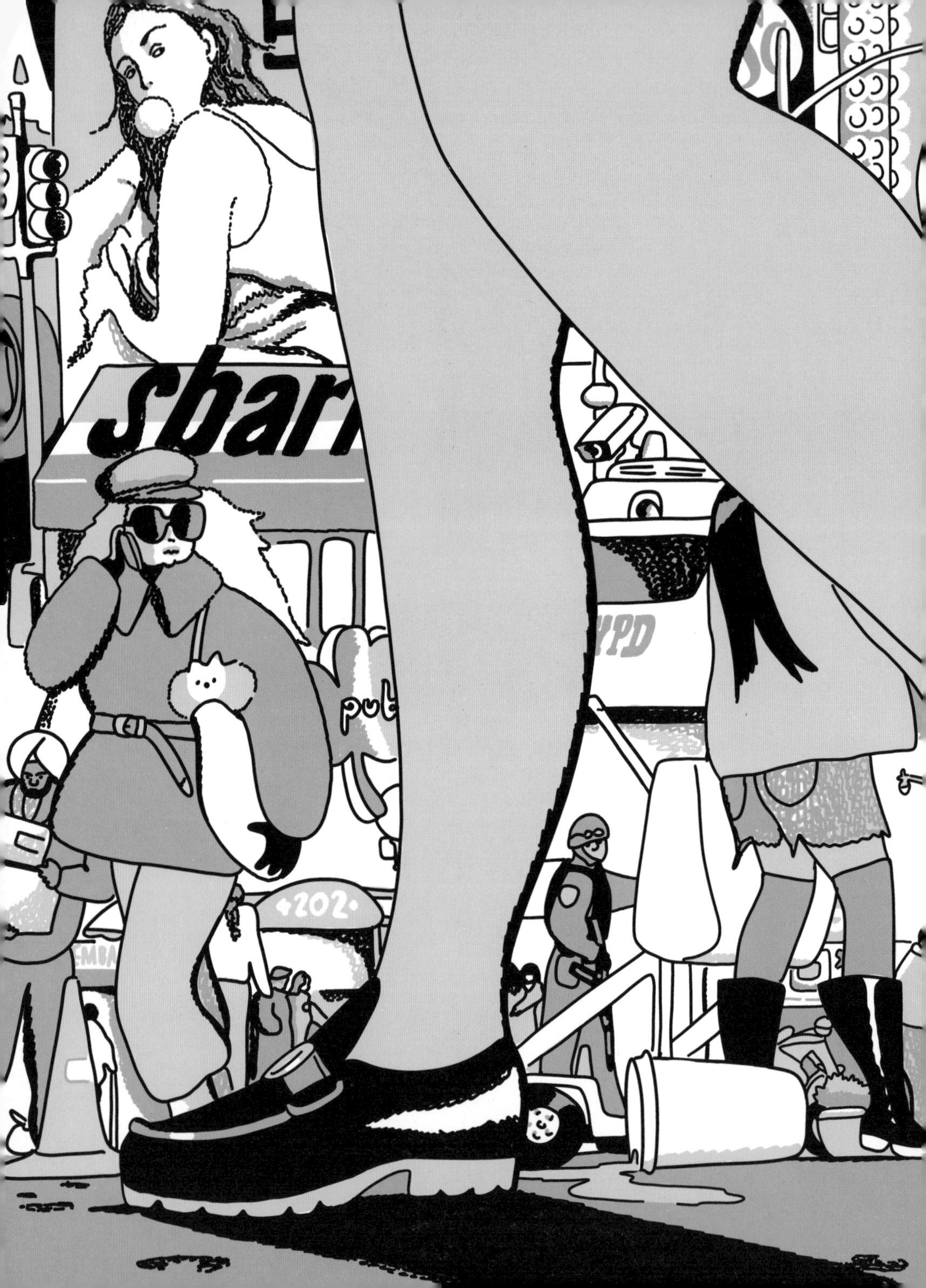
sbarr
pub
•202•
YPD

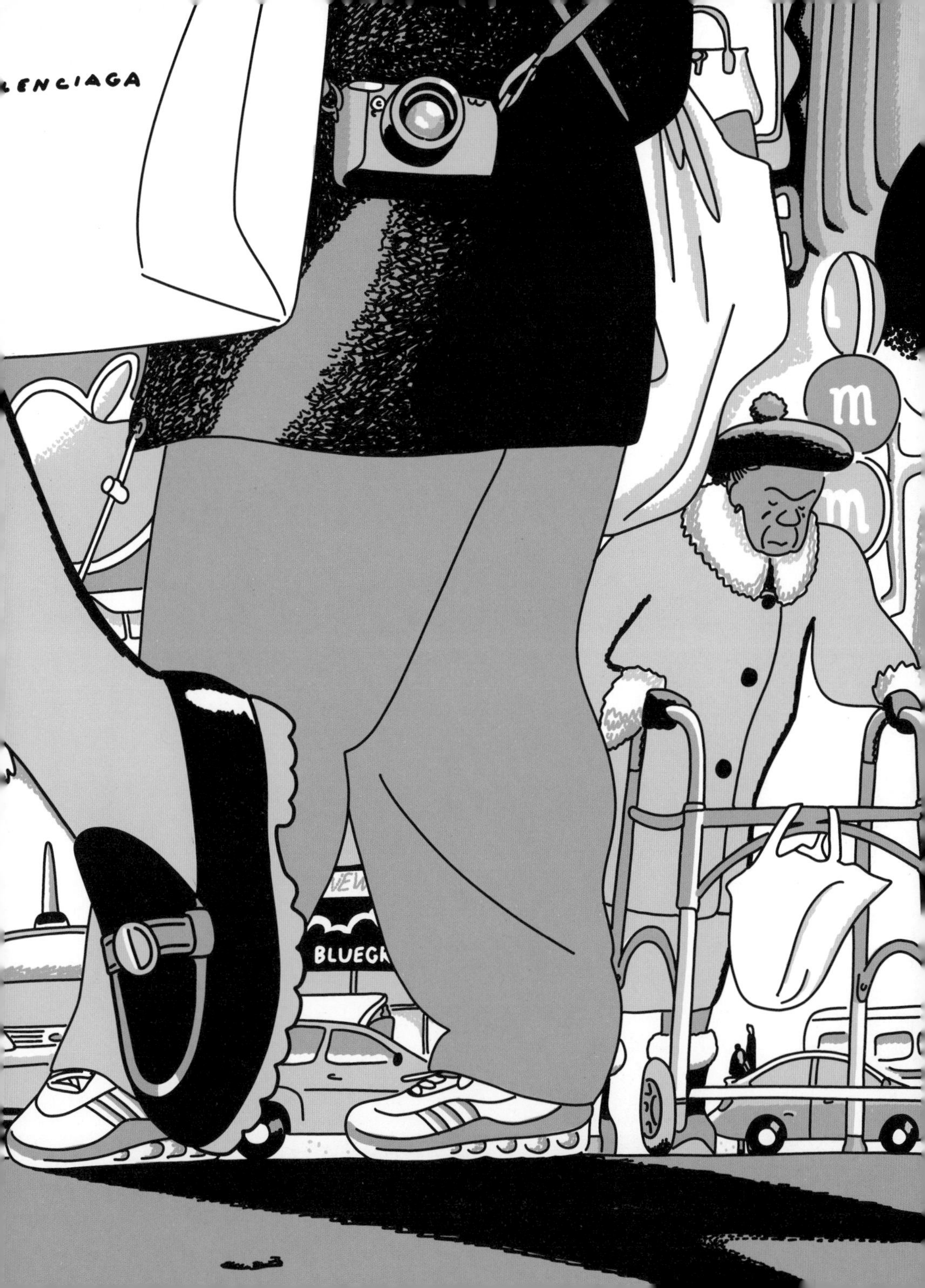
LENCIAGA
BLUEGR

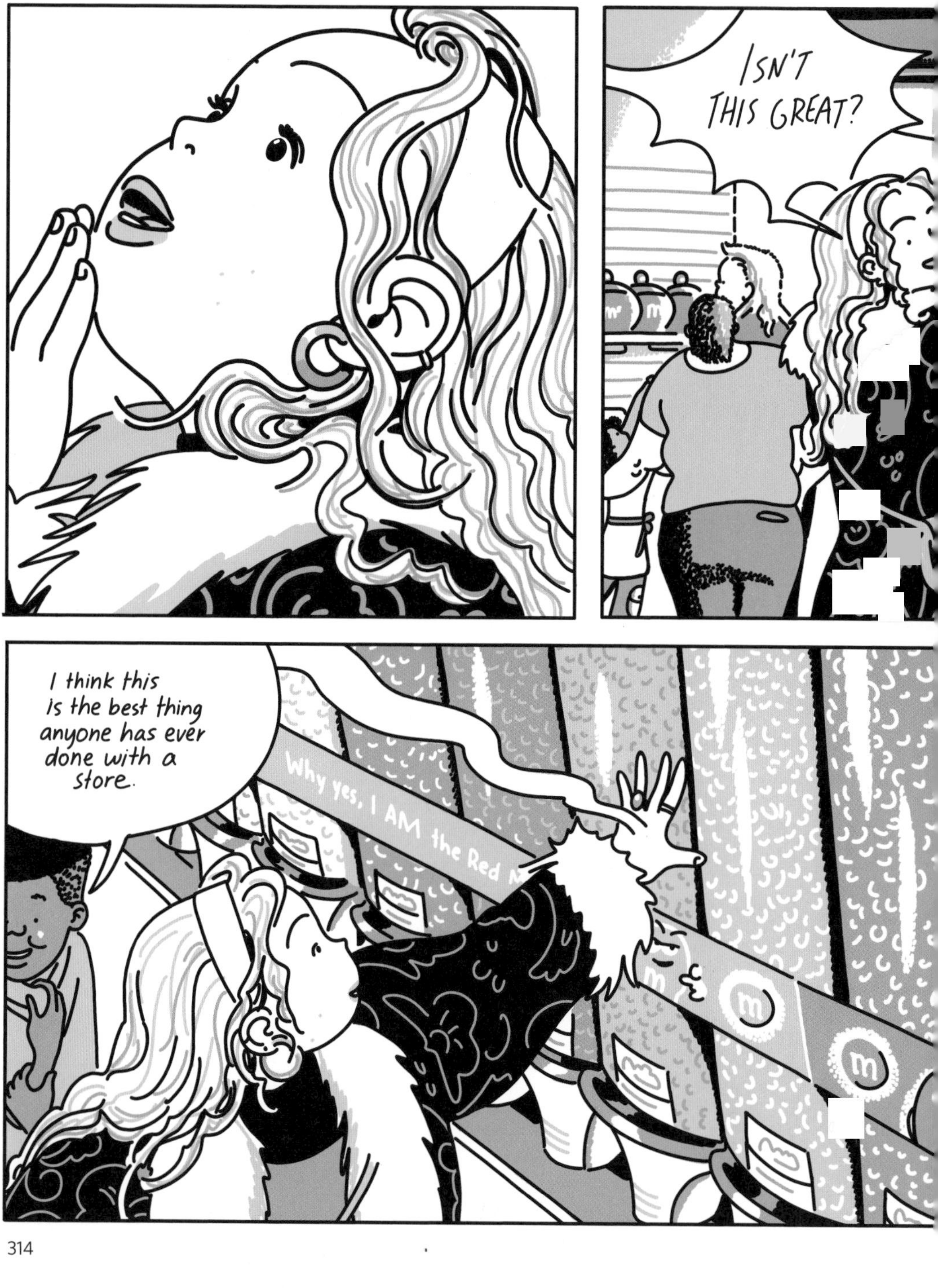
ISN'T THIS GREAT?
I think this is the best thing anyone has ever done with a store.
Why yes, I AM the Red

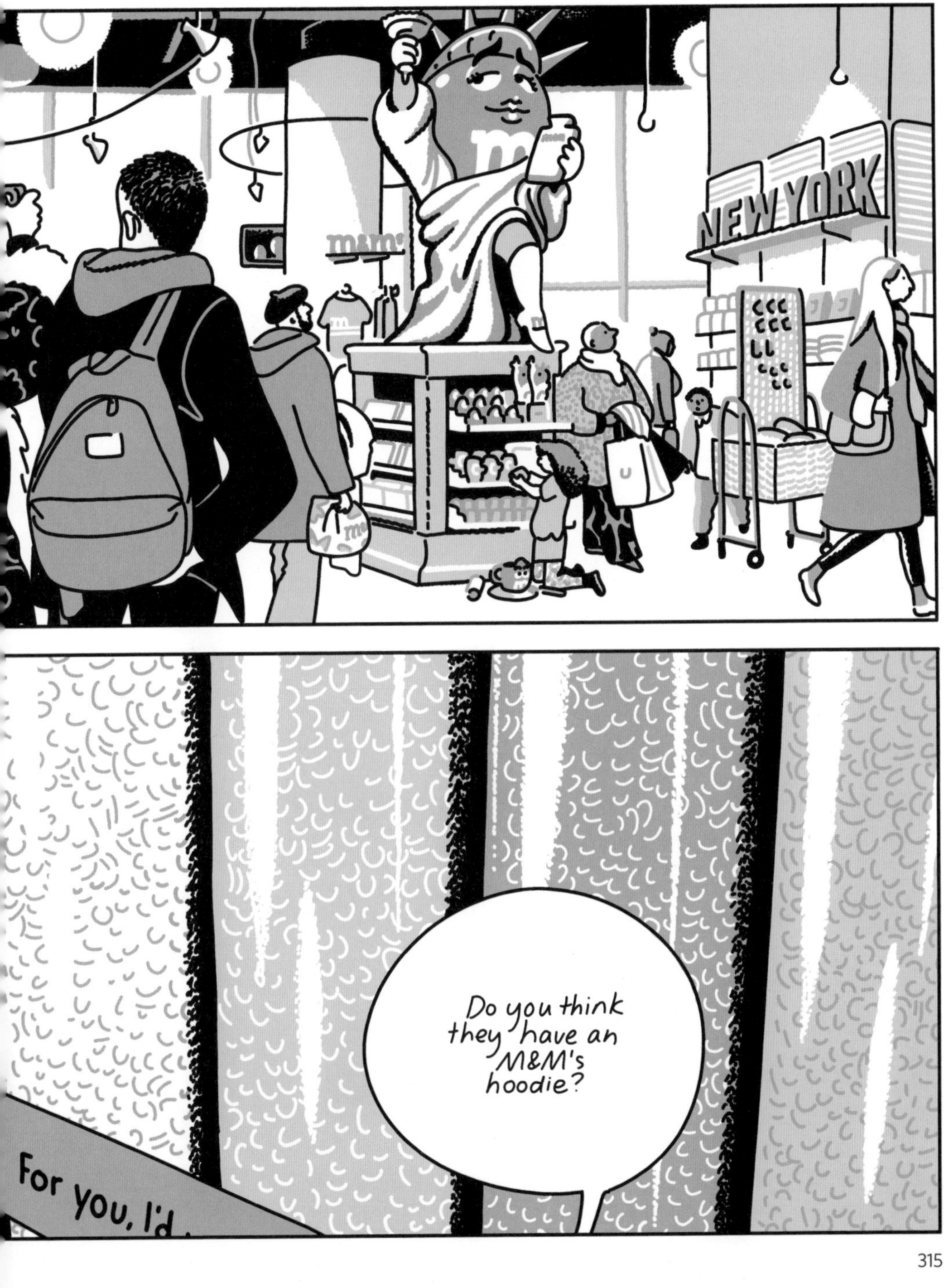
NEW YORK
Do you think they have an M&M's hoodie?
For you, I'd .

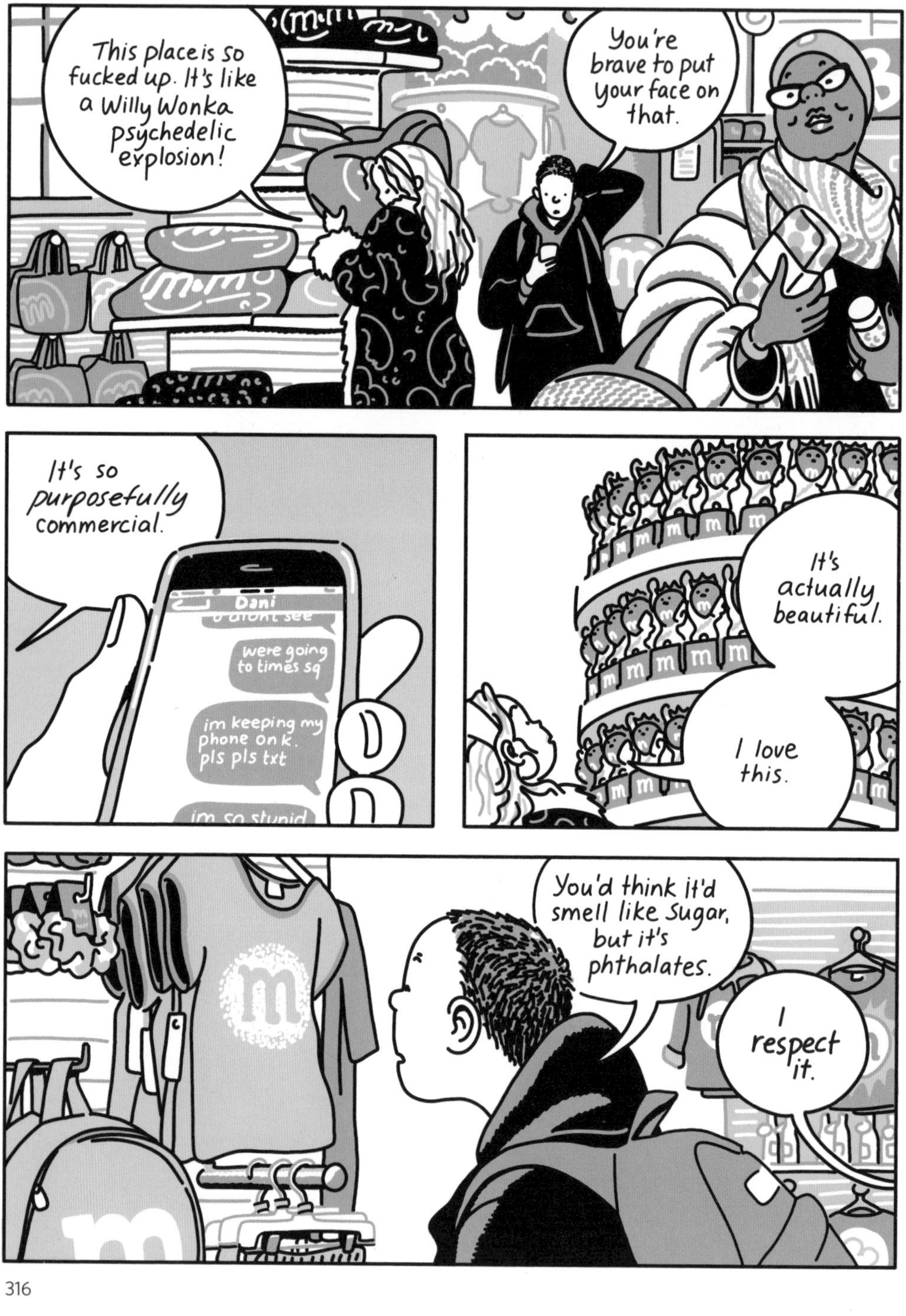
This place is so fucked up. It's like a Willy Wonka psychedelic explosion!
You're brave to put your face on that.
It's so *purposefully* commercial.
Dani
were going to times sq
im keeping my phone on k. pls pls txt
It's actually beautiful.
I love this.
You'd think it'd smell like sugar, but it's phthalates.
I respect it.

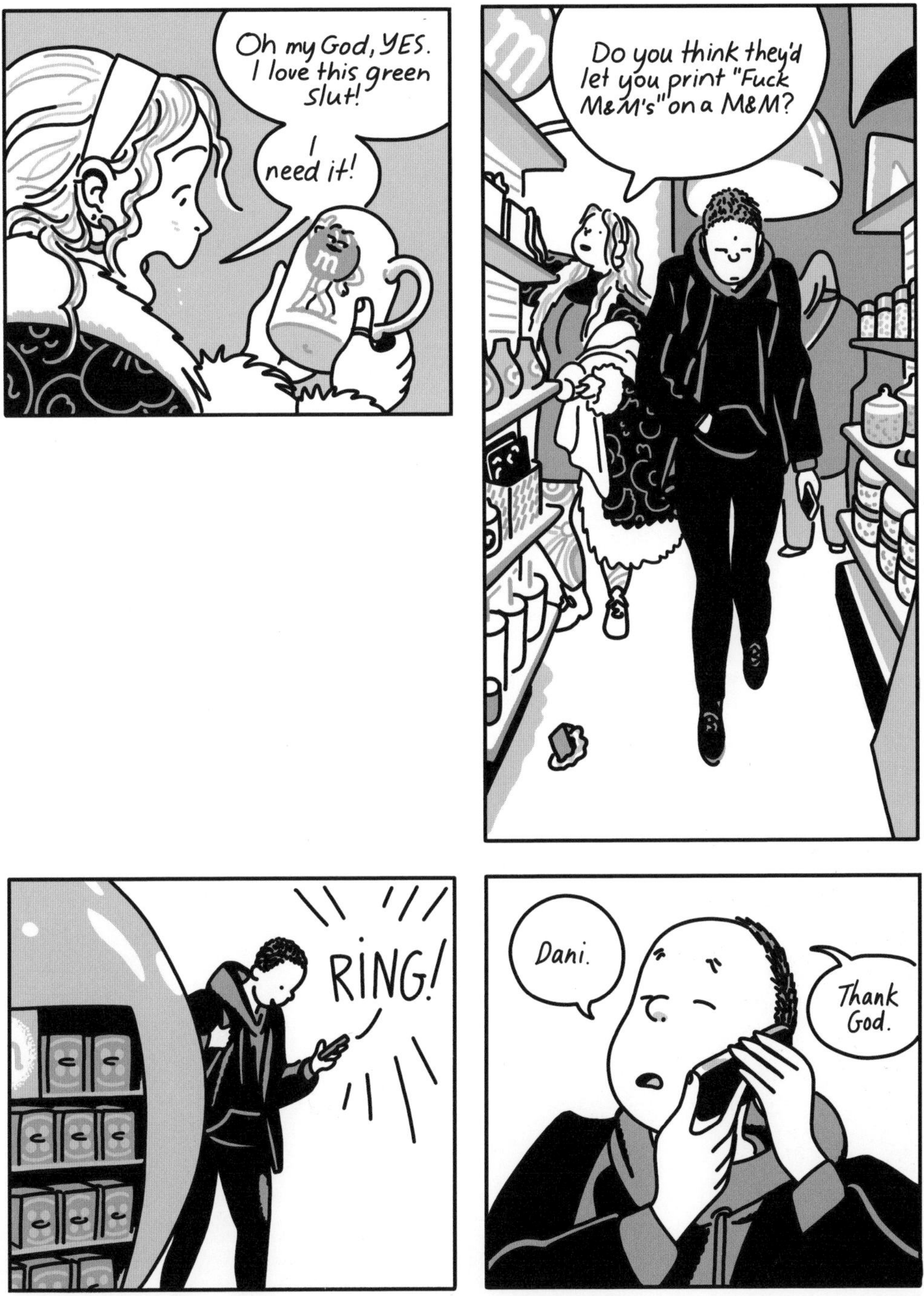
Oh my God, YES. I love this green slut!
I need it!
Do you think they'd let you print "Fuck M&M's" on a M&M?
RING!
Dani.
Thank God.

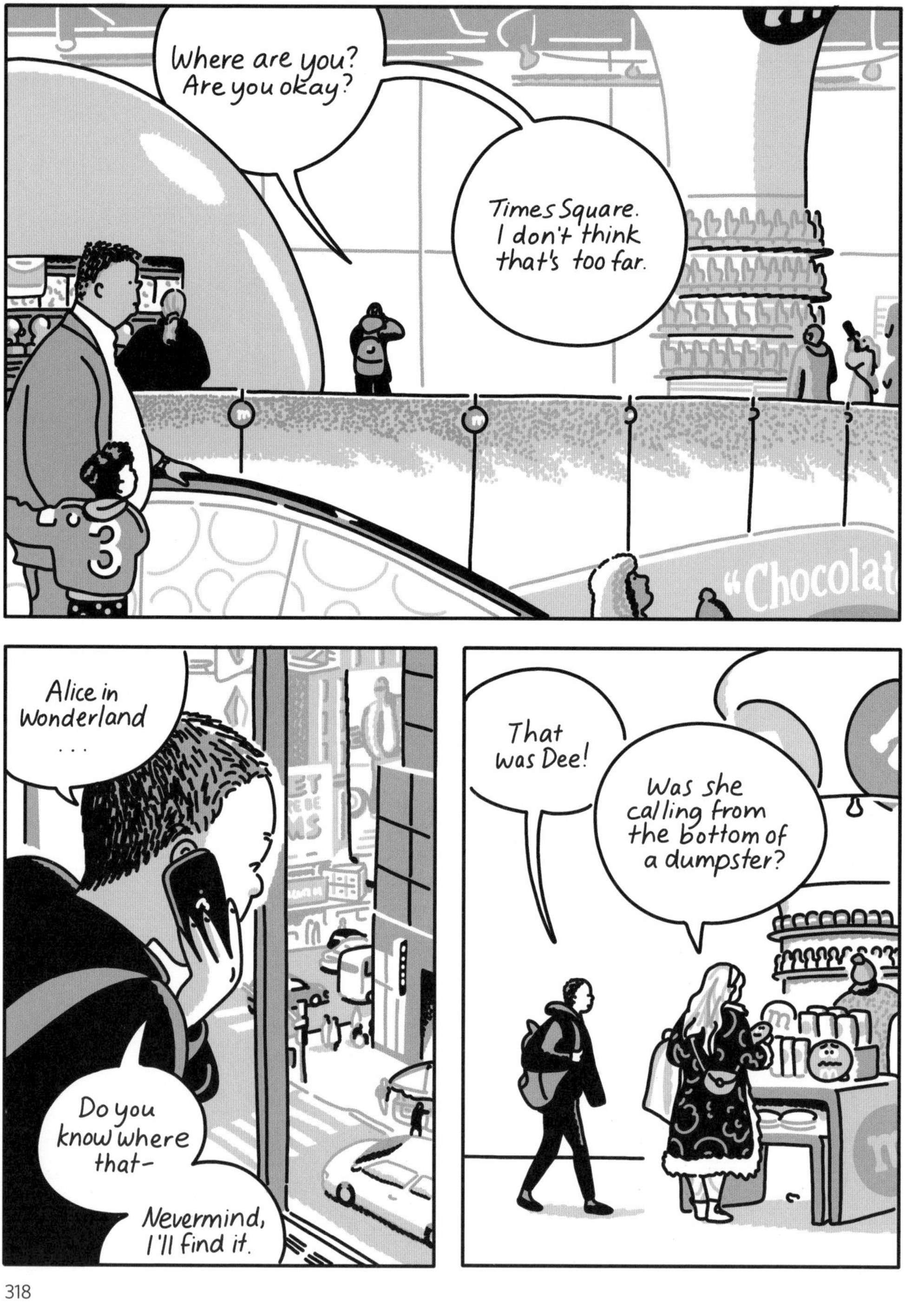
Where are you? Are you okay?
Times Square. I don't think that's too far.
"Chocolat
Alice in Wonderland . . .
Do you know where that-
Nevermind, I'll find it.
That was Dee!
Was she calling from the bottom of a dumpster?

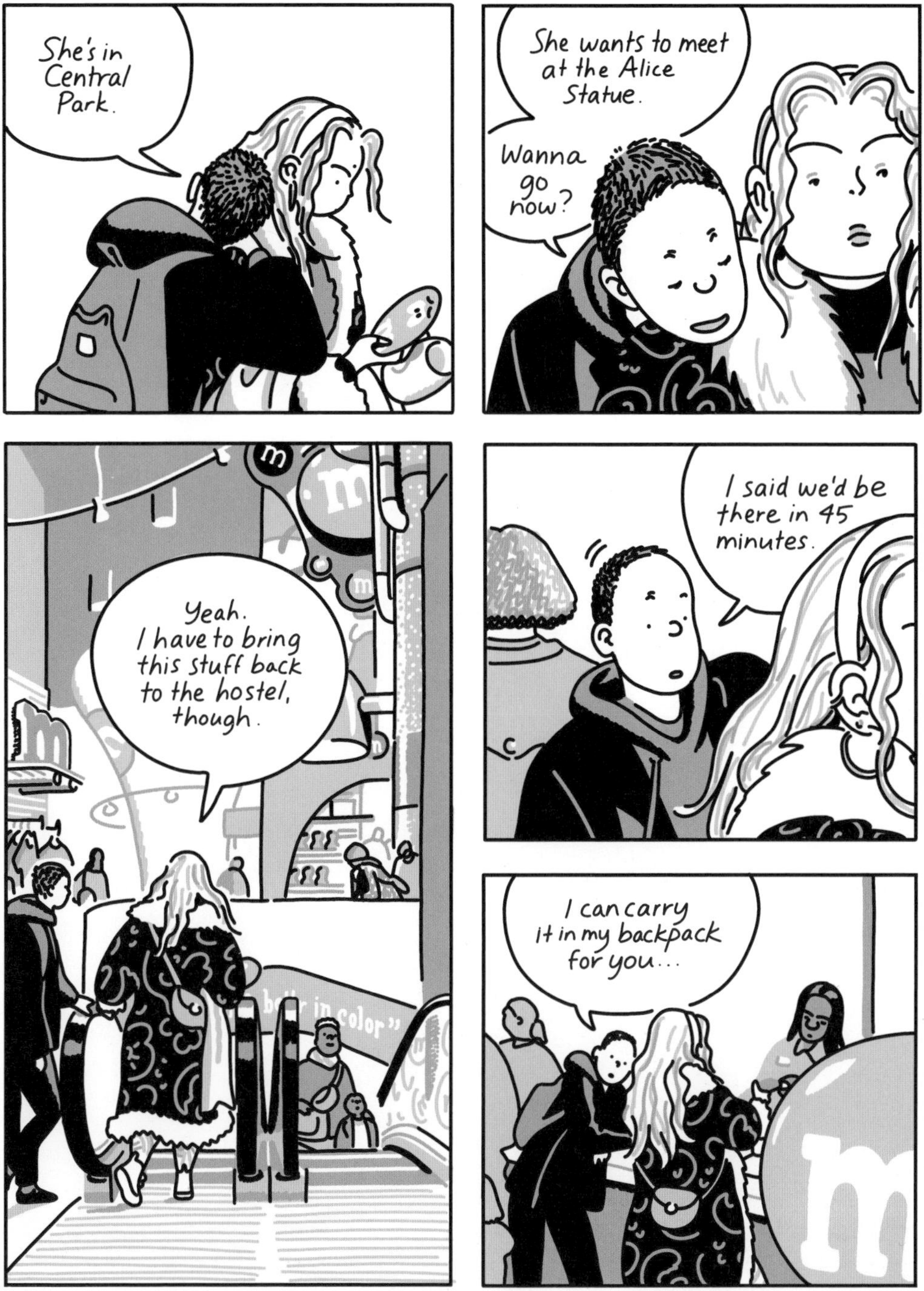
She's in Central Park.
She wants to meet at the Alice Statue.
Wanna go now?
Yeah. I have to bring this stuff back to the hostel, though.
I said we'd be there in 45 minutes.
I can carry it in my backpack for you...

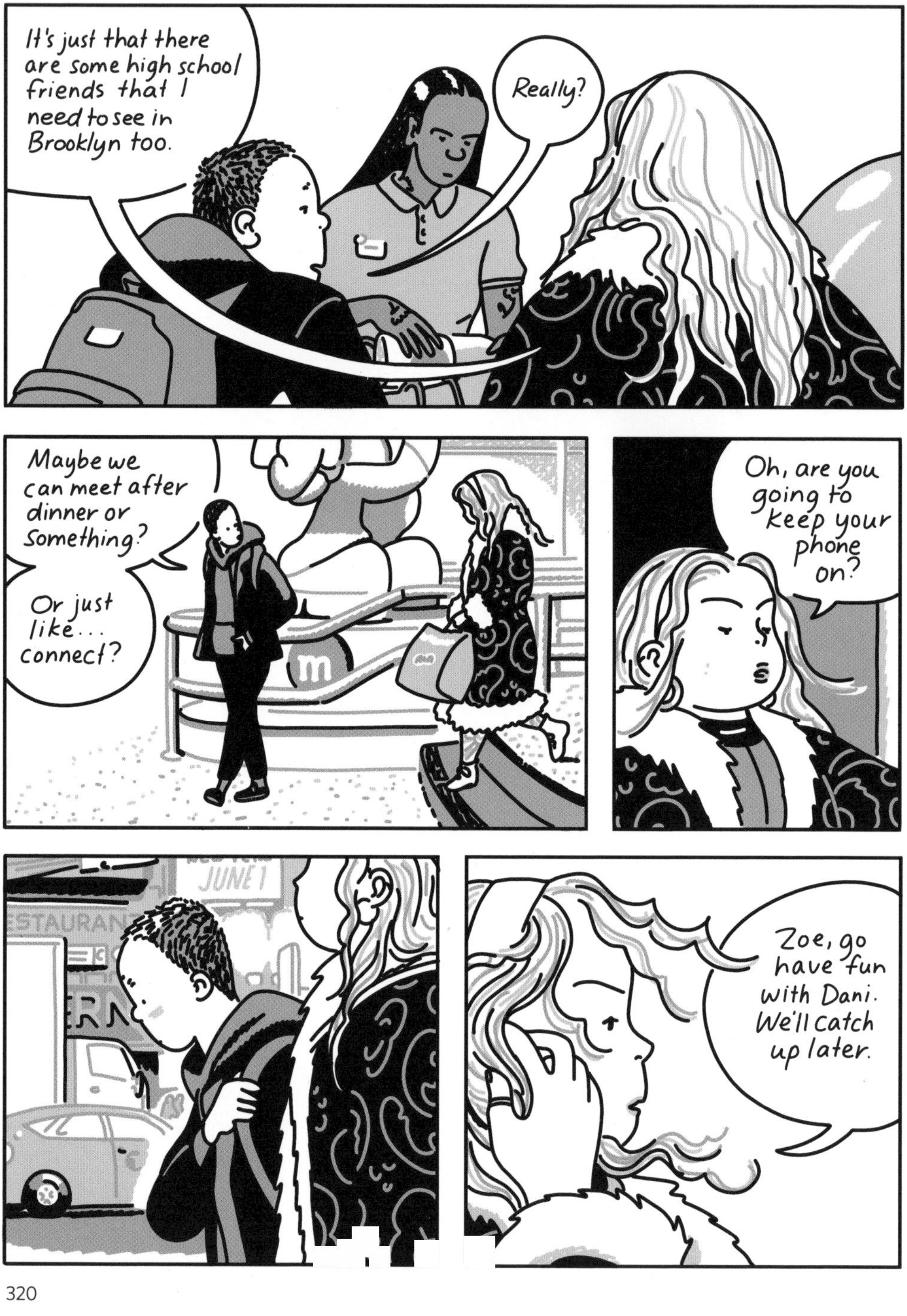
It's just that there are some high school friends that I need to see in Brooklyn too.
Really?
Maybe we can meet after dinner or something?
Or just like... connect?
Oh, are you going to keep your phone on?
JUNE 1
ESTAURAN
Zoe, go have fun with Dani. We'll catch up later.

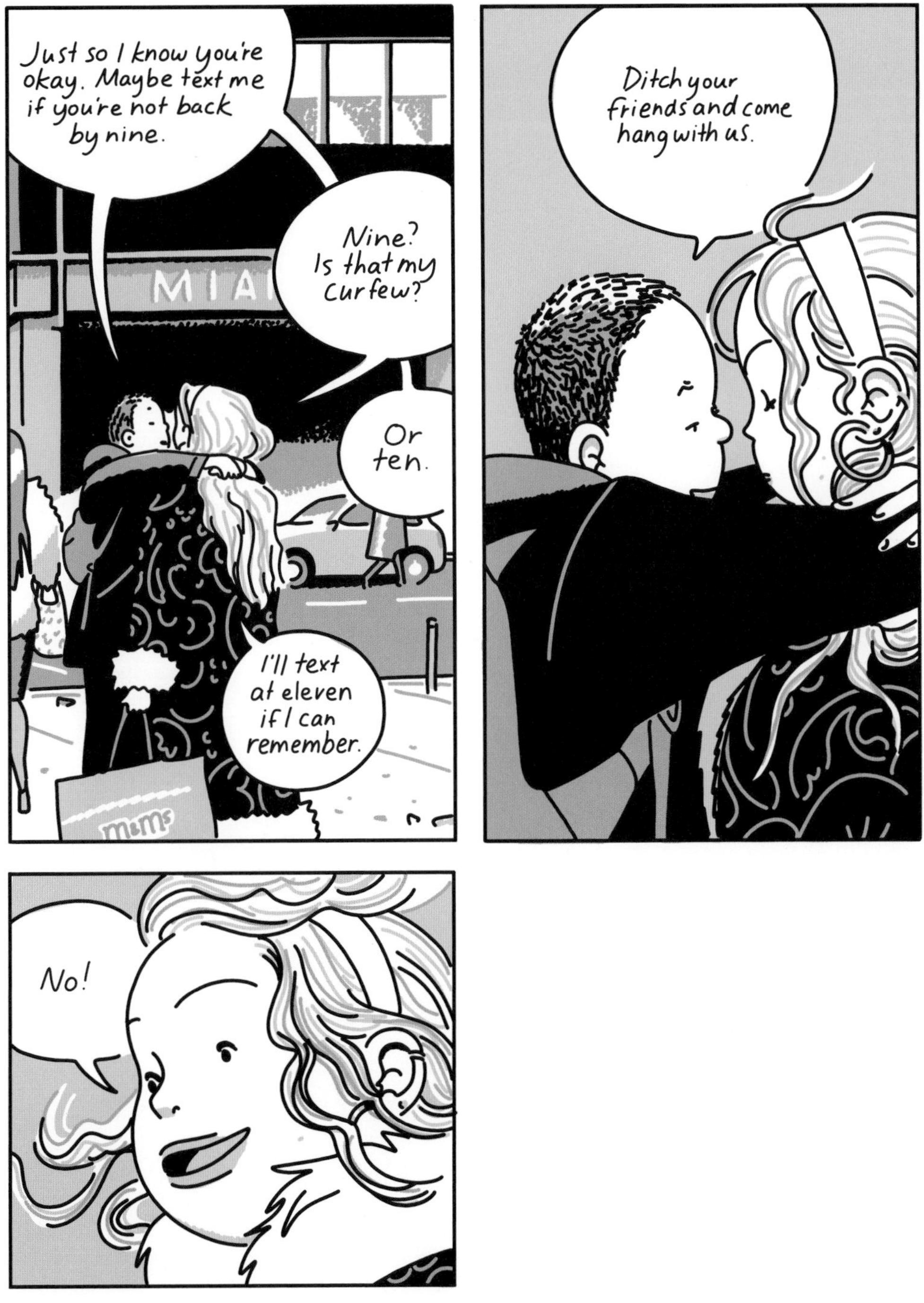
Just so I know you're okay. Maybe text me if you're not back by nine.
Nine? Is that my curfew?
Or ten.
I'll text at eleven if I can remember.
Ditch your friends and come hang with us.
No!

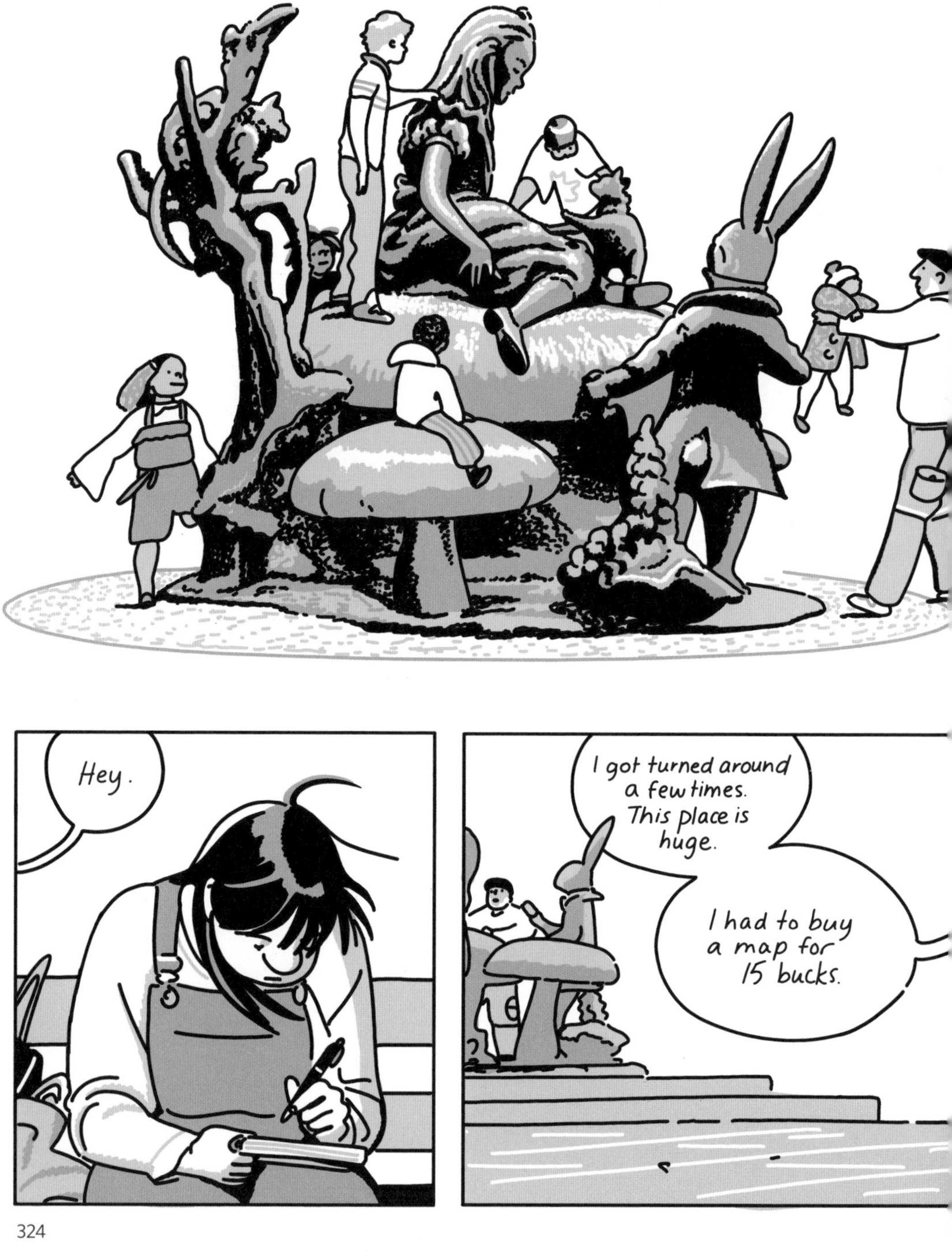
Hey.
I got turned around a few times. This place is huge.
I had to buy a map for 15 bucks.

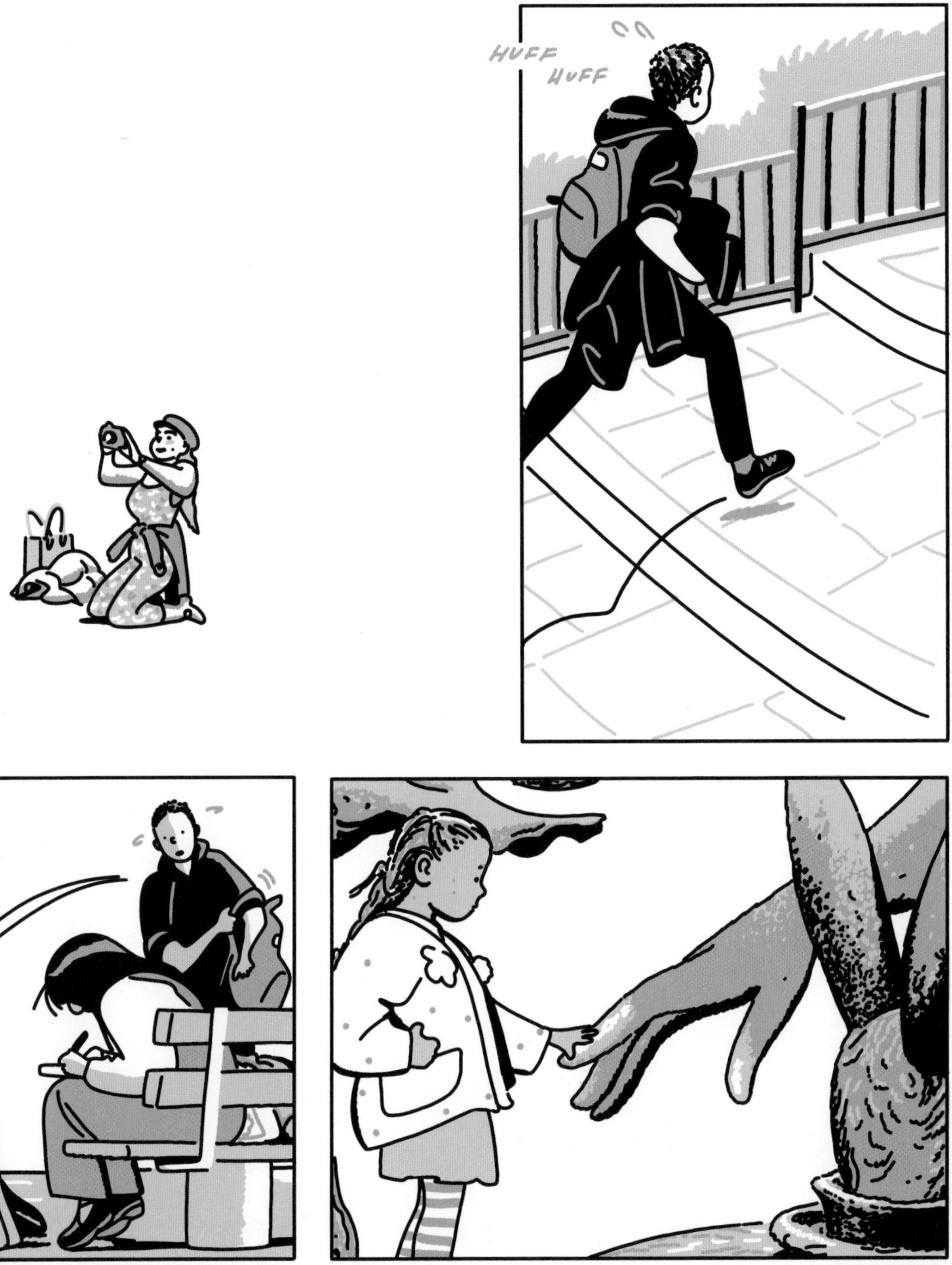
HUFF
HUFF

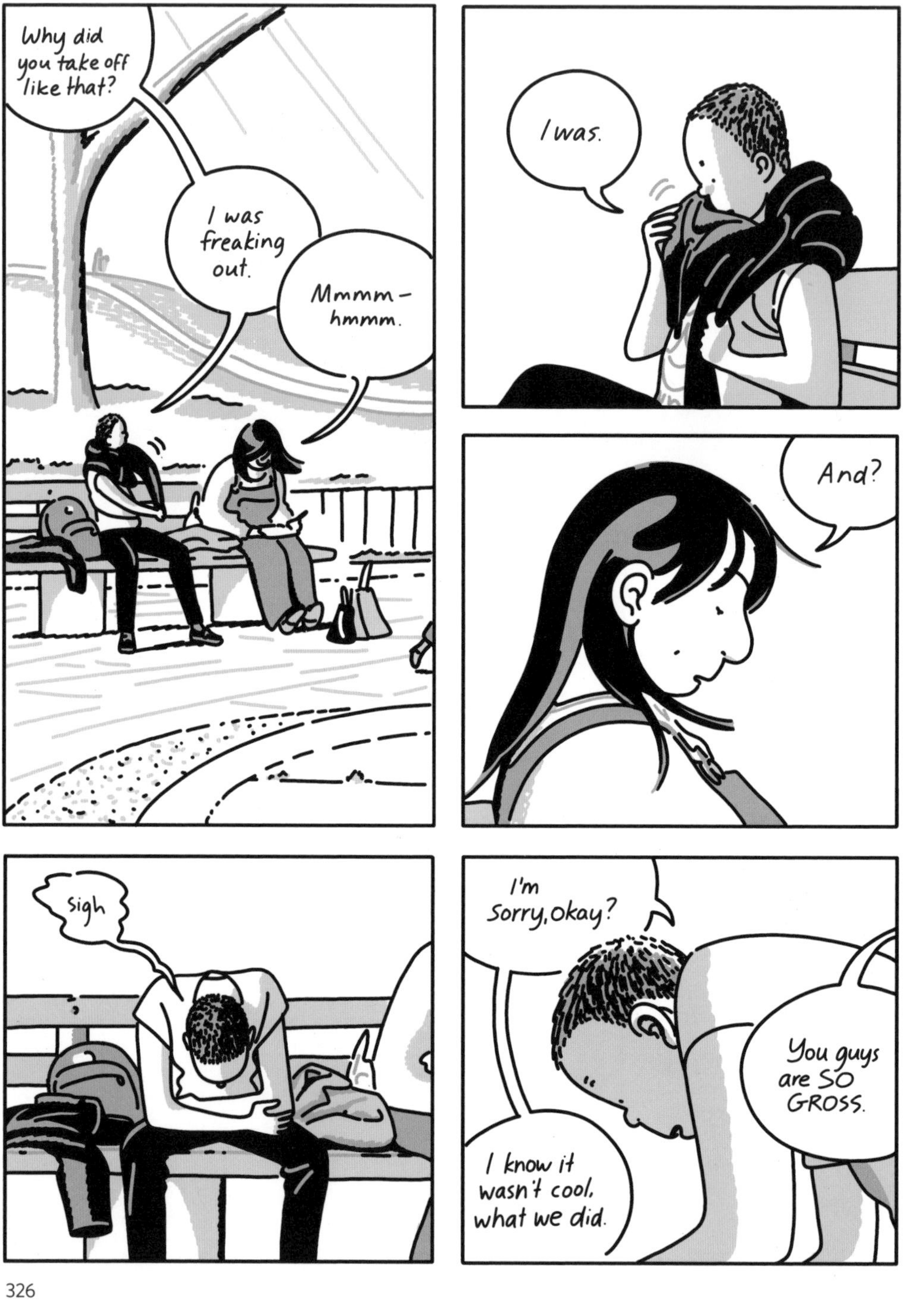
Why did you take off like that?
I was freaking out.
Mmmm-hmmm.
I was.
And?
sigh
I'm sorry, okay?
I know it wasn't cool, what we did.
You guys are SO GROSS.

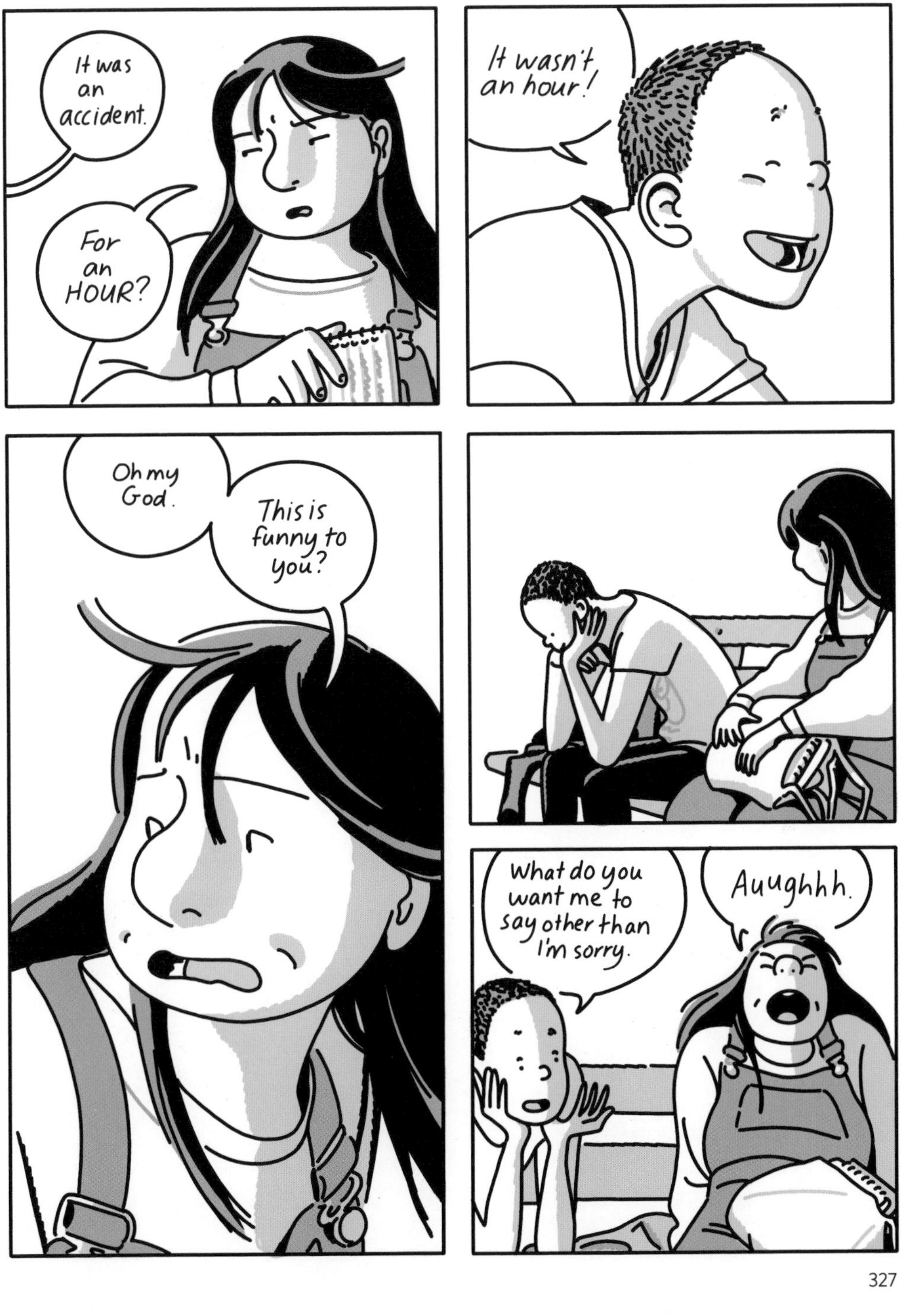
It was an accident.
For an HOUR?
It wasn't an hour!
Oh my God.
This is funny to you?
What do you want me to say other than I'm sorry.
Auughhh.

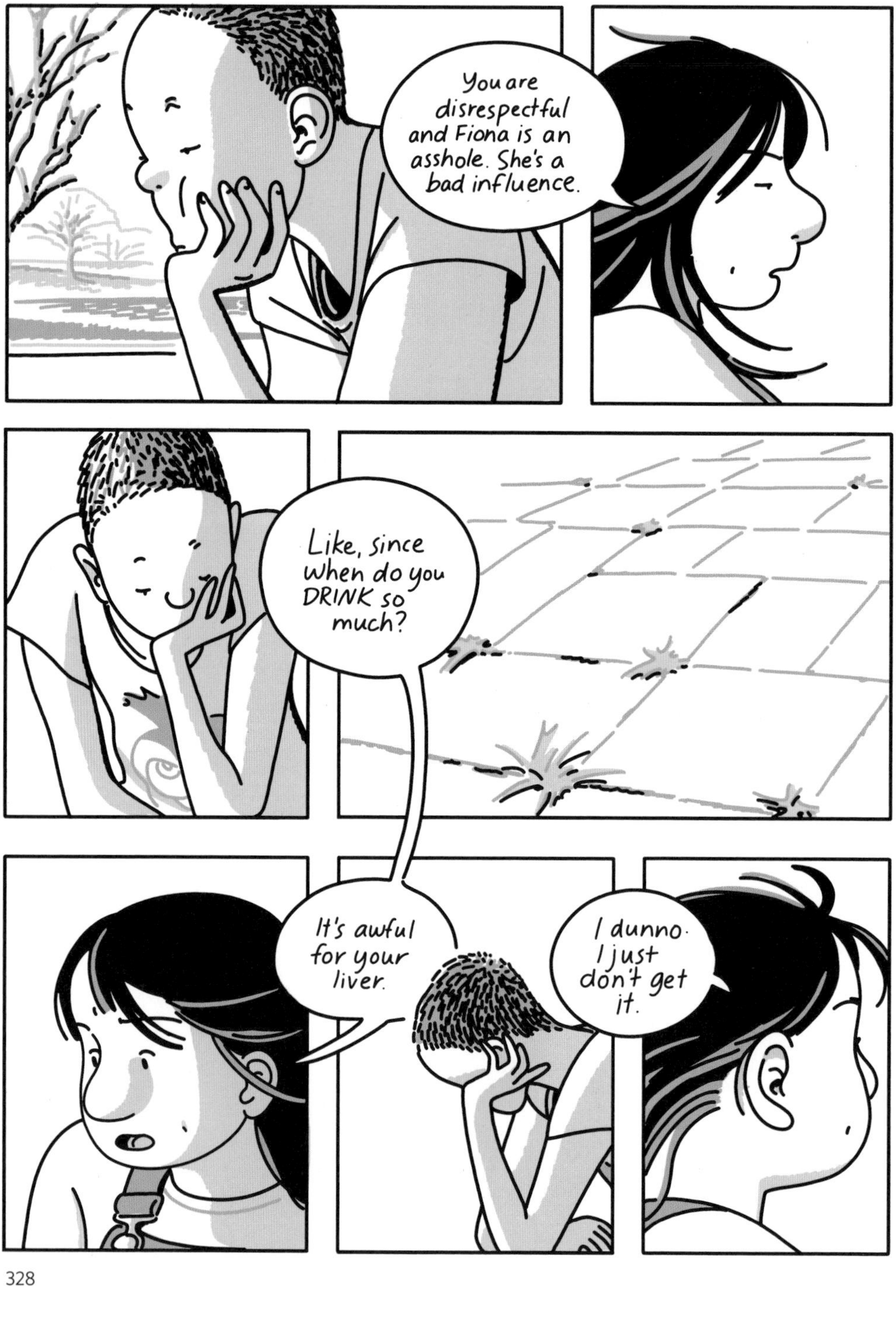
You are disrespectful and Fiona is an asshole. She's a bad influence.
Like, since when do you DRINK so much?
It's awful for your liver.
I dunno. I just don't get it.

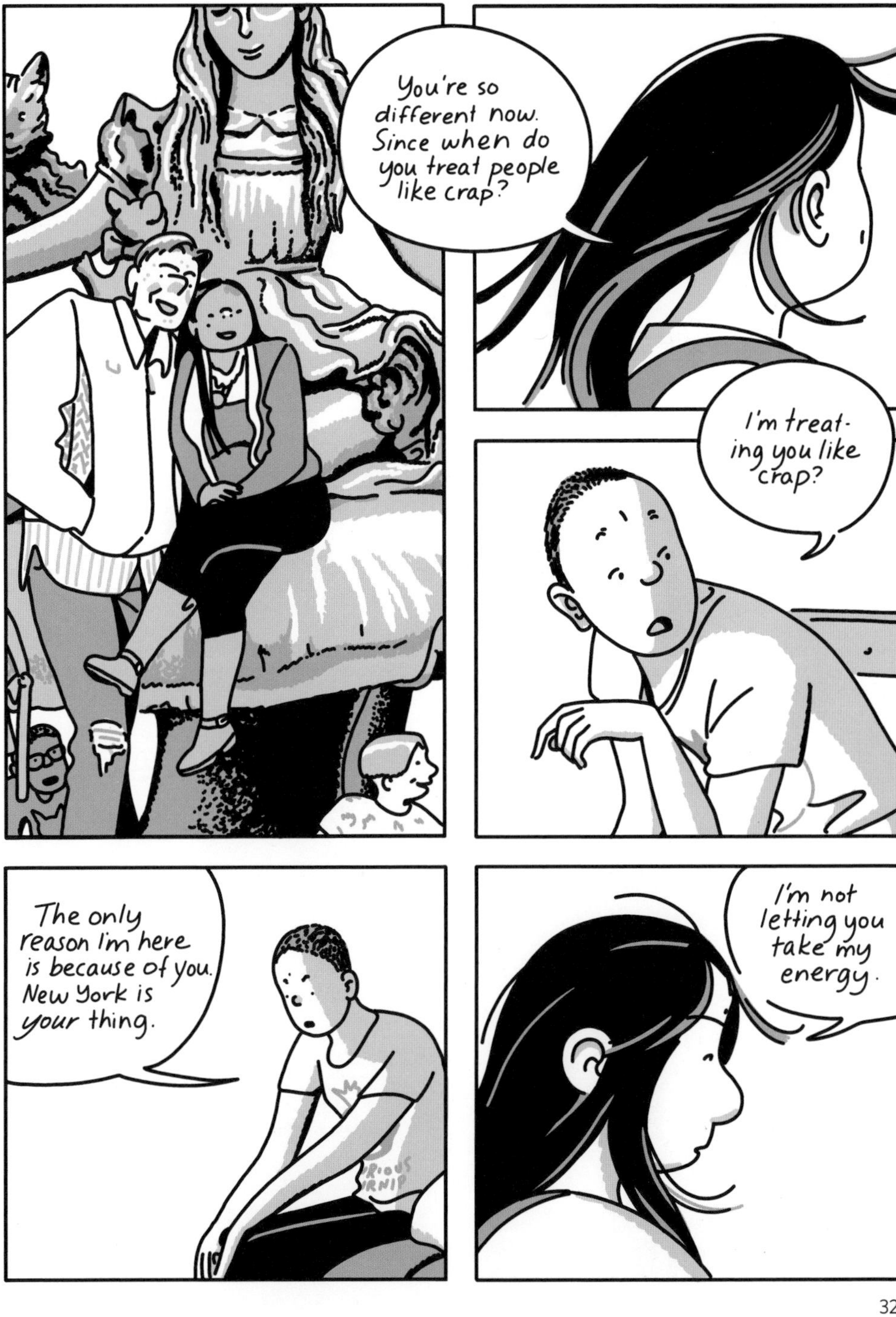
You're so different now. Since when do you treat people like crap?
I'm treating you like crap?
The only reason I'm here is because of you. New York is your thing.
I'm not letting you take my energy.

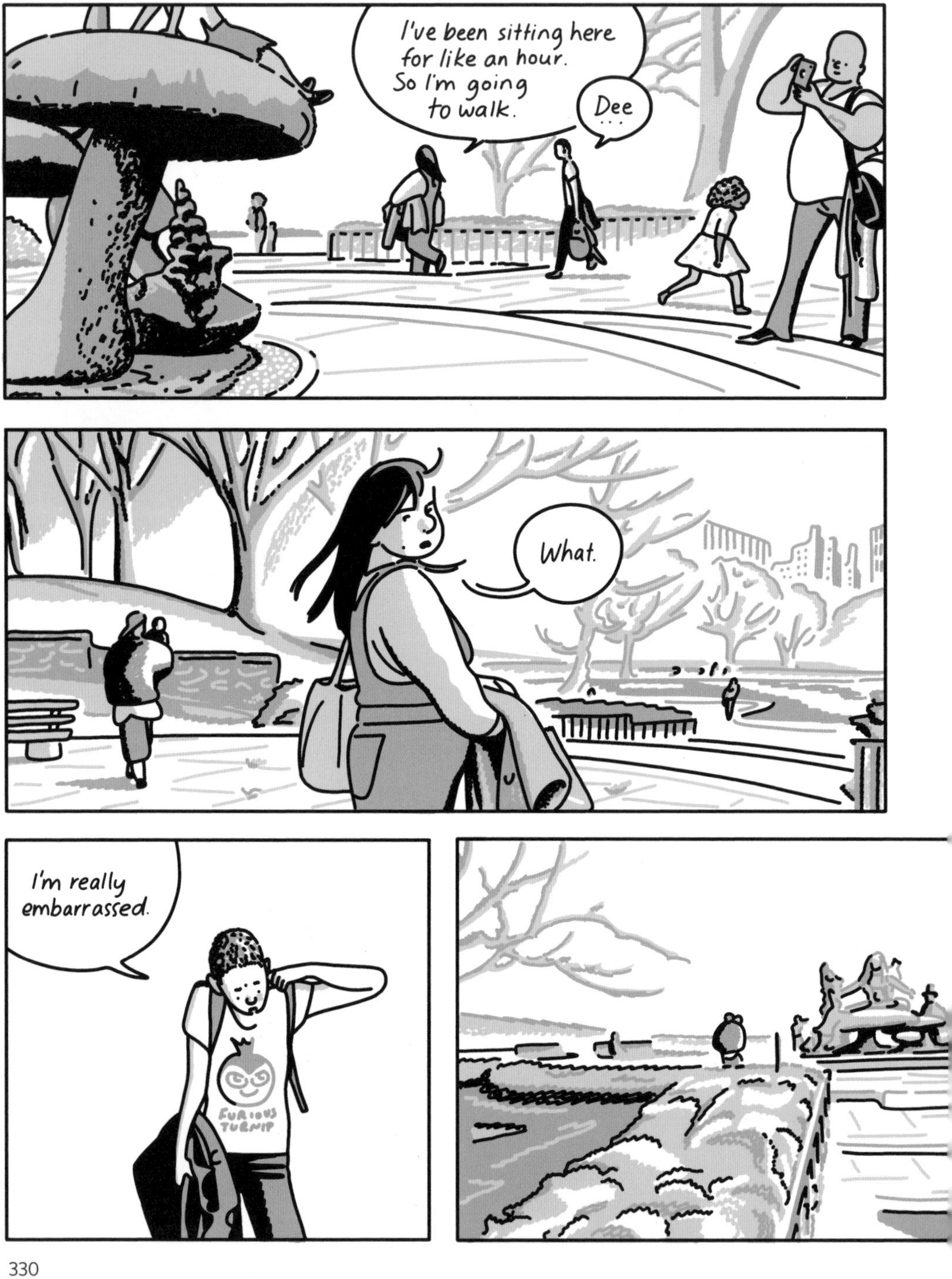
I've been sitting here for like an hour. So I'm going to walk.
Dee ...
What.
I'm really embarrassed.
FURIOUS TURNIP

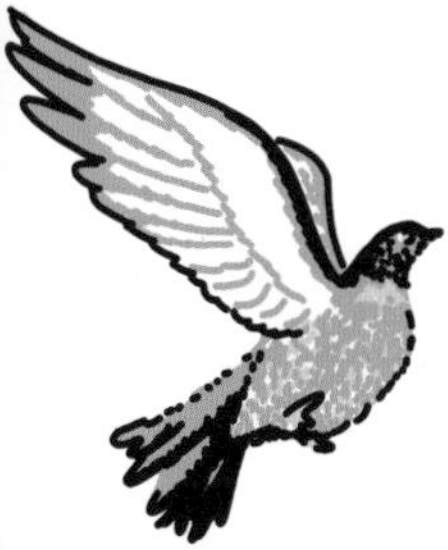

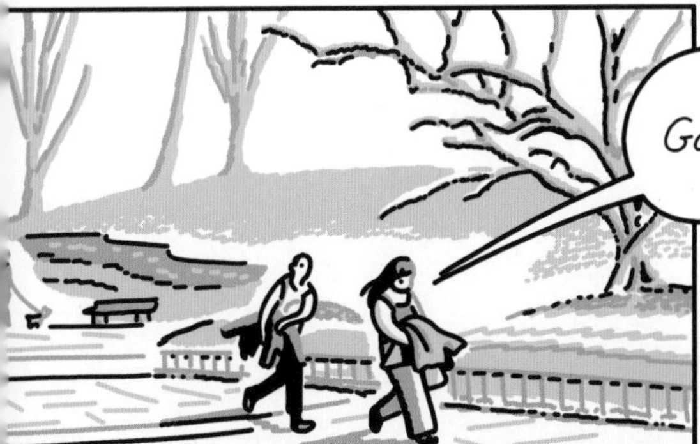
Good.

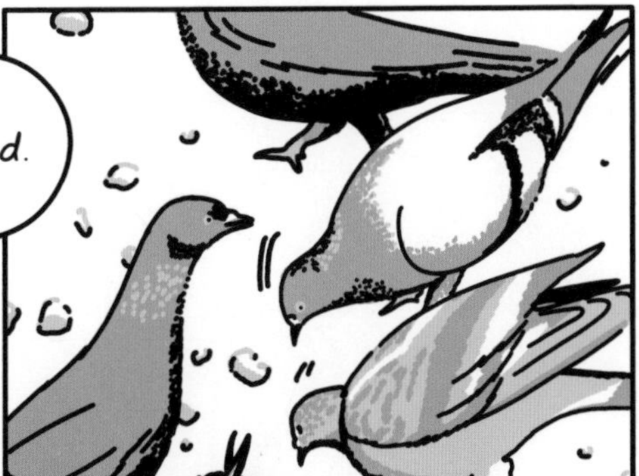

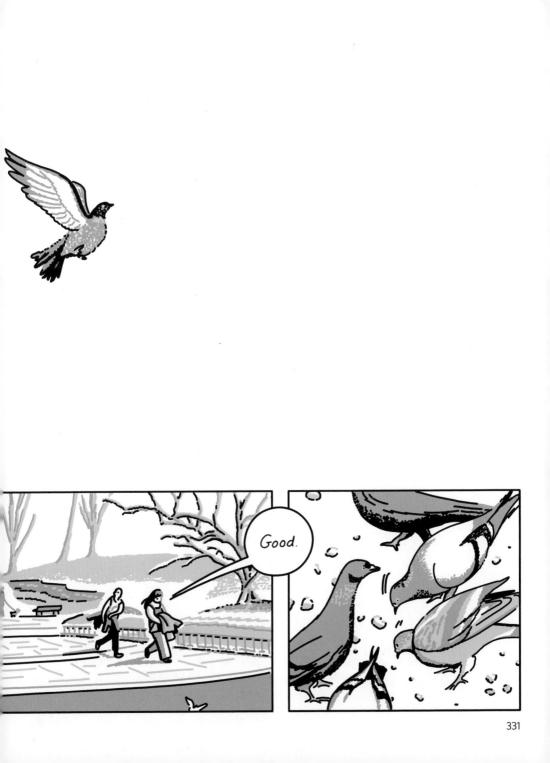

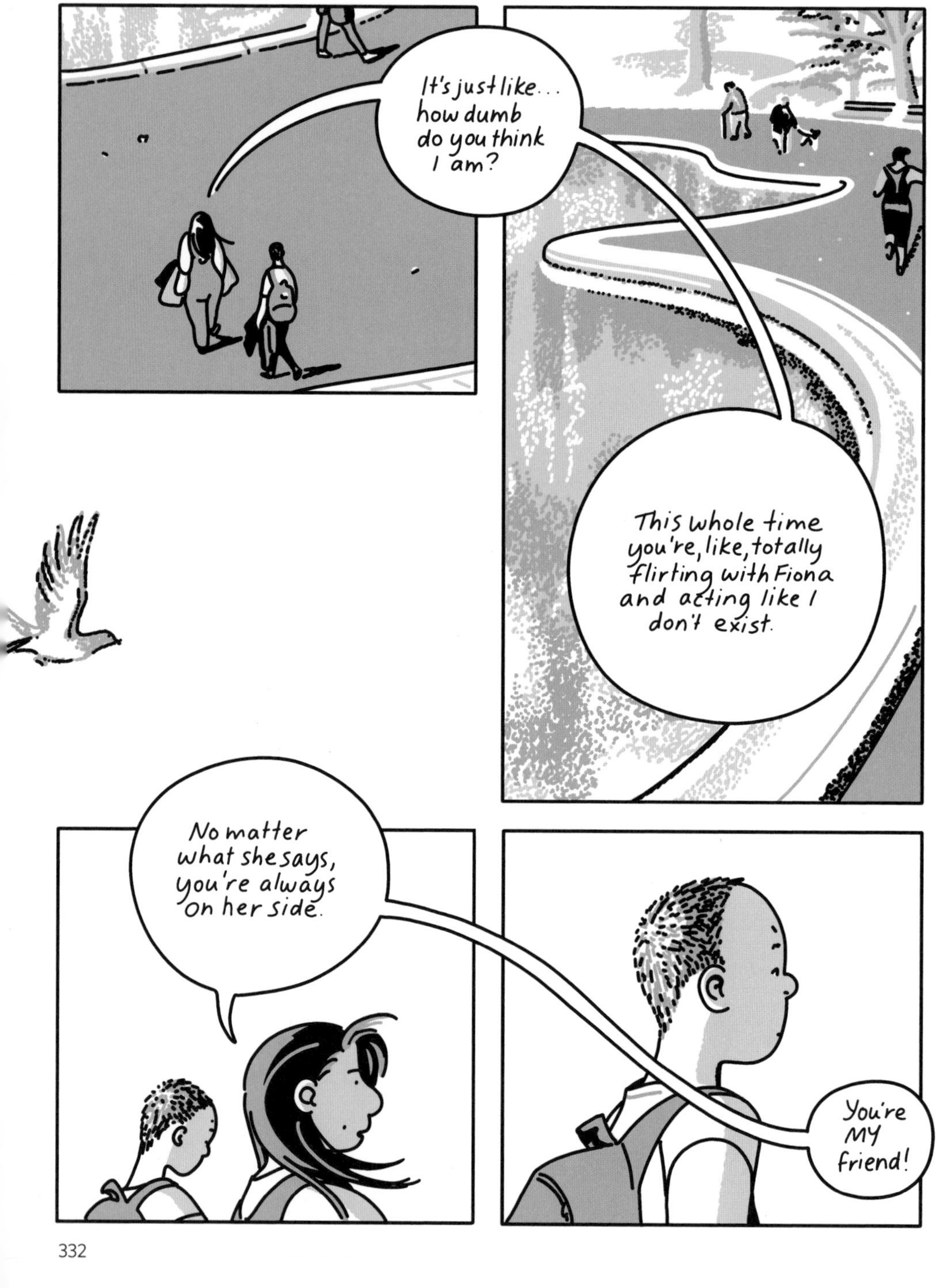

It's just like... how dumb do you think I am?
This whole time you're, like, totally flirting with Fiona and acting like I don't exist.
No matter what she says, you're always on her side.
You're MY friend!

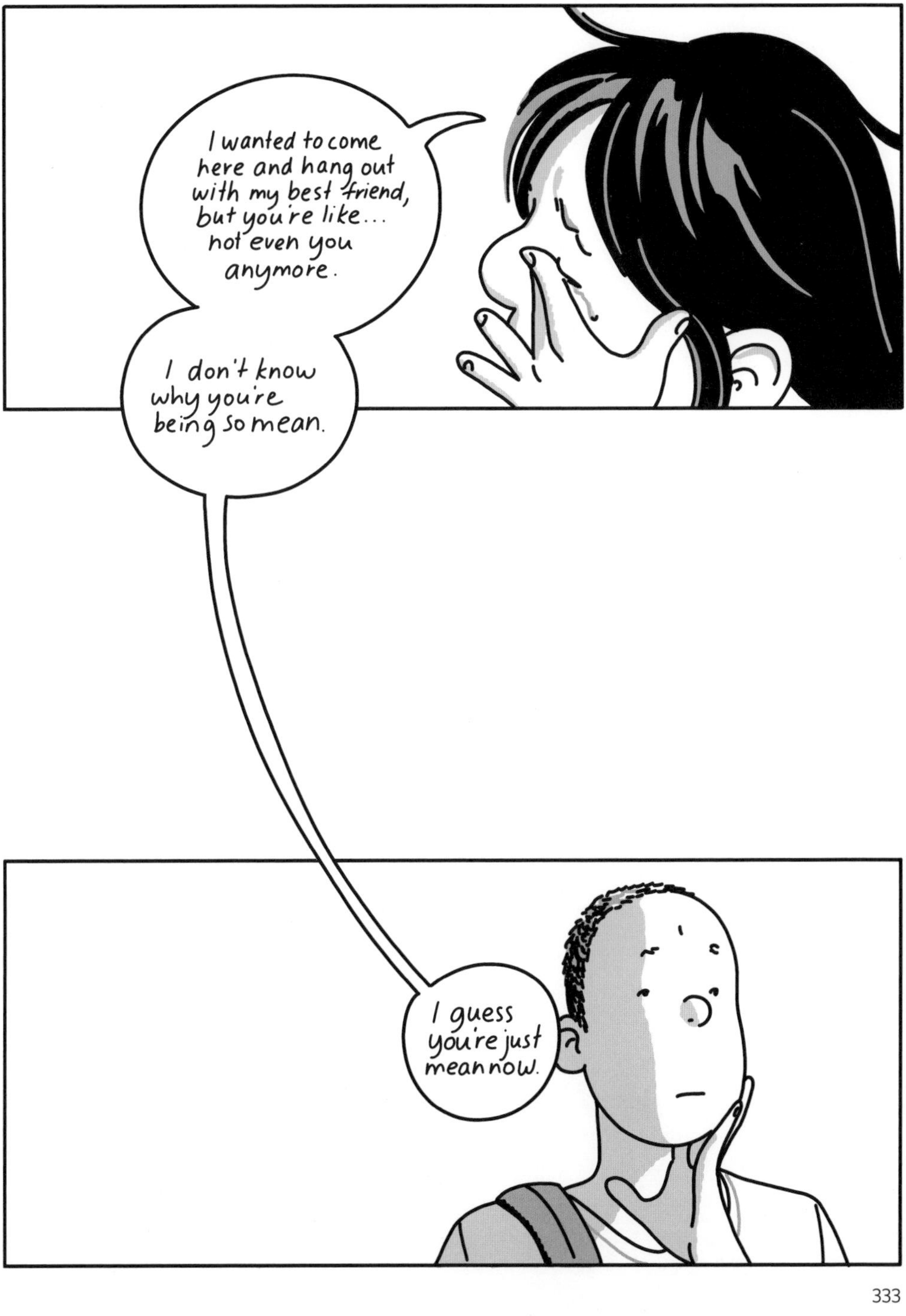
I wanted to come here and hang out with my best friend, but you're like... not even you anymore.
I don't know why you're being so mean.
I guess you're just mean now.

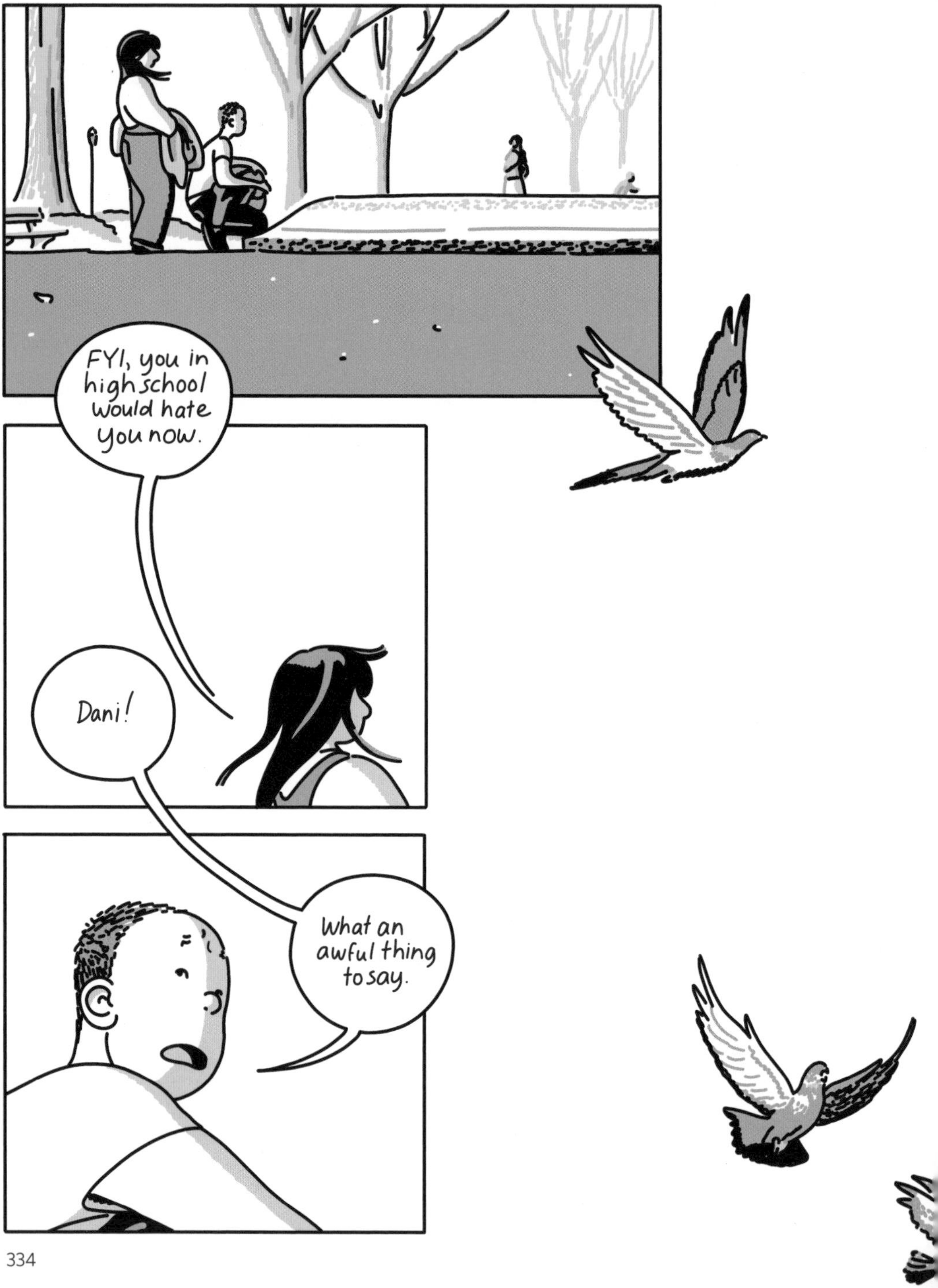
FYI, you in high school would hate you now.
Dani!
What an awful thing to say.

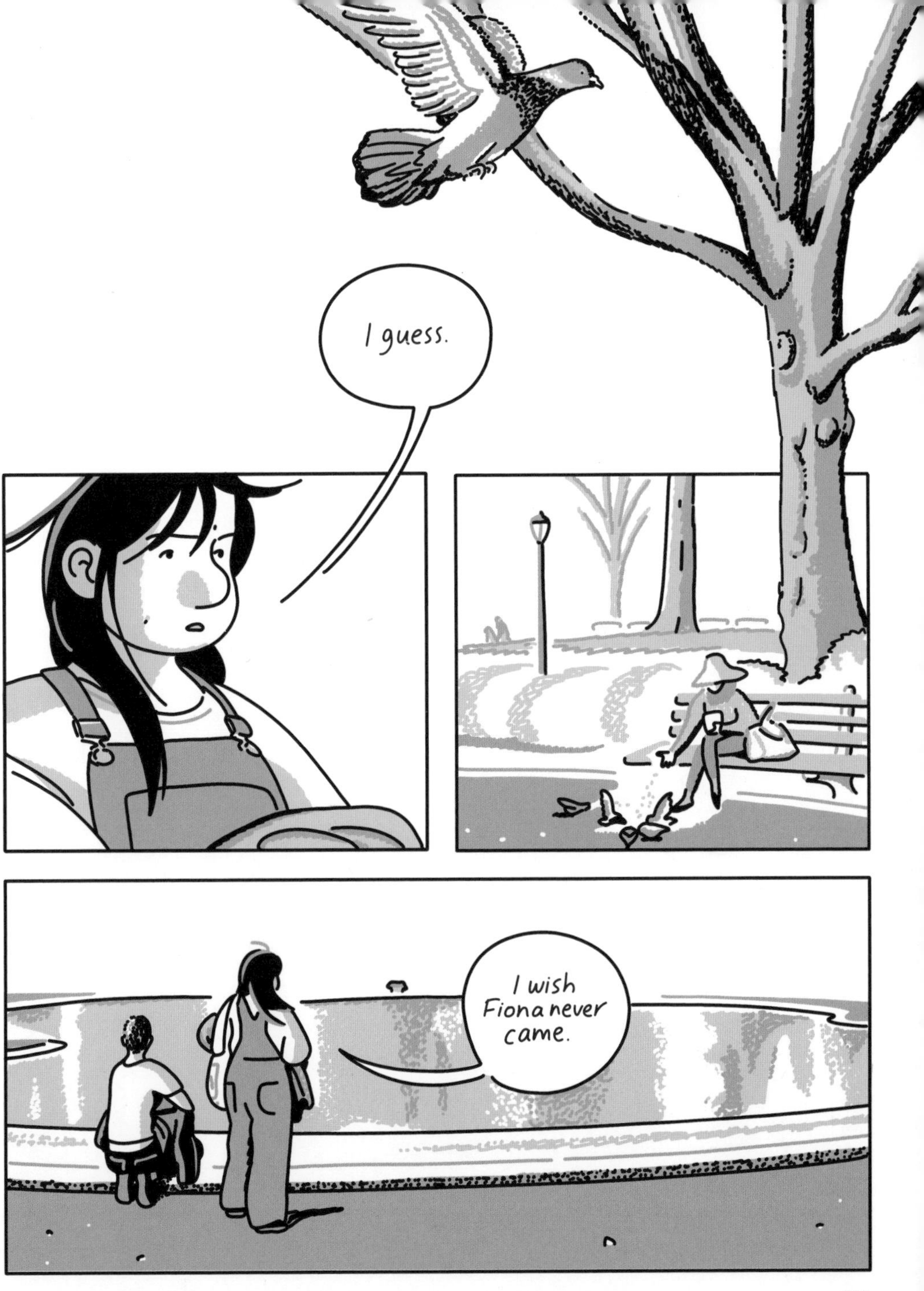
I guess.
I wish Fiona never came.

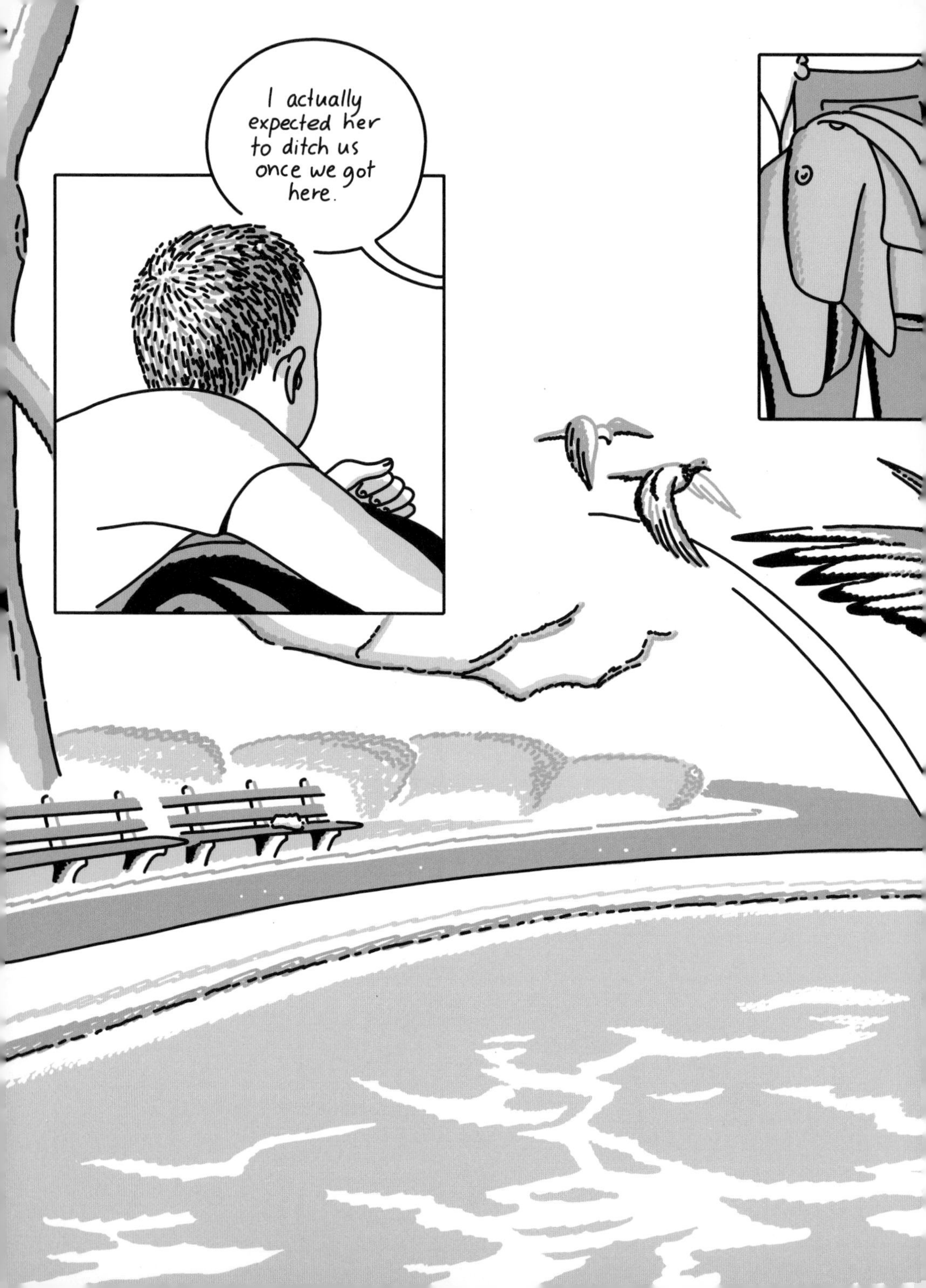
I actually expected her to ditch us once we got here.

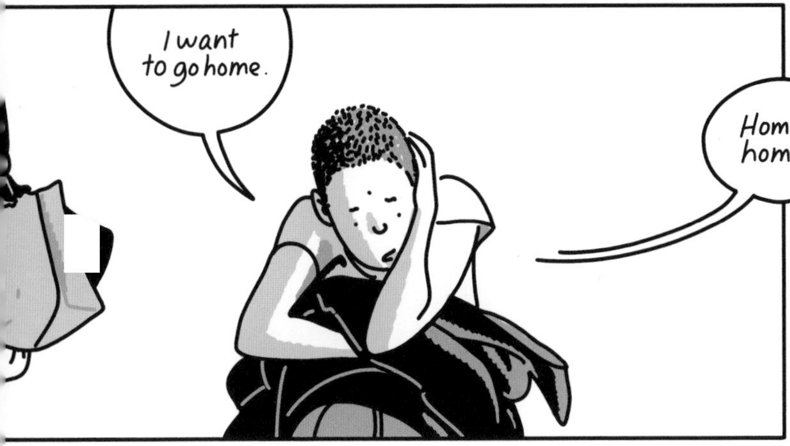
I want to go home.
Home-home.
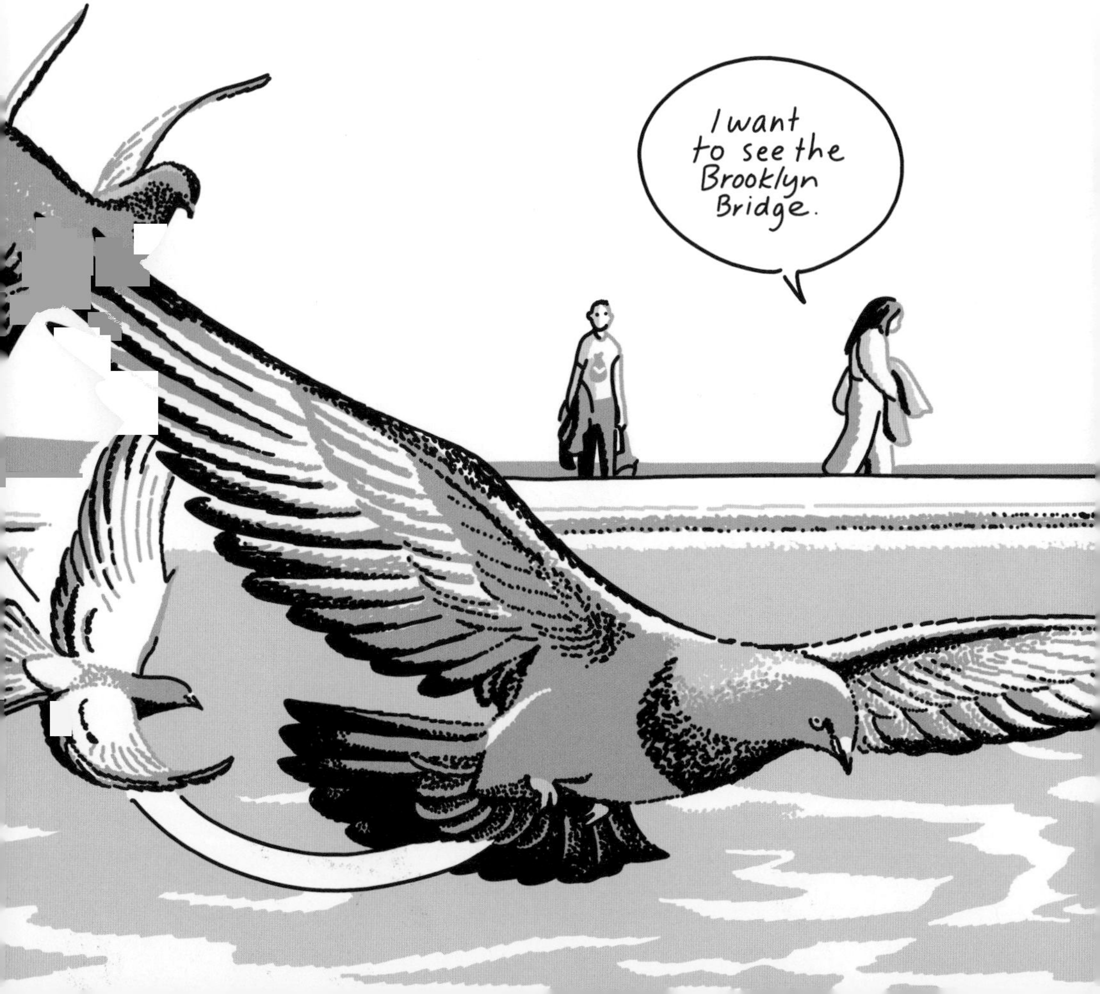
I want to see the Brooklyn Bridge.

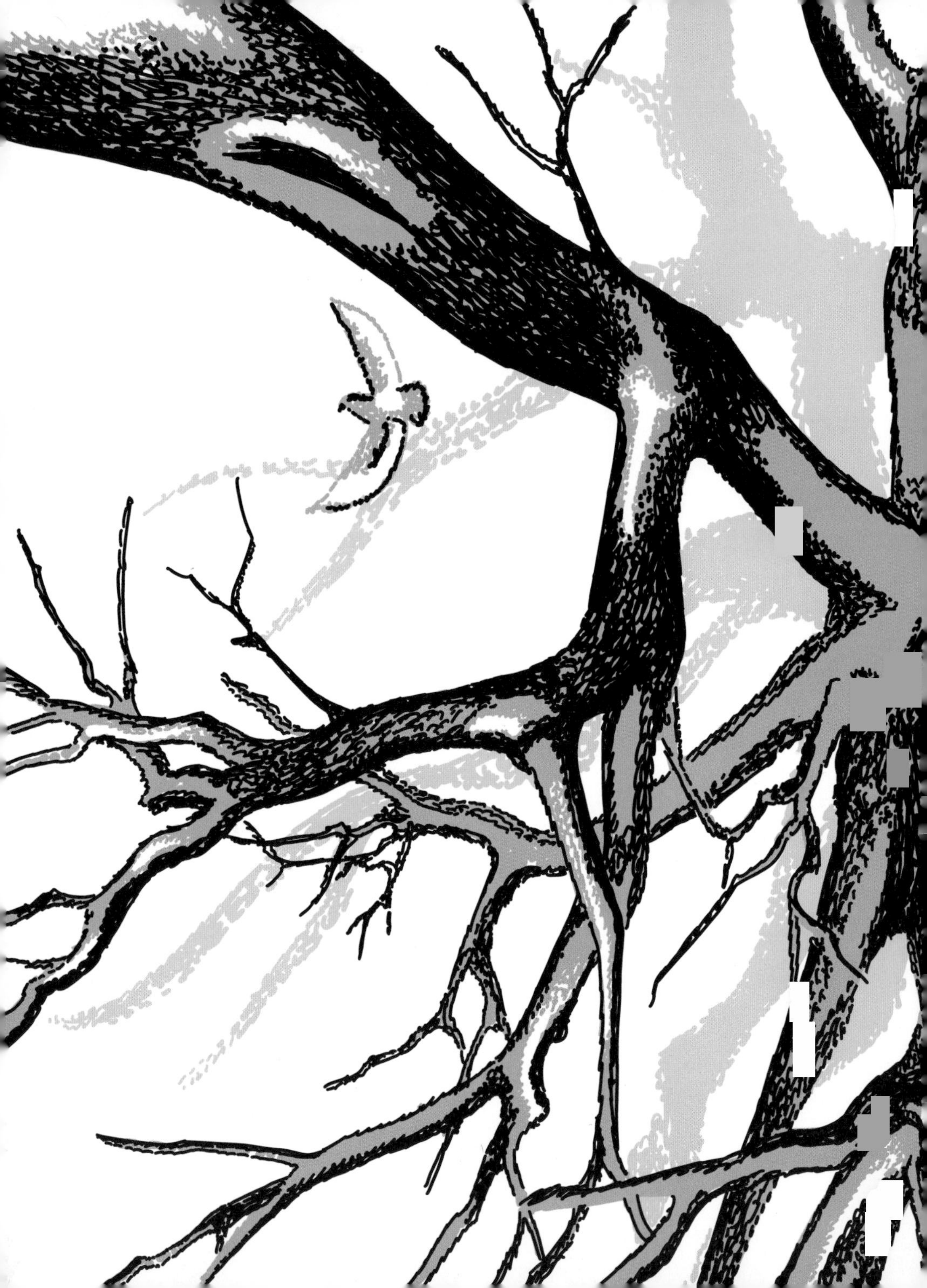

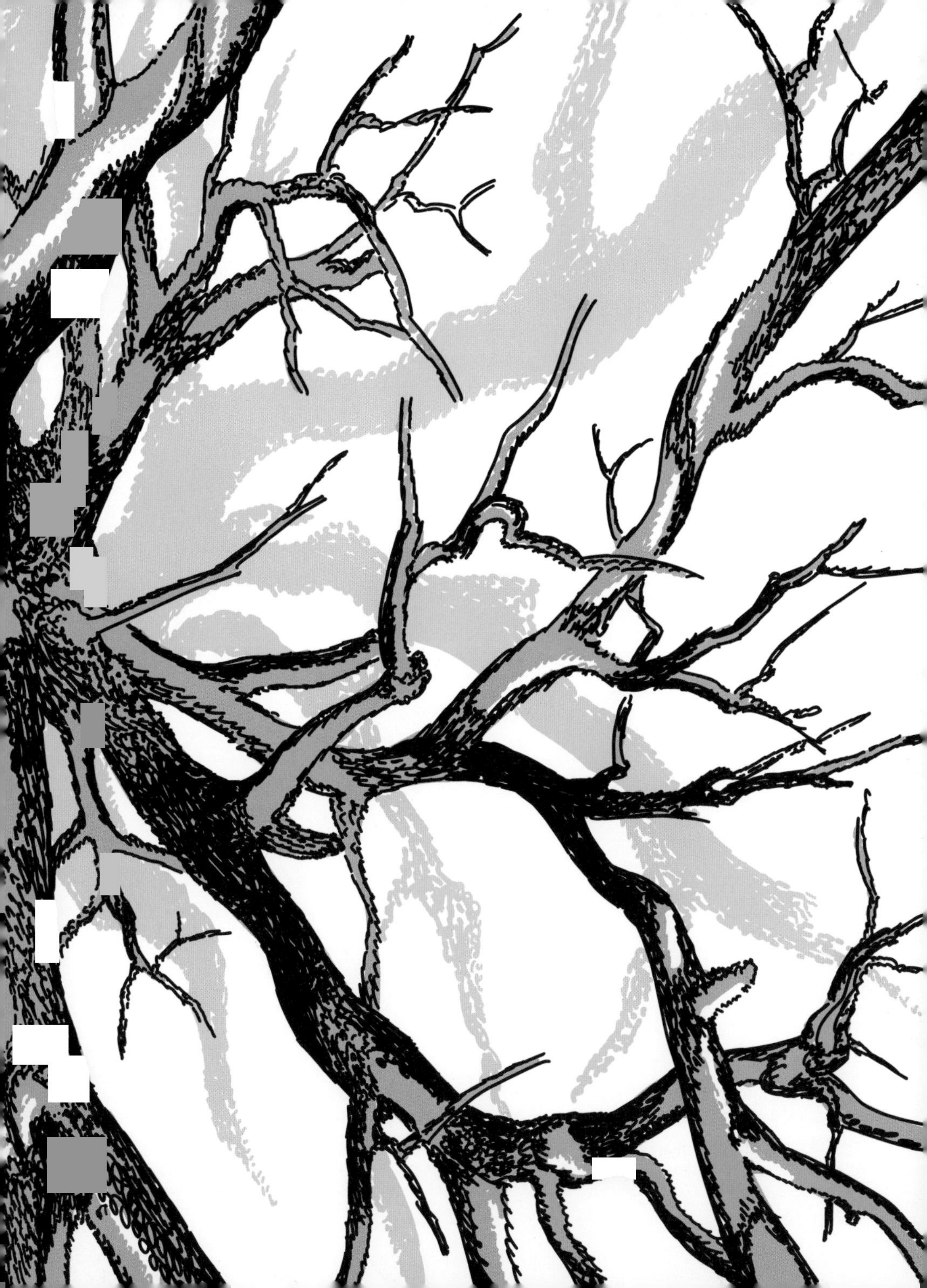

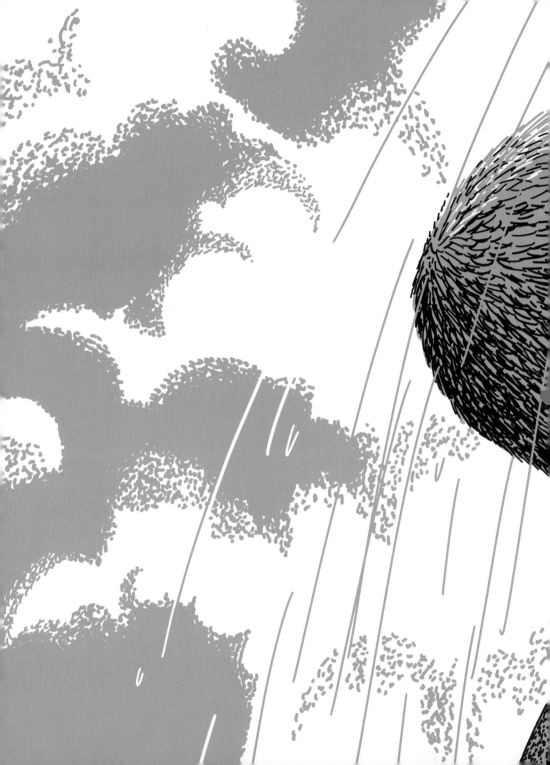

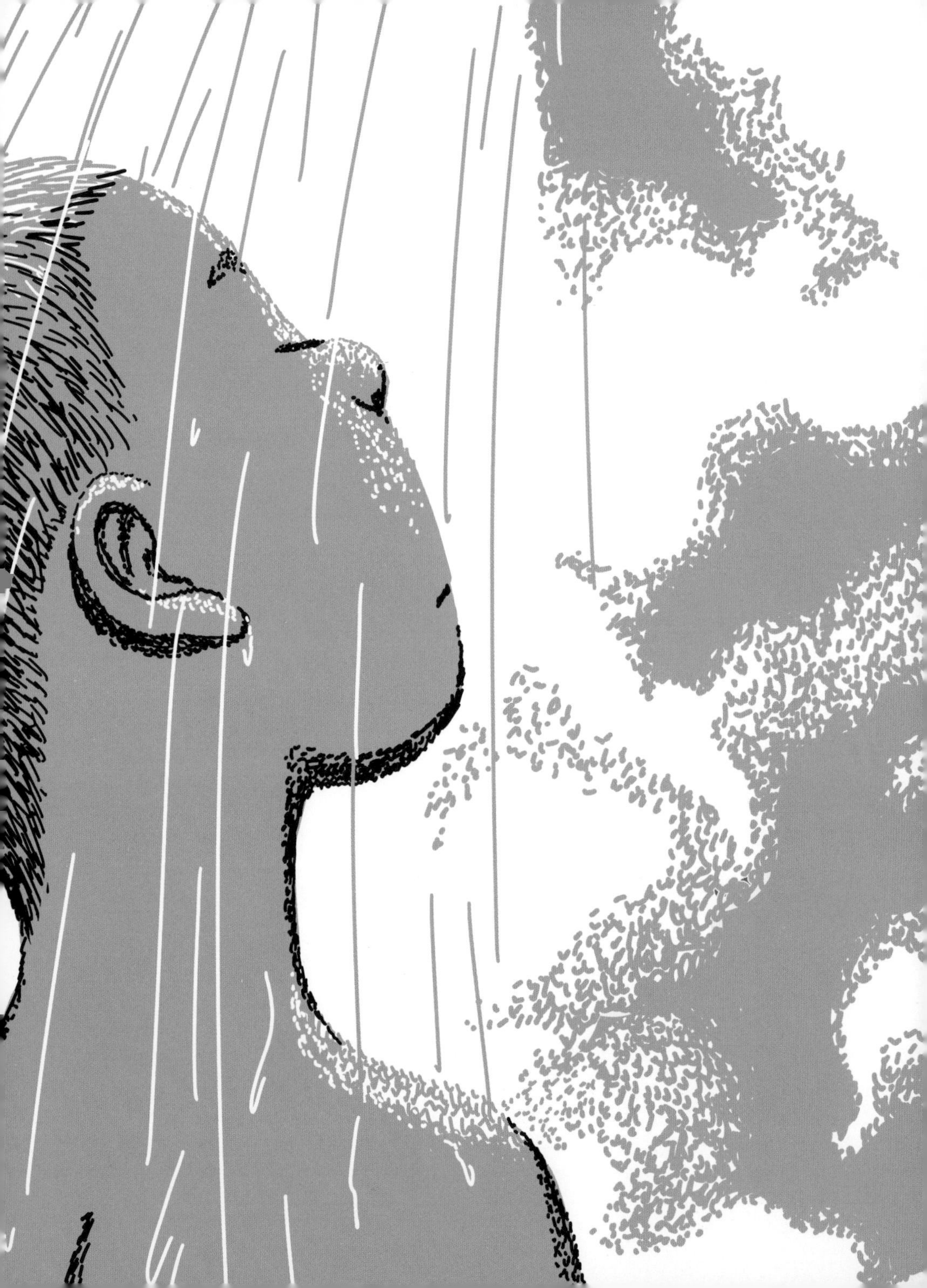

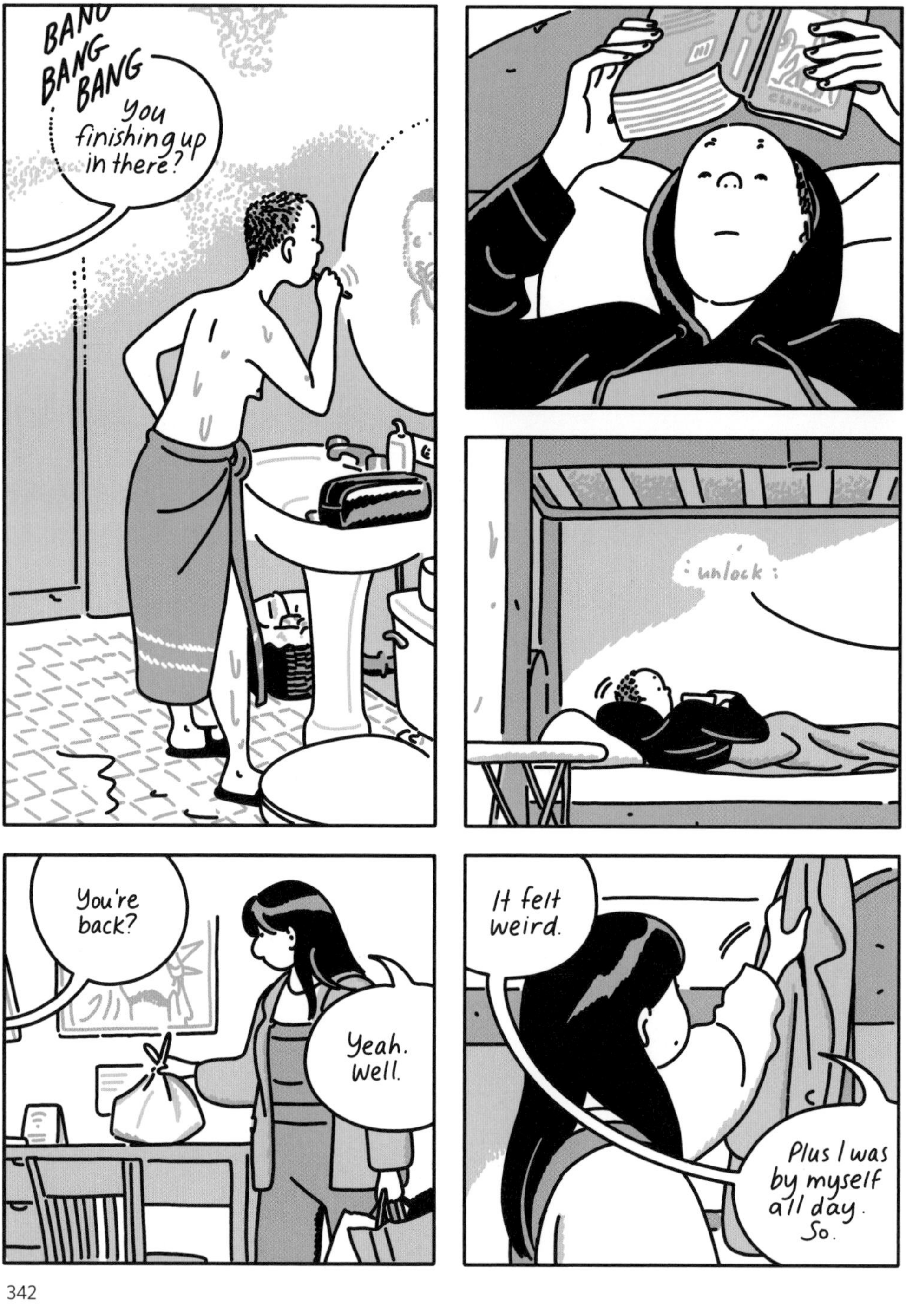
BANG BANG BANG
You finishing up in there?
:unlock:
You're back?
Yeah. Well.
It felt weird.
Plus I was by myself all day. So.

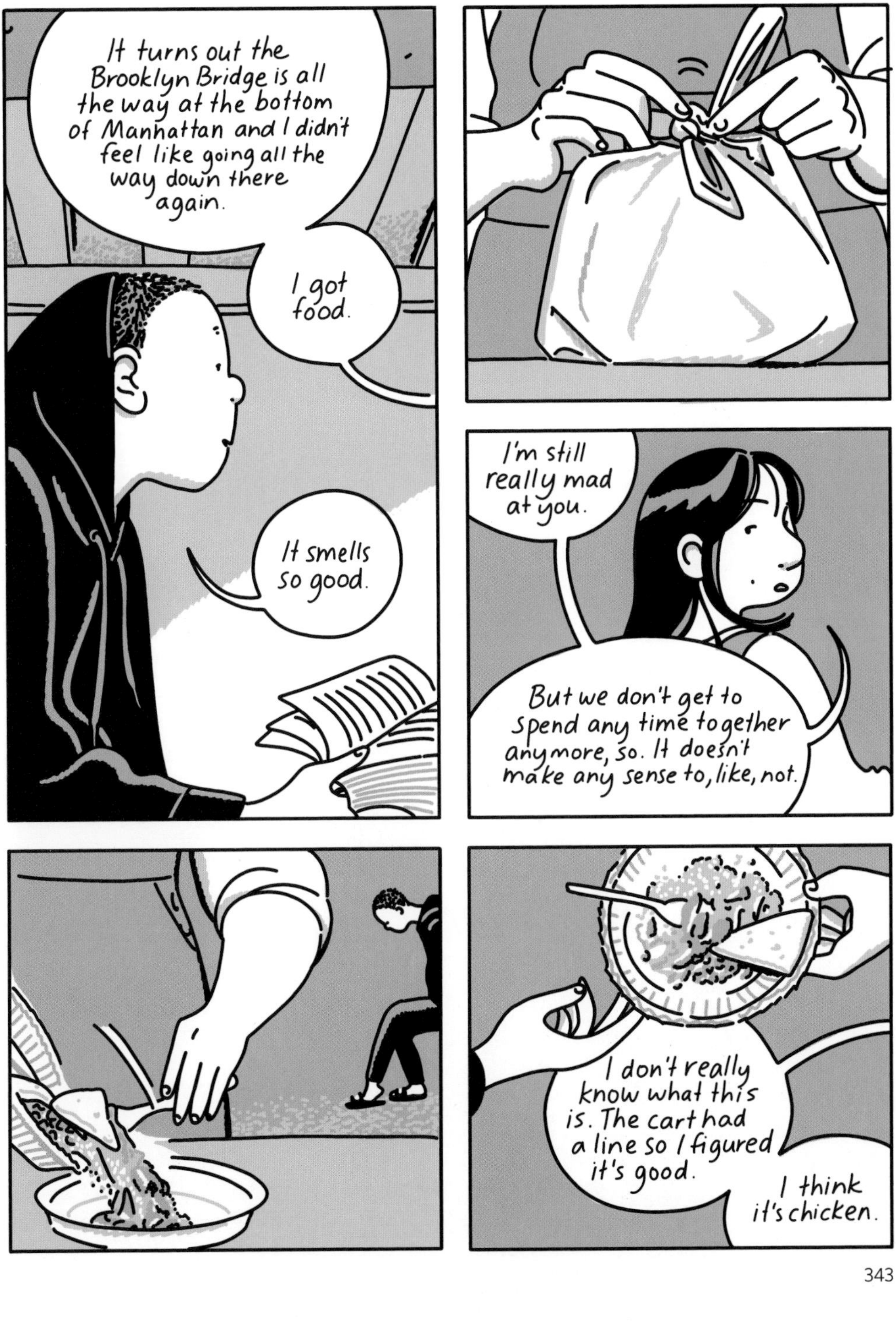
It turns out the Brooklyn Bridge is all the way at the bottom of Manhattan and I didn't feel like going all the way down there again.
I got food.
It smells so good.
I'm still really mad at you.
But we don't get to spend any time together anymore, so. It doesn't make any sense to, like, not.
I don't really know what this is. The cart had a line so I figured it's good.
I think it's chicken.

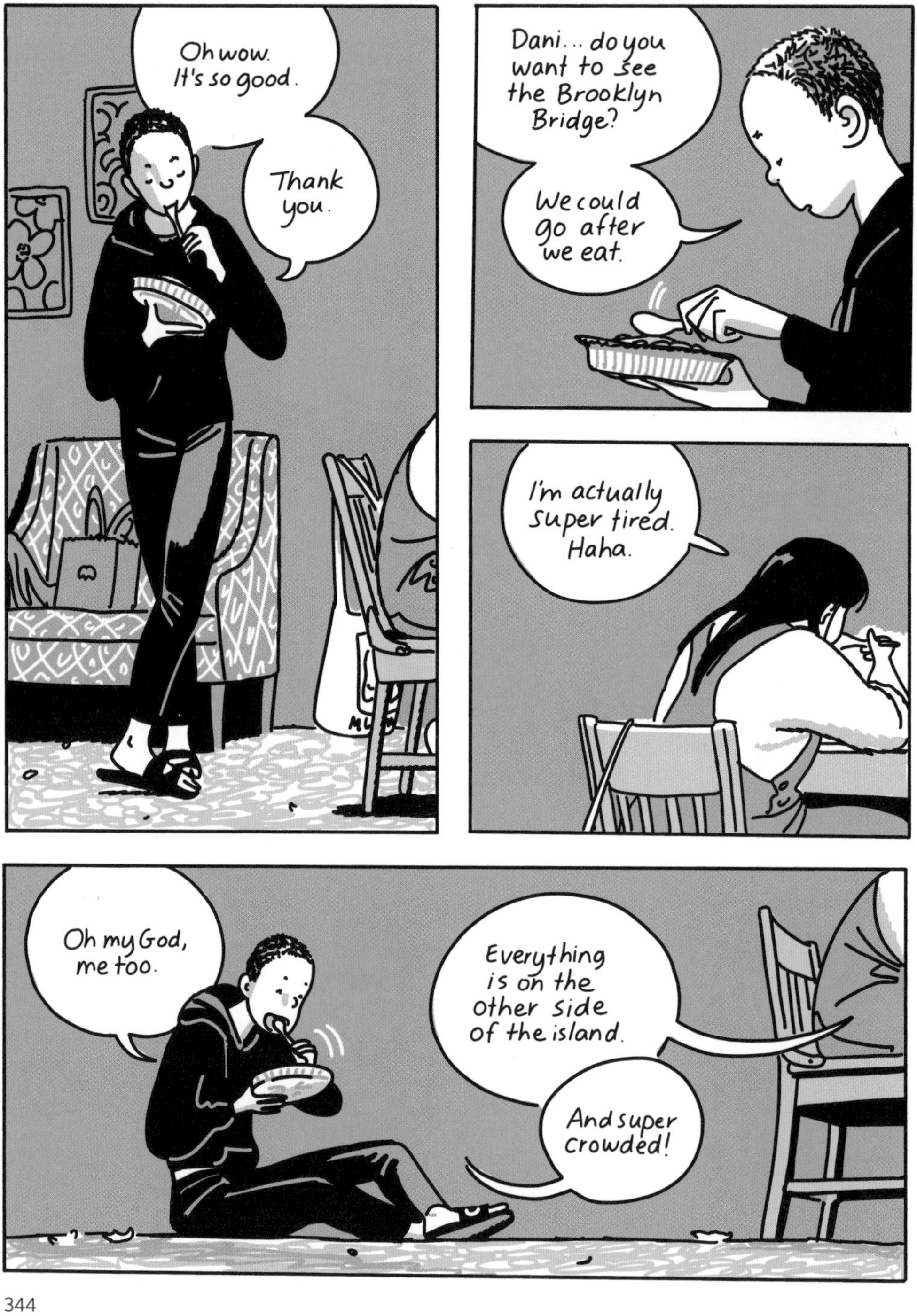
Oh wow. It's so good.
Thank you.
Dani... do you want to see the Brooklyn Bridge?
We could go after we eat.
I'm actually super tired. Haha.
Oh my God, me too.
Everything is on the other side of the island.
And super crowded!

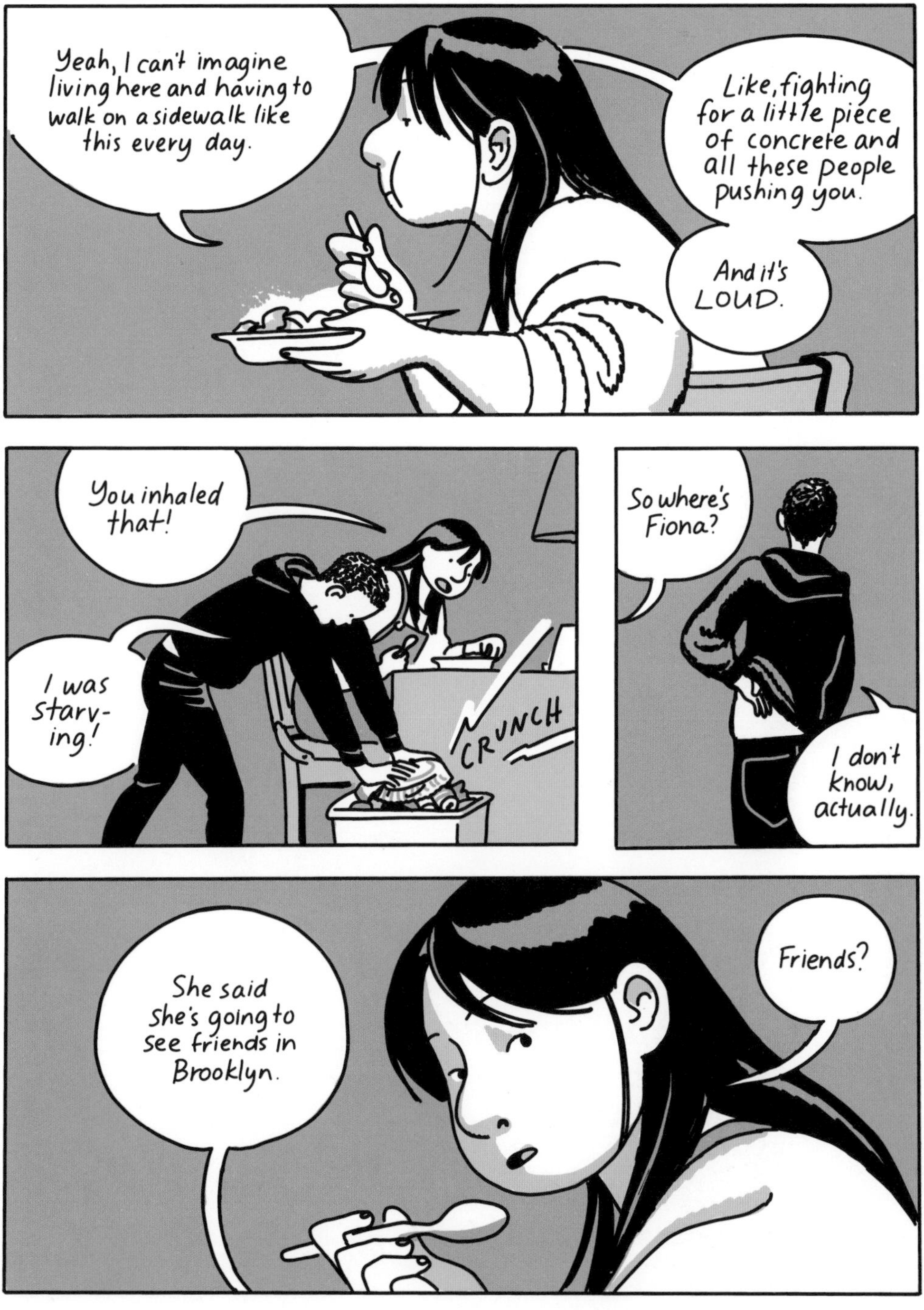
Yeah, I can't imagine living here and having to walk on a sidewalk like this every day.
Like, fighting for a little piece of concrete and all these people pushing you.
And it's LOUD.
You inhaled that!
I was starv-ing!
CRUNCH
So where's Fiona?
I don't know, actually.
She said she's going to see friends in Brooklyn.
Friends?

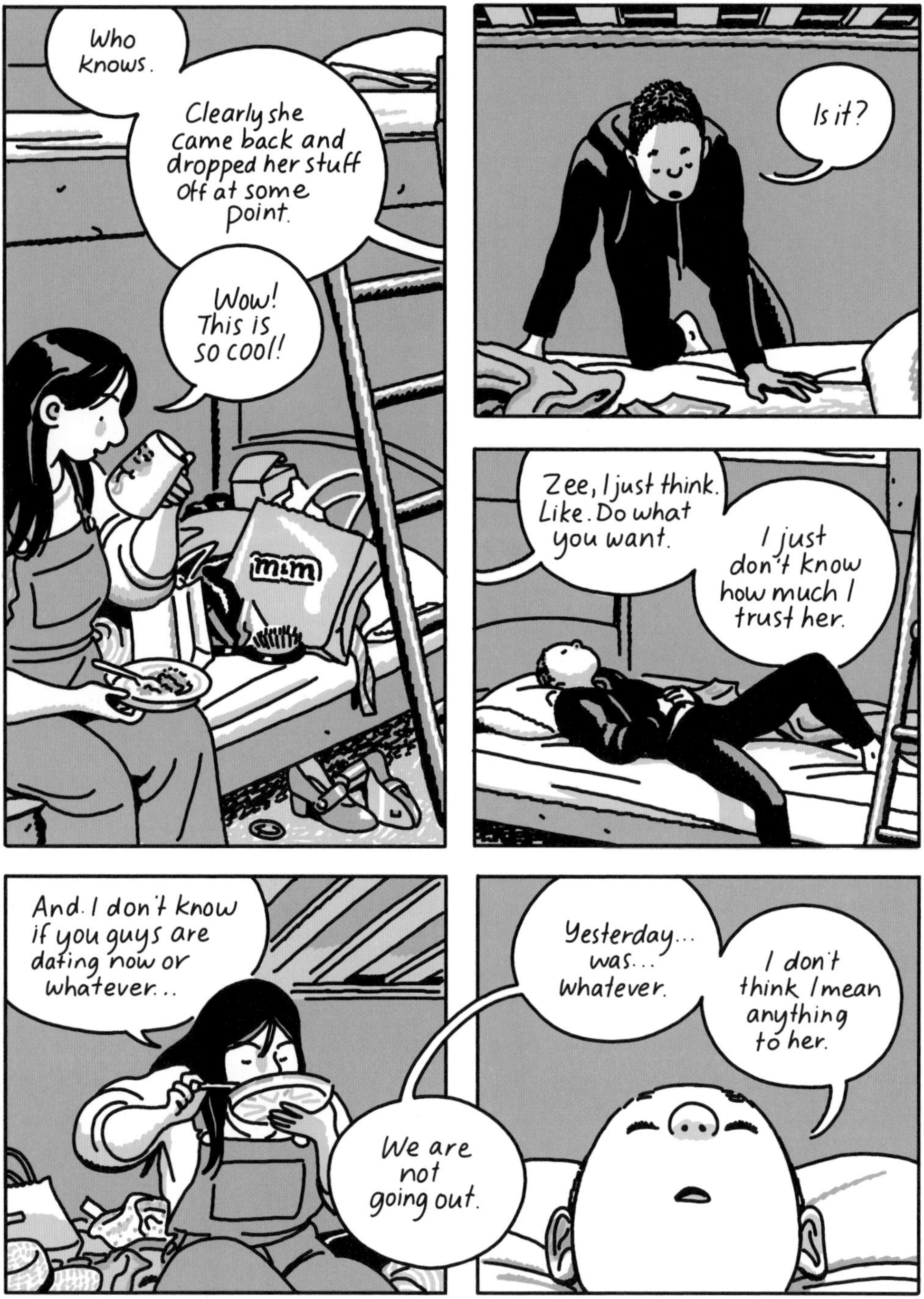
Who knows.
Clearly she came back and dropped her stuff off at some point.
Wow! This is so cool!
Is it?
Zee, I just think. Like. Do what you want.
I just don't know how much I trust her.
And. I don't know if you guys are dating now or whatever...
We are not going out.
Yesterday... was... whatever.
I don't think I mean anything to her.

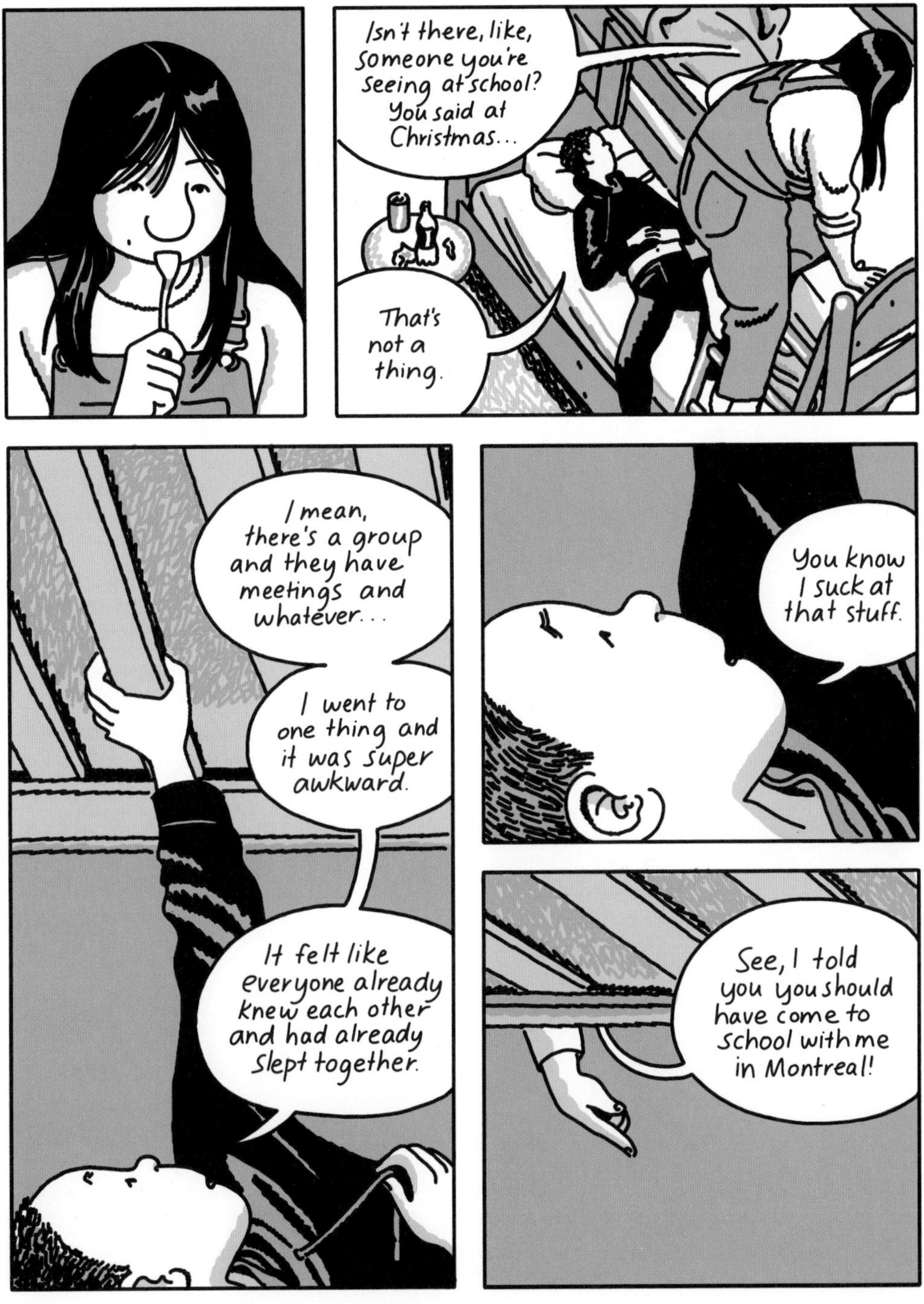
Isn't there, like, someone you're seeing at school? You said at Christmas...
That's not a thing.
I mean, there's a group and they have meetings and whatever...
I went to one thing and it was super awkward.
It felt like everyone already knew each other and had already slept together.
You know I suck at that stuff.
See, I told you you should have come to school with me in Montreal!

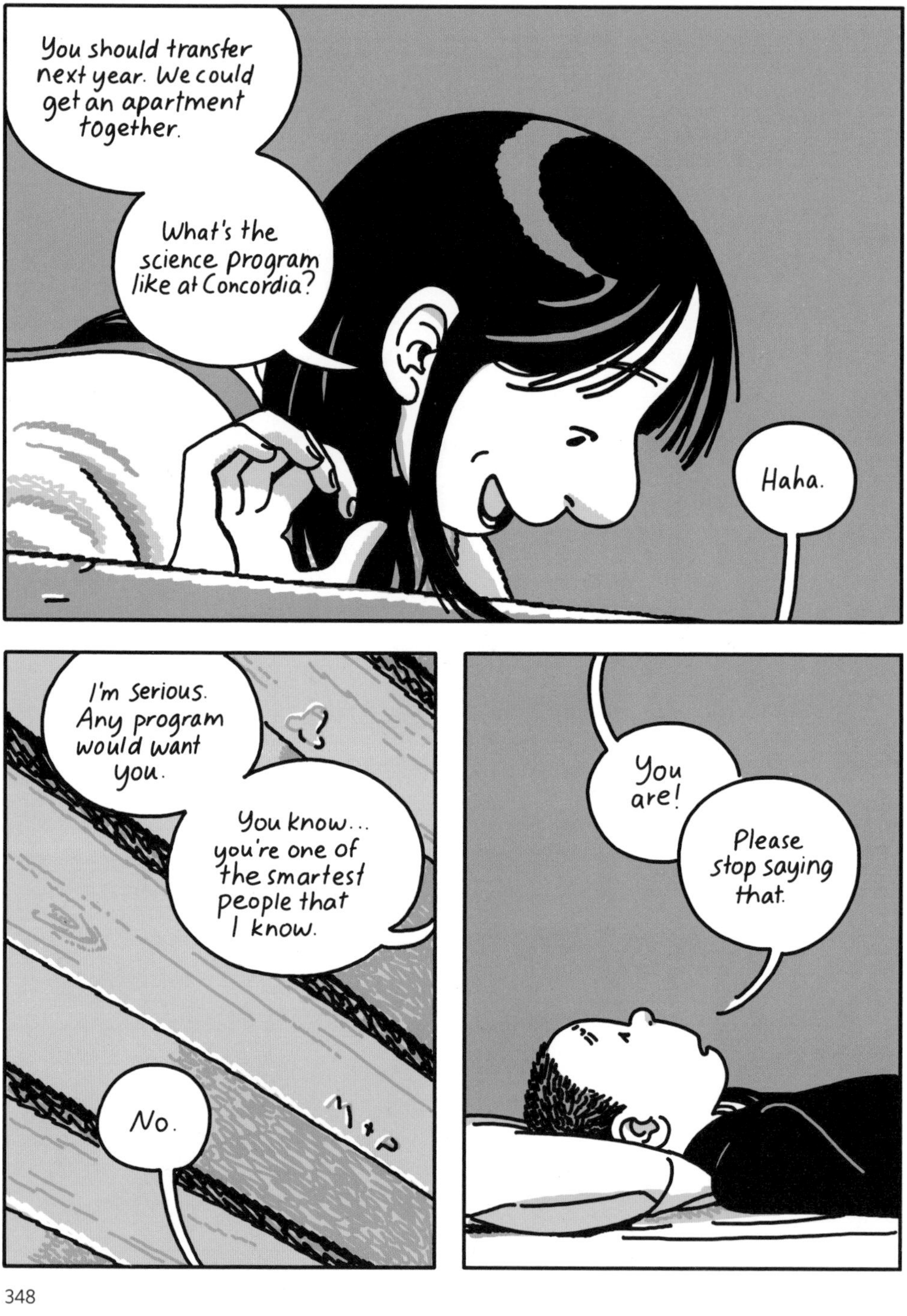
You should transfer next year. We could get an apartment together.
What's the science program like at Concordia?
Haha.
I'm serious. Any program would want you.
You know... you're one of the smartest people that I know.
No.
M+P
You are!
Please stop saying that.

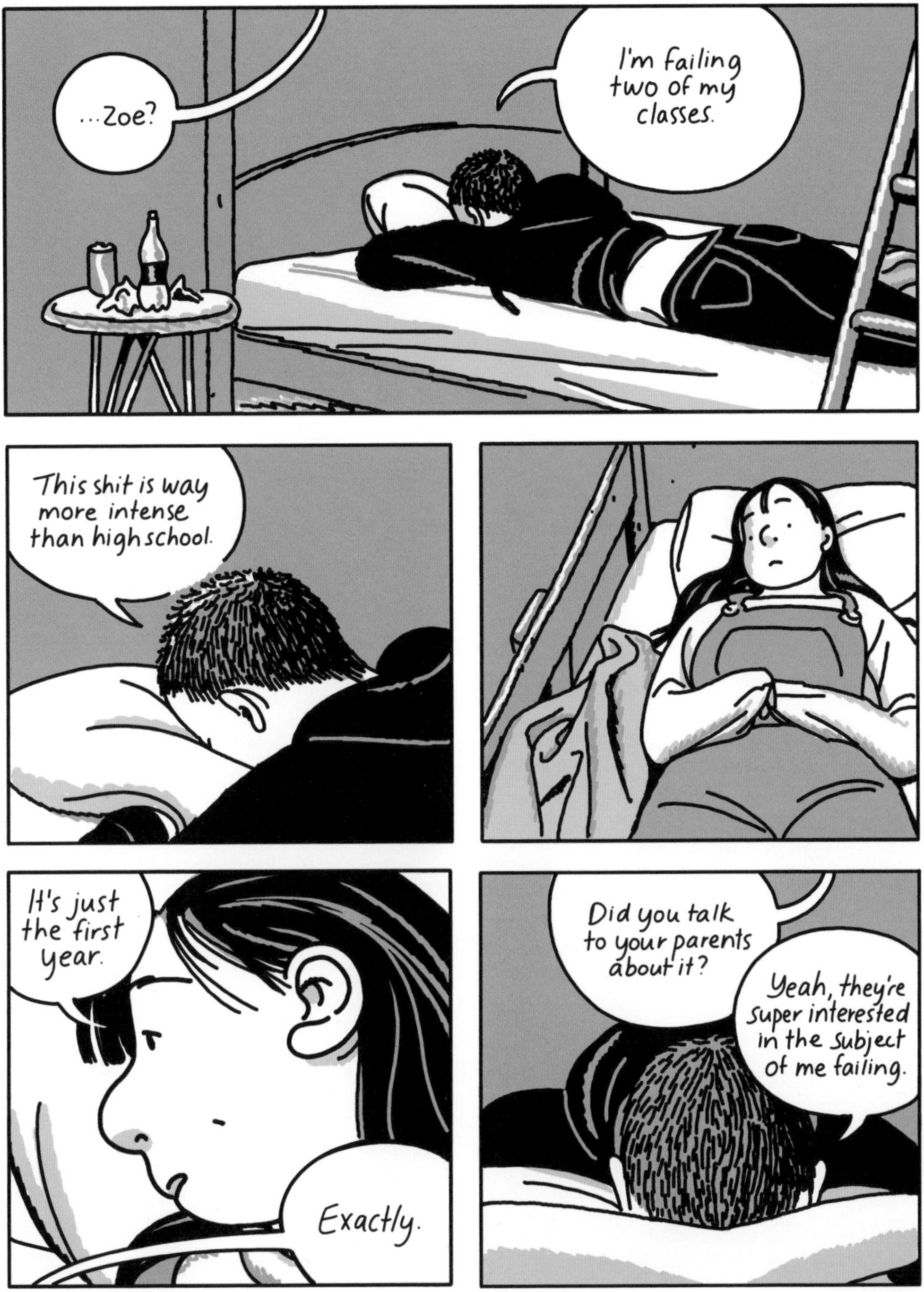
...Zoe?
I'm failing two of my classes.
This shit is way more intense than highschool.
It's just the first year.
Exactly.
Did you talk to your parents about it?
Yeah, they're super interested in the subject of me failing.

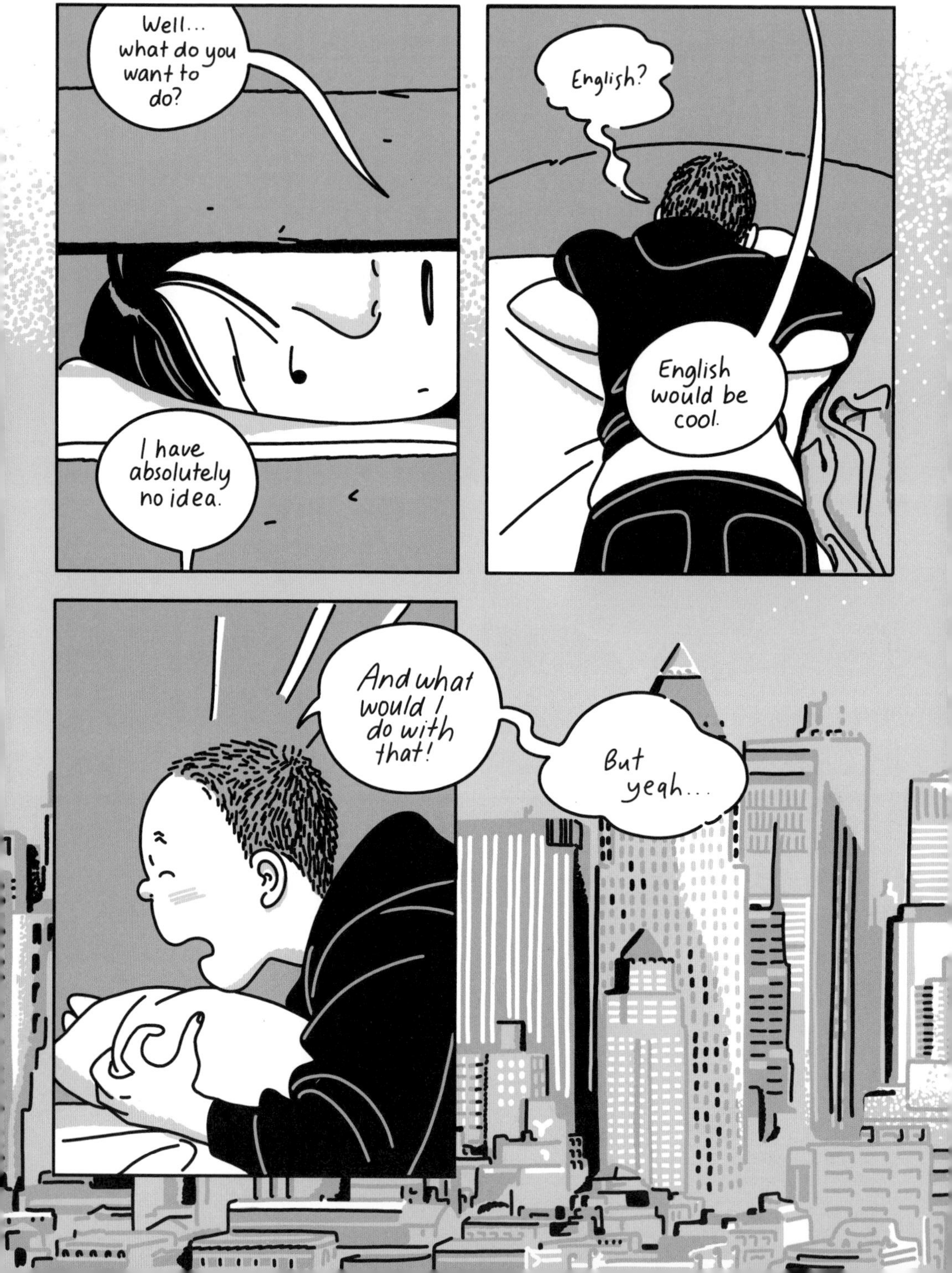
Well... what do you want to do?
I have absolutely no idea.
English?
English would be cool.
And what would I do with that!
But yeah...

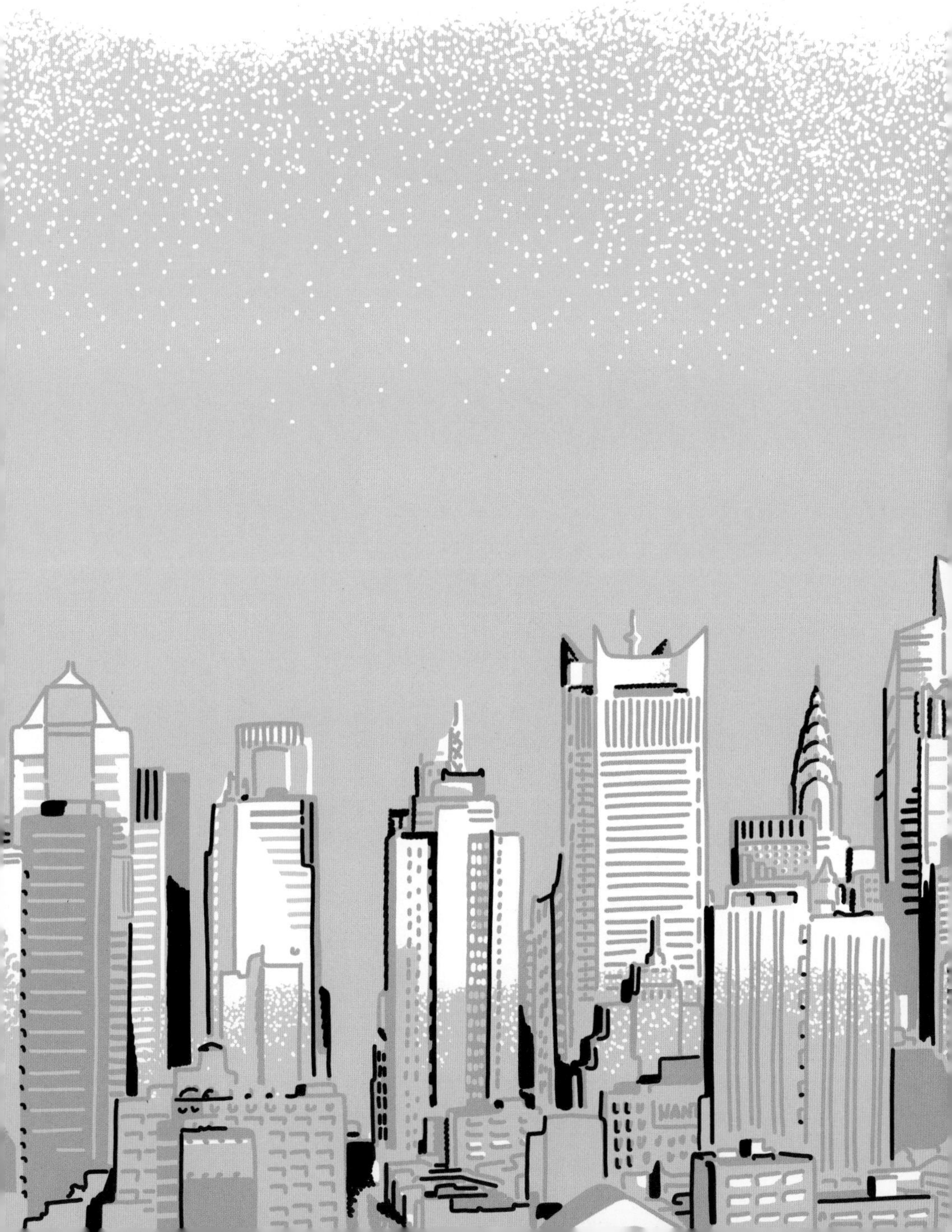

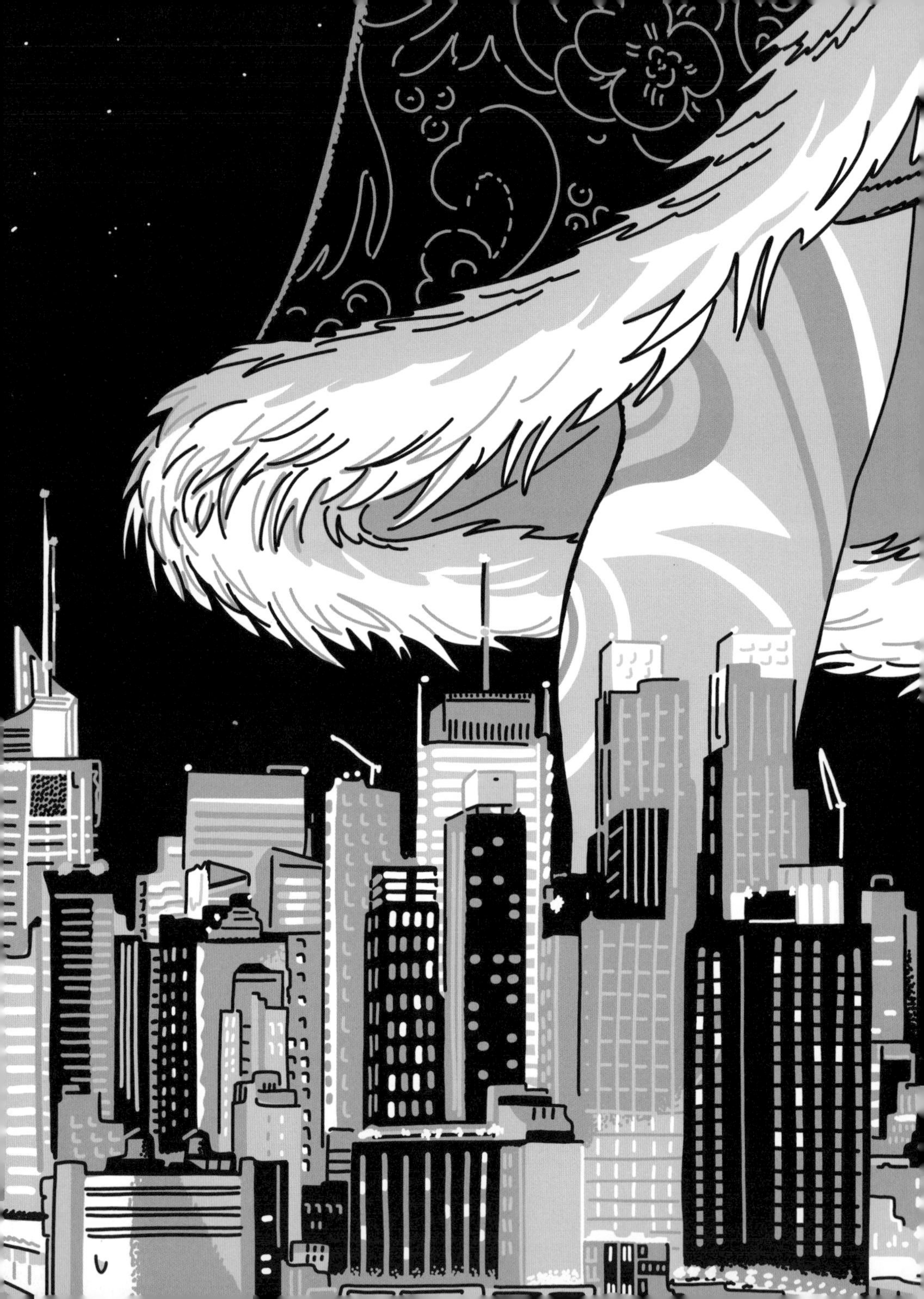

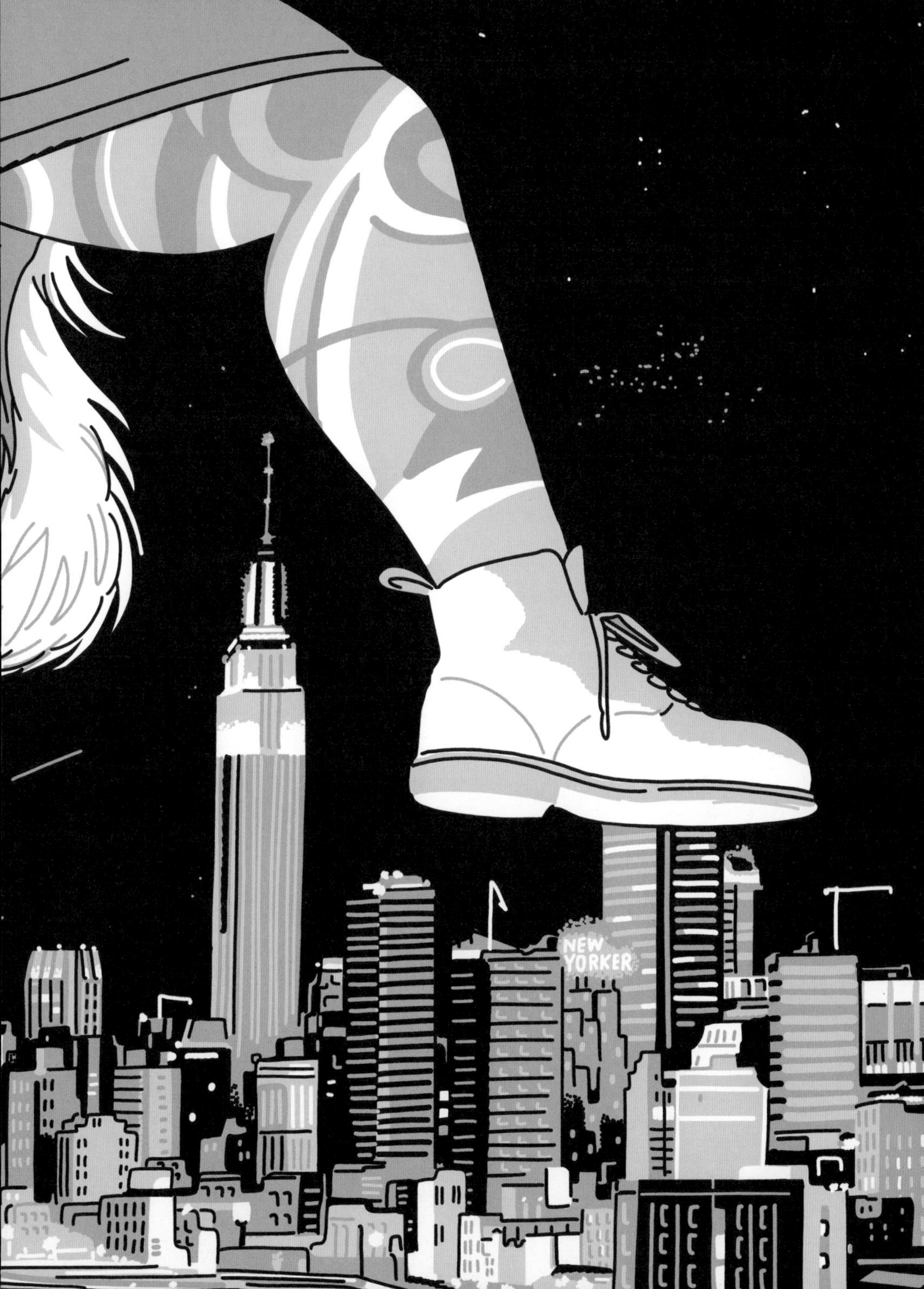
NEW
YORKER

"Over 750,000 commuters pass through Grand Central Terminal daily.
The brainchild of Cornelius Vanderbilt, the site attracts over 21 million tourists yearly thanks to its impressive beaux arts design.

Completed in 1913 by 50 artists and the input of several astronomers, the astrological mural on the ceiling depicts the sky as it appears in the Mediterranean in winter, albeit upside down.
The error was likely caused by a miscommunication during the construction of the Terminal, but—"
—Oh, this is interesting-

"a popular explanation is that it represents God's view of the ky, a style of celestial napping that was typical in the medieval period."
It's by Pisces. Can you see it?
It says when they cleaned the mural in the 1990s, they left a little spot un-touched so people could see how dirty it was from all the cigarette smoke.
Hm. I don't think so.

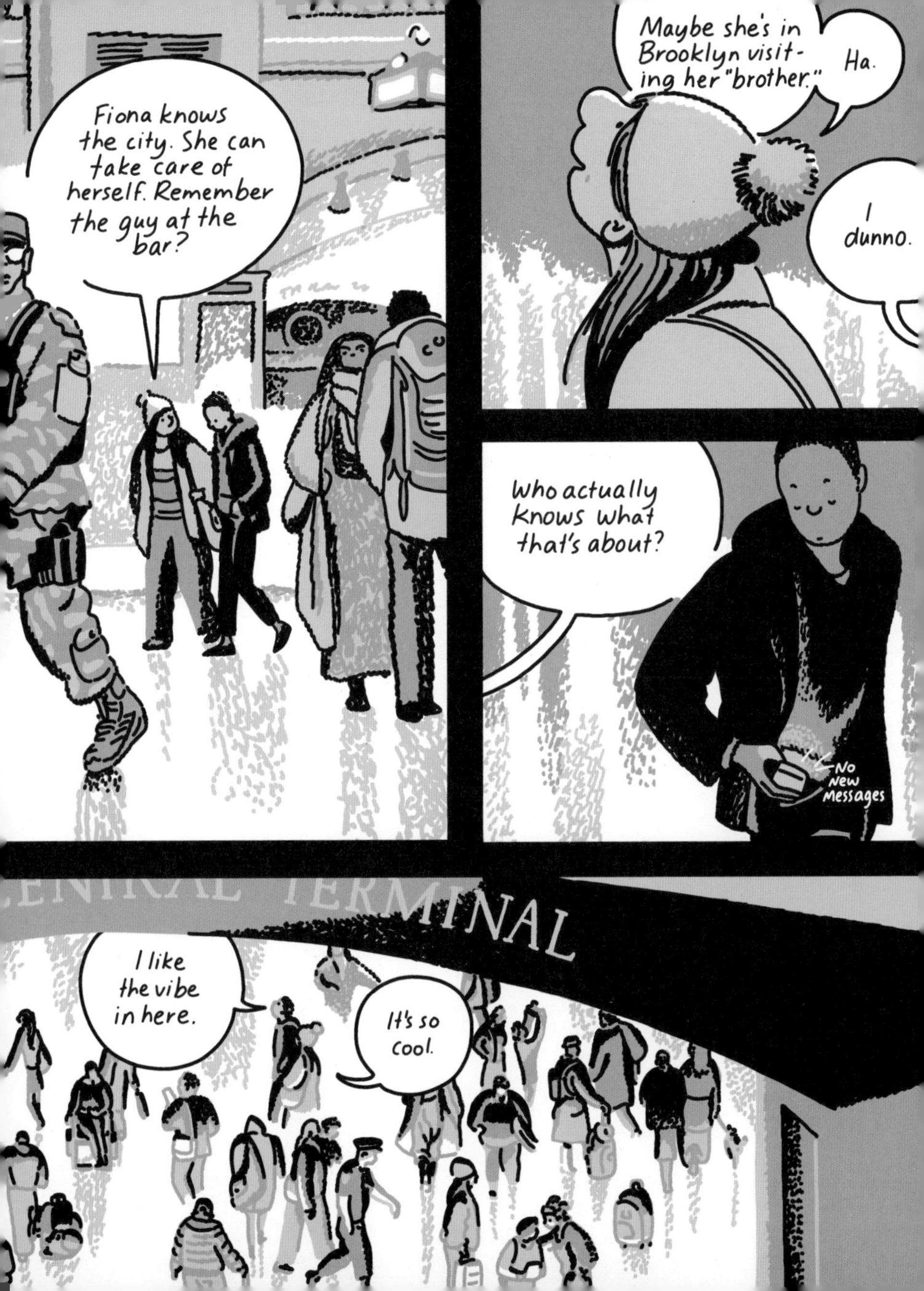
Fiona knows the city. She can take care of herself. Remember the guy at the bar?
Maybe she's in Brooklyn visit-ing her "brother."
Ha.
I dunno.
Who actually knows what that's about?
No new Messages
CENTRAL TERMINAL
I like the vibe in here.
It's so cool.

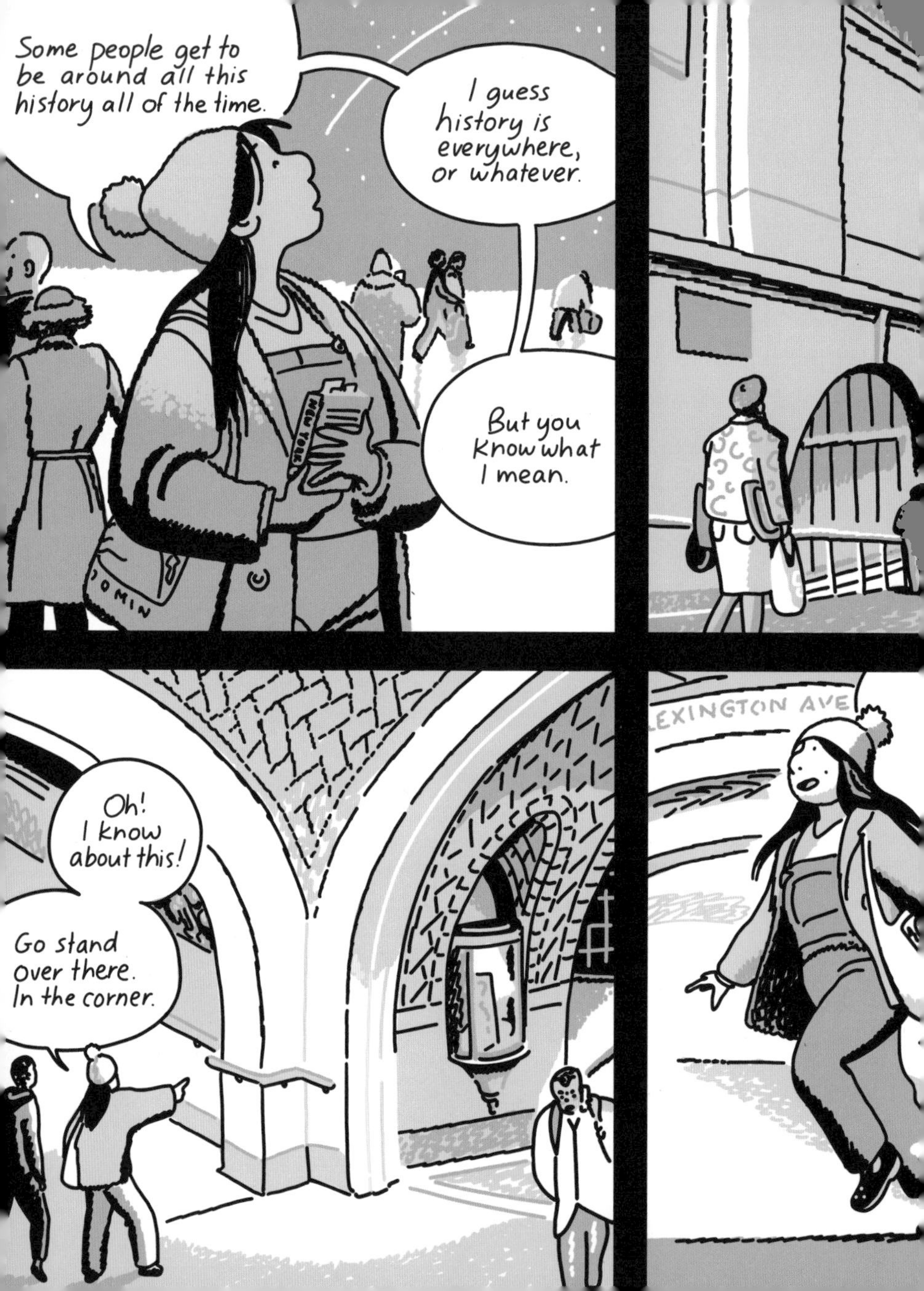

Some people get to be around all this history all of the time.
I guess history is everywhere, or whatever.
But you know what I mean.
NEW YORK
DOMIN
LEXINGTON AVE
Oh! I know about this!
Go stand over there. In the corner.

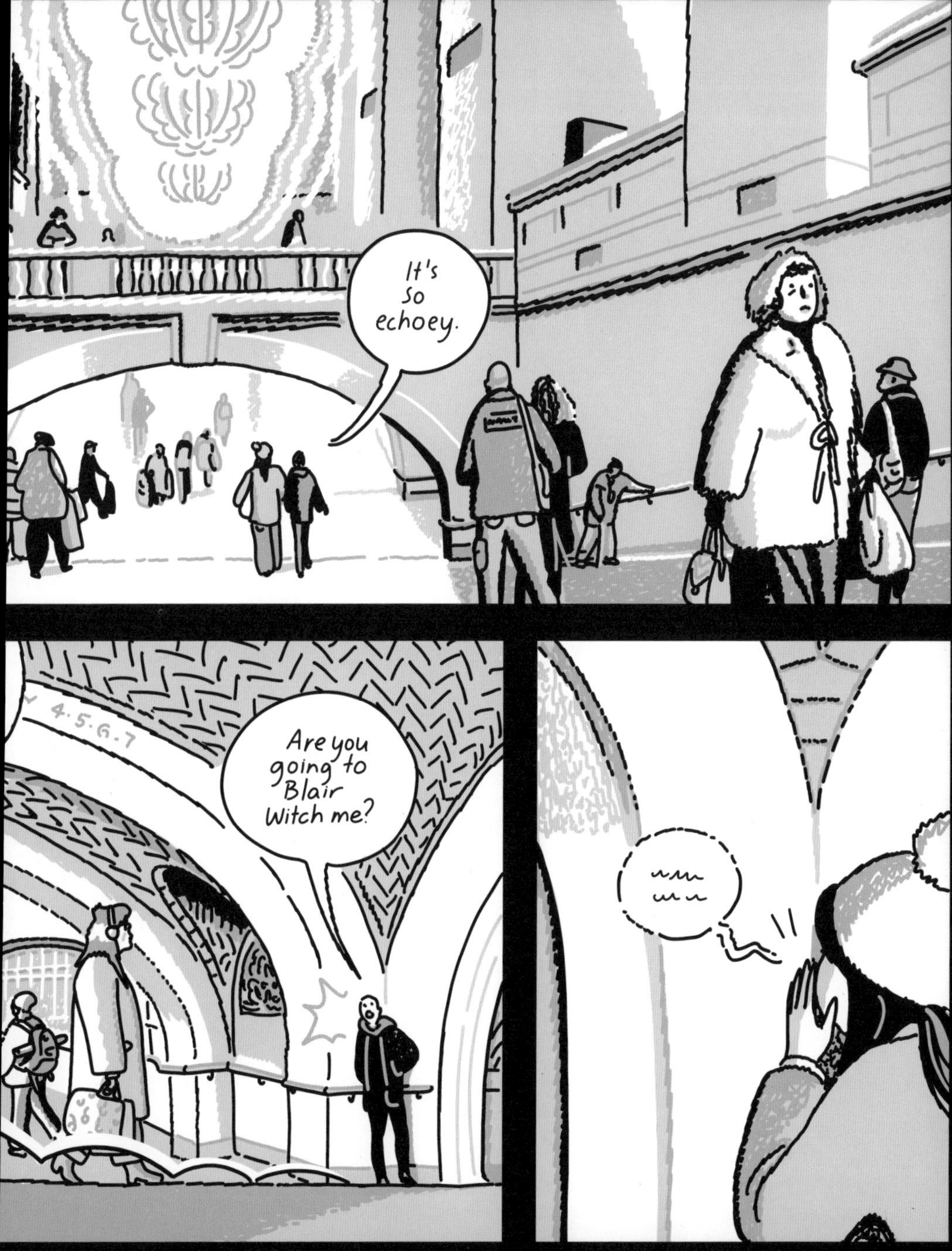
It's so echoey.
4.5.6.7
Are you going to Blair Witch me?

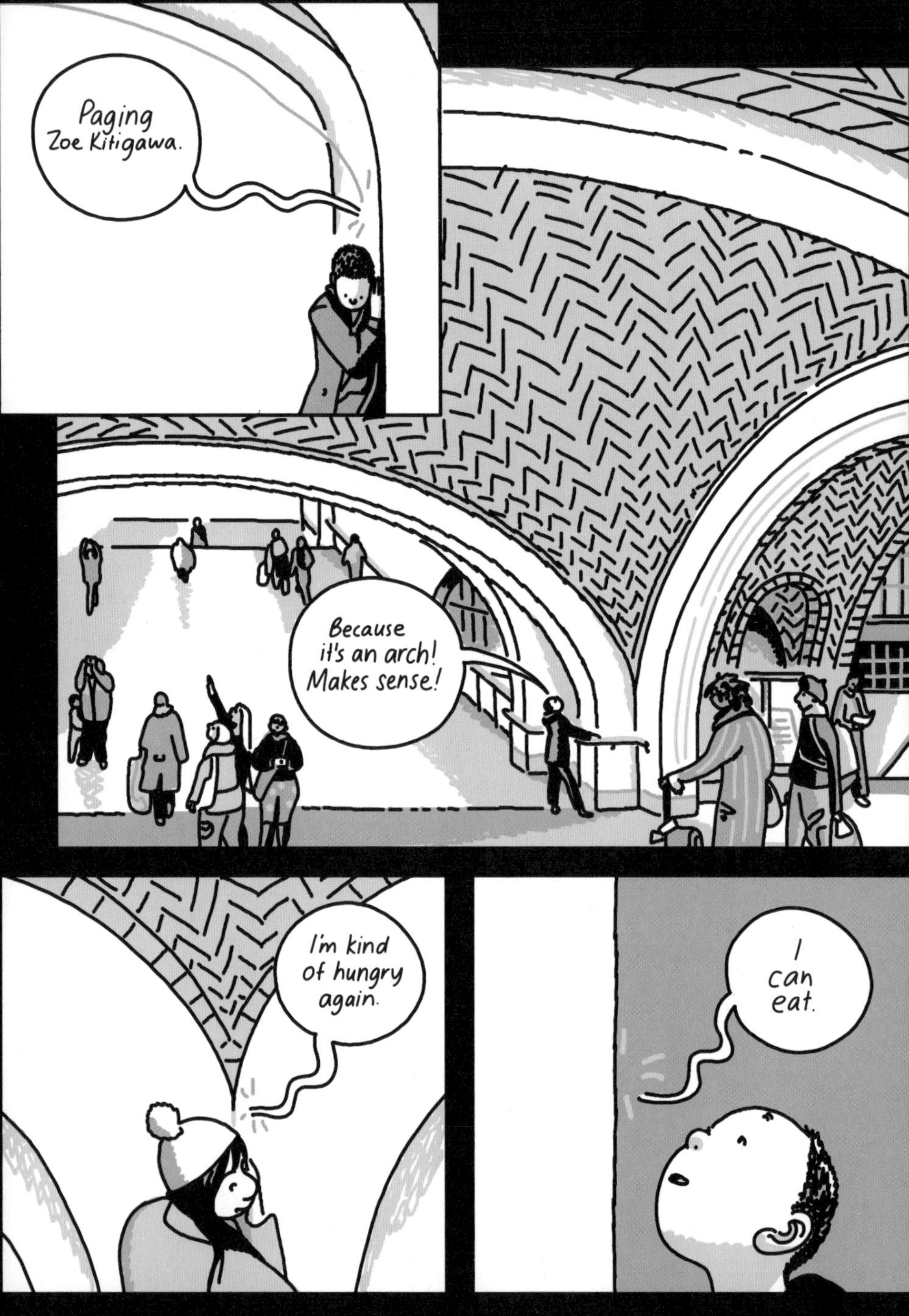
Paging Zoe Kitigawa.
Because it's an arch! Makes sense!
I'm kind of hungry again.
I can eat.

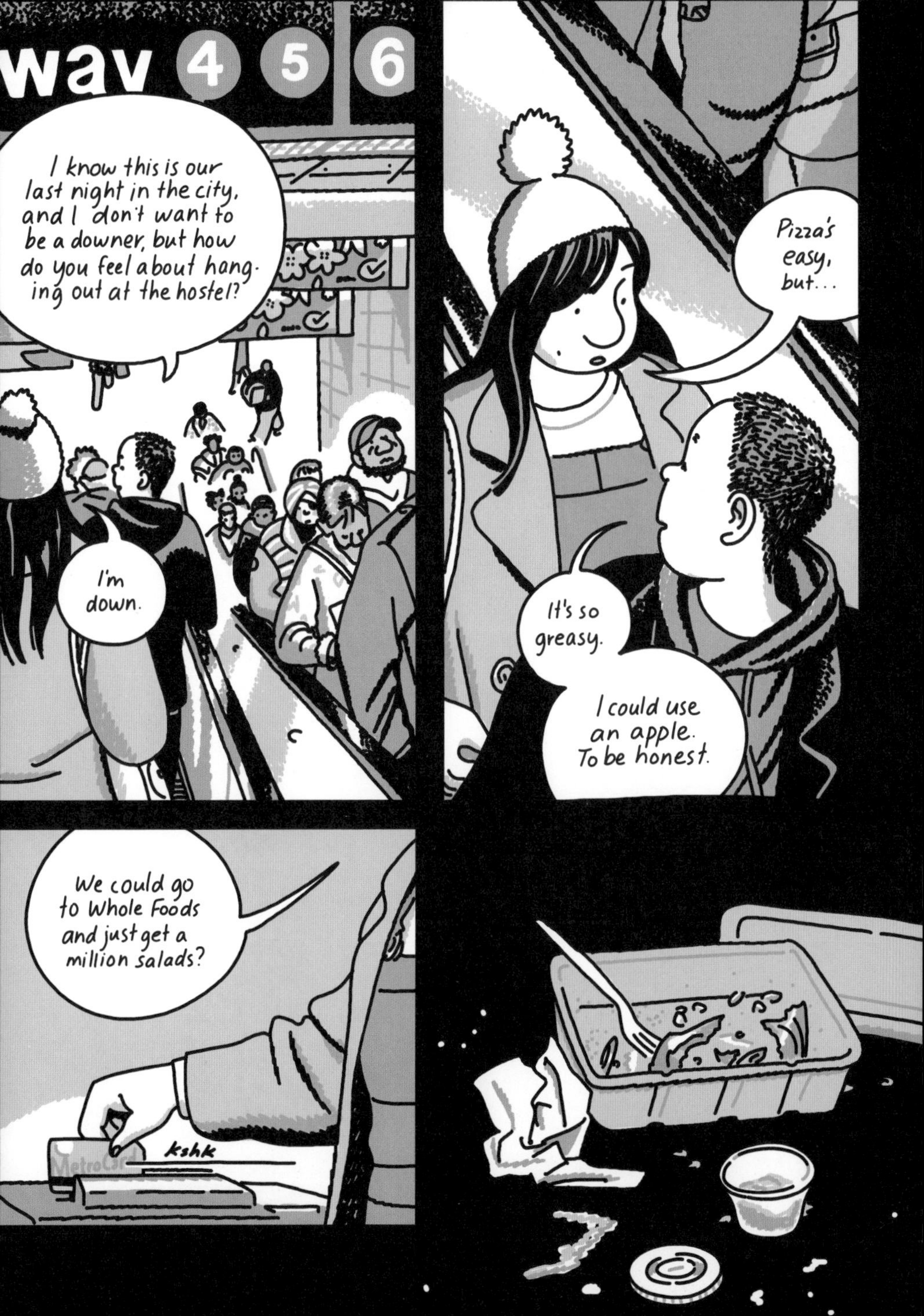
way
4
5
6
I know this is our last night in the city, and I don't want to be a downer, but how do you feel about hang-ing out at the hostel?
I'm down.
Pizza's easy, but...
It's so greasy.
I could use an apple. To be honest.
We could go to Whole Foods and just get a million salads?
kshk
MetroCard

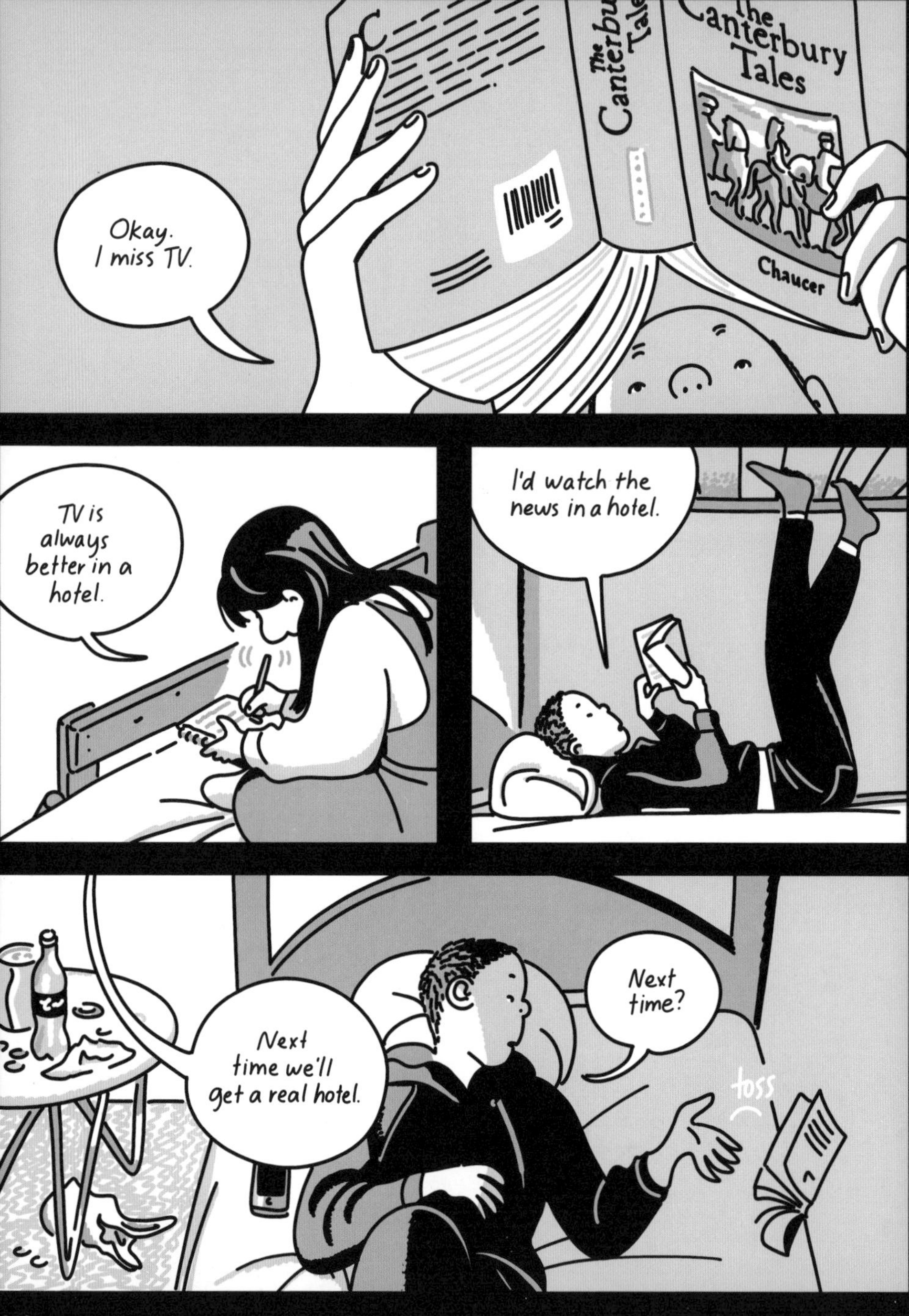
The Canterbury Tales
The Canterbury Tales
Chaucer
Okay. I miss TV.
TV is always better in a hotel.
I'd watch the news in a hotel.
Next time we'll get a real hotel.
Next time?
toss

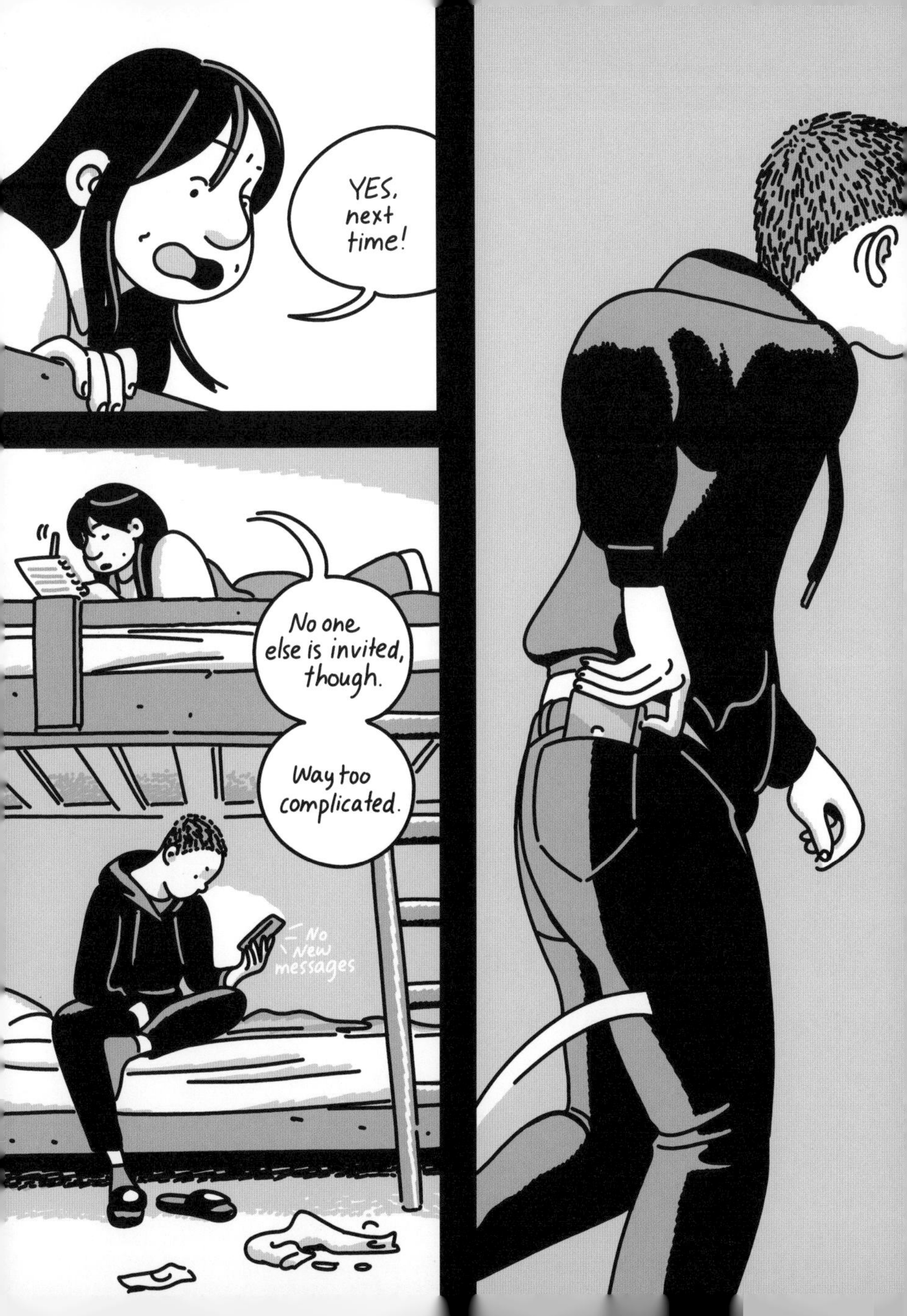
YES, next time!
No one else is invited, though.
Way too complicated.
No New messages

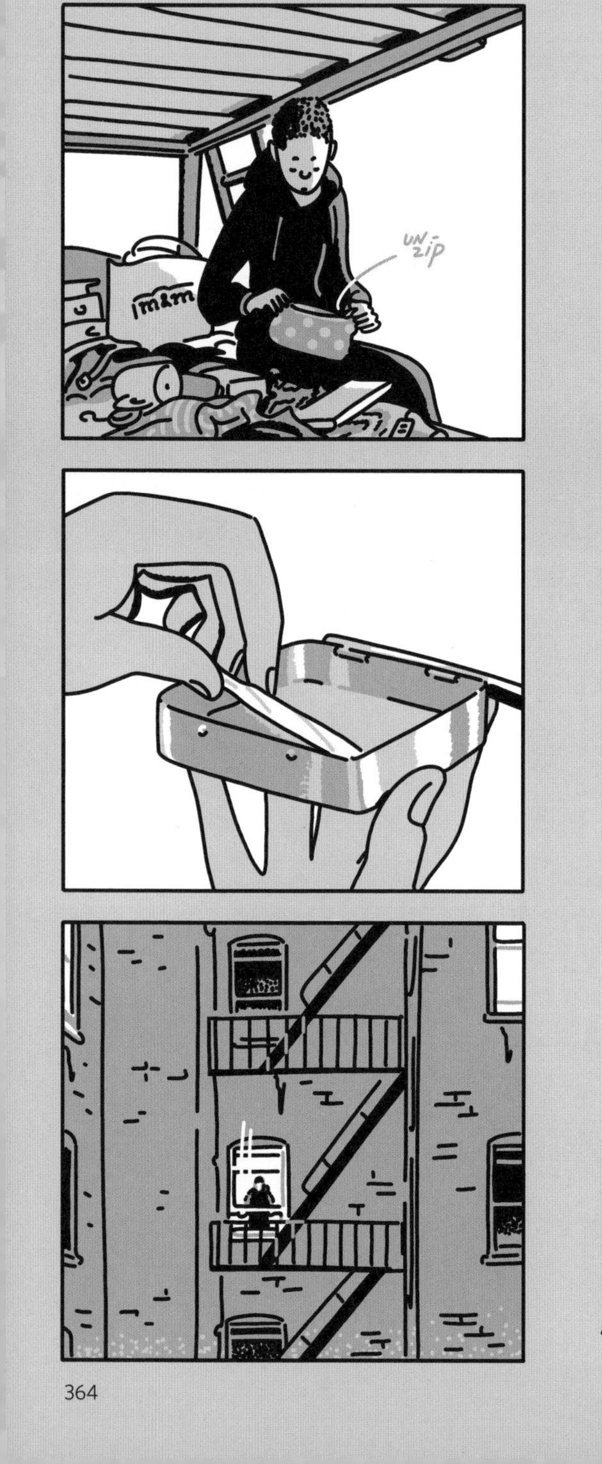
m&m
UN zip
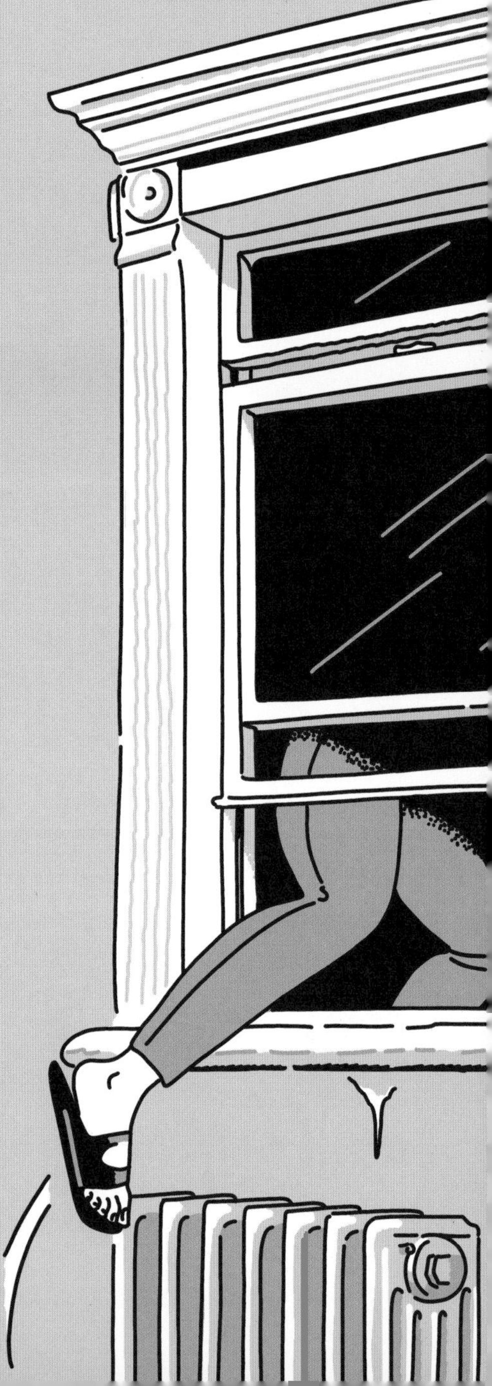

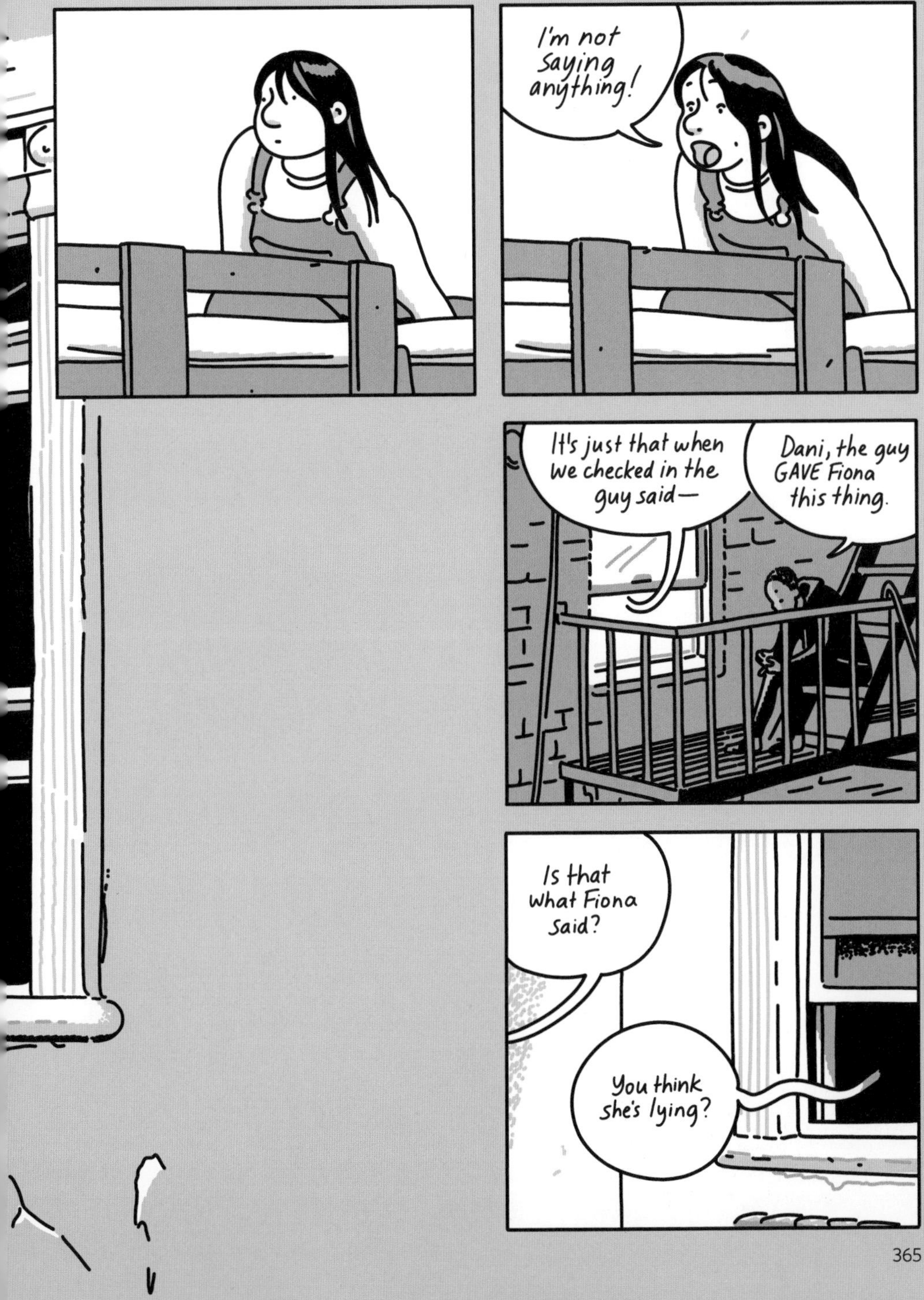
I'm not saying anything!
It's just that when we checked in the guy said—
Dani, the guy GAVE Fiona this thing.
Is that what Fiona said?
You think she's lying?

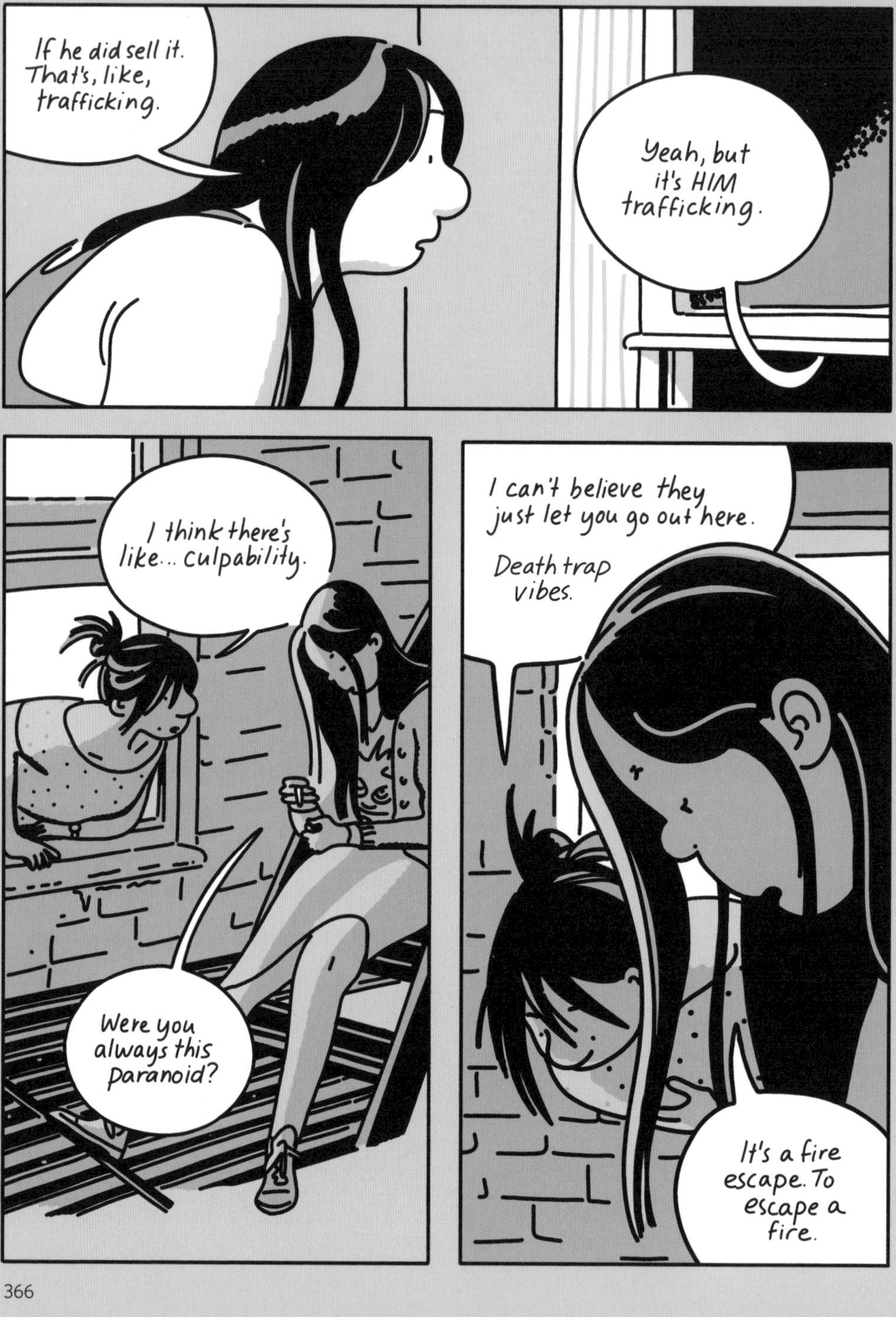
If he did sell it. That's, like, trafficking.
Yeah, but it's HIM trafficking.
I think there's like... culpability.
Were you always this paranoid?
I can't believe they just let you go out here.
Death trap vibes.
It's a fire escape. To escape a fire.

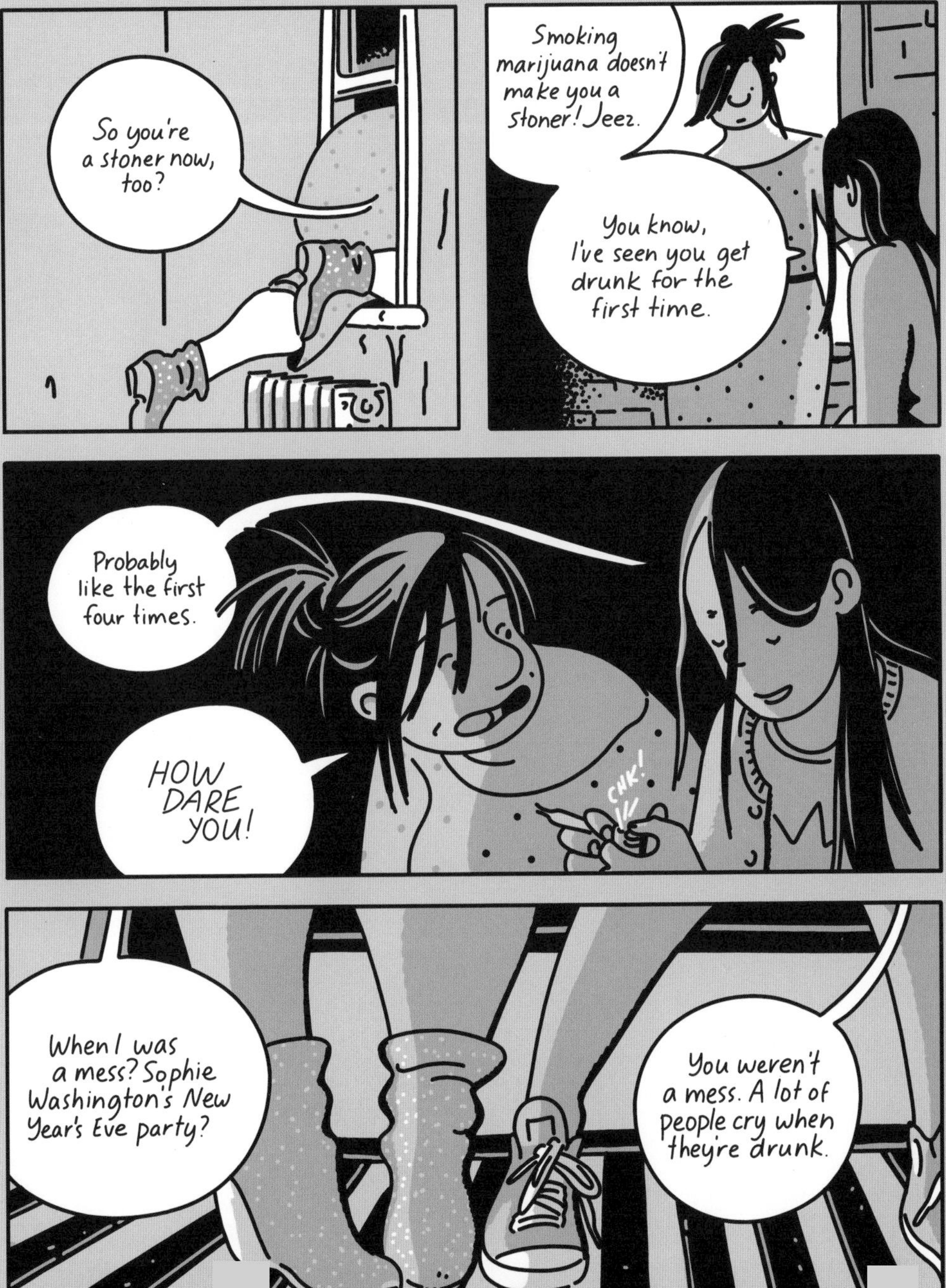
So you're a stoner now, too?
Smoking marijuana doesn't make you a stoner! Jeez.
You know, I've seen you get drunk for the first time.
Probably like the first four times.
HOW DARE YOU!
CHK!
When I was a mess? Sophie Washington's New Year's Eve party?
You weren't a mess. A lot of people cry when they're drunk.

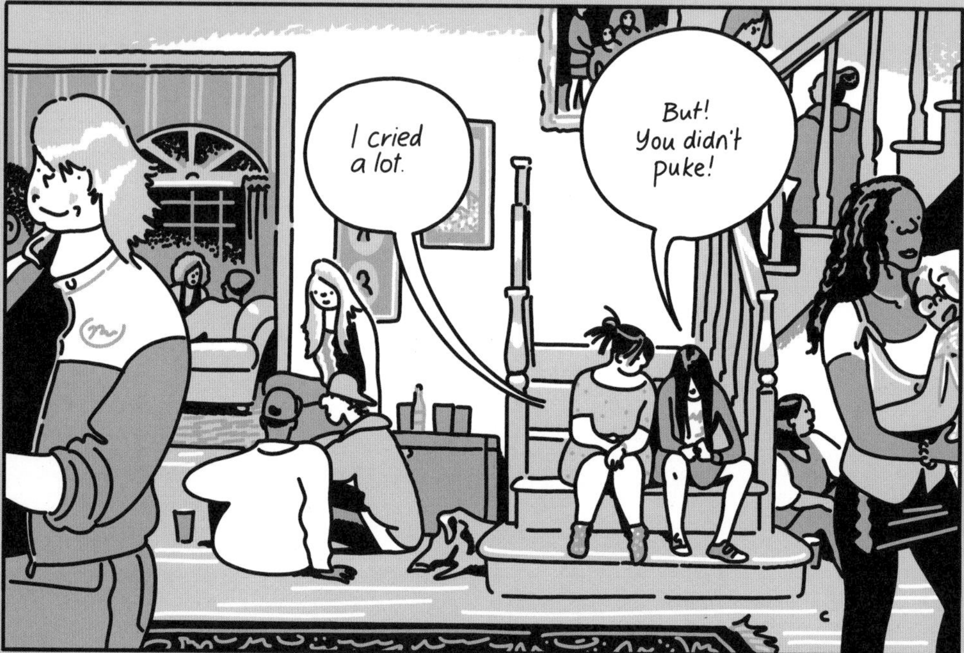
I cried a lot.
But! You didn't puke!

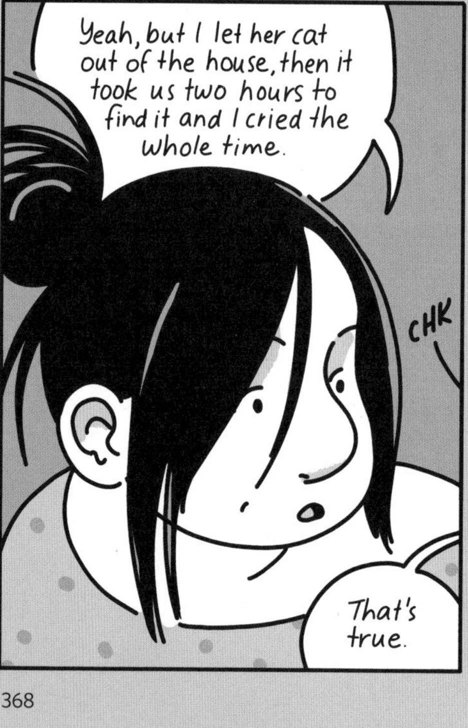
Yeah, but I let her cat out of the house, then it took us two hours to find it and I cried the whole time.
CHK
That's true.

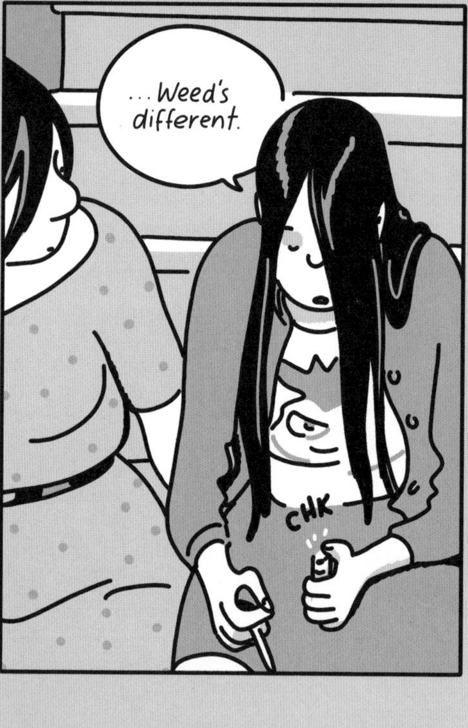
...Weed's different.
CHK

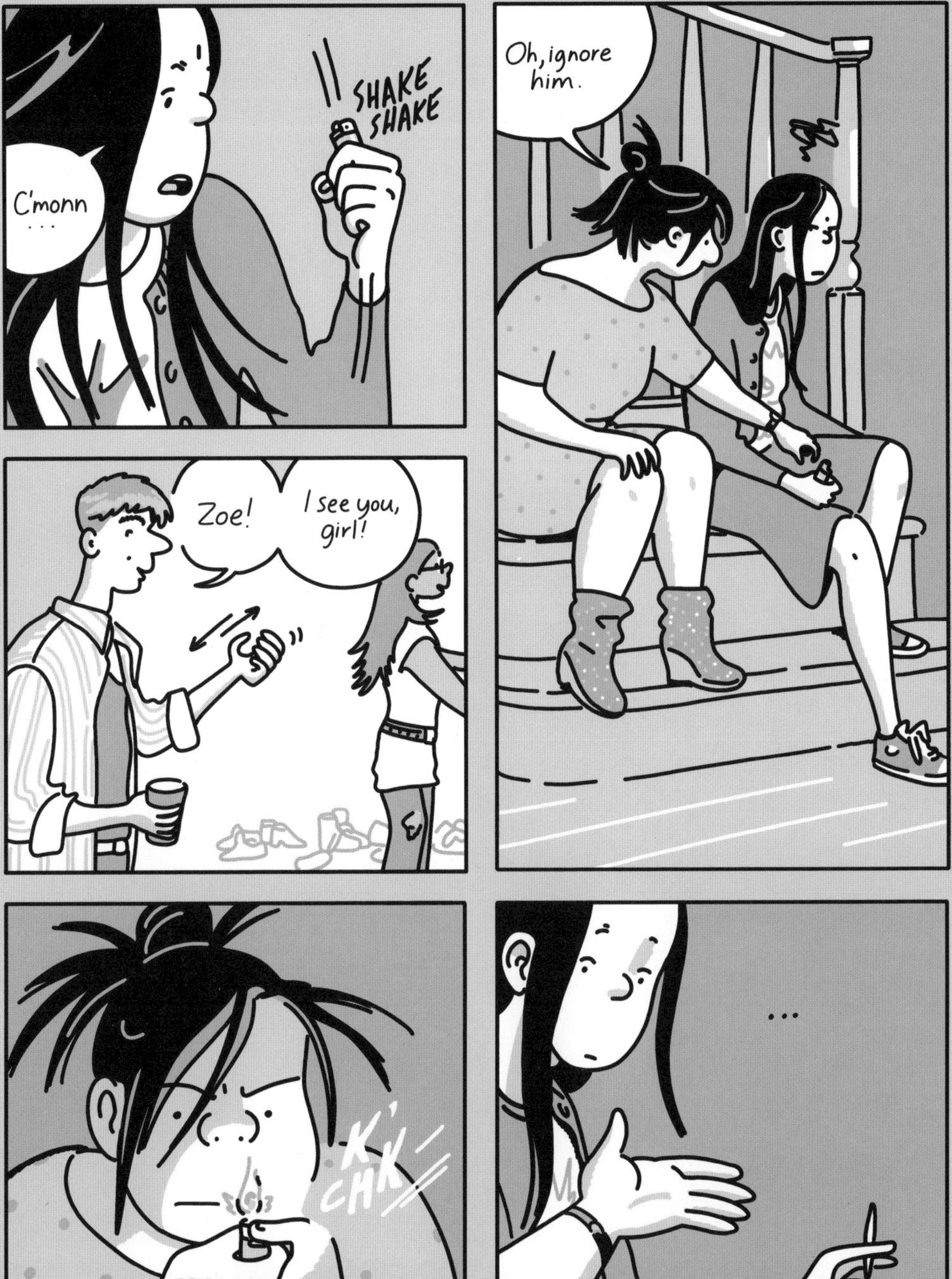
SHAKE SHAKE
C'monn
...
Oh, ignore him.
Zoe!
I see you, girl!
K'CHK
...

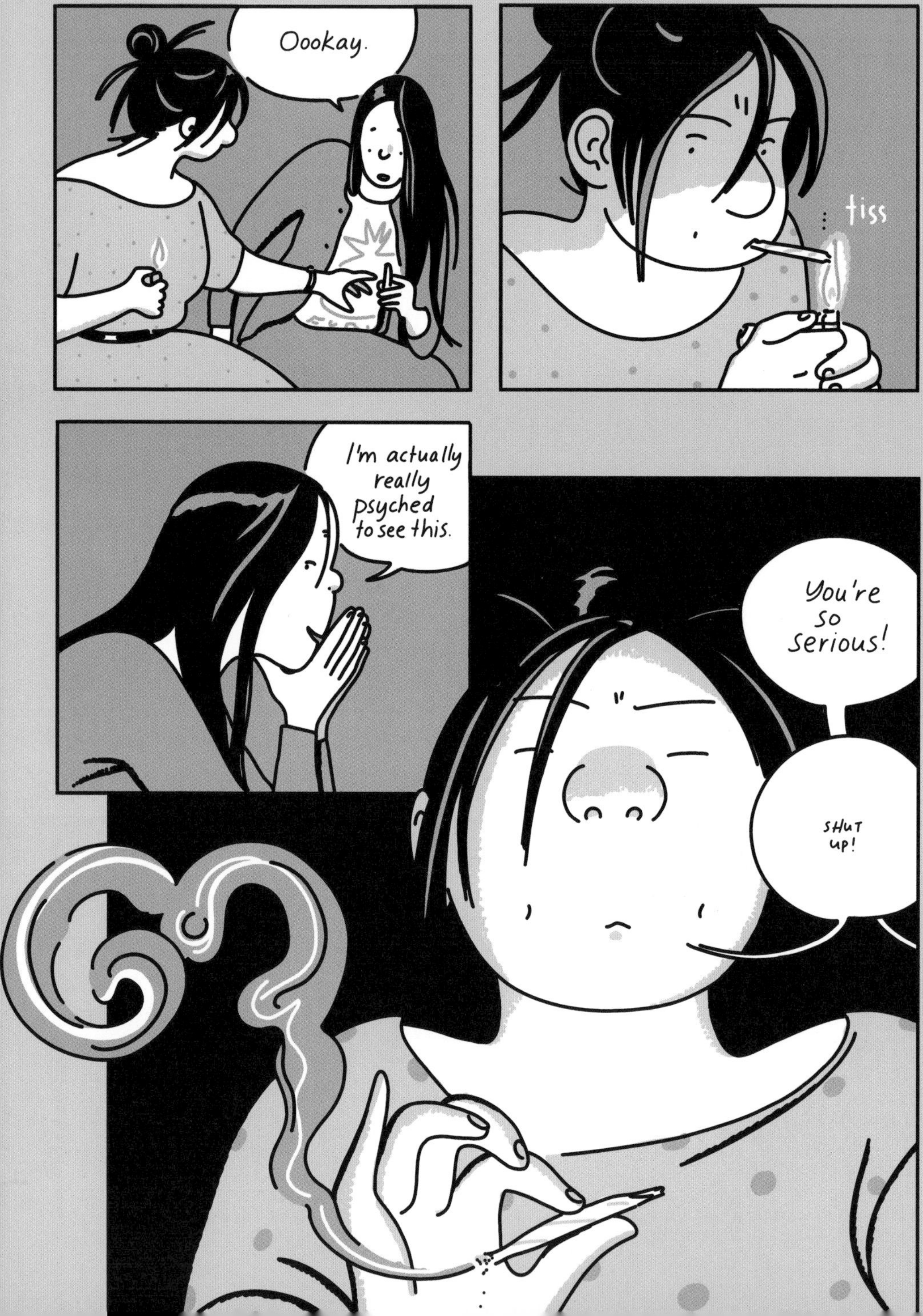
Oookay.
tiss
I'm actually really psyched to see this.
You're so serious!
SHUT up!

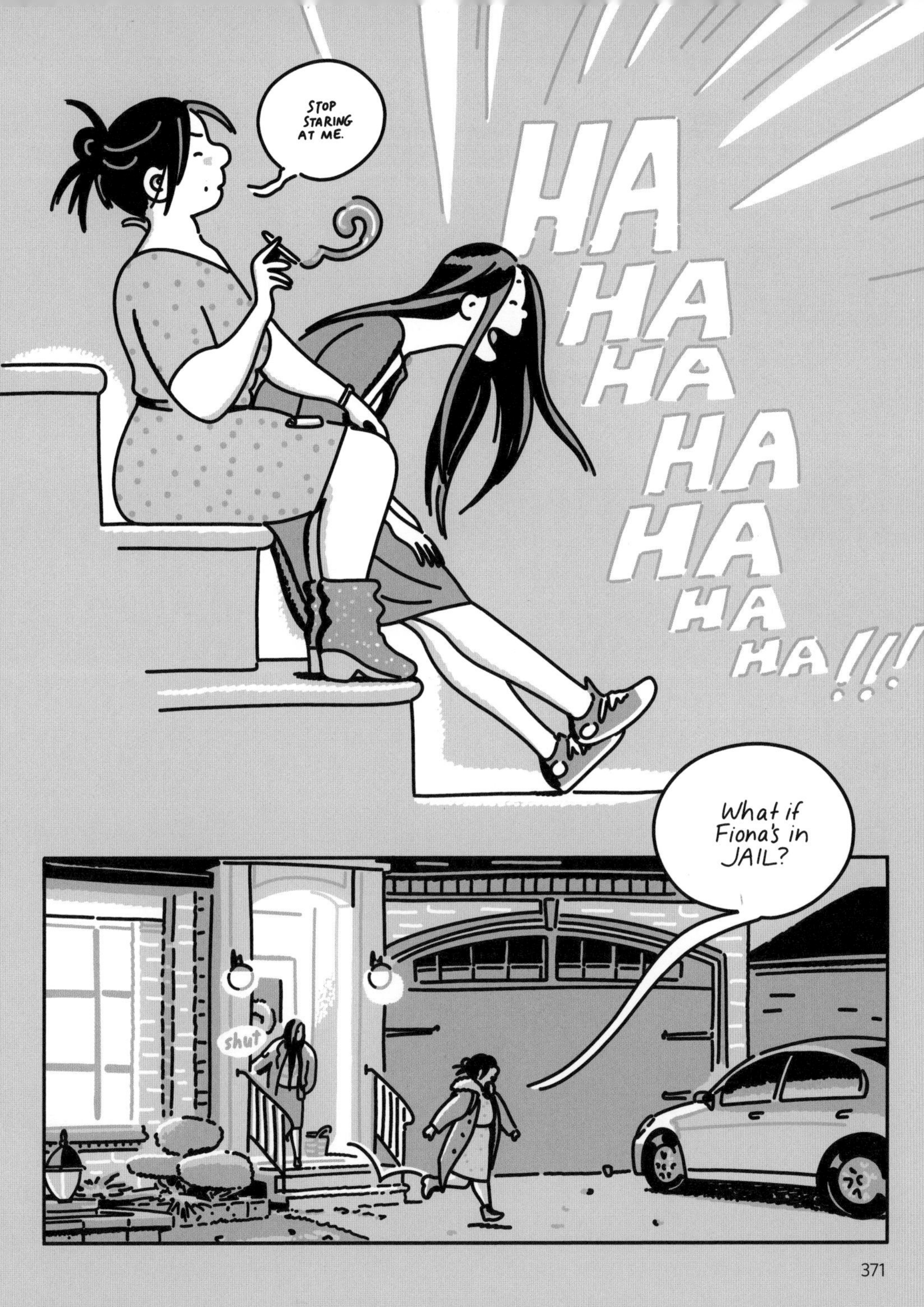
STOP STARING AT ME.
HA HA HA HA HA HA HA HA HA!!!
What if Fiona's in JAIL?
shut

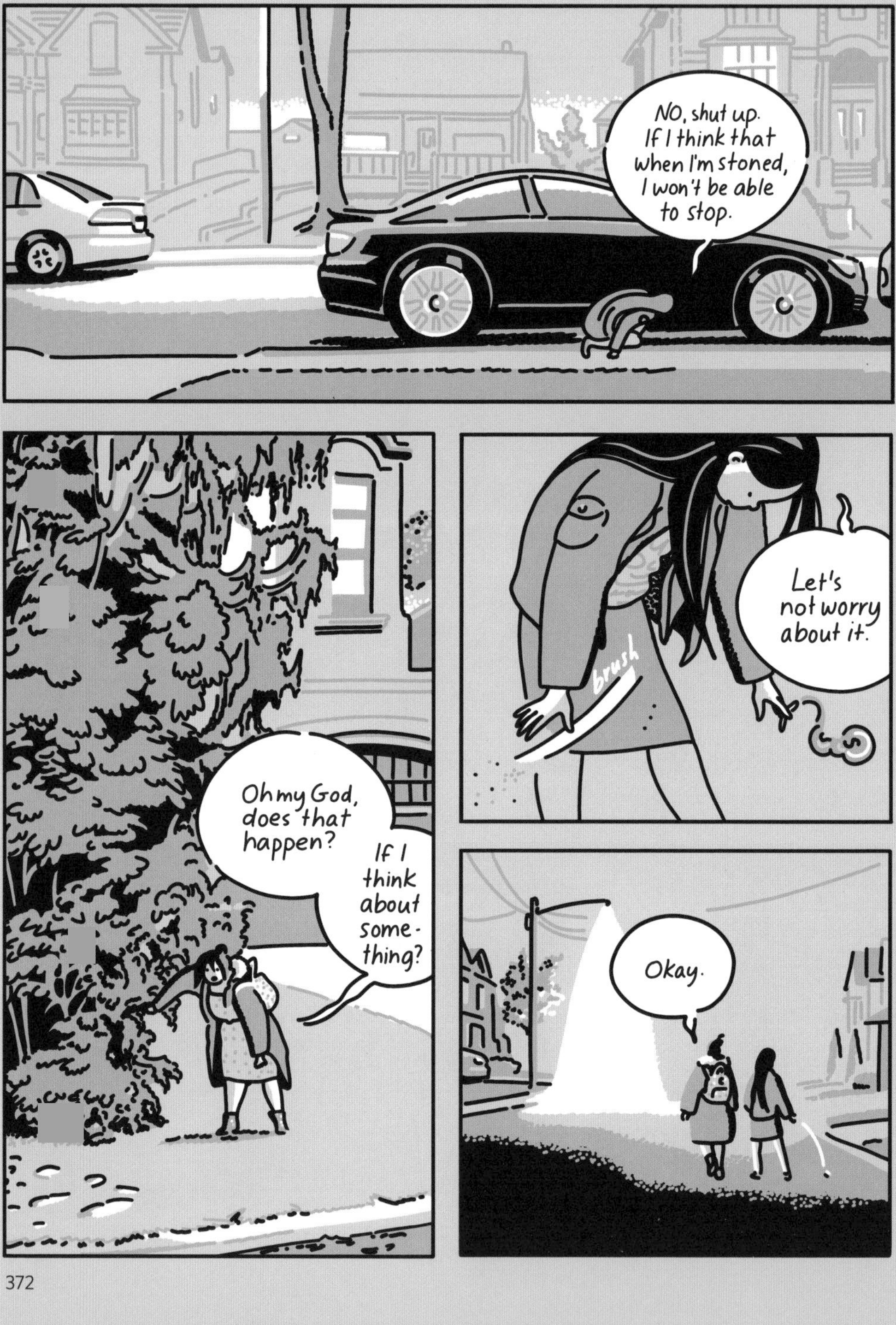
NO, shut up. If I think that when I'm stoned, I won't be able to stop.
Oh my God, does that happen?
If I think about some-thing?
brush
Let's not worry about it.
Okay.

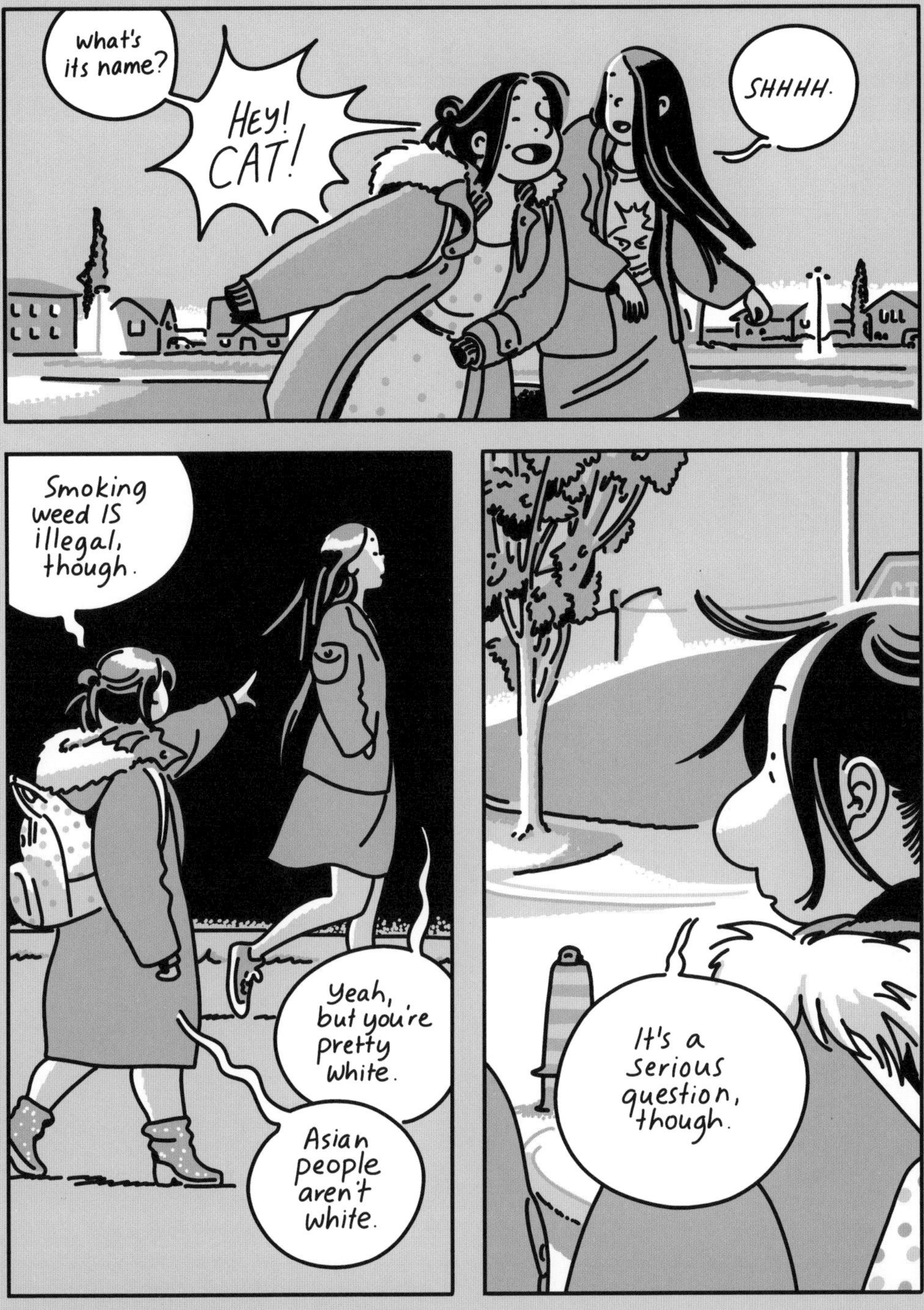
what's its name?
HEY! CAT!
SHHHH.
Smoking weed IS illegal, though.
Yeah, but you're pretty white.
Asian people aren't white.
It's a serious question, though.

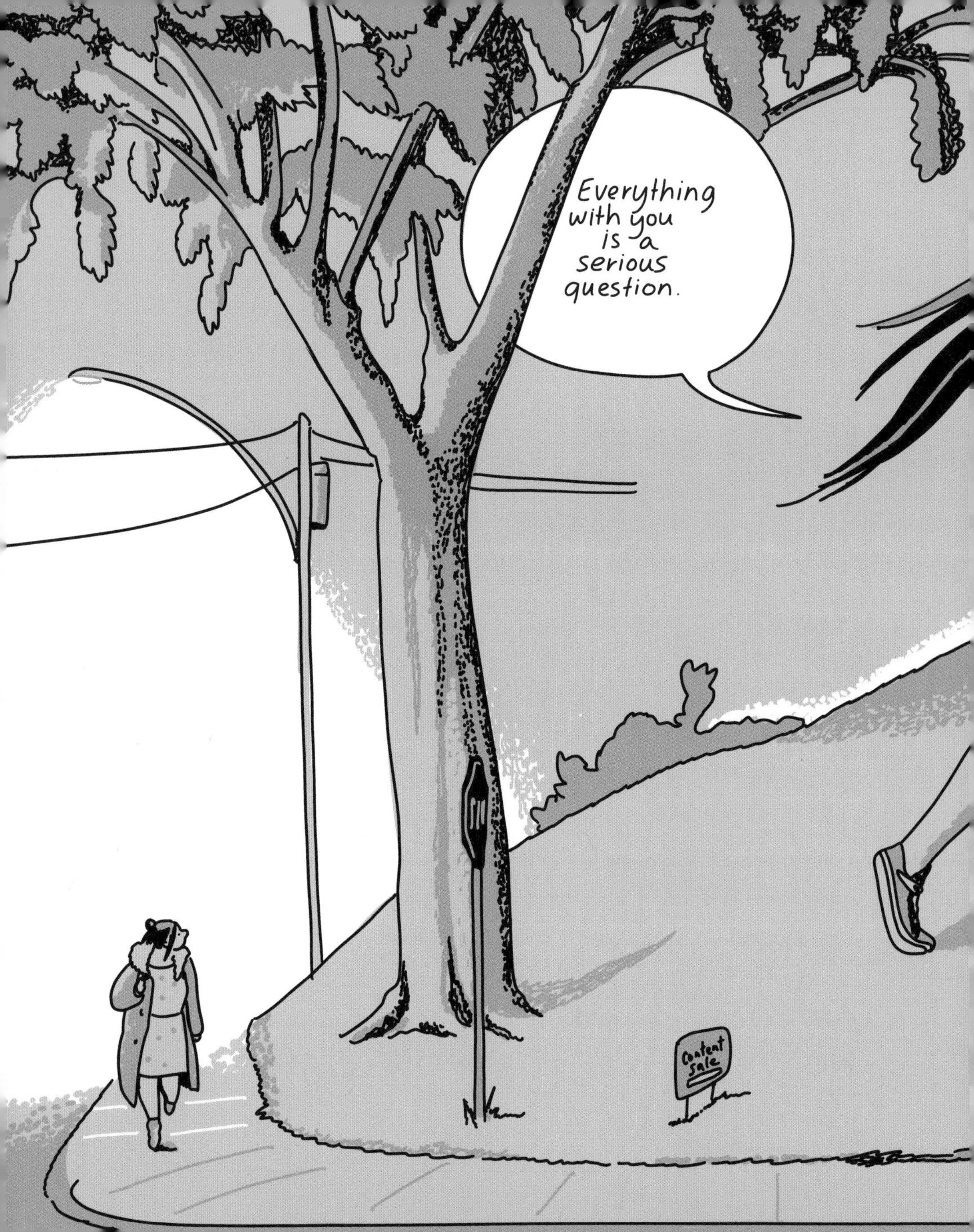
Everything with you is a serious question.
Content Sale

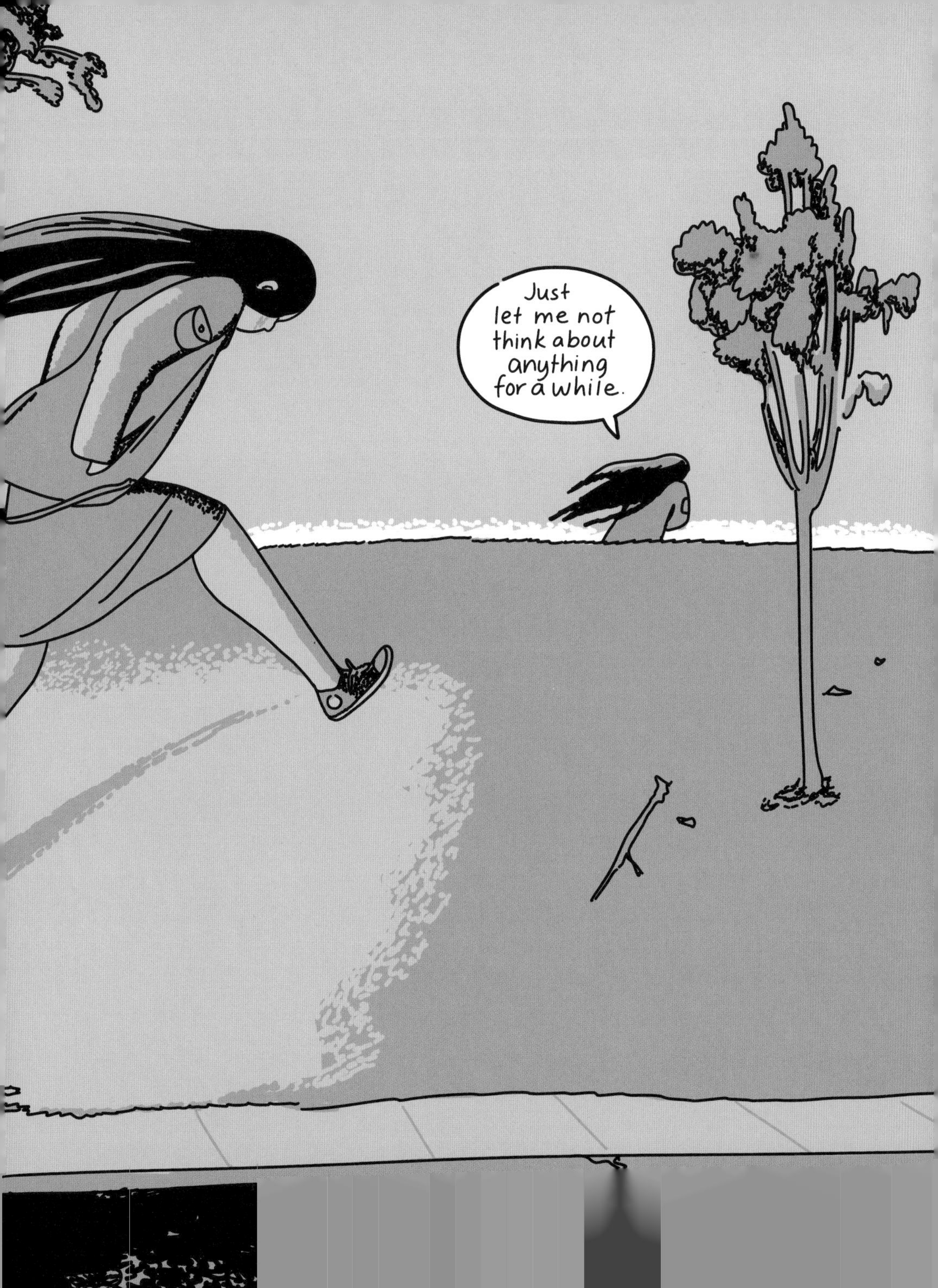
Just let me not think about anything for a while.

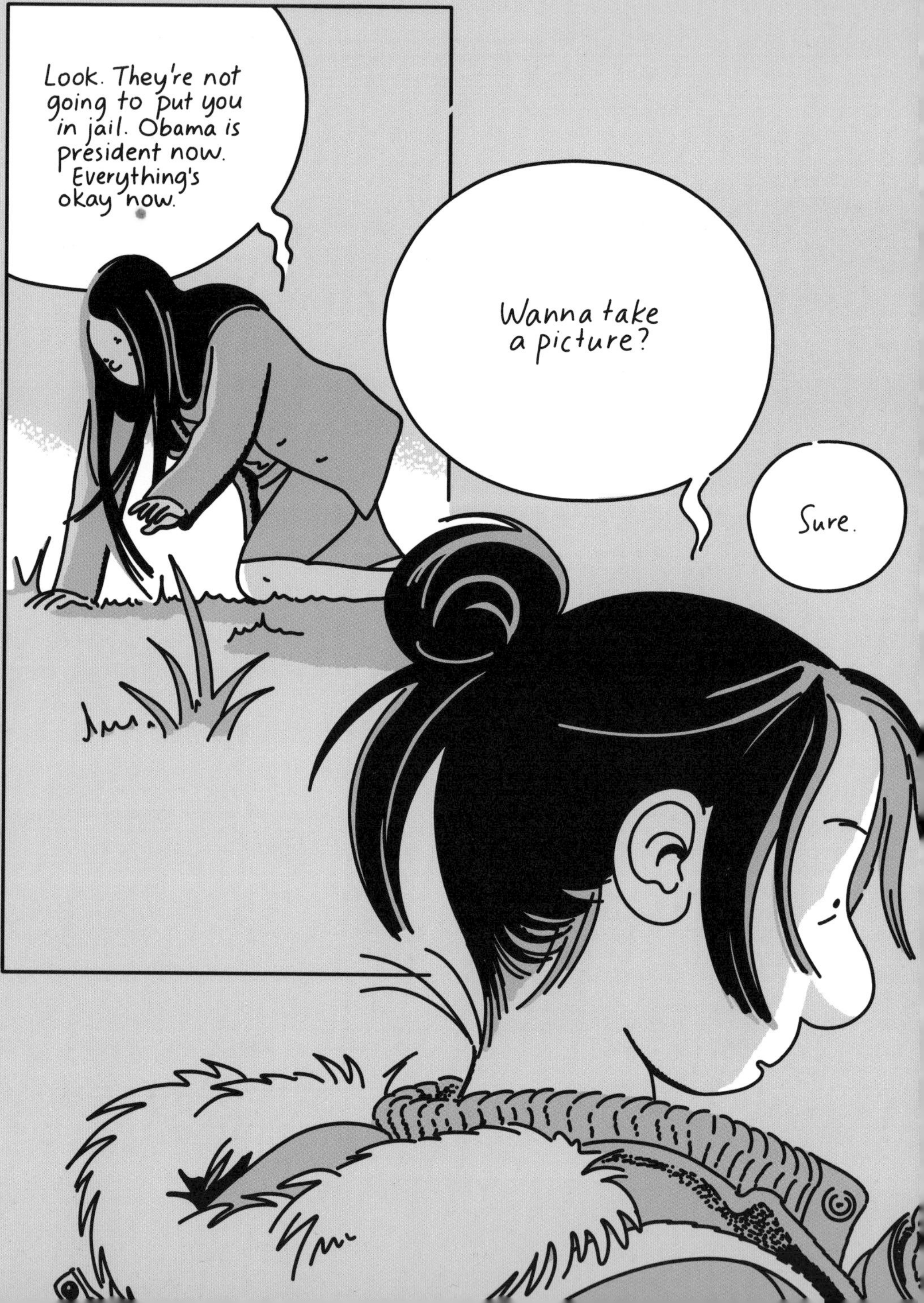

Look. They're not going to put you in jail. Obama is president now. Everything's okay now.
Wanna take a picture?
Sure.

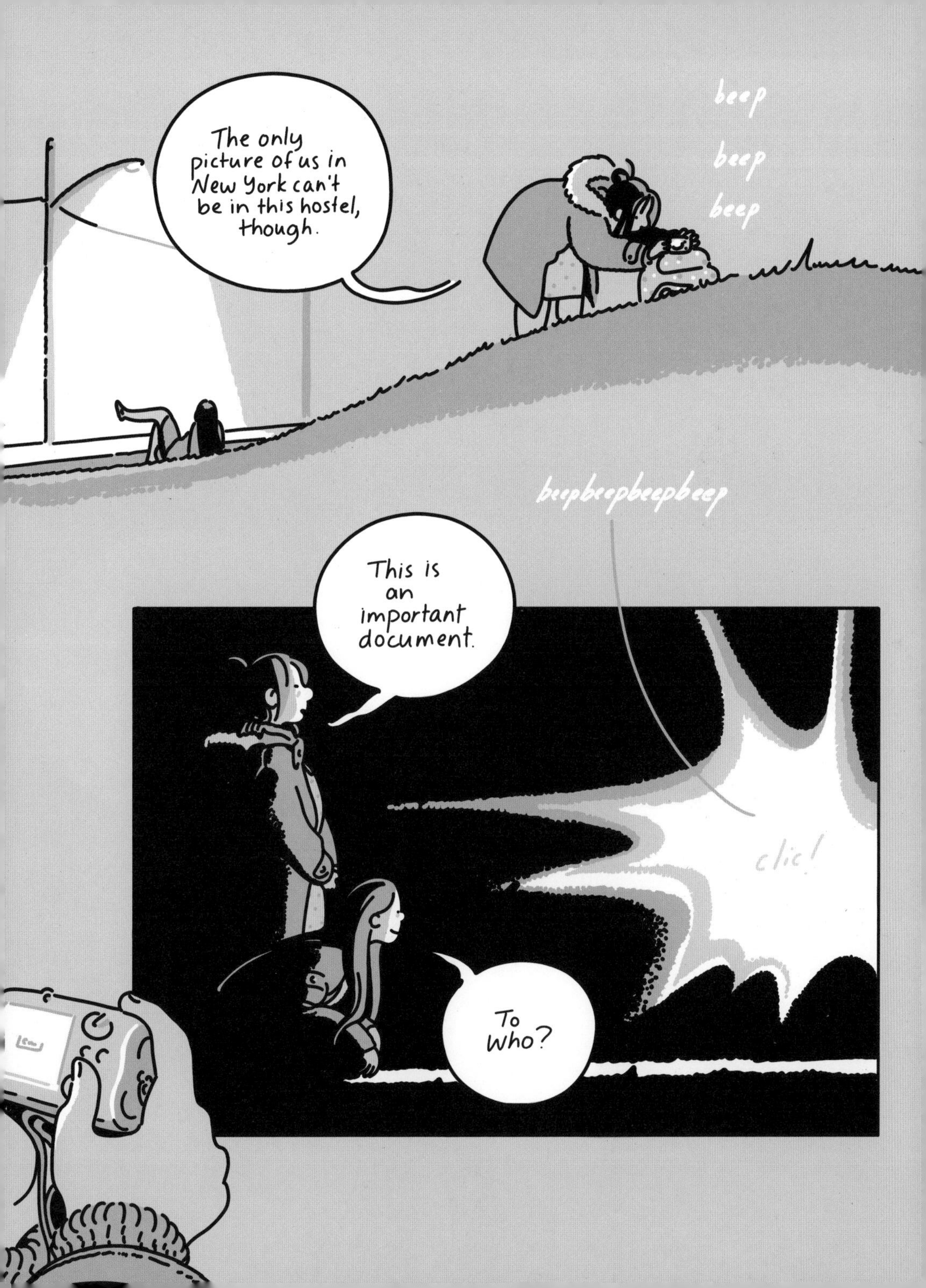

The only picture of us in New York can't be in this hostel, though.
beep
beep
beep
beepbeepbeepbeep
This is an important document.
clic!
To who?

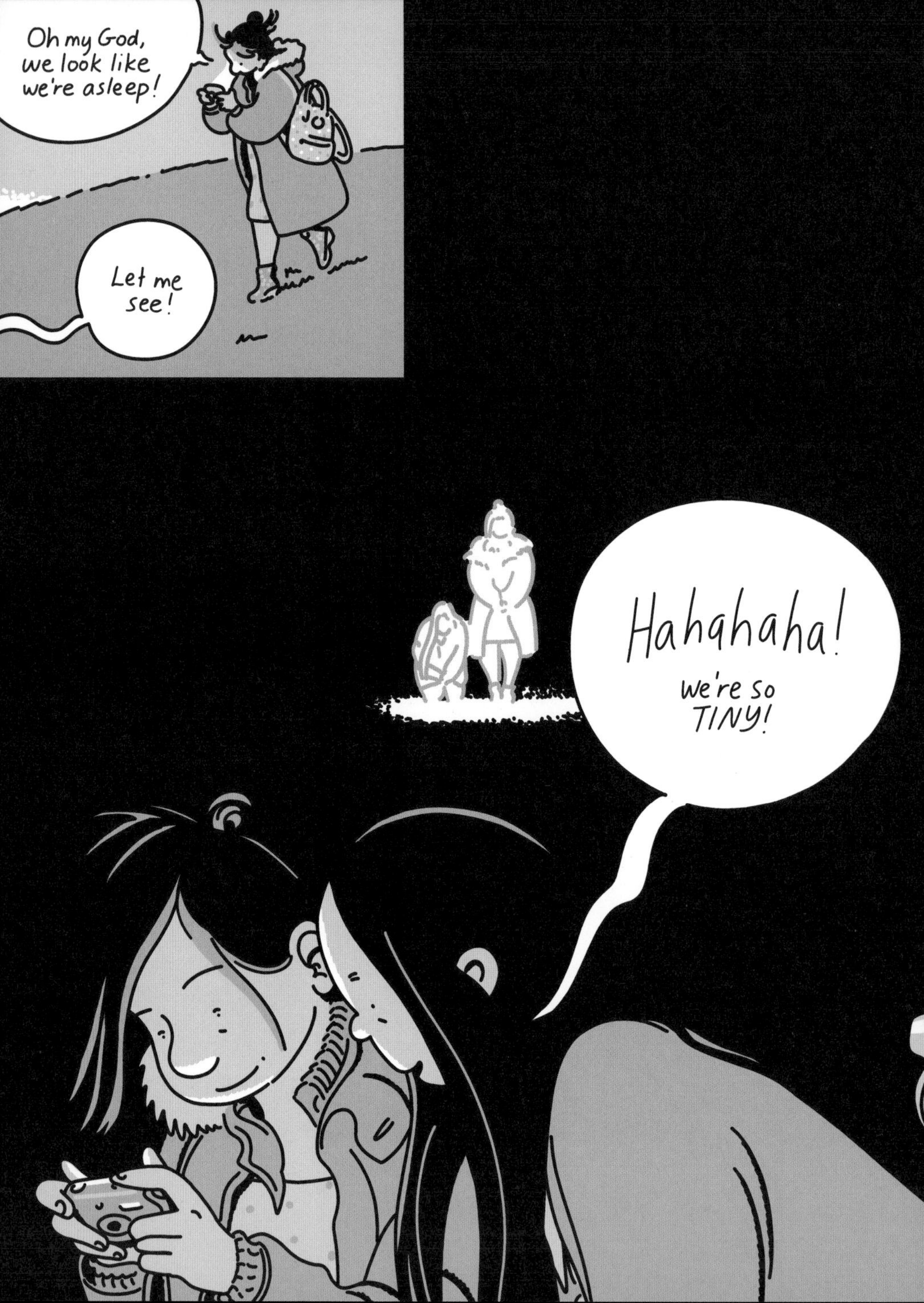
Oh my God, we look like we're asleep!
Let me see!
Hahahaha! we're so TINY!

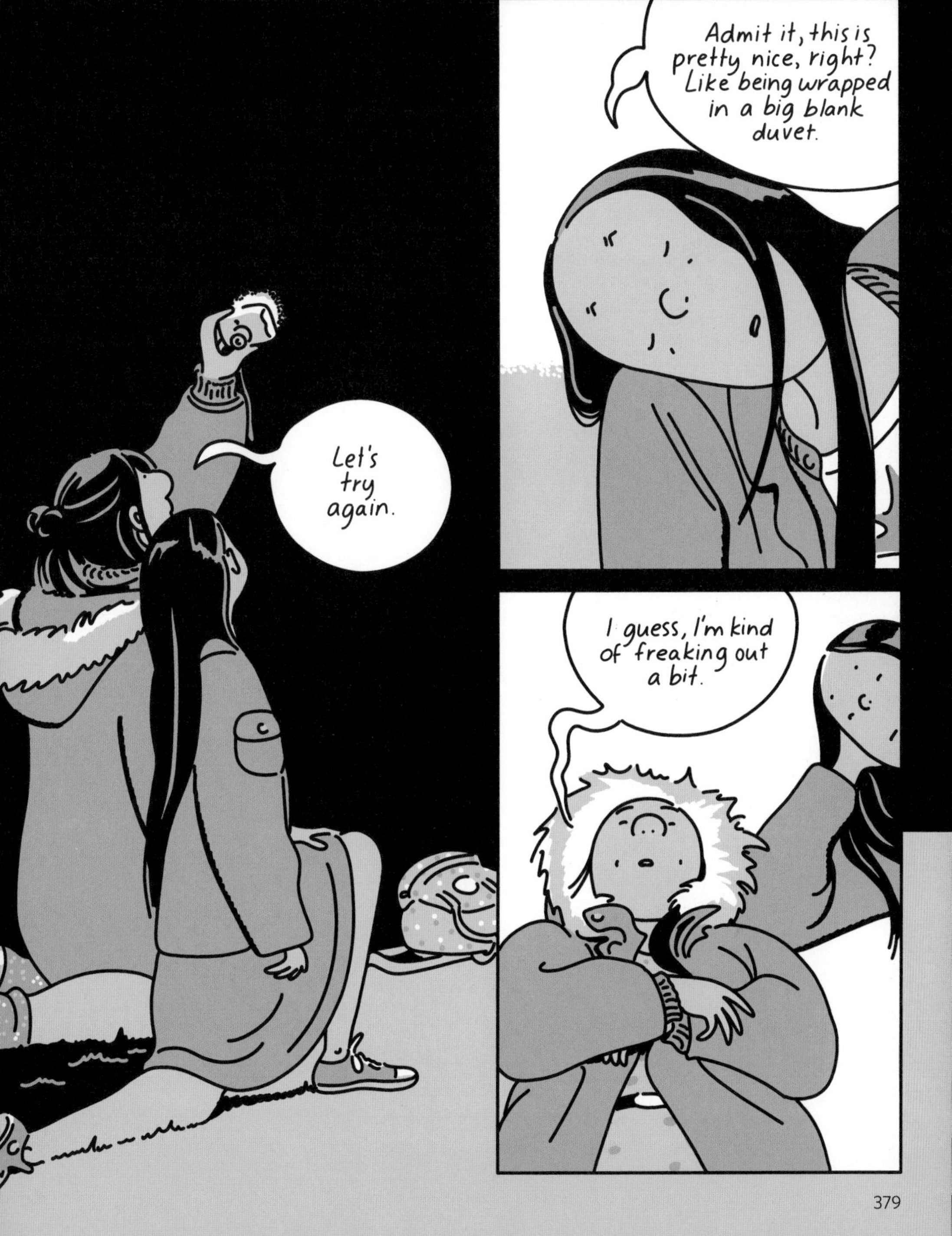
Let's try again.
Admit it, this is pretty nice, right? Like being wrapped in a big blank duvet.
I guess, I'm kind of freaking out a bit.

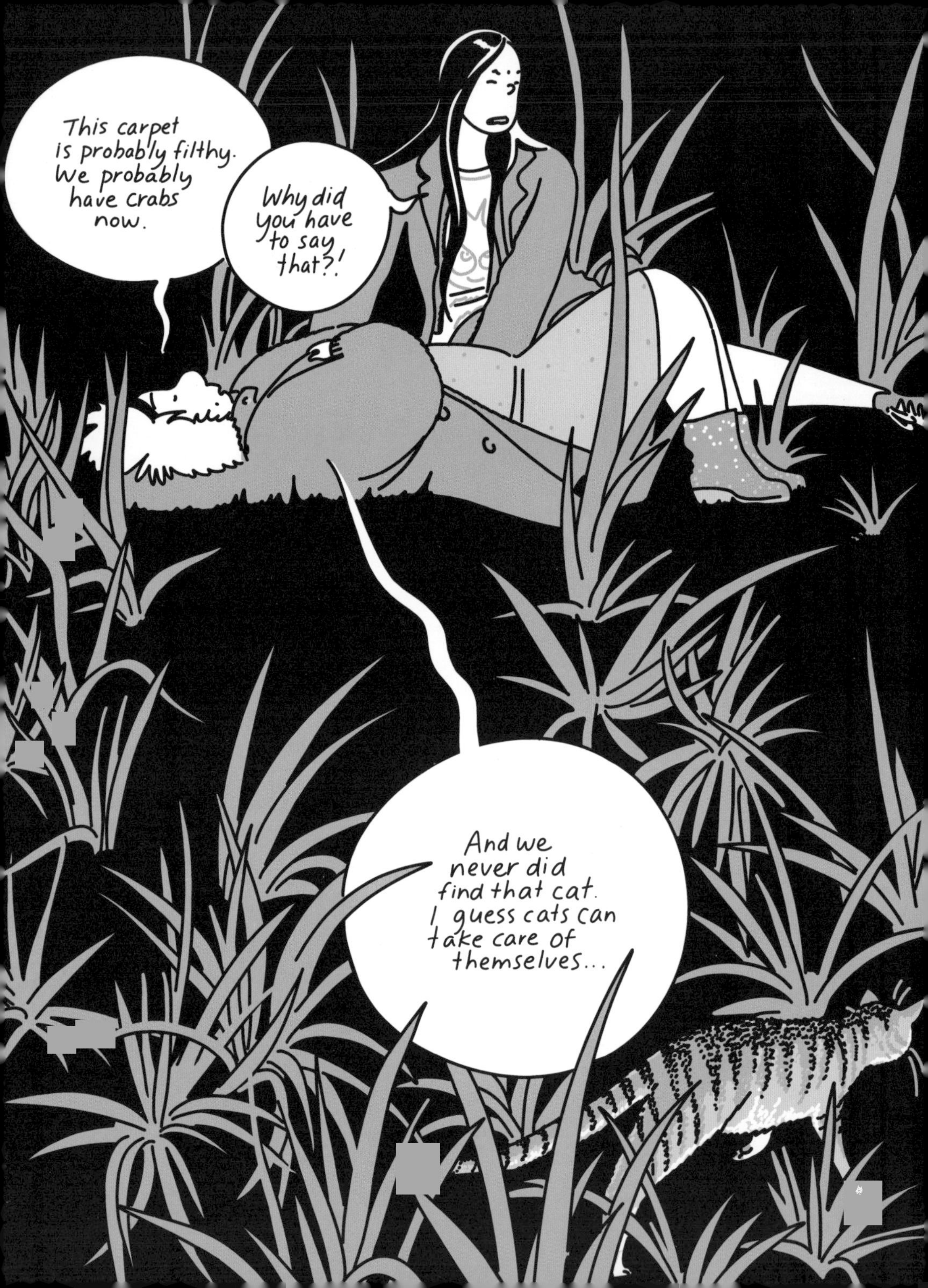
This carpet is probably filthy. We probably have crabs now.
Why did you have to say that?!
And we never did find that cat. I guess cats can take care of themselves...

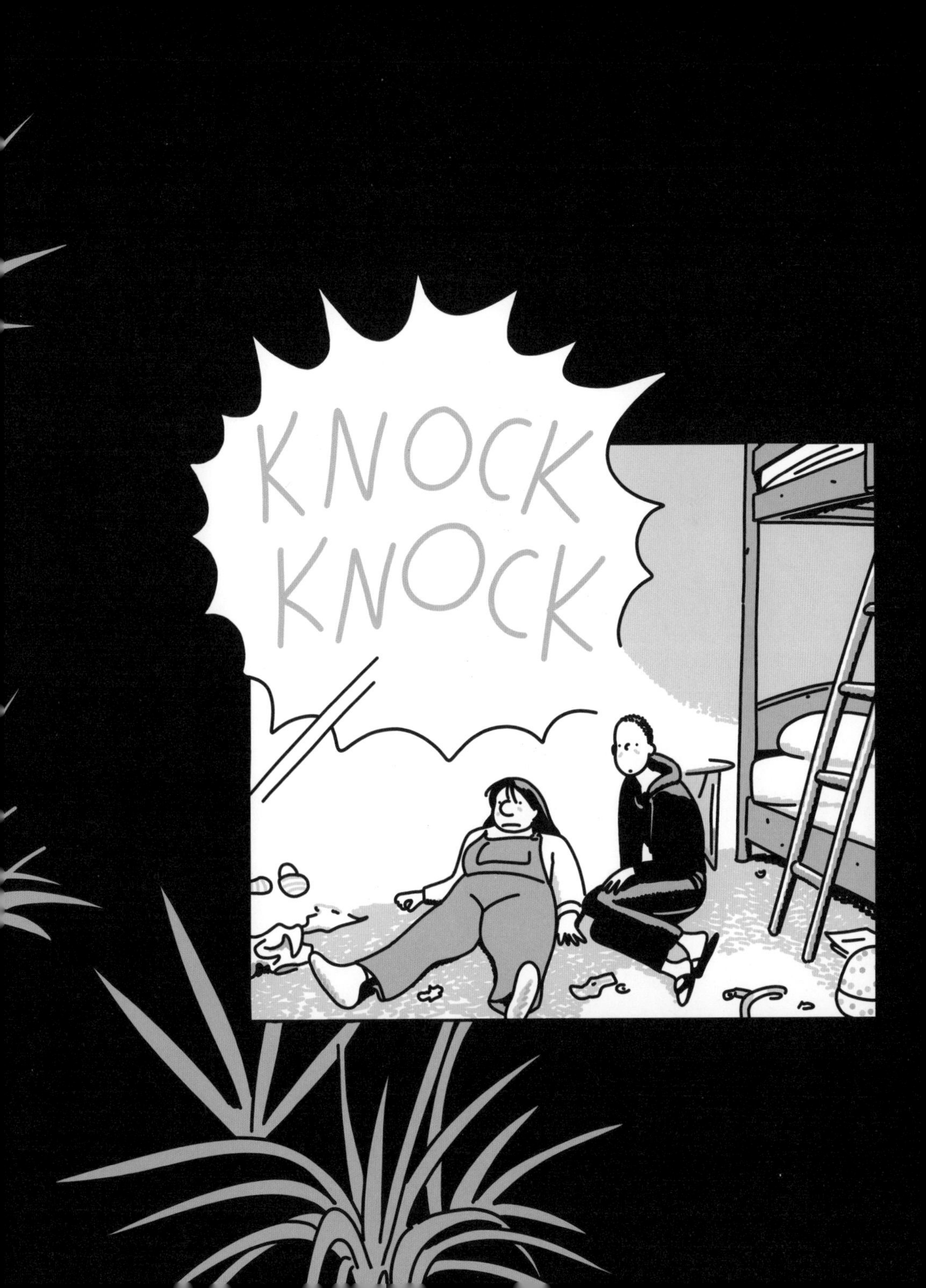
KNOCK KNOCK

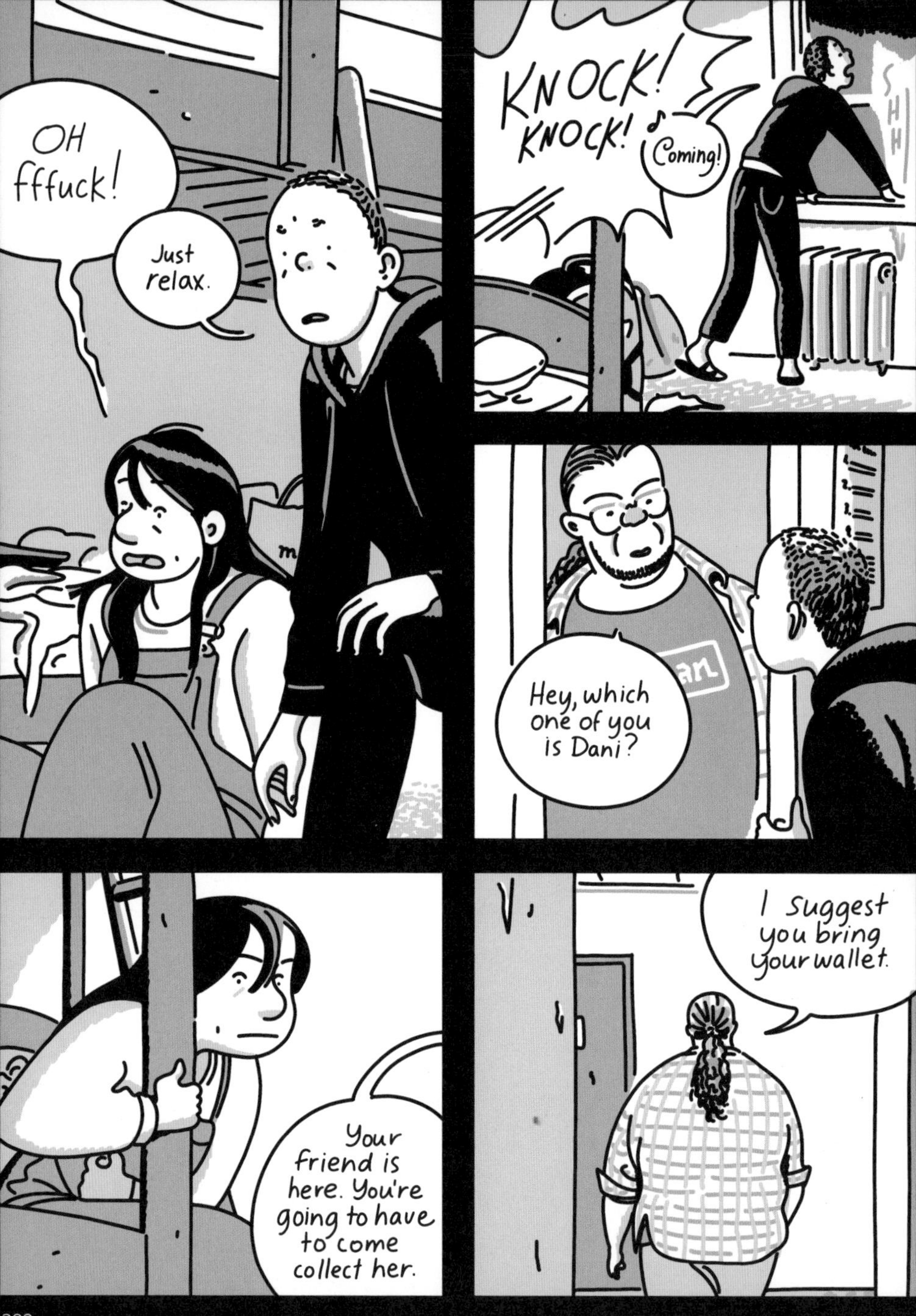

OH fffuck!
Just relax.
KNOCK! KNOCK!
Coming!
SHH
Hey, which one of you is Dani?
Your friend is here. You're going to have to come collect her.
I suggest you bring your wallet.

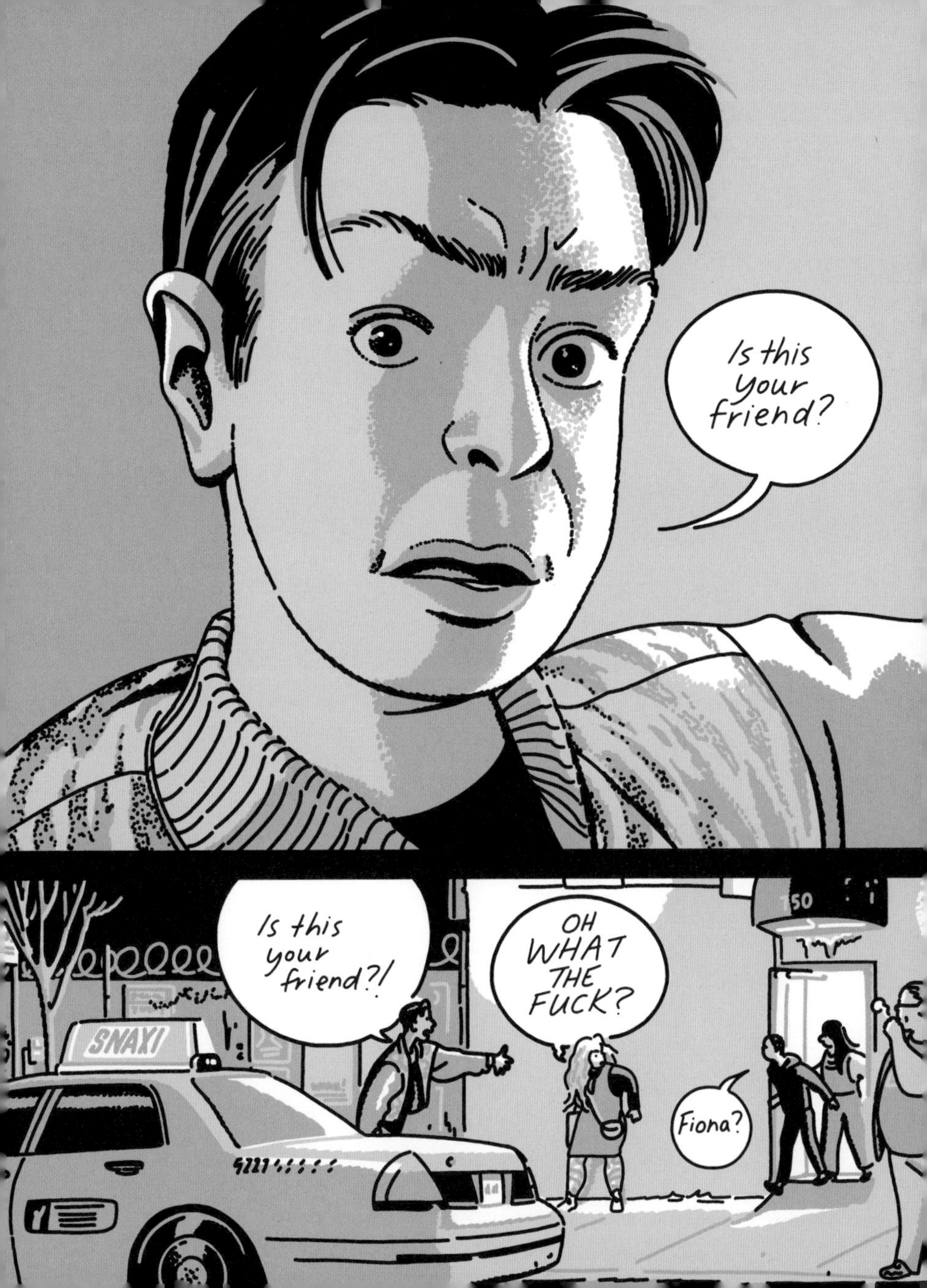
Is this your friend?
SNAXI
Is this your friend?!
OH WHAT THE FUCK?
Fiona?
150

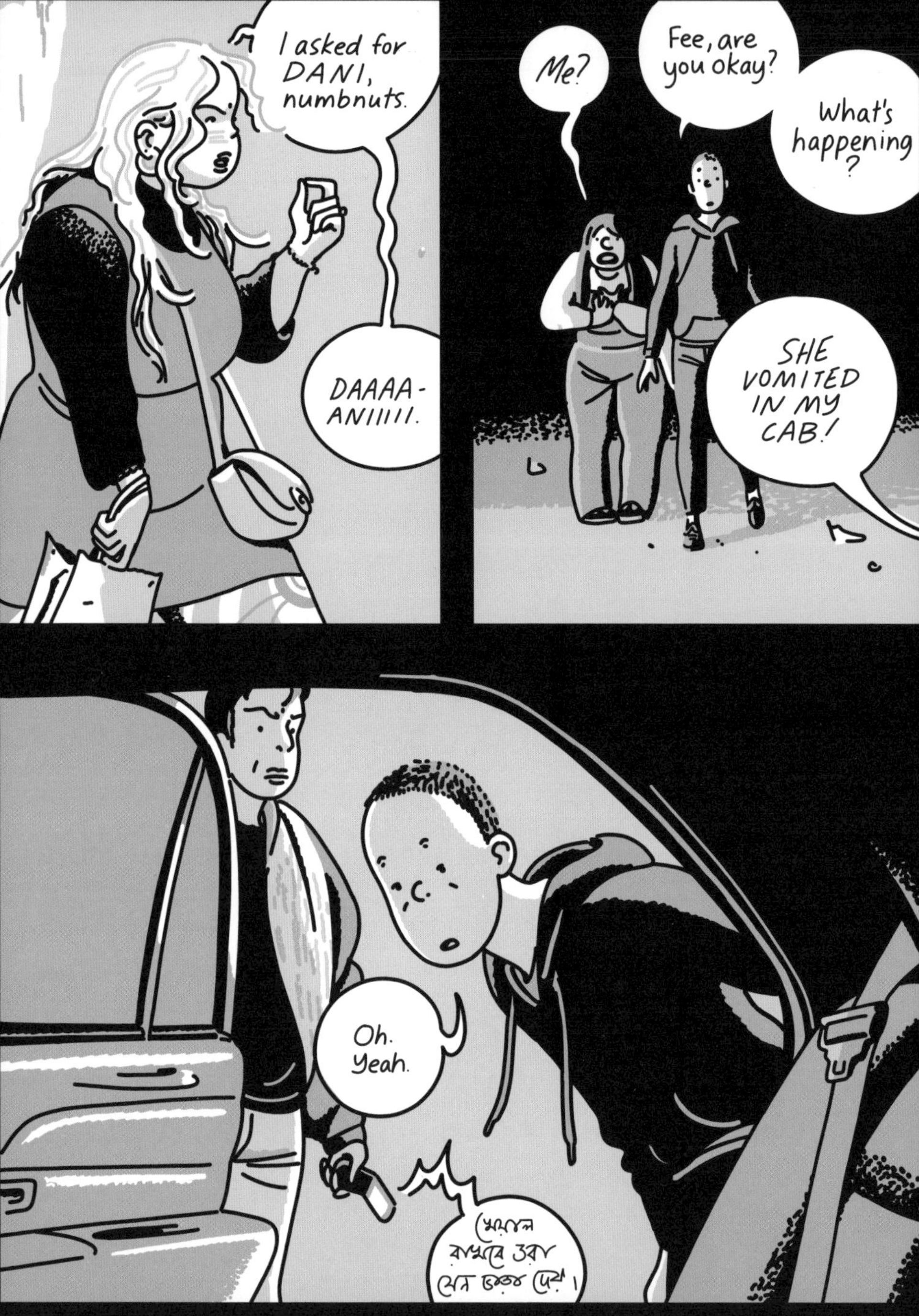
I asked for DANI, numbnuts.
DAAAA-ANIIIII.
Me?
Fee, are you okay?
What's happening?
SHE VOMITED IN MY CAB!
Oh. Yeah.

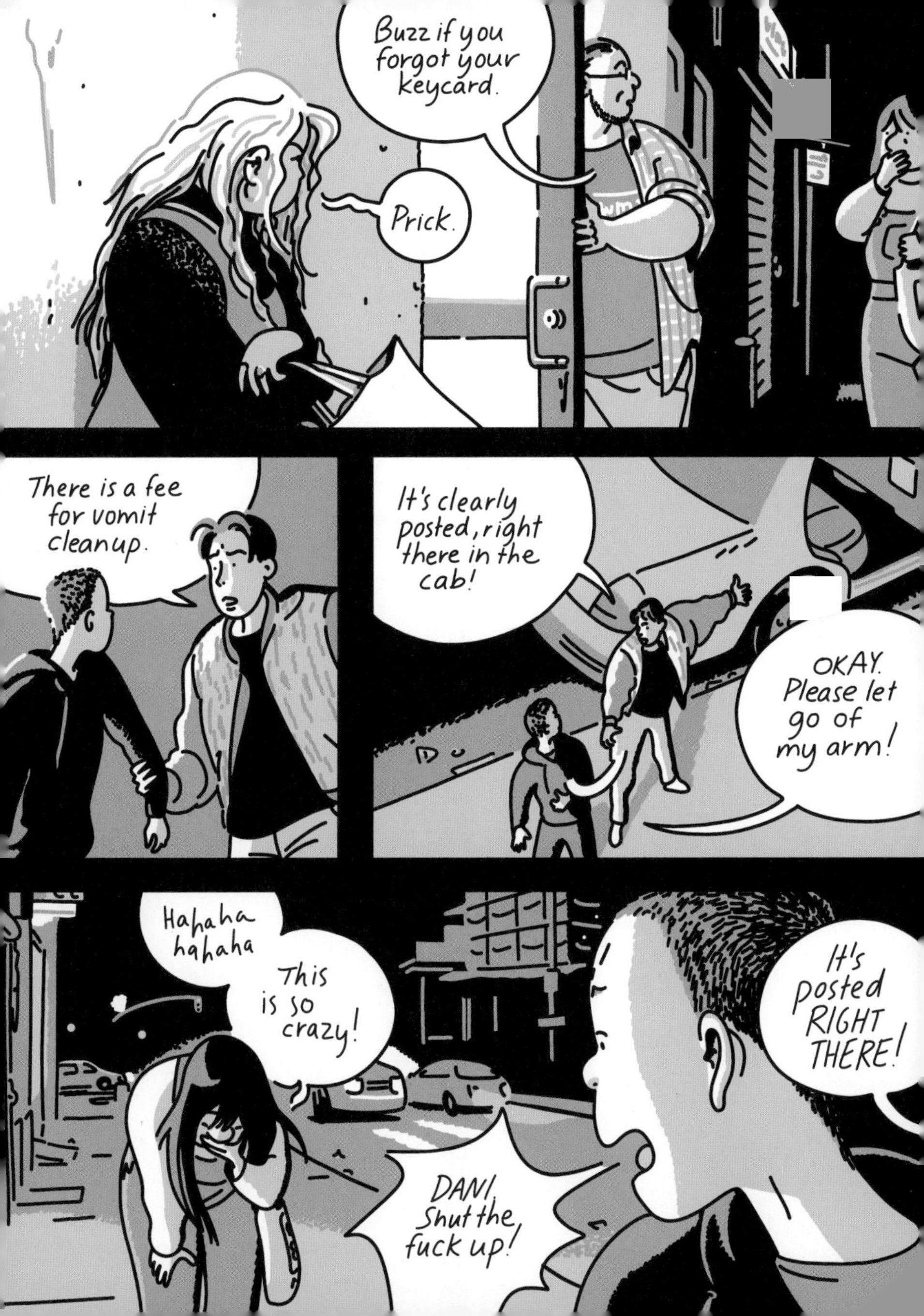
Buzz if you forgot your keycard.
Prick.
There is a fee for vomit cleanup.
It's clearly posted, right there in the cab!
OKAY. Please let go of my arm!
Hahaha hahaha
This is so crazy!
It's posted RIGHT THERE!
DANI, Shut the fuck up!

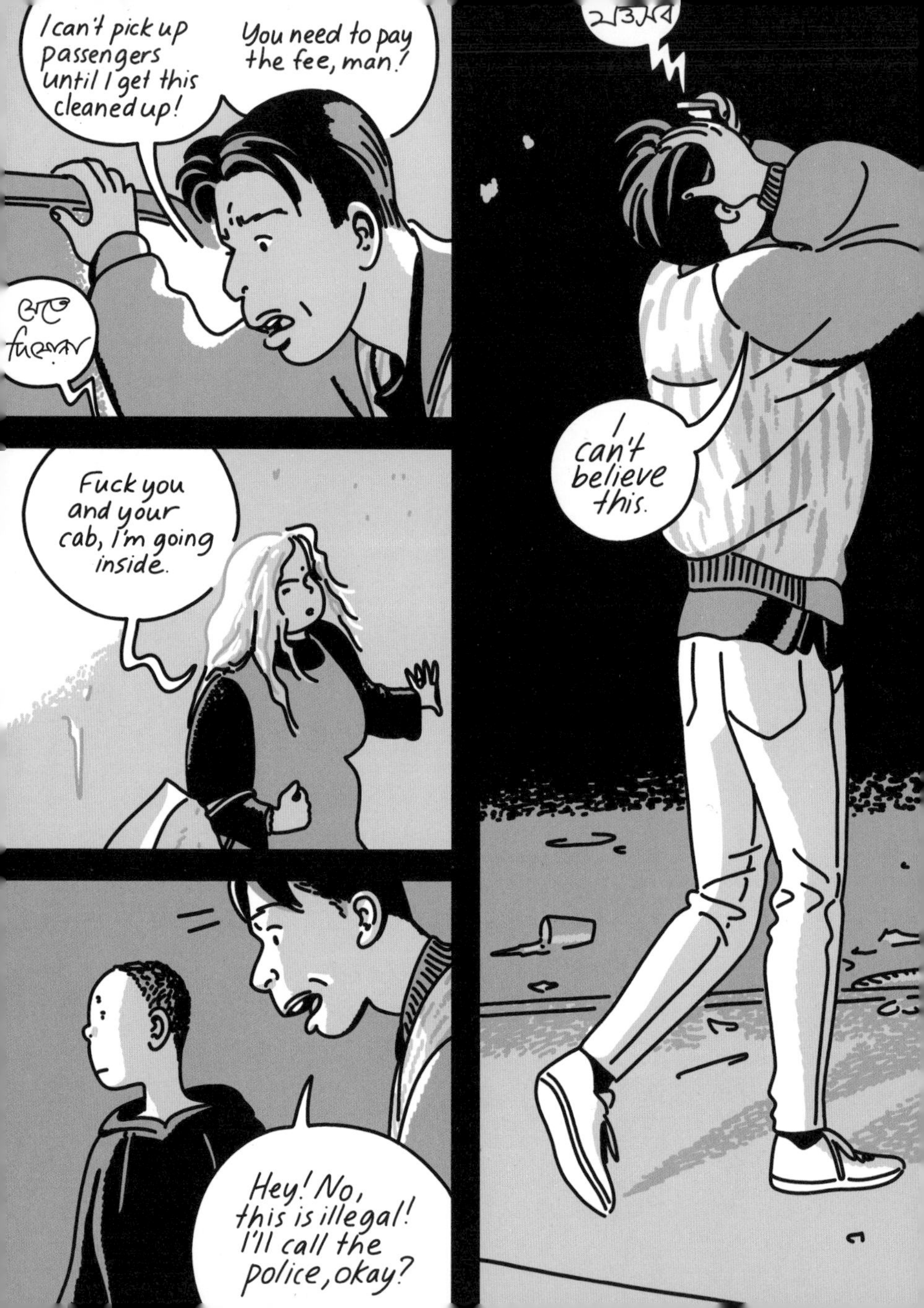
I can't pick up passengers until I get this cleaned up!
You need to pay the fee, man!
Fuck you and your cab, I'm going inside.
Hey! No, this is illegal! I'll call the police, okay?
I can't believe this.

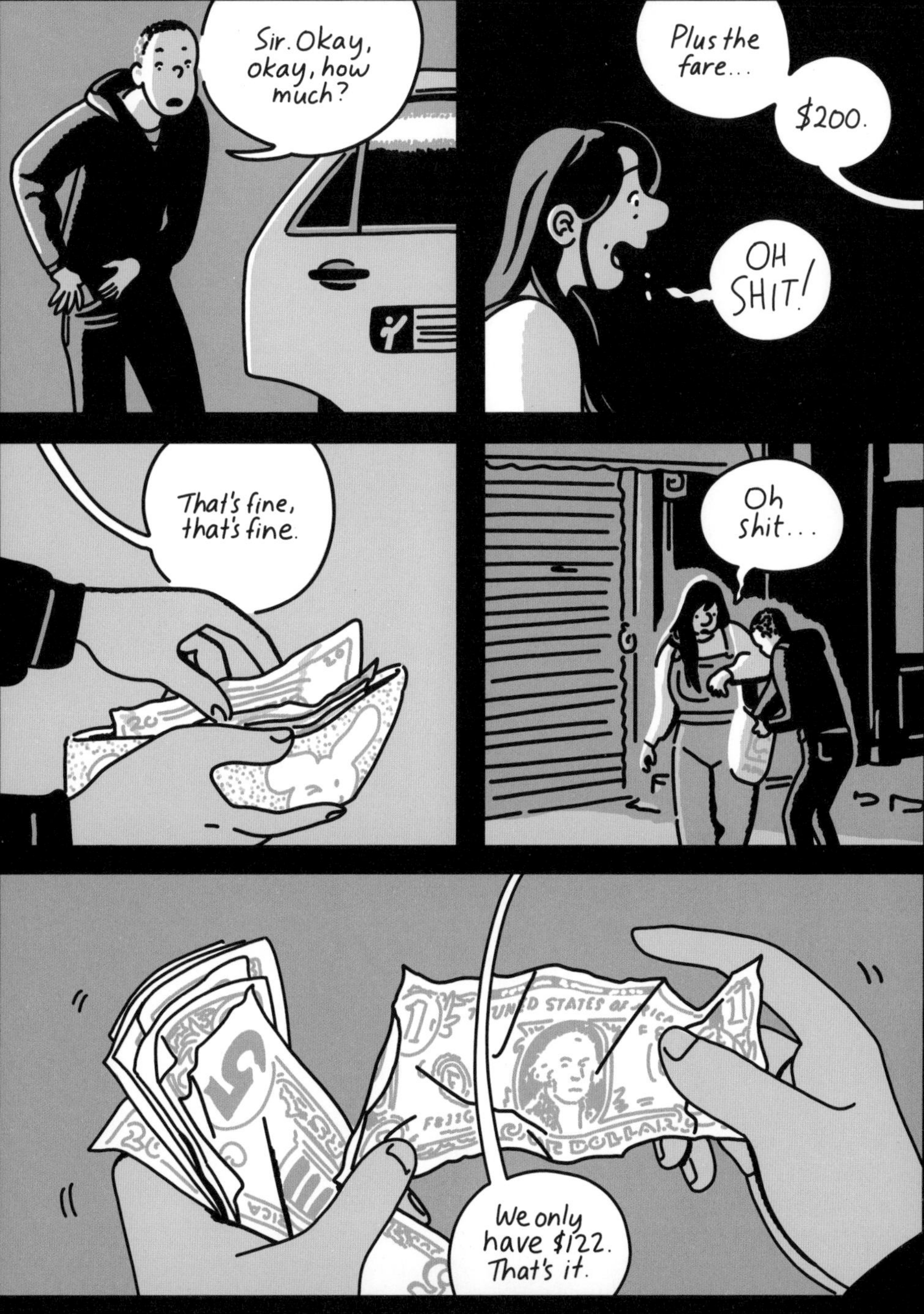
Sir. Okay, okay, how much?
Plus the fare...
$200.
OH SHIT!
That's fine, that's fine.
Oh shit...
We only have $122. That's it.

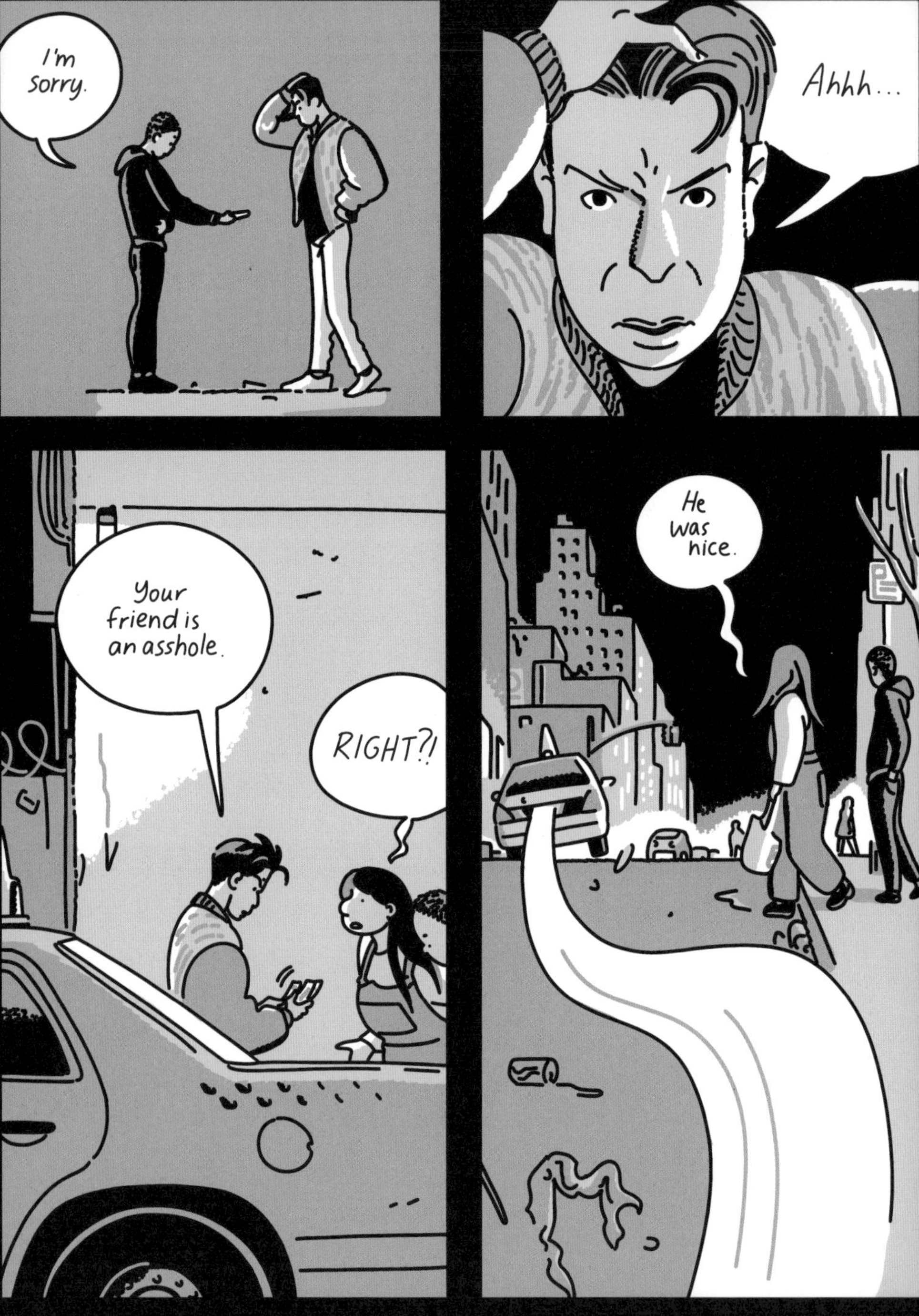

I'm sorry.
Ahhh...
Your friend is an asshole.
RIGHT?!
He was nice.

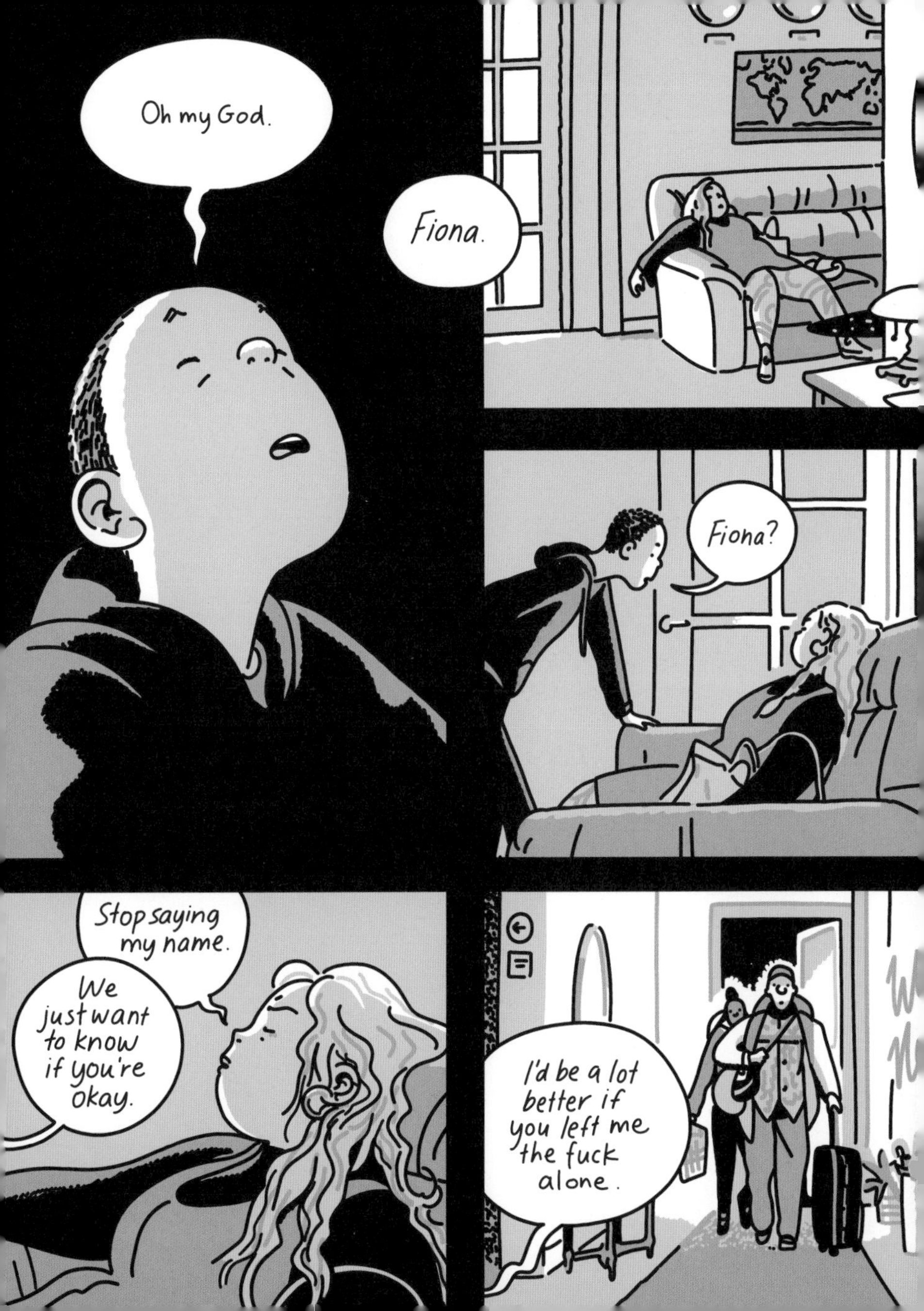
Oh my God.
Fiona.
Fiona?
Stop saying my name.
We just want to know if you're okay.
I'd be a lot better if you left me the fuck alone.

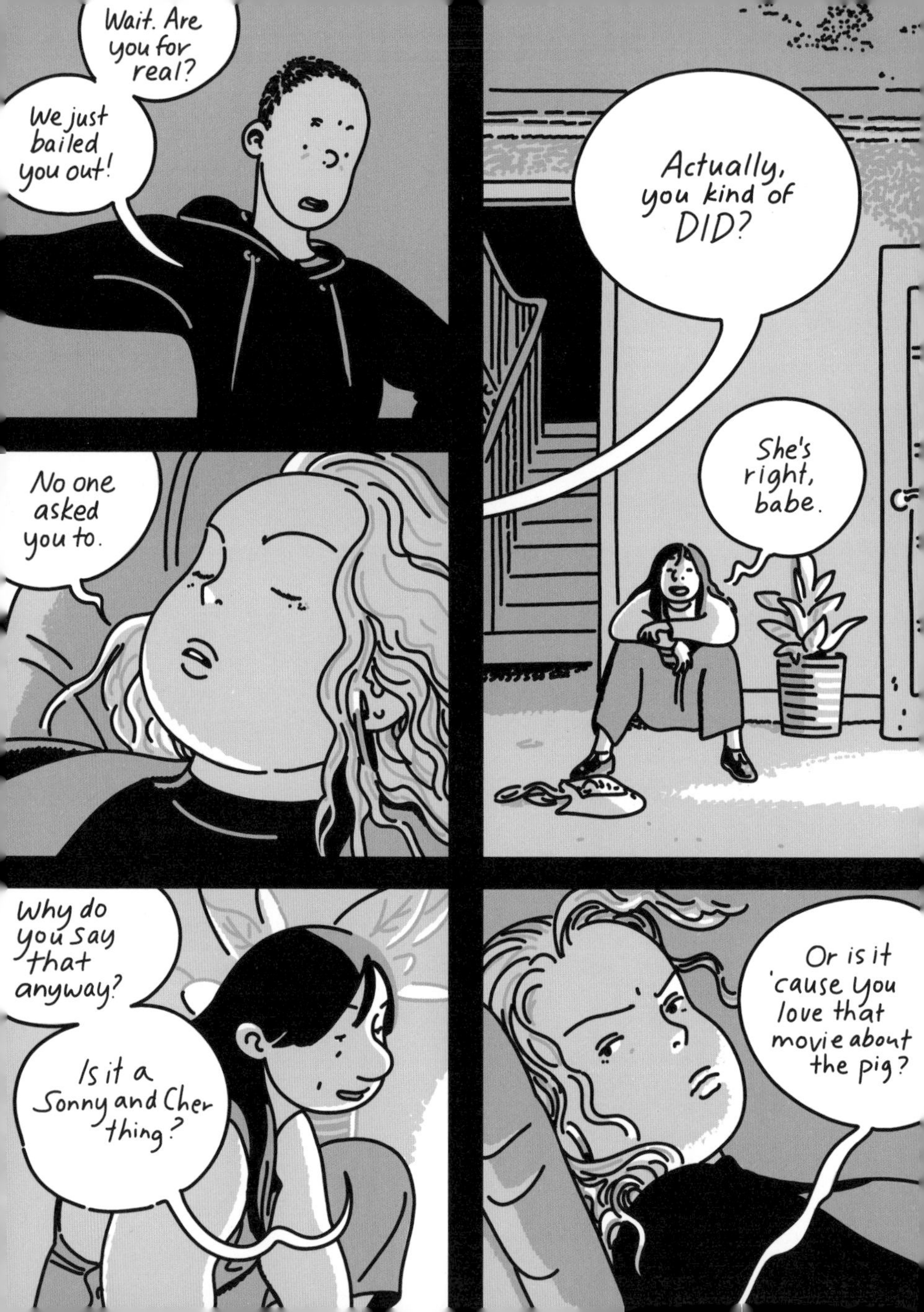
Wait. Are you for real?
We just bailed you out!
Actually, you kind of DID?
No one asked you to.
She's right, babe.
Why do you say that anyway?
Is it a Sonny and Cher thing?
Or is it 'cause you love that movie about the pig?

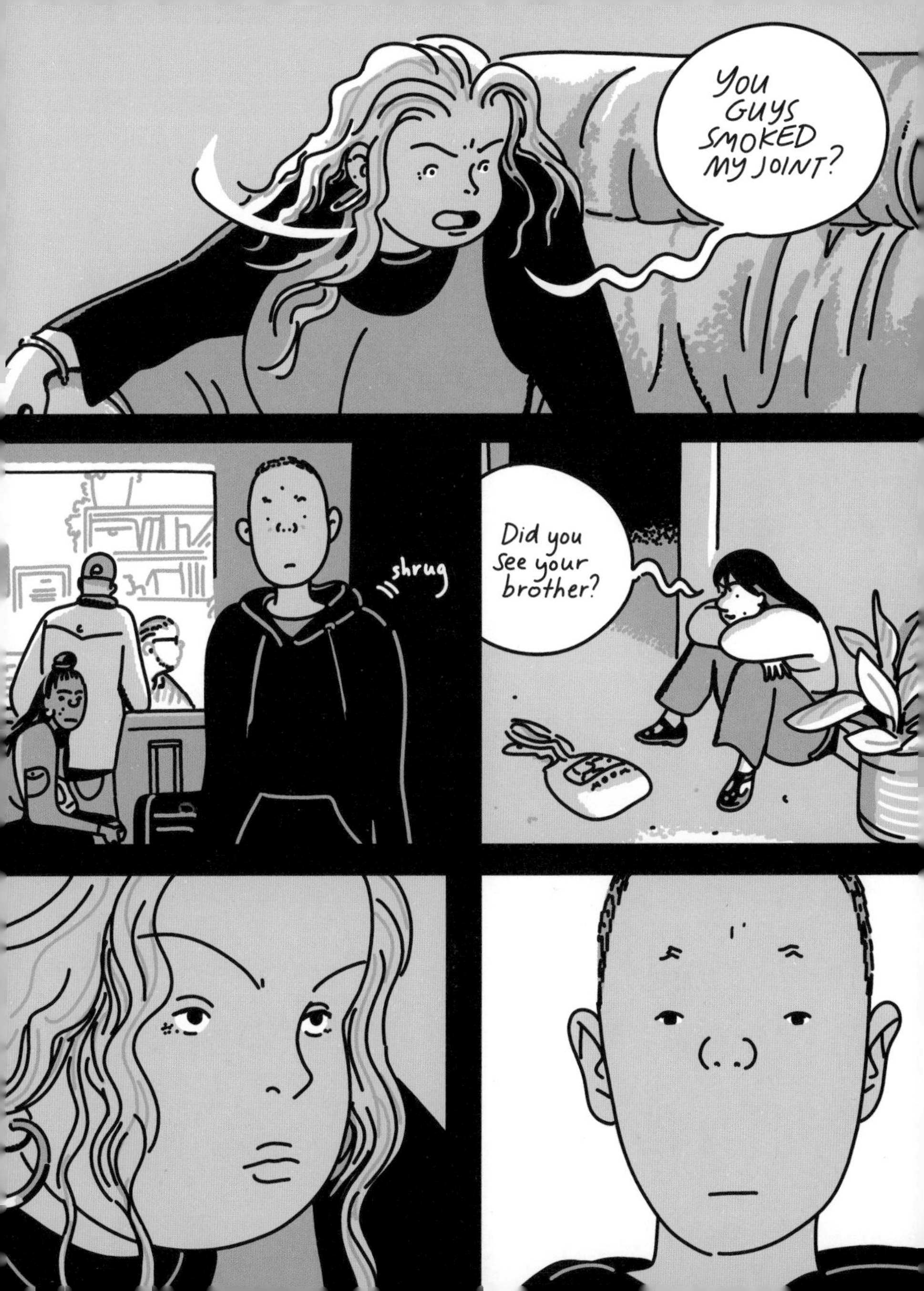
YOU GUYS SMOKED MY JOINT?
shrug
Did you see your brother?

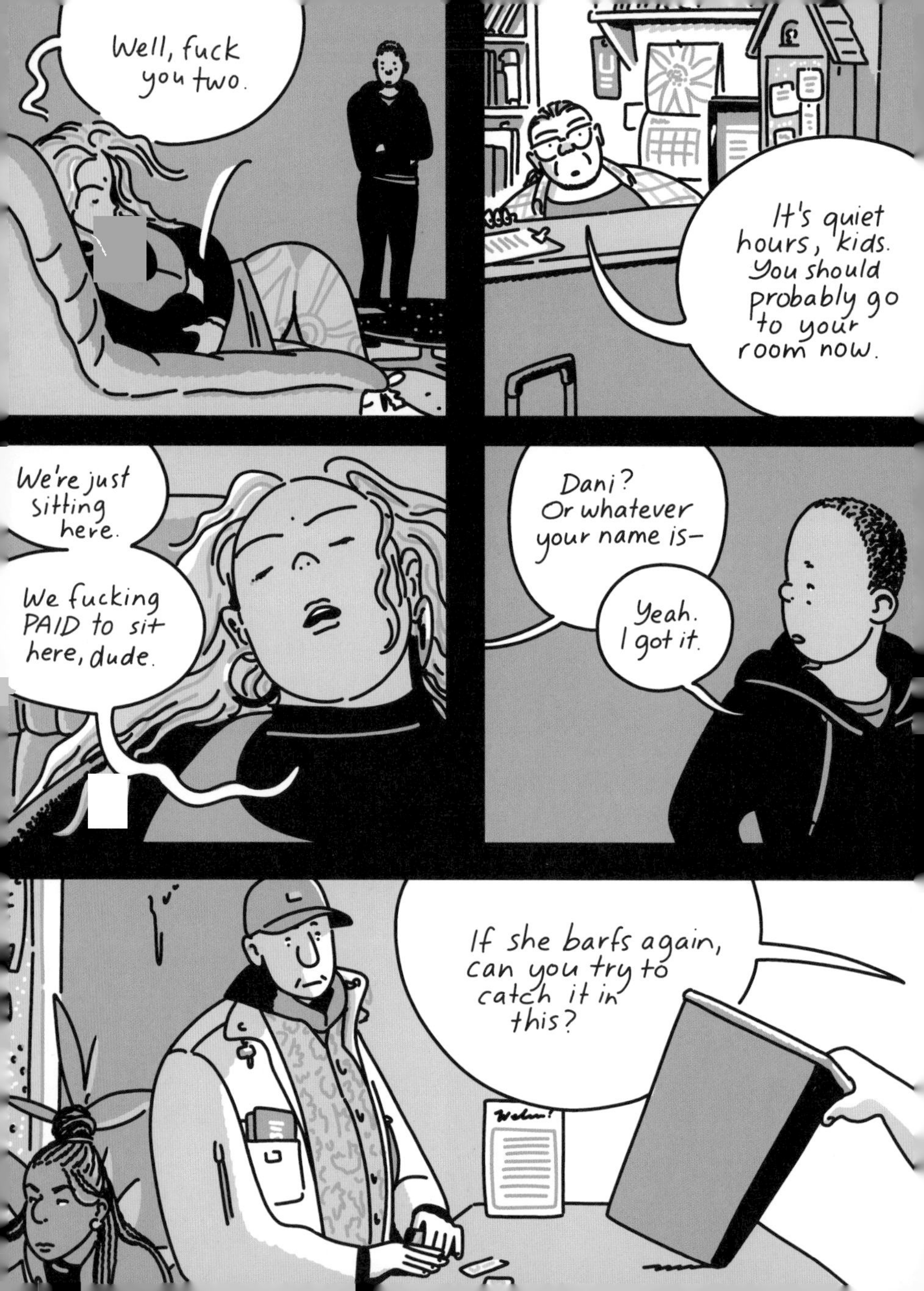
Well, fuck you two.
It's quiet hours, kids. You should probably go to your room now.
We're just sitting here.
We fucking PAID to sit here, dude.
Dani? Or whatever your name is–
Yeah. I got it.
If she barfs again, can you try to catch it in this?

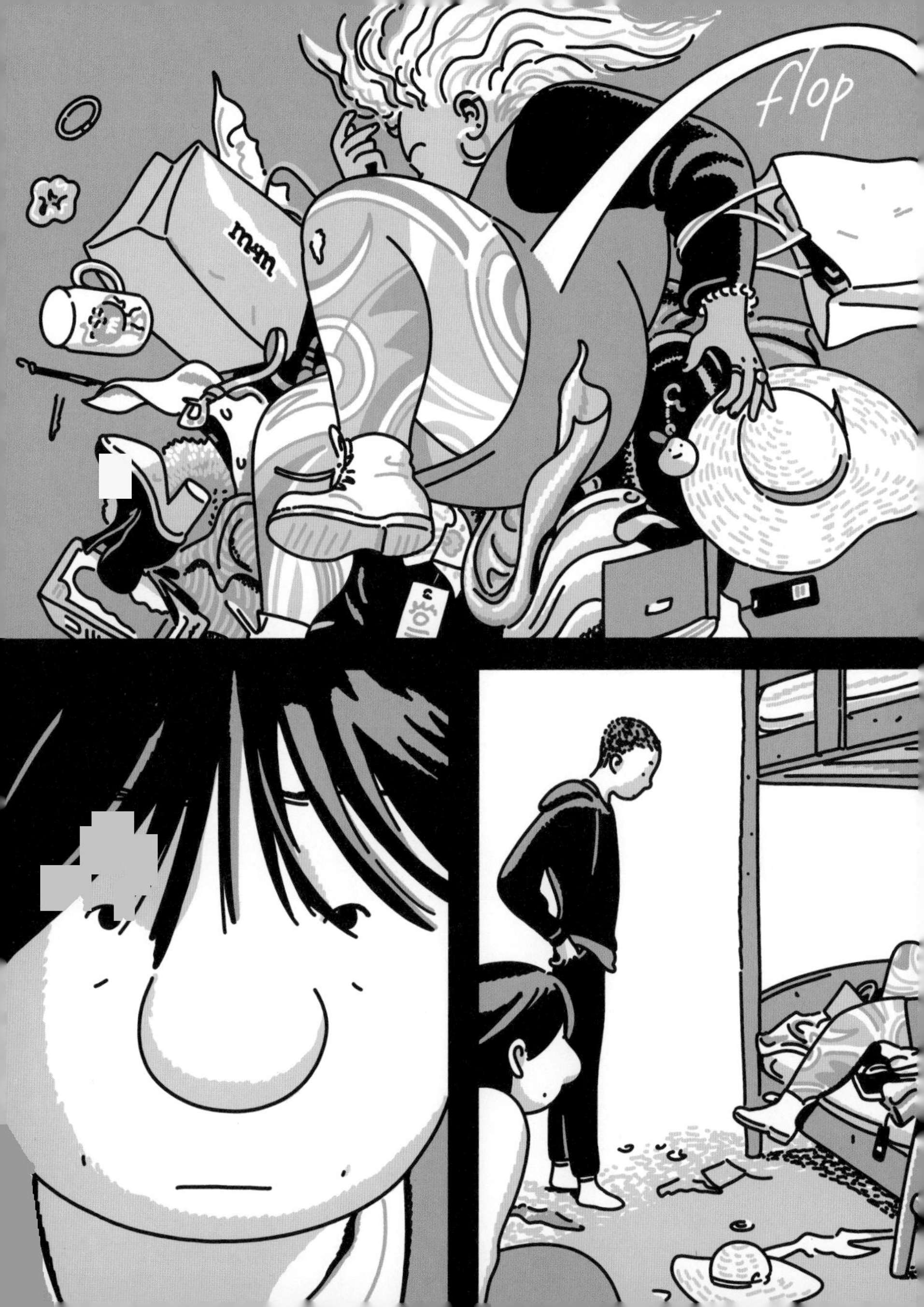
flop
m4m

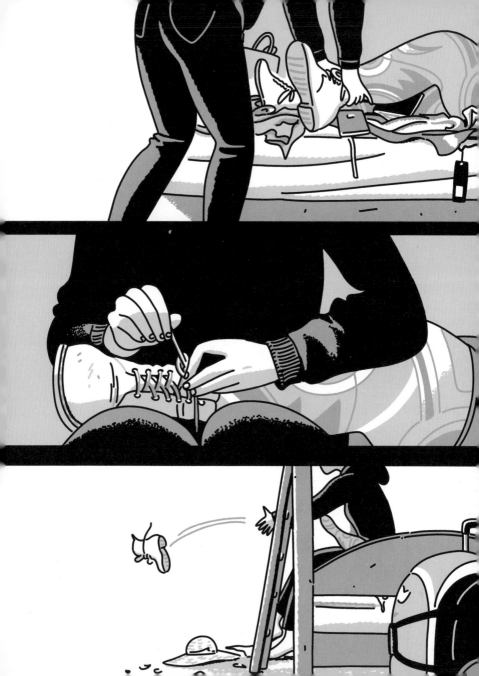

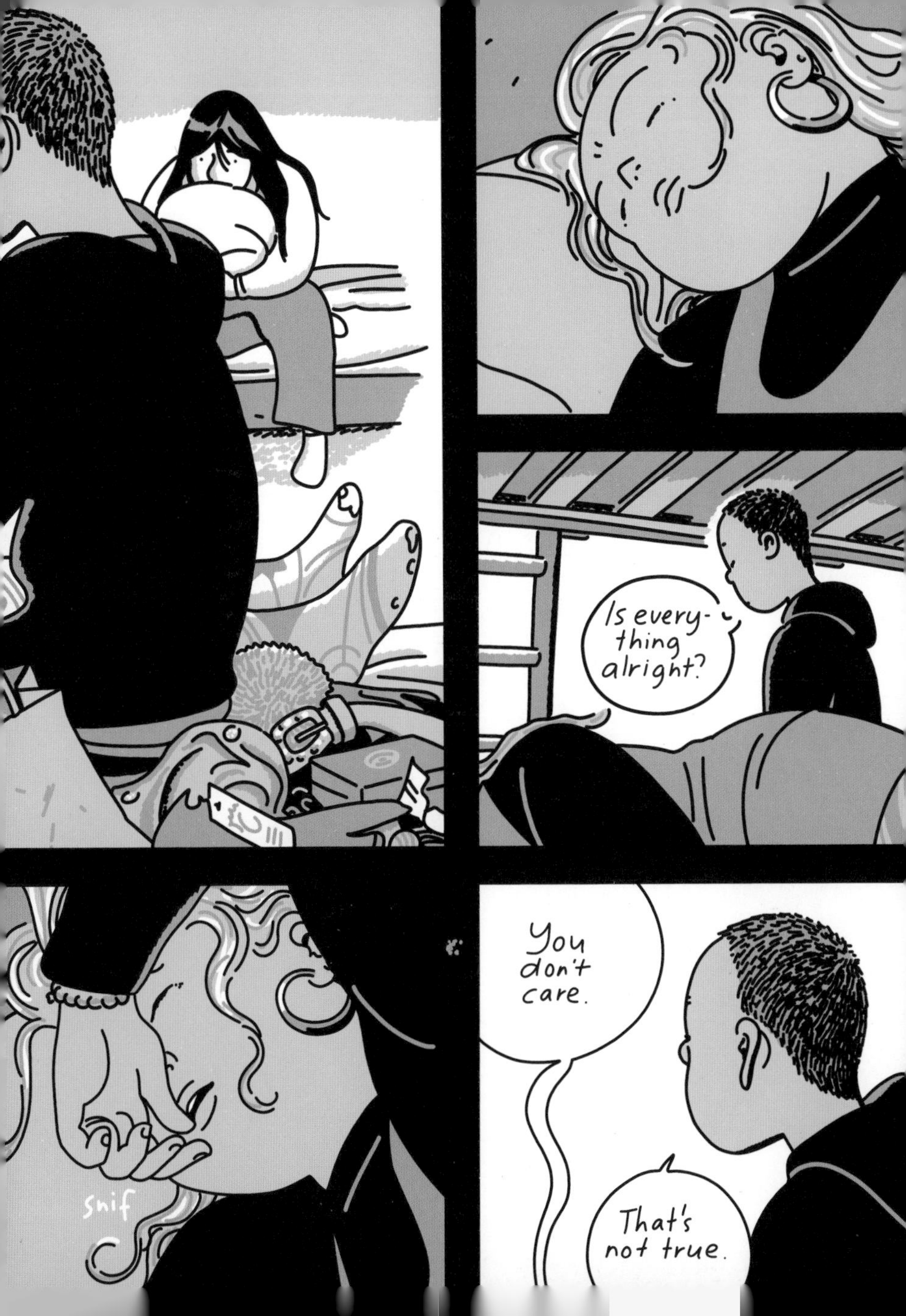
Is every-thing alright?
snif
You don't care.
That's not true.

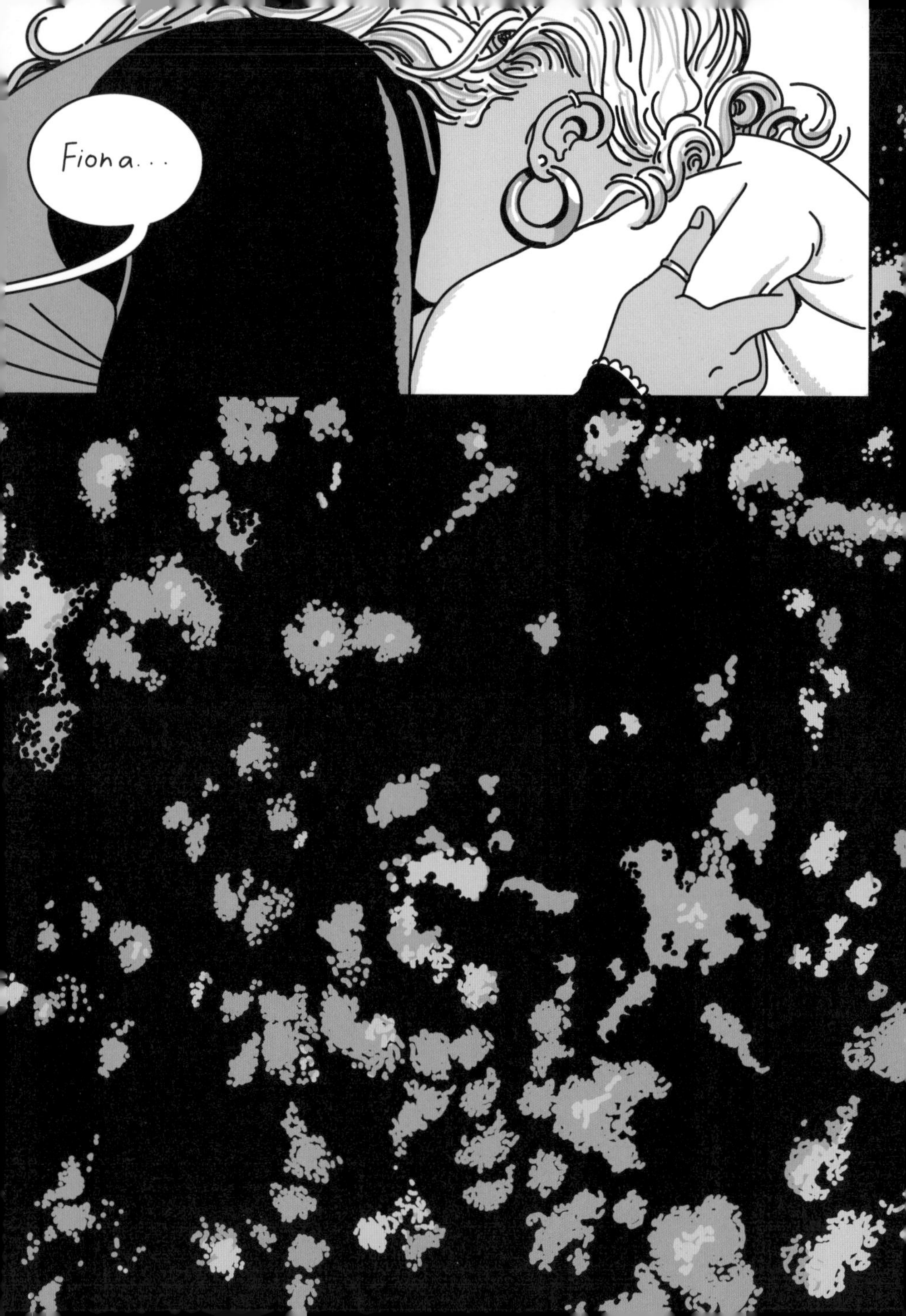
Fiona...

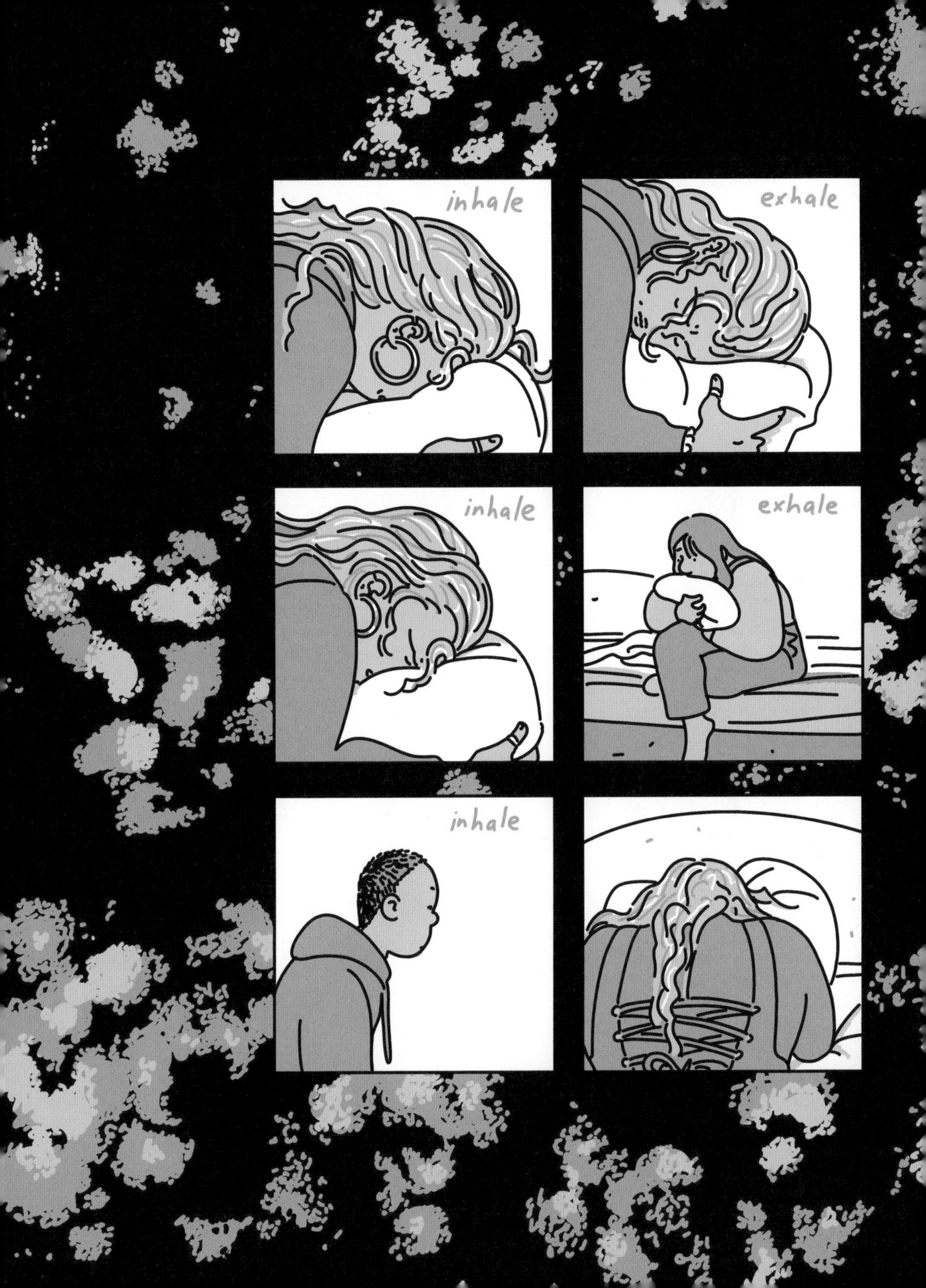
inhale
exhale
inhale
exhale
inhale

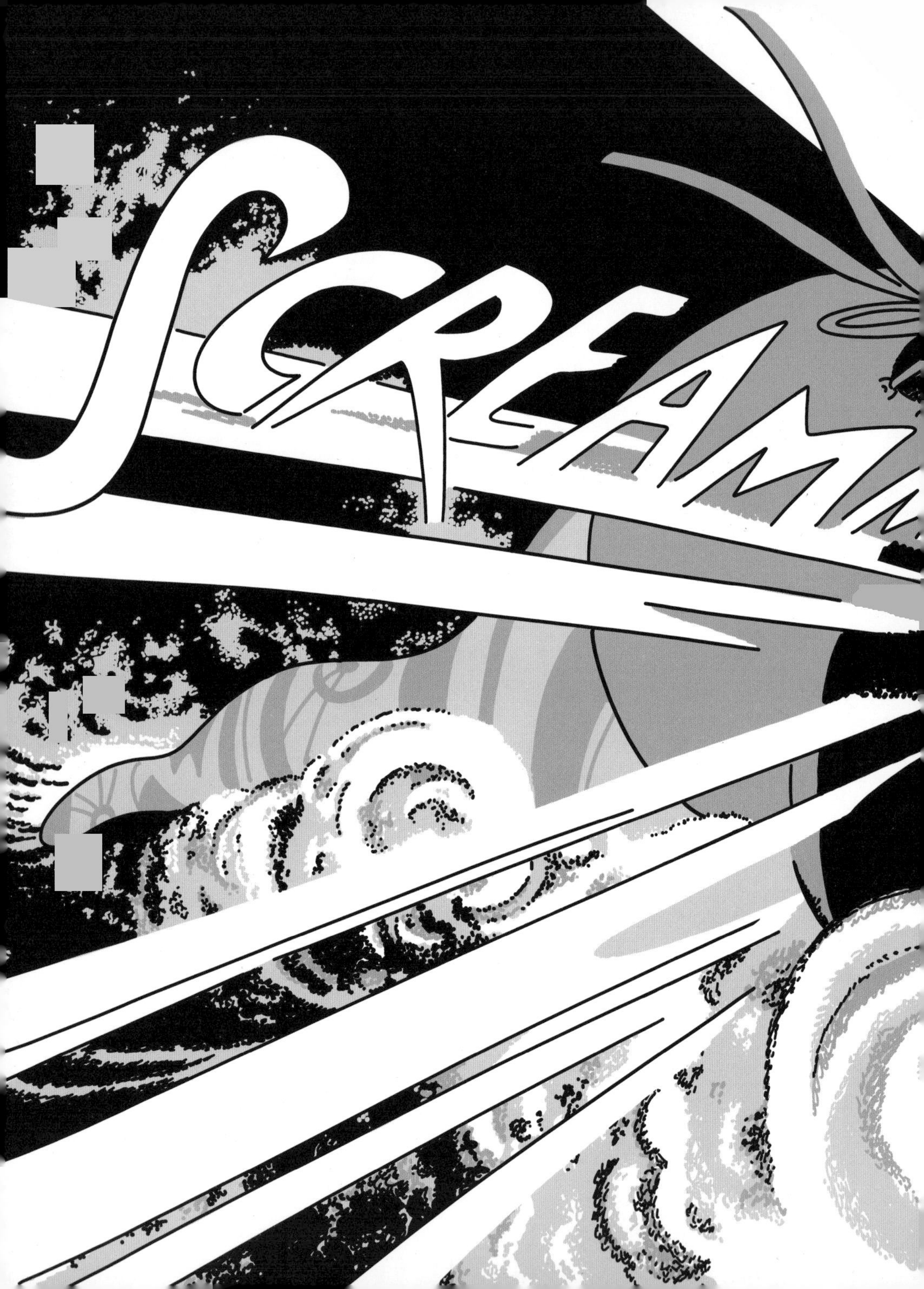
SCREAM

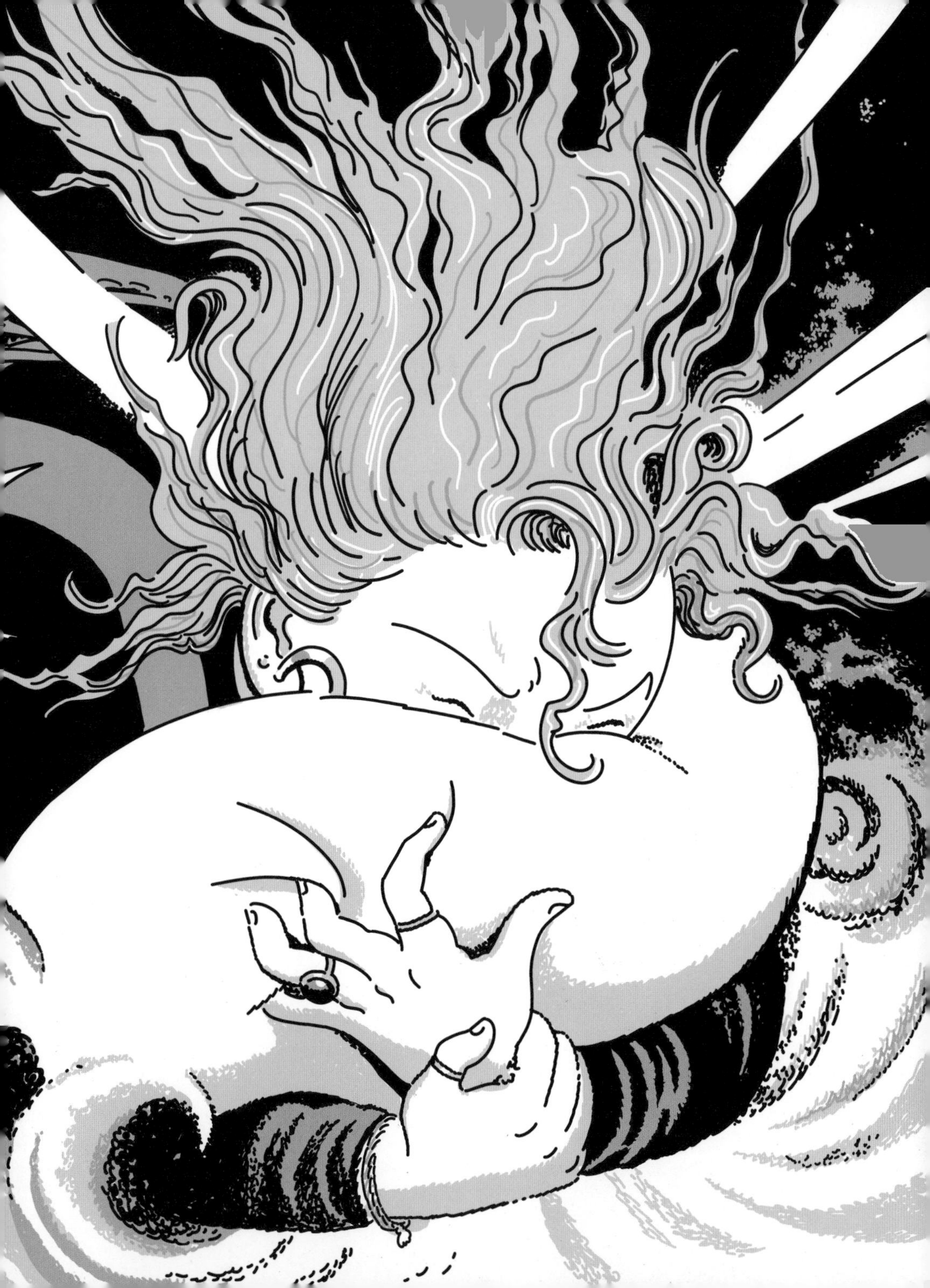

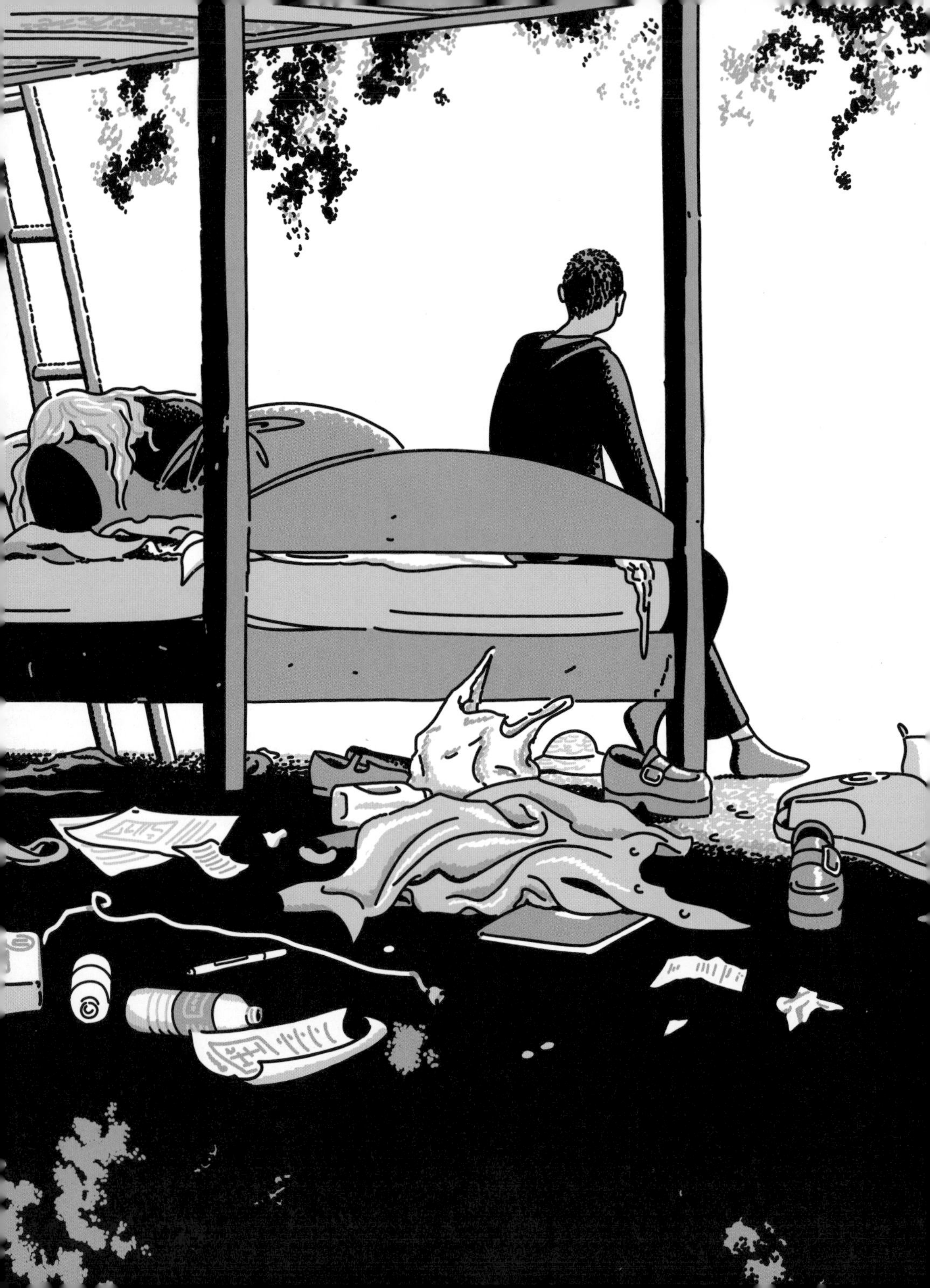

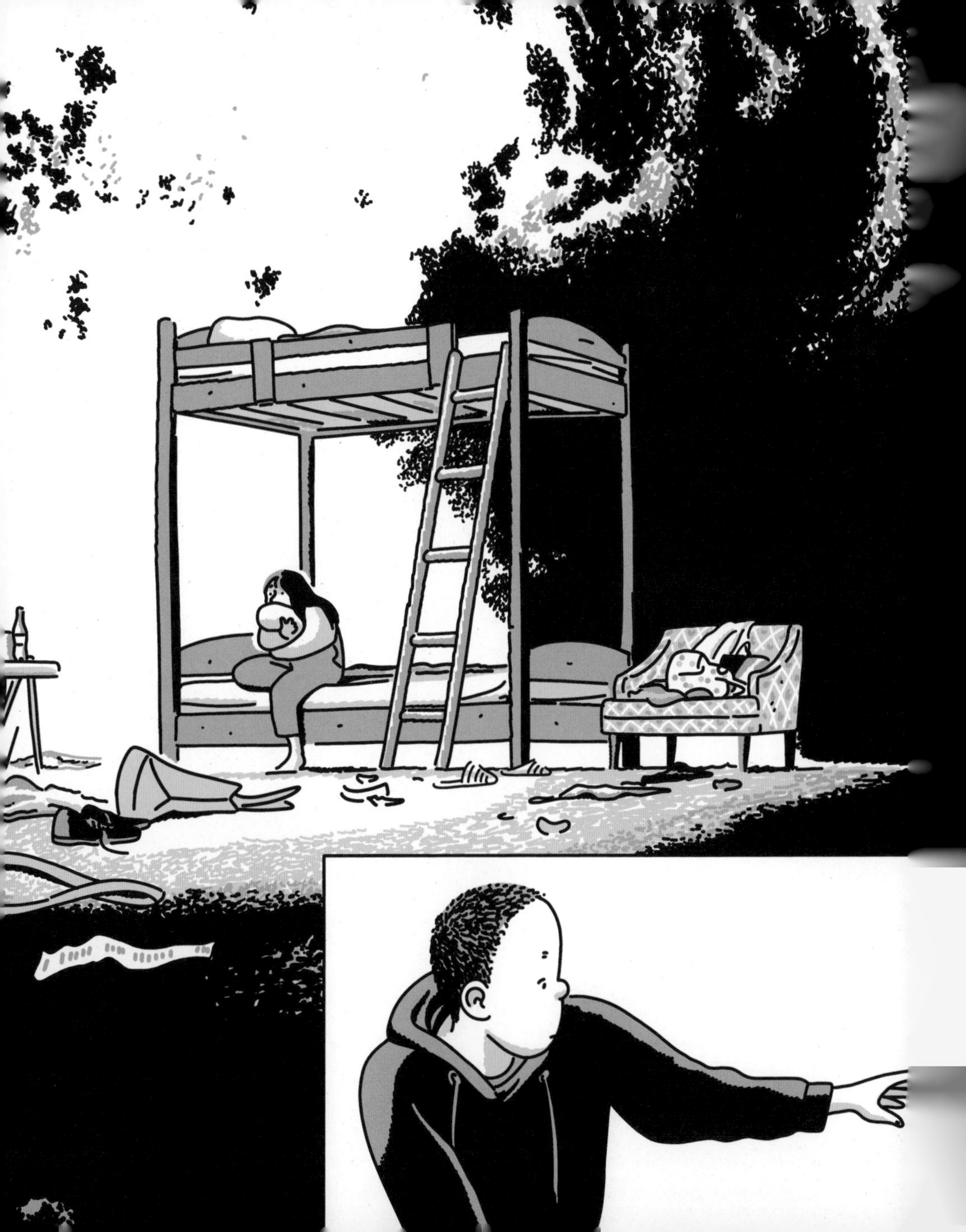

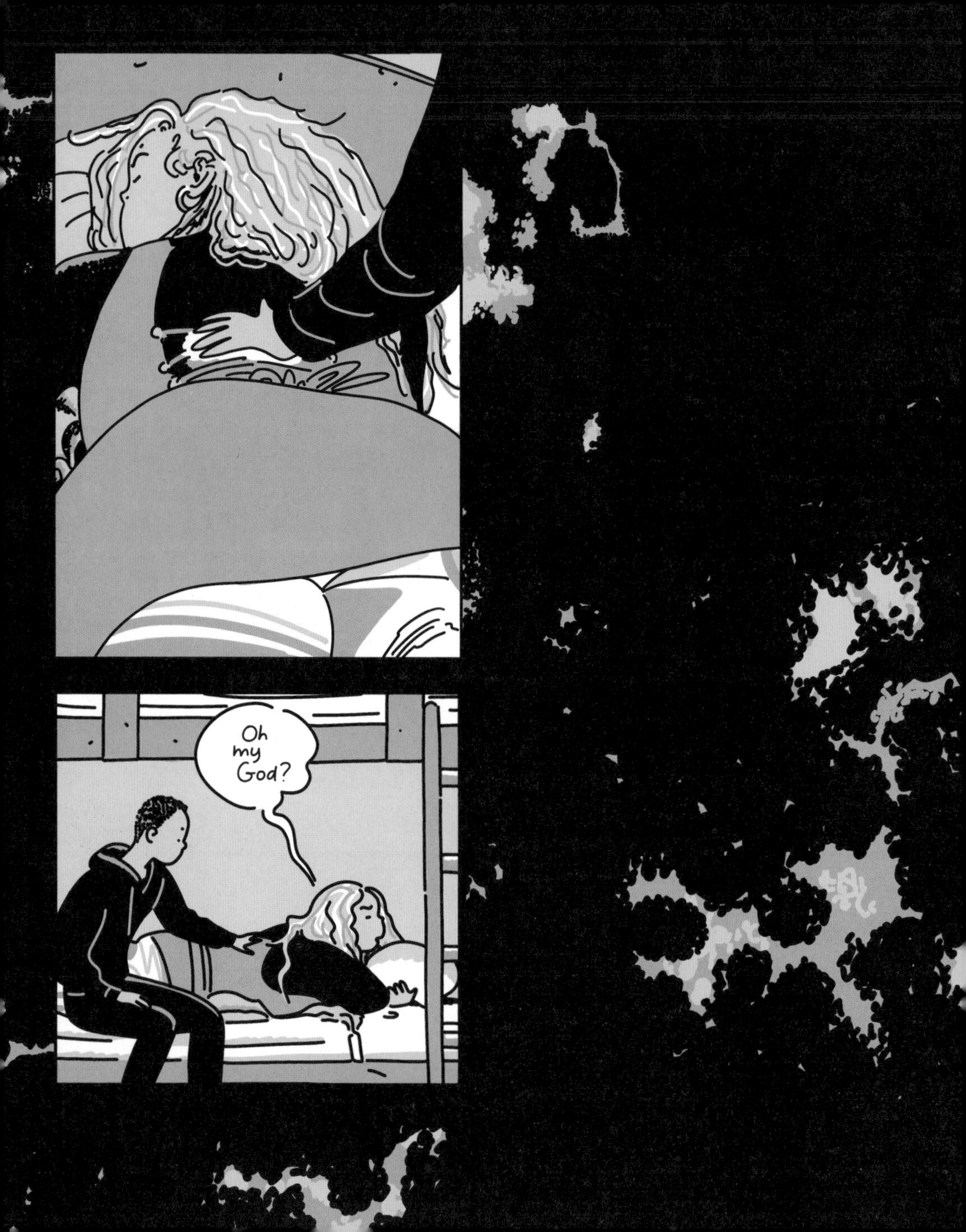
Oh my God?

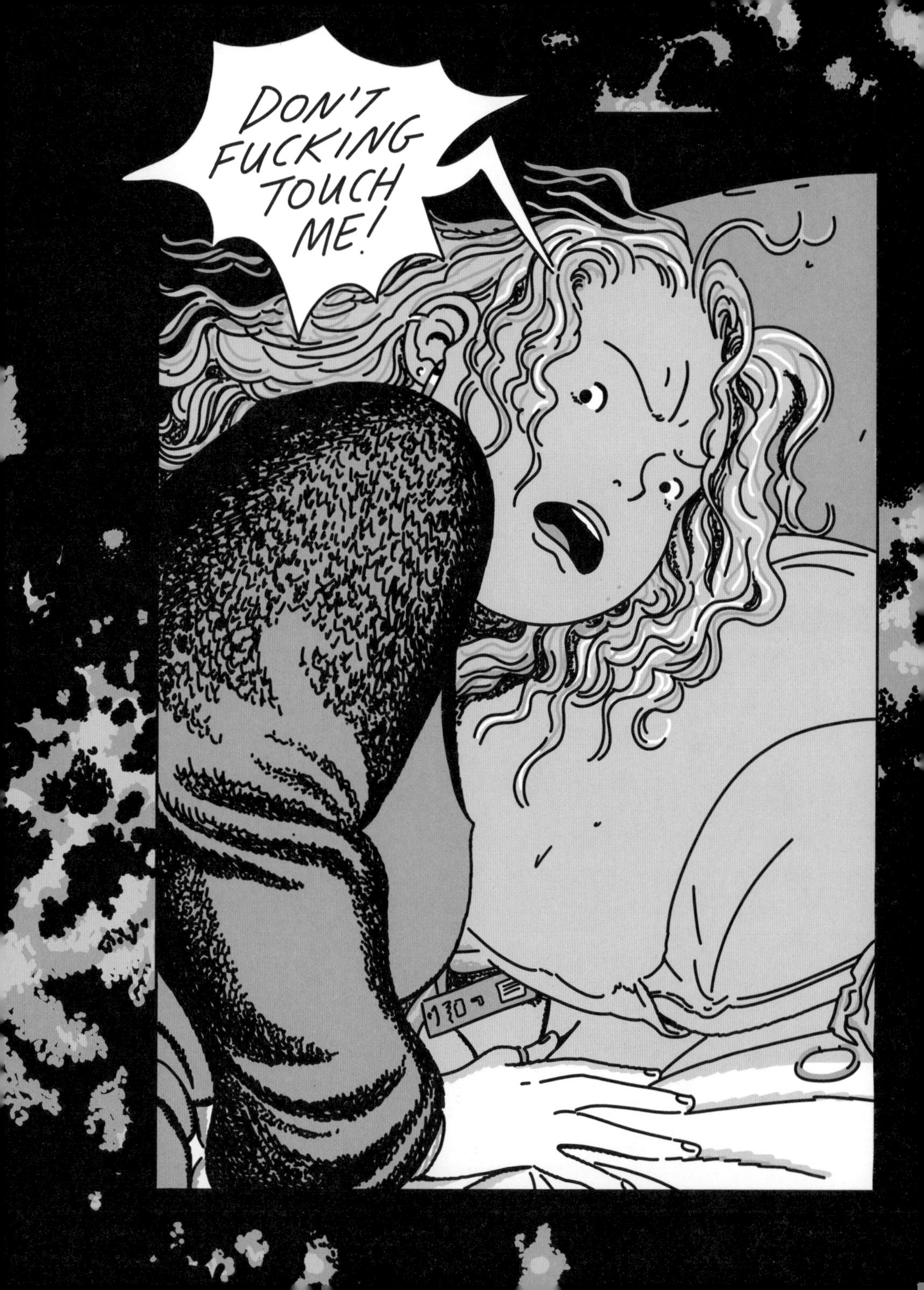
DON'T FUCKING TOUCH ME!

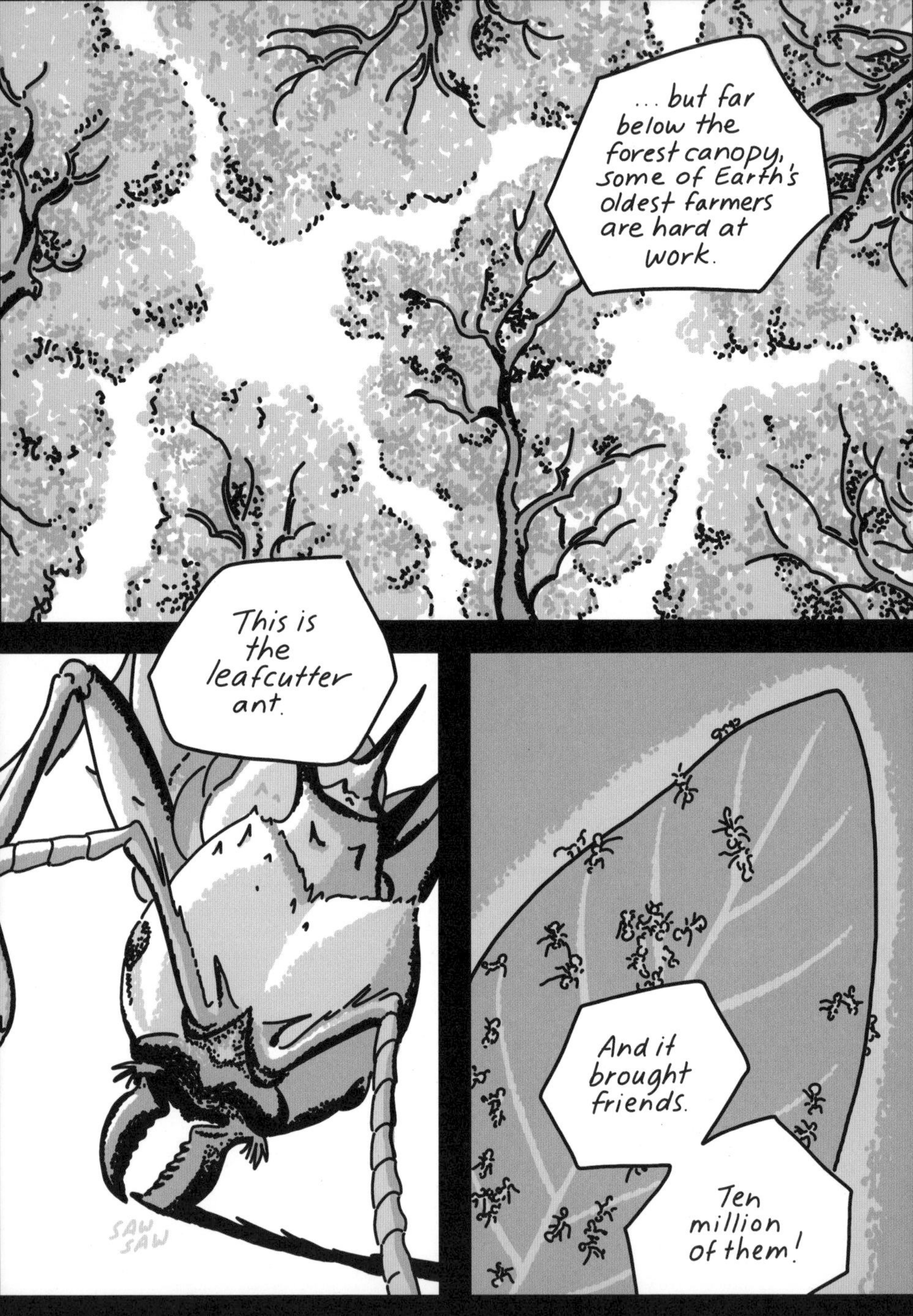
... but far below the forest canopy, some of Earth's oldest farmers are hard at work.
This is the leafcutter ant.
SAW SAW
And it brought friends.
Ten million of them!

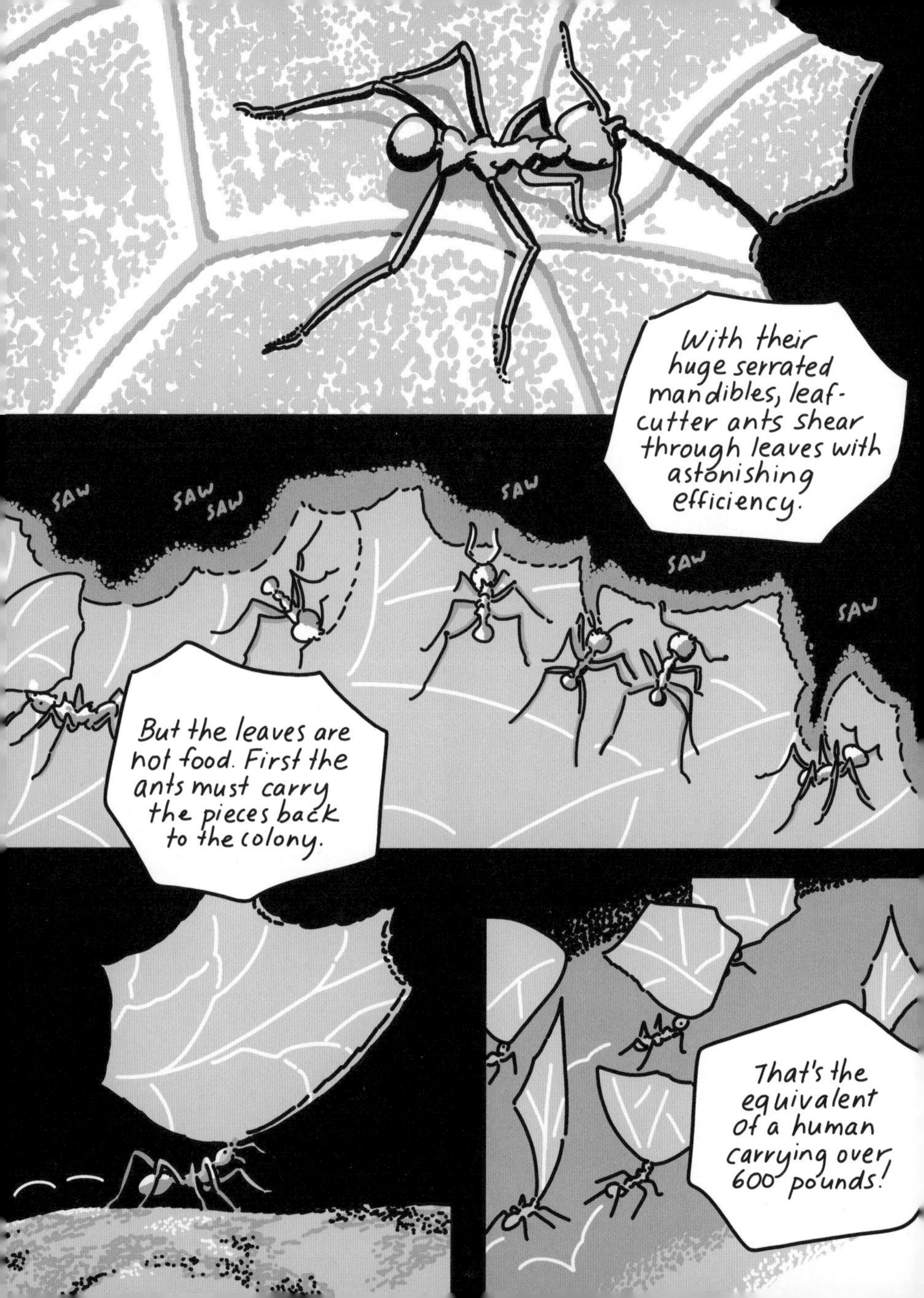
With their huge serrated mandibles, leaf-cutter ants shear through leaves with astonishing efficiency.
SAW
SAW
SAW
SAW
SAW
SAW
But the leaves are not food. First the ants must carry the pieces back to the colony.
That's the equivalent of a human carrying over 600 pounds!

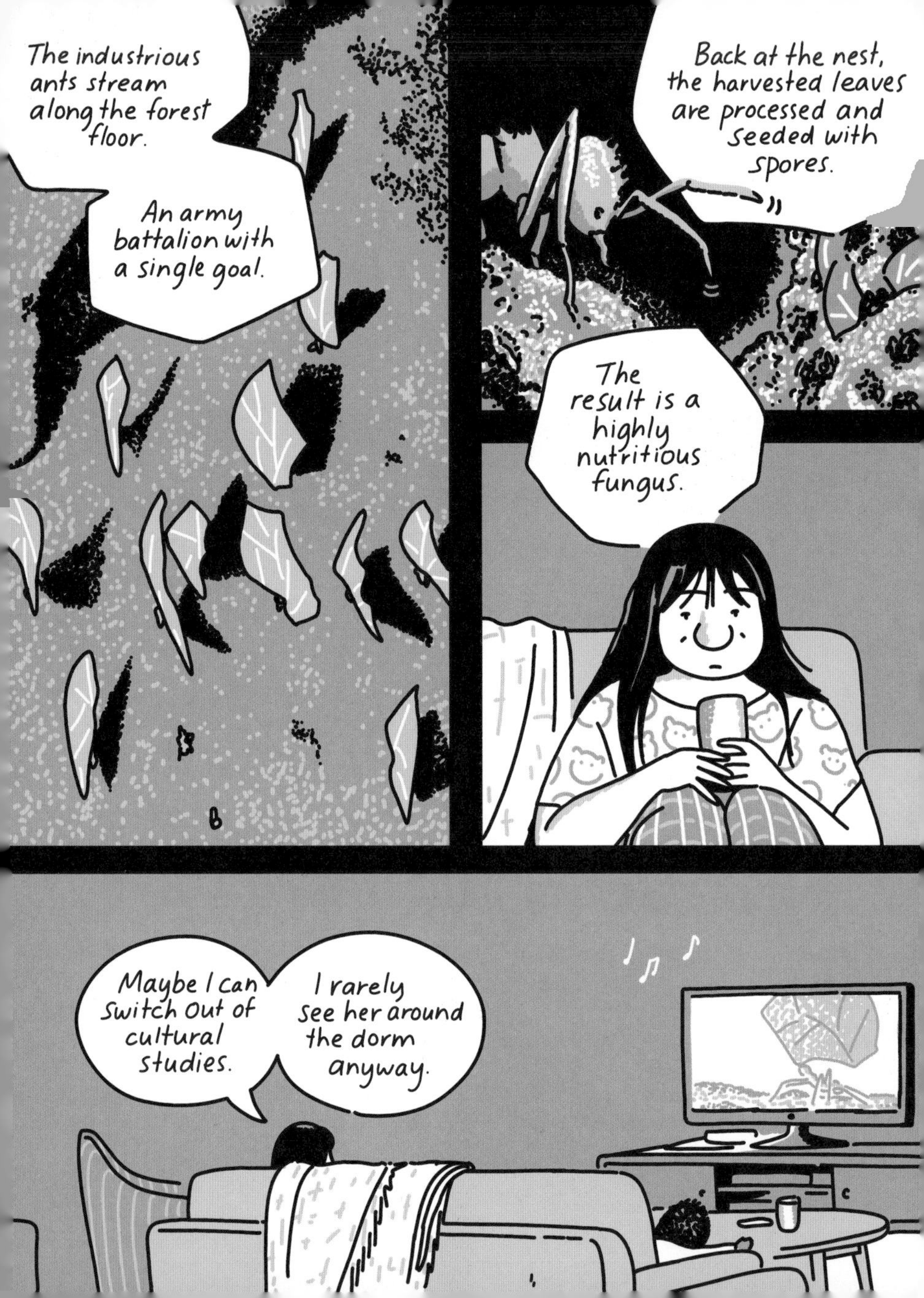
The industrious ants stream along the forest floor.
An army battalion with a single goal.
Back at the nest, the harvested leaves are processed and seeded with spores.
The result is a highly nutritious fungus.
Maybe I can switch out of cultural studies.
I rarely see her around the dorm anyway.

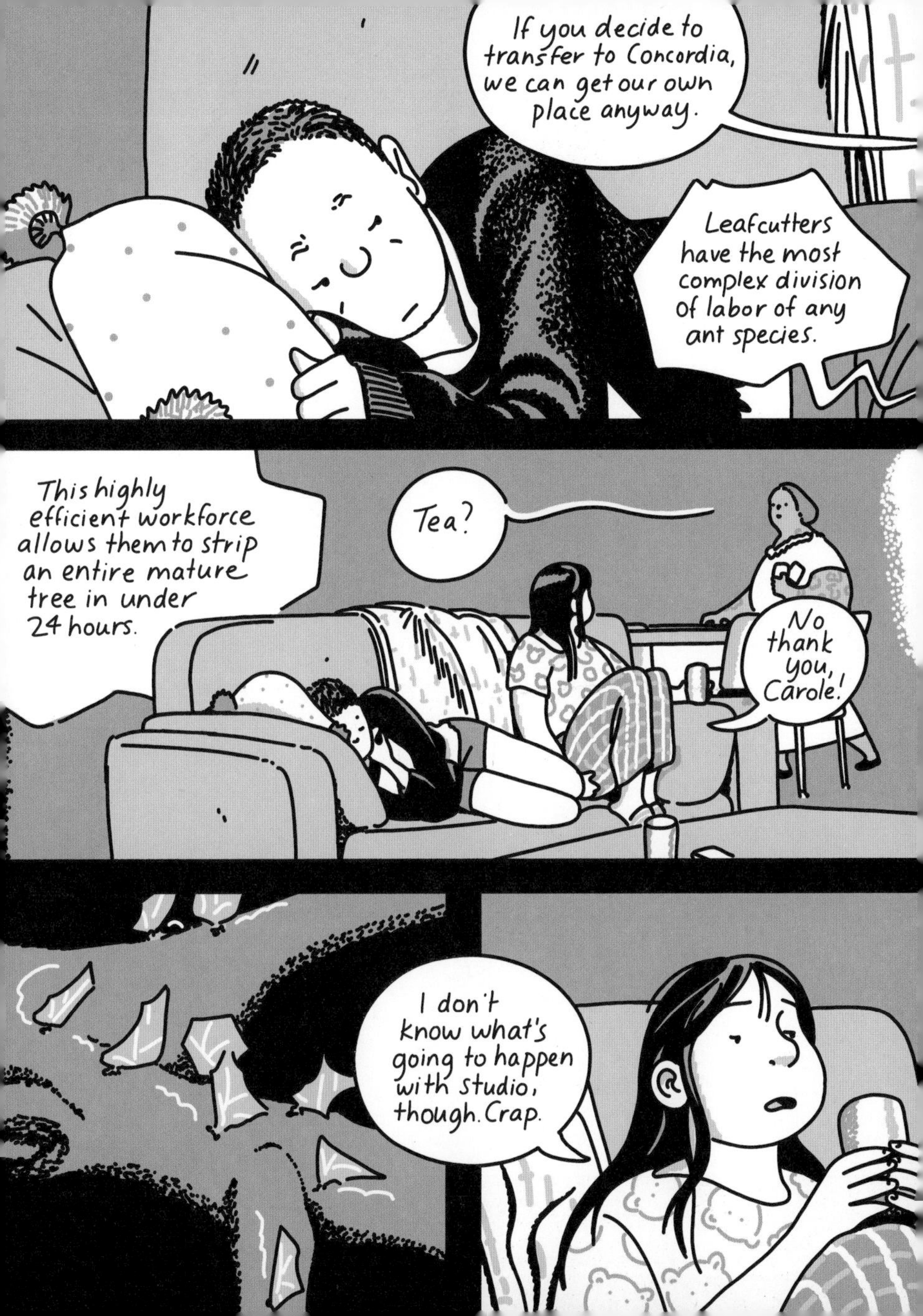
If you decide to transfer to Concordia, we can get our own place anyway.
Leafcutters have the most complex division of labor of any ant species.
This highly efficient workforce allows them to strip an entire mature tree in under 24 hours.
Tea?
No thank you, Carole!
I don't know what's going to happen with studio, though. Crap.

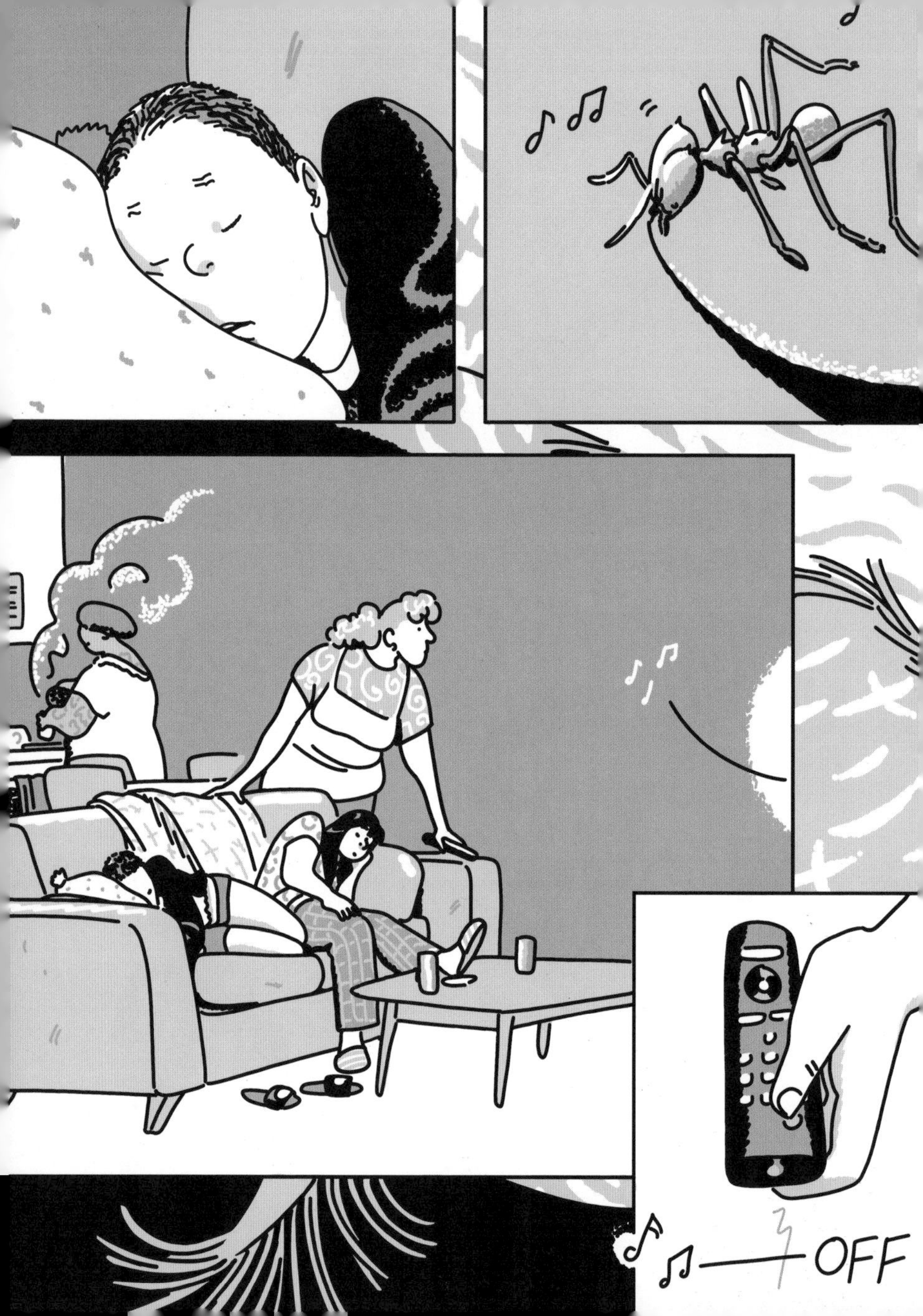
OFF

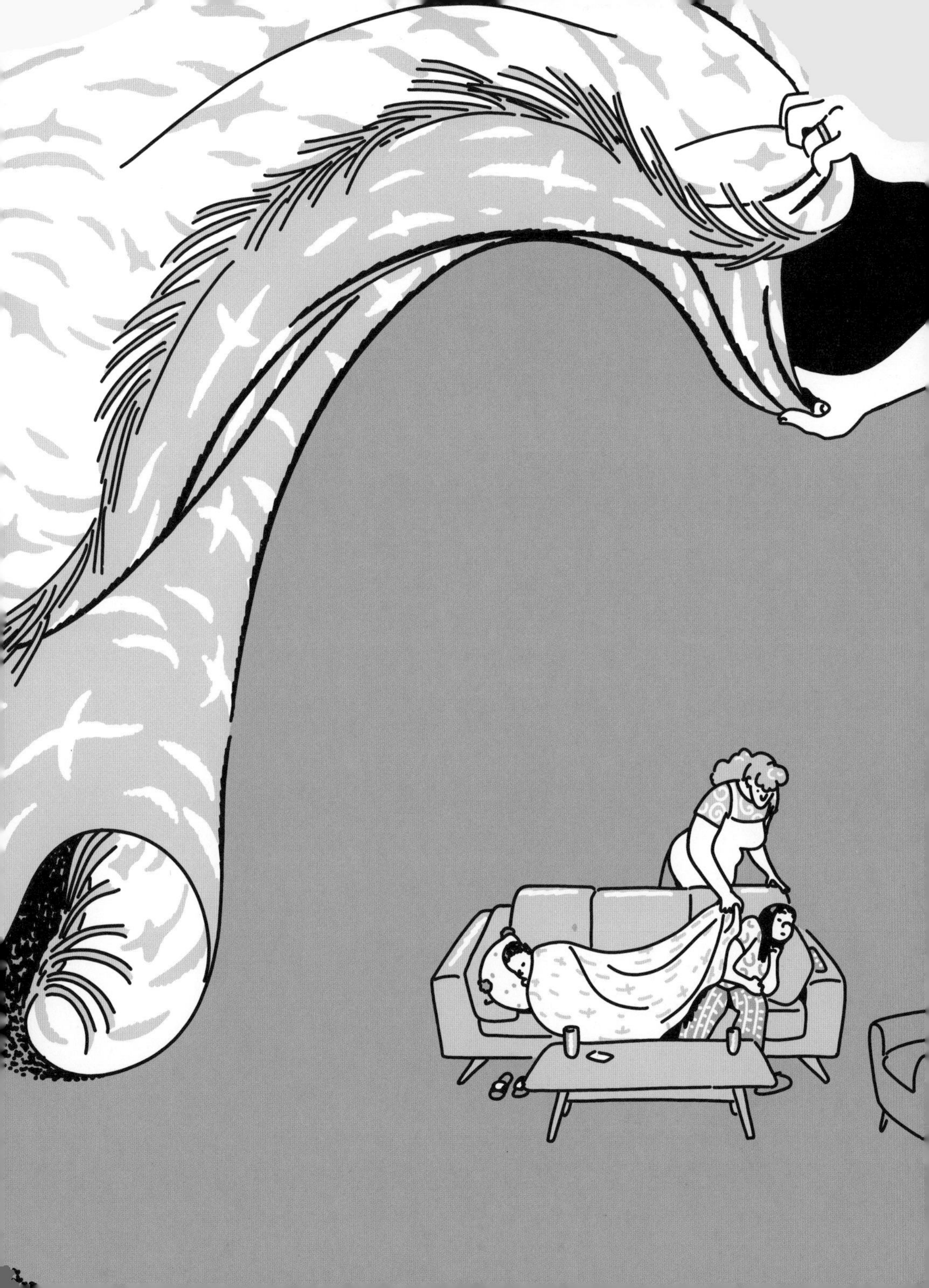

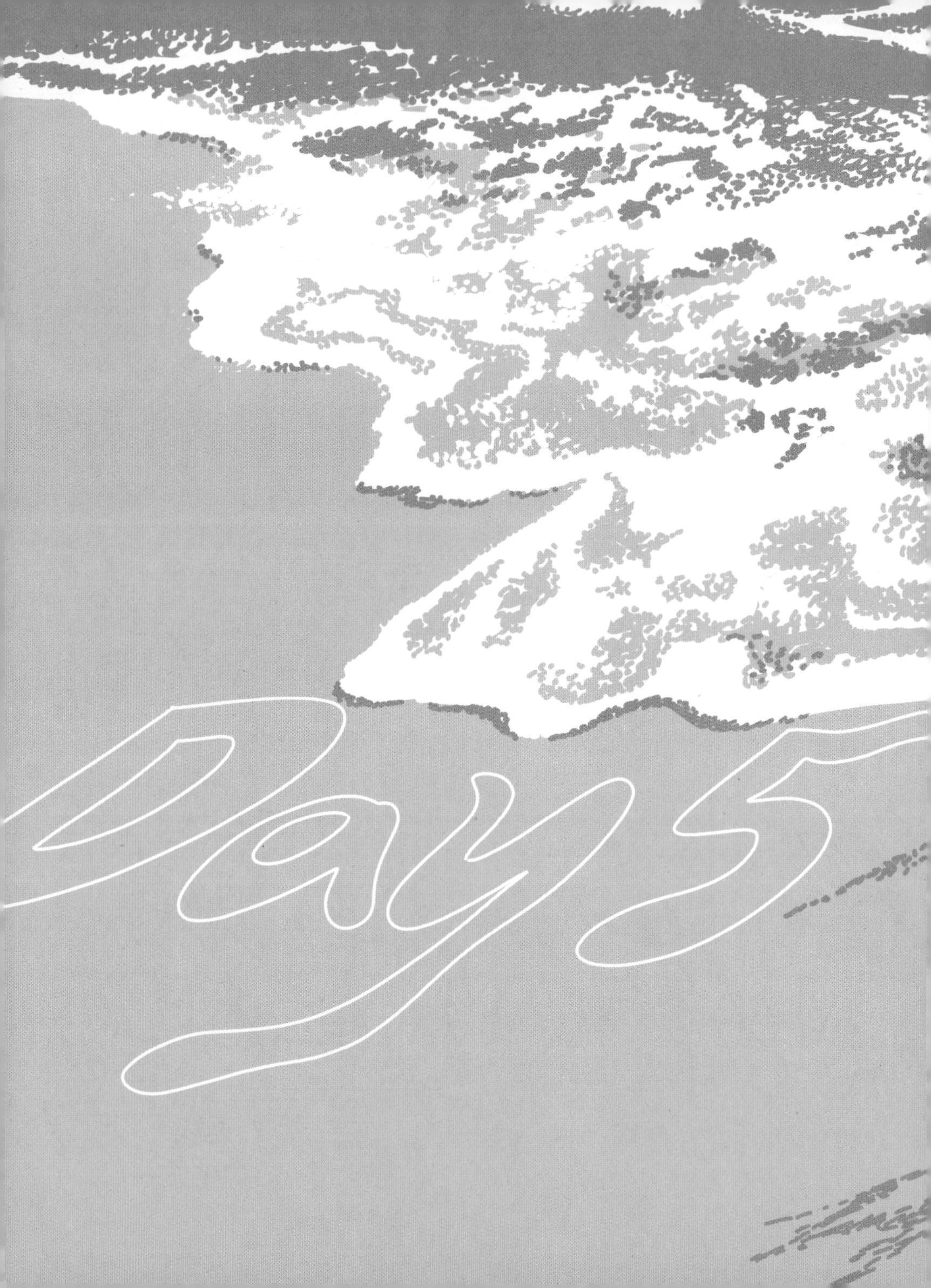
Day 5

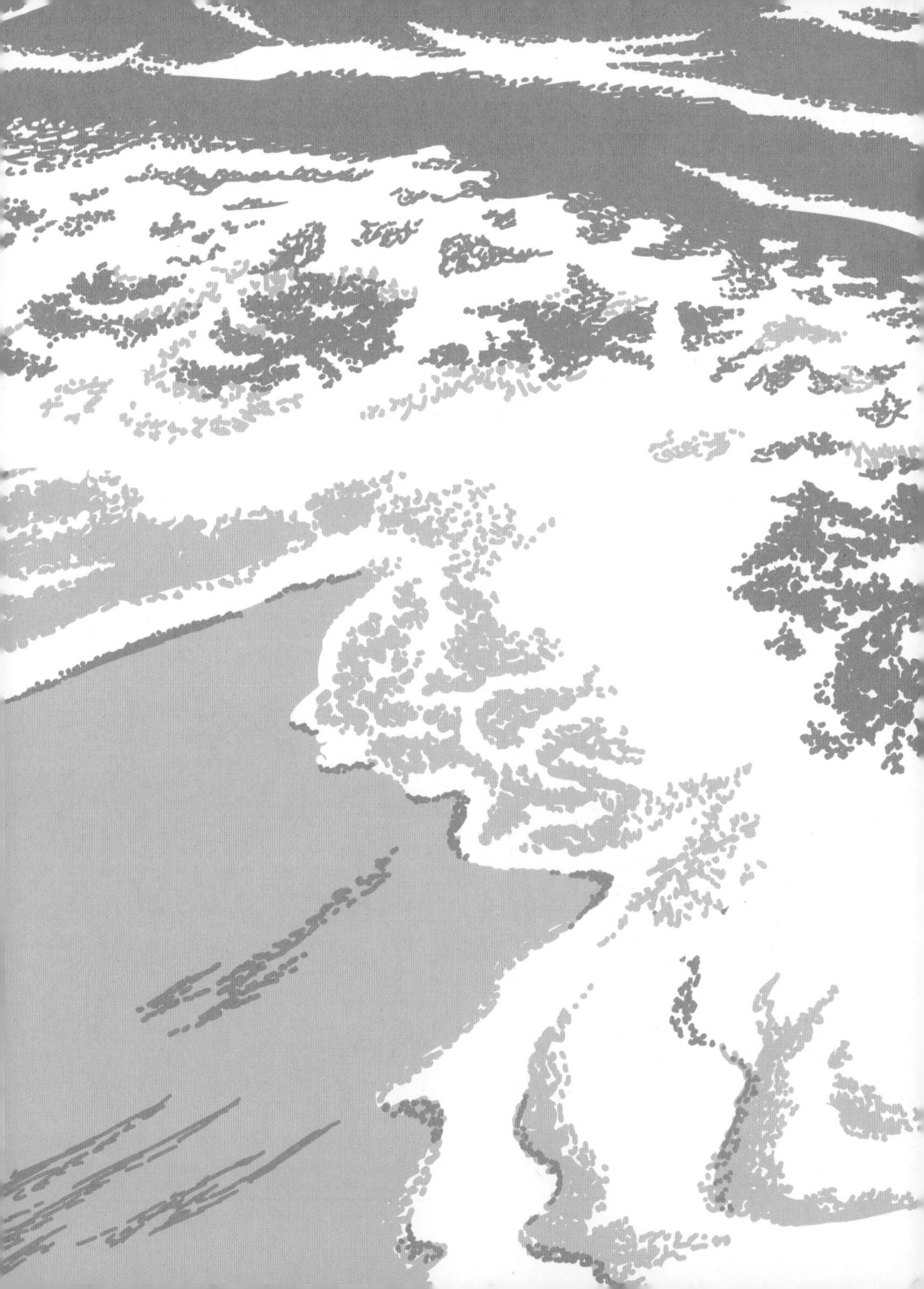

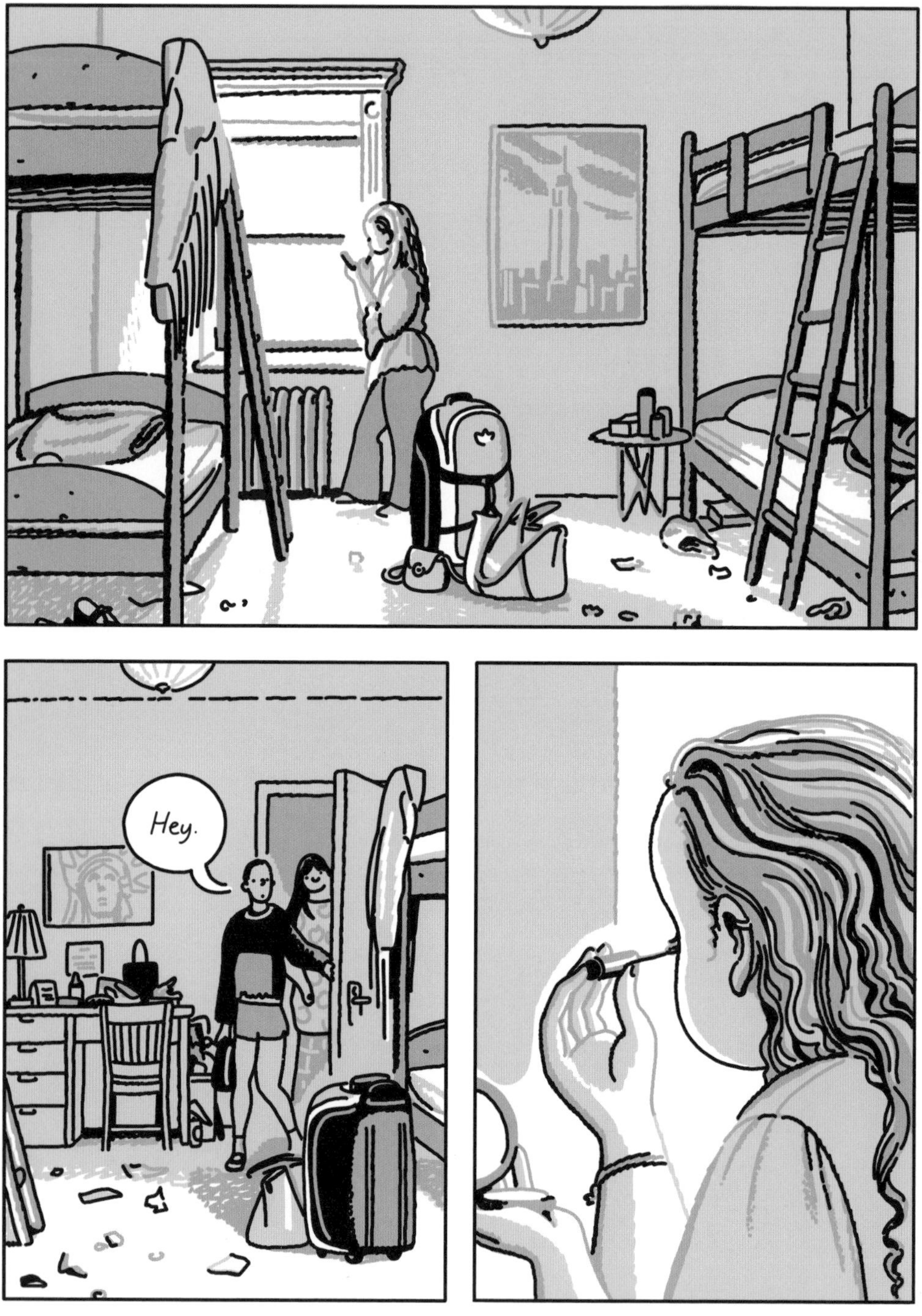
Hey.

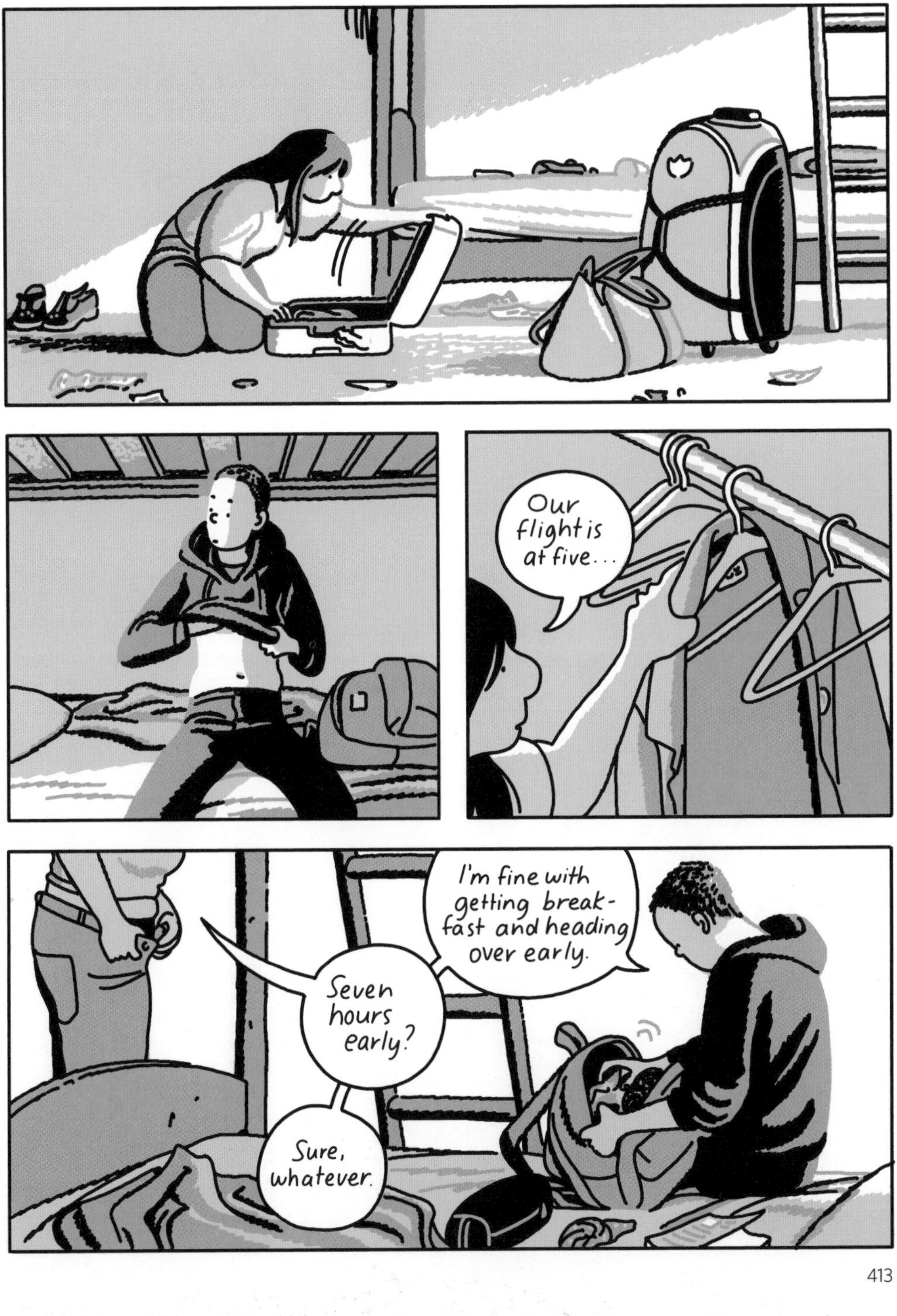
Our flight is at five...
I'm fine with getting breakfast and heading over early.
Seven hours early?
Sure, whatever.

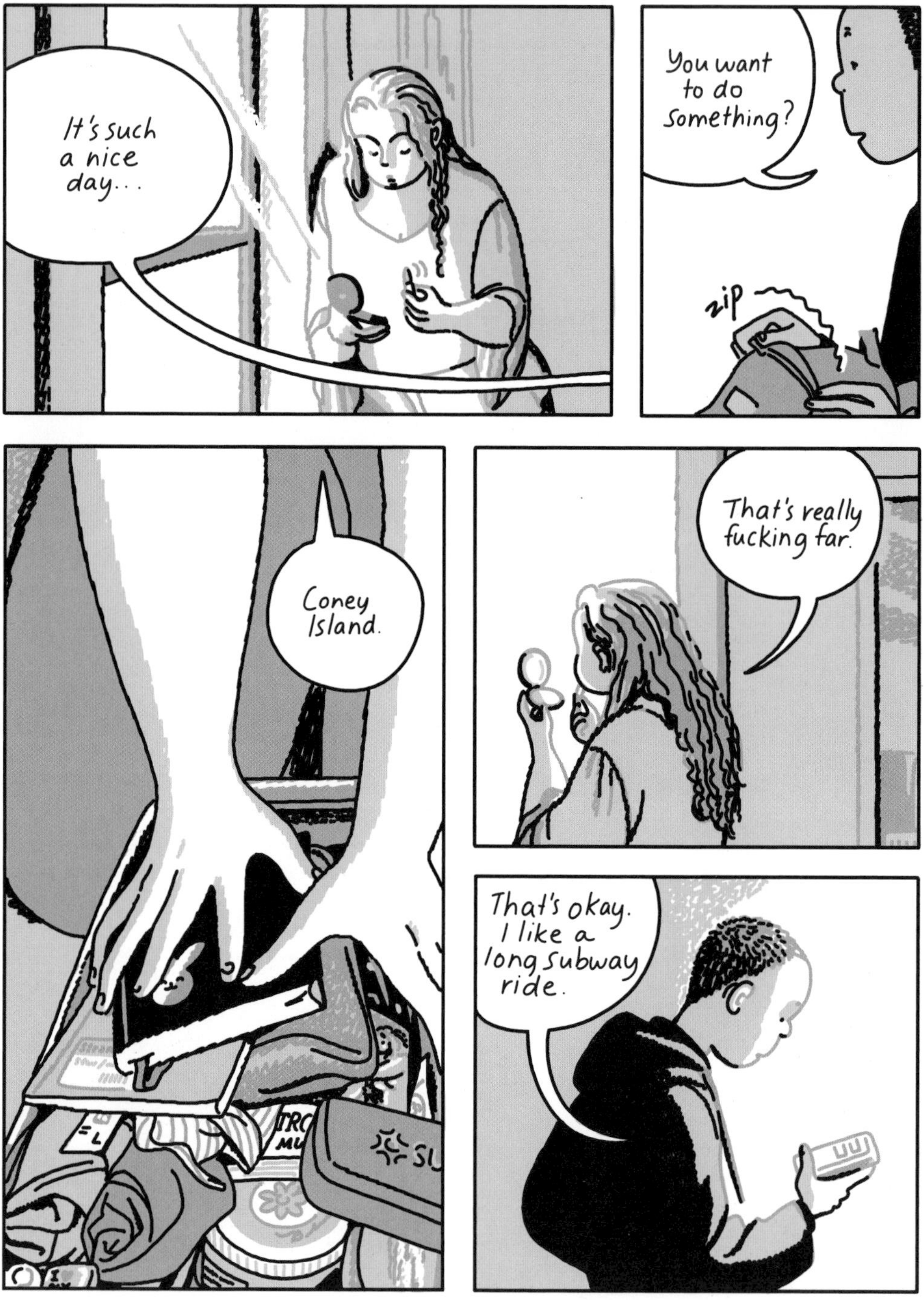
It's such a nice day...
You want to do something?
zip
Coney Island.
That's really fucking far.
That's okay. I like a long subway ride.

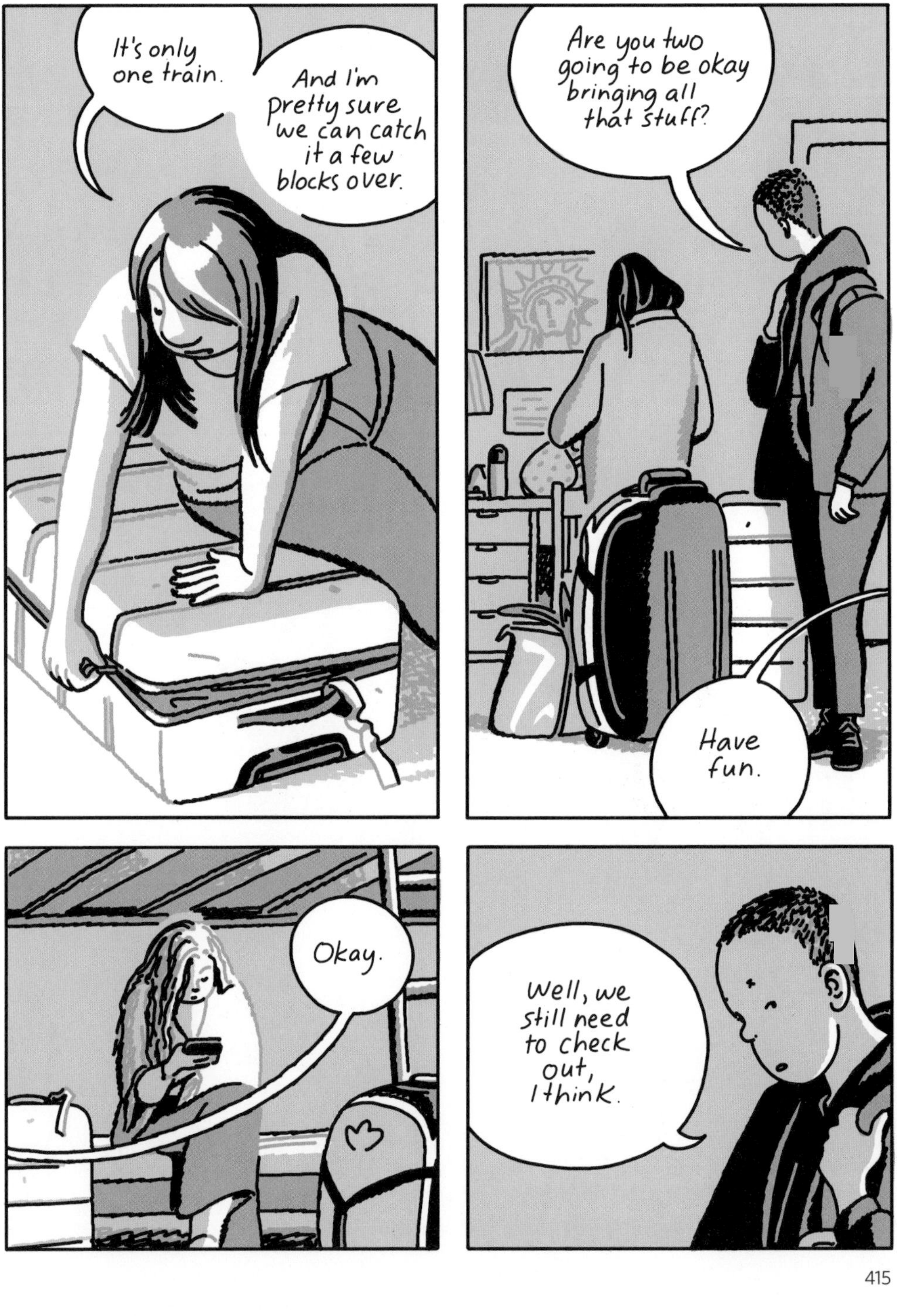
It's only one train.
And I'm pretty sure we can catch it a few blocks over.
Are you two going to be okay bringing all that stuff?
Have fun.
Okay.
Well, we still need to check out, I think.

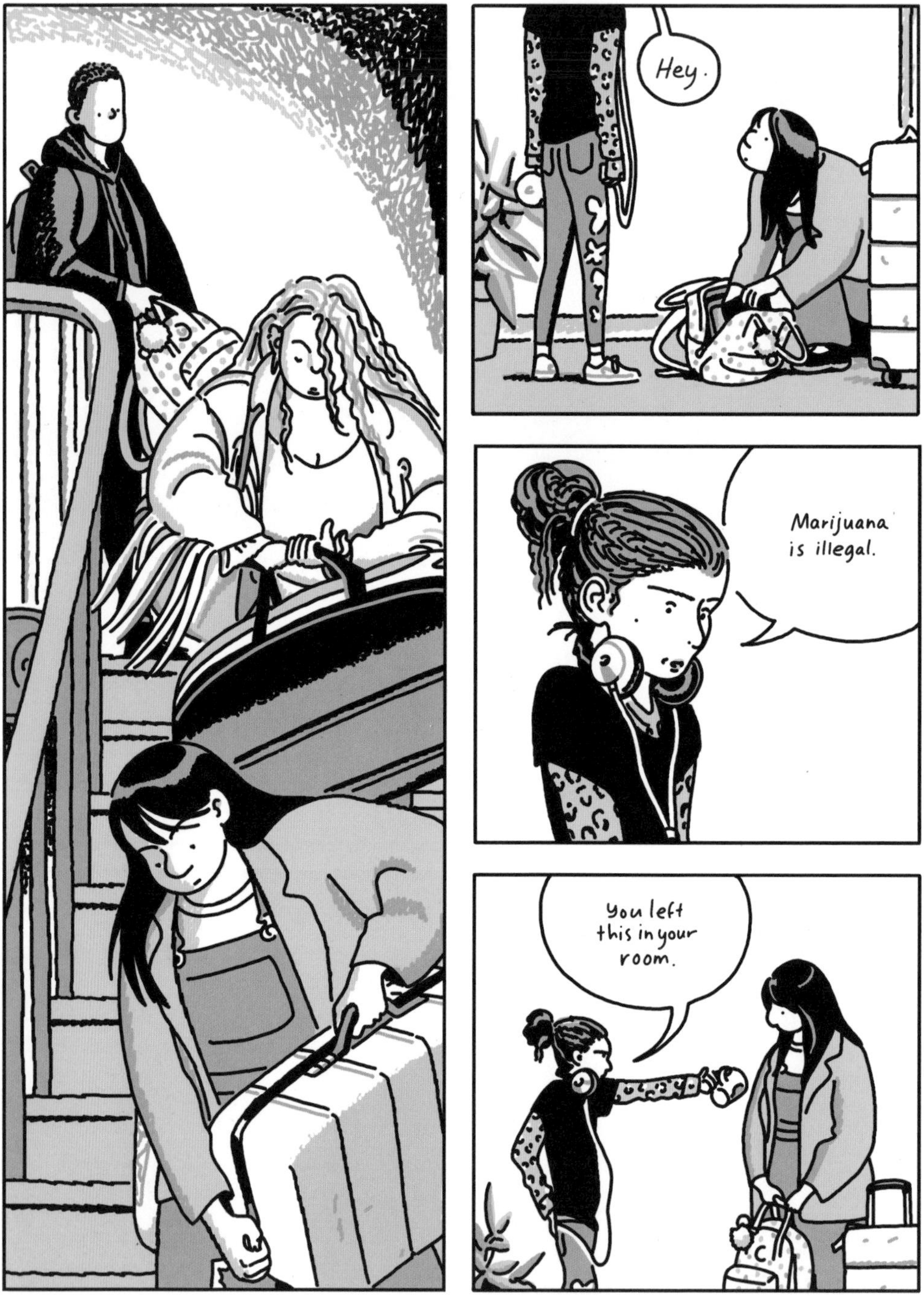
Hey.
Marijuana is illegal.
You left this in your room.

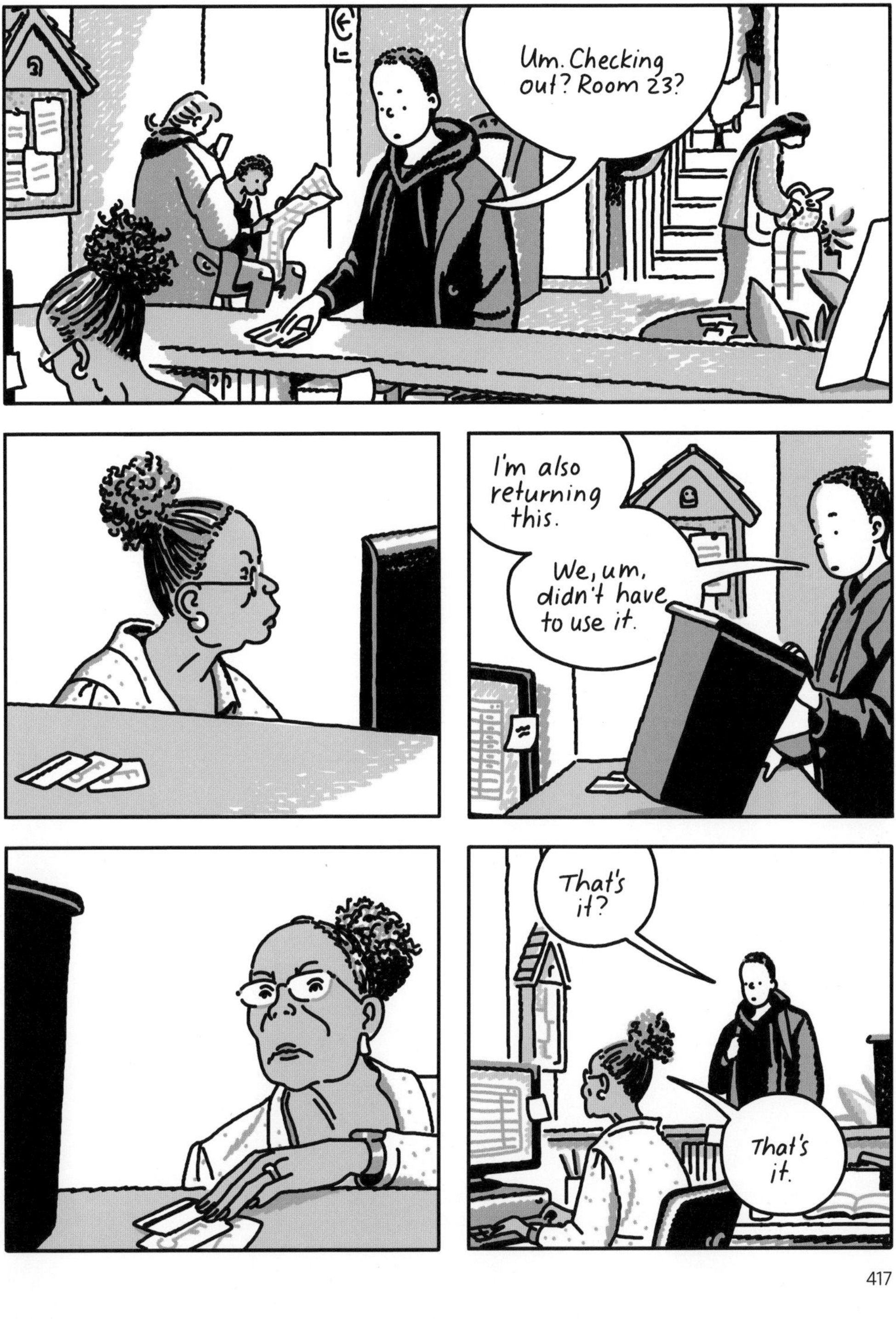
Um. Checking out? Room 23?
I'm also returning this.
We, um, didn't have to use it.
That's it?
That's it.

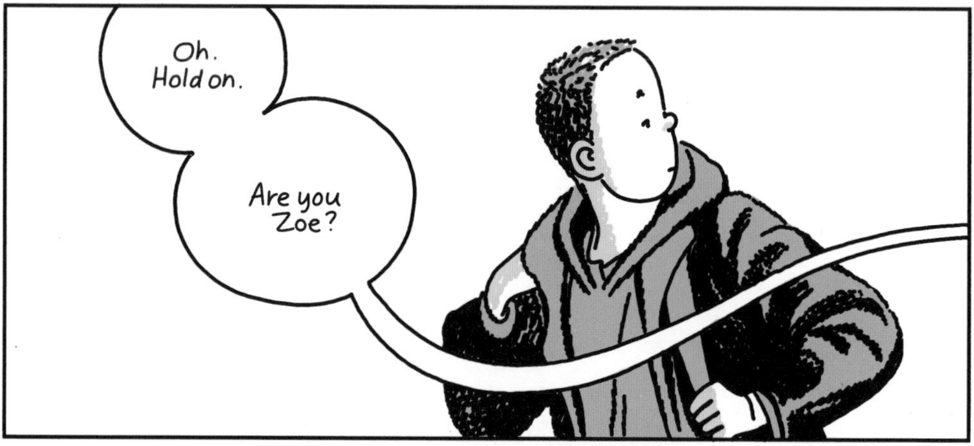
Oh.
Hold on.
Are you
Zoe?

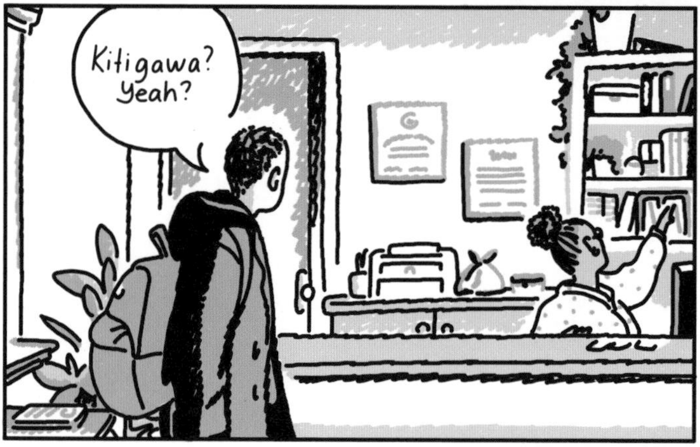
Kitigawa?
Yeah?

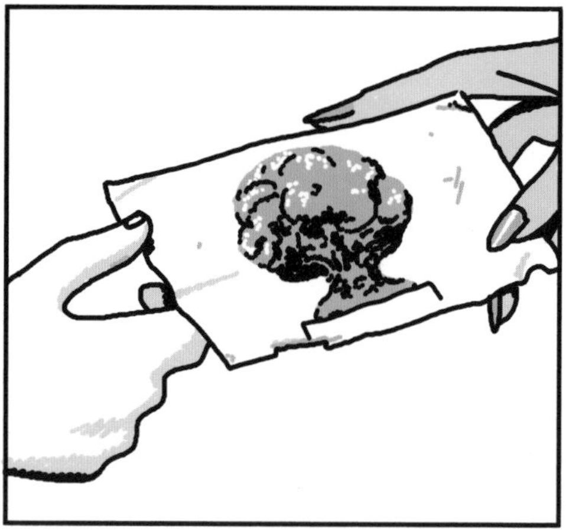

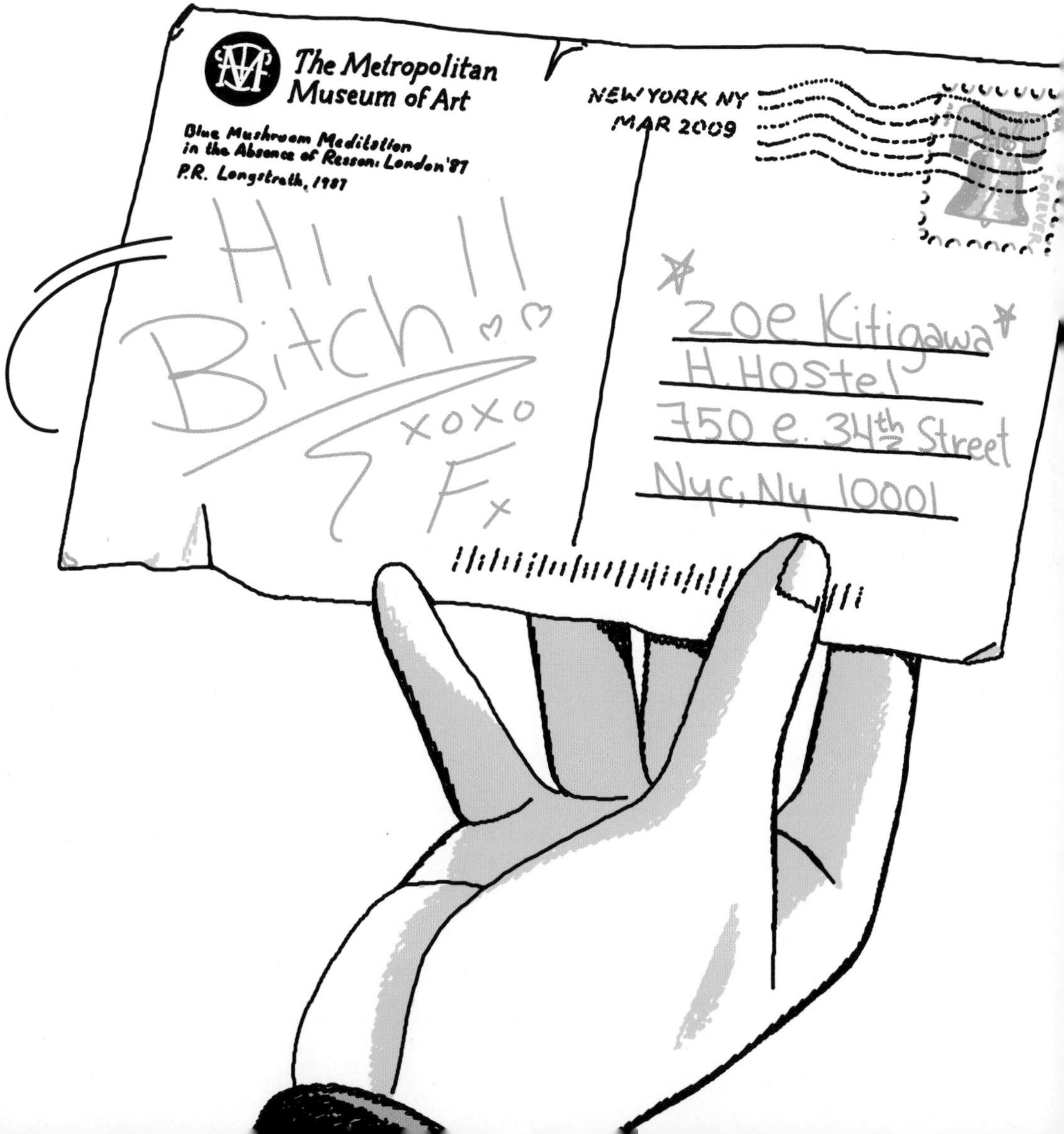
The Metropolitan Museum of Art
Blue Mushroom Meditation in the Absence of Reason: London '87
P.R. Longstreth, 1987
NEW YORK NY
MAR 2009
FOREVER
Hi !!
Bitch!!
xoxo
F x
zoe Kitigawa
H. Hostel
750 e. 34th Street
Nyc, Ny 10001

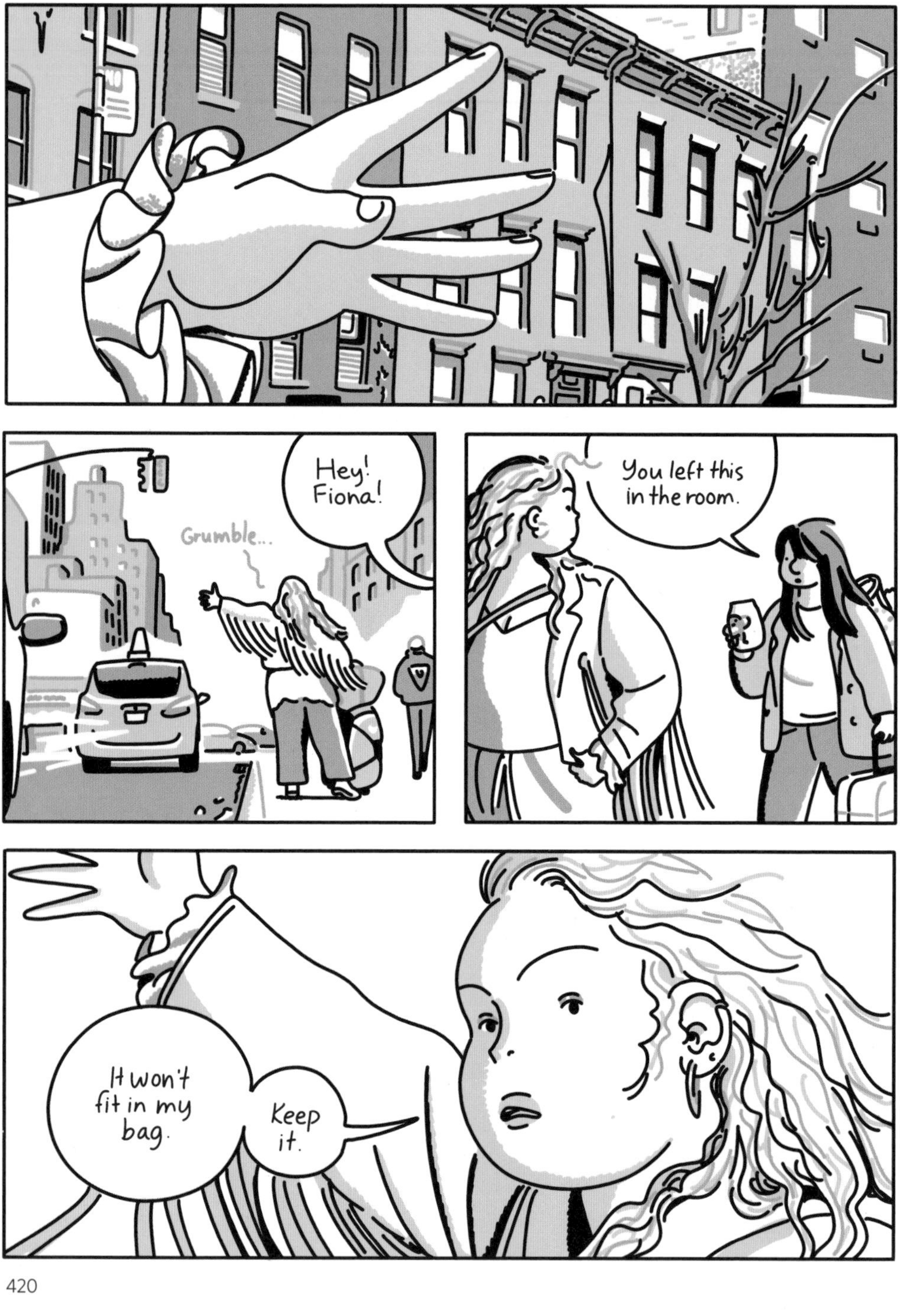
Hey! Fiona!
Grumble...
You left this in the room.
It won't fit in my bag.
Keep it.

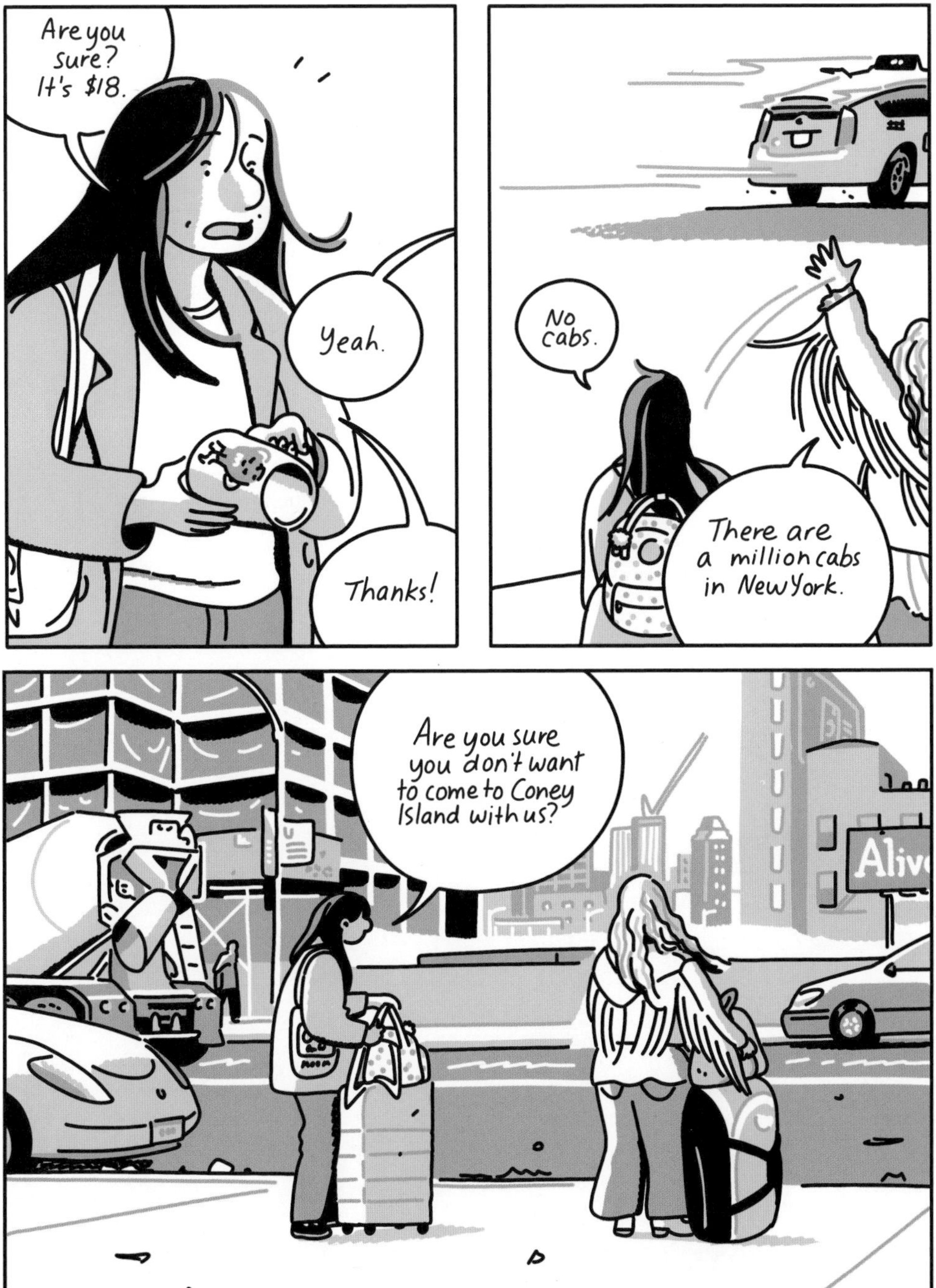
Are you sure? It's $18.
Yeah.
Thanks!
No cabs.
There are a million cabs in New York.
Are you sure you don't want to come to Coney Island with us?
Alive

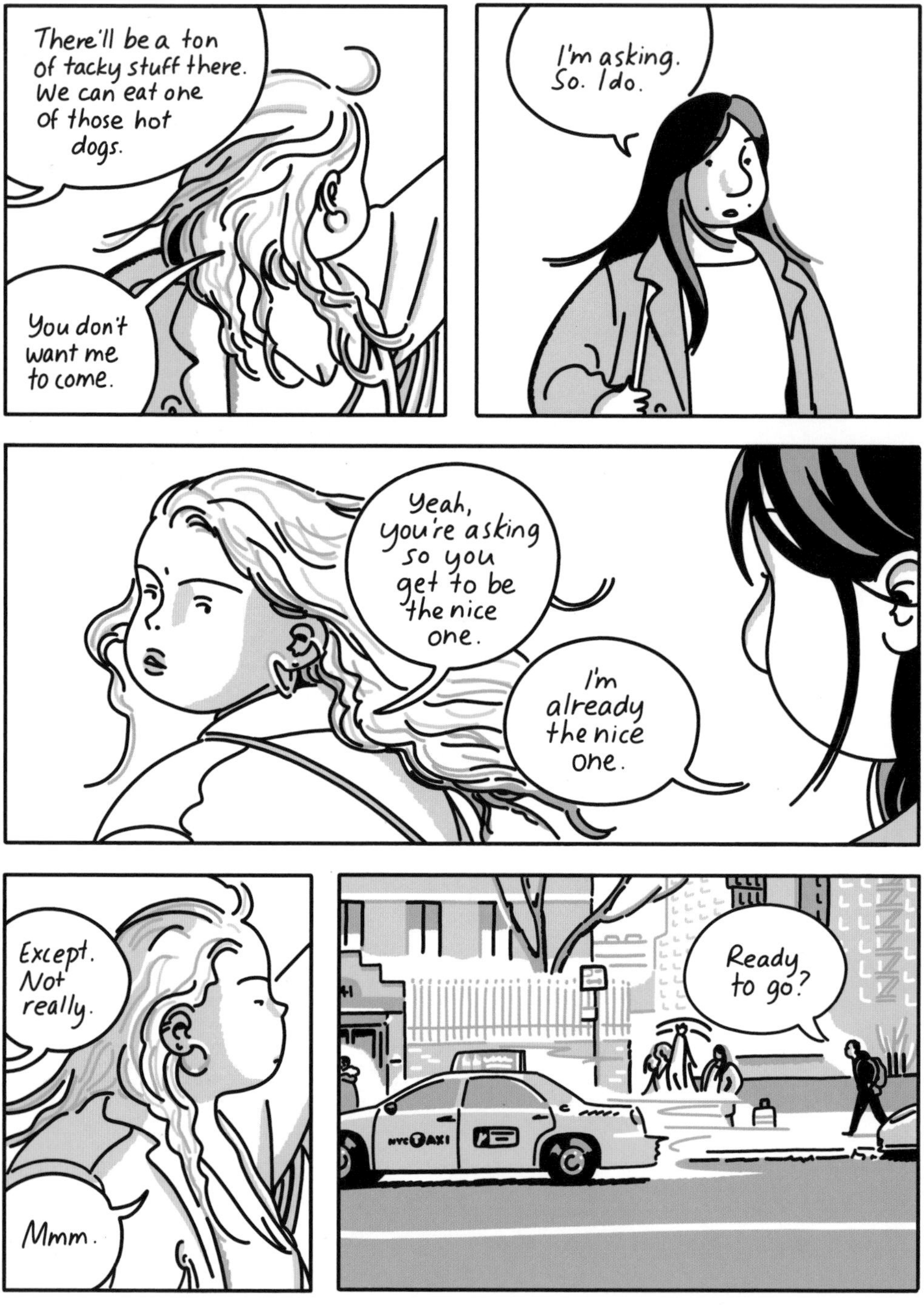
There'll be a ton of tacky stuff there. We can eat one of those hot dogs.
You don't want me to come.
I'm asking. So. I do.
Yeah, you're asking so you get to be the nice one.
I'm already the nice one.
Except. Not really.
Mmm.
Ready to go?
NYC TAXI

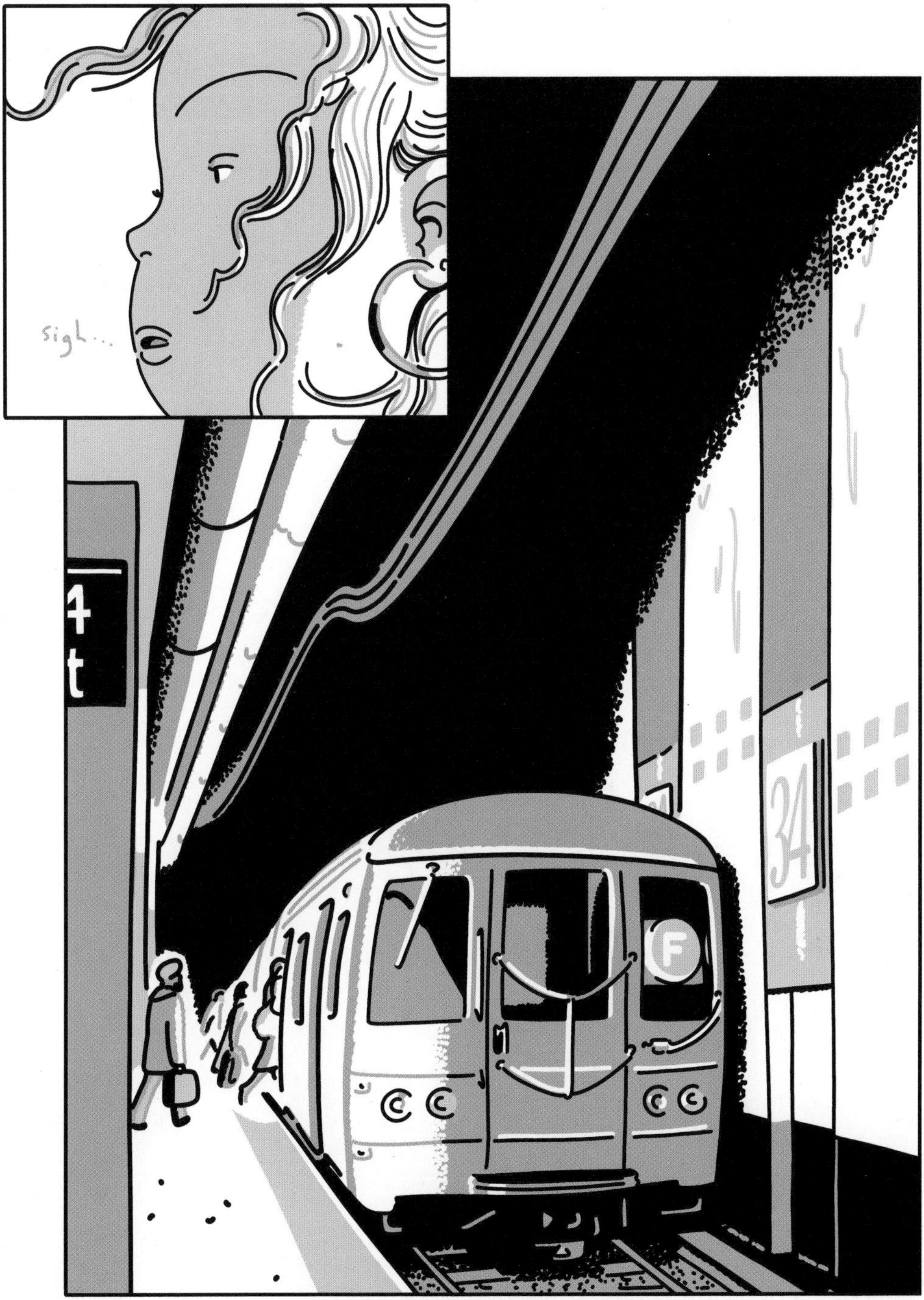
sigh...
F
34

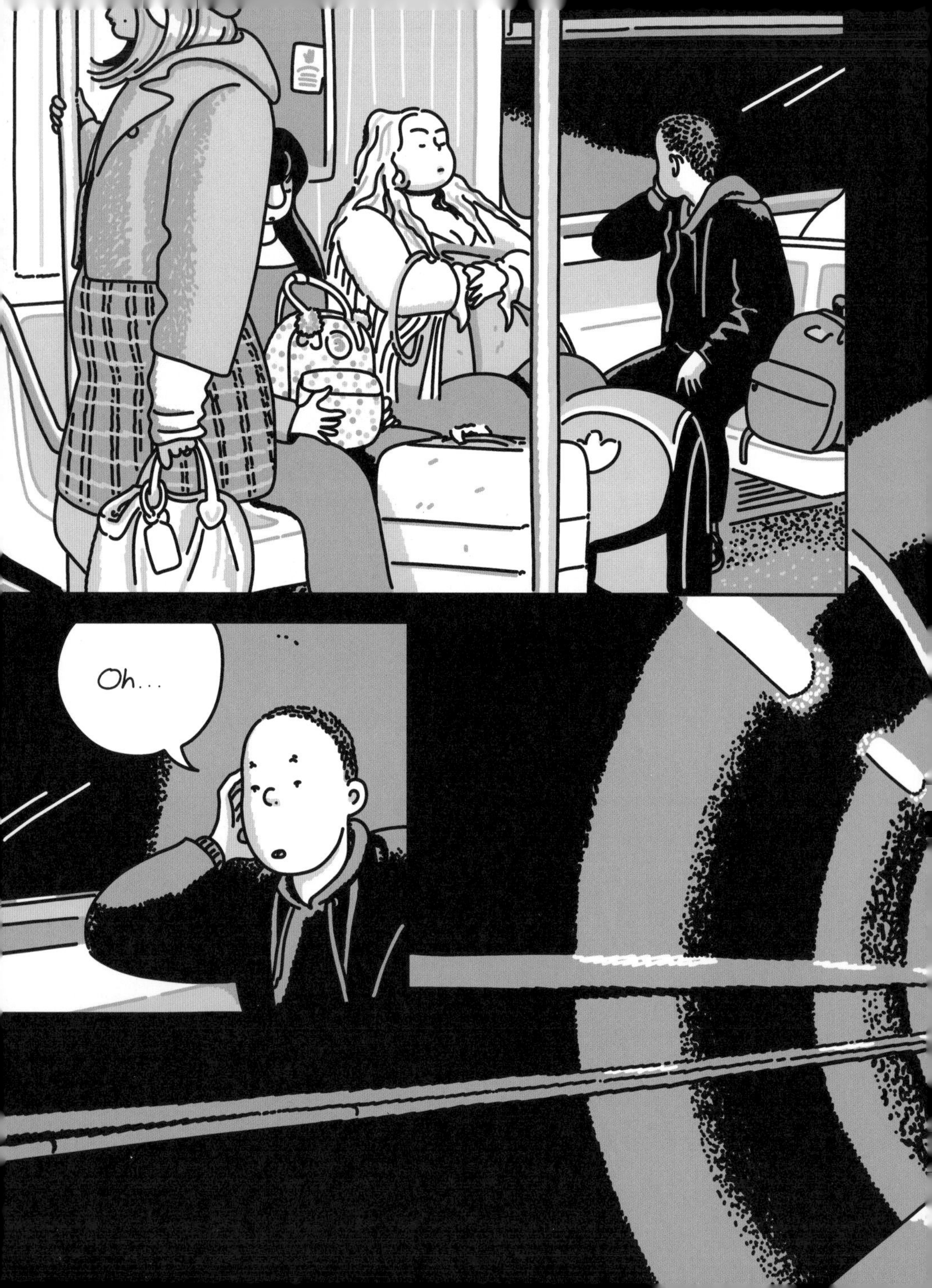
Oh...
...

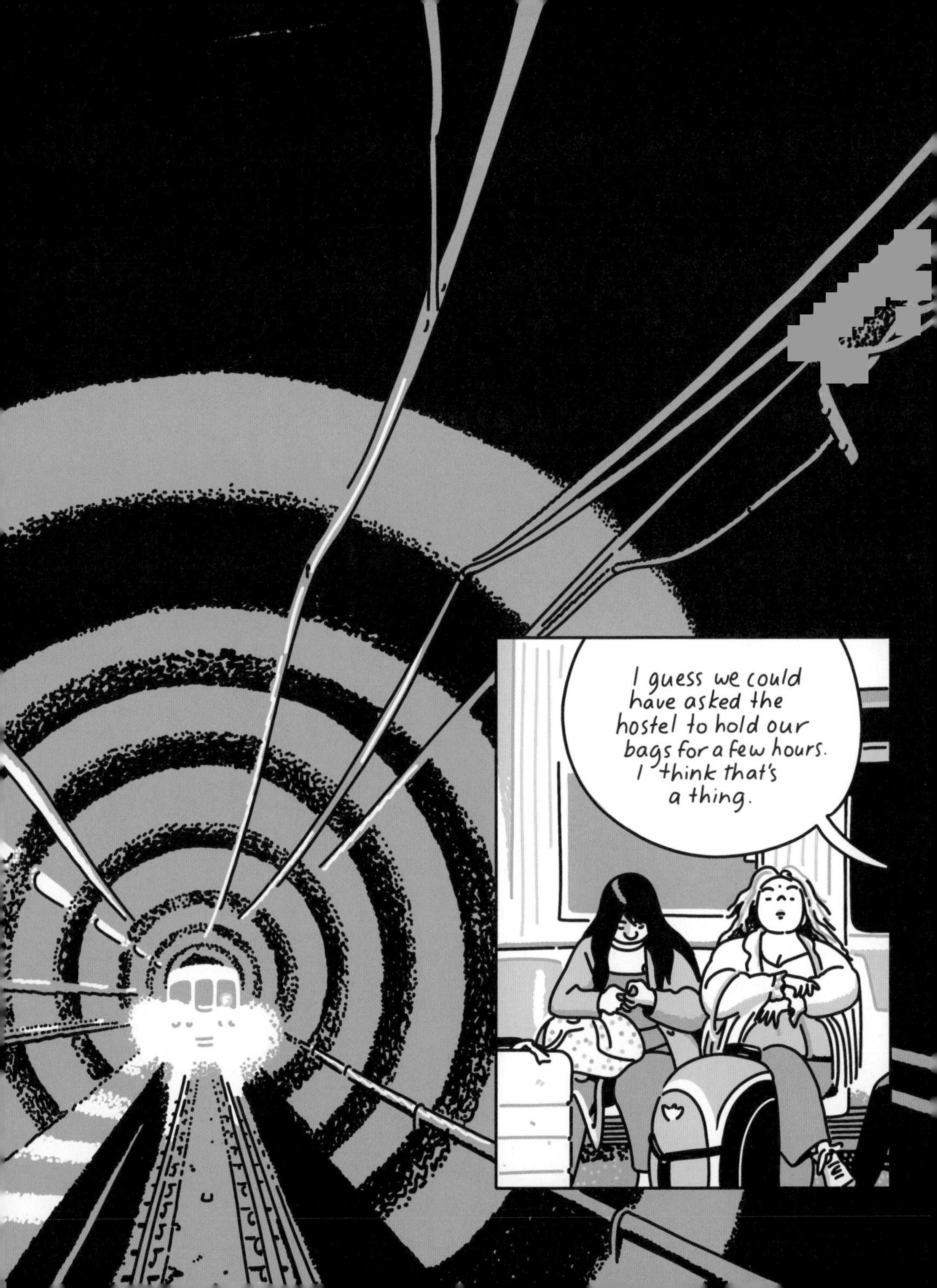
I guess we could have asked the hostel to hold our bags for a few hours. I think that's a thing.

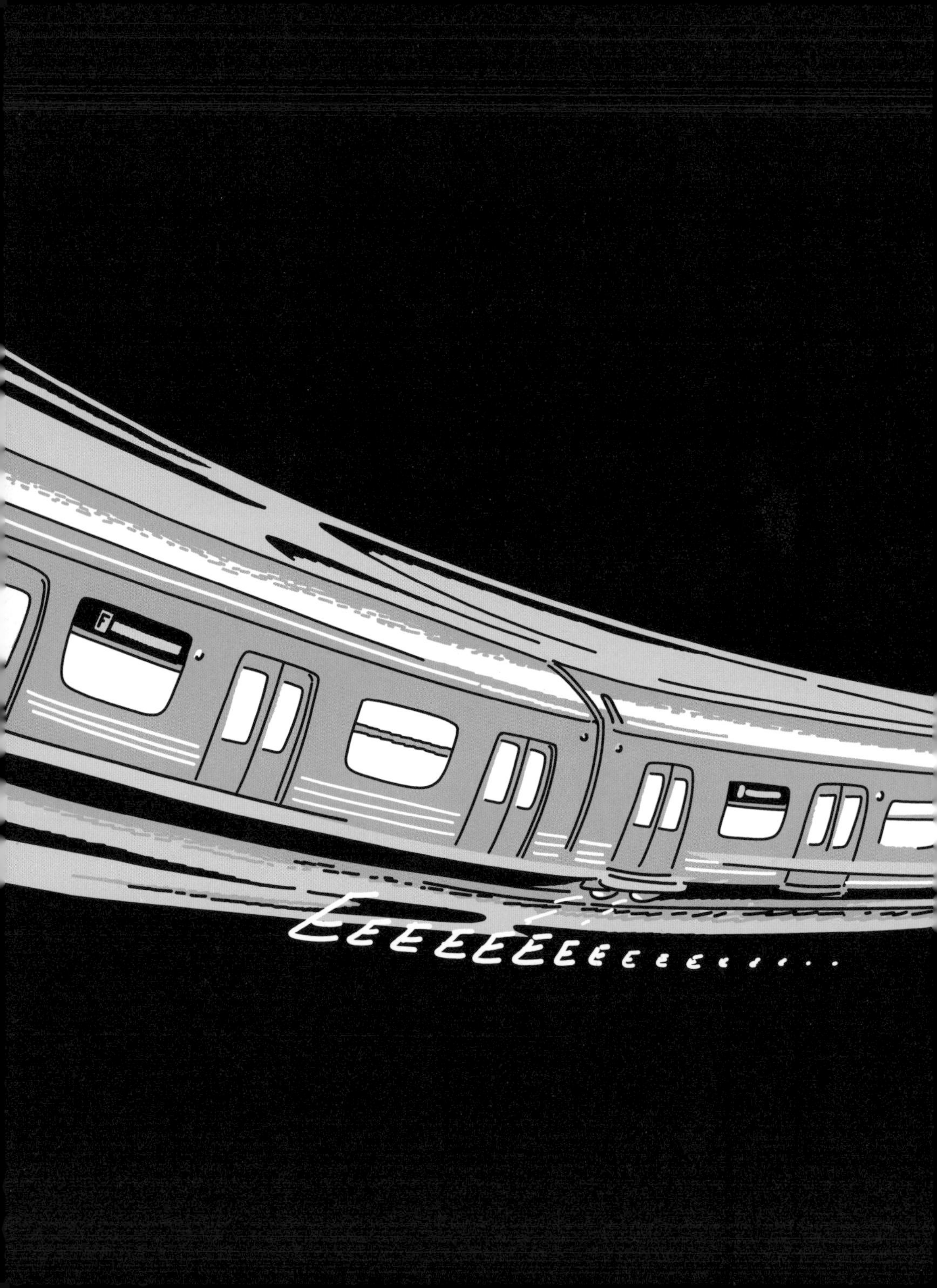
EEEEEEEEEEEe.....

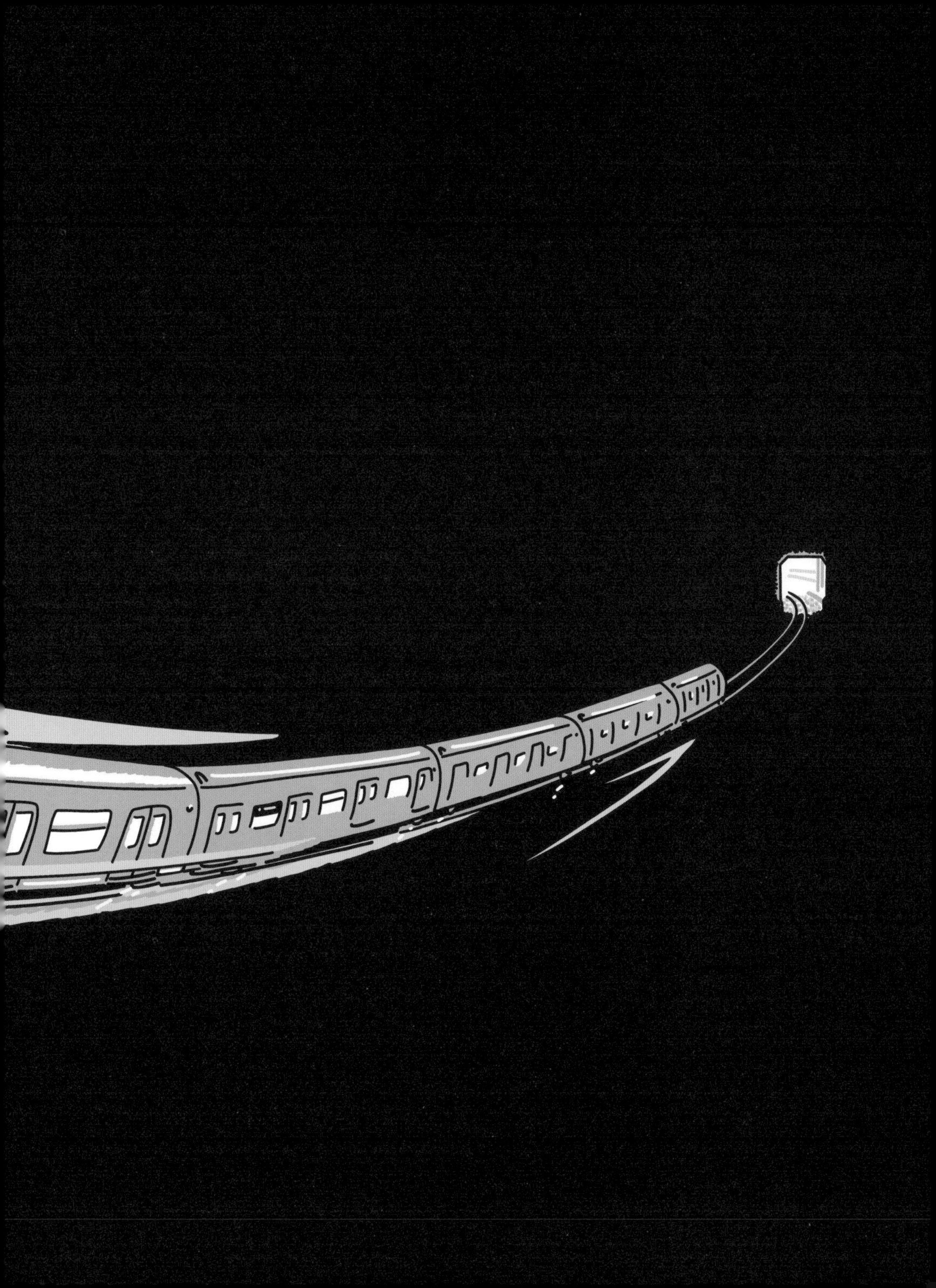

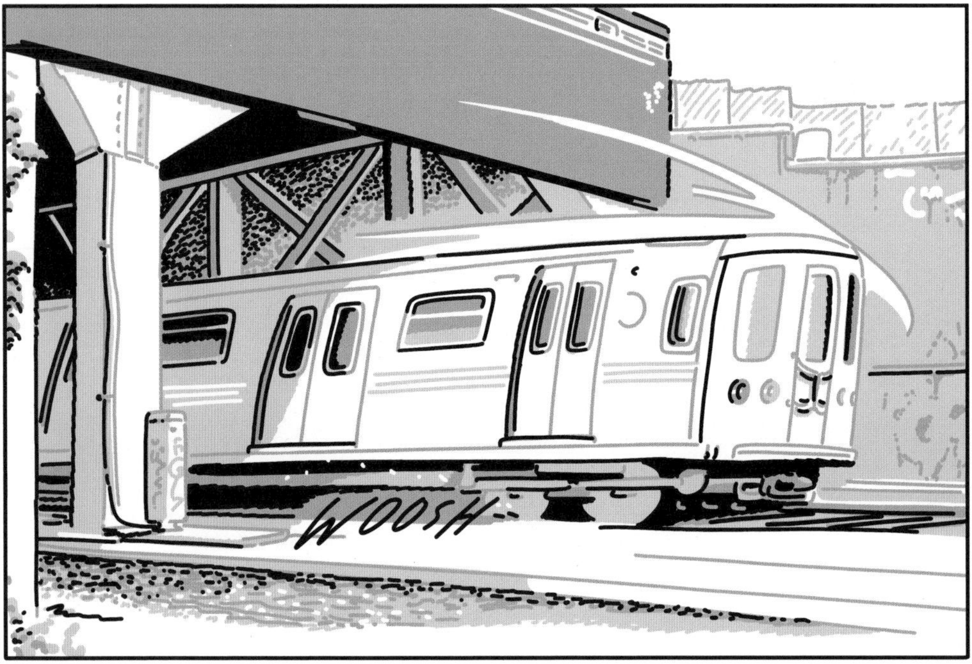
WOOSH

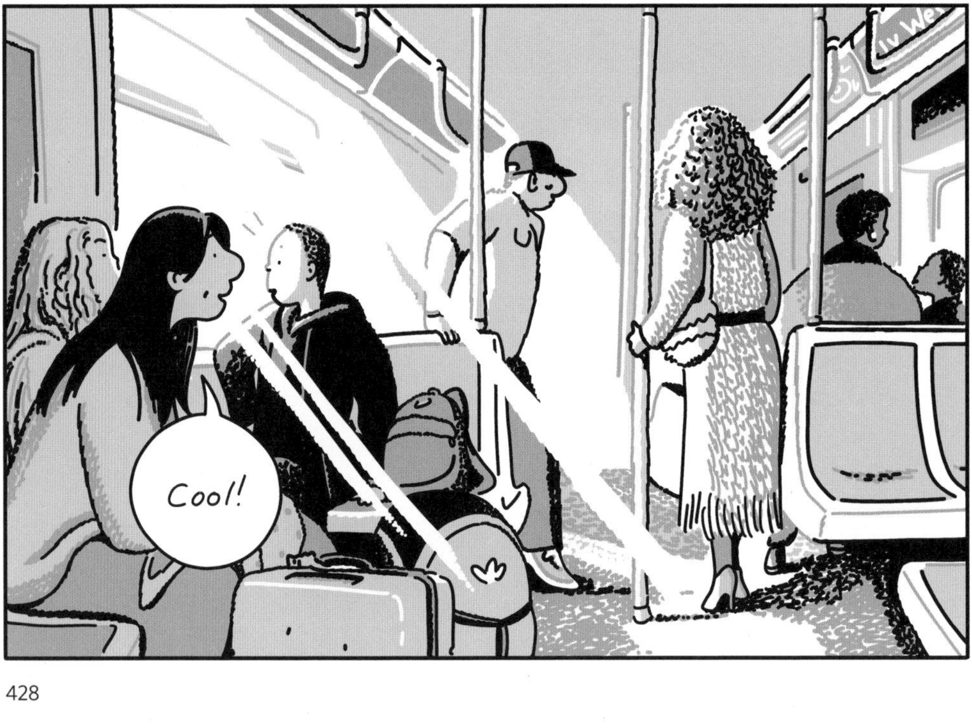
Cool!

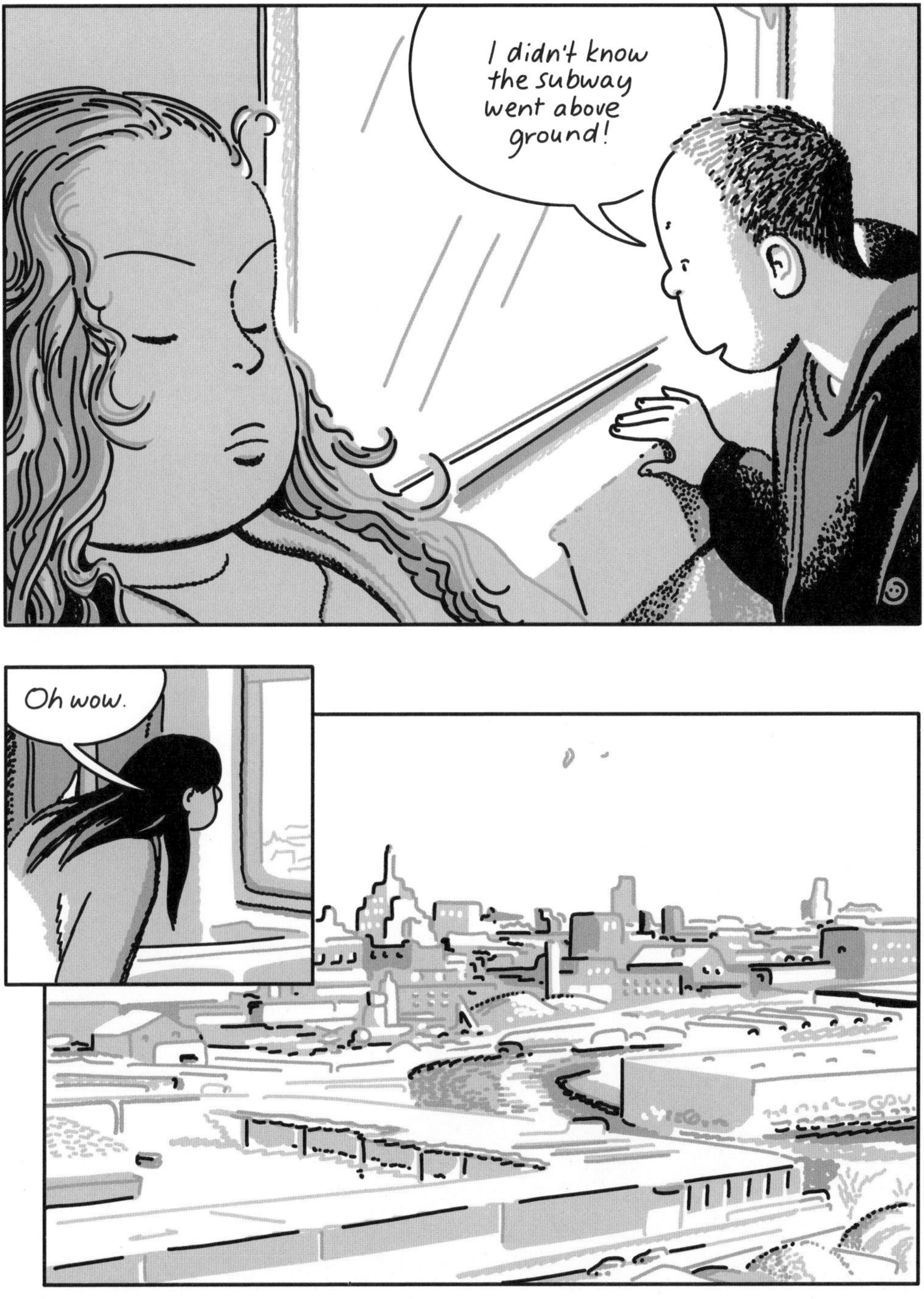
I didn't know the subway went above ground!
Oh wow.

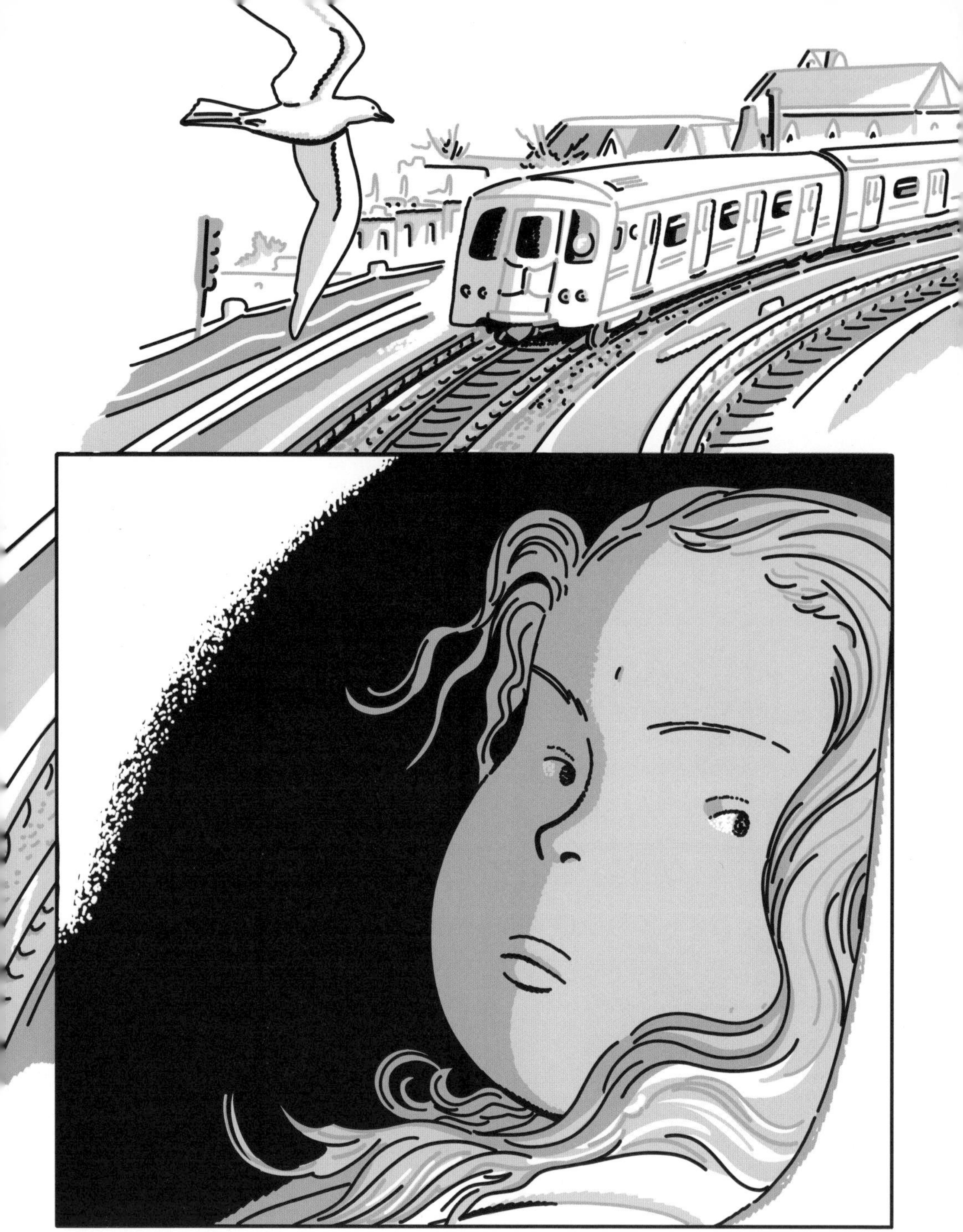

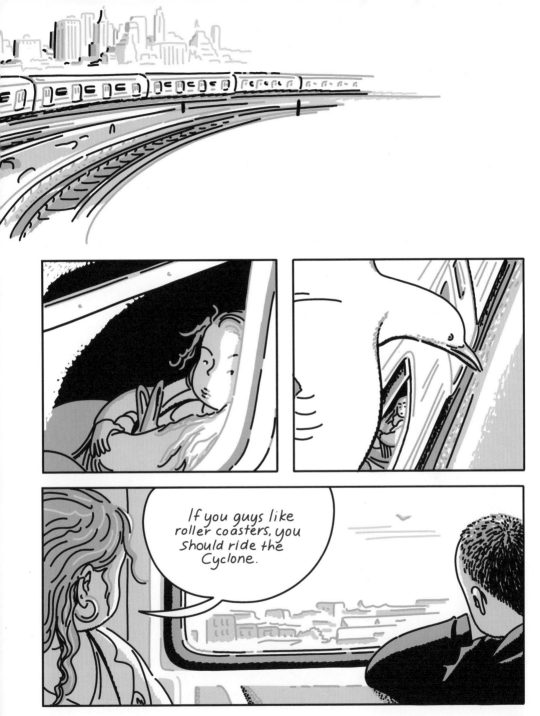

If you guys like roller coasters, you should ride the Cyclone.

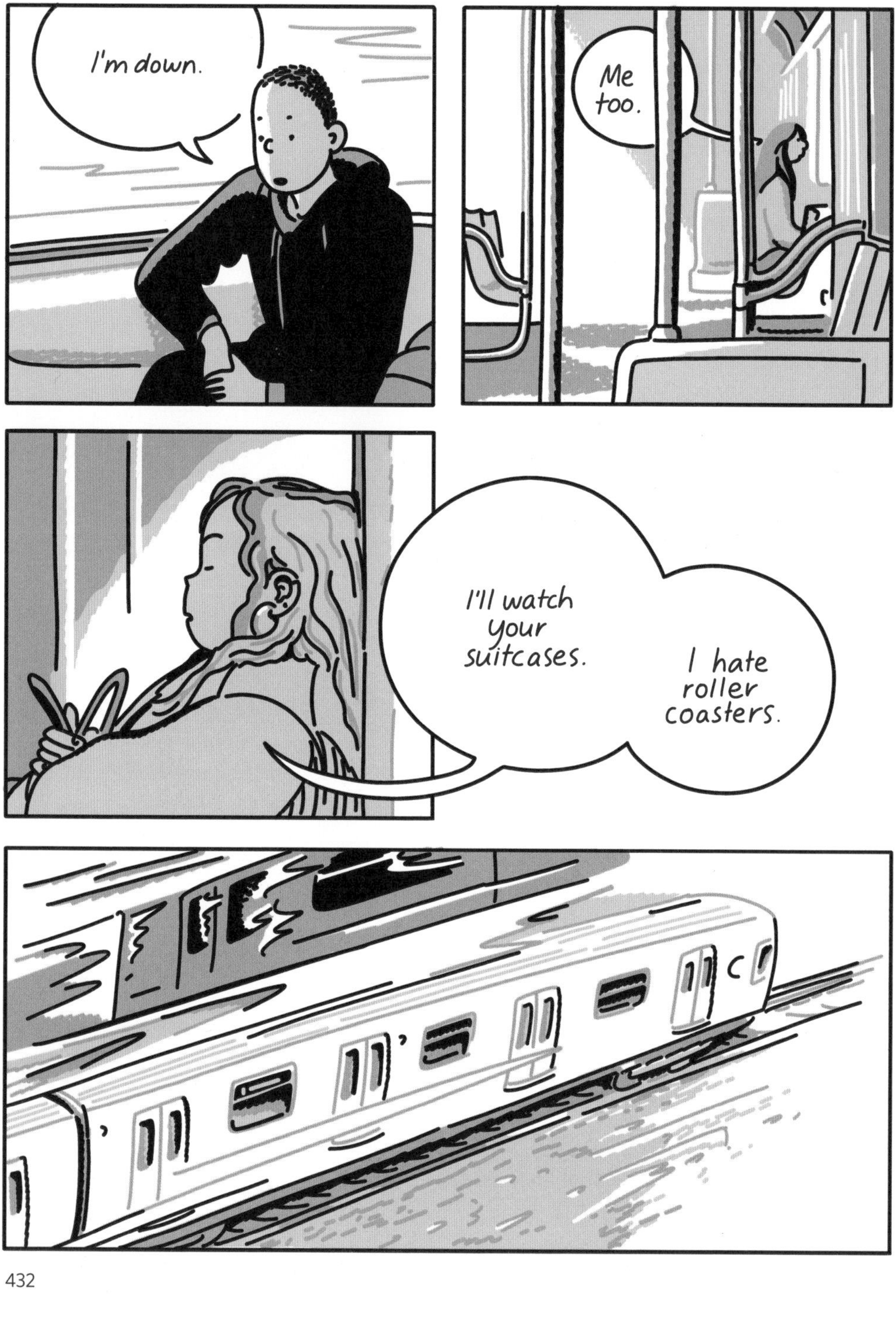
I'm down.
Me too.
I'll watch your suitcases.
I hate roller coasters.

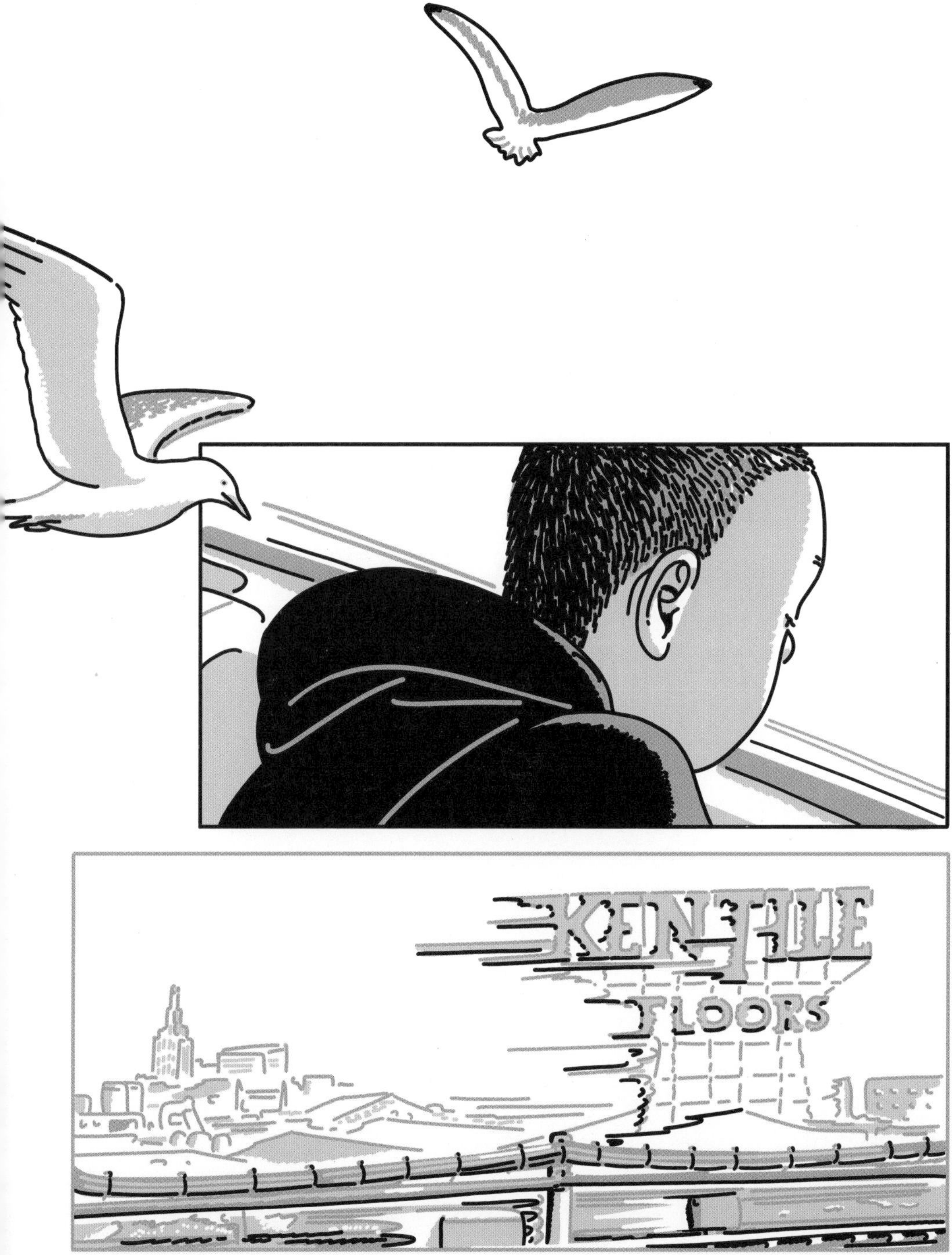
KEN-TILE
FLOORS

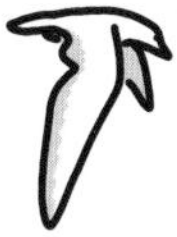

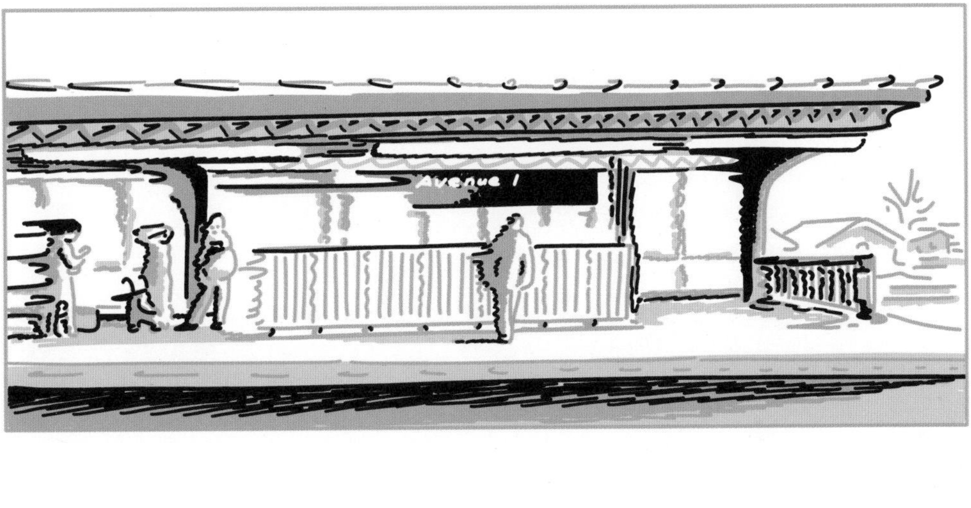
Avenue I

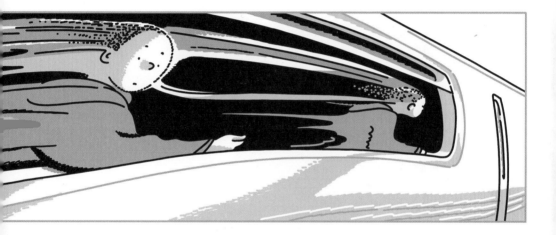

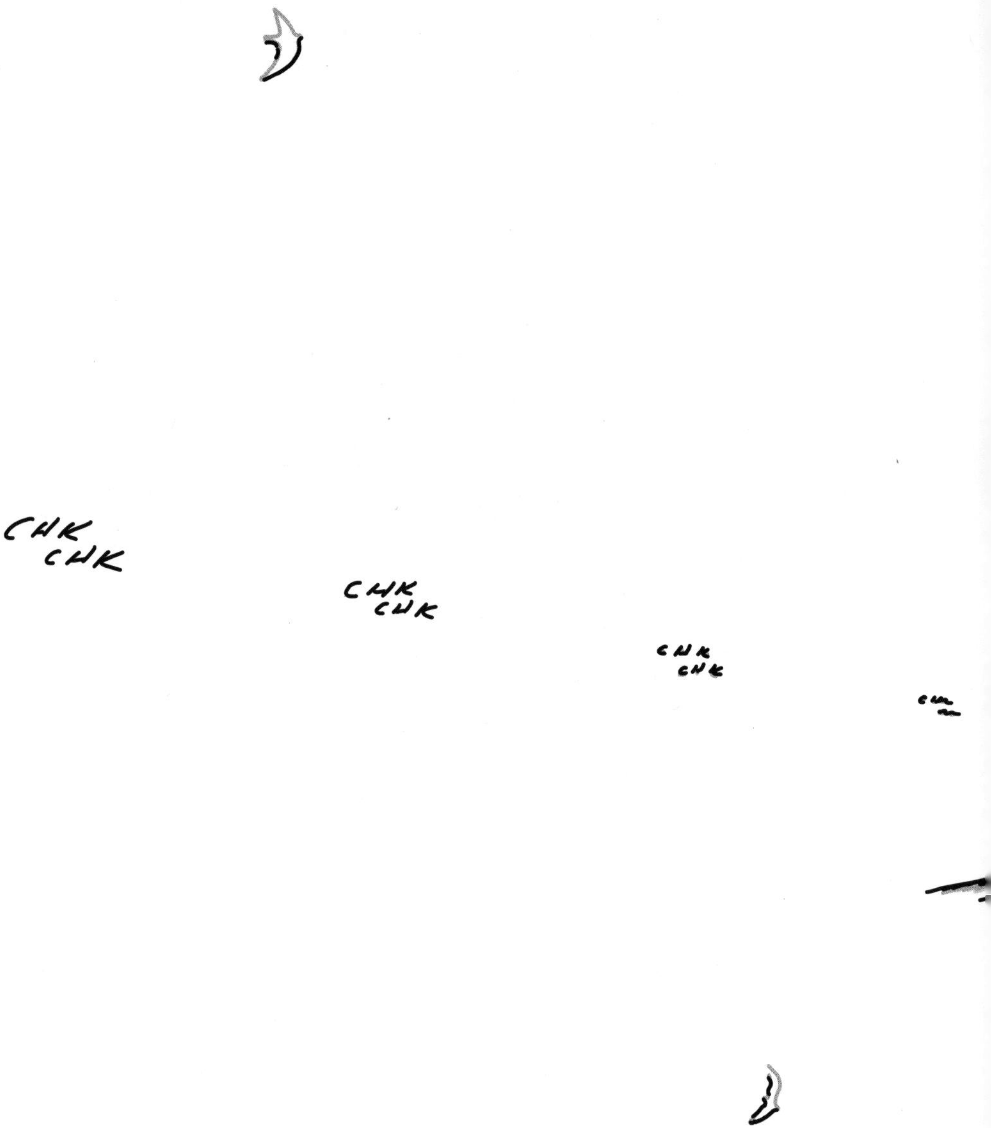
CHK
CHK
CHK
CHK
CHK
CHK

Thank you to the team at Drawn & Quarterly: Tracy, Peggy, Lucia, Shirley, Megan, Francine, Gabrielle, Kaiya, Trynne, Alison, Julia, Rebecca, and Tom. Thank you to readers E. Tammy Kim, Cory Silverberg, and Tara McGowan-Ross for their insights, and to Marjolaine Jacques, Janet Hong, Kashfia Rahman, and Mustafizur Rahman for their help with the translated text in the story.

Thank you to agents Steven Malk and Charlotte Sheedy.

As always, thank you to Michael DeForge, Heather Gold, and Lauren Tamaki.

Jillian would like to thank ST, the users of Flickr for their thorough documentation of New York City in 2009, and Google Street View. Mariko would like to thank every friend who ever went with her to New York and had a mostly fun time.

The events of this story are both too real and entirely fictional.

This book was written in the traditional territory of Huichin, the ancestral and unceded land of the Chochenyo speaking Ohlone people, the successors of the sovereign Verona Band of Alameda County (Oakland). This land was and continues to be of great importance to the Muwekma Ohlone Tribe and other familial descendants of the Verona Band. It was also written and drawn in the traditional territory of the Anishinaabeg, the Chippewa, the Haudenosaunee, the Mississaugas of the Credit, and the Wendat (Toronto). The story takes place in the traditional homeland of the Lenape (New York City).

drawnandquarterly.com | jilliantamaki.com | marikotamaki.com

MIX
Paper | Supporting responsible forestry
FSC www.fsc.org FSC™ C005748

ISBN 978-1-77046-433-9 | First edition: September 2023
Printed in China | 10 9 8 7 6 5 4 3 2 1

Cataloguing data available from Library and Archives Canada.

Published in the USA by Drawn & Quarterly, a client publisher of Farrar, Straus and Giroux. Published in Canada by Drawn & Quarterly, a client publisher of Raincoast Books. Published in the United Kingdom by Drawn & Quarterly, a client publisher of Publishers Group UK.

Canada

Drawn & Quarterly acknowledges the support of the Government of Canada and the Canada Council for the Arts for our publishing program.

Jillian Tamaki is a cartoonist, illustrator, and educator living in Toronto, Ontario. She is the author of the Eisner Award-winning graphic novels *SuperMutant Magic Academy* and *Boundless*, and the author-illustrator of two picture books, including most recently *Our Little Kitchen*.

Mariko Tamaki lives in California. She won the Eisner award for Best Writer for *Laura Dean Keeps Breaking Up with Me*, cocreated with Rosemary Valero-O'Connell. Her works have received Printz Honors, Eisner, Ignatz, and GLAAD awards. She is the curator of the Abrams LGBTQIA imprint, Surely Books.

Together, the Tamaki cousins are co-creators of the young adult graphic novels *SKIM* and *This One Summer*, which won a Governor General's Award, Printz and Caldecott Honors, as well as the Eisner for Best Graphic Novel.

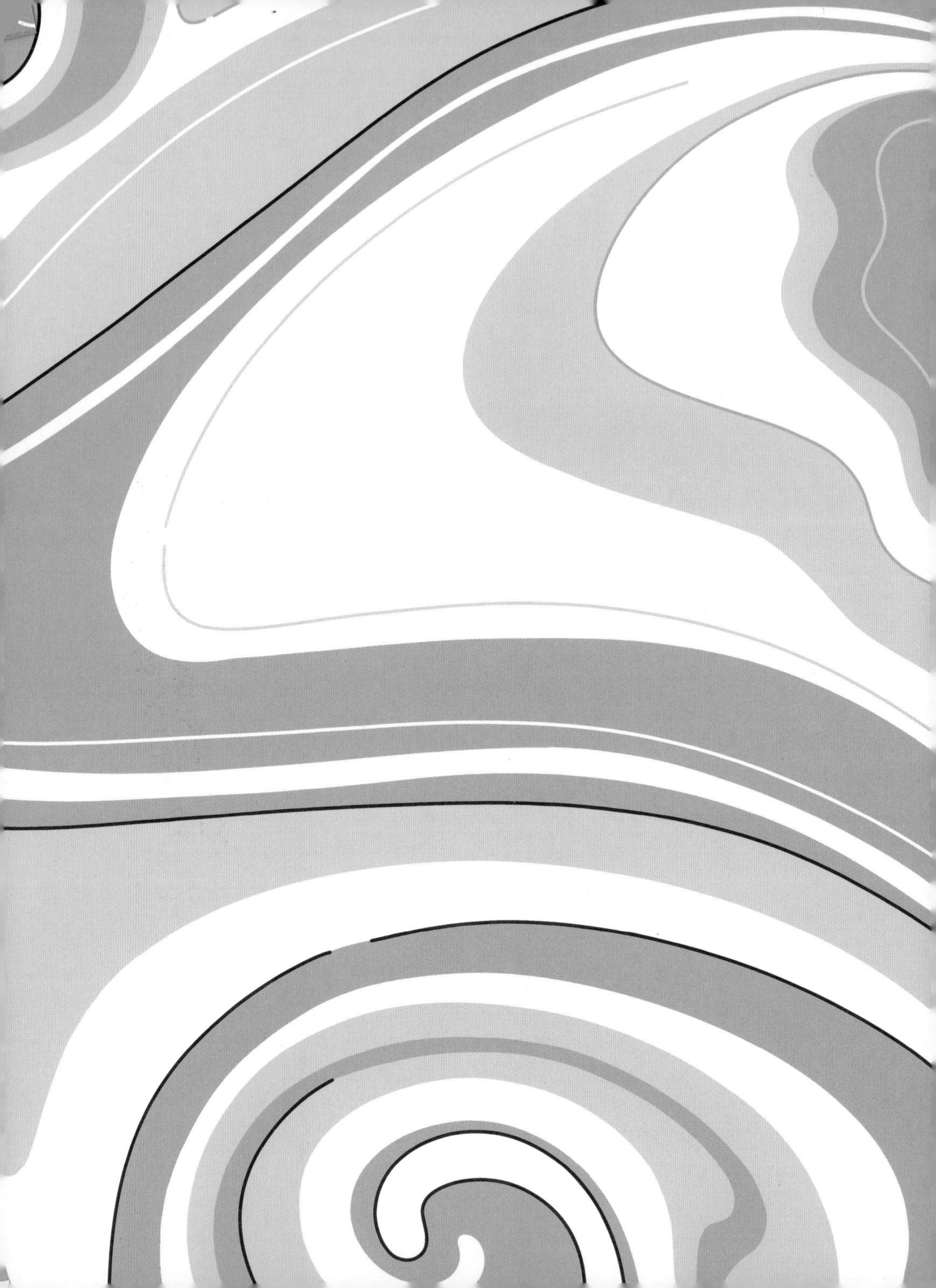